HUMAN SOCIETY

HUMAN SOCIETY

By

Kingsley Davis

University of California, Berkeley

THE MACMILLAN COMPANY

New York

Twenty-second Printing, 1966

The Macmillan Company, New York
Collier-Macmillan Canada, Ltd., Toronto, Ontario

Printed in the United States of America

R. D. McKenzie, *The Metropolitan Community*. Copyright 1933 by the President's Research Committee on Social Trends, Reprinted by permission of McGraw-Hill Book Company, Inc.

R. M. MacIver, *Society*. Copyright 1937 by R. M. MacIver. Reprinted by permission of Rinehart & Company, Inc.

Wm. F. Ogburn and Meyer F. Nimkoff, *Sociology*. Copyright 1940 by Wm. F. Ogburn and Meyer F. Nimkoff. Reprinted by permission of Houghton Mifflin Company.

Robt. E. Park and Ernest W. Burgess, *Introduction to the Science of Sociology*. Copyright 1934 by The University of Chicago.

Stuart A. Queen and Lewis F. Thomas, *The City*. Copyright 1939 by McGraw-Hill Book Company, Inc.

Joseph A. Schumpeter, *Business Cycles*. Copyright 1939 by McGraw-Hill Book Company, Inc.

To

JOE *and* WINIFRED

my Parents

PREFACE

A SINGLE book that pretended to cover all aspects of human society would be an impertinence. The present work is more limited, for it addresses itself only to certain theoretical problems and principles. It intends to raise only those questions that concern social systems as wholes. When any particular aspect of society is dealt with, it is from the standpoint of its relation to the rest of social organization. When any concrete illustration is given, it is with the intention of illuminating some point about the mechanisms of society as a whole or of social relations as such. This focus limits the scope of the volume and therefore, the writer hopes, saves it from impertinency. Whatever the merits or demerits of the exposition, the focus itself is of the greatest significance for social science.

The questions raised fall into two classes: first, those that ask about the universal characteristics of all human society, and second, those that ask about the variations from one society to another. Among the most crucial questions in the first class are the following: How does human society differ from non-human society? What enables human social systems to operate as going concerns? What, for example, do they require for their existence, and what major structures do they evolve which enable them to meet these requirements? How are these structures related to each other in the total social scheme, and how is society as a system related to personality as a system?

Among the most crucial questions of the second type—on social variation—are the following: What is the total range of variation with respect to the major elements of society? Why is the range in each case limited—what factors determine the limits? What are the major types of human society, and how strictly are the component institutions adapted to the particular type? How do social systems change in time?

Obviously such questions as these by no means exhaust the possible ones that might be asked about society and social behavior. They do not require an encyclopedia for their answer or a combination of all the social sciences from economics to criminology. Rather they represent merely a certain focus of attention. They are primarily the broadest questions that sociology, social anthropology, and social psychology have to deal with. They form the common ground but do not exhaust the data of these three fields.

The aim of the book is to give tentative theoretical answers to such central questions, and above all to try to integrate the answers into a system of thought on human society. Of course, it is easier to raise questions than to answer them. The answers given are necessarily not original, but are drawn from the literature of social science. The masters of sociological theory who are most responsible for the ideas expressed are Emile Durkheim, Max Weber, Vilfredo Pareto, Georg Simmel, Talcott Parsons, Robert K. Merton, Charles H. Cooley, Robert E. Park, and Robert M. MacIver. In social anthropology the main authors drawn upon are A. R. Radcliffe-Brown, Bronislaw Malinowski, W. Lloyd Warner, Ralph Linton, E. E. Evans-Pritchard, Margaret Mead, and Ruth Benedict. In social psychology they are George H. Mead, Ellsworth Faris, Jean Piaget, Prescott Lecky, the psychoanalysts such as Karen Horney, and the psychiatrists such as Roy R. Grinker. Others of major importance are W. C. Allee, Carl J. Warden, and Wm. Morton Wheeler in comparative sociology, Thorstein Veblen in economics, and Frank W. Notestein in population. These contributors to social science development, however, form only a small part of the total number to whom the writer is indebted.

The intention has not been primarily to evolve new theories but to synthesize the most advanced ideas bearing on the questions at issue. The book's main claim to originality, therefore, lies in its attempted integration of different schools of thought, many of which seemingly have come to the same solutions but with different terminologies and from different sets of data. In this task the writer is painfully aware of the inadequacies of the volume. Given sufficient time and resources, he would have preferred to provide more empirical evidence—growing out of the innumerable investigations reported in the literature—for the conclusions reached. He has attempted partially to overcome the deficiency in this regard by annotated bibliographies at the end of each chapter. Also, it would have been desirable to follow out theoretical implications more fully than has been done, although this would have produced a much longer and more difficult book. Finally, the writer is aware of subjects and points of view that were omitted but should have been included. These he hopes to treat in some future edition.

The book has required several years to write. In this long and toilsome task invaluable encouragement and assistance have come from students and colleagues. Among the latter it is especially pleasurable to mention Wilbert E. Moore, Robert K. Merton, Paul K. Hatt, and Harry C. Bredemeier. In addition, a subtle sort of encouragement, as well as excellent assistance in typing and proofreading, has been given by the writer's wife, Jane Davis.

It is impossible, however, to list all of those who in one way or another have contributed to making the book better than it otherwise would have been. Unfortunately, candor requires admitting that it has not been possible to correct all the faults that have been kindly pointed out by students and colleagues. This is not because the writer has failed to understand them as faults, but because it seemed necessary, for the moment at least, to put an end to an otherwise endless task. Perhaps later it will prove possible to take greater advantage of the suggestions offered. In the meantime, if the book contributes anything at all to the understanding of that most astounding and troublesome of all phenomena, human society, he will feel that the labor has been justified.

KINGSLEY DAVIS

New York

TABLE OF CONTENTS

Part I. THE NATURE OF HUMAN SOCIETY

Part II. THE INDIVIDUAL AND HIS SOCIETY

Part III. MAJOR GROUPS

Part IV. MAJOR INSTITUTIONS

Part V. POPULATION AND SOCIETY

Part VI. SOCIAL CHANGE

PART I

THE NATURE OF HUMAN SOCIETY

THE STUDY OF HUMAN SOCIETY

HUMAN VERSUS ANIMAL SOCIETY

SOCIAL NORMS

STATUS AND ROLE

THE ELEMENTS OF SOCIAL ACTION

FORMS OF INTERACTION

CHAPTER I

THE STUDY OF HUMAN SOCIETY

HUMAN beings have always regarded themselves as a unique species. They have been keenly aware of a great gulf between themselves and the rest of the animal kingdom, a gulf not matched elsewhere in the sentient world. Not only have they been aware of their uniqueness, but, after the manner of men, they have tried to explain it. They have said that man has a soul whereas the animals have not, or that man has a different order of intelligence. They have also said that man is a speaking animal and therefore not a dumb beast, or that he is a social animal and therefore civilized. Such explanations seem to be either mystical or superficial; in any case they are mere rationalizations of a deeper intuition rather than true explanations. They all agree, however, in not assigning man's uniqueness to his physical traits. As a physical specimen man is obviously related to the ape, a primate in every sense of the word. Somehow it is realized that man's uniqueness must be found on another level. But what level? Is it intelligence? Yes, but in isolation man is a very stupid animal. Is it speech? Yes, but this is only one of a general class of traits. Is it sociability? Yes, but many other animals are social. What then is the answer?

If there is any single factor explaining man's uniqueness, it is this: He, and he alone, has culture. From this all other differences flow. His intelligence, for example, is multiplied a thousandfold by the possession of culture. His speech, important as it may be, is merely a part of culture. His social life is governed by culture. Culture is therefore a profound possession that ramifies throughout human life and accounts for all of man's truly unique qualities. It adds an extra dimension to existence, and makes human what would otherwise be merely animal.

The nature of culture will be discussed later. At this point we need say only that it embraces all modes of thought and behavior that are handed down by communicative interaction—i.e. by symbolic transmission—rather than by genetic inheritance. It is what we learn from others through speech, gesture, and example, as opposed to what we acquire through heredity. The pattern of nest-building among birds, for instance, is hereditarily determined, the pattern of house-building among men is culturally determined.

The possession of culture makes not only man but his society unique. The anthropoid group out of which human society evolved is not remarkable. It is merely a variant of primate society in general and, still more broadly, of mammalian society. What has changed this basic social type to an extreme degree in the humanoid stem of the primates is the addition of culture. This, and this alone, has given human society an unmistakable and far-reaching distinctiveness.

The study of human society, therefore, involves the study of culture. No matter what aspect or part of society is considered, the presence of a cultural mode of transmission is of paramount importance. If, for instance, it is a question of the family, a sheer biological interpretation, which omits culture as a basis of explanation, will not do. Family patterns are cultural patterns, and their variations from place to place and time to time are cultural variations. It is culture that makes necessary the distinction between marriage and mating, legitimacy and illegitimacy, authority and dominance. If culture is so significant with respect to the family, how much more significant must it be with respect to such things as economic, political, and religious organization. By no stretch of the imagination can the difference between a democracy and a dictatorship, for example, be explained as a biological difference.

The analysis of human society must certainly be carried out on the cultural level, and one important part of human sociology is the study of the nature, origin, and significance of culture. But, on the other hand, social science is not, except in the broadest terms, concerned with the totality of culture. The content of culture is extremely diverse, and embraces much more than the student of society needs to encompass. It includes art, music, architecture, literature, science, technology, philosophy, religion, and a million other things. To treat culture in all its infinite detail would require a gigantic encyclopedia and an army of specialists.

Most of the sciences of man—the so-called humanistic sciences—are sciences of culture, dealing with the various and numerous branches into which the cultural heritage divides itself. This is why culture is sometimes used to refer to the fine arts—culture with a capital "C" and a sense of awe. But the social scientist's cultural interest extends only so far as culture relates to social life. He views culture, in other words, from a peculiar point of view, selecting only those aspects which throw light on social organization and behavior. If he is a sociologist or social anthropologist, he finds extremely significant the way in which culture extends the complexity, depth, and continuity of human society, and the manner in which new cultural inventions in every sphere affect the potentialities of social organization. He finds important the fact that inventions depend on the previous stage of cultural advance, and that their diffusion depends on numerous cultural conditions. Perhaps he finds most fascinating those aspects of culture which directly define the patterns of social interaction—the folkways, mores, laws, and institutions that govern conduct. Certainly he finds almost equally exciting the beliefs and ideas that go along with and are really part of these patterns; for it is characteristic of men as cultural animals that they feel it necessary not only to act but to give reasons and justifications for their acts and to pursue socially defined ends.

Does the social scientist go beyond culture? This is a hard question to answer, because the cultural element is so pervasive in human society that no behavior is free from its influence. Certainly the social investigator goes beyond what is called the formal aspects of social organization. For instance, the economist who studies the dynamic behavior of market relations is not concerned with the laws and mores of property. He assumes a certain institutional framework and devotes his attention to the interplay of supply and demand in the exchange of goods and services. This dynamic interplay undoubtedly is a creative force in its own right, not only helping to maintain the population but also operating subtly to change the very institutional setting itself. The social scientist is therefore interested in the actual day-to-day contact between individuals. He is concerned with concrete action, with the satisfaction of ends through the discriminatory choice of means in group situations. He is interested, for instance, not only in political and economic *institutions,* but also in political and economic *activities,* and in the functions these activities perform. But since in all behavior there are cultural elements, it can hardly be said that he ever escapes the necessity of considering cultural influence. It can merely be said that social science is not primarily or exclusively interested in culture as such. It is concerned first with society, and with culture only as connected with society.

One thing should be clear. The social sciences are devoted to the study of mental rather than physical phenomena. It happens, as a result of ideas and techniques in the cultural heritage, that human beings create countless physical objects: axes, wheels, vehicles, houses, ornaments, books, paintings, clothes, etc. By a common fallacy—the fallacy of misplaced concreteness—these are sometimes regarded as a part of "culture," and some of the cultural sciences, such as art and archeology, are thought of as studying them. But from a sociological point of view such physical objects are products made possible only by the transmission of principles and ideas from person to person. The essential thing, then, is the meaningful interaction between different individuals. Such things as social status, group solidarity, economic exchange, technological production, political organization, and kinship identification all involve mutual awareness, voluntary activity, and symbolic communication. Without the contact of mind with mind they would not exist. No matter by what external indices we measure them or what instruments we apply, social phenomena are primarily mental phenomena, and must be construed as such.

The Sociological Point of View

There are, as everyone knows, several different sciences busily engaged in the study of human society. The boundaries between them are vague in practice as well as in principle, and this situation, just as in the case of nations, has led to innumerable boundary disputes. From a strictly scientific point of view no one really cares where the boundaries are, because there are no boundaries in science. The disputes arise because science is pursued of necessity by organized groups and agencies, and these have vested interests in their work. Whether engaged in original research or in the diffusion of knowledge, each scientific group is in competition with others for financial support, public recognition, and personnel. Moreover, since technical competence is required in judging scientific matters, each group tries to set its own standards and resists amateur intrusion from outside. So long as sheer scientific matters are involved, no one objects to this autonomy; but it is sometimes difficult to separate strictly scientific necessities from hidden vested interests.

Neither the government nor the medical profession allows just any man to designate himself a surgeon and to operate on whoever yields to his persuasion. Our educational institutions do not ordinarily hire physicists to teach biology, or biologists to teach economics. This is all clear enough, but when the branches of learning are less distinct there may be claims and counterclaims as a means of advancing one group ahead of another. If, for example, there is a department of biology and a department of botany in the same university, they may each claim the right to give the course in genetics. A department of chemistry and a department of geology may each claim the right to give a course in petroleum. A psychology and an education department may each claim any number of borderline courses.

In the struggle for research funds, for public recognition, for jobs, and what not, each scientist stands to profit if his group as a whole is expanding rather than contracting. Consequently, in addition to the normal tendency to exaggerate the importance of whatever he is spending his life studying, he likes to have as big a scientific domain as possible. When, therefore, he is asked what his "field" includes, he is likely to give a broad definition that either includes most of human knowledge or makes his subject the foundation or the key to all the rest.

Social scientists have unfortunately been quite guilty of this sort of thing. Anthropology modestly designates itself as "the study of man." Psychology, with equal reticence, regards itself as the "science of behavior." Economics says that it studies "the ways by which man makes a living," implying that anything else, since it does not contribute to his living, is largely superfluous. Political science claims that it studies "the phenomena of power"; sociology, "society and social behavior"; history, "the significant past." Obviously they cannot all be right, or if they are, there is a deplorable amount of overlapping that would make it impossible to organize a university curriculum or establish a set of professional associations. The best way to understand the nature of the various social sciences is to pay attention to what they actually do, not what they say they do. This will show that the real basis of differentiation is not a difference in concrete subject matter, for the social disciplines are all studying the same external phenomena—the facts of social life. It is rather a difference in the point of view or focus of attention.

Each science formulates its own type of question and selects from the welter of social manifestations those data that give the most satisfactory answer. It necessarily makes assumptions, i.e. takes for granted the answers to other kinds of questions, and these assumptions may or may not be true. Each science is therefore abstract, dealing with only certain aspects of the concrete reality—aspects that are not capable of physical separation (as the limb from the tree) but only of analytical separation. It follows that, in so far as the prediction of actual events is concerned, the various social sciences are mutually interdependent because only by combining their various points of view can a complete anticipation of future occurrences be achieved. The assumptions of one are the questions at issue for the others. Economics, for example, commonly assumes rational behavior in the pursuit of individual interest. It builds its system of theory on this assumption, without, however, necessarily implying that the statement is wholly true of any flesh-and-blood person or of any total situation. Sociology makes no such assumption, but rather sets itself the problem, among others, of relating economic rationality to religious and moral non-rationality. It makes an assumption of its own—that rationality is limited by ethical and moral controls. It does not assume that this is completely true in fact, but it chooses to analyze social behavior *as if* this assumption were true. Without definite assumptions it is of course impossible to build up a system of thought because cause-and-effect relationships must always be stated in terms of the *conditions* under which they apply.

What is said here of the social sciences applies equally to the physical sciences. In fact, it applies better because the physical sciences are more advanced and hence more obviously systems of abstraction. It is clear, for instance, that a bone being eaten by a dog is susceptible to analysis from the point of view of its *chemical* content (as a set of chemical elements in relation to each other), its *physical* nature (as a system of atoms, molecules, etc.), its *biological* significance (as a kind of bone of a kind of animal, being eaten by another kind of animal), and its *physiological* importance (as a digestible or indigestible substance), not to mention its economic, artistic, moral, or other significance. (To see that it has moral or ethical significance, one has only to imagine that the bone is a human bone.) The concrete object or event is of little significance in and of itself. It becomes significant only as its connections with other objects or events, both past and future, are brought into question, and these are supplied only by the retentive and logical capacity of the mind, in other words by a process of abstraction.

There is no need here to describe the basic assumptions and points of view of the various social sciences. The present work is concerned with only one such science, and hence we need describe only its point of view—and briefly, because the entire book is the best demonstration. Fundamentally, our interest lies in societies as systems (that is, as going concerns) and in social relationships regardless of their type. This does not mean an encyclopedic approach summing up everything that the other social sciences include, but rather a special discipline devoted to the way in which societies achieve their unity and continuity and the way in which they change. It happens that this sort of analysis is usually called sociology, a name that seems as good as any, although it sometimes carries the connotation of a preoccupation with social abnormality.

What, then, are the broad problems to be discussed in the present volume? The major ones are these: First, *social structure*. How may social systems be analyzed into their essential parts or elements? What are the common elements in all social systems? What are the variable features, and what are the limits and causes of their variation? Second, *social functions*. What are the needs peculiar to social systems, and how are these needs met by their structure? Is there an intrinsic relation between organization and function, in the sense that if one varies the other must vary? How do social functions relate to the purposes men carry in their heads? What is the meaning, if any, of social efficiency or inefficiency? Third, *social interaction*. What role do conflict, competition, and cooperation play in human life? What are the dynamic aspects of group behavior—interstimulation, collective symbols, ceremony and ritual? What is the nature of human contact and communication? Fourth, *the individual and his society*. In what ways is human personality a social product? How does a society create and utilize different types of individuals? What are the subjective reactions to different kinds of social situations? Fifth, *social change*. Does social change go in cycles or in a straight line? What factors stimulate change, and what factors retard it? How is the speed of social change measured, and how fast do the different parts of society change with respect to one another?

These are fundamental problems, and the attempt to solve them is a fascinating endeavor. Many great minds have tackled them, giving solutions of one kind or another. Necessarily, our own solutions are far from final. They are neither philosophical nor religious solutions but merely scientific approximations, and science is never final.

The Hazards of Social Science

Although everybody realizes that special obstacles impede the path of social science, not everyone has a clear notion of what they are. It is sometimes said that the social sciences are "youthful" and consequently have not yet had time to achieve scientific maturity. Such an explanation, however, merely poses the problem, for it does not tell why birth should come so much later or "adolescence" last so much longer in this field than in the study of chemistry, physics, or biology. Some say that social phenomena are more complex than other phenomena and that this makes them harder to understand. But as long as any branch of knowledge contains unknown frontiers (as every field does) its degree of complexity remains infinite. The mysteries of matter, organic life, and the astral universe are as deep and unsolved as the mysteries of social life. In fact, they seem to be more complex. Nearly everyone has some notion of social affairs, but the uninitiated are abysmally ignorant of the nature of the atom. Actually we have in social matters a special avenue of knowledge that is denied the natural scientist because we experience social and psychic realities subjectively and can therefore, simply by examining our own motives, gain some insight into why people behave as they do.

What, then, can the hazards of social science be? To understand them calls for an understanding of society itself. In other words it is only through social science that the obstacles can be explained; and, in its attempt to explain them, paradoxically, social science is shackled by these very obstacles. It seems a hopeless circle, but let us try anyway, understanding that the explanation will become clearer as the succeeding chapters unfold themselves.

A social system is always normative. Its integration rests upon the fact that its members carry in their heads, as part of the cultural heritage, the notion that they *ought* or *ought not* to do certain things, that some actions are *right* or *good* and others *wrong* or *bad*. Each person judges himself and his fellows according to these subtle and ubiquitous rules; and any violation is punished by some negative reaction, be it slight or great. An evaluative attitude, an attitude of praise and blame, of accusation and justification, thus pervades every human society. To question the rules, or worse yet, to question the sentiments lying behind them, is to incur certain penalties, the least of which is controversy. The person who tries in his own thinking to escape entirely the moralistic system in order to study behavior objectively, who tries to analyze social norms and values as if they were amoebae or atoms, is quickly branded as an agnostic, cynic, traitor, or worse. Instead of public support for his work, he must count on public hostility.

To protect himself the social scientist usually accepts certain social values (the ones generally agreed upon in his society) and merely studies the means of attaining them. He thus eliminates from his inquiry the very phenomena that from a sociological point of view are the most fundamental bases of social existence. But his failure to adopt a scientific attitude may go still further. He may willingly or unwillingly get involved in controversies—i.e. disputes in which the public has taken sides—and espouse one set of values as against another. In this case he frequently winds up by becoming a special pleader, a propagandist or wishful thinker, the very opposite of a scientist. No one thinks ill of him for this, except those on the other side, because partisanship on public issues is the expected thing.

It is this dual role of the social scientist, the fact that on the one hand he is a member of a normative group and on the other an observer of this same group, that explains the main limitation on his scientific activity. It does no good to *blame* him for his limitations, to hold him responsible for his fuzzy definitions, his inexact methods, innocuous conclusions, erroneous predictions, and pompous vocabulary. These are simply the unconscious means by which he protects himself. He is expected to wear the garb of science, but is forbidden to perform its functions; therefore, he merely goes through a harmless abracadabra while reaching conclusions that everyone, or at least everyone on his side, wants to hear. If he is accused of being unscientific, he merely says that the social sciences are still in their youth and that social phenomena are very complex, or else he says that in social matters it is impossible to be neutral, not realizing, apparently, that such a statement, if taken in an epistemological sense, is self-contradictory.

In any society there are sentiments not to be questioned. They are not even to be studied dispassionately, because the mere mention of their violation in anything but a horrified tone may be taboo. More than one professor has been dismissed from an American university for inquiring into the sex life of the unmarried, for taking an open-minded attitude toward religious dogma, for teaching a course about socialism, or for adopting an unpatriotic attitude. Such subjects, if touched at all, must always be handled circumspectly, with the professor reiterating his devotion to the supreme values. The object of study should not be the values themselves, but violations of them, because violations call for action. Thus if the social scientist studies divorce, he is presumably doing so for the purpose of reducing this "evil." If he studies government, it is for the purpose of removing the obstacles to true democracy, true communism, or true fascism, depending on where he is. In any large and complex society, however, there are other matters on which public opinion is admittedly divided, and these may be discussed more freely. Yet such free discussion does not necessarily mean objective discussion. Every controversy has two sides, and both sides condemn anyone who attempts a purely dispassionate analysis. It is an ancient principle that he who does not agree, disagrees. The social scientist cannot afford to expose the assumptions, interests, and values of *both* sides alike. He must align himself with one or the other side, or risk becoming universally unpopular. If it is prohibition he must be either for or against it. If it is birth control, socialized medicine, Negro equality, labor unionization, woman's suffrage, literary censorship, legalized gambling, or higher taxes he must find reasons why it ought or ought not to be. This is the first question the public asks—which side is he on?—and the public has an exceptional ability or compulsion to read evaluative attitudes into written or spoken statements. Indeed, ordinary language is so saturated with such attitudes that it is virtually impossible to use it without laying oneself open to the charge of partisanship. An attempted dispassionate analysis merely winds up by insulting both sides, or if it is not dealing with a controversial subject but simply with human behavior, it seems satirical.

Much of what passes for social analysis is merely an attempt to assess the blame for something. *Who* is responsible for crime? *Who* is responsible for World War II? *Who* is responsible for high prices? However necessary such assessment of moral responsibility may be for the operation of society, it is not the same thing as causal analysis and often, in fact, obscures the latter.

In some ways the sociologist is faced with more obstacles than other social scientists, precisely because in trying to see society as a whole he is forced to examine the nature of human values. He must subject the mores and the basic institutions to objective analysis. He must deal with religion and the family, for example, in a spirit of secular inquiry rather than in a spirit of awe and taboo. The economist and political scientist, assuming without question the institutional framework, can deal for the most part with rational conduct and popular issues, and so escape some of the sociologist's difficulties. These specialists run into other troubles, however. The literature of political science in particular is permeated by metaphysical and moralistic concepts; sometimes it seems to be more an exercise in ethical theory than in empirical knowledge.

In view of the obstacles confronting social science, some people say there is no such thing, that at best there are merely "social studies." Others believe that social science exists but inconsistently take the view that the practitioner of it cannot be neutral, that he must inevitably take sides. If this means taking sides with reference to the matter under investigation, then it is a denial of science. Without neutral analysis knowledge is impossible. All science is neutral in the sense that the emotions of the investigator do not influence the observation and explanation of the facts. True, there are plenty of scientific controversies. Such controversies are the very breath of science. But they are controversies with reference to theoretical issues, not with reference to moral or political issues; and they are settled by observation and logic, not by propaganda and obfuscation.

Social behavior does not represent some special category of reality intrinsically impervious to systematic study. It is just as amenable to scientific investigation as any other natural phenomenon. The obstacles come, not from the subject matter itself, but from the limitations placed on the investigator by his own society. Consequently, we may look for the greatest development of social science when certain conditions are fulfilled. The first is that the society be so large, complex, and diversified that its citizens require a great amount of exact social knowledge to keep the whole thing going. In such a society the activities that are regarded as sheer means, having only a fluid relation to the ultimate ends, are quite numerous—and so long as they are regarded as means they may be studied with impunity. In such a society, moreover, the division of labor is carried extremely far, so that it seems feasible to meet the need for exact social information through a special group (always small) of persons professionally engaged in social research and teaching. Such a group is given a sort of license to investigate objectively—i.e. is given a certain amount of academic freedom, security of tenure, and scholarly seclusion. In return it is supposed to observe the canons of scientific method and the ethic of unbiased teaching. If one of the group uses his mantle of scientist to give an air of authority to propaganda, or if he converts his classroom into a political platform, he is not acting as a scientist and has no right to demand special immunity from reprisal on the part of those who disagree with him. A democratic state, for example, does not want to give a protected platform to those advocating dictatorship. It may, however, support an objective inquiry into the nature of dictatorships. If, in the classroom or in research, there is any advocacy, it must on the whole be in favor of the established values; yet under certain circumstances and in a limited sense there may be no advocacy at all, but simply analysis.

Modern industrial society favors a certain amount of social science, sociology included. Before the industrial age there was plenty of speculation about social matters, but it was primarily moralistic. Confucius, Plato, Aristotle, Aquinas were concerned with what people ought to do rather than what they really do.[1] It was not until the eighteenth and nineteenth centuries that anything like genuine social science arose. By that time the industrial revolution had created a more complicated society, forcing on scholars a new awareness of social phenomena. It had also led to a more secularized society permitting interpretations of social phenomena that were less religious and moralistic. Finally, the achievements of natural science had popularized scientific method and suggested the possibility that this approach might be applied to the data of society. For reasons mentioned, the success of the new social science was rather slight. The various branches had a slow and gradual development, and are now

[1] Robert M. MacIver, "Sociology," in *Encyclopedia of the Social Sciences.*

still limited in scope and achievement. Nevertheless, it is plain that in our type of society there can be, and is, some social science despite the obstacles.

The Value of Sociology

Of what value, it may be asked, is the study of society? Is it worth the effort it takes?

The answer seems plain. Not only does such study have a value (by almost any standard one adopts) but in a complex society it becomes indispensable. It has, in the first place, a clearly instrumental value in the sense that once certain goals are agreed upon, it helps to determine the most efficient means for reaching these goals. Social policies in a complicated society cannot be carried out simply on the basis of custom and sentiment. They require, in addition, a certain amount of knowledge about the society in question; and the larger and more diversified the society, the greater is the amount of social knowledge required. Furthermore, the broader and more inclusive the policies being pursued, the more important is a sociological as opposed to a purely political or economic type of knowledge. Suppose, for example, that a policy of increasing the birth rate is considered desirable by the majority of a nation's citizens (as in Sweden, France, and England today). The best means for achieving this goal cannot be determined in exclusively economic or political terms because matters of family organization, population dynamics, reproductive customs, and traditional values must be taken into account, and these require a sociological type of analysis.

The contribution of sociological science, in the second place, goes still deeper. In a huge specialized society we are all limited as to the amount of the whole organization and culture that we can experience directly. We each have first-hand experience of only an infinitesimal part of the life of our society. The Nebraska farmer, for instance, cannot be in his lifetime a filing clerk in Washington, a Negro in Harlem, a business man in Chicago, a housewife in Georgia, and a textile worker in Massachusetts. He can hardly know these people intimately. Yet he must live in the same nation with them and must therefore have some appreciation of them. He can get much of his knowledge from hearsay and from realistic stories and novels, but somewhere along the line either he or the people he depends upon to represent him in public affairs must have a more systematic understanding of what the lives of all these people mean to him and to one another, of how the whole is tied together. Our society is so complicated that efficient short-cut avenues to a comprehension of the parts we do not experience directly become necessary. We must have some insight into and appreciation of the motives by which others live and the conditions under which they exist. In this way intolerance, the foe of an integrated society of the modern type, is reduced. In this way decisions with reference to group policy are made more sympathetically and broadly by the ordinary citizen. In this way unity within diversity is achieved.

In the third place there is a personal as opposed to a purely societal advantage in sociological study. One of the marks of an educated person is that he has a perception and appreciation of things that ordinary individuals take for granted. He therefore has a better understanding both of himself and of others, and is more flexible in adjusting to new situations. He is capable of thinking in terms of underlying principles rather than popular stereotypes and is thus better at judging long range consequences. Finally, by a comparative grasp of societies and groups other than his own he is able to see many things as relevant to his existence which would otherwise escape notice. His life in this way becomes richer and fuller than it would otherwise be. This is doubtless why the study of social psychology, social anthropology, and sociology has such an important place today in the so-called liberal arts curriculum.

Obviously the kind of knowledge that counts is not simply descriptive. The fleeting moment, the current event, possesses no significance except as related to past and future occurrences through systematic interpretation. For social knowledge to have value, it must comprehend the basic principles of society as opposed to the mere surface phenomena. Decisions made on the basis of superficial information are likely to yield results exactly opposite to those expected.

Systematic knowledge, of course, depends on techniques of investigation. Without such techniques it is impossible either to make accurate predictions or to check those that are made. In modern society the slow process of trial and error in public policy, with no test of success other than the absence of chaos or the absence of blame, is altogether too slow and costly. Willy-nilly, in order to avoid blame and calamity, individuals and groups seek to use scientific techniques to predict results in advance. Thus every social science, including sociology, becomes increasingly technical as it goes along. Though this is an advantage from the point of view of scientific advance, it is a disadvantage from the point of view of the diffusion of knowledge, and hence special effort must be put into the diffusion process, with particular techniques developing in that sphere as well.

Let us cite a simple illustration of the predictive value of systematic social science. In our cities the construction of public school buildings represents a heavy capital investment. In order to avoid too much or too little investment, each city must know what the future number of school children of various ages is likely to be. This requires some exact knowledge about trends in rural-urban migration and birth and death rates, which in turn depend on broader social changes. The social scientist (usually in this case the population expert) is apt to reach conclusions concerning the future numbers of school children quite at variance with the more superficial opinions held by the majority of citizens. His opinion, however, is likely to save money for these citizens, whereas their opinion if carried into policy would cost them money. Therefore, they are potentially receptive to being educated in this regard, and a part of the task of the expert becomes not merely predicting the future number of school children in the city but also of demonstrating the validity of his results by exposing his techniques.

The maximum usefulness of social science is obtained, seemingly, when a dual task has been accomplished—first, a systematic study of causal relations by persons professionally dedicated to disinterested social analysis; second, a diffusion of the knowledge thus obtained to the general population. In this respect social science is perhaps no different from any other branch of scientific activity. In medicine, for example, it has become increasingly clear that the practitioner alone, guarding his medical knowledge as a private and occult monopoly, cannot insure health to a populace. Instead the public at large must share some of this knowledge; it must be educated in the necessities of general sanitation, personal hygiene, proper diet, protective immunization, etc. Perhaps the task of diffusion is more important and at the same time more difficult in the social field than in the physical sciences, but the difference is a matter of degree only.

In our type of society, then, the scientific study of social mechanisms arises and gets diffused inevitably. The question of the "value of sociology" is therefore not a question of whether or not we should have such a science but simply a question of how it is actually to be used. Clearly it has both social and individual advantages, and these explain its toleration and support despite the normative obstacles in its path.

In setting forth the necessity of social science one must be careful, however, not to imply that all knowledge is useful, or that beliefs and practices having no scientific basis are of necessity socially harmful. We shall see that the normative order itself, so necessary to society and so restrictive for sociology, inevitably contains nonlogical and nonempirical elements and therefore cannot be based exclusively on science. In other words, neither a morality nor an ethic, much less a social system, can be derived solely from science, although it can be an object of science and can profit to a degree from being such an object.

Perspective

Human society, we have said, is unique because it depends on culture. Since culture is a matter of tradition it can and does vary from one group or society to another. It is this eternal cultural variation that complicates the study of human association, particularly because of the high value each group attaches to its own way of doing things and its ignorance or contempt for other ways.

> Most of us harbor the comfortable delusion that our way of doing things is the only sensible if not the only possible one. What is more obvious than eating three meals a day or sleeping at night? Well, in Bolivia there are Indians who think otherwise: they sleep for a few hours, get up to eat a snack, lie down for a second rest, rise for another collation, and so forth; and whenever they feel like it they do not scruple to sleep in the daytime. *We* drive on the right-hand side of the road; and what is more logical for right-handed folk? But the custom of England, Sweden, and Austria is precisely the reverse, though left-handedness is no more common there than elsewhere. But surely it is natural to point with the index-finger? It is not. Many American Indians do so by pouting their lips. Again there is nothing eternally fit about weaning a baby at nine months among the East Africans and the Navaho of Arizona a boy of four or five will come running to take his mother's breast.

> In short, there is only one way of finding out whether any particular idea or custom is natural or only conventional, to wit, experience; and that means not our limited experience in Ottumwa, Iowa, or the United States, or even in Western Civilization as a whole, but among all the peoples the world over.[2]

Countless times in intellectual history a particular mode of behavior has been assumed to be "natural" or innate in man and elaborate theoretical conclusions have been built on this assumption, when in fact the behavior was merely a customary practice of the particular group. To avoid such an error one must acquire perspective; and this, as Lowie says, can be obtained only by studying societies other than our own.

Social science literature published in the United States refers primarily to events in this country. History may appear to be an exception because so heavily devoted to Europe, but the reason for this devotion is precisely that our cultural background is European. We devote far less attention to the history of China and India, though each contains almost as many people as Europe. When we study European history, therefore, we are really in the last analysis studying America. A more genuine exception to ethnocentrism in social science is social anthropology, which studies primitive peoples. But the bulk of American social investigation is investigation of ourselves.

Such localism in social science is understandable. We are naturally more interested in our own society than in any other, because we live in it. But insularity has its drawbacks. Our own folkways and institutions, our own attitudes and sentiments, are so much a part of us that we are largely unaware of them. Our attention gets focused only on the crises and the issues so that our social science is overweighted with a "problems" approach. Analysis is then pursued only to the extent that the practical and often ephemeral problem is solved. The more constant and fundamental features of our social order we take for granted; and when we do think of them, we are likely to regard them as universal and inevitable, as somehow a part of "human nature." Such an attitude is especially detrimental in sociology, which sets itself the task of understanding fundamental norms and institutions. Sociology finds itself in the embarrassing position of attempting to explain things that most people see no point in explain-

[2] Robert H. Lowie, *Are We Civilized?* (New York: Harcourt, Brace, 1929), pp. 3-4. Quoted by permission of the publisher.

ing because these things are "just there" or "in human nature." Tons of printed matter have emerged on the question of socialized medicine, but very little on the theoretical problem of the professional classes in society or the professional service as a social and human relationship. Much has been written on illegitimacy, but practically nothing on legitimacy. Much has been said about taxes, but very little about the institution of property. It almost seems that in social science, phenomena receive attention in inverse ratio to their importance.

The classical economic theory of the 19th century implicitly assumed a certain institutional order. Without this order its principles could not hold true in practice, but the theorists, unconsciously regarding the order as given in the nature of things, felt that they were describing real situations wherever found. The modern efflorescence of state socialism and totalitarian economies, not to mention labor unions, cartels, and other monopolistic controls, clearly shows the degree to which a regime of "free enterprise" depends on certain institutional arrangements that are not rooted in human nature but simply in a particular society at a particular time. In other words, the danger of *implicitly assuming* a certain institutional order is that this order is then not analyzed or explained, and generalizations based on it are given a wider applicability than they actually have.

In sociology every effort must be made to overcome the tendency toward localism, to appreciate the fact of cultural relativity. Otherwise the nature of society and culture cannot be understood. Materials on other societies than our own—on antique civilizations, on foreign nations, on primitive tribes, even on animal societies—must be utilized. Only thus can a general science of society be attained. Only thus can we get perspective and escape the shackles of our own culture.

Summary

Out of one proposition—that man's uniqueness lies in his possession of culture—grow most of the questions discussed in this chapter. For one thing, though social science is itself a part of culture, the main limitation on its development is the existence of cultural norms that may not be discussed. If there is to be a general science of society (as sociology is conceived to be) it must study, among other things, precisely these norms. There is, however, a tendency to evade this necessity by taking the basic institutions for granted and by concentrating on our own society to study the more ephemeral and practical issues of the day. In this way some of the basic problems of sociology are neglected. Also, since culture is transmitted by communication rather than by inheritance, it is not uniform for the species as a whole (as in the case of social patterns among animals) but varies from one society to another; hence the concentration on our own society to the exclusion of others makes difficult a sufficient degree of generality. A general science of society cannot be built by the study of one society alone but only by the study of many different societies. It must be able to gauge the limits of variation in social arrangements and thus to find what is characteristic of all human society as well as what is characteristic of only a few. The aim of the present volume being to present the principles of general sociology, heavy reliance is placed on comparative data. The value of such a comparative approach will, it is hoped, become clearer as the discussion proceeds.

References

Ruth Benedict, *Patterns of Culture* (New York: Penguin Books, 1946), Chap. 1, "The Science of Custom," and Chap. 2, "The Diversity of Cultures."

The comparative study of cultures as necessary to genuine social science. Very readable.

F. Stuart Chapin, "Social Obstacles to the Acceptance of Existing Social Science Knowledge," *Social Forces,* Vol. 26 (Oct. 1947), pp. 7-12.

Discusses eight obstacles to the acceptance of social science.

Emile Durkheim, *The Rules of Sociological Method* (Chicago: University of Chicago Press, 1938).

Translation of a classic statement.

Morris Ginsberg, *Sociology* (New York: Holt, 1934), Chap. 1, "Scope and Method of Sociology."

A typical armchair discussion, but rather informative. The author is a British sociologist.

E. Greenwood, *Experimental Sociology* (New York: Columbia University Press, 1944).

Shows the progress in the development of experimental techniques.

Georges Gurvitch and Wilbert E. Moore (eds.), *Twentieth Century Sociology* (New York: Philosophical Library, 1945), especially Chaps. 1-3, and 18.

Each chapter describes a branch or aspect of sociology.

Robert K. Merton, "Sociological Theory," *American Journal of Sociology,* Vol. 50 (May 1945), pp. 462-473.

This whole issue of the JOURNAL *is devoted to contemporary sociology and its various branches, together with a 50-year history. Merton's article is outstanding on the nature of sociological theory and research, lucidly set forth.*

Gwynne Nettler, "Toward a Definition of the Sociologist," *American Sociological Review,* Vol. 12 (Oct. 1947), pp. 553-560.

A concise clarification of the existing confusion about the nature of the creature, the sociologist.

Robert W. O'Brien, *Readings in General Sociology* (Palo Alto: Pacific Books, 1947), Chap. 1, "The Scientific Method."

Contains several good readings on the application of quantitative methods in social science.

Vilfredo Pareto, *The Mind and Society* (New York: Harcourt, Brace, 1935), Vol. 1, Chap. 1, "The Scientific Approach."

Trenchant exposition of the scientific method in social science. Pareto is a past master at exposing the unscientific procedures of social scientists.

Talcott Parsons, *The Structure of Social Action* (New York: McGraw-Hill, 1937), Chap. 1.

The nature of scientific method and scientific theory as applied to social action. One of the best statements in sociological literature.

Edwin R. A. Seligman, "What Are the Social Sciences?" *Encyclopedia of the Social Sciences,* Vol. 1, pp. 3-7.

A good statement of the usual definitions of the various social sciences. See also the articles on "Sociology," "Anthropology," etc. in this valuable encyclopedia.

Edward A. Shils, *The Present State of American Sociology* (Glencoe, Ill.: Free Press, 1948).

A rather brief critical assessment of current work in American sociology, by one whose eye seems somewhat jaundiced but well informed.

Louis Wirth, "Responsibility of Social Science," *Annals* of the American Academy of Political and Social Science, Vol. 249 (Jan. 1947), pp. 143-151.

Analyzes the nature of social research and the resistance offered to it. This whole volume of the Annals *is devoted to the "Social Implications of Modern Science."*

Florian Znaniecki, *The Method of Sociology* (New York: Farrar & Rinehart, 1934), Chap. 1, "The Selection and Determination of Scientific Data"; Chap. 2, "The Principles of Selection of Cultural Data"; Chap. 3, "The Data of Sociology."

An illuminating contribution to the perennial problems of how one searches for facts and constructs theories in the science of society.

CHAPTER II

HUMAN VERSUS ANIMAL SOCIETY

HUMAN beings are not the only creatures who live in societies. Ants, termites, birds, monkeys, apes, and countless other animals do the same. It would be surprising then if human society bore no relation to some of the animal societies. Indeed, the very fact that man as an organism has evolved from lower forms suggests that his society has also developed from animal prototypes. This conclusion, fully proven by scientific evidence, does not mean that human society is the same as animal society or that knowledge of the latter is an adequate substitute for knowledge of the former. It means simply that human society is a natural phenomenon like any other object of scientific investigation, and that in trying to study this society as a whole (as the present volume tries to do) one gains the broadest perspective by first viewing it in its evolutionary setting. Only by seeing what man has in common with other creatures can it be seen in what ways he is unique.

Before dealing with types of societies and with the emergence of the human type, let us first discuss the basic features of *any* society. What, in other words, are the universal characteristics of society, and what are the fundamental conditions that must be met before these characteristics can appear?

Basic Features of Any Society

All societies, whether animal or human, have certain things in common which lead to their being classed together. In the first place, they all involve a certain level of association, a level closer and more intricate than a mere aggregation but looser and less complex than an organism. In the second place, the units they bring together on this level are not cells or organs, but individuals. Before we can understand societies it is therefore necessary to know something about aggregations on the one hand and organisms on the other.

An aggregation consists of individuals collected together merely because of their passive subjection to the same external conditions. Thus a flood may bring together an accidental collection of animals or insects. Similarly, temperature, moisture, gravity, light, or any other external stimulus arousing a common tropistic reaction may draw a concentration of creatures responsive to this stimulus but not to one another. Such collections bear no more resemblance to society than does a dust storm, as anyone can see who has watched insects swarm around an outdoor light.

The same holds true if, instead of tropisms, we consider appetites as a basis of association. We are still on the level of aggregation if the appetite is satisfied directly and individually by the external environment, as with animals coming to a common water hole. It is only when other organisms in the aggregate *help* in the satisfaction of the appetite or *themselves constitute the means of satisfaction or response* that the basis is laid for a true society. If a pack of wolves kill game that could not otherwise be killed, they are to that extent constituting a society. If wasp larvae secrete a thin sweetish liquid that is sucked by the worker wasps who feed them, this mutual activity, called trophallaxis, constitutes a social relation. In short, the tropisms and appetites constitute a basis of societal association only when they knit the individuals together in a network of mutual stimulus and response. Without such mutual responsiveness there is merely an accidental aggregation which dissolves as soon as the external stimulus disappears. The aggregation thus has no power of self-perpetuation, no capacity for restitution or resistance, no force of internal unity. In actual cases, of course, the exact line between aggregation and society is sometimes hard to draw. There are societies of exceedingly low grade that resemble aggregations. These may lack some of the features we ordinarily associate with the term society, such as "mutual awareness." It is wise to bear in mind, too, that a social relationship—i.e. one of mutual stimulation—is not tantamount to society. It is only when there is a *system* of such relationships that we may properly use the term.

Since a society embraces organisms that mutually stimulate each other, the idea may arise that it can be understood by studying its constituent individuals. This idea contains a germ of truth, but it also contains a fallacy. To see the difficulty requires a brief examination of the difference between organism and society.

The organism is a complex system of relationships between cells. Being nothing more it is dependent on the cells for its existence; and yet it has a unity and structure of its own that cannot be grasped purely in terms of its cells. The latter, indeed, live and die while the organism continues for a much longer period. The organism has a life history running through the stages of growth, maturity, decay, and death. It has two primary needs: nutrition, so that it may have the energy to live, and protection, so that it may have the chance to live. The ultimate resultant in nature, however, is not the perpetuation of the particular organism itself, which must soon die, but the perpetuation of the species. So the organism has still another fundamental need which, as it were, is built into its structure. This is the need for reproduction. After reproduction has been fully accomplished the organism decays and disappears. Clearly, since part of its nutriment has gone to the offspring, the nutritional need of the organism is partly subservient to the reproductive need. Also, since the protective system helps the organism not only to find and guard its own nutriment but also to accomplish its reproduction, the protective need is similarly subservient. In fact the three needs—protection, nutrition, and reproduction—are mutually dependent, all being contributory to the perpetuation of what is really an emergent reality, the species.

Like an organism, a society is a system of relations, but relations between organisms themselves rather than between cells. It has like the organism a determined structure; and the parts of this structure when in operation contribute to the existence of the whole, giving it a continuity apart from that of the constituent individuals. It is this possession of a continuity and structure of its own that makes it impossible to reduce the study of society merely to a study of its individual members. It is like a house which, though composed of bricks, nails, mortar, and pieces of lumber, cannot be understood purely in terms of these materials; it has a form and function as a complete house.

Life in society serves as one mode of adjustment to the environment, giving the strength of numbers and of specialization to the associated individuals and thus aiding them in protection, nutrition, and reproduction. It is of benefit not only to its members but also to the species. Some of the individual members may be readily sacrificed in order that the society and hence the species may go on. Its value as a mode of adjustment is attested by the frequency with which it has emerged in evolutionary history. Wheeler, for example, has found that a societal mode of existence has emerged independently in erstwhile solitary species of ants no less than thirty times.[1] Among mammals it is virtually impossible to find any species that is completely solitary. A societal mode of existence therefore seems to have considerable survival value.

The frequent emergence of society in evolutionary history should not, however, blind us to one fact: The organism, by definition, is essential to the survival of any species. Society, on the other hand, is essential to the survival of only those species that have become adapted to a social mode of existence. Species of solitary bees have survived as long as social species, yet apart from their communal hives the social types could not now exist.[2] Similarly *Homo sapiens*, who has been a social animal ever since he became a species, inheriting this trait from his animal ancestors, could not exist apart from his own peculiar kind of society. Once it has emerged in a line of descent, society thus becomes a biological necessity and affects the direction of organic change.

The emergence of society may be viewed as one of the great steps in evolution—a step that some species have taken and others not. It ranks with the emergence of the cell, with the emergence of the multicellular organism, and with the emergence of the vertebrate system as one of the crucial advances in living development. Like the other steps it represents a new synthesis of old materials, possessing unique qualities not to be found in the old materials considered separately. It is thus a true example of what is called emergent evolution.

To realize that society is a true emergent, one need not trace its independent origin in countless animal types. One need merely grasp the difference between it and the organisms of which it is composed. Several decades ago it was fashionable to compare society to an organism, the idea being to demonstrate that a social system is, after all, a system. The analogy was helpful but never perfect. The cells

[1] Wm. Morton Wheeler, *Essays in Philosophical Biology* (Cambridge: Harvard University Press, 1939), p. 155.

[2] Wm. Morton Wheeler, *The Social Insects* (New York: Harcourt, Brace, 1928), pp. 81ff.

of the organism are too rigidly fixed in their mutual relations, too completely subordinated to the organism, and too specialized to be called members of a society. They are not so spatially detached and independently mobile as are the latter. So the organism is not, strictly speaking, a "society of cells." The organism possesses a sensorium and (in the higher forms at least) consciousness, which no society possesses. Moreover, the rather fixed life history of the organism is not characteristic of society. Undoubtedly there are societal stages somewhat similar to growth, maturity, and decay, but as one would expect from the lesser unity of society, they are not nearly so definite as the organic stages. Finally, the types of organisms are clearer, more numerous, and easier to classify than the types of societies. For these reasons the analogy between organism and society is always at best an analogy and not an identity. It is a poorer analogy in the case of mammalian than in the case of insect societies [3] and for this reason is of no particular value in studying mammalian sociology. In the case of human society it is a completely false trail despite its occasional revival by a popular writer such as Oswald Spengler. If, then, society is different from the organisms that compose it, it must be something added to these. It must be a new emergent.

By way of summary we can say that association in the sense of spatial and temporal togetherness occurs throughout the living world. It is found in the cell, which is an organization of complex molecules; in the organism, which is an organization of cells; and in the society, which is an organization of organisms. What we call society then is merely one level of association. It involves a closer and more mutual system of interaction than does the accidental aggregation, but still a looser and less defined system than the organism. The fact that it is an association of organisms makes it qualitatively different from the organism. It adds a new element to the species and is thus a true emergent.

Societal Necessities

As going, living systems all societies have certain common needs that must be met if they are to continue. At the most general level these needs are independent of the particular kind of society and may therefore be regarded as primary needs. They define the necessary

[3] Wheeler has carried the parallel between an ant society and an organism to a brilliant and extreme perfection. See his *Essays, loc. cit.*, pp. 3-27.

conditions for the existence of any society no matter what the species or the circumstances.

The primary societal needs may be classified under four major categories as follows: first, those having to do with the individuals in society, viewed as physical organisms; second, those having to do with the division of function as between the different individuals; third, those having to do with the mutual cohesion of the individuals within the society; and fourth, those having to do with the perpetuation of the society through many generations. We may characterize these categories more briefly as needs for population, specialization, solidarity, and continuity.

The first kind of need arises from the fact that a society is composed of separate organisms. Without these organisms—that is, without a population—it could not exist, any more than an organism could exist without cells. Therefore any society, whether insect, animal, or human, must take care of the three needs previously mentioned as characterizing the organism. It must make suitable provision for the nourishment of its population by exploitation of the natural resources of the habitat and division of the fruits of this exploitation. It must provide for the protection of the members against natural dangers and parasitic or predatory enemies. And it must provide for the continual replacement of its population by facilitating contact between the sexes and care of new offspring. These are needs that each creature provides for itself in solitary species. All that a social system does is to facilitate their satisfaction through group interaction of some kind. The very introduction of group coöperation, however, creates new needs that refer not to the individual organisms but to the maintenance of the social system. These additional needs are not present in solitary species, but they are present in every social species.

To begin with, if there is to be group coöperation there must be some mode of dividing the labor, some mode of specialization among the group's members. The degree of specialization may be very slight, as in a herd of cattle, or it may be very great, as in a beehive. The degree of specialization is one important measure of the intricacy of the social system, but in any case, if there is a society at all, there is some division of labor. Furthermore, in any society there must be some mode of contact between the members and some motivation for such contact. Above all, there must be mutual tolerance among the societal members as well as some way of distinguishing members from nonmembers. Otherwise there would be no essential cohesiveness in the group. Finally, the group itself, or at least its structure and character, must be perpetuated. There must be some mechanism by which the system of relationships is continued beyond the lifespan of any one individual or generation.

So important for general sociology are these universal necessities, applicable as they are to every kind of society from insect to man, that a brief summary outline is now given:

I. Maintenance of the population.
  a. Provision of nutriment
  b. Protection against injury
  c. Reproduction of new organisms.

II. Division of function among population.

III. Solidarity of the group.
  a. Motivation of contact between members.
  b. Motivation of mutual tolerance and resistance to outsiders.

IV. Perpetuation of the social system.

It must be stressed that the needs listed under Class I are characteristic of solitary as well as social species. All that happens under social conditions is that these same needs—for nutriment, protection, and reproduction—are met with the aid of a new mechanism, social organization, which in turn has certain needs of its own if it is to perform its instrumental function.

One could make the list still simpler by speaking of only one need—the need for societal survival—all the rest being instrumental to this one. Or one could go further and say that the final need is for the survival of the species, society itself being purely instrumental. Our interest, however, lies not so much in the final result as in the societal mechanisms and conditions by which the result comes about. Lest the term "need" seem to involve us in evaluation or teleology, let us say that all that is meant by it is a necessary condition for the existence of society. It is not meant to imply that the members of a social group realize and strive for these requirements or that they should do so. We simply say that societies, like everything else, require certain conditions before they can exist; and our interest attaches to the various kinds of mechanisms that have been evolved to supply these conditions.

Bio-Social Systems

The fact that different kinds of societies manifest extremely diverse means of satisfying the societal needs gives us a fundamental basis for classifying the types of society. The broadest division, as indicated in the previous chapter, turns on whether the social patterns are determined by heredity or by culture. Societies having patterns fixed by heredity may be called bio-social, whereas those having patterns fixed by culture may be called socio-cultural. The division is an uneven one, however, because all social species except man exhibit the first general type (the bio-social) while only man exhibits the second (the socio-cultural). Yet since man is so widespread and culture so variable as to permit wide variation *within* the species, the classification is not so unbalanced as first appears. In other words, each of the two classes contains many subtypes; those of the bio-social class are associated with different species, those of the socio-cultural class with different cultures. The rest of the present chapter deals with bio-social types and handles the socio-cultural simply as a general class in contrast to the bio-social. The remainder of the book is then devoted to socio-cultural, or human, society in detail.

In the nonhuman world every social system meets its basic needs primarily through mechanisms determined by heredity. The social responses of each individual spring from an inherited tendency to react in a fixed manner to stimuli provided by other members of the group. The totality of these responses, exhibited by all the members in the interacting group, constitutes the social system. Not every member reacts in the same way, however, because the physical characteristics of the various individuals differ in predetermined ways. The division of labor is accomplished by the physiological specialization of the members. Since the perpetuation of the social system is accomplished through the transmission of the genes, any change in the social order must come primarily from a change in the germ plasm. The society is therefore a function of organic evolution. It is fundamentally biological in character and for this reason the name bio-social is applied.[4] Organic evolution, as we know, is a matter of continuous modification of the hereditary structure of the organism. In the case of bio-social species the hereditary structure has simply been modified so as to adapt the organism to life in society. The chief way to understand bio-social systems is therefore to investigate the hereditary mechanisms built into the structure of each individual member.

The fact that all nonhuman societies are bio-social in type does not mean that they are all alike. The variety of patterns capable of being transmitted by genetic inheritance is astounding. The obvious difference between a termite and a bird society, for example, is so great that the two can be classified together only on the very broadest of principles. The termites have an elaborate division of labor, a tight cohesiveness, and a socially-constructed environment. The birds have a minimum of each of these and manifest a greater amount of flexibility in individual behavior. Yet in both cases the social reactions are primarily inherited.

Although bio-social systems exhibit astounding differences as between species, they are, within the same species, quite standardized. Being hereditary, each kind of society is characteristic of the species as a whole. Human society, on the other hand, shows no such uniformity. Though all human beings today are members of the same species their social patterns differ remarkably from one time and place to another. This is because their patterns are determined not by genetic inheritance but by cultural transmission.

MAMMALIAN SOCIETY

It should not be inferred that heredity has nothing to do with human society. The fact that socio-cultural groups appear only among human beings should itself dispel this notion. The humanoid stem alone has shown that it has a biological capacity for the development of culture, and the general traits of this stem determine at least in part the limits of cultural variation. It is not that on the human level the socio-cultural system has entirely displaced the bio-social, but rather that the element of culture has been added. Culture has been built onto and has fundamentally modified a previously existing bio-social system. Indeed, human society with all its cultural

[4] Carl J. Warden, *The Emergence of Human Culture* (New York: Macmillan, 1936), pp. 17ff.

trappings developed out of an ancestral anthropoid group that was bio-social and which had itself arisen from the general mammalian type of group. Strictly speaking, therefore, one should designate human society as bio-socio-cultural, although the term is clumsy. In any case one must keep the characteristics of all mammalian societies in mind if one is to understand the particular kind found in either apes or man. The bio-social matrix is just as important to the understanding of human society as is the cultural matrix, although the latter is the element that gives human society its uniqueness.

One characteristic of all mammalian social groups as distinguished from those of the insects is the minimum degree of bodily differentiation among their members. Any permanent bodily specialization that occurs is along sex lines, and even this is not great. The difference in size, strength, and shape as between a cow and a bull, a tomcat and a female cat, a male chimpanzee and a female chimpanzee, and a man and a woman is not pronounced. There are plenty of mammalian species in which it is difficult to tell the male and female apart until the genital organs are examined. In the case of human beings there are occasional instances in which a woman has dressed and passed for years as a man without detection. Highly developed insect societies, on the other hand, show a greater differentiation between male and female than any mammalian group. But they do not stop there. As is well known, they go on to differentiate each sex into two or more castes. The females are commonly divided (by hereditary and dietary mechanisms) into queens and workers, and the difference between the two is so great that unsuspecting naturalists have sometimes described them as different species. Among the Carebara ants, for instance, the queen is several thousand times larger than the workers. In some ant societies the sterile female workers themselves are split up into additional castes. There may even be distinct kinds of queens and distinct kinds of males in the same species.[5] But nowhere among mammals does such polymorphism within the same sex occur.

The absence of structural specialization within the female sex has profound importance for mammalian society, because it rules out the possibility of limiting the function of reproduction to a few females only, freeing the rest for other functions. There cannot be any mam-

5 Wm. Morton Wheeler, *Social Life Among the Insects* (New York: Harcourt, Brace, 1923), pp. 136-143, 158-161.

malian queen who is structurally adapted for continuous reproduction and nothing else, or any sterile female workers. Instead each female must normally both work and reproduce. It will appear later that in a human industrial society the core of the "woman problem" lies precisely in the difficulty of integrating the reproductive with the nonreproductive functions. Furthermore, since every mammalian female is normally capable of reproduction, the basis is laid for sex to play a wider role in mammalian than in insect society. The ants, for example, have succeeded in relegating sex to a minor episode preceding the founding of a new colony. Once mated, the queen carries a lifetime store of sperm in her spermatheca, these being kept alive in her body and used as needed for fertilizing her tremendous egg production. In this way the social insects have virtually eliminated sex relations from group life and have thus given greater emphasis to the food appetite as the driving and integrating force. It should be added that because of the reproductive capacity of the queen most insect societies are simply one tremendous family, the members of which sometimes run into tens of thousands. The mammalian family is much smaller; and in contrast to the insect system the society is often, at least in the higher forms, composed of more than one family.

A second important characteristic of mammalian groups is the degree to which social responses are learned rather than completely inherited. In the case of the subhuman mammalian types this may seem to contradict what was said previously about nonhuman groups being biologically determined, but it is more of a qualification than a contradiction. The truth is that the higher nonhuman mammals are capable of a good deal of learning, and part of what they learn is acquired in the social group. But such learning is not cultural in character. It does not involve symbolic communication but rather direct experience, and is therefore much more limited in scope and importance than cultural learning. It may be that "the chimpanzee mother, apparently with definite intent, encourages and in many ways aids her infant to . . . walk, climb, and eventually to run about and play," [6] but she does not *tell* her infant how she walked when she was herself an infant or say to him what kind of a chimpanzee he

[6] Robt. M. Yerkes and A. W. Yerkes, "Social Behavior in Infrahuman Primates," in Carl Murchison (ed.), *Handbook of Social Psychology* (Worcester: Clark University, 1935), p. 1013. Social learning in animals is discussed at length in Otto Klineberg, *Social Psychology* (New York: Holt, 1940), Chap. II.

should be when he grows up. The social learning of animals is more by example than precept. It cannot convey the past or the future and cannot therefore achieve an accumulated tradition of techniques and ideas. Nevertheless, the fact that it occurs shows that there is in mammalian society a basis for the emergence of culture as occurred in the human stem, and that there is a marked contrast between mammalian and insect society in the amount of learning exhibited.

The greater flexibility of mammalian social behavior is due to several factors. Mammals are complex organisms with a resulting capacity for modification. They have, comparatively speaking, a long life-span and hence an extended period of immaturity during which the complex organism can adjust its innate responses to the demands of the environment. Being warm blooded and viviparous they require an extended contact between parent and offspring; the nursing of the young from the *mammary* glands gives the entire class of animals its name. During its slow maturation the organism gradually learns through trial and error the patterns for which it has the inherent capacity. This is why the phenomenon of play is so prominent in mammalian childhood. Part of each individual's experience lies in its social contacts with others, particularly its parents, and it therefore has an opportunity to learn social responses by repeated trials and by example. The mammalian social group thus does not rest on the strictly fixed innate patterns of social behavior that the insect society manifests. More is left to conditioning. The social system exhibits a greater degree of indeterminacy. This means that it is less integrated. It also means that every mammalian species is to some extent social, whereas many insects, even some bees and wasps (though no ants), are solitary. Yet the looseness of mammalian society makes it possible in most species for the mature animal to shift for himself; hence mammals have a greater capacity than insects for being social part of the time and solitary another part of the time.

If mammals have such a superior capacity to learn, the question may be raised as to what compensatory advantage the insects have. Nobody believes that in the struggle for survival the insects really have their backs to the wall. The answer is that they have taken one direction, the mammals another. The insects are small creatures and therefore can exist in great numbers. They are also short-lived. This means that they are rapid breeders. In some species of African termites, for instance, the queen can lay eggs at the rate of 30,000 per day. Necessarily the insect mortality is exceedingly high, the turnover of generations very rapid; but since the fertility is also enormous the result is that biological adaptation through mutation and natural selection can be achieved rapidly. It has been noted in this connection that insects soon tend to develop strains that are immune to certain insecticides. The advantage the insects have, then, is that their hereditary mechanisms can change speedily. They can experience and try out thousands of mutations in a short span of time. For them heredity offers a flexible instrument for environmental adaptation. In the case of the larger, longer-lived, slower-breeding mammals, on the other hand, fixed hereditary mechanisms are a stumbling block. The mammals have relied more and more heavily on learned responses. They have not won the battle with the insects but they are holding their own. They have evolved a type of society which features learning, and in the case of man at least, this mode of adjustment has paid rich dividends.

PRIMATE SOCIETY

Since the primates are the highest order of mammals, they all (including man) exhibit certain bio-social traits that represent simply exaggerations of basic mammalian characteristics. The exaggerations, however, have the effect of producing a more complicated and in the case of man a greatly different type of society. By way of illustration let us begin with the reproductive function.

Monkeys, apes, and men, in common with other mammals, are not separated into anatomically distinct castes. Not only is there an absence of physical specialization within the same sex, but the sexes themselves are not sharply different. This absence of organic specialization within and between the two sexes, together with a roughly equal sex ratio at birth, has the effect of giving all mature members of the society a chance to participate in reproduction. Sex therefore becomes an important element in group cohesion. So much is true of all mammals, but the primates have gone one step further. They, as distinct from the other mammals, have neither a definite mating season nor a continuously repeated cycle of oestrous and anoestrous—that is, no period of rut in the male or heat in the female. Instead, the female like the male is capable of sexual intercourse at all times; she has a menstrual rather than an oestrous cycle. It is true that in some species (e.g. baboon, macaque, howler, chimpanzee) there is a definite period of enhanced desire at the time of ovulation—a time marked by swelling and coloration of the sexual skin, which acts as an erotic stimulus to the male; but in practically all species, despite this periodicity, both male and female are capable at all times of responding to sexual stimuli. As a result the constant association of the two sexes is assured and sex is made a continual and pervasive basis of group cohesion.[7]

In addition, as compared to the lower mammals the primates possess a more complex sensori-motor equipment. Their eyes are keener, their brains more developed, their behavior more flexible and intricate. As we might expect their stage of immaturity lasts longer. These traits—neural complexity and long infancy—mean that the primates have a greater chance of being *conditioned* within the group environment. The continually present sexual drive, for instance, receives extensive conditioning, with the result that among the primates sexual behavior is not simply automatic and reflexive but is associated with numerous stimuli that are themselves nonsexual. A study of the chimpanzee's sex development indicates that this animal must, like human beings, learn the sexual act.[8] From his earliest days he gradually masters all the assorted movements that later make possible the coördinated act of intercourse, and by engaging in sexual play he perfects this act long before reaching sexual maturity. The primates also learn to adapt the sexual response to the exigencies of group life. They "prostitute" themselves by introducing sexual stimuli into intrinsically non-sexual situations.[9] In such cases their sexual responses have no connection with libidinous appetite but are used instead as a means of obtaining certain advantages.

So much for the primate *capacity* to be conditioned; what produces the *necessity* for it? Zuckerman points out that monkeys and apes live in a society characterized by a system of dominance.[10] Each member of the group enjoys a precarious position determined by the competitive interaction of his dominant characteristics with those

[7] S. Zuckerman, *The Social Life of Monkeys and Apes* (New York: Harcourt, Brace, 1932), Chaps. III, IX.

[8] Harold C. Bingham, "Sex Development in Apes," *Comp. Psych. Monographs,* Vol. V (Baltimore, 1928). Among feral men—i.e. persons long isolated from their fellows as children—an almost complete lack of sexual interest has been noted. See J. A. L. Singh and Robert M. Zingg, *Wolf-Children and Feral Man* (New York: Harpers, 1942), pp. 187, 239.

[9] Zuckerman, *op. cit.,* p. 152.

[10] *Op. cit.,* pp. 312-314.

of his fellows. The degree of his dominance determines how his bodily appetites will be satisfied—the number of females he will possess, the amount of food he will eat, the freedom from attack he will enjoy. Combined with the constant presence of sexuality the system of dominance produces the "prostitution" mentioned above. Whether male or female, young or old, each animal adapts himself to his competitive social system partly through sexual reactions. By the use of sexual stimuli he can sometimes obtain an advantage that would otherwise be denied him by more dominant members of the group. For example, if a weaker baboon secures food and a stronger one comes to take it away from him, the weaker animal may present himself sexually, no matter if his sex is the same as that of the aggressor. If he thus succeeds in diverting the more dominant animal's attention, he can swallow his food.

Dominance characterizes all mammalian social groups. The primates are peculiar only in the pervasiveness and flexibility of it. All of their activities tend to be oriented with reference to it; and the larger the social group, the more noticeable is the phenomenon. It is most extreme in large groups such as those of baboons, least noticeable in the stable family groups of the gibbons.[11]

Within the family group dominance is structured in terms of age and sex. It is therefore more fixed and less competitive, and for this reason the family group operates to a certain degree to protect its members from the wider system of dominance. But in order to understand how the family group is held together, it is necessary to refer again to the constant sex attraction. It is this sex factor that helps to hold not only the entire simian group together but also the "marital" group. In most primate species the share of females going to each male is determined by the scale of masculine dominance. The male and his female or females tend to move together either alone or as a part of the larger horde.

In the lower mammals the link between male and female is constantly broken and remade, the sexual bond becoming effective only at oestrous periods and the intervening time being taken by pregnancy and lactation in the female and by preoccupation elsewhere in the male. Hence the lower mammalian family usually consists of

[11] C. R. Carpenter, "A Field Study in Siam of the Behavior and Social Relations of the Gibbon (Hylobates Lar)," *Comp. Psych. Monographs,* Vol. 16 (Baltimore, 1940), pp. 184ff.

mother and offspring. Even this, however, is of fairly short duration because the offspring quickly become self-sufficient. In the primates the long period of infancy insures a more protracted mother-child relationship; and since the female does not have a litter but generally only one offspring at a time, her family group is small. With the constant sexual attraction holding the male to the female, the simian or anthropoid family therefore differs from the lower mammalian family in being a bi-parental unit more durable, more balanced, and less numerous. Usually there are "bachelors," males that have not been able to secure any females. These may be attached to some particular family group by their interest in the females, with whom they commit "adultery" when the "overlord" is not looking, or they may live in a bachelor group.

The primates, as against the other mammals, show a noteworthy development of communicative mechanisms. They manifest a wide range of vocalization, facial expression, bodily posture, and manual exploration. It is their complex sensori-motor equipment that makes possible this diversified interactional behavior. They are able to *learn* that particular sounds or movements coming from another monkey or ape indicate certain probable behavior in the future. Any mammal can do the same, but the primates can do it better.

Carpenter describes how the infant learns to orient itself with reference to the mother by distant signals.

> The mother prevents the infant from clinging to unsuitable parts of her body and forces it to cling in such a way that it will be comfortable for her and will not interfere unduly with her movements. After a short period of training, the infant clings consistently in positions . . . which fittingly relate to the mother's behavior. . . . During exploratory responses of the very early gibbon infant, it leaves its mother for short distances. If the mother needs to move away while the infant is separated from her, she reaches for the infant, grasps it and puts it on her belly and it assumes a position suitable for being carried. Gradually the mother's motor components of these interactive responses with the baby are reduced. . . . When the mother is ready to move, she merely looks for the infant, assumes a suitable posture for receiving it and then the infant comes and climbs to its position. Later the stance of the mother, a quick look in the direction of the infant or a limited movement of the hand is sufficient. In time, the control of the mother may be effected through patterns of sound, signaling the anticipated movement.

> . . . This is one example of how contact control is replaced, through learning, by more symbolic control.[12]

Zuckerman points out that apes and monkeys "rival us in the interest, at any rate the immediate interest, they show in their environment. They are the only other animals that have hands—which, as Watt wrote, 'like the stereoscopic eye, can go round and through things. . . .' Kohts found that the Rhesus monkey very nearly equals us in the variety of minute movements which its fingers can make." Zuckerman adds that in their environment the most interesting thing to monkeys is other monkeys, and that this interest "in the movements of their fellows is an obvious outcome of their social lives." The individual "enjoys only such social and material advantages as he is able to withhold from his fellows. For this reason a monkey usually reacts in some degree to every movement of neighboring animals."[13] It is not strange, then, that he learns to respond in an appropriate way to social situations no matter whether the cue is vocal, gestural, postural, or all three.

But a peculiarity of primate "communication" needs to be noted. Monkeys and apes learn to respond much better than they learn to stimulate others. The cries they emit, the postures they assume, the expressions they wear are for the most part unlearned or at least automatic responses. This is proved by the fact that the vocalizations of each species are specific for that species. Within the same species as between one group and another there are no differences in range or type of vocalization. The members of one species cannot acquire the mode of vocalization used by the other. They can learn to respond to the typical vocalizations of the other species, just as a dog can learn to respond to human words, but they cannot learn to "speak" this new "language." In sum, the vocalization of the subhuman primates is apparently inherited rather than acquired, although its application in specific situations is seemingly learned.

Additional evidence for this conclusion is that several investigators have tried without success to teach anthropoids to speak. One set of animals learned "to brush their teeth, to spit, to eat with a spoon, to go to bed, and a hundred other things which the family was doing." But they did not learn to speak. In another case an orangutan had her tongue repeatedly pressed back with a spatula for

[12] *Op. cit.*, p. 166.
[13] *Op. cit.*, pp. 156, 169.

articulation of the hard "d" or "k" sound. "Almost pathetic was the way in which the docile little animal was trying her best to cooperate without apparently grasping the point. After a time she offered to push the spatula against her tongue with her own hands. . . . But what it was all about, or that she might utilize the lesson, quite likely never entered her consciousness." The investigator properly concluded "that the apes do not possess the faculty of language in the proper sense of the word." Similar results were obtained by another investigator who, working with the gibbon, concluded that its sounds, like those of other mammals, merely express emotions and do not convey objective meaning. "Utterances relieve the utterer; there is no semblance of their being purposive as regards conveying information. The chimpanzee, in fact, does not confine himself to vocal utterances: when frightened he rattles a tin pan or thumps the wall of his cage. It is clear that we are beyond what can profitably be construed as language when we are driven to include the rattling of pans.

"All in all, the data at hand are unanimous to the effect that the speech faculty of the apes is substantially on a par with that of a normal six-months old human infant; namely, nil. When we inquire why this is, it seems likely that however we may paraphrase it in more technical terms, the old reason literally holds: animals do not talk because they have nothing to say." The structure of the ape's mouth parts is so similar to man's that he could undoubtedly make close approximations to human speech. "Yet he never tries to speak, nor apparently can he be induced to try, no matter how close his associations with humans." [14]

Clearly there are different levels of communication in terms of the degree to which symbolism is carried. One level involves what may be called the anticipatory symbol. Through past experience the animal learns that an initial part of an action can stand for the completed action. The dog may know what is coming when the master picks up the whip or the gun; the infant ape may know what to expect when its mother puts herself in a position to carry it. Another level is the expressive symbol, in which the internal state of the animal is accompanied by a characteristic cry, gesture, or expression. The members of the group learn to associate these expressions with

[14] Quotations and paraphrased material taken, with permission, from A. L. Kroeber, "Sub-Human Culture Beginnings," *Quarterly Review of Biology*, Vol. 3 (Sept. 1928), pp. 328-330. References to original research will be found in this excellent article.

the moods and acts of their fellows, and they adjust their behavior accordingly. With animals as complex as apes and monkeys the deliberate use of both anticipatory and expressive symbols is to be expected. The mother may deliberately glance at and motion to the infant in order to get it to come to her. An animal may simulate anger in order to bluff another one. The other animals in turn, noting these symbols, adjust their behavior accordingly, but they do it in view of the existing social situation. It often happens, for example, that the animal reacts not simply to the symbol automatically but to the intention behind the symbol. He infers this intention in part from the social situation. Thus he may know that another animal is bluffing and may elect to call that bluff. On this level the primate group exhibits an exceedingly wide and complex range of interrelated stimuli, and these give the group its structure. The group, indeed, seems almost human.

It is another, or third, level of symbolism that is missing in non-human groups. This is the level of what may be called the arbitrary symbol. Whereas the anticipatory symbol is intrinsically tied to its meaning by the structure of the completed act, and the expressive symbol is so tied by its physiological connection with the internal state, the arbitrary symbol has no intrinsic connection whatsoever with the thing symbolized. The word *lie,* for example, no matter whether it is spoken, written, or spelled on the fingers, is purely indifferent so far as the various events and actions that it signifies are concerned. This is shown by the fact that it has several diverse meanings, each having no connection with the others, and that in other languages an entirely different word or set of words is used to designate these same meanings. The only reason this word conveys the meanings it has, is that the people who speak English are arbitrarily agreed on these meanings.

The absence of arbitrary symbolic communication in animal groups is a grave limitation. It means that such communication as exists must always be tied to the *present* situation. Anticipatory and expressive symbols, by virtue of their intrinsic connections with their meanings, are not pure symbols. They cannot be used, therefore, to depict situations that do not exist as a part of the current situation. An animal may simulate anger in order to bluff his companion, but he cannot describe to this companion another situation in which bluffing occurred. He may by his manifestation of fear indicate to his fellows that an enemy is approaching, but when no enemy is near he cannot describe what an enemy is like and teach his fellows what the appropriate behavior would be. It is only by a system of arbitrary symbols that absent situations can be handled, that the environment can be manipulated in mental or imaginary terms, and that a cumulative body of group knowledge can be built up. In short, it is only through the use of such symbols that what we call culture becomes possible.

Being incapable of symbolic communication in its purest sense, the apes and monkeys of one generation are incapable of transmitting their acquired knowledge and attitudes to the next generation. Each generation must through its own actual participation in experience acquire the same knowledge and attitudes all over again. Infant apes cannot be told that Chinamen wear pigtails; they cannot know anything about it until they actually see a Chinese wearing a pigtail, and then they will not know what it is until they actually pull it. They cannot be told without seeing a snake that snakes are dangerous. They cannot be told about gods, spirits, and ghosts, or about patriotism, truth, and beauty.

Simian and anthropoid groups epitomize in a general way the fundamental bio-social mechanisms of human groups, because *Homo sapiens* is just a high-minded type of primate. But their lack of culture introduces a tremendous gulf between them and human society. In fact, the gulf is so large that on the human level we may regard the presence of culture combined with the typical traits of primate society as creating a new social emergent—a type of society found in no other animal species. Strictly speaking this new kind of society is bio-socio-cultural. In the interest of brevity we call it socio-cultural or merely human society.

HUMAN SOCIETY

Human groups as bio-social systems exhibit the same general traits as primate society, just as the latter in turn manifests the same general traits as mammalian society. But whereas in ape and monkey groups the exaggeration, modification, and complication of the more general traits occur primarily on a physiological basis, they occur in human society on a cultural basis.

For instance, human beings like the other primates and mammalians, are structurally homogeneous. There are fat and lean women, pretty and ugly ones, lazy and hardworking ones, but there are no innate castes of women born with anatomical characteristics suited to their caste functions. Neither are there men so born. Yet human society, as we know, is a complex affair requiring an elaborate division of labor. Here culture steps in. Through culture it becomes possible to *train* persons for specific tasks. Human society thus creates its own castes, not by organic but by cultural modification. And since these human "castes" are not organically determined they may not be castes at all—i.e. they may not be hereditary. They may be merely classes or occupational groups.

Again, human society has continuous sexuality and the constant association of the sexes as one of its basic elements, because *Homo sapiens* possesses the same reproductive physiology as the anthropoids. But the conditioning of this sexuality, its utilization in a system of dominance, goes much farther than anything to be found among apes and monkeys. The phenomena of repression and sublimation; of marriage, adultery, and incest; of commercial and religious prostitution bear eloquent testimony to this fact.

Homo sapiens, furthermore, carries to an extreme the primate trait of neural complexity and the consequent capacity to learn. As a result we find that man alone is capable of evolving a system of arbitrary symbolic communication. It is this system, enabling man to transmit attitudes and knowledge from one generation to the next, that makes possible the elaborate conditioning of the anthropoid biosocial traits. Whereas among apes and monkeys all conditioning must take place in the actual situation and the range of what they can learn is thus greatly restricted, "men, thanks to the possession of language, can convey to one another a clear idea of situations which are not present and of the behavior appropriate to such situations." [15] People who have never been shipwrecked, who have never even seen a ship, may understand what it is like to be shipwrecked and may know the proper response.

Cultural learning has the advantage that it enormously speeds up the process of learning. For instance, if each musician had to learn the techniques of making music simply by watching others do so, there would be very little music. There are certain principles involved in music which can be transmitted by word of mouth or re-

[15] Ralph Linton, *The Study of Man* (New York: Appleton-Century, 1936), p. 83.

duced to writing, and a comprehension of these principles facilitates the learning. Also, the musician may play pieces that he does not know by heart, simply by following the written score; and in this way he may play ancient as well as modern pieces. Furthermore, he does not have to make his own musical instrument. It is made for him according to principles that are again handed down by cultural tradition. To be sure, the budding musician has to practice; there is still an element of trial and error. But the acquisition of principles from others reduces the trial and error part to a minimum. He profits not only from the techniques that the generation before him acquired out of its own experience, but also from those acquired by the generation before that, and so on. Having reduced to a minimum the reliance upon instincts and carried to a maximum the reliance upon learning, human beings have evolved an exceedingly rapid shorthand method of acquisition.

Not only does learning become more rapid under a system of symbolic communication but the total volume of things learned is increased many thousand times. If we take into account the techniques, rules, rituals, beliefs, names, vocabulary, attitudes, anecdotes, statuses, and facts that each person learns, we see that the total amount even for the most primitive society is infinitely beyond what an anthropoid—or, for that matter, a cultureless human being—could acquire. In short, culture has the capacity to accumulate. Each generation can add to the cultural heritage on the basis of its own peculiar experience. In this way the group may come to have not only more but also better knowledge. This capacity for accumulation does not always result in steady progress. There may be decay and retrogression. But in the long course of human evolution the capacity for cultural improvement has on the whole been realized in practice.

The amount that any one man can learn in the lifetime allotted him, even under cultural conditions, is limited. Yet a peculiarity of human society is that the members of the group need not learn the total culture in order to profit by it. A socially determined division of labor allows different persons to acquire different parts of the cultural heritage. Putting to work the part they do learn, they perform useful functions for the entire group on the basis of their special knowledge. A man does not have to know carpentry in order to have a house, or to understand combustion motors in order to drive a car. Since there is apparently no limit to the amount of specialization that may take place, there is no conceivable limit to the amount of cultural accumulation that may occur. The total culture is that of the group as a whole rather than that of any one person. In this way human society gets around a possible limitation on the growth of culture—the finite capacity of the single individual to learn.

When it is seen that the total culture belongs to the society as a whole rather than to a single member, an important conclusion emerges. Survival depends not so much on the talents and strength of particular individuals as upon the culture of the group as a whole. Since, moreover, different human groups possess different cultures, the perennial conflict of these groups has led to what one may call a struggle for survival on the cultural level. The group that is most efficiently organized and has the most advanced techniques tends to dominate over the others, and the others must either borrow from it (in which case the superior culture is spread) or lose out in the struggle. This process of natural selection on a societal rather than an individual level has been one of the factors forcing an ever greater specialization and accumulation of culture in human history. There is a sense then in which we can speak of the evolution of culture without committing ourselves to social Darwinism. The latter theory would have us believe that social advance is determined mainly by the natural selection of physically inherited traits on the part of individuals rather than by the natural selection of cultural traits on the part of groups. But the fact that the Spaniards could conquer and impose the bulk of their culture on the Indians of South America was not due to the biological superiority of the Spaniards. It was due, rather, to the superiority of their culture for military purposes.

Although specialization overcomes the limitation which individual capacity would otherwise place on cultural advance, there are other social inventions which also help. One of these is writing. Throughout most human history the transmission of the cultural heritage has been accomplished through *verbal* communication. This word-of-mouth process, however, has several disadvantages. It taxes the human memory to the utmost; it requires the physical presence of teacher and pupil; and it makes the high points of intellectual and inventive endeavor difficult to retain. Primitive societies are primitive primarily because they have no system of writing, which explains why the term "preliterate" has been so widely used as a synonym for such societies. Writing, in contrast to verbal communication, allows ideas to be "stored" apart from the immediate communicating situation. This gives a spread to communication since the persons communicating can be miles or centuries apart and one person can communicate his ideas to millions of others. The fixing of ideas by writing has another advantage in that the highest achievements of thought can be set down once for all. Everyone knows that at times as a result of long concentration on a problem he has a series of ideas which are far above average and which, if not set down in writing, are apt to be forgotten and lost forever. By setting things down in writing, therefore, men can insure that the greatest contributions will be incorporated into the cultural heritage. The best thinkers of each generation communicate almost directly with the best thinkers of succeeding generations, without their ideas having to pass through the deleting effect of transmission through dull intellects. Also, with the best thoughts thus captured and fixed, duller minds can work on them at their leisure. Such fixation, furthermore, aids the process of specialization previously mentioned. Written ideas on the same subject can be stored together, as in libraries. A specialist can learn from this stored knowledge, imbibing not only the contributions of the living masters in his field but also those of the dead masters as well. By having before him the major contributions made up to his time, he can with ease investigate the still unsolved problems. Thus he can expand the frontiers of knowledge, and by dividing the labor with others he can become a specialist within a specialty. In this way writing intensifies the degree of specialization.

Writing, then, extends the effectiveness of symbolic communication in human society. There are many other inventions that do the same, such as printing, radio, and telephone. Present-day civilization would be impossible without these techniques, for civilization is a matter of the quality and quantity of what is culturally transmitted.

One of the outstanding peculiarities given to human society by symbolic communication—a peculiarity unknown to monkeys and apes—is what we may call *legitimacy,* or *the normative.* In every human situation there are two elements—the facts and the attitude or sentiment toward the facts. The latter are conveyed as a part of the cultural heritage, so that they are there in advance of the actual situation. Perhaps the most powerful of these attitudes and sentiments are those relating to what ought and ought not to be. People tend either to approve or disapprove of the facts, particularly the actual behavior of the participants, in accordance with received judgments. In this way a new dimension is given to social existence, a new and pervasive instrument of control over individual conduct. The normative ideas exist in the minds of the group members, and by being communicated as judgments on conduct they influence the course of external events. For example, human beings must distinguish between mating, which occurs as a fact in every mammalian species, and marriage, which is a special kind of mating that is normatively but not biologically defined. In the same way a man can eat, sleep, walk, or do almost anything else legitimately or illegitimately, depending on the kind of socially defined situation in which he does it.

If individuals were not responsive to the judgments of others, this normative control could not exist. But human beings as members of a group that depends on symbolic communication cannot help but be responsive to such judgments, because their minds and their personalities are formed by the transmission of attitudes and ideas. The judgments that others make about them and their fellows, are therefore their own judgments about themselves. As the phenomena of conscience and feelings of guilt testify, they approve or disapprove of their own acts along with the acts of their fellows. Also, the success or failure of the individual in attaining his own ends is influenced to a great extent by the opinions that others hold toward him. Hence he is motivated by both subjective and objective forces to pay attention to the communicated feelings of others concerning his own conduct, just as he is motivated to express his feelings concerning the conduct of others. In short, he is motivated to seek the esteem of his fellows. Thus human society has not only a factual order but also a moral order, and the two are causally interdependent.

The presence of the normative factor complicates every bio-social trait handed down from our anthropoid ancestors. For instance, the pattern of dominance, fundamentally similar to that of monkeys and apes, is greatly modified—in some ways enhanced, in other ways softened—by the cultural definition of legitimate and illegitimate dominance. There arises in human society a system of normatively sanctioned power which we call *authority*. This overlays and sometimes conflicts with other bases of power, such as strength, ability, personality. which may consequently give rise to unsanctioned power.

Furthermore, persons in authority may use their legitimate power in illegitimate ways, as the phenomena of graft and corruption universally testify. It becomes clear that the study of human society must always keep in mind not only the facts but the normative attitudes toward the facts; for both are embraced in the reality that we call socio-cultural.

Societal Needs and Instrumentalities

What has just been said about human society is meant simply as a brief characterization to set it off from other types of society. The features mentioned, along with others, will be discussed more fully in the chapters that follow. The present chapter has attempted to show that all societies of whatever species have certain basic needs that must be met if they are to continue as societies. These needs, however, can be met in fundamentally different ways, and it is in terms of these different ways of meeting them that one type of society can be distinguished from another. The greatest differentiation is that between social groups whose needs are met by inherited mechanisms and those whose needs are met by cultural transmission. The former class (bio-social) embraces all animal societies, the latter (socio-cultural) only human society. Within each of these categories, however, further distinctions are possible. The insect societies exhibit rigid instinctive patterns and great organic differences between their members. Mammalian societies, on the other hand, manifest a relative absence of organic specialization and a greater degree of learned behavior. The primate groups in particular show a very high degree of learned behavior, and it is in this type of group that culture and hence human society had their origin. Although human society is of one general type, the possession of culture allows for remarkable variation in social behavior from one human group to another. This variation sets the stage for what amounts to a struggle for survival and a natural selection of cultures, and furnishes a constant stimulus for the fulfillment of the capacity for progressive accumulation inherent in the nature of culture.

It should be apparent that the different mechanisms for meeting societal needs, as manifested in the various types of society, all contain evolutionary advantages peculiar to themselves. The short-lived, fast-breeding insects have made genetic inheritance a flexible means of adjusting the society to the environment. The long-lived, slow-breeding mammals have utilized learned behavior as a quicker mode of adjustment. In human beings this reliance upon learning has led to the emergence of culture, involving the transmission of knowledge and attitudes through a system of arbitrary symbols. This emergent has enormously deepened and complicated the original anthropoid society out of which human society grew. It has constituted a protective envelope, so to speak, separating the human being from his physical environment and creating within his society an interdependence that superficially bears more resemblance to insect communities than to the looser mammalian groups. Among the peculiarities that it introduces are specialization on the basis of training and control on the basis of moral conformity.

Needless to say, each type of society, having developed a structure for meeting the primary societal needs, inevitably acquires secondary needs relating to its particular kind of structure. As the result of a cultural mode of adaptation, for example, human society has developed a great many necessities that apply to socio-cultural systems but to no other kinds. These secondary needs we have not discussed, but so far as human society is concerned they will figure prominently in the subsequent treatment.

References

W. C. Allee, *The Social Life of Animals* (New York: Norton, 1938), Chap. 3, "The Aggregations of Higher Animals"; Chap. 5, "Group Behavior"; Chap. 7, "Some Human Implications"; Chap. 8, "Social Transitions."

An outstanding authority on animal ecology here deals with the problem of group formation and social behavior in the animal world. Readable and interesting.

C. R. Carpenter, *A Field Study in Siam of the Behavior and Social Relations of the Gibbon,* Comparative Psychology Monographs, Vol. 16, No. 5 (Baltimore: Johns Hopkins Press, 1940).

Somewhat technical and not well written, but one of the best field studies of any species of great ape.

Carl J. Warden, *The Emergence of Human Culture* (New York: Macmillan, 1936), Chap. 1, "The Meaning of Culture"; Chap. 2, "Do Animals Possess Culture?"; Chap. 3, "The Emergence of Man and Culture."

A brief, incisive treatment of the nature of culture and its relation to human evolution, by a student of animal behavior.

Carl J. Warden, *The Evolution of Human Behavior* (New York: Macmillan, 1932), Chap. 1, "Some Problems of Human Evolution"; Chap. 2, "The Natural Kinship of Man and Animal"; Chap. 3, "When Anthropoid Became Human"; Chap. 5, "The Coming of Modern Man."

The evolution of man and of human society is here treated with broad sweep and imagination.

Wm Morton Wheeler, *Emergent Evolution and the Development of Societies* (New York: Norton, 1928).

An excellent brief presentation of the appearance of new emergent levels (including the societal) in evolution.

Wm. Morton Wheeler, *Essays in Philosophical Biology* (Cambridge: Harvard University Press, 1939), Chap. 1, "The Ant-Colony as an Organism"; Chap. 4, "The Termitodoxa, or Biology and Society"; Chap. 7, "Emergent Evolution and the Development of Societies"; and Chap. 12, "Animal Societies."

No biologist has contributed more to the understanding of insect society and its bearing on the theory of human society than has this great entomologist. His more technical works on the social insects, especially the ants, are invaluable.

S. Zuckerman, *The Social Life of Monkeys and Apes* (New York: Harcourt, Brace, 1932).

A classic account of social behavior among the infra-human primates. Mostly devoted to baboons in captivity, it nevertheless gives information on other species and on the scant studies of primates in the wild.

CHAPTER III

SOCIAL NORMS

According to the last chapter the unique trait in human society—the thing which transforms the primate grouping into a new emergent reality—is the system of symbolic communication. By such a system situations can be depicted, thought about, and acted on even when they are not present. This makes possible, as pointed out, a distinction between legitimate and illegitimate conduct; so that always in human society there is what may be called a double reality—on the one hand a normative system embodying what *ought* to be, and on the other a factual order embodying what *is*. In the nature of the case these two orders cannot be completely identical, nor can they be completely disparate. The normative order acts, for example, as a determinant (though not the only determinant) of the factual order. Whereas for insects and subhuman mammals actual behavior is determined by the interaction of inherited traits and the external environment (including other members of the same society), human behavior is determined in addition by culturally acquired patterns. A strong element in the culturally acquired patterns is the normative element—the feeling that the culturally acquired patterns *ought* to be followed. The factual order is what it is, therefore, partly because the normative order is what it is. This becomes plainer when we realize that the norms often (though not always) conflict with biological inclination. They are *controls*. It is through them that human society regulates the behavior of its members in such ways that they perform activities fulfilling societal needs—even, sometimes, at the expense of organic needs.

In turn the factual order exercises an influence on the normative system, for the norms must always refer to events in the real world and take into account the factual situation. Although norms represent in a sense an imaginary construct, although they are matters of attitude and sentiment, they must nevertheless if they are to have any effect represent correctly the relations between real events. A rule requiring all men to have three wives would be valueless if the sex ratio did not permit. A rule for which there is no real sanction often fails for that very reason. Similarly, a rule requiring everybody to bathe in salt water in order to prevent tuberculosis would be valueless if bathing in salt water had nothing to do with curing this disease. The normative system, since it aims to achieve results in the factual world, is subject to constant modification by events in that world.

When we speak of human society, therefore, we have in mind not merely the objective set of relationships between the members but the subjective set of norms as well. Unless we know both we cannot understand the society; for since they are not identical the normative order can never be completely deduced from knowledge of the factual order, nor vice versa. If there were no normative order there could be no human society; for the innate equipment of the human organism is not sufficiently comprehensive or integrated to give automatic responses that are functionally adequate for society. In fact, *Homo sapiens* has so long lived under conditions of social integration that he is in the same condition as the social insects—i.e. incapable of existing alone. No human being can be entirely solitary from birth and survive. Only after he has enjoyed the fruits of social life, only when he has already become socialized, can he in rare cases exist apart from his social group. Man's dependence on society, unlike that of the insects, is not derived from fixed innate responses to mechanical social stimuli but rather from learned responses to meaningful stimuli. Hence his dependence on society is ultimately a dependence upon a normative order. The normative order makes the factual order of human society possible.

It is only in imagination that we can talk about a human group apart from norms, and such a group to say the least would be characterized by Hobbes' hypothetical state of nature, a war of all against all, "solitary, poor, nasty, brutish, and short." The human organism has become biologically specialized for life in a group where normative regulation prevails. The central nervous system, notably the cerebrum, has been developed to a point where the individual has enormous powers of learning; and in turn the inherited mechanisms have undergone degeneration to the point where they are inadequate in themselves for survival. The human organism must consequently participate in a normatively regulated social system in order to maintain its life. This fact alone would indicate that the normative element in human society is millions of years old. It gives to human society a marvelous cohesion, but a cohesion based on a different principle from that found in any other society.

Though millions of years old, normative society is not yet so old that the human organism has become completely passive in its adjustment. On the contrary the organism is still resistant to normative control; and one of the great unsolved problems of human life is the conflict between organic inclination (mainly appetitive) and social restraint (mainly normative). This is by no means the only unsolved problem, for as we shall see there are conflicts between norms themselves, but it is nevertheless a fundamental one inherent in the nature of cultural society.

The influence of the normative order in social life implies, of course, that human beings do not simply act but that in addition they reflect upon, have theories about, and pass judgment on their acts. Inevitably then, and ironically too, they reflect not simply on their acts but also upon the very normative order which forces them to reflect. Thus in all human thought there is an attempt to explain the *source of authority* or *power behind* the norms. Why is it that mere imaginings, mere feelings that things should be so, have so powerful an effect upon reality? The explanations have been many and various. Modern thinkers have frequently professed to find the source of the norms in biological nature, to treat the norms as if they were instincts, but this cannot be the real source because as we have just seen it is man's organic nature that is controlled by the normative order, rather than the normative order being derived from the organism. Other explanations have been in terms of ethics or religious beliefs, but ethical and religious notions are themselves a part of the normative order and hence require rather than provide an explanation. Rarely have the explanations of normative order been sociological, but according to our view it is only by sociological analysis that the source and nature of normative rules can be discovered. Such an analysis would point out that normative control has arisen concomitantly as human society has arisen. It has been made possible by man's capacity to learn and by the development of symbolic communication. At the same time it has been made necessary by the exigencies of societal survival in the struggle between human groups.

In the last analysis, then, the normative order has evolved as a part of human society because it helped to satisfy the fundamental societal needs, thus enabling societies and hence the human species to survive. To put it differently, it would be impossible to control the natural environment by means of culture without also controlling man himself. Those groups which did not maintain a normative control over their members could not generate enough internal coöperation to survive.

So thoroughly have norms become a part of the human mode of existence that they are to a high degree internalized. For the individual growing up in a society each norm is not necessarily an external rule which he may obey or try to evade; it may be a part of himself not regarded objectively at all or understood and felt as a rule, but simply a part of himself automatically expressed in behavior. Such internalized norms guide and determine his intuitive judgments of others and his intuitive judgments of himself. They lead to the phenomena of conscience, of guilt feelings, of striving, of elation and depression. They are more personal than habit, deeper than consciousness. Many of the problems of personality as well as of society can therefore be formulated in terms of norms and departures from the norms. On the other hand it is true that many norms do not become internalized. Many of them, indeed, do not even become habitual, and some of them are not even obeyed.

Actually, however, a norm need not necessarily be carried out to the letter in order to influence behavior. The fact that an individual has striven to achieve an expected pattern alters his behavior from what it would have been had he never striven at all. It has been a frequent mistake of moralists and social theorists alike to imagine that absolute fidelity to the normative order is essential to society. Rather, it is primarily respect for and endeavor to fulfil the normative patterns that are necessary. Complete achievement would not only be impossible in the case of many norms but would be disadvantageous for the society. In order to get what it needs a society asks for more than it expects, in much the same way that a mother requests better behavior from her child than she really expects or desires. The precise ratio between requested, functionally advantageous, and actual levels of performance depends of course upon the situation. Often a particular line of activity is required as a "duty" and the individual is definitely expected to "do his duty." But in this case the required activity may involve a moderate rather than a maximum level of performance. The maximum may indeed be recognized as more desirable but not stipulated as a duty. An excellent illustration is seen in the army where decorations for heroic behavior—i.e. behavior "beyond the call of duty"—are given.

It should obviously be borne in mind that norms do not apply equally to all members of a society or to all situations. They are adjusted to the positions people hold in the social order, to the occupations they practice, etc. What is proper for a woman is not always proper for a man. Thus expectation and performance are always qualified in view of the socially defined situation in which the norm applies.

The conception of a norm implies by definition a sense of obligation. The individual in a given situation should, ought, or must follow certain behavior. Unless he makes an effort to carry out the required pattern, the condition that the norm requires will not come about. The idea of resistance, of some obstacle to the norm, is clearly implicit in the definition. Unless there were some obstacle to overcome there would be no need of a sense of obligation about doing the thing required. Indeed, the behavior would be forthcoming anyway without effort, automatically; and no offering of rewards or threatening of punishment would be necessary. A norm, therefore, admits that the stipulated pattern requires effort, and says that the effort should be made.

One can argue that all culturally transmitted behavior patterns carry a sense of obligation and are therefore normative. If an individual learns to speak a language there is an obligation to speak it correctly, and if he lives among people who possess that language there is an obligation to use it rather than some other tongue. Similarly, if a man learns to practice medicine there is a slight obligation to engage in that practice, and a strong obligation, once he is practicing, to use the most effective methods available. Most cultural transmission thus imparts to the learner a sense of obligation. Yet it is certainly true that any culture permits in certain situations alternative modes of behavior, and that in some of these cases the amount of approval attached to the various possible patterns is approximately equal. In contemporary American culture a man in polite society is expected to shave, and he meets some disapproval if he fails to do so; but whether he shaves with a safety razor, an old style razor, or an electric razor is largely a matter of indifference. In other words, the *choice* between different patterns is sometimes left free. More frequently, however, the normative system prefers that one pattern be chosen rather than another but without absolutely insisting on it. A Hindu is not supposed to travel to a foreign country, but under modern conditions he is permitted to do so.

Classification of Norms

One cannot discuss for long the general subject of norms without making some distinction between the different types. Yet there are so many distinctions which cross one another that a systematic classification is difficult. One way is to differentiate norms on the basis of the kind of sanctions applied. Some rules are supported merely by mild disapproval of the violator, while others are supported by physical force. This distinction is correlated to some extent with another one—namely, the degree of importance attached to the rule in the society—and with still another, the manner by which the rule comes into being (whether by deliberate legislation or by unconscious growth). Finally there is apparently a slight correlation between these criteria and the degree of spontaneity with which the rule is followed as well as the rapidity with which the rule changes. These correlations, however, are very rough. What sociologists have done is simply to group norms into several broad classes, admitting that the various criteria of distinction overlap considerably and that the classification is therefore crude. In this way they usually distinguish what are called folkways, mores, and law, and sometimes differentiate fashion, fad, convention, etiquette, and honor. We shall follow this same procedure.

Folkways

Most of the patterns applied in everyday behavior consist of folkways. These are relatively durable, standardized practices regarded as obligatory in the proper situation but not absolutely obligatory, enforced by informal social controls (gossip, ridicule, ostracism) rather than by formal complaint or coercion, and originating in an unplanned and obscure manner rather than by deliberate inauguration. The grammar and vocabulary of a language, for example, form a system of verbal folkways, of most of which we are entirely unaware. Likewise such things as the number of meals per day, the modes of preparing food, the kinds of food chosen, the regular brushing of the teeth, the use of tables, chairs, beds, etc. are all folkways. It is through the folkways that the business of living in a socio-cultural environment is made possible, and their unreflecting character makes for efficiency and frees our minds for the more problematic events of life. Those folkways that are repeated often enough become habits—habits of thought as well as of action—and they come to form the unstated premises in our mental life. They provide a high degree of predictability both of our own and of others' behavior, so that we feel some security and some order in life. To violate some of the folkways is usually possible, but it is impossible to violate all of them, for then the individual would find himself virtually excluded from social contact. Survival in such a circumstance would be extremely difficult, not merely from an external or physical point of view but also from an internal or mental point of view. The very reasons for nonconformity in one particular situation are apt to be, for the individual in question, the folkways prevailing in most other situations. If the alpha and omega of human existence are to be found anywhere it is in the folkways, for we begin with them and always come back to them.

Some folkways are less arbitrary than others. The folkways connected with driving a car, for example, such as steering, handling the knobs on the instrument panel, using the clutch, changing a tire, etc., are determined by the nature of the object that is dealt with. They are technological folkways. But there are other folkways connected with driving a car, such as staying on the right or left side of the road, signaling at a turn, resisting backseat driving, offering the neighbors a ride, and keeping the vehicle clean, which are arbitrary in the sense that out of a number of alternatives, all either possible or irrelevant from a technological point of view, some are seized upon and made *the* way of behaving simply by fiat of usage. Some of the folkways may be made into laws, as we shall see in a moment. The most arbitrary folkways are of course those which relate to pure symbols. Thus in language, as we have seen, there is no intrinsic connection between sound and meaning; hence the connection as established in the folkways is purely arbitrary; out of the tremendous assortment of possible sounds and their combinations certain ones are selected and made to apply to particular objects or ideas.

The sanctions of the folkways are themselves folkways. It can be said that societies are not caught napping, because for each violation of a norm there is usually some standardized procedure for punishing or otherwise discouraging the violation. But the sanctions of the folkways are by definition comparatively mild, consisting generally in informal retaliations (usually direct or indirect expressions of adverse opinion). It should be noted, however, that sanctions are cumulative. If the same norm is persistently violated by the same person the retribution grows accordingly; furthermore, if the same person violates a large number of different norms the punishment for the violation of each is likely to be greater than if he violated one alone.

Like the folkways which they uphold, sanctions are limited to particular groups. Hence it follows that informal sanctions may not be effective if the person against whom they are directed is not a full-fledged member of the group. Thus the city fellow who wears loud sport clothes in a local hamlet is likely to be criticized, but the criticisms may be ineffective because he does not value the good opinion of the village yokels. Physically he is in the local world, but mentally in terms of his normative system he is in the city.

Mores

Whereas each folkway is not considered tremendously important and is not supported by an extremely strong sanction, each *mos* is believed to be essential for social welfare and is consequently more strongly sanctioned. There is a greater feeling of horror about violating a *mos,* a greater unwillingness to see it violated. Presumably, therefore the mores relate to the fundamental needs of society more directly than do the folkways—or it would be better to say that the emphasis put upon a given *mos* is proportional, first, to the importance of the need which the behavior serves and, second, to the obstacles (either in the organism or in the environment) to meeting that need.

Folkways and mores are similar, however, in being of remote and obscure origin, unplanned, unquestioned, and relatively unchanging. They are also similar in that the sanctions are informal and communal in nature, depending on the spontaneous reactions of the group rather than on the reactions of officials acting in some special capacity. The mores represent the hardest core of the normative system. The folkways are, so to speak, the protoplasm of the cell, the bulky part, while the mores are the nucleus, the essential part. It is only when the mores are called into question that people reflect upon them. Ordinarily the mores are taken for granted as being a highly important part of the nature of things. Belief rationalizes them in the form of myth, ritual expresses them in the form of symbols, and action embodies them in the form of right conduct. The mores are morally right, their violation morally wrong. Hence the profoundest measuring rod of right and wrong is found precisely in the mores, which fact has given rise to the expression that the mores can make anything right or anything wrong.[1] In public opinion there is no higher court than that of the mores themselves, and in many simple societies no further type of norm is needed for the proper regulation of the membership. The mores have no need of justification, because they exist of their own right. They are not subject to deliberate change or to analysis, and criticism of them draws down strong punishment upon the head of the critic. The members of society, in short, share sentiments highly favorable to the mores. There is a sense of unreflecting solidarity among people who share the same mores because their sentiments are alike; and there is a sense of resistance and antagonism towards anyone with different mores. Whereas foreign folkways are merely disconcerting because they upset old habits and familiar grooves, foreign mores are deeply disturbing because, in addition, they offend profound sentiments.

Taboos are mores expressed in negative form. The rules against incest, for example, are in the mores, but they tell us not so much what relationship should prevail between parent and child, brother and sister, as what relationship should *not* prevail. On the other hand the rule regarding the wife's sexual relations with men other than her husband is stated both positively (a wife must be sexually faithful to her husband) and negatively (she must not commit adultery); it thus involves both an exhortation and a taboo.

Some mores refer to a relationship between two persons in a given situation—e.g. between husband and wife, doctor and patient, priest and confessor. Others, more general in character, presumably

[1] Wm. Graham Sumner, *Folkways* (Boston: Ginn, 1906), Chap. 15.

relate to a great number of different relationships and situations—e.g. the admonition to be honest, or brave, or industrious. In some cases the rule becomes so general that it does little more than state the desirability of observing the mores whatever the situation—e.g. when people are told that they should lead a good life, be free from sin, think no evil, or follow the golden rule. Thus we have not only specific mores requiring behavior of a particular kind but also general ones saying that whatever the specific rule, it should be obeyed. In this way the mores try to guarantee their own enforcement.

Are the Folkways and Mores Sufficient?

A question that has often been raised is this: Are the folkways and mores sufficient by themselves to provide social control for a society? At bottom this question really aims to inquire about the status of law and may be rephrased as follows: Is law an indispensable element in social control; and is it, therefore, like the folkways and mores, found universally in human society?

The answer depends to some degree on the matter of definition. Law may be so broadly defined that it includes the mores. But as defined in the present work (see the next section) it is different from the mores, and the question is therefore relevant. Looked at in this way it seems there are certain kinds of societies—namely, isolated primitive and peasant communities—where the folkways and mores are sufficient in themselves to regulate conduct. In these societies, often embracing only a few dozen or at most a few hundred individuals, the people know each other well, and anything that happens receives the attention of the whole community. Furthermore, since they are not exposed to a different culture but all grow up in the same tradition, they tend to take a common attitude towards whatever happens. Finally they are conscious of the fact that they take the same attitude toward any event, and this places a feeling of group strength behind whatever action they may take. Now, a would-be violator in such a community is faced with formidable obstacles. To begin with, he is very likely to be detected. It is difficult to steal property and try to use or dispose of it in a group where everybody knows intimately the simple objects possessed by each individual. It is also difficult to murder a man without having one's motives shrewdly suspected. If the offender is detected, he stands to lose a great deal. He lives his life in the community, and consequently the opinion of his fellows means a great deal to him emotionally. Also, since the community is capable of acting spontaneously and unanimously, he may run the risk of economic and physical injury. Consequently we find that small isolated societies often do not have anything we would call law. The folkways and mores are alone sufficient to provide the necessary amount of control. Indeed, the social control may be much more complete than in societies having a well developed legal system.

A few examples will illustrate the point. The Indians of Labrador depend greatly on the trapping of fur-bearing animals for a livelihood.

> Accordingly, for one trapper to take the game from another's traps . . . is a serious misdeed. For this, however, there is no stated punishment. The victim of such theft usually takes his own means of attempting to identify the thief, and when his mind is made up he is apt to talk freely about the robbery. The discovery soon reaches the ears of the offender and the consequences thenceforth remain a matter of individual concern. There may be only suppressed ill-feeling or perhaps threats by the offended party. This is generally sufficient to check further poaching. . . .
>
> In every band there are met those whose status among their associates is that of the undesirable. The visitor, like myself, is warned against reposing trust in them. Their relatives are often ashamed of them. Being avoided, they forfeit the satisfaction of friendship; hence this becomes their punishment. As mild as all this appears to us, it is serious enough in these lonesome societies. And should resentment lead the ostracized to further deeds intensifying his unpopularity, he may develop into being an offender of greater magnitude—ultimately to become a social outcast. This is a more serious situation. If he becomes morose, it is worse for him, and he may take steps to get even with his associates; to take vengeance on society and finally be murdered.[2]

The Ibans, or Sea Dyaks, of Borneo seldom infringe the mores of their society,

> because of the dread every person has of being cursed by someone he has injured. This fear operates particularly in cases of theft,

[2] Quoted in Wm. I. Thomas, *Primitive Behavior* (New York: McGraw-Hill, 1937), p. 516, from Frank G. Speck, "Ethical Attributes of the Labrador Indians," *American Anthropologist,* Vol. 35 (1933), pp. 578-579, 565-566.

which is consequently very infrequent. A liar is punished during his life, and after death by an ingenious method called *tugong bula.* Soon after his dishonesty is discovered, the people begin to pile twigs and branches near the place where the offense occurred, and always thereafter all passers-by throw their contributions of sticks on the heap. Some of these "liars' heaps" are very old, but the name of the offender is not forgotten, living on in perpetual disgrace as the name of his monument of shame.[3]

The African Bushmen, when untouched by civilization, apparently enjoyed an entirely informal system of social control.

This absence of any organized system of public control does not imply that the Bushmen have no laws. On the contrary all their institutions, manners and customs serve to regulate the relations between the members of the band, and thus to maintain law and order. The child at birth comes into a world where there already exist definite forms of organization and behaviour, of ceremonial, of manners and fashions, and as he grows up he falls more or less unconsciously into acting and thinking like those around him, and in this way comes to conform to social norms. There are moreover more or less deliberate means of impressing upon young people the social sentiments necessary for the maintenance of the law and order of the community. The education they receive in the households of their parents and out in the veld, and above all the highly-important teachings at the puberty ceremonies for boys, instruct them in tribal lore and tradition, inculcate social norms, and determine their activities accordingly.

There are, further, various sanctions by which non-fulfilment or the breach of any recognized custom is penalized, . . . In this category we may place ritual sanctions, where any departure from a prescribed rule of conduct is followed automatically by evil results, without any direct interference on the part of the community. The breaking of a taboo, for instance, is held to produce serious consequences, such as death or disease or ill-luck in the chase . . . Girls who do not observe the restrictions imposed upon them at the time of puberty are believed to change into frogs, while men who are seen by the girls at this time become permanently fixed in whatever position they then occupy, and so on. And again there are numerous observances and avoidances associated with hunting, which if neg-

[3] Thomas, *op. cit.,* p. 517, quoted from a manuscript by Raymond Kennedy, *The Ethnology of the Greater Sunda Islands,* pp. 463-464.

> lected will result in ill-success, the loss of a wounded animal, etc. . . .
>
> Other breaches of custom, however, involve the direct intervention of the members of the community. In general, when disputes arise between the members of the band . . . there is no appeal to any supreme authority, for, as we have just noted, there is no such authority. . . . The only remedy is self-help. . . . Blood vengeance indeed is the principal, if not the only recognized way of dealing with serious offenses committed against a person even by members of the same band.[4]

In this last quotation the author uses the term "law" evidently to mean any custom that has any sanction whatever. But it is clear that the society in question has no legislative body, no judicial body, no central authority, and no special enforcement agency. In short, it lacks practically everything that we associate with law as distinct from mere custom. We must conclude, then, that it is regulated by folkways and mores, and not by law. If the term law were used to cover such phenomena we should be obliged to distinguish different types of law—as folkways law, mores law, law law, etc.—which would be clumsy usage.

Customary Law

There are not many societies like the African Bushmen which entirely lack special organization for the enforcement of the social rules. Most societies, including many primitive bands and all peasant communities, have some elements that are associated with what is generally called law. Usually the first such element to appear is a judicial body which renders judgment when cases of infraction or conflict arise. Thus the Hottentots, an African people closely related to the Bushmen, have or did have a tribal council. Among the offences tried before this council were murder, manslaughter, treason, theft, incest, adultery, and sodomy.

> As soon as a man was known or suspected of having committed such an offence, every member of the kraal considered it a duty to arrest him at the first opportunity, unless he succeeded in making his escape. Once captured he was safely held until the council assembled, which

[4] I. Schapera, *The Khoisan Peoples of South Africa* (London: Routledge, 1930), pp. 151-152.

> was always as soon as possible. The councillors sat in a circle, and the accused was placed in the centre, where he could hear all that was said and himself be heard by everybody around. The accuser then stated his case, and produced all his proofs, supported by witnesses. The prisoner, in return, offered all means of defence the case would suggest, advancing any contradictory evidence at his command, and his answer was listened to with undivided attention. The matter was then thoroughly discussed by the councillors, the verdict being arrived at by the decision of the majority. If the accused was acquitted, a few head of cattle from the herds of his accusers were adjudged to him as compensation. But if he was found guilty, and the headman, in whose hands the final sentence lay, pronounced in favour of death, the sentence was immediately executed. The headman, as chief executioner, rushed towards the criminal and felled him to the ground with a heavy blow of the kirri; all the other men then violently attacked him until he was beaten to death.[5]

It is clear that the Hottentots did not have specialized policemen. Every man in the community was supposed to exercise police functions. It is also clear that they did not have a legislative body or a constitution. They had only an informal judicial body, a council of elders. This judicial body enforced certain of the communal rules—rules that, were it not for such specific enforcement, would be simply mores. In short, the first step in the emergence of law is generally the emergence of some kind of organization for judging guilt and pronouncing punishment. The community as a whole can do the rest. The norms are not enacted but are simply part of the immemorial tradition of the community.

When the mores thus come to have some special organization for their enforcement, we may call them laws. Seldom are all the mores thus enforced, but only the more important ones. Since, however, there is no legislative body for the enactment of new rules not previously part of the cultural heritage, the law in this case should be called "customary law." This category then includes everything between sheer folkways and fully developed law. In so far as human societies have had any law at all, this is what they have generally had. Only with the development of large-scale political organization, extensive specialization, and writing has complete or genuine law come into existence.

[5] Schapera, *op. cit.*, pp. 339-340.

Enacted Law

In complex societies mere public opinion, informal force, and moral conscience cannot ensure order. Some form of special political organization becomes necessary. At first it may be nothing more than a headman assisted by the clan or tribal elders, but it helps to mobilize the group for war and to settle disputes that threaten internal unity. The greater its role, the more such government must command, interpret, and enforce a system of rules governing social relations. At first it utilizes the rules already there (the mores) and simply undertakes to interpret and apply them in the name of the community at large. It must decide what the mores are, which ones apply in a given case, and what the penalty should be. In the face of growing social complexity and increasing group size, however, this judicial function ceases to be sufficient. The community at large can no longer be expected to apprehend the criminals and carry out the penalties, for the people may be too scattered and too preoccupied with other matters. There must be created some enforcement agency—persons authorized to use force if necessary—which will assume police duties. Also, with conditions changing rapidly and life becoming more complicated the old mores no longer suffice to give complete guidance. Here one of two paths may be adopted: (1) There may arise no concept of enacting new rules and hence no legislating agency, but the courts may rely on past decisions embodying new applications of the old mores. Here precedent is supposedly king, but through legal fiction and new interpretations the law actually changes. Laws that are not formally enacted but are formally decided and enforced are sometimes called customary law, and in the case of Anglo-American countries, "common law." (2) On the other hand the chief, king, or other governing official may frankly make new rules; or a special body—a legislative council, parliament, or what not—may be created for this purpose. In this case the old mores are not necessarily overthrown. They may be embodied in an unwritten constitution, a written constitution, or a continuing body of "common law." They supposedly remain effective unless definitely overruled by the new enacted laws, and usually the enacted laws are conceived as somehow carrying out the spirit of the ancient mores.

The manner of deciding what the law is depends on how it is made. If it is enacted law the exact wording of the statute must be examined and interpreted in the light of a given case. If it is not enacted law its exact nature is determined by precedent, the decisions of prior tribunals being taken as final. In either case a written language is almost indispensable, in the one case to preserve the exact wording of the statute and in the other to store the prior decisions of the courts. For this reason what we regard as fully developed law is hardly to be found apart from the use of writing.

It can be seen that law is a more deliberate, more clearly stated thing than folkways or mores. It is a product of conscious thought and planning, of deliberate formulation and voluntary application. It is not only necessitated by a complex society but it also makes such a society possible. Like most of the conscious and rational aspects of social life law is in one sense superficial. It does not determine the fundamental sentiments but is rather a product of them. For instance, the things that are first enacted into law usually began as mores; so that law is sometimes defined as mores given the specific sanction of governmental enforcement. And laws which are not supported by the folkways and mores usually have little chance of being enforced. Yet superficial as they are from this point of view, laws perform a genuine function in giving precision, scope, and a means of formal enforcement to the mores in societies where multiplicity of groups and interests, accumulation of culture, and improved means of communication have broken down the solidarity of the small community and substituted for it a larger, more dynamic, and more secularized society.

Being deliberate, the law is also highly adaptable to changing conditions; hence the more dynamic the society, the less is reliance placed on traditional customary rules and the more it is placed on newly enacted regulations. Thus with the coming of railroads and automobiles to the United States, it was impossible for their regulation to be exclusively in terms of the old folkways and mores because, while these provided general rules of fairness and social organization which could remain the same, they did not provide specific application to these new modes of transportation. Consequently a whole system of law sprang up to regulate them—the clearest example being the system of traffic rules governing automobiles. True, a great number of folkways and some mores also came into being surrounding these new devices, but the point is that the society became so complex and the devices were so new that deliberate regulation became necessary—regulation in many cases devised by specialists, enacted by legislators, interpreted by courts, and enforced by policemen. Such new law which follows current conditions lacks the aura of sanctity that surrounds the mores or the customary law. It is essentially a secularized type of norm.

But it must be noted that there are sentiments of sanctity and awe with reference to the law itself as a total body. The rituals surrounding the court, such as the robe and elevated position of the judge, the swearing of the oath, the presence of a clerk and the formulae of debate and evidence, all encourage and express a sacred attitude toward the law as such. The judge must be addressed as "your honor." "Contempt of court" itself is punishable. Undue noise or unseemly behavior in court is not tolerated. There is little doubt, however, that the new regulatory laws are in themselves regarded from a secular point of view, which encourages a tendency to violate them whenever a suitable opportunity offers itself. A man does not lose social esteem because he violates a speed law; at the most he merely loses time and money. Thus the law may or may not give official sanction to folkways and mores; if it does not, it loses a certain force of sentiment which the folkways and especially the mores have behind them. Generally, however, the legal system is buttressed by an indirect if not a direct connection with the mores, since the very conception of legality, of respect for authority, of justice and right, are inherent in the mores. Yet when the laws are somehow out of line with the folkways and mores, these very selfsame attitudes are used as a justification for disobedience to the law.

If we ask how laws ever become instituted which are contrary to the folkways and mores of a society, the answer is "pressure groups." Law, by definition, is enacted or at least interpreted and enforced by special agencies. These special agencies *represent* the total society or total political unit. Wherever there is representation there is also the possibility that certain parties will gain greater control over the representative body than other parties. Hence particular groups, in line with their own interests, their own folkways and mores, may engineer laws through the official channels which offend the sentiments of the rest of the society. A good illustration is the eighteenth amendment to the Constitution of the United States. The American public, for whom drinking is rooted in the folkways, was somewhat passive during the process of enacting this amendment. But the prohibitionist lobby was very active. It is safe to say that the law never represented the majority of public sentiment. Soon, however, the majority felt the effects of the law and a reaction began to assert itself which did not stop until the amendment was repealed. Of course, the greatest pressure group is the government itself. The governing group wishes to stay in power and is thus tempted to use the legislative machinery in its own interest. In a dictatorship the yielding to this temptation is painfully apparent. But all governments, whether democratic or dictatorial, depend to some extent on support and coöperation; and they try to please the organized interests in the body politic according to the amount of legitimate or illegitimate help these may be able to give. These interests may often be far from representing the sentiments of the public at large.

It has frequently been asserted that in a period of change the law lags behind other aspects of society. This is not necessarily true. Often the law is utilized as an instrument of social reform and, if successful, of social change. The eighteenth amendment after all was regarded as "forward looking" when it was adopted; it was certainly ahead of the mores. The Wagner Labor Relations Act was probably ahead of the general sentiments of the public at the time it was enacted. In Latin America much "enlightened" legislation has been passed in the 20th century, not because the bulk of the people were insisting on such changes but because the governing and intellectual elite, which alone ran the government, was nourished on European and American models. How fast the law moves ahead depends on which pressure groups are pushing it. If the pressure group is a reform league an attempt may be made to "reform society by passing laws." In that case the attempt may fail because the mores are lagging behind the law. If the pressure group is conservative an attempt may be made to "set back the clock" by passing "reactionary" legislation. If the attempt fails it is because the mores are ahead of the laws.

The only law that is likely to be always behind the times is customary or common law, precisely because it is closest to if not identical with the major mores of the community. But even customary law may undergo changes—often by the process of legal fiction and reinterpretation—which very nearly keep step with social change generally. Enacted law on the other hand is an important means whereby a complex and changing society maintains stability despite the rapid alterations. Such law helps the society assimilate the changes by adjusting group advantages and injuries resulting from them. It inaugurates some types of change that can come only from legislative action. Finally, by affecting the framework in which social relations can take place, law may become an advanced instrument of social change on a national and international level. The dogma that the law always lags behind the times is like most other unqualified generalizations about social change—strictly untrue.

Institutions

At the beginning of this chapter we spoke of a normative order. So far, however, our classification of norms has not included any discussion of the orderly relationships between norms. It is now necessary to point out that the totality of folkways, mores, and laws in a society are related in a systematic fashion and that consequently a fruitful approach to understanding social structure is in terms of the normative system.

Too often we are inclined to think of normative order in terms of logical consistency. Actually the verbal statements of the norms may be highly inconsistent one with the other. Admonitions may direct the individual to do exactly opposite things. For instance, members of the same group may be told on the one hand that the meek shall inherit the earth, and on the other that only the brave deserve the fair; that celibacy is holy, yet that marriage is sacred; that a little knowledge is a dangerous thing, yet that half a loaf is better than no bread at all; that everyone should hitch his wagon to a star, yet that uneasy lies the head that wears the crown. These verbal formulations, however, are apt to be superficial and their inconsistencies unimportant, for two reasons: First, most folkways and mores are not stated in sufficiently accurate verbal forms to be subjected to analysis of their logical implications with relation to other norms. They are vague and hide many of their assumptions. It is only the laws, by virtue of their more deliberate character, which can be discussed from the point of view of logical consistency, and it is well known that bodies of law applicable to whole societies are *systems* in the sense that they permit logical analysis and tend toward mutual compatibility of the numerous particular laws constituting the system. Second, most folkways and mores in contradistinction to laws are not stated verbally anyway. The verbal statement is not the important thing, but rather the sentiments and unconscious attitudes which underlie any verbal statements that may be made. It follows, therefore, that the place to look for consistency, for the order in the norms, is not in the verbal statements but in the applications to behavior. We may, for example, view the consistency of the norms from the point of view of the system of positions which each person holds and the relation of these positions to those which other persons in the society hold. This will be done in the next chapter. Or we may look at the normative order from the point of view of the elements of action—ends, means, and conditions—with a view to understanding how the norms embody themselves in action. This will be done in the chapter after the next. For the present it is sufficient to lay down the principle that in norms as applied in the factual world there is a certain amount of mutual dependence and order, and that on the purely normative level the concept of *institutions* serves better than any other to convey the notion of segments or parts of this normative order.

An institution can be defined as a *set* of interwoven folkways, mores, and laws built around one or more functions. It is a part of the social structure, set off by the closeness of its organization and by the distinctness of its functions. It is therefore inclusive rather than exclusive of the concepts previously defined; for without folkways and mores there could be no institutions. Marriage, for example, embraces the complex of folkways surrounding the approved mating of men and women, including in our culture engagement and wedding rings, rice throwing, the honeymoon, lifting the bride over the threshold, showers, etc. It also embraces certain mores—premarital chastity, postmarital fidelity, taking of the vows, obligation of support, etc. Finally, it embraces certain laws—license, record, right of divorce for cause, protection against fraud, proper age, absence of prohibitive kinship bonds, etc. All of these norms taken together form a definite structure—the institution of marriage—which has meaning as a whole and which, when operative in behavior, results in the performance of certain social and individual functions such as reproduction and child rearing on the social side, sexual gratification and affection on the individual side. Similarly it can be said that economic, political, religious, and recreational institutions each represent a distinguishable set of interrelated folkways, mores, and laws coherently organized and capable of performing distinct functions. In later chapters each major type of institution will be analyzed with this conception in mind.

The quickest way to envisage the total social order of a society is to understand its major institutions and the relations between these institutions. Thus if a person can grasp the basic economic, political, religious, familial, and recreational complexes in the culture of the United States and can see how they are mutually interdependent, he has mastered the most salient features of our social organization. The rest, even including the class structure and the population distribution, is a matter of filling in the details. Often the specialist deals with only one institutional complex, ignoring the rest. The economic historian, for example, deals only with that part of history which is relevant to economic organization. Such specialization has the advantage of being broad enough to give us a substantial view of the social order and yet narrow enough to deal minutely and realistically with the facts. It does not, however, give us the total picture. The latter—an over-all view of the entire normative structure—is apt to seem vague and abstract, particularly when the society under consideration is a great and heterogeneous one. Yet the over-all view is equally essential, and there must be some social scientists (not merely philosophers or literateurs) who are willing to undertake it.[6] The social anthropologist who goes out and studies a small isolated primitive society has an easier task. It is easier for him to determine what lies in the society and what not, to pick out the essential features, and to grasp their interrelations; furthermore, since he is not describing a society of which his readers are members, he cannot be checked and criticized so readily. The sociologist describing his own society can scarcely satisfy any of his readers because they all tend to look at the whole from the point of view of their own experience within it.

Custom, Morality, and Religion

In any language there are words vaguely designating different kinds of norms. English has many such words, including "custom," "convention," "etiquette," "morality," "usage," "fashion," and "fad." The meanings overlap but they are sufficiently distinct to indicate

[6] One such attempt is Robt. C. Angell, *Social Integration in the United States* (New York: McGraw-Hill, 1941).

that there are many kinds of folkways and mores. It would be possible to differentiate the various kinds according to the institutional complex of which they form a part. Thus we speak of family customs, economic customs, religious customs, linguistic customs, etc. This is commonly done and will be relevant later when we consider the major institutions. For present purposes, however, another line of distinction seems more appropriate. This is the line of distinction conveyed by the common words of our language and already used in the present chapter, resting upon the degree of permanence, the amount of awareness, the strength of the sentiment, and the kind of sanction characterizing the norm.

"Custom" is a broad term embracing all of the norms classified as folkways and mores. It connotes long established usage and is therefore frequently contrasted with what is new, as when we speak of "the customary way of doing things," or say that a given innovation is "contrary to custom." Custom refers primarily to practices that have been oft-repeated by a multitude of generations, practices that tend to be followed simply because they have been followed in the past. The term is therefore closer to folkways than to mores, but it tends to convey the traditional, automatic, mass character of both of them.

"Morality" on the other hand lays stress upon the inner sense of obligation, the feeling of right and wrong. It implies real sentiment behind the observance of the rule and a certain amount of principle and firmness of character in one's conduct. The norm is observed not simply because it is traditional, not simply because others around one observe it, but because it conforms to an abstract principle of justice, purity, fairness, truth, etc. It is more self-conscious, abstract, and consistent than sheer custom. It is therefore closer to the mores, although it stresses the sentiment, rationalization, and consistency behind the mores. On an extremely intellectual or philosophical level morality becomes an "ethic." The latter is often related to the norms of special groups (as when we speak of "medical ethics") or is reserved for the speculative systems of outstanding thinkers (as when we speak of the ethics of Aristotle).

Every major religion stands in intimate relation to the morality of the people who profess the religion. Certain of the moral tenets are explained as having a supernatural origin; the powers of the other world are conceived as supporting and cherishing these principles, being ready to punish their violation and to reward their observance; and salvation and blessedness are interpreted in terms of the individual's relation to the moral ideals. Religion therefore adds something to morality and strengthens it by connecting it with the world lying beyond the senses. It often happens that not all the moral rules are embodied in religion. Some of the lesser rules may be conceived in purely secular terms. Nevertheless, there is usually a feeling that the supernatural world somehow is connected with the whole of group morality as a system. In other words the sense of guilt at having violated a moral principle is very close to the sense of sin even when the specific norm is not religiously sanctioned. When, therefore, we speak of Christian morality we mean something much broader than merely the Ten Commandments.

Convention and Etiquette

Convention and etiquette are both special kinds of folkways, distinguished by a certain awareness that they have no deeper meaning but are merely matters of convenience in social relations. In this sense they stand at an opposite pole from morality, though they share with the latter an element of traditionalism. Because of their intrinsic meaninglessness both convention and etiquette often acquire an invidious symbolism that plays a part in class relations.

Convention is more a matter of principle and less a matter of adornment than etiquette. It prescribes rather rigid forms which social relations in given situations must follow. It thus eliminates trial and error and hence confusion in human interaction. The rule that motorists must drive on the right side of the road is a convention. Nobody considers this a sacred rule or one involving some mystic principle. It is merely an agreed-upon procedure, and when one is in England one adjusts quite readily to driving on the left instead of the right. Everybody recognizes that without some such rule the highway would be a much more dangerous place than it is. The essential thing is not the particular rule but some standardized procedure by which mutual activities are regulated and prevented from interfering with each other. People are constantly forced to adjust to the presence of others in going about their daily business. They must go through the same doorways, get on and off the same public conveyances, patronize the same shops, seek the same goods. The conventions afford a modus vivendi in all these situations. The fact that the relationships go as smoothly and automatically as they do, with a minimum of confusion and friction, suggests that the conventions are generally satisfactory. The mental subtleties as well as the physical conveniences of social interaction are subject to convention. In conversation, for example, certain topics are ignored by tacit agreement because they might create tension if openly expressed. Certain forms of speech and behavior are used to keep a relationship on a superficially friendly basis, when underneath there is a real antipathy or conflict of interest. One does not say to a man's face what one says to his friends, and one does not say to his friends what one says to his enemies. A humane conspiracy prevails by which, except in extraordinary circumstances, a man is permitted to cherish his own illusions about himself. In make-believe, in humor perhaps, a person may tell the truth, but only because it is assumed not to be true. Without these conventions human intercourse would indeed be uncouth and unbearable.

Etiquette, or "good manners," is concerned with the choice of the proper form for doing something. It implies that a choice is possible and that there is a hierarchy of the possible alternatives. For this reason it serves as a ready if superficial device, an external symbol, by which a person's class status may be identified. From the point of view of social efficiency and convenience it makes little difference how one disposes of one's knife, fork, and napkin, introduces two strangers, or dresses for the evening meal. But from the point of view of punctilio it makes a great deal of difference, because it is by a proper or improper choice in these little matters that one's standing in the social hierarchy is often judged. Etiquette is thus mainly a discriminating device, although it also serves as an external manifestation of good intentions toward others, as in greeting, well-wishing, and other behavior classified under the heading of politeness.

Fashion and Fad

When we speak of folkways and mores, customs and morals, convention and etiquette, we think of them as relatively fixed. We know that they do change, but the change comes so slowly that it is hardly perceptible. There was no precise moment, for example, when the pronunciation of English in the United States became suddenly different from the pronunciation in England. The divergence evolved gradually and unconsciously, yet it has now reached such a stage that the two peoples have difficulty in understanding each other. When philologists look back over the history of language, they find that such changes occur persistently and regularly; but within a single lifetime they are hardly discernible. Thus the bulk of the folkways and mores remain relatively permanent, and any attempted change in them tends to arouse emotional resistance in the public at large. People feel insecure, confused, and angry when established custom is "flouted" or "outraged."

Man does not live, however, by security alone. He yearns for something new, for variety and novelty. At first it might seem that this desire could not be satisfied through social norms, because the norms emphasize obligation and conformity. Yet curiously, the human animal manages to be a conformist even when he is seeking change. He achieves this strange anomaly by a set of norms that demand an intense conformity while they last but which endure only a short time. These norms go by such names as "fashion," "fad," and "craze."

Time is the very essence of fashion. The same style of dress that was in vogue three years ago may appear ridiculous today, and the style that seems so beautiful, so exquisitely appropriate today will inevitably appear ludicrous a few years hence. A set of old photographs arouses our laughter. We wonder how we could have worn such foolish hats, such peculiar trousers, such ugly dresses, and we congratulate ourselves on showing much better taste now. Since we cannot visualize what changes the future will bring, the standard of today seems somehow perfect and ultimate, and so we do not hesitate to stand once more before the camera.

The rapidity with which fashion changes introduces a certain emulative and invidious possibility. The new mode cannot be adopted simultaneously by everybody in the society. Somebody has to start it and somebody has to be the last to adopt it. Just how it starts is still something of a mystery requiring more sociological research to solve than has yet been given it. Many fashions seem to appear first in the upper classes, presumably started by persons who cater to these classes. People lower in the social scale then imitate the new mode and thus acquire a transient identification with the elite. Being in fashion of course involves considerable cost; one shows his affluence, alertness, and good taste by keeping up with the latest mode. Fashion seems to be most prominent in an open class society, where the symbols of status are not fixed by custom but are changeable and hence subject to imitation. Many fashions, however, seem to have little relation to class prestige. They are started by those who are skillful at catching the mood of the moment and are imitated simply because they arouse interest or give a minor degree of personal distinction. The new song hits, for example, are adopted most quickly by adolescents of all classes, and they are produced by writers and composers who have talent and who have access to the channels of mass communication. Doubtless the individuals who learn a new tune ahead of others in their group, if the group is interested in that sort of thing, derive a bit of personal esteem from their alacrity; but many start singing the new song just because it appeals to them. Others of course, including many adults, acquire the new melody mainly because it is forced on them through endless repetition. In general most people are content to follow along. They are not the leaders of fashion, nor are they the hopeless laggards. To be completely out of fashion in many particulars is to lose much social esteem, and few people care to run such a risk.

Though fashion plays a role in the dynamic interplay of class relations, though it satisfies simultaneously the contrary desires for novelty and for conformity, it still pertains to the more superficial aspects of social life. The deep and abiding patterns defined in custom and law lay down the essential structure of a society. Within the interstices of this structure, within the areas of indifference, fashion holds sway. Fashion pertains to things that can change because they are trivial, whereas custom pertains to things that cannot change because they are important. Fashion stresses the change itself, not what changes. "It turns the desire for novelty into social practice," and "makes novelty the right and proper thing for the group." [7]

Fashion is necessarily more prevalent in modern civilized society than in primitive tribes or peasant communities. Modern society has gone farther than any other in its positive evaluation of change, in its tolerance of differences, and in its cultivation of individual taste. It therefore places few shackles on the cycle of fashion. At the same time its mobile class structure with numerous ill-defined strata gives

[7] R. M. MacIver, *Society* (New York: Rinehart, 1937), p. 366.

individuals a powerful incentive to be "in the swim." Urban life with its fleeting and specialized contacts makes the individual's rating depend on readily observable externalities and thus magnifies the importance of fashion as a status device. A man is judged not so much by his ancestry, his character, or his genuine accomplishments as by his automobile, his clothes, his use of English, and his manners. If he can keep up-to-date in these matters, though not too up-to-date, he will assure himself of a certain *éclat*. Modern society also possesses a greater economic surplus and more leisure than other societies, and hence furnishes its members with the means and time to play with luxuries, to occupy themselves with superfluities. "We do not think of fashion in overalls; there is more of fashion in the body of an automobile than in its chassis; there are no fashions in steam shovels. Consequently, the higher the standard of living, the more material there is for fashion to operate upon." [8] Finally, the means of mass communication are more rapid in modern society. A novelty invented anywhere among the millions may soon be known everywhere. And there are countless specialists whose talent consists precisely in creating novelties. Custom reigns most where isolation is greatest; fashion predominates where contact is easiest. The potpourri of cultural forms in industrial civilization, the cumulation of technological invention and ideological inquiry, the rapid transmission of "news," all diminish the area of life controlled by custom and increase the area controlled by fashion. The margin of moral indifference is thus tremendously expanded, giving great freedom to the play of fancy and the vagaries of fashions, fads, and crazes.

> In extreme cases, among frivolous or very sophisticated groups, fashion may become the main guide of life. In decadent civilizations it may usurp the place of morals. Thus Tacitus, in deploring the decline of morals in the Rome of his day, declared that 'to corrupt and to be corrupted is called the fashion.' Within its proper sphere fashion serves a useful social function. It introduces a common pattern into the area of indifference, an appearance or sense of likeness which enables people of very diverse interests and dispositions to meet on common ground and which makes it easier for them to retain beneath that surface, in harmony with one another, their essential individual and group characters. It has on that account a special significance in the extensive range of a diversified democratic

[8] MacIver, *op. cit.*, p. 367.

civilization. But when its control passes beyond the superficialities of life, it offers a poor substitute for the more established sanctions. For its rule is shallow and inconsequent, concerned with the form and not with the substance of living, devoid of conviction and of stability.[9]

What we have said about fashion is true *a fortiori* of fads and crazes. The latter are merely special cases of fashion distinguished by the quickness with which they alternate, the utter superficiality of their content, and the irrationality and intensity of the temporary fascination with them. The famous dancing mania of the Middle Ages was a craze; the late and unlamented dance step called the "Lindy Hop" was a fad. By virtue of their extremity fads and crazes are generally limited to a smaller proportion of the population than is fashion. When skirts become longer, nearly every woman feels obligated to lengthen her own; but a new puzzle, a new game, a trick dance step that becomes all the rage is likely to involve the participation of only a small segment of the populace. Correspondingly, the societal importance of fads and crazes is less than that of fashion in general. We hardly think of them as norms at all but rather as examples of crowd behavior.[10]

Society and the Normative Order

It should now be clear that social norms are extremely varied and extremely pervasive, that they are a peculiar feature of human society, and that they are an essential part of what we call social order. They have arisen as a feature of cultural adaptation. The individual acquires them through a process of indoctrination. Some of them he internalizes and these become part of his personality. Some of them he respects because of their consequences. Regardless of whether or not he obeys the norms completely, they influence his behavior and his thinking. It is largely through them that his conduct is regulated and integrated with the conduct of his fellows. It is through them that a society acquires a coherent structure and manages to get the business of group life tended to.

It follows that one of the most fruitful approaches to the study

[9] MacIver, *op. cit.*, pp. 367-368. Quoted with permission.

[10] Edward A. Ross in his *Social Psychology* (New York: Macmillan, 1921) treats fads and crazes in a chapter called "Mob Mind."

of society is through the analysis of norms. When we understand the normative system of a society, when we know the folkways, mores, laws, and institutions, we know a great deal about that society. Consequently, the study of social norms represents one of the fundamental desiderata of the science of human sociology.

In any tribe, community, or nation, however, the number of specific norms is so great that a mere catalogue of them would never be finished. What the sociologist looks for is not such a catalogue but an understanding of the *system* of norms. He wants to know the more fundamental rules, to comprehend the relations between them, and to trace their connection with other aspects of group existence. He wants to understand the basic stresses and cleavages, the conflicts between norms and the means by which these are overcome. Therefore, he usually centers his attention upon the major institutions and views the more specific norms as integral parts of these institutions. In this way he is able to see the normative order as a whole; he does not miss the forest for the trees.

Throughout the rest of this volume the "normative approach" (in the sense of analyzing norms and institutions, not in the sense of laying down moral imperatives) will be employed and will be integrated so far as possible with other fundamental approaches. The present chapter must be regarded as an incomplete discussion of normative phenomena. It has not gone far into the connection between the individual personality and the normative order; it has not said much about religion and the moral system; it has not canvassed thoroughly the subject of social change in relation to normative rules; nor has it discussed the major institutions. These things will be treated later. The discussion at this point has been concerned with describing the nature of social norms and classifying some of the main types. It is merely an introduction to the analysis of norms as an approach to sociological understanding.

References

Ruth Benedict, *The Chrysanthemum and the Sword* (New York: Houghton Mifflin, 1946).

Lucid analysis of Japanese morality and its relation to the behavior of the Japanese in World War II.

A. Radcliffe Brown, *The Andaman Islanders* (Cambridge: Cambridge University Press, 1922; Glencoe, Illinois: Free Press, 1949).

The social customs and institutions of a primitive society, analyzed from the point of view of their functional interrelations. An outstanding contribution to the literature of social anthropology.

Morris R. Cohen, *Law and the Social Order* (New York: Harcourt, Brace, 1933), Parts 2 and 3.

Essays by a legal realist on various aspects of the law as a social phenomenon. Readable and provocative.

Jerome Hall, *Theft, Law and Society* (Boston: Little, Brown, 1935).

The evolution of the law and practice of theft during the development of modern society. An excellent study.

Walter Lippmann, *Public Opinion* (New York: Macmillan, 1922).

Popular myths, stereotypes, and the ways of their enforcement. A book that will never grow out-of-date.

Robert M. MacIver, *Society* (New York: Rinehart, 1937). Chap. 18, "The Mores and the Social Structure"; Chap. 19, "The Major Social Codes"; Chap. 20, "Social Codes and the Individual Life."

An excellent brief treatment of the normative aspect of social phenomena.

Bronislaw Malinowski, *Crime and Custom in Savage Society* (London: Paul, Trench, Trubner, 1932).

Rules and their violation as seen in the Trobriand Islands. Stresses the reciprocity of social obligations, the readiness to disobey rules, and the spontaneous nature of punishment.

Karl Olivecrona, *Law as Fact* (London: Humphrey Milford, 1939).

A lucid and incisive discussion of the nature of law as seen in its social context.

Roscoe Pound, "Sociology of Law," in Georges Gurvitch and Wilbert E. Moore, *Twentieth Century Sociology* (New York: Philosophical Library, 1945).

A scholarly account of various writers and their contributions to the sociology of law, by the foremost of contemporary legal theorists.

Edward A. Ross, *Social Psychology* (New York: Macmillan, 1921).

A very readable account of public opinion, conventionality, fashion, fad, etc. In some ways this book anticipates and excels Lippman.

Wm. Graham Sumner, *Folkways* (Boston: Ginn, 1906).

The classic account of folkways, mores, and law from the point of view of comparative sociology. Still vivid and informative.

Wm. I. Thomas, *Primitive Behavior* (New York: McGraw-Hill, 1937).

Comprehensive treatment of all kinds of social obligations as found in primitive societies, with liberal quotations from the field literature of social anthropology.

N. S. Timasheff, *An Introduction to the Sociology of Law* (Cambridge: Harvard University Press, 1939).

This textbook is comprehensive and scholarly, though not altogether successful as a systematic and scientific treatise. It contains an extensive bibliography on the subject.

Max Weber, *The Theory of Social and Economic Organization* (New York: Oxford University Press, 1947), Chap. 1, "The Fundamental Concepts of Sociology."

Deals with the concept of legitimacy in relation to social organization, especially in relation to authority.

CHAPTER IV

STATUS AND ROLE

ALL approaches to social phenomena may be drawn together in terms of the interacting situation in which two or more persons are in contact. If, for example, one's scientific interest is focused primarily on social norms, it is worthwhile looking at the situations in which these norms apply. Similarly, if one's interest is directed toward status and role, as is the case in the present chapter, it is worthwhile asking how statuses and roles figure in the concrete situation. Let us therefore, in beginning our discussion, seize the opportunity to introduce the interacting situation as the meeting ground of all sociological abstractions.

The Interacting Situation

The essence of any social situation lies in the mutual expectations of the participants. These expectations rest to a great extent on the norms applicable in the situation. Every culture evolves folkways and mores to cover typical situations, thus furnishing a pattern for the mutual expectations of the interacting parties. In this sense almost every situation is socially defined. Each actor has some conception of what he himself expects of the others, and believes he has some notion of what they expect of him and of what they expect that he expects them to expect.

Each party's action on the basis of the definition of the situation has the effect of testing the validity of his own anticipations as well as the anticipations of his co-actors. If his behavior seems "natural" in the situation—i.e. if it fits the anticipations of the others—they respond as they had planned to respond. If he in turn was correct in guessing their response, he then responds to their behavior in the manner foreseen by himself and them. Assuming that everything "goes smoothly" according to the mutual expectations, the interaction usually achieves a previsioned end and gets something accomplished. But should the action at any step prove different from that which was expected, the situation must be *redefined*--that is, the expectations must be altered to meet the new turn of events. With the situation thus redefined the interaction may go on smoothly to a conclusion (a conclusion not originally foreseen but nevertheless subsequently provided for), or it may have to be redefined several times before the sequence of interaction is complete. The redefinitions of the situation may involve increasing pleasure and compatibility on the part of the actors, or they may involve growing displeasure and impatience. If, for instance, a traveling salesman walks into a store and the proprietor mistakes him for a customer, the relationship must be redefined by the salesman. If the goods recommended by the salesman are disliked by the proprietor, an unfavorable redefinition will have to be made. If, however, it is subsequently discovered that the salesman went to the same college as the proprietor, a slight and pleasurable further redefinition will take place. Any number of incidents of this sort may transpire before the business is transacted and the interaction terminated. In some cases the situation may be progressively redefined in the direction of unpleasantness. Indeed, the behavior of a participant may be such as to require a redefinition in terms of punishment; the response of the others then takes the form of retaliation.

The actual behavior thus plays a dynamic part in the social situation. It is through a chain of overt responses (either symbolic or literal) that the process of interchange moves along, each act testing the various mutual expectations and forcing a constant redefinition. The overt behavior is always begun with respect to a defined situation. No circumstance under which different people come together is totally undefined. At the very worst there are general rules capable of being applied to such situations—as when strangers meet. Often, it is true, the details of action are not very clearly defined, so that there is an air of tentativeness about the contact. When a student first goes to college he experiences a certain amount of disorientation because he does not know exactly how to behave toward all the people he must somehow deal with. It is quite true of course that no situation is completely defined in the sense that all the interaction is totally predictable. The nearest approach to total predictability is found in formal occasions, when the behavior is minutely regulated according to convention and when any deviation from the prescribed pattern is carefully avoided. Although such situations are totally defined ideologically, the concrete action may at any point introduce unexpected elements.

The expectations involved in a situation are based in part on the norms applying to that situation. In so far as this is true the reasoning runs as follows: "If such and such an act occurs, then such and such a response *must* (or *should*) follow." This is similar to scientific inference, but the difference lies in the term "must" or "should." In science the result follows because it could not possibly fail to follow. In normative thought the result follows only if *the actor tries to achieve it.* The result required by a normative rule is therefore a matter of intention and effort. Traffic laws lay down the necessity of obeying certain signals. When the policeman gives a signal one's car must behave in a certain way—not because the signal automatically affects the car like wind turning a windmill but because the driver, having perceived the signal, knows what is expected and feels a necessity of acting accordingly. The actor knows that if he disappoints the policeman's expectations the situation will be redefined by the policeman in appropriately unpleasant terms.

Not all expectations are normative in character, however. There is a certain factual element that helps define what will happen. One knows, for example, that a child of two years cannot do the things that an adult of thirty can do. One knows that people have motives for acting differently from what the norms call for, and that one must take account of these motives in predicting the behavior of one's co-actors. The policeman trying to apprehend a man thought to be a criminal must be prepared to see the man resist arrest. The parent must admit the possibility of misbehavior on the part of the child. By definition the concrete situation is one in which all of the factors determining behavior come together. The normative element is only one such factor. But even this element hinges on another—namely, the status of the persons involved in the situation—which brings us to the subject of social status, position, and role.

Identity within the Situation

Essential in the interacting situation is the identity of each participant, for not everybody is supposed to expect the same thing. A husband expects sexual response from his wife, but not every man has the right to expect such a response from her. A president expects certain advice and help from his cabinet ministers, but nobody else may expect these things from them. A person therefore enters a social situation with an identity already established. His identity refers to his *position,* or *status,* within the social structure applicable to the given situation, and establishes his rights and obligations with reference to others holding positions within the same structure. His position and consequently his identity in the particular situation result from all the other positions he holds in other major social structures, especially in the other structures most closely related to the one he is acting in at the moment.

To aid in establishing the identity of the person, external symbols are frequently utilized. A common indicator, for example, is the style of dress. When different members of the armed services happen to meet, their relationships are regulated in advance by the military code. The individuals may be absolute strangers, yet from the uniform and badges worn they can tell at a glance what their respective positions are and can behave accordingly. Similarly, men and women wear distinct costumes, and in many societies the married and unmarried, the old and young, the merchants and craftsmen do the same. If the entire costume is not distinct it may be that a badge or emblem, style of haircut, quality or color of cloth, or some other minor device serves to identify the individual's social position.

Undoubtedly there are many mistakes and many frauds possible in this matter of identification, as when an unauthorized person wears the costume or insignia to which he has no right. A married man may pretend to be unmarried. A civilian may impersonate an officer. A layman may practice medicine without a license. The mores and laws of the society usually condemn such fraudulent practices and punish the pretender when he is caught.

In the course of an individual's life very broad positions are first acquired. He begins with a general identity—such as that of class, sex, and family—which will later govern his position in many particular situations. As he goes through life he acquires more specific positions, and his actual behavior in the various situations to which these positions apply serves to refine and modify the initially assigned identity. Thus as time goes by he has for each new situation a more complete and more unique identity. Such progressive refinement gives a dynamic, developmental character to his positional history. For instance, a male acquires certain broad rights and obligations simply because of his quality of maleness, and these enter to some degree into nearly every situation in which he participates. But his subsequent personal history in day-to-day interaction contributes further to his social identity and differentiates him in many respects from other males.

The normative system lays down the formal rights and obligations in connection with a position. Though it permits a certain amount of legitimate variation within the limits imposed, it also lays down rules to be followed in case the individual oversteps the limits. A right is a legitimate expectation entertained by a person in one position with respect to the behavior of a person in another position. From the point of view of the other person this claim represents an obligation. "Right" and "obligation," therefore, are simply different definitions of the same relationship.

Although many norms are expressed independently of particular positions and situations—like the simple exhortation to be honest—they must, when applied in behavior, vary according to the status of the actor and the situation he is in. Absolute honesty in the sense of speaking the truth on all occasions is an impossible ideal; there are many occasions when persons do not wish to hear the truth, particularly about themselves, and will penalize the person who tells it to them. The same is true of other absolute or abstract norms. All norms, no matter how expressed, are relative to the particular situation. Which norm applies in a given case depends upon the relations between the statuses of the interacting persons.

The Organization of Statuses

An individual carries his social position around in his head, so to speak, and puts it into action when the appropriate occasion arises. Not only does he carry it in his head but others also carry it in theirs, because social positions are matters of reciprocal expectation and must be publicly and commonly conceived by everyone in the group. An individual who has a purely private conception of his status is insane and socially useless.

Each person occupies many different statuses. We sometimes speak of *the* status or *the* social position of a given individual, meaning the sum total of his specific statuses and roles, especially in so far as they bear upon his general "social standing." More often, however, we qualify our statement by giving at the same time the context to which our statement applies. Thus we may say that Dr. Jones has a high standing *in his profession,* or that Mrs. Jones is well known *as a clubwoman.* In other words we rate the person's behavior according to the norms applying to a specific status. We implicitly recognize that he has many statuses and that we are singling one out for particular mention.

All the positions occupied by a single individual constitute when taken together an important element in his personality. Since each person has but so much time, energy, and ability, and since his activity must achieve results and satisfy needs, his system of statuses must be to some degree integrated. His personal efficiency, his mental stability and contentment depend to a large extent on the integration of his various social positions.

Similarly, the total system of positions in the entire society or group must be reasonably well integrated. Otherwise the society or group could not carry on its existence. Ordinarily the various statuses —occupational, familial, political, religious—are so bound together in terms of interlocking rights and obligations that their manifestation in behavior gets things accomplished and the collectivity is perpetuated. One of the things that is perpetuated, of course, is the system of positions itself. Basically the positions tend to remain the same; it is mainly the occupants of the positions who change.

STATUS AND OFFICE

For clarity one should recognize that some social positions are, so to speak, in the folkways and mores whereas others are merely in the by-laws and rules of specific organizations. Some are generalized and known to everybody; others are limited and known only to a few. Perhaps it will aid understanding if we give a name to each half of this continuum, calling the one *status* and the other *office.* The term status would then designate a position in the general institutional system, recognized and supported by the entire society, spontaneously evolved rather than deliberately created, rooted in the folkways and mores. Office, on the other hand, would designate a position in a deliberately created organization, governed by specific and limited rules in a limited group, more generally achieved than ascribed. An example of a status in our society would be "skilled laborer"; of an office, "head carpenter of the Blank Construction Company." Another example of status would be "professor"; and of a corresponding office, "professor of government at the University of Arizona."

It can be seen that holding an office may at the same time give one a status. The kind of status it gives depends upon the importance, scope, and function of the organization of which the office is a part, as well as the importance of this particular office within the organization. A general and a private both occupy a niche in the army, but because of the great difference of rank their respective positions give them a quite different status with the public at large. Furthermore, in wartime when the function of the army is supremely important the prestige attached to all army positions tends to rise, whereas in peacetime it usually falls again.

Conversely, holding a particular status may help one acquire a certain office. Statistics in the United States prove definitely that sons of professional people and wealthy businessmen have a better chance of attaining high positions than do sons of other kinds of men. One study found, for example, that "52 per cent of the children of professional people go to college, as contrasted with only 6 per cent of the children of unskilled laborers."[1] The difficulties that United States Negroes have in securing skilled and well paid jobs are notorious.[2] In countless ways a man's more generalized statuses determine his specific offices, and the latter in turn affect his statuses. Between these two kinds of social position there is necessarily a close interdependence. Occupational position, for instance, is often a status and office both, the first when viewed from the standpoint of the general public, the second when viewed from the standpoint of the particular business or agency. The same is true of many other concrete social positions.

POSITION AND ROLE

A position, whether status or office, defines a minimum of obligatory behavior for the incumbent, but it cannot insure that the incum-

[1] Works Progress Administration, Division of Social Research, *Urban Youth, Their Characteristics and Prospects,* Publications, Series 1, No. 24. Cited in Wm. F. Ogburn and Meyer F. Nimkoff, *Sociology* (New York: Houghton Mifflin, 1940), p. 314.

[2] See Gunnar Myrdal, *An American Dilemma* (New York: Harpers, 1942), Part IV.

bent will carry out this behavior perfectly. If it is a position on a baseball team it calls for certain responses when the ball comes within reach of the player, but the player may perform poorly or skillfully. If it is a position in a business office it calls for intelligent responses when certain questions arise, but the person occupying the position may respond wisely or unwisely—so wisely that he may be promoted or so unwisely that he may be dismissed. How an individual actually performs in a given position, as distinct from how he is supposed to perform, we call his *role*. The role, then, is the manner in which a person actually carries out the requirements of his position. It is the dynamic aspect of status or office and as such is always influenced by factors other than the stipulations of the position itself. This means that from the point of view of the social structure it always contains a certain novelty and unpredictability.[3] When we elect the mayor of a town we have a fair idea of what he is supposed to do in the office, but we can never be sure just what he will do. If he falls too far short of the expected behavior we may impeach him or we may simply fail to re-elect him. If he does more than the office really requires we praise him and perhaps elect him to a higher post.

What leads an individual to do less or more than his duty in a position? One consideration is how hard he *tries*. We assume he will try to carry out at least the minimal requirements. If he does not try at all or for some other reason falls completely short, he does not occupy the position at all in a functional sense (though possibly in a purely formal sense). The fact that he tries is due to the normative element in the position. Without some *feeling* of obligation, some desire to try, there would be no effectiveness to the so-called rights and obligations. How devoted the person is to the given norms of his position and hence how hard he tries, depends of course on the other demands on his time and loyalty. Holding other positions with rights and obligations attached to them, he is forced constantly to avoid giving everything he has to the one status or office under consideration. He must somehow lead a balanced life, rendering both to Caesar and to God. The laborer may deliberately do less than he

[3] *Cf.* G. H. Mead, *Mind, Self, and Society* (Chicago: University of Chicago Press, 1934), pp. 173-178. What Mead calls the "me" is the internally perceived position while the "I" is the actual behavior in the position. "The response to that situation as it appears in his immediate experience is uncertain, and it is that which constitutes the 'I'." (P. 175.)

can because his job and self-satisfaction depend not solely on how well he performs but on how well he stands with his union, and his union may be advocating a go-slow and extend-the-work policy. The businessman may give less than fair value received because he identifies himself more with the profit of his company than with the benefit of the community at large. The father may neglect his wife and children because he wishes to put most of his time into his professional advancement.

But the fact that even when trying the individual always manifests variations from the expected norms, shows that a factor other than effort influences performance. This is the factor of capacity, determined both by experience and by heredity. Experience involves cumulative learning in previous situations; it builds up in the individual the integrated habit systems that influence capacity to perform at any current moment. Heredity influences the effect that experience has. A feebleminded person cannot ordinarily perform well the duties of husband, teacher, or leader, whereas a well-endowed person may perform them much better than average. Some kinds of statuses and offices require special talents, while others require merely the expression of attitude and conformity to vague rules of behavior. The status of "grandmother" requires relatively little capacity while that of a concert pianist requires considerable. The degree to which hereditary or acquired capacity plays a part therefore varies considerably from one position to another in the social structure.

Taken as a whole the statuses and offices of a society represent a distributive system in which the talents and habits of the population are allocated to different kinds of functions. It is through them that the division of labor in human society is accomplished. An efficient society so trains and distributes its individuals that the rewards held out as rights are sufficient to induce them to try to fulfil the obligations of their positions; the obligations are proportional to individual capacities; and the expectations of different positions held by the same individual are not contradictory.

STATION AND STRATUM

Since any single individual occupies not one but many statuses and offices, and since for his personal and social efficiency he must find some coherence in the several positions he fills, we could expect that in any society certain positions will tend to adhere together in different individuals. Such is actually the case and so we may speak of a *station,* meaning by this term a cluster of statuses and offices that tend to be combined in one person as a locus and are publicly recognized as so combined in a great many cases. Whereas a single status or office defines one's position with reference to a limited sector of social interaction, a station embodies one's generalized status (the sum total of one's major positions) in the over-all social structure. A station is therefore a recurrent combination of statuses having a certain degree of fixity.

The name that is given to a particular station often comes from one of the major statuses constituting it. For instance, we sometimes speak of the "landowning class" by which we mean more than simply landownership. We mean a whole group of rights and privileges which happen to be associated with landowning but are not necessarily a part of it. A man may own no land and still be a member of the landowning class, because he has all the other positions that landowners in the given society generally have; and contrariwise a man may own land without being a member of the landowning class. Furthermore, the particular position that gives a name to the whole station may not itself be uniform; it may be really a name for a class of positions which are roughly similar and which tend to have the same associated positions. Thus doctor, lawyer, and professor are each different occupational positions, but are on about the same level of evaluation and accompanied by similar allied positions. A common name, "professionals," designating a station is therefore given the incumbents.

For a mass of persons in a given society who enjoy roughly the same station, we can use the word *stratum*. Any population is commonly divided into strata. In fact, specifying the strata is one of the most convenient and frequently used ways of giving a shorthand description of a social structure. Such a procedure implies the existence of relative rank. Different stations are felt to be unequal in the public estimation and hence a hierarchy of strata is recognized. It is also known that individuals occupying the same station and hence falling in the same stratum tend to look at the world from the same point of view. They have like interests and common problems. Sometimes though not always they stick together, manifesting a solid front towards persons in other strata. We may speak of this collective front, when it occurs, as stratum solidarity.

Several types of stratified organization may be distinguished according to the kinds of positions constituting the station, the degree of stratum solidarity, the methods by which persons reach and leave the station, etc. The best known types are the caste system at one extreme and the open class system at the other. Discussion of these types, however, must be deferred until the chapter on social stratification.

Prestige, Esteem, and Rank

An essential ingredient of social norms, it will be recalled, is the selective approval and disapproval of modes of behavior in accordance with what is expected of an individual in his social position as applied in a particular interacting situation. Now, however, it must be realized that there is still another level of invidious distinction. A person may perform all the duties of his position and may even be praised for doing this, and yet be held in low regard. A slave, for example, may obey his master well, yet in spite of his excellent behavior he will occupy a low position. A charwoman may perform her tasks unusually well and receive the praises of her employer, yet scarcely anybody will envy her status. A ghostwriter may do all the work on a book that comes out under another's name, but he will not receive the plaudits of the crowd. Truly there is a dual sense in which people are regarded, and a clear understanding requires that the two aspects of the appraising process be separated.

The secret of the matter is this: We attach an invidious value to the status or office as such, independently of who occupies it or how its requirements are carried out. At the same time we attach another kind of value to the individual according to how well or ill he fulfills the duties of whatever status he happens to be in. The first kind of invidious value—the kind attached solely to the status or office, or combination of them—we may call *prestige*. Public opinion tends always to rank positions, to refer to them as high or low, good or bad, elevated or depressed. A job is spoken of, for example, as giving high prestige to its holder. The status of the M. D., of the federal official, of the scholar and scientist is said to be high. A class is spoken of as "low" or "middle," a caste is designated as "pariah" or "Brahmin" with obvious implications. An individual is insulted if he is identified with what he feels is a lower station, as when an M. D. is mistaken for a dentist or a chiropractor. Such evaluation has purely to do with the social structure—i.e. it attaches to the status, station, or stratum in abstraction from the individual. Anybody who happens to hold the position enjoys the prestige that goes with it.

But it has already been pointed out that different incumbents of the same status or office do not fulfill its duties equally well, and that consequently these incumbents are not equally acclaimed by their associates. Since their prestige is the same by virtue of their occupying similar positions, we must call by some other name the evaluation of their role (their actual behavior in the situation). This evaluation we call *esteem.* It refers to the invidious value attached to any given role or combination of roles. A person may hold a position of high prestige and yet, by virtue of his behavior in that position, enjoy little esteem. If in various positions he behaves at variance with the expectations then he earns the reputation of buffoon, ne'er-do-well, lunatic, simpleton, blackguard, or what not. Esteem is thus always related to the expectations of a position, yet it is attached not to the position itself but to the success or failure in carrying out the stipulations of the position.

All positions carry a certain amount of prestige, either high or low. But it does not follow that between any two positions there is an invidious distinction; they may carry the same amount of prestige. Sometimes the prestige scale is referred to as a scale of *vertical* differentiation (as implied by such terms as "high," "low," "middle," "upper," "bottom class"). Accordingly, any two positions having a different rank are sometimes said in sociological literature to be separated by *vertical social distance,* and a person moving from one to the other is said to have manifested *vertical mobility.* Conversely, two different positions having the same prestige are said to be separated only by *horizontal social distance.* While often convenient, this technical usage should not be taken as being anything more than an illustrative analogy. To speak of "social space" is like calling an automobile a "mechanical horse." The analogy brings out certain truths, but if taken literally it leads one astray.

Power and Position

By *power* as applied to social affairs is usually meant the determination of the behavior of others in accordance with one's own ends. The distribution of power is intimately bound up with the distribution of statuses and offices and hence with the configuration of stations and strata. Usually, for example, the line of power corresponds roughly with the hierarchy of prestige. Thus the whole social structure, the whole system of positions, may be viewed as a legitimate power system.

Power, however, attaches in actuality not merely to the status or office but also to the individual independently of his position. In other words an individual acquires power through his role as well as through his position. This can be aptly illustrated in those numerous situations where a reversal of the alleged power relations occurs—in family relations, for instance. Thus, although the status of the *pater familias* in Roman society gave him certain rights and hence power over his wife, her intelligence and energy, if superior to his, could in fact reverse the relation and force him to play the subordinate role. Similarly in our own society, where parents are supposed to have authority over their children, we find the latter frequently tyrannizing over their gullible fathers and mothers.

It becomes necessary, then, to distinguish between what may be called structural or positional power and all other kinds of power. The first variety may be called by its usual name, authority, and the other may be referred to simply as naked or unauthorized power. The power that goes with authority is most clearly manifested when behavior is determined solely by one's status or office—for instance, in formal legal relationships as contrasted to immediate and informal relationships. Indeed, social distance (especially of the vertical sort) bolsters structural authority at the expense of personal power; intimacy, on the other hand, bolsters personal power at the expense of structural power as indicated by the saying that familiarity breeds contempt.

If, therefore, we ask what the source of a man's power is in a given case, the answer is that part of it comes from his statuses and offices and another part from his roles in these statuses and offices. The problem of the source of power, however, does not end here. It can be pushed to a more fundamental level by raising two extremely significant questions: First, how does a particular individual happen to occupy a given position and thus enjoy the authority and power that it conveys? Second, why does the position carry the power that it does? The latter question will not be fully treated until we reach the chapters on stratification and political institutions, but the first will receive its major treatment in the following paragraphs.

How Positions Are Filled: Ascription and Achievement

The process by which the statuses in a society are constantly being filled by the infiltration of new personnel to take the place of the old is sometimes called, by organic analogy, social metabolism. Such metabolism is fully as important to a society as digestion is to an organism. In both cases raw materials are being absorbed and made to furnish the energy that gives life to the whole structure. In the case of the organism it is food substances that are taken in, whereas in the case of society it is new individuals.

Faced with a constant stream of raw material in the form of new babies, which it must so process and so distribute that the variegated system of interlocking adult statuses will be filled and the business of group living accomplished, every society is caught on what Linton regards as the horns of a dilemma.[4] On the one hand, as we know, the formation of the individual's habits and attitudes begins at birth; consequently the earlier his training for specific statuses can begin, the more complete will be his eventual adjustment. For this reason there arises a tendency to ascribe the individual's status at birth and to begin fitting him at once for the duties that will subsequently be his. On the other hand, we know that no two individuals (not even identical twins) are inherently the same at birth. Their capacities differ from one to another and there is as yet no way of telling, short of subsequent experience, what their peculiar capacities are. For this reason there arises a tendency to postpone the determination of adult statuses until each individual has shown which statuses he is peculiarly fitted for.

Here, then, are two opposite possibilities—the ascription of status independently of individual qualities or the achievement of status according to individual accomplishment—each with societal advantages and disadvantages on its side. Every society is confronted with the necessity of making an unconscious but difficult choice between the two. It is possible to imagine one type of society in which status is exclusively ascribed and to deduce the qualities that such a society would have. In fact, there are some societies that go far in this di-

[4] Ralph Linton, *The Study of Man* (New York: Appleton-Century, 1936), p. 115.

rection. It is equally possible to imagine another type of society in which status is exclusively achieved and to deduce the qualities that it would have. But the truth is that no human society seizes either horn of the dilemma completely. Every known society makes some use of both principles. The question really boils down, then, to what is the degree of ascription and achievement in any given case, and also what types of statuses lend themselves to one or the other kind of recruitment.

Ascribed Status [5]

The fabrication of the infant for future positions must begin as soon as possible. Socialization is at best a long and tedious process, one that is never perfectly achieved. It pays to begin the training as soon as possible when the child is in its most plastic stage. Furthermore, the child cannot be left culturally vacant for any extended period of time. Except in complete isolation he will acquire culture one way or the other whether he is deliberately trained or not. Nor can he be trained for his more general initial statuses without some regard for the narrower ones that he must eventually fill. The process of socialization must begin at once.

Paradoxically, however, the fabrication of the child for future statuses cannot begin until he already has a status. This is due to the fact that the work of socialization, if it is to be accomplished, must be assigned to particular persons whose responsibilities and rights with respect to the infant are clearly defined and who are motivated by various social mechanisms to perform the appropriate tasks. Such assignment, such arbitrary connection of the child with persons who already have a status in the social structure, immediately gives the infant membership in the society and a specific place in the system of statuses. The statuses he receives at this time, some temporary and some permanent, are clearly ascribed statuses because the infant has certainly not achieved them.

These initial statuses, since they are ascribed at birth, are of course given at precisely the time when society knows least about the potentialities of the individual concerned. Indeed, the human raw material seems discouragingly homogeneous whereas the statuses con-

[5] Parts of this section are taken almost verbatim from Kingsley Davis, "The Child and the Social Structure," *Journal of Educational Sociology,* Vol. 14 (Dec. 1940), pp. 217-229.

stituting the social structure are highly differentiated. Although there are undoubtedly differences of capacity between infants, these lie hidden only to be revealed by the subsequent process of socialization which itself requires that the child first be placed. It follows then that the placing of the infant is arbitrary, a matter not of pure accident certainly but at least of blind social rule. And it is no mitigation of this fact to realize that the statuses thus ascribed, precisely because they come first, tend to be the most important in the individual's life. They determine and limit the range of statuses which he may subsequently achieve or try to achieve.

However blind and arbitrary the ascription of statuses may be from the point of view of innate capacity, it is nonetheless done according to a certain unconscious order—an order varying from one society to another and yet everywhere having an underlying uniformity. The rationale of the process can be seen by raising this question: What is there about the infant that a society *can* use as a basis for the arbitrary assignment of status? The newborn baby is so undifferentiated, so inscrutable as to its future capabilities that one wonders what a society does or *can* seize upon as a basis for immediate status ascription. The answer is that there is little indeed to serve such a purpose. What little there is can be reduced to four categories, viz. sex, age, age relationship, and kinship. Let us discuss each of these.

SEX

The infant's sex is a definite, highly visible physiological fact which appears at birth and remains fixed for life. It provides a universally applicable dichotomy for dividing all individuals into two permanent classes, male and female. It also denotes on the part of each class a differential but complementary system of biological traits and processes which during a long period of the person's life will be associated with reproductive functions. The biological system, furthermore, is characterized by the peculiar primate reproductive physiology previously mentioned, leading to continuous sexual interest and elaborate sexual conditioning and harboring a libidinous urge tremendously significant in human motivation. Sex difference is consequently a very convenient, not wholly fortuitous basis for the ascription of lifetime statuses. This is why in every society it is utilized not only for assigning definite statuses but also for giving monopolies on achieved statuses—which means in effect that many otherwise achieved positions are at the same time sex-ascribed.

Given this functional ascription on the basis of sex it seems inevitable that an evaluative ascription should also be made, one sex receiving more prestige than the other. Social position, as we have seen, is seldom merely a matter of prescribed activities. It is usually also a matter of invidious judgment as well.

The great error in interpreting the ascription of status on the basis of sex (as in other cases of ascription) is to assume that the ascribed behavior springs from the biological qualities of the groups concerned. In many societies the male-female division of statuses is rationalized in terms of the alleged inherent traits of men and women. In Western culture, for instance, women were long pictured as naturally more stupid, delicate, emotional, intuitive, religious, and monogamous than men. This notion justified women's exclusion from higher education and better occupations, their disbarment from certain property rights, their submission to the double standard of morality, and their subordination to men generally. Psychology once talked of masculine and feminine "instincts."

Such ideas do contain a grain of truth, since the division of status is related to the different function of the two sexes in reproduction. But they go too far in assuming that each sex possesses biological attributes that explain directly the behavior ascribed to it. The error in such an assumption can be shown by two facts: first, that the genetic differences between men and women are not great enough to explain the social differences between them; second, that the social differences themselves are not fixed but change from one society to another and from one time to another. When these facts are understood it becomes plain that sex is in many respects merely an arbitrary device, a convenient peg for the ascription of status, and is used in social organization simply because it is apparent at birth and remains fixed for life.

In spite of obvious physiological differences it is easy to exaggerate the hereditary disparity between men and women. The heredity of the female, after all, is the same as that of the male in 46 of the 48 chromosomes, and just how much effect the female's extra "X" chromosome has is a matter of dispute.[6] Above all it is easy to exag-

[6] For an excellent popular summary of recent knowledge on sex differences, see Amram Scheinfeld, *Women and Men* (New York: Harcourt, Brace, 1943).

gerate the number of physical differences between the two that could in any way determine social behavior. There seem to be only two: the female's lesser physical strength and her bodily specialization for reproduction. In the matter of physical strength there is considerable overlapping, but the average man can whip the average woman; perhaps this is a factor in the general prevalence of masculine dominance in both human and anthropoid societies. Yet human society has long been institutionalized to the point where individuals do not get their status simply by virtue of physical strength. The president of the United States is not invariably a prize fighter. Also, the institutional subordination of women seems in some cases more complete than sheer physical dominance would make it. The binding of women's feet in old China or the seclusion of women in India was done according to moral prescription, not according to physical coercion. Furthermore, such practices were not thought of as "subordination" by the parties concerned. They did not necessarily imply a conflict of wills such as physical combat assumes. This is proved by the fact that women are often the staunchest supporters of the very customs that "liberals" consider to be "enslaving" them. It is thus a mistake to think that a dependent position is always resented by the dependent person. The women whose feet were bound in China or who were shut up in the *zenana* in India did not feel "enslaved." Instead they felt proud of their condition, because both footbinding and *purdah* were regarded as marks of upper-class position.

One should remember, too, that formal authority does not always mean actual dominance. Insofar as women have qualities that men desire and for which men compete, they can procure advantages for themselves despite their social position. Indeed it is astonishing how much they are able to gain in the face of physical and institutional dominance by men. They do it through shrewd manipulation of the male, often controlling through him the organization that he himself is supposed to control. Catherine the Great was not the only mistress to rule an empire, nor Helen the only woman to cause a war.

The secret both of woman's physical weakness and of her usual assignment of status is her child-bearing function. Forced to carry the parasitic embryo in her body for an extended time and to nurse the helpless young for a period thereafter, she is limited as to what she can do. As in most mammalian species her whole body is specialized to some extent for reproduction whereas the male, with his readier strength but shorter life-span, is specialized for fighting. It is not surprising, then, that the tasks usually associated with womanhood are those most compatible with reproduction. Keeping house, cooking, gardening, sewing, making pots, etc., all fit with bearing and rearing children. Hunting, fishing, fighting, herding cattle—particularly if they require long trips and great physical exertion—are not so compatible and tend to be allocated to men.

To explain such a recurrent though by no means universal division of labor, one does not need to assume that males and females have hereditary traits directly expressing themselves in social behavior. Possibly there are sex differences in personality and mentality; this is a matter of dispute and research. But if they exist they are so slight that social organization need not conform to them, and in fact their relevance to social organization is questionable anyway. The fact that women's occupations are more frequently those that can be pursued in or near the home does not mean that women have a "home-making instinct." It means simply that social efficiency is served by ascribing to women such occupations as will not interfere with child-bearing. Nobody inherits a social position biologically. It seems plausible, then, to regard woman's reproductive function rather than her alleged personality traits as the key to her assignment of status. She is given the kind of tasks that accord with this function, not the kind that agree with her "feminine personality." Femininity is defined by the ascribed status, not vice versa. Seldom will women be placed in armies as regular fighting personnel; seldom will they be given occupations that take them far away from home for long periods; seldom will they be assigned to violent tasks requiring physical exertion, exposure to bodily injury, and sheer physical strength. Rather, they will be assigned to tasks that permit them to remain close to home, do not seriously interfere with pregnancy, require routine endurance rather than sudden exertion, and relate most closely to the care of children. (Today in the United States a few women become practicing physicians, but they generally specialize in obstetrics or children's maladies.) For this reason female work is more uniform and more circumscribed from society to society than is that of men.

Actually, however, the division of labor is never precisely the same in any two cultures. In some cultures the men build the houses, in others the women do so. In some cases the men dress killed animals, in others the women dress them. In some tribes the men serve as magicians, in others the women do so. The only universal fact is that everywhere there is specialization on the basis of sex, and that this specialization tends to be compatible with child-bearing and child-tending on the part of women. The following description of the people of Lesu in the South Seas is fairly typical:

> Men have one kind of work and women another, and a third may be done by either one of them or jointly. . . . It is the men who have the strenuous job of clearing the dense jungle ground, and it is the women who come later and plant on it. It is the women who cook, while the men bring in the firewood and make the fires. Even in the cooking there is a division, for the men prepare the animals to be baked, while the women's cooking is restricted to the vegetable portions of the meal—taro and yams. It is the men who go forth into the sea with the nets and spears to catch the fish, while the women content themselves with catching crabs off the reef. It is the women who feed the pigs, carry the water, and keep the house clean, while the men go into the bush and hunt wild pigs. It is the men who build the houses and keep them in repair, but the women carry the heavy burdens on their backs. There are joint occupations such as taking care of the children, the making of magic, and minor detailed work like the basket-making. Carving and most of the objects of material culture are made by the men. . . .
>
> On the major occupations this demarcation is rigid. No woman ever goes fishing and no man ever scrapes taro. But in some of the less important tasks there may be exceptions. If a woman is very tired her husband may go to the beach and fill the hollow bamboo stems with water for her. This was taken for granted, and when I saw it happen several times there was no ridicule.[7]

In our own culture the particular statuses assigned to women have changed greatly, but the fact of a division of labor between the sexes is still with us. Today in the occupational sphere it is not so much that women are categorically excluded (though that is the case in coal mining, structural steel work, underwater tunneling, etc.) as it is that they are handicapped in competition (e.g. in medicine, law, college teaching) and must accept lower wages and less prestige for the same amount of work. In other words, their ascribed statuses limit their attainment of achieved statuses. It seems doubtful that the

[7] Reprinted from *Life in Lesu* by Hortense Powdermaker, by permission of W. W. Norton & Company, Inc.

ascription of status according to sex will ever disappear from society or that any particular kind of division by sex will persist forever.

AGE

Among the various bases for the ascription of status, age holds a peculiar place. Like sex, it is a definite, highly visible physiological fact apparent at birth. The baby's zero age does not distinguish him from other infants but it does separate him from older persons. Unlike sex, however, age is a steadily changing condition and therefore cannot give rise to permanent lifetime statuses. Each individual, if he lives, must eventually abandon any given category. The only way age can give a permanent status is in terms of an *age relationship* between given persons (e.g. between parent and child, elder brother and younger brother, senior member and junior member) in which case it is the time interval between the parties and not age itself that remains fixed. The feature of variability makes age totally impractical as a basis of caste and, in contrast to race or sex differentiation, minimizes the development of a characteristic personality for each rung in the scale.

Furthermore, except in terms of an age relationship, age is not a dichotomy but a continuum which can provide a basis for several rather than two general statuses. It is a continuum with infinitely small gradations, yet if too many distinctions are made within this continuum age loses its character of high visibility (small differences of chronological age being hard to detect) and its character of intrinsic social relevance (for only in terms of broad age grades can there be an intrinsic connection between the physical condition and the social condition associated with age). Hence there are usually only a few age statuses—fixed in the culture but not permanently for the person—through which, if he lives, every individual passes. These stages must usually be characterized by definite manifestations such as those of infancy, childhood, puberty, maturity, and old age. No matter how broadly they are conceived, however, the grades overlap and the classification becomes arbitrary. Most age statuses that purport to be based on physiology are in reality dependent to an equal or greater degree on social events and attitudes that have at best only a rough correlation with actual age.

There are often various specialized series of positions which are assigned somewhat on the basis of age but which involve the participation of only limited groups. Some of these, including many occupational careers in modern society, lead through well-established age rungs in some particular direction such as higher pay and responsibility. More abundant in complex societies, such sequences are not quite so much a matter of age as the more generalized age statuses, because achievement plays a greater part in the attainment of each rank. In a bureaucratized business concern, for example, a man is usually promoted according to seniority; but a person who is far below the average in ability may not be promoted at all, while one who is far above the average may go ahead more rapidly than usual. Similarly, universities usually select for a president a man with a long distinguished career behind him, but sometimes they seize upon an unusually talented younger man and hope that his youthful drive will more than compensate for any errors of judgment that he may make.

Mention of these specialized age series brings us back to our original problem, for at the inception of an individual's life there is no intrinsic evidence as to which series he should traverse. The initial statuses ascribed to him are all on the basis of traits such as sex, age relationship, and kinship, which are arbitrary so far as the actual potentialities of the individual are concerned. The kind of age status involved in the seniority principle as seen in organized labor, business establishments, and government agencies implies that a type of career line has already been chosen by the individual and that, by staying on the job, he has acquired at least a minimum aptitude. But the statuses given at birth are purely ascribed; the element of choice and the element of experience do not enter. The baby's zero age is taken as a reference point simply because it is an obvious physical fact of great social significance. At later ages, like other ascribed statuses given later in life, the age statuses begin to have a more definite content and a greater diversification. In other words, the statuses ascribed to the developed individual inevitably have in them an element of experience and perhaps of achievement which the statuses ascribed at birth cannot have.

All societies recognize age as a basis of status, but some of them emphasize it more than others do. It is well known, for example, that in the old culture of China and Japan a great deal depended on the person's age whereas in modern Western society much less depends on it.

> Many generations of Chinese children were brought up on *The Twenty-Four Examples of Filial Piety*. Wu Mang, who let himself be eaten by mosquitos in order to divert them from his parents; Lao Laitze, who at the age of seventy put on his gaily colored child's clothes and played with toys to make his parents happy; Wang Hsiang, who during the summer fanned his father's bed and during the winter warmed it with his body, and twenty-one other equally filial characters were presented in this book as models for imitation.[8]

Contrast the following attitude of Japanese women in the late nineteenth century with that found among American women today:

> No Japanese woman is ashamed to show that she is getting along in years, but all take pains that every detail of the dress and coiffure shall show the full age of the wearer. The baby girl is dressed in the brightest of colors and the largest of patterns, and looks like a gay butterfly or tropical bird. As she grows older, colors become quieter, figures smaller, stripes narrower, until in old age she becomes a little gray moth or plain-colored sparrow. By the sophisticated eye, a woman's age can be told with considerable accuracy by the various little things about her costume, and no woman cares to appear younger than her real age, or hesitates to tell with entire frankness the number of years that have passed over her head.[9]

Age status would be exhibited in its purest form if it were not limited by any other basis of status. As a matter of fact, however, it is always limited by sex status since in all known cultures men and women of the same age are treated differently. It tends also to be limited by kinship status. In the Chinese and Japanese cases it was clearly tied to kinship, for the stress was upon filial piety and in particular upon the father-son relationship. In some primitive tribes, however, everybody of roughly the same age and sex is regarded as belonging to a certain organized social group, a phenomenon called *age-grading* by the social anthropologists.

Among the Masai (an African people) for example, every male passed through three recognized stages: boy, warrior, and elder. The status of boy was lost when he passed through the puberty rite

[8] Olga Lang, *Chinese Family and Society* (New Haven: Yale University Press, 1946), pp. 24-25.

[9] Alice Mabel Bacon, *Japanese Girls and Women* (Boston: Houghton Mifflin, 1891), pp. 119-120.

(circumcision). During his initiation and the healing of the wound he was regarded as a neophyte ("recluse"), and for two years thereafter as an apprentice ("shaved one"). Then until age 28 or 30 he figured as a full-fledged warrior, the most coveted status in the tribe. During the bachelor-warrior stage the young men lived together in a separate kraal, being thus spatially separated from the rest of the community. Living with them, however, were their paramours, the immature girls. Each warrior had his favorite mistress who tended his cattle and made his personal ornaments but who was never identical with the girl betrothed to him in his childhood. Finally, at about age 30 each man settled down in a separate establishment, taking his fiancée as wife provided she had not in the meantime suffered the disgrace of pregnancy. He then held the status of an elder until his death.

The Masai women passed through a roughly corresponding series of age statuses. As an equivalent of the boys' circumcision they underwent clitoridectomy after the first menses and were known as novices until the wound healed. After that they acquired a new status involving marriage and lasting until the menopause. With the menopause another age status was entered—a status that lasted until the woman's hair turned white.

The different age statuses were associated with distinctive usages. Unrelated persons addressed one another by terms signifying their respective age statuses. Married women were distinguished by iron necklaces, iron earrings, long garments. The bachelor warriors carried the sword, spear, club, and shield distinctive of their rank, wore a special costume, subsisted entirely on meat, milk, and blood, abstained from intoxicants, and lived in a special compound. Among the elders those old enough to have circumcised children were privileged to wear a special kind of earring.

The use of age as an organizing principle did not stop here, however, for the Masai had something roughly corresponding to the phenomenon of "class spirit" in American private colleges. Circumcisions did not take place regularly but occurred only during alternate quadrennia. Individuals circumcised during one quadrennium were regarded as those of the "right-handed" circumcision, while those circumcised during the subsequent quadrennium (roughly eight years later) were of the "left-handed" classification. A right-handed age class and the immediately following left-handed one together constituted a "generation." As soon as a circumcised group had recovered from the experience they tried to secure a name for themselves, a distinctive design for their shields, and a separate kraal. No sooner, however, did the novices attempt this than the older warriors would swoop down on them. There would follow a struggle, and if the older warriors were victorious the establishment of the new group would take a longer time. When all members of the older age-class had married and discarded the bachelors' kraal, they would collectively assume the rank of elders, leaving their successors in sole possession of the warrior's status. Throughout their subsequent life they would stick closely together. The customs of the Masai emphasized the solidarity of the age-class. For example, girls initiated during a certain quadrennium were reckoned as belonging to the age-class of the boys circumcised during that period; consequently the boys of that class could freely have sexual relations with them whereas it was forbidden to have such relations with a woman of the father's class. A visitor from another district at once entered the kraal of an age-mate who withdrew from the hut leaving his guest to sleep with his wife; there was no choice in the matter, for an unobliging host incurred the curse of his age-mates. A wife mistreated by her husband could seek refuge with one of his age-mates. A widow or divorcee could consort with her husband's fellow class members but with no one else.[10]

Generally a society recognizes at least four age periods: infancy, childhood, maturity, and old age. Many societies have in addition two other peculiar age periods to which they attach importance—namely, the unborn and the dead. The unborn may be believed to be the spirits of departed ancestors. The primitive Australians, for example, thought these spirits dwelt in the clan's totemic water hole and that one entering the womb of a woman was later born as a member of the clan. The Hindus think of the unborn in a vague way as the spirits of persons or animals who lived in former incarnations. Sometimes unborn children are betrothed to other unborn children according to some pattern of arranging marriages.

10 This account of the Masai age-grading system is paraphrased from Robt. H. Lowie, *Primitive Society* (New York: Liveright, 1920), pp. 50-51, 270-275. Lowie took his material from the works of Hollis and Merker, to which he refers. Reliance upon age-grading is very prominent in African societies and has figured in tribal military affairs. Cf. I. Schapera, *A Handbook of Tswana Law and Custom* (London: Oxford University Press, 1938), pp. 28-30, 185-187.

The transition from the status of the unborn to the status of the living is marked by ceremonies and taboos surrounding the act of birth. Among the Chinese and Greeks as well as many other peoples the infant was not thought to be a member of the society until he had been ceremonially recognized by the father. Before that moment he could be killed (infanticide) with little compunction if circumstances warranted.

The transition from infancy to childhood is a smooth one and is seldom socially stressed. The change from childhood to adulthood, however, is marked by rather rapid and obvious physiological changes and by a change from an attitude of absorbing the culture to one of active participation in it. This change is therefore very widely recognized in ceremony, custom, and law. An extreme recognition is represented by so-called puberty rites (as seen in the case of the Masai) by which the entire status of the person is changed during a comparatively brief but dramatic round of ritual observances. In many cases marriage follows almost immediately upon this change, and so increases the social importance of the transition. In other cases, as among the Masai and in most civilized societies, marriage comes later —giving rise to a brief and often conflictful period of unmarried adulthood. Modern society places a great strain upon the transition from childhood to adulthood for four reasons. First, the culture is so complex that the period of learning and of dependence is prolonged far beyond the period of physiological maturation, often into middle age. Second, the recognition of social competence does not come all at once in every sphere of activity but arrives in a disjointed and partial fashion. The age at which a young person can marry, for example, is usually prior to the age at which he can vote; the age at which he can make a legal contract is often different from the age at which he can take a job or finish his education. Third, the emancipation from parental authority is not marked by a universally recognized and publicly expressed series of steps, but is a matter of private definition in each family. As a result there is often competition and conflict, the parents attempting to hold on to their authority for the good of the children, the children trying to free themselves from parental dominance and yet hold on to the advantages—financial and otherwise—which the parents still have to offer. Fourth, the interval between sexual maturity and marriage is prolonged but an attempt is made to prevent premarital sexual relations. In Ireland, Sweden, and England, for example, the average age of marriage is in the late twenties or early thirties—about fifteen years after puberty. The prolongation of the unmarried state and disapproval of premarital intercourse introduce an element of sexual strain that complicates an otherwise difficult situation. All in all, then, the so-called period of adolescence in our society is defined as a major problem, whereas in some other societies it is no problem at all.[11]

The passage of individuals from adulthood to old age is so imperceptible and so variable from one individual to another that it seldom receives explicit social recognition. The menopause in women and the gradually lessening sexual power in men usually come several years or even decades before physical vigor is lost. Nevertheless, there are societies in which the transition to the old age status is definite and the status itself socially distinguished. In Japan, for example, it was customary for the father to surrender his powers formally to his son and after this to enter a period of voluntary retirement. Many American universities have adopted the custom of compulsory retirement at a given age. The arbitrariness of such social definitions can be seen from the fact that some men are senile long before their retirement, others mentally vigorous long afterwards. Among some peoples the aged are made to work hard and are disesteemed and neglected. In extreme cases they are simply abandoned and hence meet death (although, as among the Eskimo, this is not necessarily a sign of disrespect). In cases at the opposite extreme, as in China, the old receive a reverence and deference that place them in a very high position.

In settled cultures where sedentary rather than warlike or predatory pursuits are followed, there is a tendency for an individual's power and prestige to increase with age. The young person despite his greater physical and mental capacity is forced to defer to people whose organic capacities are less than his. The latter, by virtue of having held a position early in life, are able to continue to hold it later in life and by virtue of it to acquire other positions of even greater influence. Furthermore, because of the endlessness of the

[11] For further analysis of the status of the adolescent in our society, see Kingsley Davis, "The Sociology of Parent-Youth Conflict," *American Sociological Review*, Vol. 5 (August 1940), pp. 523-535; and "Adolescence and the Social Structure," *Annals of the American Academy of Political and Social Science*, Vol. 230 (November 1944), pp. 8-16. Citation to the literature will be found in these articles. See also Chap. 8 of the present volume.

educational process in a complex culture they are in a way better qualified for responsible positions. Their qualification, however, is a socially acquired and not a biologically maturing qualification. It is based on knowledge and experience, both necessary for successful political and administrative decisions. Thus in a sense (the physical sense) the community does not utilize its great men until they are already past their prime; but in another sense (the social sense) it utilizes them at the peak of their greatness—in what one might call their administrative or sociological maturity. The principle of seniority is therefore no accident. The charge is frequently made that the old hang on to their positions as vested interests and that this is the explanation of the subordination of youth to age. That older persons seek to hold their power is generally true, but their desire does not explain the fact that they *can* do so. They are able to hold their power because they have a kind of superiority—a superiority developed and buttressed by the ascription of status on the basis of age in an organized society, but a superiority nonetheless.

Because the living are descended both physically and socially from the dead and because they too will soon be among the dead, there is an inevitable tendency to give the dead a status in society. In Western society the dead are memorialized primarily in relation to their achievements while living. Their status is therefore to a large extent an achieved status. In other societies, however, they are given a status in death that depends simply on their being dead. This is true in those cultures where ancestor worship is practiced and where the dead are thought of as hovering near and taking a continued interest in human affairs.

> Thus a Tanala clan has two sections which are equally real to its members, the living and the dead. In spite of rather half-hearted attempts by the living to explain to the dead that they are dead and to discourage their return, they remain an integral part of the clan. They must be informed of all important events, invited to all clan ceremonies, and remembered at every meal. In return they allow themselves to be consulted, take an active and helpful interest in the affairs of the community, and act as highly efficient guardians of the group's mores. They carry over into their new status the conservatism characteristic of the aged, and their invisible presence and constant watchfulness does more than anything else to ensure the good behavior of the living and to discourage innovations.[12]

[12] Linton, *op. cit.*, pp. 121-122.

KINSHIP

In addition to sex and age another characteristic of the raw infant which can be utilized in giving him an initial status is kinship, his relation to his parents and siblings. The simplest form of ascription on this basis is the identification of the infant's status in the community with that of his parents. Even more than in the previous cases mentioned, such ascription is highly arbitrary. There is no necessary relation between the capacities of the parents and those of the offspring. Brilliant parents may have stupid children and vice versa. The socially ascribed identity between parent and child is therefore more complete than the genetics of inheritance would warrant. Consequently the universal tendency to ascribe status on the basis of this identity cannot be explained in terms of biological fact, as the apologists of class rigidity have sometimes attempted to do. It must be explained in terms of sociological principles; and the first of these is that it is socially convenient. The family appears as a universal social institution, and in it the child is closely associated with the parents and is initially socialized by them. In view of this close association and the fact that the parents are given responsibility for the child, it is a matter of pure economy to identify the child's status with them rather than with someone else. This is what was meant when it was said earlier that the rearing of the child requires that he be given a status at the very start; somebody must be made responsible for him and hence must be given a status with reference to him. The first responsibility and hence the first status connection, accordingly rests with the parents.

The child may take the parent's status immediately as in a caste system, or he may acquire it later but begin training for it at once (as in succession or inheritance). In the latter case we may speak of the process as "delayed ascription." Finally, the child may seek achieved positions that are different from those of the parents but with a competitive advantage or disadvantage provided by his parents (as in open-class occupational placement). This we may speak of as "fluid ascription," understanding that in this the element of achievement has reached a rather large proportion but has not entirely displaced the element of ascription. In any case, through identification with the parents the child becomes automatically related to the rest of the society and is trained accordingly. So important, indeed, is this *jus sanguinis* principle that a wide number of important statuses depend upon it. The ascription of citizenship, religious affiliation, and community membership, for instance, is in most cases a matter of identification with parents who are already citizens, communicants, and members. From an ethical point of view the most controversial type of status transmitted from parent to child is that of class position. The child inevitably derives an advantage or disadvantage according to his parents' rank in the social scale, and in some societies his position is fixed for life. This aspect of ascribed status will be treated below in the chapter on class and caste.

The child at birth not only acquires some elements of the parents' status in the larger society but he acquires a position in the family itself. He acquires an individual status as son or daughter. Since his parents are kin to other individuals his relation to his parents defines his relation to these more distant kinsmen. Thus he is not only a son but also a grandson, a nephew, a brother, a cousin, etc. Human societies universally recognize rights and obligations in accordance with these kinship connections. In some cases much of social life is governed by them. In other cases, as in our own society, the extended kinship ties have dropped into the background but the immediate family ties remain socially important. Although there is great variation in the precise kinds of rights and obligations associated with kinship statuses, the fact of such association is universal.

OTHER BASES OF ASCRIPTION

Sex, age, and kinship do not exhaust all the bases for the ascription of status. The newborn infant, for example, manifests the physical stigmata of his race. It is therefore possible to assign him a status on the basis of his racial traits and thus create in the society a system of racial castes. Since racial features are inherited, however, this basis of ascription is very similar to ascription on the basis of the parents' status. In fact, even when a racial basis is assumed there is a tendency to assign the child's position on the basis of his parents' position. In the United States a child of "Negro" parentage tends to be defined as "Negro" regardless of the fact that he may be almost totally white in a physical sense. Some of the Southern states define as a Negro any person who has a drop of Negro blood in his veins. Such a definition is obviously more sociological than racial.

There are still other circumstances affecting the child's status.

Illegitimacy, for example, prevents full identification with the parents. Plural birth in some societies gives the children so born a peculiar status, occasionally resulting in death for them. The total number of children born in the family, the fact of adoption, the fact of the death of a parent, the occurrence of divorce—all these can affect the infant's status independently of his will. One can see that the so-called "accident of birth" is ubiquitous and extremely important in society.

The Achievement of Status

In any society, no matter how rigid, there is knowledge of individual accomplishment and individual failure. The give and take of everyday life, the intimate play of personalities in the interacting situation, provide a setting for the irrepressible expression of natural differences. People assess one another with shrewd and practiced eyes and give their private allegiance to those who are kindly, capable, talented, and original. The role and the role personality are never governed solely by the status and the status personality but are determined by individual differences of many kinds. It follows that esteem and prestige are not necessarily synonymous, that an ascribed status system is never able to hold all individuals in complete fixity. There are always men who are so cunning, so gifted, so energetic, and so drivingly ambitious that they become leaders despite every known obstacle. The history of all lands and all times is studded with their names, for they are the men who make history. They are the men who can use the institutional machinery whatever its form to control other people and can subtly change the system in order to give themselves a place in it.

Our present interest, however, lies not in the exceptional individual but in the institutional order itself. Though we know that personal accomplishment always plays a part in interaction we still must ask to what extent the social system institutionalizes the recognition of achievement. To what extent does it provide for an orderly and legitimate change of status according to the individual's manifestation of talent and effort? If the social system encourages its members in this way it will not drive the exceptional person into illicit channels but will make use of his capacities for common social ends. It will also make use of people who would not have the genius to overcome great obstacles but who, with encouragement, can put into effect very useful capacities that would otherwise be suppressed. Finally, by providing for an orderly change of status the social system can prevent the filling of high positions by incompetents who would become simply tools in the hands of sharp-witted but unscrupulous and irresponsible men.

It is not easy to say why some societies institutionalize achieved status and others do not, but it is possible to cite some interesting correlations between these factors and other societal traits. In primitive society an emphasis on achieved status apparently goes with warfare and dangerous occupations such as hunting, raiding, and deep sea fishing. The following account of coup-counting on the part of the warlike plains Indians will illustrate the point:

> After subsistence, war was the most important pursuit of certain plains tribes. Among the war customs one of those best known was counting coup. Coming in actual contact with the enemy by touching him with something held in the hand or with a part of the person was the bravest act that could be performed. It was a proof of bravery—a feat which entitled the man or boy who did it to the greatest credit.
>
> When hunting, it was not unusual for boys or young men it they killed an animal, especially if it was an animal regarded as dangerous, to rush up and count coup on it, to see who could be the first.
>
> The Cheyenne counted coup on an enemy three times; that is, three men might touch the body and receive credit according to the order in which this was done. It is evident that in the confusion of a large fight, such as often took place, many mistakes might occur and certain men might believe themselves entitled to honors which others thought were theirs. After the fight was over, then, the victorious party got together in a circle and built a fire of buffalo chips. On the ground near the fire were placed a pipe and gun. The different men interested approached this fire and, first touching the pipe, called out their deeds, saying, "I am the first," "second," or "third," as the case might be. Some man might dispute another and say, "No, I struck him first," and so the point would be argued and the difference settled at the time.
>
> Very commonly a party returning from war would give one or more scalps to a group of old men and old women who would paint their faces black and carry the scalp about all through the village dancing

at intervals, singing the praise of the successful warriors, making speeches in their honor, and generally rejoicing.[13]

In civilized society a tendency toward commerce, an extreme division of labor, urban conditions of life, and rapid social change seem to be correlated with an emphasis on achieved status. Whether such social characteristics are the result or the cause of the prominence of achieved status is virtually impossible and perhaps not important to decide; but the functional relations are easy to see. Commercial activity implies that economic behavior has won some independence from noneconomic controls; and since it deals with scarce commodities purely as means to greater gain, it offers the individual a prime opportunity to advance by the use of his native capacities. An extreme division of labor gives a competitive advantage to the person who is talented in his work; but it is possible to overemphasize this point, because a person trained from childhood to perform the duties of an ascribed status may develop a high skill despite a merely average talent. By concentrating a large population in small territory and supporting itself by varied enterprises, the city enables individuals to be readily selected for particular positions according to their manifest achievements. Finally, rapid social change provides continually new statuses which, precisely because they are new, cannot be filled by ascription.

It is interesting to ask not only what kinds of societies emphasize achieved status but also what kinds of statuses are likely to be thrown open to achievement. Obviously one would expect that those statuses requiring the possession of unusual talent would be the first to be thrown open. All the education in the world will not make of a mediocre person a great violinist or a great mathematician, a great actor or a great writer, a great prize fighter or a great track star. Next one would expect that those statuses depending on the informal and spontaneous approval of the populace would be predominantly achieved. For this reason the theatre and the sports arena, the rostrum and the printed page have long been avenues by which persons of humble birth could advance themselves socially. Finally, one would guess that those statuses requiring such long and costly education that private resources cannot supply it and hence necessitating public pro-

[13] Condensed from Geo. Bird Grinnell, "Coup and Scalp Among the Plains Indians," *American Anthropologist*, Vol. 12 (1910), pp. 296-310.

vision of training, would be thrown open to achievement. The training of the doctor or lawyer in modern society cannot be accomplished within the family. It requires large schools with elaborate resources and professional faculties. Anyone who can get himself into these schools and show enough effort and ability to pass through them is in a fair way to becoming a doctor or a lawyer. The schools are therefore channels of vertical mobility.

The Relation of Ascribed to Achieved Status

Both ascription and achievement are found in every culture. Each, though opposite in principle, is complementary in function and therefore essential to society. In order that the infant be fabricated for specialized statuses his socialization must start at the earliest possible moment. For this he must be initially placed in the social structure. Yet it is precisely at this point that least is known about him The initial placement, therefore, despite its tremendous subsequent importance is a matter of arbitrary social rule based on the few available external characteristics. Later the individual's achievements must also be recognized, and not long after birth each child's accomplishments begin to set him off from others. These accomplishments, however, are already partial products of statuses ascribed at birth, so that differences of achievement can never be interpreted purely as differences of inherent capacity. Ascribed statuses, coming first in life, lay the framework within which the transmission of the cultural heritage is to take place. They determine the general goals (e.g. the adult statuses) toward which training shall aim and the initial persons who shall carry it out. When, accordingly, we know the child's sex, age, age relations, and the class, religion, region, community, and nation of his parents, we know fairly well what his socialization—indeed, his life—will be.

Ascribed statuses also give a feeling of security that purely achieved positions can never give. All of life cannot be thrown open to competition. One cannot feel that every person is a competitor for whatever status one holds. Above all one cannot feel that there is no limit to the sheer manipulation of means, no rules and principles that are fixed beyond the power of the ambitious to change. Hence laborers, bureaucrats, and professionals each band together to lessen competition among themselves. Businesses enter collusive agreements to hold up prices. Producers advocate tariffs to protect themselves from foreign competition. The community frowns on easy divorce, on repeated changes of religious belief, on rapid change of citizenship, on outright and open opportunism in all things.

On the other hand, within the framework of authority and security laid down by the system of ascribed statuses there must necessarily be some achievement. The value of achieved status is not only that it places the right persons in the right place but that it stimulates effort. The duties connected with statuses are often onerous and exacting and cannot be accomplished without hard training. Without competition there would be an inevitable tendency to demand the rewards of the status without adequately fulfilling its duties. The lassitude of monopoly and the stimulation of competition are too well known to require documentation.

The usual condition in society, then, is that broad outlines of status are laid down by ascription while many specific statuses are open to achievement. Even an ascribed status requires, unless it is purely passive, some degree of training. A king who rules by divine right must nevertheless know something about the behavior required of a king. Even an achieved status is usually limited in one way or another by ascription. The usual mode of limitation of achieved status is through limitation of the number of competitors. In a sense the presidency of the United States is an achieved office, since no one can get there without going through the competitive process of winning an election. But the Constitution forbids anyone to compete for this office who is not a native born citizen, not thirty-five years of age or over, and not at least fourteen years a resident within the country. Furthermore, we know that there are certain customary limitations that are as effective as if they were written into the Constitution. No woman, no Negro, no Oriental, no Catholic, no Jew has ever been president. It is conceivable that one of these might someday get the office, but it will be only by overcoming a great handicap. Thus approximately 120 million out of a total of 140 million people in the United States are effectively excluded from becoming president of the United States. Nearly always there are such limitations on achieved status, so that any concrete social position can generally be said to be partly ascribed, partly achieved. In this sense ascription and achievement are abstractions, but they are nonetheless real.

References

Kingsley Davis, "The Forms of Illegitimacy," *Social Forces,* Vol. 18 (Oct. 1939), pp. 77-89; "Illegitimacy and the Social Structure," *American Journal of Sociology,* Vol. 45 (Sept. 1939), pp. 215-233.

These articles treat illegitimacy as an ascribed social status. They delineate the kinds of illegitimacy and attempt to explain why the illegitimate child is treated as he is in society.

John F. Embree, *Suye Mura* (Chicago: University of Chicago Press, 1939) Chap. 5, "Social Classes and Associations"; Chap. 6, "The Life History of the Individual."

Description of the social structure in a Japanese village. The different statuses are clearly described.

Isacque Graeber and Steuart H. Britt (ed.), *Jews in a Gentile World* (New York: Macmillan, 1942).

Membership in a minority ethnic or religious group is one of the major problems of the modern world. Here the status of the Jew is considered from many angles by experts in different fields.

E. T. Hiller, *Social Relations and Structures* (New York: Harper, 1947), Part 6, "The Structure of Society: Statuses."

Devotes 220 pages to a discussion of status in general and of different bases of status. Contains separate chapters on childhood, youth, old age, sex, vocation, profession, office, and class as bases or types of status.

Everett C. Hughes, "Dilemmas and Contradictions of Status," *American Journal of Sociology,* Vol. 50 (March 1945), pp. 353-359.

A well-written analysis of situations involving incompatible statuses—e.g. the Negro physician vis-a-vis white patients or the female engineer. The nuances and subtleties of status contradictions are neatly handled.

Ralph Linton, *The Study of Man* (New York: Appleton-Century, 1936). Chap. 8, "Status and Role."

An excellent presentation which has had wide influence. The present chapter owes a great deal to Linton's pioneer analysis.

Robt. H. Lowie, *Primitive Society* (New York: Liveright, 1920), Chap. 4, "The Family"; Chap. 5, "Kinship Usages"; Chap. 8, "The Position of Woman"; Chap. 11, "Theory of Associations"; Chap. 12, "Rank."

Condensed description of varieties of patterns in primitive society, describing types of kinship, sex, age, and class positions. Lowie's best book, recently reprinted.

Margaret Mead, *Sex and Temperament in Three Primitive Societies* (New York: Morrow, 1935).

Three different primitive communities were studied to find out how they assign positions to and interpret the temperaments of men and women. Dr. Mead writes up the results in beautiful prose with sharp clarity. Would another observer have seen the same things she saw? One who doubts it is Jessie Bernard whose article, "Observation and Generalization in Cultural Anthropology," American Journal of Sociology, *Vol. 50 (January 1945), attacks the book unmercifully but effectively.*

J. J. Nieboer, *Slavery as an Industrial System* (The Hague, 1900).

A classical study of the institution of slavery. A good description of the nature and variety of a particular kind of status.

Amram Scheinfeld, *Women and Men* (New York: Harcourt, Brace, 1943).

A popular but accurate summary of what is known about sex differences, both social and biological.

Georg Simmel, "Superiority and Subordination as Subject-Matter of Sociology," *American Journal of Sociology,* Vol. 2 (1896-97), pp. 167-189, 392-415.

Probably the most penetrating essay on this subject ever written. Translated from the German.

Everett V. Stonequist, *The Marginal Man* (New York: Scribners, 1937).

In the case of minority racial or religious groups there are people—emancipated from the minority religion or racially mixed—who have a marginal status. They are full-fledged members neither of the minority community nor of the larger community. Professor Stonequist's book analyzes this situation acutely in the light of historical cases; he has done much to popularize the concept of the "marginal man."

Max Weber, *The Theory of Social and Economic Organization* (New York: Oxford University Press, 1947), Chap. 3, "Types of Authority"; Chap. 4, "Social Stratification and Class Structure."

Conceptual analysis of kinds of authority, class relations, traditional structures, and social change. Translated from the German but still heavy going.

Logan Wilson, *The Academic Man* (New York: Oxford University Press, 1942).

The sociology of the academic profession written in a readable but systematic manner by a former professor of sociology and now a dean. An excellent example of status analysis, with observations on prestige, competition, and the definition of the situation.

CHAPTER V

THE ELEMENTS OF SOCIAL ACTION

ANALYSIS of social phenomena purely in terms of norms and statuses leaves something to be desired. It runs the danger of treating the individual as a wooden automaton whereas we know that such things as choice, thought, emotion, and perception are inextricably involved in everything that could be called social. The usual procedure in social science is to assume the existence of a subjective mentality, to assume that it has certain characteristics, and to place the main attention on objective indices of social behavior and their causal relationships. Thus the political scientist when he analyzes the *forms* of government does so in terms of the constitutions and laws in which these forms are objectively (albeit symbolically) embodied; when he studies political *behavior* he does so in terms of election returns, new legislation, judicial decisions, and administrative acts; and when he studies the *causes* of political events he usually does so by relating these phenomena to others on much the same level—i.e. to economic, religious, military, and technological trends as found embodied in external results. The eye of the political scientist is therefore on government as the object of study, not on the person; and this is as it should be since somebody has to center his attention on government. Nevertheless, like any other social investigator the political scientist inevitably makes some assumptions about the internal workings of the human mind with reference to political matters. Since political manifestations such as votes, enactments, debates, appointments, etc., all involve symbols, they must be associated with some sort of mental activity. Also, since predictions of future political behavior frequently rest on estimates of how given classes "think" or what some leading figure like Stalin, Truman, or Peron "will do," we know that assumptions are inevitably being made about the way the human mind works in political situations. It is not suggested here that the political scientist should become a psychoanalyst and take the personality as his object of study, but merely that he should bring into the open whatever assumptions are being made so that they can be integrated with the general body of political theory in systematic fashion. What is said for political science goes also for other social scientists. The sociologist more than any other social scientist must necessarily give attention to the behavior of the person, because he is interested in the nature of social action as such and hence is interested in human motivation at its deepest level.

Our view is that *any* theory of social behavior, in so far as it allows for the existence of subjective phenomena at all, must take into account the irreducible components of human action; and that, having done so, it is capable of being more systematic and more flexible than would otherwise be the case. The present chapter undertakes to defend this view by describing and discussing the components of action.

Definition of the Elements

The simplest way of putting our task is to say that we must adopt the point of view of the actor. We must ask how he regards the social relations in which he participates, how he is socially motivated, how his mind works. In a sense we have done this already when we discussed the feeling of obligation and the necessity of effort in connection with the observance of norms, and when we discussed prestige and esteem in connection with status and role. But there we were going only so far as was necessary from the point of view of the norms and statuses themselves, not from the point of view of the actor. Now we must look at social relations through the eyes of the participant. Let us start with the single act in which the actor is involved.

A single act, from the subjective or voluntaristic point of view, can be analyzed in terms of four indispensable and inseparable factors, as follows:[1] (1) An *actor*. (2) An *end,* a future state of affairs toward which in the mind of the actor the process of action is aimed. (3) A set of *conditions,* aspects of the situation over which the actor has no control. (4) A set of *means,* aspects of the situa-

[1] The conception of action and its elements given here is derived with some modifications from Talcott Parsons, *The Structure of Social Action* (New York: McGraw-Hill, 1937), especially pp. 43ff.

tion over which the actor does have control. (The existence of the actor himself as an indispensable factor could be taken for granted and the list thus reduced to three, but it seems better in the interest of greater clarity to keep the actor as one element.)

In analyzing social behavior whether as scientists or as casual observers, we unavoidably use these concepts. Introspection inevitably reveals to us the four elements and the problematic relations between them. We analyze our own behavior in such terms and we assume that the same considerations apply to the behavior of others—especially since the things they tell us indicate that this is so. As political scientists, economists, sociologists, or social anthropologists we use the same set of concepts either implicitly or explicitly, systematically or unsystematically. Each of the four is indispensable in the sense that it cannot be derived from another: Ends cannot be derived from means, or means from conditions. They are analytically distinct, and no one can make sense in discussing action without using all four concepts.

ACTOR

When we speak of the agent of action it is not the body of the actor we have in mind but the "ego" or "self." It is the "I" or the "me" rather than the "it." The ego, then, is the subjective entity that possesses *awareness* and has *experience,* which makes decisions and then reflects on the decisions it has made, which holds together past events and imagines those that are to be. Parts of the body may be lost (an arm or a kidney) without a part of the ego being lost; qualities of the body (its color or its weight) may change without the ego changing. To the self the body is a part of the situation, a means or a condition of attaining ends (as any one can see who watches a girl primp). Though a necessary condition for the existence of the self, the body is not a sufficient condition. There are undoubtedly organisms without self-awareness but there are no selves without an organism. The ego is an emergent quality characteristic of highly integrated organisms, a quality most completely developed in man because of man's capacity for symbolic communication and hence his ability to judge himself as others judge him.[2]

The true observer of human life cannot be satisfied with merely

[2] George H. Mead, *Mind, Self and Society* (University of Chicago Press, 1934), Part III.

recording the external behavior of an individual. He must go beyond this to the internal subjective experience which accompanies the behavior. He cannot stop with observing simply the impingement of external events upon his body but must discover also how the individual *perceives* them. The way a person perceives his world, the way he feels and thinks, is an indispensable clue to his behavior. True, it is the organism which behaves, but it is the ego which acts.

END

The end that the self conjectures is the "x" factor in the algebraic equation of social action. It has reference to the future, to a state of affairs which does not exist now. Its representation therefore requires the use of imagination and its realization the use of effort and will. It exists over and above the immediate world of fact and thus resembles the normative order, which also is mental and is additional to the world of external fact. In fact, between the system of ends and the system of norms there subsists an intimate and multidimensional relationship of the greatest significance, as we shall presently see.

When the end has been attained the act is finished, because by definition the act pivots on the end. An end, once attained, is displaced by another end which initiates a new line of action. In this way, from the subjective point of view, each person's behavior consists of an interrelated series of acts. Although the end is by definition subjective, it may be conscious or unconscious. If unconscious it is at least capable of becoming conscious and it has the self as its refererence point. The psychoanalysts, among others, have succeeded in demonstrating that unconscious ends are important in determining behavior. If we add that social scientists have also demonstrated the importance of conscious ends, it becomes plain that the end element cannot be neglected in interpreting behavior. Indeed, those theories which have attempted to ignore it (such as behavioristic psychology and social Darwinism) have fallen far behind common sense in the effort to reach the truth.[3] Obviously not all activity of the human organism is motivated in the sense of having an end in view, but much of it is—especially that which is social in character. A useful device is therefore to analyze behavior *as if* it were motivated and to formulate a theoretical system on that basis, realizing of course that in keeping with all scientific theory this device represents an abstrac-

[3] Parsons, *op. cit.*, pp. 110-121.

tion from concrete reality and hence, taken alone, is not adequate for complete explanation.

An end should be distinguished from a sheer resultant. If a future state of affairs is bound to come about anyway regardless of the actor's intervention, it is not an end. The end, strictly defined, is that part of the future state of affairs which would not eventuate if the actor did not want it and did not exert himself to attain it. A farmer may want it to rain next week, but whether or not it actually will rain is beyond his control. Rainfall next week is not therefore one of his ends. But if he plants corn on the assumption that if it rains the corn will grow, the future growth of the corn is an end that he has; and if things turn out well in fact and the corn does grow, it is partly because he has acted to attain his end.

In due time we shall discuss the sources of ends, but for the moment it is sufficient to note that ends are *chosen*. They are chosen with reference to *values* in the first place. A value is that which is considered desirable, which is thought worthy of being pursued regardless of whether or not it is actually being pursued. In a given situation it influences what is chosen as an end. The source of the value in turn lies chiefly in the *sentiments,* broad backgrounds of feeling which makes some things seem valuable, others not valuable. Such feelings arise partly from organic urges, partly from internalized norms. The transition from sentiment, to value, to end is one of increasing specificity. In a sense the end is the particular application of a sentiment or value to a given situation as perceived by the actor.

It should be recalled that both end and value must be carefully distinguished from function. The latter has already been defined as a contribution to the existence of a given structure, be it a personality, an institution, or a society. Why the two (end and function) do not necessarily correspond should now be clear. The actor's perception of the world is so limited in countless ways that he cannot know all the consequences of his behavior. The latter may therefore have functions which he in the pursuit of his end does not see. Furthermore, since the actor initiates his behavior with an end in view and justifies one end always by a value or another end, it is possible for his conduct to be controlled by controlling his ends; and such control may in some cases be more effective if he grasps only the end and not the function as well. Even when the self or ego is the structure in question, the end may not correspond to the function. Thus a man who rationalizes his failure in his profession as due to his wife's extravagant desire for amusement can save his ego more effectively if he does not realize that the function of his rationalization is precisely to hide from himself his own weakness. If he knew clearly the function of his explanation, the explanation would be worthless to him. When the structure in question is a social system the advantage of not having the actor grasp the function (assuming that he could) is often greater still. It is doubtful whether a man who makes a sacrifice to his god would make the sacrifice if he knew the social function of his act, because the situation to which his end is oriented would be altered and the end itself would disappear. Some of the ends that are farthest from any knowledge that a social function is being performed are of the greatest functional importance.

CONDITIONS

An end implies not only effort and will but also obstacles in the way. Were there no obstacles the desired state of affairs would arrive without any help from the actor, and so there would be no need of an end or of any action. On the other hand the concept of action clearly implies that obstacles can be overcome. If they were all insuperable every effort to reach the end would fail and the actor would soon quit trying (acting). Those obstacles that are insuperable we call conditions. They set the stage within which action must take place. If a traveler wishes to reach a distant city he cannot by a wave of the hand reduce the distance until it reaches zero. He must take the distance as a given condition and compensate as best he can for it with other means.

The conditions imposed on the actor may not all be external. Some of them may lie in the actor's own organism. Many who aspire to be great violinists fail because they lack the talent. Some of the conditions may lie even nearer to the personality, as when a man loses a great opportunity because he is timid. Other conditions are social but not internalized, such as laws which we obey only because a penalty greater than the desired end is attached. In sum, the conditions limiting our attainment of ends arise from three general sources: physical environment, innate capacity, and society. These, however, also represent the only sources of the means. Whether something is a condition or a means therefore depends upon the situation.

Human beings do not pursue ends they regard as impossible. They often cherish values that are incapable of realization and profess sentiments that lean toward the unattainable. But the specific ends they pursue in concrete situations are felt to be attainable. If action always failed or for that matter if it always succeeded, the personality would disintegrate. Man's lot is to be eternally striving because men are end-pursuing animals. The amoeba may be safely regarded as free from striving, not because it is free from the necessity of securing food to live but because it has no awareness of the process. Lacking this awareness it cannot visualize the end and undergo the agony of failure or the joy of success. Human beings are more complex than the amoebae, but less fortunate than the gods. Their flights of imagination, howsoever sustained, are weighted and brought to earth again by bleak reality. Theirs is the necessity of perpetual compromise. They dare not wish for too much and they must not wish for too little.

MEANS

To reach any end some means must be employed. In some situations the means may be something simple like speech, in others it may be an elaborate apparatus like a factory. Often the same end is attainable by more than one means, giving the actor considerable choice as to which he shall utilize. This makes possible one type of error, for the means chosen may not be the most efficient. This and other potential errors give rise to an element of uncertainty in action. The actor can seldom be absolutely sure of reaching his goal.

What is a means for one actor may be a condition for another. In the same situation one man, for example, may feel obligated to tell the truth while another will feel privileged to tell a lie. Again, for a man who knows how to operate a machine it may be a useful tool, but for one who does not know how, it may be an insuperable obstacle. Whether or not a given part of a situation is a means or a condition depends not so much upon the part itself as upon the actor. He brings to the situation not only an end but also his natural and acquired capacities. Of course, the end itself is not dependent upon the objective situation, for it is brought into the situation by the actor and may be completely different according to who happens to be in the given objective situation. Thus the presence of a teetotaler in a saloon has a very different meaning from the presence of a habitual drunkard in the same place.

Furthermore, what is a means in one situation may be a goal in another. If a man wishes to own a home he may adopt the means of saving part of his salary, in which case saving his money becomes an immediate goal and budgeting or some other expedient a means of reaching it. The actor's total behavior is thus a complicated network of interrelated means and ends, of interwoven chains of action. At the bottom of the network are things seldom viewed as ends in themselves but always primarily as means (such as taking distasteful medicine), while at the top are things seldom viewed as means but primarily as ends (such as art). Between the two extremes are the bulk of activities regarded as means in one context and as ends in another. Because of man's limited intelligence he cannot easily visualize all the steps required to reach an exceedingly distant goal, and because of his limited will power he cannot readily bring himself to pursue such a goal. Instead he visualizes the distant goal only vaguely —more as a sentiment or value than as a specific goal—and in the meantime regards each step as an end in itself which may be immediately achieved. It is in this manner that unintelligent weak-willed *Homo sapiens* manages to accomplish great things. He does better when the steps are neatly planned for him, the rewards carefully adjusted to the difficulties in the way. In much of his social life he is encouraged to pursue temporary ends placed there for the purpose in order that he may ultimately reach more distant and important ends. In the grading system of our schools, for instance, classroom marks become ends in themselves for the students; and so weak is the goal of scholarly achievement that the grades are also made a means to many things really irrelevant to grades—such as fraternity membership, late-hour privileges, cutting privileges, etc.

SUMMARY

Extremely important in human behavior is the subjective universe. The center of this universe is the self or ego, and the direction of activity is determined by the end which the ego brings to the situation. Those aspects of the situation that the actor may control are his means and those that he cannot control are his conditions; but which aspects he can control and which not is a matter determined partly by himself. The elements of action are therefore distinct from one another yet mutually dependent, and if behavior is to be analyzed from the subjective point of view at all, no one of them may be ignored.

The Relation of Means to Ends: The Problem of Rationality

Since the achievement of an end requires that the means be somehow adapted to that end, there is an element of rationality or attempted rationality in all human action. There is also, as we have said, an element of potential error, for the means adopted often have unanticipated consequences—consequences which pleasantly or unpleasantly surprise the actor. It is natural in a "striving species" that the ideal type of action should be rational and that the causes of error should be one of the most persistent problems in the history of thought. If we review a few of these causes we shall understand better not only why error occurs but also how social life contributes to it.

SUPEREMPIRICAL ENDS

The first source of trouble lies in the ends themselves. A peculiar thing is that the ends men strive for are often imaginary in a double sense: they are not simply future states that do not exist now, but they are future states that never will exist in this world. Thus a major goal for countless individuals is some sort of "salvation"—a goal not to be realized until the "next life" and therefore transcendental.

Since such ends visualize a future state of affairs in the superempirical world, it is impossible to prove or disprove in logico-empirical (scientific) terms that *any* means chosen is adequate. Hence there is no rational basis of choice among possible means—indeed, no way of deciding what is a means or what is a condition—with the result that rationality becomes irrelevant and the action is nonrational in character. The Hindu who adopts a male child because he wants a son to perform the *sraddha* ceremony and thus to speed him heavenward after death through successive reincarnations, is adopting a means to his end, to be sure; but his choice of means has arisen from *no* knowledge of cause and effect but rather from arbitrary tradition. He undoubtedly *believes* that there is an intrinsic cause and effect relation, but the very strength and necessity of this belief indicate that the connection between means and end is not one that can be rationally perceived. He simply accepts the connection on faith rather than on evidence.

Later discussion will show that these transcendental or superempirical ends are no accident in human society. They are instead a permanent feature, for they motivate people to behave in a way useful to societal survival. They represent a constant source of nonrational conduct. In a sense the question of error is not relevant to such conduct. Since the means is related to the goal only by traditional fiat, since proof and disproof are ruled out, there can be no demonstrated error except that of mistaking such action for rational action (which the actor generally does). The only other kind of error is to employ the *socially wrong means.* A Methodist minister who sprinkled water on the bride and groom as a part of the marriage ceremony would be condemned as having used the wrong means to the right end. But so far as cause and effect are concerned the connection between marrying a couple and placing the bride's hand in that of the groom is purely arbitrary and has no more intrinsic character than sprinkling their heads with water would have. The error in this case is not a mistake as to cause and effect but a mistake as to the proper social form.

HAZINESS OF THE END

A second source of nonrationality derives from the frequently hazy and nebulous character of the end. By this is not meant that no end is in view as in purely reflex or instinctive behavior (such behavior falls outside our present consideration and excludes the problem of rationality). What is meant is an end of the sort that Thomas and Znaniecki call the "wish for new experience" in which "unforeseen consequences actually constitute the purpose of the action" with the tacit assumption that these consequences will be desirable.[4] The boy who starts a fire on the living room rug "just to see what will happen" is a case in point. Even in more ordinary cases there is a certain haziness about the end—that is, a failure to distinguish carefully between the future state of affairs as it would be with or without effort, a failure to differentiate between different ends involved in the same action, etc. Such haziness makes it diffi-

[4] Robert K. Merton, "The Unanticipated Consequences of Purposive Social Action," *American Sociological Review.* I (Dec. 1936), p. 899, footnote.

cult for the actor to gauge accurately the effect of the means he utilizes; he may succeed or fail without knowing why.

IGNORANCE

A third source of deviation from rational behavior is lack of knowledge. The actor can utilize only what he knows, and he never knows all the possible means in his situation. He may wrongly perceive something that would be of use to him, as when a traveler reads a timetable wrongly and misses his train. Again, he may be ignorant of something that he *could* have known because it is in his culture but which he either never learned or has forgotten—as when a man is bitten by a snake or has a severed artery but fails to remember any first-aid techniques applicable in such a situation. Such errors are often regarded as blameworthy because the individual is "expected to know." But if the person is ignorant of something he could *not* have known because it is not in his culture (as when a primitive fails to predict an eclipse) or is not in his special field (as when a physicist proves uninformed on the latest development in literary criticism), he is not condemned. The distribution of knowledge and ignorance according to position in the social system is a definite part of the social system itself, so that many forms of ignorance are tolerated or praised rather than condemned. In any position, however, a certain amount of knowledge is required, and if a person does not have it or makes an error that shows ignorance, he is judged to be lazy, careless, or stupid.

NORMATIVE RESTRICTIONS

A fourth source is not so much a cause of error as of failure. Error assumes that the person has chosen the wrong means among those from which he was free to choose, while failure may mean simply that he was not free to choose a means which was effective. For instance, the folkways and mores necessarily exercise control not only over what ends shall be pursued but also over what means shall be utilized to attain those that are pursued. The actor is debarred from using certain means which would gain the end but which are taboo to him as a member of society or as an occupant of a certain position. This forces him to select his means from a fairly narrow range of possibilities. A Catholic, for example, who wants to have no more children is limited to two out of hundreds of possible methods of preventing conception. The taboo may and often does extend to the knowledge as well as the use of a given means. The Catholic is not even supposed to know about the "unnatural" methods of contraception. Such normative restrictions placed on the use of means tend to lead to and coalesce with ignorance, but they do not necessarily rest upon it. The Catholic is not supposed to use the "unnatural" methods even when he knows about them. Fundamentally, whether it is use or merely knowledge that is in question, he is supposed to avoid mechanical contraception out of a feeling of obligation. The limitation is basically normative.

Why do the norms thus limit the actor's available means? In answer, let us first point out that even without norms the actor would be forced to limit his means in the pursuit of any one end; he has a multiplicity of ends and consequently has to see that the means he uses to gain one do not injure his chances of gaining others. He has to balance his means for the benefit of his total system of ends. A man with a limited income wants to buy innumerable things. Yet since he cannot buy them all he has to decide what he will spend his money on and what not. Similarly but even more crucially, in a society the total system of ends of all the individuals must somehow be balanced and maintained. Means are scarce and ends are limitless. The normative order so operates that the pursuit of his ends by each individual cannot limitlessly inconvenience other individuals in the pursuit of their ends. To take an extreme example, murder is generally excluded as a means to legitimate ends, as are also force and fraud. Any member of a family knows how the attainment of his ends must be modified in the light of the attainment of ends by other members of the family.

In addition to limiting the available means the normative system also *increases* them. It multiplies the requirements for attaining ends. For instance, if a man is hungry he cannot simply grab whatever food comes within his vision. He must go through an elaborate process of securing some money by working for it, begging for it, or borrowing it; of going to a place where food is known to be served; of ordering the food; of eating it with particular instruments; of paying for it; and of using the proper verbal expressions. It is in this sense that the normative order, as expressed in the behavior of individuals occupying the system of positions, constitutes an elaborate environment for the individual, an environment which not only restricts means but also defines the ends themselves and creates artificial but socially necessary means for reaching them.

Both by restricting means and by creating artificial ones the normative order controls behavior. In either case the control may be of the internalized or the externalized type—internalized if regarded as right in itself, externalized if treated as a mere necessity. Society is so organized that unless the individual chooses his means from those normatively available, he will be injured in reaching some of his other ends, as by fine, public censure, or what not. The individual may perceive this in a perfectly rational manner. But in addition he generally internalizes many of the norms as well, or at least has sentiments and values which support them. To this extent normative regulation and rationality are opposed. To an observer outside the society, for example, it seems almost that the actors are blindfolded or walking in a daze, because they do not see the possibilities that lie at hand for the realization of their desires; or else it seems that they are doing things which seem elaborately unnecessary for such realization. In addition, not content with simply observing the norms which limit means, human beings also give reasons for the existence of the norms. These reasons seldom truly explain the function of the norms and hence are fallacious as explanations of why the means are limited.

CONCLUSION ON RATIONALITY

In one sense all human action has at least a rational element. The actor tries to select among the means at his disposal the one most appropriate to his end. But whether or not he realizes it the range of means at his disposal is often quite narrow as compared with what it *might* be. There are many ways in which what would otherwise be means are removed to the status of conditions in the actor's situation. Those we have mentioned are the following: First, the actor acquires ends that are superempirical, with the result that his only source of evidence concerning the adequacy of means is social tradition which specifies one or two devices out of an infinitude of possible symbolic means. Second, the actor's conception of his ends is sometimes vague and confused, making it difficult for him to relate means to them in strictly cause and effect terms. Third, the actor is ignorant of means which, were he more careful, more learned, or more fortunately situated as to position or culture, he would know. Fourth, the actor is controlled by normative rules which limit the means that he may use to reach his ends and which create additional means that he must use.

In spite of these four prolific sources of nonrational conduct the actor generally has the illusion of rationality. This is because his attention is concentrated on those means that are at his disposal, not on those that might be used. The Hindu who with cattle all around him starves to death rather than eat meat, may think of himself as acting quite rationally. Beef eating is for him not a possible means. The disinterested observer, however, free by definition from cultural bias and possessed of the latest scientific knowledge, sees that the means on which the actor is concentrating do not exhaust the possibilities. He may point out that a means ignored by the actor because unknown to him or unconsciously accepted as forbidden will actually work better. Doubtless the actor's illusion of rationality is a protection both to his ego and to his society. No social order could be composed of persons willing to use any means whatever to gain their ends. This proposition suggests that no social order could be entirely made up of rational behavior, nor could it be as rational as it seems to the members of the society. So pervasive is the illusion of rationality in fact, that it permeates the social sciences and prevents their taking an entirely clear view of their own milieu. Much social science analyzes human behavior only in so far as such behavior can be assumed to be rational. Many errors with reference to industrial relations have been made, for example, because it was assumed that laborers seek only their economic gain and that they use only rational means of attaining this goal.

Of course, an action does not have to be rational to succeed. It may succeed without the actor knowing why—as with "hunches," "luck," "intuition," etc.[5] Nevertheless there is a correlation between rationality and success which would be perfect if the actor were omniscient and omnipotent. The fact that the correlation in practice is not perfect is due to the circumstance that in any man's behavior rationality is only an element; there are always other variables which influence the result.

[5] Robert K. Merton, *op. cit.*, p. 896.

The Elements of Action and the System of Positions

Action as we have been thinking of it, is an abstraction. It is that behavior which is initiated with an end in view, but not all behavior is so initiated. Much human behavior, especially of the autonomic part of the organism, is *caused,* to be sure, but not motivated. The process of digestion, of blood circulation, of pupillary dilation, is not ordinarily action in the sense of taking thought and exerting effort. It happens that behavior in which ends are involved is extremely important in understanding society, whereas purely reflexive or instinctive behavior is not; because it is through symbolic communication and the related mental processes—through ends and the perception of means—that human beings are socially influenced. One way of seeing the importance of action as we have defined it is to consider its relation to the system of social positions.

The duties of a status will not be carried out unless they become ends for the incumbent. How they do become ends for him is plain. Indoctrination may lead him to regard the duties as a sacred obligation or as a just repayment for the "rights" of the position. Experience may teach him to regard them as necessary means to ends required in other statuses. In any case it must be remembered that the community distributes its esteem according to the manner in which the positional mandates are carried out. Finding himself *publicly* identified with a position, the individual winds up by subjectively identifying himself with it as well. The state of his ego then depends on how well he satisfies the requirements of the status in his own eyes as well as those of his fellows, but his own view reflects theirs.

The occupant of a status is limited in the performance of his duties by the presence of obstacles. To overcome these obstacles he is expected to use only such means as the society provides and permits. Although prevented from exercising too much ingenuity, he usually has some choice between available means. It is through the determination of this choice that factors outside the position influence his achievement and hence affect his esteem. He gets esteem in proportion to how well he manipulates such means as are offered him in his position.

Levels of Integration of Ends

So far the discussion has dealt mainly with the elements of a single act (the pursuit of a single end). Let us now consider how different acts and hence different ends are related to one another. This requires separating different levels of integration according to whether it is the individual's or the society's ends, the instrumental or the ultimate ends that are being considered.

TECHNOLOGICAL INTEGRATION

Every person's behavior embraces thousands of separate acts related to one another like the strands of a web. Consequently, what is an end in one context may be a means in another context. A barber sharpens his razor so that he may shave his customer efficiently. He shaves the customer for money. With the money he buys clothes. With the clothes he keeps warm and looks well. By keeping warm he feels comfortable, and by looking well he receives the approval of others.

Some ends are never ultimate but are always intermediate. The goal of having a sharp razor, for instance, is hardly an end in itself, but simply a necessary means to a clean-shaven face. When an actor is viewing his ends merely as instrumental and is not raising the question of balancing independent ends against each other, he is thinking technologically. On this level the ends are devoid of emotional appeal and the means are judged in a matter-of-fact way according to the canons of efficiency. If the whole means-end chain is viewed as crowned at the top by ultimate values, then the technological sector is at the bottom. The technological is by definition purely instrumental. It involves the use of scarce resources to achieve an immediate end in the most efficient manner possible; it does not involve any distribution of resources among different ends.

ECONOMIC INTEGRATION (INDIVIDUAL)

Many actions are not instrumental solely to the next end in the means-end chain but are instrumental to several different ends at the same time. Thus the money the barber receives for shaving a man is not instrumental solely for buying clothes but also for purchasing hundreds of other commodities. In this situation the individual cannot assume a purely technological attitude, for he must balance one end against another and distribute his scarce resources among them according to some order of preference. The order of distribution is determined by how important he *feels* the ends to be relative to one another.

This process of allocating scarce means to various ends we call *economizing* and refer to the motivation as *economic*. On the technological level the question of balancing various independently valuable ends is not raised, but on the economic level it is. Once, however, the individual has decided on the relative importance of his competing ends he can proceed quite rationally to allocate scarce technological products to them. Economic action, like technological action, is therefore basically rational. It attempts to make the scarce goods serve as many different purposes as possible.

Our hypothetical barber, we shall say, receives an average monthly income from shaving his customers. With this amount he must purchase all sorts of things. In addition to clothes he must pay out sums for rent, light, laundry, food, entertainment, tobacco, transportation, and all other standard items on the budget. Most of these ends are in part intrinsically valuable in themselves, in part simply means to other ends. Scarcely any of them can be met as completely as he would like from his average monthly income. Rent, for example, gives him an apartment or a house and thereby satisfies his needs for comfort, rest, and shelter; but he cannot pay enough rent to secure the kind of dwelling he would like to have. He would like to have one that would be *more* comfortable and convenient and also one that would *look* better and give him more prestige. If he paid his whole monthly earnings he could have a much better house; but in this case he would have no money for anything else. There are other things which he not only must have but which he wants as well. He therefore must make his income "go as far" as he can, he must "economize." In doing this economizing he is guided by his feeling in regard to the relative importance of the various ends, his conception of how intensely he wants each kind of good. His subjective feeling in the matter is not capricious; on the contrary it is based on realistic knowledge of how his body makes him feel when its needs are not met, how others make him feel when he does not come up to their expectations or standards, and how the intrinsic aspect of his ends is damaged if he neglects their instrumental aspect (e.g. concentrates on the gratification which food gives him without regard to how he will feel and look later). Years of living have taught him, as it teaches all persons, that no act, no moment, is without its consequences for future acts and future moments. The consequences of his acts are related in cause and effect fashion. The ends which he strives for must and do bear some systematic relation to one another; they must strengthen rather than weaken one another.

The individual's subjective fund of knowledge, sentiments, values and ends reflects the systematic needs of the two levels of his nature—the organic on the one side and the social on the other; and when he uses his scarce resources for his various and competing ends his sense of balance, of the relative importance of his ends, is no matter of caprice. In short, the very concept of economic action implies that the actor's different ends are systematically interrelated. They are potentially limitless but are in fact tied down by the reciprocity of relationships and the scarcity of means.

INTEGRATION OF ENDS WITHIN THE SOCIETY

The problem of the integration of ends, complex enough when there is only one actor, becomes much more complicated when a multiplicity of actors is involved. Just as the single actor's ends must be organized in some way, so the ends of a plurality of individuals must be balanced one against another and arranged in some kind of order. The community, like the single individual, is faced with the necessity of allocating scarce goods and services to the different ends represented. The only difference is that this time the competing ends are those of different individuals rather than those of a single individual.

This may look at first glance like a small difference but it is really a crucial one. To see how crucial it is one has only to reflect that in the allocation of his scarce means among his various ends, the individual has a guide. The guide is his own subjective impression of the relative importance of his ends. They are, after all, his own ends and he alone knows how strongly he holds each of them. A society, on the other hand, has no such guide. There are no ends which the society as an entity has in view. Ends are by definition subjective and hence private. It is therefore only individuals who have ends, and as between one individual and another there is no independent basis for judging whose ends should prevail. Each person feels the validity of his own ends, not that of other people's ends. The very fact that others pursue their ends vigorously may lead him to redouble his efforts to seize the scarce means and satisfy his own ends first.

This absence of any inherent basis for allocating scarce goods among the different members of the community is the fundamental impasse of human society. Yet many people refuse to recognize it as a fact. They seek to find or to put their faith in some absolute basis for comparing and judging the ends of different persons. But what can such an absolute basis be? Where is the entity that can compare the ends of different individuals and judge that some should get a certain amount of scarce means and others a different amount, or for that matter that they should all get the same amount? An inanimate object could not do it, because inanimate objects do not compare and judge. Another individual could not do it, because he would merely be influenced by his own subjective feelings no different from the competing feelings of the others. Biological instinct could not do it, because the ends determined by such instincts are among the most fiercely competitive that we know of, as the phrase "nature red in tooth and claw" indicates. Society could not do it, because society is not a person but rather an organization of persons. To think of society itself as having ends or as comparing and judging, is to think anthropomorphically. Such an idea assumes society to be a sentient creature, to have a mind, and therefore is guilty of committing the group mind fallacy. Perhaps God gives an absolute basis for comparing the ends of different individuals, but this is a mystical explanation which science cannot utilize. Besides, the next question would be who is it that knows God's laws. If different persons thought they knew God's laws but had different conceptions of such laws, we would be back at the same problem again, no better off than we were before.

The truth is that in practice, as we know from the actual observation of social life, there is in each society a distributive order. Some people do get more and some people do get less, and the thing hangs together somehow as a system. We saw in the chapter on position and role that there is an order in society—an order that works only through the minds of the constituent members. So without a doubt, despite the absence of a societal mind, every social structure achieves and could not survive if it did not achieve an integration of the ends of its members. Our question is then really concerned with how this integration is actually accomplished. Unless we can discover the way in which such integration occurs, we shall miss utterly the secret of the human type of society. Let us try to unravel that secret by analyzing the problem on different levels—economic, political, and moral.

ECONOMIC INTEGRATION OF ENDS (SOCIETAL)

When a group of people have competing ends, as they are bound to do, there are theoretically no limits to the means that they may use. For instance, control over others is a particularly valuable aid to the satisfaction of one's ends. In pursuing one's ends in a rational and vigorous manner, therefore, one has the possibility of treating others purely as means and of employing force and fraud on them. The others also have the possibility of retaliating in kind. This would lead to anything but an orderly distribution of goods. It would lead to a state of utter conflict—a war of all against all—in which the strongest would win satisfaction of his needs and the weakest would die. Yet no group could remain intact in this way. It would represent a state of social chaos very different from the societies that we actually observe.

What we do find is that there is certainly competition but that there are limits on the means that may be utilized. In this connection we ordinarily think in terms of economic exchange wherein each person, by giving up something that someone else wants, gains something in return. This works all right so long as the power of the two individuals is roughly equal, but it seldom is equal. When differences of power arise one individual can force the bargain by offering the other person the choice between giving up something or suffering sheer coercion. It is this sort of thing that the rules governing economic exchange are designed to avoid. Our fictitious barber, for example, may advertise his barber shop, may boast of his prowess, may buy many papers and magazines for his customers, and may do any of a thousand other things to attract trade. But at the same time there are many devices he may not use. For example, he may not go around to all the other barber shops in town and cut off the heads of the competing barbers. He may dream of doing it because it is a simple and effective method of eliminating competition; but he may not actually do so or seriously threaten to do so. Neither may he throw bricks through the windows of the other shops, offer his customers opium to smoke, or allege that his competitors use poison on their razors. Many of the means for satisfying different ends, then, are distributed through competitive exchange of services and commodities, but the exchange is always regulated by a system of rules or norms. Who enforces these rules and by what right? Where do the rules themselves come from? These questions take us to the political and moral level, for they cannot be answered in economic terms. Adam Smith to the contrary notwithstanding, there is no wizardry by which the rules that limit the economic pursuit of self-interest can be derived from that pursuit itself.

POLITICAL INTEGRATION OF ENDS

Those who enforce the rules of competition as well as other kinds of rules, are the political authorities. How are these individuals to be distinguished from the rest of the group? They are certainly not any different in a biological sense; they are just ordinary specimens of *Homo sapiens* like the rest. Their only distinction is that they are incumbents of socially defined positions. In their actions they represent or claim to represent the group as a whole. Therefore they are given or assume the right to use force and fraud (firearms, imprisonment, propaganda, censorship, etc.) in order to see that the rules of the group are observed. But the great difficulty is that once they get into this position they have the possibility of using their command of all means (including means that are forbidden to the private citizen) not simply to enforce the rules of the group but also to satisfy their own ends. Hence come the graft, corruption, nepotism, and hypocrisy that we ordinarily associate with political office. The spoils may be so great that other men wish to attain political office in order to share in the loot, and this partly explains the fierce effort to attain political office by any means whatsoever, including revolution. Whoever controls a monopoly of force controls the society and is *ipso facto* the political head.

In view of the danger of having a political head, in view of the corruption and abuse, one would think that societies would dispense with government altogether. In fact, some Utopians have suggested exactly this. But it is not realistic because it overlooks the problem we are trying to solve. If a society is to have any degree of integration of ends it *must* enforce some rules, because the ends of different individuals do not simply harmonize automatically. With any degree of social complexity, as we have seen, the rules must be enforced by persons specialized for the purpose, for a heterogeneous community cannot enforce them spontaneously. Therefore there *must* be a political organization and there *must* be people in authority. A society can exist with a tyrant, a king, an elected president, or a gangster at the top; it cannot exist with nobody at the top (unless it be an isolated primitive village). In cases of dispute as to ends the political authority is in a position arbitrarily to say who is right and who is wrong. It can make and interpret the rules. It thus accomplishes an integration of the ends of different individuals by fiat, with force in the background to make the fiat acceptable. The fact that it does accomplish this integration of ends explains the functional necessity of government.[6]

It is doubtful, however, if there is any society in which the members obey the rules solely because they fear the arm of the law. As suggested in the chapter on social norms many of the folkways and mores are internalized, rooted in sentiment and emotion. Even political authority tends to be emotionally conceived and obeyed because a value is attached to it. The political authorities themselves are often guided by a strong attachment to the folkways and mores. The very structure of government may stand as a highly valued institution—as is true, for example, of the Constitution of the United States. These facts suggest that we have not yet reached a full solution of our problem.

RELIGIO-MORAL INTEGRATION OF ENDS

The truth is that up to now we have been laboring with the implicit assumption that the ends of different individuals are competitive. So in a sense they are, and in so far as they spring from purely biological urges—that is, in so far as their origin is purely individual—they are surely competitive. But the real question concerns another possible origin of ends. We know in fact that people acquire their ends through communicative interaction with other members of their society. It thus follows that they can acquire a set of *common* ends—common in the sense that the ends are shared by the whole community and are known to be so shared. Furthermore, these ends can refer not so much to a future state of the individual himself as

[6] Political institutions will be discussed more fully in a later chapter. The present reference to the role of political authority in the integration of ends must necessarily be brief.

to the future state of other individuals and, in the last analysis, to the group itself. Common ends oriented with reference to the action of others are virtually identical with the mores. They are simply the manifestation of the mores in the subjective sphere of individual action. The behavior called for in the mores and the enforcement of the mores by the members of the community at large would not take place unless the mores stood in the minds of the people as ends to be achieved. Common ends oriented with reference to a future state of the group as a whole simply express how the people think the group should be organized and what results it should produce as a corporate entity. Such ends can of course be extremely competitive when they are not held in common. Some of the bitterest struggles of mankind have been with reference to ideals of conduct and social organization which differed as between one group and another. But so long as a community holds such ends in common they are not competitive, because they do not refer to a future state of the individual taken separately but to the behavior or the future state of the group taken collectively.

The mores require, in effect, that persons occupying such and such a status, in such and such a situation, should act in a certain way because such action is "good," "right," and "essential for social welfare." They clearly involve a judgment as to the actions of others. Thus a person who believes that it is wrong for a mother to marry her son is not satisfied merely with avoiding such a marriage in his own case. His mother may be dead. The rule is conceived by him to apply generally, and his end is to see that nobody violates it. His means of reaching this end is to exercise whatever control he can over the behavior of others to see that they are prevented from forming such a relationship and are punished if they do. He considers this end more important than many others, since he himself would rather go hungry, do without warm clothing, and work hard than marry his mother, and since he would not tolerate other persons marrying their mothers for money or for any particular end that he can think of. He is willing to pay money to special people occupying the position of policemen to see, among other things, that people do not marry their mothers; and he is personally ready to express his opinion of anybody who does and thus throw his weight on the side of right. He is also ready to transmit to his children the view that such a thing is horrible to conceive.

Ideas as to the proper organization and functioning of the society as a whole are often less clear-cut, but they are nevertheless present. The citizens of a nation may hold with virtually one accord that the nation should gain a place for itself in the sun, even if this involves acquiring more territory by armed conquest. They may be willing to sacrifice for this ideal, to subordinate nearly everything else to it. They may be willing to suppress and ostracize anyone who does not agree with this policy or lend a hand in it.

It is clear that such ends are not only noncompetitive when held in common by the group, but they are ultimate. There are no ends above them. They are simply held to be good in themselves, for no ulterior reason. Other ends, and above all those that relate to the individual's own satisfactions taken distributively, are subordinated to them. For this reason we should call the ends we have been describing the *common-ultimate* ends possessed by the members of the society.

We are now nearing the end of our quest. It is the possession of common-ultimate ends that gives the key to the integration of ends in human societies. Such ends stand at the top of the hierarchy of ends and hence control and regulate the rest. It is in terms of them that a distributive order is sanctioned and maintained. It is on the basis of them that a standard is found for judging the relative merits of lesser ends as held by different individuals. As between two different groups holding an entirely different set of common-ultimate ends, there is no recourse. But within the same community this type of ends constitutes the integrating feature. In fact, we tend to define a society or at least a community as a collection of persons adhering to the same set of ultimate values and pursuing the same set of common ends.

But one more question remains. What is the source of these common-ultimate ends?

If one asks the ordinary person about them he is likely to say that they are simply a part of "human nature," that they are "handed down from the past," or that they are "God-given." None of these answers is satisfactory from a scientific point of view. The human nature response is ambiguous, but it usually implies a biologistic view which does not square with the variability of ends from one society to the other. The second answer is all right as far as it goes, for we know that the common-ultimate ends are transmitted by communication, but it does not explain how the generations "in the past" came to share these ends. The third answer is religious and goes beyond empirical knowledge, yet it is worth noting how frequently in society the common values are connected with religious belief.

Our answer can be brief. It will be elaborated further in later chapters. We hold that the possession of common-ultimate values by the members of different societies arose in the process of societal evolution. It resulted from the process of natural selection on a societal basis. In the struggle against nature and in the struggle between one human society and another, only those groups survived and perpetuated their culture which developed and held in common among their members a set of ultimate ends. The important thing was not so much the particular content of the ends but rather the fact of having ends in common. Viewed in this light the possession of common ends must be virtually as old as human society itself. Such possession is necessary for cohesion and group coöperation in any socio-cultural system.

In a sense such ends are figments of the imagination. They control behavior and often lead to a severe limitation of biological satisfactions on the part of the individuals who hold them. Yet it is nobody but the individuals themselves who hold, perpetuate, and enforce these ends. Furthermore, the ends have a future reference and never correspond perfectly with conditions in the factual world. It follows that the strength with which they are held must be derived from the influence of group interaction in some way. This is where religion enters the picture. It seems generally true that religious belief explains and makes real the common-ultimate ends, and that religious ritual strengthens and renews these ends in the minds of the participants. This is why the ordinary man quickly refers to religion when pushed for an explanation of his ultimate values. The very feeling of profound conviction that surrounds these values is itself religious in quality.

Conclusion

It should now be apparent that a systematic differentiation of some of the major institutions can be made in terms of the integration of unit acts and their elements. Technological action is that in which the means are purely instrumental to immediate ends; hence the choice of means is made solely on utilitarian grounds. When the question arises as to the allocation of scarce means to different ends, the economic level has been reached. The individual adjusts means to his various ends on the basis of his subjective evaluations, but as between different members of a society the allocation must be made in terms of exchange based on free rational choice between individuals. Such exchange, however, is regulated by mores and laws that limit the means each individual may use to gain his own ends at the expense of others. The mores and laws are effective partly because they are enforced by political authority, which can compare the ends of individuals arbitrarily, and also because they have been internalized and thus transformed into ends, values, and sentiments in the minds of the people. Such ends and values are common in the sense that they are noncompetitive and ultimate in the sense that there are no other ends above them. One individual does not lose by another individual's observing the mores and the laws. On the contrary, he gains; it is to his interest to see that others obey. Behind political authority, therefore, stand the sentiments of the people which justify the authority in the name of the ultimate common ends; and justifying the ultimate common ends in turn, are religious belief and practice. Ends are in themselves nonrational. This is why the religio-moral realm is at the opposite extreme from the technological. It is in the religio-moral realm that the unity of society is primarily to be found.

A later section of the book is devoted to the major institutions in society—technological, economic, political, and religious. The reader will do well to keep the present discussion in mind when he approaches that section. The elements of action are essential to an understanding of these institutions.

References

Ives Hendrick, *Facts and Theories of Psychoanalysis* (New York: Knopf, 1939).

Psychoanalysis is concerned with the system of means and ends as contained in the individual mind. The book by Hendrick is one of several good summaries of psychoanalytic theory. See also Part II of the present volume.

Robt. M. MacIver, *Social Causation* (Boston: Ginn, 1942), Chap. 7, "Cause as Incentive"; Chap. 8, "Cause as a Responsible Agent."

The role of subjective factors in the causation of events, and how we observe those factors.

Robt. K. Merton, "Social Structure and Anomie," in Ruth Nanda Anshen (ed.), *The Family: Its Function and Destiny* (New York: Harper, 1949).

In this theoretical analysis of social disorganization, a revision and extension of an earlier article, the means-end schema is absolutely central.

Talcott Parsons, *The Structure of Social Action* (New York: McGraw-Hill, 1937), especially Chaps. 2 and 3.

Extremely hard to read but exceptionally rewarding when the material is mastered. The present chapter draws heavily on this great work.

CHAPTER VI

FORMS OF INTERACTION

MUCH of the thinking about society is in terms of social relationships. One thinks of the relation between father and son, employer and employee, leader and follower, merchant and customer; or of the relation between friends, between enemies, between children, etc. Such relationships are among the most obvious features of society, and consequently it seems an elaboration of the obvious to inquire into their nature. But sociology must analyze and classify social relationships because they represent not only a common but also a fundamental way of organizing social data. In short, a society may be viewed, if one wishes, as a system of relationships.

In analyzing social relationships one soon finds them more complicated than they first appear. It turns out, in fact, that to understand them requires the conceptual tools set forth in the previous chapters; for obviously these relationships involve norms, statuses, and ends. They involve *reciprocal obligations, reciprocal statuses, and reciprocal ends and means* as between two or more actors in mutual contact. They refer to a form or pattern of interaction between these individuals, and this is why the school of sociology which has attempted to systematize its thought in relationship terms (Simmel, von Wiese, Park, Burgess, Becker) has been called the "formal school."

By a sort of shorthand description, social relationships are often spoken of as subsisting not only between two or more individuals but also between two or more groups. Thus one hears that two nations are "at war," that two social classes are "antagonistic," or that two business firms are "competing." What does such usage mean? It may mean simply that whenever members of the two groups come into contact, a certain mode of interaction transpires—as when one remarks that the Dinwoodie and the Rutledge families are "not speaking." It may mean, however, that the groups as corporate units are sustaining a certain kind of relationship with one another, in which case it is not every member but only the duly constituted representatives of the group as a whole who create the relationship. Not just any citizen may declare his nation at war with another, but only those citizens who are authorized to speak for the nation as a whole. In fact the citizens of two nations may be fighting each other without the nations being at war. The most important members of a group, so far as intergroup relations are concerned, are those specifically empowered to represent the group as a whole. Interaction between them must be less personal than would otherwise be the case, because they represent not their "own" interests but those of the group. For this reason the contacts between diplomats are governed by protocol to a much greater extent than the contacts between private citizens. This distinction between two kinds of group relationship should be kept in mind; a failure to do so leads to loose thinking about human affairs.

Obviously any society contains hundreds and perhaps thousands of socially defined relationships. The immediate family alone may contain as many as fifteen.[1] How many relationships a society utilizes is simply a matter of how many criteria it takes into account in defining behavior between individuals. The fifteen relationships of the immediate family rest on only three criteria—age, sex, and generation. Outside the family an infinite number of criteria may be used, so there is no limit to the number of possible relationships.

It follows that to catalogue all the meaningful relationships in which human beings are involved would be a never-ending task. Instead they must be classified and dealt with as general types. Any classification, however, must have some point to it. In social science, as in all science, classification is worthless unless it seizes upon traits that are significant, traits that facilitate causal analysis. For this reason social relationships have been classified and discussed in terms of the *kind of interaction* they manifest. The most important kinds

[1] Father—elder son
" —younger son
" —elder daughter
" —younger daughter
Mother—elder son
" —younger son
" —elder daughter
" —younger daughter
Husband—wife
Elder brother—younger brother
" " —elder sister
" " —younger sister
Younger brother—elder sister
" " —younger sister
Elder sister—younger sister

of interaction singled out for consideration have been conflict, competition, and coöperation. Each of these has several subtypes, but mention of the main ones alone is enough to demonstrate that a proper understanding of the forms of interaction is essential to the understanding of society. The remainder of this chapter will be devoted to the main types of interaction. It will begin by a brief reconsideration of the nature of interaction itself; then, by a process of reasoning from opposites, it will discuss isolation (the absence of social relationships); and finally, it will consider conflict, competition, coöperation, and their interrelations.

Social Contact

Social interaction by definition involves contact, and contact necessarily requires a material or sensory medium. It need not of course require the impingement of one body directly upon another, but it does require the occurrence of direct or indirect sensory stimulation between the interacting parties. The material medium, however, is only a necessary, not a sufficient basis of contact. Individuals can be in material contact without being in social contact. For example, two tribes living on opposite sides of a swamp and having nothing to do with each other may nevertheless be bitten by mosquitoes that continually carry malaria from one tribe to the other. It is not mere physical contact that counts, but meaningful or symbolic contact. Good will may be expressed by either a handshake or a spoken phrase, a letter or a smile. Added to the sensory stimulus is a meaningful stimulus. A dead man's will is an indirect and tenuous material link with his heirs, but its physical character is far less important than its meaning. Until material or sensory contact acquires meaning for the subjective selves of the persons concerned, it is not social in the human sense. The social behavior of human beings consists of acquired responses to the meaningful responses of others. Human interaction, in other words, is communicative interaction.

The essential feature of communication is that one person infers from the behavior of another (whether speech, gesture, or posture) what idea or feeling the other person is trying to convey. He then reacts not to the behavior as such but to the inferred idea or feeling. The other person then reacts to his response in terms of the idea or feeling—the meaning—behind it. When a girl receives flowers she looks at them and smells them, but her main interest is in *who* sent them, and *why*. Were they sent to end a quarrel, to mark an anniversary, to cement a promise, to say farewell, to brighten an illness? Unless she can answer such questions she will feel at loose ends, not knowing what to do. It is the meanings behind the behavior that are involved in the system of mutual expectations previously described as being present in the interacting situation.

It should now be clear that a significant classification of the kinds of interaction must keep in view the meaningful character of social contact. A classification of all social relationships into two types, one involving the physical approach of the individuals toward each other and the other involving the physical withdrawal of the individuals away from each other, would have no sociological significance. Such a crude procedure would group together, as being alike, two men engaged in a fist fight and two lovers engaged in an embrace, and this would not make sense.

Isolation

The quickest way to see the significance and nature of social contact is to consider the absence of such contact. Absolute isolation in the sense that one individual has no contact whatsoever with other individuals at any time, is of course purely hypothetical. The close parental care that the human infant requires for five or six years in order to survive, is not simply automatic and innate on the part of the parents but is meaningful—i.e. is normatively defined. The child is thus a social object for the parents; if he were not he would not receive the physical care necessary for life. The child's response to the social situation in which he is placed is at first mediated through physical tension and gratification. As he responds socially he becomes aware of the symbolic significance of events around him, adopts certain values and ends that are transmitted to him, and through these comes to control his behavior in conformity with certain normative patterns. Through this process of socialization he comes to be a social personality, a responding, modifiable unit in a web of social relationships. Even if the child is feeble-minded he acquires some inkling of communicated meanings, some degree of socialization. Only if he is a mere senseless bundle of cells in human shape will he remain immune to communicative contact, and even then he will be, and will survive only as, an object of attitudes and meaningful contacts on the part of others.

The nearest thing to absolute isolation of an individual is the case of so-called feral children who at an early age are separated from human company and manage to survive alone. These children, scores of whom have been reported, demonstrate the enormous extent to which the traits of human beings are socially acquired [2] and hence the necessity of meaningful contact for the development of human nature as we understand it. Their isolation, however, is so near to the hypothetically absolute kind that it is not itself a part of the social order. The kind of isolation we are interested in is the type of which the participants are aware, the type that is integrated with other social relationships.

Instances of meaningful isolation are the following: solitary confinement in a prison cell, lonely pursuit of a solitary occupation (e.g. shepherd), friendless anonymity in a city, voluntary retirement from human company, etc. It seems difficult to say anything about such instances as a class of phenomena, because they differ so greatly according to the social context in which they are found. Thus there is little similarity between solitary confinement in a prison cell and voluntary retirement to an ivory tower; the differences seem more important than the likenesses. But we can say this: Regardless of the significance attached to it in the given situation, isolation of the individual is always considered to be a negative value that may or may not have compensatory advantages. Even the voluntary retirement of the anchorite is thought by the anchorite himself, and certainly by those less devout, to be a terrible price to pay for virtue; unless this were the case it would hardly be regarded as worth doing, for it has the nature of a sacrifice. The voluntary retirement of a scholar is hardly a bona fide case, because he is really retiring from the crowd of living persons in order to be free for the indirect communicative contact with distant or departed thinkers through the medium of books; he is therefore being merely selective in his choice of company.

Our question is why prolonged and relatively complete individual isolation is viewed by the isolate as a negative value. In the first place, other people constitute and provide the means to most of one's

[2] See Chap. VIII.

ends. Members of human society are so interdependent that their native appetites, even after the period of infancy, are difficult to satisfy without human company; and there is a wide range of acquired tastes and goals that are dependent on others for their satisfaction—such as a liking for drama, for songs, for a variety of foods, for news of the outer world, etc. In addition, the structure of the human personality is so much a product of social interaction that when this interaction ceases it tends to decay. The deleterious effect of solitary confinement on mental balance is notorious, and is one reason why this sort of treatment has been abandoned except as extreme punishment. The individual protects his personality as best he can by imaginary social relationships; he converses, plays, fights with himself. But since in his imagination the responses of the others are always what he expects, the element of novelty, of surprise and challenge, and hence of real stimulation is lacking. Finally, it seems that apart from any instrumental value they may have, social relationships become ends in themselves. Not every social relationship is thus endowed, but many are, so that the isolated individual comes to have almost a craving for human company. This fact has given rise to the popular belief that there is an innate social tendency, a "gregarious instinct," in human beings, but we need no such mysterious entity to explain what is more easily explained in terms of the social system. A society that did not teach its members to value the social relationships constituting its structure would be missing a necessary aid to social cohesion. Indeed, since the main forms of interaction in a society are laid down in the mores, these forms are *ipso facto* valued by the societal members as ends in themselves.

Plainly the reasons for the negative evaluation of enduring and complete isolation are profound ones. Most individuals who have a poetic conception of solitude could not stand complete isolation for a day, much less a week. They would do well to read the following lines from Cowper:

> I praise the Frenchman, his remark was shrewd,—
> How sweet, how passing sweet, is solitude!
> But grant me still a friend in my retreat,
> Whom I may whisper, Solitude is sweet.

The kind of isolation considered desirable is always temporary and partial, such as being away from a crowd or being alone for an hour.

It is then called "solitude." When, however, it begins to pall it is called "loneliness."

The fact that total isolation is disvalued, together with the reason for this disvaluation, explains the use of it in social organization. Its occasional use as severe punishment implies that for the time being the person is beyond the pale of society, an object of desire to nobody else, permitted to live only in a physical sense. His range of means for the satisfaction of his ends is forcibly narrowed to almost zero with the implication that his ends are unimportant, i.e. are ends for nobody else. Voluntary isolation is seldom if ever complete. The extreme instances bear an underlying similarity to the involuntary cases, in that they assume a lack of common ends with the other members of the society. The anchorite presumably cherishes transcendental values—values to which the common herd pays merely lip service, values for which isolation is a necessary condition. His separateness may be highly praised by his contemporaries as an example of extreme devotion to transcendental values, but if he is truly isolated he will not hear this praise. He can be sustained in his endeavor only by the values he has previously imbibed in a social relationship but for which he now believes the social relationship to be a hindrance. In either case, whether voluntary or involuntary, the isolation of an individual as a part of the social organization is only temporary and partial. The longer the isolation the more it signifies a deep hiatus between the ends of this individual and those of the group. Removal from social contact makes it impossible to share ends with others.

PARTIAL ISOLATION AND SOCIAL DISTANCE

An extreme form of punishment for public crimes in simple societies is often banishment from the tribe. The culprit is not necessarily isolated from all mankind but only from the society of which he has been a part. So dependent is he upon kinsmen and fellow citizens, so hard is the lot of the stranger in other areas, that such banishment is often tantamount to a sentence of death. Among the early Greeks, for example, the most severe punishment for a crime committed against one's own group was expulsion from the kinship group. The clothes of the culprit were taken from him; he was followed to the boundary of the clan's territory by a wrathful crowd; and in the earliest times it was a matter of chance whether or not he was killed by the crowd before he could get away. Such individuals, called "wolves," led a precarious existence in new lands if they escaped alive.[3]

If banishment separates the individual from a given society, excommunication separates him from the religious community. In the simplest societies banishment and excommunication are practically synonymous and are widely practised. In somewhat more complex social systems the religious aspect of life is differentiated from other aspects, so that an individual can remain in contact with his fellows and still be excommunicated, i.e. excluded from the sacred rituals that are the highest expressions of devotion to the group's gods. To the degree that religion is paramount, this punishment is severe. "Excommunication was the earliest punishment inflicted by the Christian church upon its members and, although in the course of time its original character was altered, it has always remained the foundation of the criminal law of the church."[4] Today, of course, excommunication means less than it did in the Middle Ages, but to the devout Catholic it means a good deal. In the early days of a proselyting religion when civil authority does not reinforce the religious authority, excommunication is one of the few devices that may be employed by the worshipers to punish one of their members. As distinct from banishment, excommunication usually allows for the readmission of the culprit after penance is done.

It is only a short step from excommunication to ostracism, in which a secular group simply refuses to associate with an individual either because of something he has done or because of the position he occupies. With reference to that particular group he is cut off from all satisfactory association, though he may retain his position in other groups.

Excommunication and ostracism, as opposed to total isolation and banishment, apply mainly to particular sectors of association. A boy who is labeled "sissy" may be ostracized by the neighborhood gang, but his relationships with his parents, his teachers, his Sunday school class, etc. may remain completely normal. Ostracism is thus closely related to the sense of solidarity of particular groups or classes

[3] Gustave Glotz, *La solidarité de la famille dans le droit criminel en Grèce* (Paris: 1904), pp. 22-25.

[4] H. D. Hazeltine, "Excommunication," *Encyclopedia of the Social Sciences* (New York: Macmillan, 1937), p. 671.

rather than of the community as a whole. In one form or another it is therefore a pervasive and effective element in maintaining conformity to group norms and group organization.

Deliberate exclusion of an individual from one type of association may arise, however, not as retaliation for unorthodox behavior but simply as a taboo implying no fault on the part of either party. This might be called mutual avoidance. A well-known example is found in the case of customary avoidances between kinsmen, especially kinsmen by marriage. In a large number of primitive societies the husband, more rarely the wife, assumes an attitude of distance toward the parents-in-law. Either no direct intercourse is permitted between the man and his parents-in-law or it is hedged about with numerous restrictions. Son-in-law and mother-in-law may be forbidden to see each other, to speak directly to each other, to use the name of the other, to undress in the presence of the other, etc. "There is an anecdote of a Kirgiz woman who was prohibited from employing the usual words for lamb, wolf, water and rushes because they formed part of the names of her relatives by marriage. Accordingly, in telling her husband of a wolf carrying off a lamb through the rushes on the other side of the water, she was obliged to paraphrase: 'Look yonder, the howling one is carrying the bleating one's young through the rustling ones on the other side of the glistening one!' "[5]

Another form of mutual avoidance is that between men and women. As we saw in discussing the ascription of status on the basis of sex, men and women are encouraged to associate in some respects, discouraged in other respects. Our most complete taboo, for example, is the separation of the sexes for excretory purposes. Another is the taboo on incest. Sexual intercourse is generally limited to well defined situations. Still another type of mutual avoidance is that between members of different social classes or of different castes. Untouchability in India means that for purposes of marriage, eating, drinking, smoking, and physical contact in general, certain low castes are to be avoided.

When isolation from mutual contact becomes a prescribed rule affecting only certain sectors of relationship, we see that it then forms a basic principle of social organization. Social distance as well as social nearness is therefore a structural principle in society. The

[5] Robert H. Lowie, *Primitive Society* (New York: Horace Liveright, 1920), pp. 84-85.

systematic distribution of avoidance is as necessary as the systematic distribution of contacts. Such avoidances, however, are quite distinct from absolute isolation.

ISOLATION OF SOCIETIES AND GROUPS

Few societies have ever been totally separated from all others for any great length of time. Human contact, at least in recent millenia, has ringed the globe. Yet there are some instances which impress moderns as representing an extreme degree of societal isolation. The northernmost inhabitants of the earth, the Polar Eskimos, for example, "occupy a narrow fringe of coast . . . in North Greenland. . . . Less than a thousand miles from the Pole itself, this remote tribe of 271 persons (in 1926) is separated by hundreds of miles from its nearest neighbors, the Eskimos of West Greenland and those of North Baffin Land."[6] Yet these Eskimos must not have been completely isolated for any great length of time, for their dialect is so similar to the other Eskimauan dialects that they can make themselves understood as far away as Alaska. We find instances of far greater linguistic barriers among peoples who live much closer together. On the island of New Guinea, for example, the aborigines were split up into groups speaking twenty or more entirely different languages. In North and South America there were, according to traditional scientific linguistic classification, 150 different languages.[7] Such linguistic differences constitute effective barriers to social contact among peoples geographically near as well as those remote from each other.

Other things equal, the more isolated a society the slower it is to change. It remains dependent upon tradition, upon ascribed rather than achieved status, upon sacred values and transcendental ends. It misses the stimulating effect of cultural cross-fertilization. Even our own mountain communities, shut off from contact by physical barriers, show the effect of such isolation.[8]

Stultifying as societal isolation may seem, it is nevertheless an aid to social solidarity and is sometimes an important adjunct of the ethnocentric attitude. The shunning of the foreigner goes hand

[6] Geo. Peter Murdock, *Our Primitive Contemporaries* (New York: Macmillan, 1936), p. 192.

[7] A. L. Kroeber, *Anthropology* (New York: Harcourt, Brace, 1923), pp. 98-100.

[8] Mandel Sherman and C. B. Key, "The Intelligence of Isolated Mountain Children," *Child Development*, Vol. 3 (1932), pp. 279-290.

in hand with a love of one's own ways. Within the society, likewise, the integrity of particular groups is reinforced by maintaining social distance (avoidance) toward other groups. By this route we return again to the point that partial isolation is a significant element in social organization. An important form in which group avoidance manifests itself is in *residential segregation.* Such segregation may arise from uncontrolled competition for housing in a free market (thus separating people according to their wealth), from the undirected operation of the ethnocentric attitude (thus congregating people of a given nationality, religion, or occupation), or from the deliberate segregation of persons by law (as in the ghettos of Medieval or of Fascist Europe, the separation of married from unmarried adults in many primitive tribes, the segregation of male and female college students in separate dormitories).

Partial isolation, whatever its specific form, tends to be associated with the individuals' social positions and to be expressed in the rights and duties of these positions. It implies that between the individuals occupying different statuses there is a difference of ends. It is therefore one of the means by which societies are organized. Some mutual avoidance, some social distance, some ethnocentrism seems inevitable.

Conflict

Conflict is an ever-present process in human relations. It may be solved on one level, as when there is agreement on ends, and break out anew over the question of means. Such partial conflict, however, is different from total conflict. The latter implies that there is no level of agreement at all, and that consequently the only method of solving the disparity of interest is through the resort to physical force.

One may raise a profound question by asking why conflict, both in its partial and in its total form, is such a constant feature of human society although it is everywhere deprecated. The answer goes back to matters discussed already. Human society is not a tightly compressed affair but instead has a loose integration. The integration is not on a biological but on a mental level. It must be created anew and constantly maintained through psychic processes such as indoctrination, inspiration, and repetition. It must somehow rest on the possession of common and extra-personal ends on the part of its members. These ends cannot come from man's biological nature but only from communicative contact with his fellows; they thus differ greatly from one society to another because they are associated with differences of culture. This, then, gives the first great basis of conflict—ethnocentrism—the dislike of people with different culture and different ultimate ends from one's own. Those with the same set of ultimate ends cling together and identify themselves with one another, while those with a different set do the same. A social group, furthermore, has a corporate character: a name, a common leadership, a determinate structure, a sense of familiarity. Individuals identify themselves with this corporate entity and conceive their ultimate duty as loyalty to it, whether it be a clan, a tribe, a city-state, a religious sect, or a nation.

The kind of group conflict we are most familiar with is war between nations, and we recognize that nationalism forms an essential basis of such conflict. Let us illustrate with the case of Japan. As is well known the Japanese have expressed their nationalism in the form of emperor worship. The emperor has been regarded as divine, as the supreme head of the state, as the supreme priest of the state religion (Shinto), and as the symbol of the nation. Respect for him has been the deepest sentiment, and devotion to him the supreme duty for each Japanese. The following passage describing the reaction when the Emperor Mutsuhito died at the end of a forty-five year reign, illustrates perfectly the depth of the sentiment.

> The doctors issued bulletins several times a day and people waited anxiously for encouraging news. But the news grew worse and worse. All the citizens of Tokyo worried. They suffered because their great father suffered. Streetcars ran slowly, trying not to make a noise. The populace gathered around the palace moats under the green willows or in the huge front grounds. During the ten days that His Majesty was ill, more than ten thousand men and women, old and young, assembled every day, looking anxiously toward the palace beyond the white walls of the ancient castle of Yedo. . . . We, the infants of His Majesty—we spoke of ourselves in this way, prayed to the gods, the ancestors of Japan, to bring back the royal health. Day and night his subjects stayed around his palace praying silently. Ten thousand people gathered without making a sound. The masses whom even thousands of policeman could not hold in silence when they did not want to keep quiet, were here under the hot July sun hushed with one accord in real prayer. Papers reported that many men com-

mitted suicide in the hope that their ancestors would accept the offering of a private life as a substitute for that of His Majesty the Emperor Mutsuhito!

At last the great spirit of the Meiji Emperor ascended to heaven, and darkness fell upon the nation. The imperial mourning lasted an entire year, divided into three terms. . . . During this period we moved quietly, at school, on the street, even at home. We did not laugh. We played no music. Even marriages were postponed until the year was over.

Nothing could be more impressive than the funeral of the Emperor. . . . [It] was performed strictly after the manner of two thousand years ago, except that its scale was enlarged by the enhanced splendor of the modern nation. . . . [We] were carried back in sentiment and atmosphere to ancient Japan . . . All the streets along which the funeral cortege was to pass were cleaned beforehand, and kept in the utmost cleanliness and quiet. Electric lights were turned off and pine torchlights substituted. . . . The high officials who were given the honor of following the imperial hearse practiced walking long beforehand in their ancient robes, wearing crowns and lacquer shoes. . . . We spectators all bowed low to the coffin, murmuring eternal farewell to our beloved Mikado in our hearts but not with our voices, although quiet weeping was heard here and there. Thus we continued our silent prayer until the second gong told us that the son of the late Mikado—the new Emperor of Japan, who was already at the temporary shrine built on a field just outside the city for the purpose—had received the coffin and was now going to read his words of grief in the presence of his father's spirit.[9]

This noble and sincere description appeals to us as any devotion to ends outside ourselves always does. It seems to have nothing to do with conflict, and indeed it greatly helps to prevent conflict *within* the nation. It can be seen, however, that people so devoted to the national idea are ready to fight for this idea if it is conceived to be endangered or dishonored in any way. The world seems too small to contain different peoples who feel this way about the national entities to which they belong. It is hard for absolutes to dwell together in peace. The glory of Japan, the glory of Germany, the glory of Russia, the glory of France, the glory of America—these

[9] Baroness Shidzue Ishimoto, *Facing Two Ways* (New York: Rinehart, 1935), pp. 68-69.

cannot be pursued indefinitely without getting in each other's way. The nation is a definite organized entity capable of being symbolized and made the focus of attention. Japanese children were taught from infancy to revere the emperor, to believe the myths about his divine ancestry, to worship his portrait, and to be willing to sacrifice and die for him if necessary. Other nations glorify themselves by roughly similar means. Each nation gains cohesion and strength through emphasizing its own destiny as against that of other nations. It suffers least from internal conflict precisely when it is engaged in external conflict with an enemy. Internal harmony and external conflict are therefore opposite sides of the same shield. This is why war is held to be inevitable in a world of sovereign nations. As yet the world as a whole is not organized as one social entity, and for this reason cannot be made the object of sentiment in the same way as a nation.

As for internal conflict, every organized group strives to eliminate it as far as possible, because conflict precludes that degree of coöperation necessary for societal efficiency. The elimination is achieved by the possession of common ends by the members. It is not possible, however, to eliminate all conflict because, despite the presence of common values, there are also ends that relate to the person himself. Only individuals have ends, and some of these ends have to do with the satisfaction of personal needs—needs for food, sex, comfort, recreation, social standing, etc. Such ends are insistent; in one way or another the individual tends therefore to rationalize their gratification. Since the means are scarce one man gains his ends at the expense of another, and conflict easily arises unless it is controlled somehow. It is controlled partly by banning outright physical conflict and internecine warfare. The organized group reserves for itself the use of force and forbids its use for purely private ends. Any permissive use of force, such as occurs in legal dueling, is apt to be highly ritualized and seldom results in death. Sporadic outbursts of open conflict do occur, however, and in weak societies they occur frequently. The effort to eliminate them is never entirely successful.

The suppression of open conflict within the group does not mean the elimination of partial forms of conflict. It means simply that the conflict is not of the all-out variety. There are many ways of getting the best of an enemy without actually doing him bodily harm. He may be fired from his job, put in his place, given a feeling of insecurity. Partial conflict is forever occurring, whether in family, school, factory, or neighborhood. It is an inescapable part of social life.

Whether of the total or partial kind, conflict captures the attention. It is the stuff that drama feeds on. It assumes that between the two parties there is no common ground, no end higher than the interests that divide them, and that the only solution is the elimination of one or the other—either by death, banishment, avoidance, or some conclusive economic or social victory. The effort of a social system is always in the direction of controlling violence in the interest of common ends, yet as a matter of fact society itself engenders conflict situations and cannot avoid doing so. By alloting different statuses to different people it lays the basis for envy and resentment. By giving authority to one person over another it sets the stage for the abuse of authority and for retaliation by force. By instilling ends that are competitive it makes it possible for competition to spill over into violence.

There are of course social mechanisms that smooth over conflict. One of these is humor, which removes the tension that might otherwise expend itself in physical violence. Another, mentioned above, is social distance or avoidance. A third is sentiment formation, which overcomes the conflict of interests by making harmony seem a greater goal than the separate interests of the antagonistic parties. A fourth is variety and change, for an existing situation is more tolerable if it is known that it will not last long. A fifth is organized rivalry, which provides an opportunity for simulated battle, for intense group loyalty, for the manifestation of prowess in vanquishing others, and yet because the interaction has a set form and definite conclusion it allows the energies to be expended either harmlessly or to the advantage of the society.

It is clear, however, that such mechanisms are not universally successful. Humor, social distance, noble sentiments, social change, organized rivalry—these may on occasion provoke rather than prevent conflict. The truth is that there are elements of conflict in all situations, because the ends of different individuals are always to some extent mutually exclusive. Conflict is a part of human society because of the kind of thing human society is. There is no social mind, but only the minds of particular individuals; no social end, but only the ends of concrete persons. In so far as harmony is attained it is through the agreement of individual minds, and this agreement thrives best when there is an external danger—when the common ends of the group are pitted over against (and therefore in conflict with) the common ends of another group. Thus internal harmony depends to some extent on external conflict (war). At the same time the agreement on ends within the society can never embrace all ends. Individuals, as separate organisms and egos, inevitably have ends that are mutually exclusive. They push for the attainment of their own ends as against the ends of other individuals, sometimes using illegitimate and definitely hostile means to bring success. Since human groups are loose units as compared to the cell, the body, or even the insect colony, the human type of cultural adaptation depends upon the interplay of diverse interests within the group. Such interplay cannot escape all conflict. The miracle is not how much conflict there is, but how little.

Competition

In contrast to conflict, which aims to destroy or banish the opponent, competition simply aims to out-do the competitor in achieving some mutually desired goal. It is thus a modified form of struggle. It implies that there are rules of the game to which the competitors must conform and that behind these rules, justifying and maintaining them, is a common set of values superior to the competitive interest. It also implies an absence of coercion. The rules are so arranged that the ends must be obtained by other methods than fraud or physical force. If the chain stores take business away from the local merchants by offering better goods at cheaper prices, that is competition. If, on the other hand, the small merchants induce the government to tax the chain stores out of existence, that is not competition because the state has the power of coercion. If a metropolitan paper employs thugs to smash newsstands selling a competing paper, that is not competition either. The rules of competition limit the means that may be used to gain the competitive end; they tend especially to eliminate force and fraud. When competition breaks through the rules it transforms itself into conflict.

It follows that there is no such thing as "unrestricted competition." Such a phrase is a contradiction in terms. As usually used, it means a maximum number of goods open to competition and a minimum restraint upon the means to be used. But in no society are all goods distributed on a competitive basis. Today in the United States, for example, utilities are distributed by quasi-monopolies under government control; membership in the army in wartime is not determined by competitive bidding but by military draft; and the capitol in Washington is not for sale. Every society limits the goods open to competition and the means to be used. Competition is never entirely "unrestricted."

But neither is competition ever completely eliminated. As the black markets during a period of rationing clearly show, it has a tendency to spring up and flow around the barriers erected against it. It always appears in one form or another no matter what the institutional order.

Competition cannot therefore be identified with laissez-faire, free enterprise, etc. These are simply types of economic systems that give great scope to competition. They are not identical with competition but embody a set of mandatory institutions that facilitate it. Competition is only an element in such systems. On the other hand, a so-called non-competitive system is not one that has no competition but rather one that limits it to a much greater degree than does a laissez-faire system. An essential part of any social system, competition varies as to scope, intensity, and type from one system to another. Soviet Russia has plenty of competition. So does the United States, but in a different way. The American variety is molded by the economic institutions of private property, contract, and the open market and by the political institution of representative government. These not only define the type of competition but give it great scope as well. They open the door to the pursuit of wealth through entrepreneurial ability and the pursuit of office through oratorical ability. One can go further and say that even our courtship institutions are competitive, not to mention our science, our education, and our sports.

Competition is extremely dynamic. It stimulates achievement by lifting the level of aspiration, by threatening failure as well as promising success, and by adding an element of rivalry. For this reason it becomes particularly strong in complex and changing societies. In fact its obvious connection with what is called progress has led to its enthronement in some circles as the essential feature of modern civilization. The most thorough statement of this point of view occurs in classical economic theory, succinctly if ironically paraphrased in the following passage:

> The actors are human beings, impelled by the utilities which articles of consumption possess to overcome the disutility of personal effort. Each must take his mite of service or his property to market and fetch away the wherewithal of his living. In the market goods and services are all tagged with prices and personal wealth comes by way of careful and shrewd calculation. In disposing of goods and services each has to compete with others who have like goods and services to sell. In seeking what one would have each has to bid up against others who would take it away. As a result value is a sovereign in the great competitive economy; an upward dart of price or a downward drop allows those who will pay most to purchase, gives a market to those who will sell for least and effects a neat adjustment between supply and demand. Under the double competitive process of seller against seller and buyer against buyer it cannot well be otherwise. For if it chances that a price is too low to effect a balance, a flood of bids speeds it to the proper level; and if too high, a host of offers brings it down. The domain of competition is almost universal. The march of invention opposes new wares to old: motor busses to street cars, electric refrigerators to ice, radio to the phonograph. Wants even vie to create a competition between unlike goods: a modern car and an antique coach, an evening down town and a Sunday in the country . . . With price as a guide competition continuously accommodates the production of goods to the changing demand for them. A delicate structure of responsive prices must keep on effecting the best mediation that may be between the wants of the people and the productive capacity of industry. . . .
>
> The industrial system is an automatic self-regulating mechanism which must continuously secure from a niggardly nature just such goods as yield the largest surplus of pleasures over pains. It is a Newtonian economic system wherein matter is replaced by wealth, attraction and repulsion give way to utility and disutility, the phenomena of the market like those of the heavens are given an equilibrium, a system of checks and balances keeps the machine in order, and the theory of the conservation of energy finds a parallel in the law of the economic maximum.[10]

[10] Walton H. Hamilton, "Competition," *Encyclopedia of the Social Sciences,* pp. 143-144.

Not only did the classical theorists come to regard the competitive system as automatic and self-regulatory, but they thought it explained the whole social order. "The individual man, in seeking his own profit, will necessarily seek to produce and sell that which has most value for the community, and so 'he is in this, as in many other cases,' as Adam Smith puts it, 'led by an invisible hand to promote an end which was no part of his intention.' "[11]

In their enthusiasm for competition these men overlooked certain things that are plain to see. They overlooked the institutions and rules which alone enable competition to work—the protection of property, the enforcement of contracts, the prevention of fraud. They overlooked the common ends and values which are not competitive but which are superior to those that are. They overlooked the limitations on means. They forgot that competition can be vicious as well as beneficent, that it can lead to starvation in the midst of plenty,[12] to fear and insecurity, to instability and panic. They forgot that competition treats others purely as means and in itself is devoid of sentiment. They forgot that unlimited competition leads inevitably to monopoly, that the very success of the strong leads to gigantic power over the weak and creates such inequality that a mockery is made of free contract. Above all, they forgot that few are willing to pay the full cost of competition, that security as well as opportunity is a universal human motive.

Nowhere do we find people submitting themselves to complete competition if they can help it. Business men seek to erect tariff barriers against foreign competition—the Maginot line psychology in economic affairs. They seek to agree among themselves on prices and thus prevent "cut-throat" competition, at the same time trying to exclude newcomers from entering the charmed circle and sharing in the increased profits. They seek to buy out their competitors and expand and consolidate their holdings until they possess an impregnable economic empire. Labor unions strike and picket for higher wages, limit membership by charging exorbitant entrance

[11] Robt. E. Park and Ernest W. Burgess, *Introduction to the Science of Sociology* (Chicago: University of Chicago Press, 1924), p. 504.

[12] The Bengal famine of 1943, for example, was an inflationary famine. There was just enough food to go around, but the rising prices caused hoarding, the hoarding caused scarcity, the scarcity caused more hoarding, and the increased scarcity caused starvation. The remedy was not more competition but an efficient system of rationing. This, however, was not provided because the government was weak.

fees, plead for a guaranteed minimum wage, demand the exclusion of foreign laborers, call for tariffs to protect union-made products, advocate the closed shop, oppose technological advances which replace manpower, use violence to prevent nonunion laborers from working, and hold to the principle of seniority. Bureaucrats seek to protect themselves by civil service rules, by attention to protocol, and by subservience to superiors. Wives and husbands want security from possible rivals. White persons seek to limit competition by forcing the blacks into a fixed inferior position.

Everywhere there is an effort to fetch security by erecting a barrier. Everywhere there is an effort to grab an opportunity by breaching a barrier. A social system is thus a neat balance between competitive and noncompetitive forces. The capitalistic interlude between the Industrial Revolution and the Second World War was unusually competitive. It could not endure. The demand for stability and security is pulling it back to the more usual condition of fixity and authority. Looked at in one way, competition is nothing else than our old friend achieved status. Its opposite is ascribed status. We have already found that no society can rest exclusively on one or the other but that it can emphasize one against the other. Many who denounce competition today are not yet willing to admit that they are asking at the same time for fixity of status.

Coöperation

Coöperation is commonly believed to be the opposite of competition. This is not true if it means that in a given situation one necessarily excludes the other. A coöperating group is one that is working together to accomplish a goal that all desire. In many cases it is realized that competition will aid the attainment of this goal, and so a system of competition is allowed or deliberately instituted. The Soviet government learned early in its history that competition for high pay has a stimulating effect on productivity. Since Russia's great need was to increase production by leaps and bounds, it developed an ingenious system of "socialist competition."

Unless competition enhances the overall goals of the society it will find critics aplenty. So long as it is controlled and institutionalized, it is presumably a means by which the coöperation of all is accomplished. In reality it is conflict rather than competition that is the opposite of coöperation. Yet coöperation may occur without making internal use of competition, and between two competitors the overarching element of coöperation may be lost from sight. In fact, each of two competitors trying to outstrip each other may view its own organization as coöperating within itself but not coöperating at all with the other organization. Often, therefore, the ultimate coöperative effect of competition escapes awareness; the closer and more intimate coöperation of the organized group is the center of attention. This is what gives the illusion that competition and coöperation are necessarily opposed.

The Interrelation of the Forms of Interaction

It should be clear that the forms of interaction discussed here—conflict, competition, and coöperation—are all interdependent. They are ever-present aspects of human society. Any social system, in fact any concrete situation, will manifest all three in a complex and intertwined manner. There is no coöperating group, no matter how harmonious, which will not contain the seeds of suppressed conflict. There is no conflict, no matter how bitter, which will not have some hidden basis of compromise. There is no competition, no matter how impersonal and ruthless, which cannot claim some contribution to a larger coöperative cause.

It should also be clear that an analysis of social behavior in terms of the forms of interaction is an indispensable mode of approaching social phenomena. Since it is the last of the fundamental approaches that we shall consider, the way is now open for a summary of the four modes of analysis dealt with.

The Four Fundamental Approaches: A Summary

If the last four chapters have any validity, they indicate that sociological study involves several different but mutually supplementary points of view. Four such points have been discussed here, chapter by chapter. The first and broadest of the four concentrates upon the social norms—the folkways, mores, laws, and institutions of different societies. The second, analyzing the application of these norms in particular statuses and situations, views a society as a system of social positions occupied by the members of the society.

Both of these modes of study have to do primarily with social structure. The third approach, however, centers its attention on the elements of action—the ends, means, and conditions in terms of which the norms and statuses enter the motivation of each individual. It gives a more dynamic view of social phenomena. The fourth approach is also dynamic, for it studies the processes of interaction—conflict, competition, and coöperation—that take place within the social framework.

These points of view do not represent the entire range of possible approaches in sociology. They do not include for instance the functional point of view (the over-all and inclusive approach of the present volume), the evolutionary and deterministic approaches with their emphasis on social change (to be considered later) or the so-called "problems approach." The combination of the four basic approaches discussed here, however, does provide a rather complete foundation for the analysis of social systems within what may be regarded as a functional framework. Different schools of thought in sociology have each tended to emphasize one or the other of the four orientations. The approach of William Graham Sumner represented primarily a concern with social norms.[13] The approach of Marx, and in a different way Linton, represented mainly an interest in status.[14] The work of Talcott Parsons, drawing upon Max Weber and economic theory, focused its interest on the elements of action.[15] And the orientation of Robert E. Park and the so-called "Chicago school" of sociology directed its attention mainly to the processes of interaction.[16] The works of all of these men (some are still living) have become classics in the field, and the authors have inspired many followers. Furthermore, each of the four points of view, taken as a central starting point, is capable of very wide application and can take into account nearly everything stressed by the other approaches. The concepts of one approach are capable of translation into the concepts of another. For this reason many of the authors mentioned

[13] Wm. Graham Sumner, *Folkways: A Study of the Sociological Importance of Usages, Manners, Customs, Mores, and Morals* (Boston: Ginn, 1906).

[14] Karl Marx, *Capital: A Critique of Political Economy,* first published in Germany (without completion) in three volumes between 1867 and 1894. Ralph Linton, *The Study of Man* (New York: Appleton-Century, 1936).

[15] Talcott Parsons, *The Structure of Social Action* (New York: McGraw-Hill, 1937).

[16] Robt. E. Park and Ernest W. Burgess, *Introduction to the Science of Sociology* (Chicago: University of Chicago Press, 1921).

would not like to be so narrowly classified as they have been here. They view themselves as having covered the field. But in generalizing each point of view so as to represent the entire range of social phenomena, these men tend to proceed by assumptions and residual categories in order to cover what their central point of departure does not readily embrace. For this reason it is better to state the different modes of analysis explicitly and then to combine them in a more complete system of thought.

If the present work has any originality, it lies primarily in the effort to combine these explicitly stated modes of analysis in an over-all functional approach. In this task, perhaps, the work lays itself open to the charge of eclecticism; but the answer to such a charge is a pragmatic one: if the combination of approaches leads to a more rounded and more flexible view of the social system, this is proof enough of its acceptability. If all approaches are put to work, and if the relations between them are systematically kept in mind, the superficiality of eclecticism will be avoided. The rest of the book is essentially an effort to apply these four approaches to social phenomena. The main analytical part is contained in the chapters that have been covered. The future chapters represent an effort to apply these analytical tools to the relation of society to the person, the analysis of groups, the study of major institutions, and the understanding of social change. The success or failure of the undertaking can be judged by the reader himself.

Before approaching the larger problems just mentioned, it seems wise to give the reader a brief example, by way of illustration, of how the sociological analysis of a specific phenomenon can prove illuminating. For this purpose a topic has been chosen which ordinarily would not be thought of as lending itself to social science study. The topic is jealousy; the discussion of it is presented in the next chapter.

References

Chester Alexander, "Antipathy and Social Behavior," *American Journal of Sociology,* 51, (January 1946), pp. 288-292.

A brief but relevant discussion of antipathy in interpersonal behavior.

Crane Brinton, *The Anatomy of Revolution* (New York: Norton, 1938).

An attempt by a historian to set forth the uniformities, the typi-

cal stages and elements, of revolutionary conflict. Based on the study of four popular revolutions: French, American, English, and Russian.

Arthur R. Burns, *The Decline of Competition* (New York: McGraw-Hill, 1936).

An outstanding analysis of the ways in which competition is weakening in economic life and in economic theory.

Lyford P. Edwards, *The Natural History of Revolution* (Chicago: University of Chicago Press, 1927).

"Unpretentious, suggestive, tentative. One of the best introductions to the subject available in English. Mr. Edwards does not pretend to do more than sketch the essential problems and indicate possible further work. Admirably free from special pleading."—Crane Brinton's comment.

Margaret Mead (ed.), *Cooperation and Competition in Primitive Societies* (New York: McGraw-Hill, 1936).

A discussion by anthropologists of coöperation and competition in various primitive societies. Promises more than it delivers, but it does bring together some comparative materials on this topic.

Wilbert E. Moore, *Industrial Relations and the Social Order* (New York: Macmillan, 1946), Chap. 17, "Labor Organization"; Chap. 18, "Collective Bargaining"; Chaps. 19-20, "Industrial Conflict."

Sociological analysis of labor relations. Each chapter has an extensive bibliography.

Georg Simmel, "The Sociology of Conflict," *American Journal of Sociology*, Vol. 9 (1904-05), pp. 490-525, 672-689, 798-811.

A masterpiece of theoretical formulation. Translated from parts of the author's great German treatise on sociology.

Hans Speier and A. Kähler (eds.), *War in Our Time* (New York: Norton, 1941).

A symposium on social aspects of warfare. The senior editor is an outstanding authority on the sociology of war.

Edgar T. Thompson (ed.), *Race Relations and the Race Problem* (Durham, N. C.: Duke University Press, 1939).

This whole volume approaches race relations from the interactional point of view, but two articles, those by E. B. Reuter and Guy B. Johnson, deal particularly with competition and conflict in race relations.

W. Lloyd Warner and J. O. Low, *The Social System of the Modern Factory; The Strike: A Social Analysis* (New Haven: Yale University Press, 1947) Chap. 1, "The Strike—Why Did It Happen"; Chap. 2, "Prelude to Conflict"; Chap. 3, "The Natural History of a Strike."

A sociological analysis of a strike which throws light on the nature of social interaction and especially on the development of conflict. See also the article by Scott and Homans, Chap. XI.

Kimball Young, *Sociology* (New York: American Book, 1942), Chap. 24, "Competition"; Chap. 25, "Conflict"; Chap. 26, "War as Conflict and Institution"; Chap. 27, "Cooperation."

Textbook presentation. Each chapter has a classified bibliography.

PART II

THE INDIVIDUAL AND HIS SOCIETY

JEALOUSY AND SEXUAL PROPERTY: AN ILLUSTRATION

SOCIALIZATION

PERSONALITY INTEGRATION

PERSONALITY DISORGANIZATION

CHAPTER VII

JEALOUSY AND SEXUAL PROPERTY: AN ILLUSTRATION

AT FIRST glance jealousy may seem an unlikely topic for illustrating the value of a sociological approach. It is usually regarded as an emotion, an individual or psychological phenomenon having little to do with culture and social organization. This very conception of jealousy, however, makes it a useful illustration. If a sociological mode of analysis can be shown to throw new light on the subject, the value of such analysis will be demonstrated.

Actually, all of the types of sociological analysis set forth in the previous chapters seem applicable to jealousy. First of all, it turns out to be a reasonable assumption that jealousy has a function not only with reference to the individual's emotional balance but also with reference to social organization. Secondly, it appears that the manifestations of jealousy are determined by the normative and institutional structure of the given society. This structure defines the situations in which jealousy shows itself and regulates the form of its expression. It follows that unless jealous behavior is observed in different cultures, unless a comparative point of view is adopted, it cannot be intelligently comprehended as a human phenomenon. Thirdly, the situations in which jealousy occurs involve the statuses and roles of various persons with reference to one another. It is through the definition of these statuses and roles that the institutional framework governs the manifestations of jealous emotion. Fourthly, since the various participants in the love entanglement (and it is only sexual jealousy that we are considering) are pursuing ends by various means, an understanding of their behavior requires analysis in terms of means, ends, and conditions. Finally, jealousy involves certain processes of interaction—competition, rivalry, and trespass.

These processes, too, must be understood in their social context, for they are institutionally regulated and culturally variable. All in all it would seem clear that a sociological approach holds definite possibilities of contributing to a knowledge of this peculiar kind of emotion.

Sexual Property as an Institution[1]

Descartes defined jealousy as "a kind of fear related to a desire to preserve a possession." If he had in mind what is customarily called jealous behavior, he was eminently correct. In every case it is apparently a fear or rage reaction to a threatened appropriation of one's own or what is desired as one's own property. Later, in Chapter XVII, we shall deal with economic property as a social institution. Sexual property differs from economic property in many respects but nevertheless bears some resemblance to it. Among other things, sexual property is institutionally defined and regulated. Let us begin, then, by viewing jealousy in relation to sexual property.

Conflicts over property involve four elements: Owner, Object, Public, and Rival or Trespasser. If the conflicts are in the nature of competition rather than trespass, Ego is a would-be owner and his enemy is a rival instead of a trespasser. A popular fallacy has been to conceive the jealous situation as a "triangle." Actually it is a quadrangle because the public, or community, is always an interested element in the situation. The failure to include the public or community element has led to a failure to grasp the social character of jealousy. The relationships between the four elements are culturally regulated. They are current in the given society and constitute the fixed traditional constellation of rights, obligations, and neutralities that may be called sexual property. They are sustained and expressed by the reciprocal attitudes of the interacting parties.

Since property, however, is not always actually in the hands of the owner, ownership must be distinguished from possession, the one being a matter of law and mores, the other a matter of fact. Possession by a person other than the owner may be either licit or illicit. Illicit possession bears witness that the rules of property are susceptible of evasion. Licit possession by one not the owner, as with

[1] This and succeeding sections of the chapter first appeared in *Social Forces*, Vol. 14 (March 1936), pp. 395-405, under the title, "Jealousy and Sexual Property." The article has been only slightly modified in the present version.

a borrowed or rented piece of property, emphasizes the strength of these rules.

Acquisition of property proceeds usually according to socially established norms of competition and, in many cases, by stages. In the initial stage the field is generally open to a class of persons, anybody in this class being free to put in a claim. The qualifying rounds of a golf tournament or the sudden entrance of a strange but attractive young woman are cases in point. Gradually a few competitors take the lead. Social order then requires that others recognize the superiority of these, quit struggling, and turn their attention elsewhere. Finally, after continued competition among the favored few, one competitor wins. This is the signal for everyone who was initially interested to drop all pretense of a claim and take his defeat in good spirit. The end is no longer a legitimate one for him because competition for this particular piece of property is now, by social edict, either temporarily or permanently over. It is owned by one man, behind whose title stands the authority of the community.

Values, however, do not invariably change hands in any such orderly fashion. The unscrupulous stand always ready to take possession in defiance of the rules, to replace the orderliness of rivalry with the disarrangement of trespass. They may at any stage, under peril of organized retaliation, upset the procedure and seize physical possession of the property.

There are thus two dangers which beset any person with regard to property. The first is that somebody will win out over him in legitimate competition. This is the danger of superior rivalry. The second is that somebody will illegitimately take from him property already acquired. This is the danger of trespass.

Most malignant emotions are concerned with these two dangers; they are directed either at a rival or trespasser or at someone who is helping a rival or trespasser. Such emotions may be either suppressed by the group culture or utilized for maintaining the organized distribution of property. In general fear and hatred of rivals are institutionally suppressed, fear and hatred of trespassers encouraged.

In the initial stages of acquisition fear of rivals is frequently paramount. Such fear is merely the obverse side of strong desire to win. In so far as a society fosters the desire to win and builds up an emotional drive in the individual to that end, it inevitably fosters the fear of losing. By the same token, when defeat actually occurs it implies a frustration of strong desire, hence an inevitable emotion. This emotion occurs frequently, since most competitors cannot win. Yet once the property is in the winner's hands, social organization requires that such emotions be curbed. Society tends necessarily to suppress them and to encourage one-time rivals to be "good sports," "graceful losers."

The successful rival, however, need not suppress these emotions. Once established as owner he is encouraged by the culture to express them toward any trespasser. Free expression of malevolent emotion against a trespasser protects the established distribution of property and maintains the fixed rules for its competitive acquisition.

Types of Property Attitudes

Can the relationship of affection between two persons be conceived as a property relationship? This is a question not to be answered glibly. The affectional relationship is certainly not identical with *economic* property, although sheer sexual gratification (as in prostitution) may be. Affection assumes that the object is desired in and for itself. It therefore cannot be bought and sold; it is not a means to something else, not an economic thing. Yet the affectional relationship has features that are characteristic of property in general. It is, above all, highly institutionalized; it involves some sort of institutionalized exclusiveness, hedged about with rights and obligations. There is competition for possession, a feeling of ownership on the part of the successful competitor, a "hands-off" attitude on the part of the public, and a general resentment against anyone who tries as a trespasser to break up the relationship by "stealing" the object. In view of these considerations it seems possible to apply the term property to the institutionalized possession of affection. There apparently exists no other term that will describe those types of sanctioned possession that are not economic. Nevertheless the distinction between economic and non-economic property must be made clear. This can be accomplished by a more detailed consideration of types and sub-types of property, mainly in terms of the means-end schema.

Economic property is that type in which the object possessed is a means to an ulterior end. Noneconomic property is that type in which the object is an end in itself. Several sub-types can be distinguished under each head, but we shall rest content with distinguishing three kinds of economic and one kind of noneconomic property, calling them by the attitude which Ego takes in each case toward the object—respectively, *need, vanity, pride,* and *love*.

1. *Need*. Some objects of property satisfy organic needs. Food, shelter, prostitute, or servant may fall into this category. The object is not valued for itself, but simply as a means of satisfying the need; it may be bought, sold, and substituted. The attitude of the public is subsidiary. A person desires the public to regard the object as his property, but only because he needs it.

2. *Vanity*. When an object is valued not for the satisfaction of a need but for the response it elicits from one's neighbors, and when the only connection between the owner and object is mere possession, a new property situation is apparent. The attitude of the public is no longer subsidiary but paramount. An expensive diamond, a top hat, a long automobile are useless except as tokens and instruments of the owner's social status. The ulterior end is the envious approval of the community.

Whereas in the need situation a rival or trespasser could proceed only by gaining possession of the actual object, he may in the vanity situation employ an additional procedure. He may gain the ulterior end by possession of a different but superior object.

Vanity is often condemned on moral grounds because there is no necessary relationship between merit and the possession of an enviable object. A fool may inherit a crown; an ignorant farmer acquire riches in oil; a silly girl possess incomparable beauty. When such people attribute merit to themselves for such possessions they are vain, and such vanity is in the public's opinion thin and unlovely.

3. *Pride*. This type is characterized by an intrinsic relation between owner and object. The object represents some form of accomplishment and reflects the owner's professional ability. There is thus a necessary connection recognized by the public between the qualities of the owner and the nature of his possession. The ownership is indeed more a matter of accomplishment than of legal technicality. All that the law or the public can do is recognize and protect it when it comes by copyright, patent, and other rules; it cannot create it.

4. *Love*. In the three previous cases the object, while not necessarily inanimate or completely passive, takes no dynamic part in

the equilibrium. In the present case, however, the end desired consists in a personal attitude, an attitude of affection. Since affection is a phenomenon of will, the question of possession is thereby placed largely in the hands of the object one wishes to possess.

Out of this peculiarity grow the other idiosyncrasies of love-property. We find, for instance, that a jealous lover (assuming for the sake of illustration that he is masculine) often attacks the love-object herself, seeking to restrain her from directing her affection elsewhere or to retaliate against her for having already done so. Having control over the vital element in the situation—the goal being sought by the other party—she is in a position to decide the issue. She can bestow affection either on Ego or on his rival, as she chooses. A man might destroy his food in order to keep another from getting it; he might destroy his jewels or other emblems of prestige; he might even renounce and forsake his profession—but unless indulging in an anthropomorphic fit of temper, he would not thus destroy his possession out of resentment against the possession itself. A man who breaks his golf club after a bad shot knows perfectly well that the club had no volition in the matter. Yet in the case of sexual jealousy the resentment may be more against the object of love than against the rival. Everybody is familiar with the various forms of aggression practiced against each other by those in love, varying all the way from outright murder to mental cruelty.

In the situations of both vanity and pride we noted that the thing really desired was the envy or admiration of the public—in other words, an attitude. The object actually owned was a means to this end. The same is true of the love situation, where an attitude of affection is desired. To this extent the three property situations—vanity, pride, and love—are similar, and we do find that the term "jealousy" has at one time or another been applied to all of them, especially to the pride situation, as when we speak of "professional jealousy." Only to the need situation does the term jealousy seem totally inapplicable.

But, as noted, the love-property situation stands out from the others in that the attitude desired is an attitude of the object itself, not of the general public. This has a profound effect on the attitudes involved. Not only does the object become subject to jealous aggression because it is a human object, but there is a mutuality to the relationship that is lacking in the other forms of property. The affectional relationship implies a reciprocal, mutual interchange between owner and object which is not true of the other forms. Indeed, both are owners and both are objects at the same time. The love relationship, unlike other property relations, is an end in itself. The object of affection plays a dynamic role in determining the direction of the conflict situation by his or her ability to determine the character of this relationship. This doubtless explains why conflicts over love generate more emotion than other kinds and exhibit a more dramatic quality. When the object possessed is another person, the universal tendency of the possessor to identify himself with the thing possessed (transmuting "mine" into "I") is given the greatest opportunity to express itself. The lover feels that his love is a part of himself and that his existence would be meaningless without her. Still, simply because the object of love is not inert but willful, this personal identification is probably most tenuous of all in the love situation. The object possessed has it within her power to nullify the possession. This means that the love relationship is at once unusually close and unusually instable or tenuous. As a result it is doubly intense and highly charged with emotion.

Each type of property-situation described here is of course an abstraction, an ideal-type. Motives and attitudes in actual life situations are nearly always mixed. Need, vanity, pride, and love will be present in practically every concrete situation. Rarely in the vanity situation, for example, is sheer possession the reason for the public's envy and respect. Usually the secret of such envy and respect is that possession conveys power. Such power may be valued merely for the envy it commands, in which case the relationship remains within the vanity type. Or it may be valued because it enables one to satisfy needs, to succeed in love, or to acquire skills, in which case it falls by implication into one or the other of the three non-vanity types. In actual life several or all of these attitudes are present in the same situation. In the relation of man and woman there may well be and usually is an attitude of need, of vanity, and of pride (or their opposites), as well as an attitude of love.

The Dynamic Sequence

In depicting the four types of property relationship we have stopped four processes in mid-air. They are not static but dynamic;

they are instable conflict situations tending inevitably toward their own solution. Fidelity to fact would require that some notion be given of their processual sequence from *début* to *dénouement*.

A complete sequence in love-property conflict would begin with the rivalry phase. It would depict the changing attitudes of the rivals, and of the object of affection and the public, as some of the competitors are eliminated and one finally wins. The next phase would show the winner in secure possession at some level of ownership such as the "sweetheart," the "fiancée," or the "spouse" level. He is no longer jealous because rivalry is finished and no trespasser is in sight, and the public has an attitude of "don't disturb." The third phase, trespass, would describe the attitude of Ego as he becomes aware of an enemy—his feelings toward the trespasser, the love object, and the public. It would describe also the attitudes of the trespasser, and since the direction of the sequence hinges largely upon the woman (at least in our culture), it would describe her attitudes toward lover, rival, and public. If she favors the trespasser and is willing to risk Ego's and the community's wrath, Ego may lose. On the other hand if she does not favor the trespasser, if he himself is not willing to take the risk, or if Ego or the public uses irresistible force, Ego may win. The multiplicity of attitudes between the four interacting parties grows amazingly complex. Innumerable combinations are possible. To describe them all would be a fascinating adventure into the anatomy of dramatic reality, but it would also require a complete volume.

One attitude that seems dependent upon the stage of conflict is envy. Envy is the attitude not of the owner but of an observer or a potential rival. It implies that a person would like to have what another has but that he is at the moment making no effort to wrest it from the other. It can hardly be present in one's mind at the same time as jealousy, because the latter implies some claim to possession or at least a right to compete. Envy is in a sense inevitable. In so far as the desire for certain valuables is instilled in the mind, the person who does not possess these values will inevitably wish that he were in the place of the one who does, and will sometimes secretly wish that the other were not there. But since envy usually goes contrary to the established distribution of the world's valuables, it is frowned upon by the group as a whole.

Jealousy and Intimacy

Since in love-property the object of possession is the devotion of another person we may expect jealousy to have a direct connection with the sociology of intimacy. The nature of intimate, or *primary*, relationships is dealt with in Chapter XI. We shall not anticipate that chapter here, but will simply raise the question of how jealousy is related to the intimate type of social bond.

Although jealousy can appear only when there is a presumption of *primary* association in the past, present, or future the fact should be noted that jealousy also indicates at least a partial negation of that rapport between persons which we commonly ascribe to intimacy. It admits that affection has strayed or may possibly stray in the direction of a rival or trespasser. Even when the affection has not actually strayed, jealousy shows on the lover's part a mistrust inimical to the harmony of perfect intimacy.

What, then, is the function of jealousy in intimate association? As a fear reaction in the initial stages of rivalry it is simply the obverse side of the desire to win the object. The desire to win being institutionally cultivated, the fear of losing is unavoidably stimulated also, though its expression is publicly frowned upon. But after ownership has been attained, jealousy is a fear and rage reaction fitted to protect, maintain, and prolong the intimate association of love. It shelters this personal relationship from outside intrusion. This is not to say that it never defeats its own purpose by overshooting the mark. So deeply emotional is jealousy that its appearance in the midst of modern social relationships (which are most profitably manipulated by self-composed shrewdness) is like a bull in a china shop. Nonetheless its intention is protective. It is a denial of the harmony of intimacy only in so far as its presence admits a breach; and is destructive of it only in so far as it muddles its own purpose.

Jealousy stresses two characteristics of the primary relationship: its ultimate and its personal qualities. The relationship is for the jealous person an ultimate end in itself, all other considerations being secondary. This explains the bizarre crimes so frequently connected with jealousy—crimes understandable only upon the assumption that for the criminal the affection of a particular person is the supreme value in life. It also explains the connection between extreme jealousy and romantic love. The "personal" quality of the relationship is manifested by the unwillingness of the jealous person to conceive any substitute for the "one and only." He insists upon the uniqueness of personality. Were the particular person removed, the whole relationship and its accompanying emotion of jealousy would disappear.

An old debate poses the question whether or not affection is divisible. Is it possible to love two people sincerely at the same time? Most authorities on sex relations answer that it is possible and cite cases as proof. Iwan Bloch, for example, asserts that simultaneous passion for several persons happens repeatedly.[2] He adds that the extensive psychic differentiation between individuals in modern civilization increases the likelihood of such simultaneous love, for it is difficult to find in any single person one's complete complement. Bloch gives numerous examples from history and literature, particularly cases where one aspect of a person's nature (usually the intellectual) is satisfied by one lover, another aspect (usually the sensual) by a different lover.

The conclusion invariably deduced from this is that jealousy is harmful and unjustified. But to end the discussion with this ethical argument is to miss the point. Even though love, like any other distributive value, is divisible, institutions dictate the manner and extent of the division. Where exclusive possession of an individual's entire love is customary, jealousy will demand that exclusiveness. Where love is divided it will be divided according to some scheme, and jealousy will reinforce the division.

Rivalry, Trespass, and Social Class

While the love-property situation contains a relationship of intimacy and is therefore illuminated by the sociology of primary association, it also contains a diametrically opposite kind of relation—namely, that of power—which concerns the sociology of dominance and subordination. This relationship which obtains between the lover and his rival or trespasser is not a value in itself but a means to an ulterior end; and it connotes an absolute opposition of purpose in the sense that if one succeeds the other fails. The rival or trespasser

[2] Iwan Bloch, *Sexual Life of Our Time* (New York: Allied Book, 1926), pp. 206-207. Havelock Ellis, *Studies in the Psychology of Sex*, VI (Philadelphia: F. A. Davis Co., 1914), pp. 568-569 agrees. Also Joseph K. Folsom, in his *Social Psychology* (New York: Harper, 1931).

may be a stranger or a close friend; in either event, so far as the common object is concerned he is an enemy.

Here as elsewhere in the discussion it makes a difference whether the enemy is a trespasser or a rival. Rivalry is most acute in the early stages of acquisition, and jealousy is at this point a fear of not winning the desired object. Toward one's rival one is supposed to show good sport and courtesy, which is to say that society requires the suppression in this context of jealous animosity. Regulated competition constitutes the *sine qua non* of property distribution and hence of stable social organization. But as one person gets ahead and demonstrates a superior claim, his rivals, hiding their feelings of jealous disappointment, must drop away. If any rival persists after the victor has fortified his claim with the proper institutional ritual, he is no longer a rival but a trespasser.

Jealousy toward the trespasser is encouraged rather than suppressed, for it tends to preserve the fundamental institutions of property. Uncles in our society are never jealous of the affection of nephews for their father. But uncles in matrilineal societies frequently are, because there a close tie is socially prescribed between uncle and nephew. The nephew's respect is the property of the uncle; if it is given to the father (as sometimes happens because of the close association between father and son) the uncle is jealous.[3] Jealousy does not occur in the natural situations—and the "natural situations" are simply those defined in terms of the established institutions. Our malignant emotions, fear, anger, hate, and jealousy, greet any illicit attempt to gain property that we hold. We do not manifest them when a legitimate attempt is made, partly because we do not then have the subjective feeling of "being wronged" and partly because their expression would receive the disapprobation of the community. The social function of jealousy against a trespasser is therefore the extirpation of any obstacle to the smooth running of the institutional machinery.

Discussions of jealousy usually overlook the difference between rivalry and trespass. A case in point is the old problem of whether one can be jealous of a person not one's equal. If the person is a trespasser the answer is that he can be any distance away in the social scale. But if he is a rival he cannot be too far distant. Rivalry

[3] Bronislaw Malinowski, *Crime and Custom in Savage Society* (London: Paul, Trench, Trubner, 1932), pp. 100-111.

implies a certain degree of equality at the start. Each society designates which of its members are eligible to compete for certain properties. While there are some properties for which members of different classes may compete, there are others for which they may not compete. In such cases the thought of competition is inconceivable, the emotions reserved for a rival fail to appear, and the act is regarded not as rivalry but as a detestable thrust at the class structure. Thus it happens that for a given lover some people cannot arouse jealousy as of a rival. If the love-object yields to a member of a distinctly inferior social class, jealousy will turn into moral outrage, no matter if the lover himself has no claim on the love-object. It is for this reason inconceivable that a Negro could be the rival of a Southern white man for the hand of a white girl. The white man would have him lynched. Southern society does not permit Negroes as a class to compete for the affection of white girls. It is almost equally inconceivable that a white man could be a Negro's rival for the hand of a colored girl. The Negro has either too much advantage in the likelihood of social ostracism for the white man or too little advantage in that the white man, if immune to ostracism, can take the property by employing the weight of his caste position.

But jealousy against a trespasser is another matter. Since a trespasser by definition is a breaker of customary rules, the more he breaks, including the rules of class structure, the more of a trespasser he is. A violator of property rights may for this reason occupy any position on the social scale.

The fact that men of native races sometimes prostitute their wives to civilized men without any feeling of jealousy while they are extremely jealous of men of their own race,[4] is sometimes pointed out as showing that men are jealous only of their equals. This is true only in so far as jealousy of rivals is meant. The civilized man is not conceived by the natives as a rival, nor as a trespasser. He *may* be conceived as a trespasser—if, for example, he attempts to retain the wife without paying anything. In the case mentioned he is not a trespasser but merely one who has legitimately paid for the temporary use of property. His very payment recognizes the property rights of the husband. The following case is much more illustrative:

[4] Bronislaw Malinowski, *The Sexual Life of Savages* (New York: Harcourt, Brace, 1929), p. 271.

"A Frenchman of position picks for his mistress a girl who is not his social equal. You can see for yourself that his wife is not jealous. But let him choose a woman of his own social rank—then you'd see the fur fly; . . ."[5] Among some social spheres in France, if we are to believe what we hear, women of different classes customarily exercise proprietary rights in the same man without feeling jealous of each other. But since it is not customary for women of the same rank to share a man, such a condition would be either rivalry or trespass and would arouse intense jealousy.

One may argue that the nearer two people are in every plane, the more intense will be the jealousy of rivalry; while the further apart they are, the greater the jealousy of trespass.

But between the lover and the object of his love the relationship is not one of power. If a woman is regarded simply as a pawn in a game for prestige the pattern is No. 2 in our typology, not No. 4. It is a question of vanity rather than jealousy. In the love situation the jealous person values the affection for itself. It is his fear of losing this intrinsically valuable affection to a rival or a trespasser, rather than his fear of losing prestige in the eyes of his public and his rival, that paralyzes him.

The Social Function of Jealousy

Into every affair of love and into every battle for power steps society. The community has an inherent interest in love not only because future generations depend upon it but also because social cohesion rests upon the peaceful distribution of major values.

A question that all authorities feel compelled to settle concerns the social or anti-social character of jealousy. Forel declares that jealousy "is only the brutal stupidity of an atavistic heritage, or a pathological symptom,"[6] while Havelock Ellis calls it "an anti-social emotion."[7] The chief arguments are that it is an inheritance from animal ancestors, a hindrance to the emancipation of women, and an obstacle to rational social intercourse.

The hasty readiness to praise or condemn prevents a clear understanding of the relation of jealousy to the social structure. Careful

[5] Benjamin B. Lindsey and Wainwright Evans, *The Companionate Marriage* (New York: Boni & Liveright, 1927), p. 88.

[6] August Forel, *The Sexual Question* (trans. by C. F. Marshall) (New York: Rebman, no date), pp. 118-119.

[7] Havelock Ellis, *op. cit.,* Vol. 6, p. 564.

analysis is cut short by the quick conclusion that jealousy is instinctive. The assumption is that certain stimuli call forth a stereotyped, biologically ingrained response. Jealousy is therefore regarded as an animal urge and denounced as anti-social. Such condemnation instead of comprehension illustrates once more the tendency of the moralistic bias to take precedence over the scientific attitude in the handling of social phenomena.[8]

The instinctive view fails to analyze jealous behavior into its different components—to distinguish between the stimulus (a social situation having a meaning only within the culture where it is found) and the physical mechanism involved in the total response. It puts all constituents into the undifferentiated category of instinct. Doubtless the physiological mechanism operating in the jealously aroused person is inherited. But the striking thing about this mechanism is that it is not specific for jealousy, but appears to be exactly the same in other violent emotions such as fear and rage. The sympathetic nervous system seemingly plays the usual role: increased adrenal activity speeding the heart, increasing the sugar content of the blood, toning up the striated muscles and inactivating the smooth muscles.

If we are to differentiate jealousy from the other strong emotions we must speak not in terms of inherited physiology but in terms of the type of situation which provokes it. The conflict situation always contains a particular content, which varies from one culture to the next. The usual mistake in conceiving jealousy is to erect a concrete situation found somewhere (often in the culture of the author) into the universal and inherent stimulus to that emotion. This ignores the fact that each culture distributes the sexual property of the society and defines the conflict situations in its own way, and that therefore the concrete content cannot be regarded as an inherited stimulus to an inherited response.

[8] The logic of social ethicists at times becomes badly scrambled. Frequently it is clear that what they call "instinctive" are merely the institutions to which they are habituated and to which they lend their approval. The biological basis of the institutions is thus assumed to justify them, for if a thing is instinctive, like love, it must be good and should not be suppressed but given full expression. On the other hand the inveterate propensity to derive all social phenomena from the genetic qualities of the individual leads the ethicists to infer that certain disapproved behavior like criminality, war, or jealousy is also instinctive. In this case the assumption that it is biological becomes, not a justification, but a reason for condemnation. It is "atavistic," "barbaric," "animal-like." The biologistic interpretation thus seeks to have its cake and eat it too. It is like the appeal to "human nature." It can serve as a prop to whatever attitude one wishes to take, whether of praise or of condemnation.

This mistake is made, I think, by those theorists who seek to explain certain human institutions on the basis of instinctive emotions. In the field of sexual institutions Westermarck is the outstanding theorist who has relied upon this type of explanation. He disproves the hypothesis of primeval promiscuity and proves the primacy of pair marriage largely on the basis of allegedly innate jealousy.[9] He assumes, indeed, that all types of sexual relationship other than monogamy (as he knows it in his own culture) are native stimuli to instinctive jealous retaliation.

As soon, however, as we admit that other forms of sexual property exist and that they do not arouse but instead are protected by jealousy, the explanation of monogamy breaks down. Whether as the obverse side of the desire to obtain sexual property by legitimate competition or as the anger at having rightful property trespassed upon, jealousy would seem to bolster the institutions where it is found. If these institutions are of an opposite character to monogamy, it bolsters them nonetheless. Whereas Westermarck would say that adultery arouses jealousy and that therefore jealousy causes monogamy, one could maintain that our institution of monogamy causes adultery to be resented and therefore creates jealousy.

Had he confined himself to disproving promiscuity instead of going on to prove monogamy, Westermarck would have remained on surer ground. Promiscuity implies the absence of any sexual property-pattern. Yet sexual affection is, unlike divine grace, a distributive value. To let it go undistributed would introduce anarchy into the group and destroy the social system. Promiscuity can take place only in so far as society has broken down and reached a state of anomie.

The stimulus to jealousy, moreover, is not so much a physical situation as a meaningful one. The same physical act will in one place denote ownership, in another place robbery. Westermarck appears to believe that it is the physical act of sexual intercourse between another man and one's wife that instinctively arouses jealousy. But there are cultures where such intercourse merely emphasizes the husband's status as owner, just as lending an automobile presumes and emphasizes one's ownership of it.

We may cite, for example, the whole range of institutions whereby in some manner the wife is given over to a man other than her

[9] Edward Westermarck, *The History of Human Marriage* (New York: Allerton, 1922), Vol. I. Chap. 9.

husband. These run from those highly ritualized single acts in which a priest or relative deflowers the wife (the so-called *jus prima noctis*) to the repeated and more promiscuous acts of sexual hospitality and the more permanent and thoroughgoing agreements of wife-exchange; not to mention the fixed division of sexual function represented by polyandric marriage. In societies where any institution in this range prevails, the behavior implied does not arouse the feeling of jealousy that similar behavior would arouse in our culture. Jealousy does not respond inherently to any particular physical situation; it responds to all those situations, no matter how diverse, which signify a violation of accustomed sexual rights.

The Internal versus Overt Manifestation

Possession of a thing of value without any right to it is a prevalent condition in sexual behavior; affection is evidently difficult to govern. The converse—ownership without possession—is equally prevalent. At least in our culture the instances are countless in which there is no overt transgression of convention and yet affection has strayed. Wives and husbands abound who have little or no affection for their mates but who would not actually sully the marriage tie. Their affection is owned by their mates, but not possessed.

Our discussion seems to have associated jealousy exclusively with ownership, with outward conformity rather than with actual possession. This has not been due to ignorance of a possible discrepancy between the two, or to ignorance of the fact that many lovers, especially the romantic variety, profess to care only for the possession of affection and nothing at all for conformity to senseless tradition. Our focus of attention has been due, rather, to a conviction that so-called outward conformity, either through speech or overt behavior, must always be taken as the symbol of the inward state. If a woman never by word or deed let the fact appear that she did not love her husband, he would never have cause to feel jealous. She must say or do something contrary to a wife's institutionally sanctioned role before jealousy will be justified. If she says she loves her husband and yet does things contrary to the mores, such as going out with a prohibited man, actions will be presumed to speak louder than words and jealousy will be in order.

For those who conform outwardly to many meaningless and secretly detested conventions and perform an even greater number of routine technological acts which try their patience, a close correspondence between inner feeling and external act seems questionable. Yet if we analyze the less conspicuous because less conscious aspects of behavior, we find the correspondence frequently quite close. In situations where people are supposed to feel ashamed they tend actually to feel ashamed—and prove it by their outward manifestation of embarrassment. In situations where people are supposed to show respect they usually feel respect. In only a few civilizations is the distinction between external act and internal feeling sharply realized, and even then the two spheres are not far apart. In any case action which conforms to the institutions of property is the symbol of genuine possession, and contrary action the symbol of lack of possession.

It is true that conformity at any particular time may be a deception, but the deception is hardly significant unless it manifests itself at some time in nonconformist behavior. Whether or not it is a deception depends, of course, upon the internal state, which is the motivating factor. So the aim of the lover is always to control the inner state of affection, not simply to enforce a present outward conformity which guarantees nothing concerning future behavior. This in spite of the fact that his only clue to the true feeling is the loved one's external conformity or nonconformity.

Unless through each stage of progressive ownership actual possession also progresses, inconvenience will result. A girl who becomes engaged to a man without caring for him and without intending to marry him is in an uncomfortable position. She cannot complain if her fiancé's legitimate jealousy and the public's interest in morality restrict her actions. She knows that when she breaks her engagement she must have a good excuse wherewith to avoid social censure. At all times she is constrained to feign an affection she does not feel. On the whole the inconvenience of a hiatus between real feeling and institutional status is in this case greater than the advantage. Moreover, most girls are trained to think of such a hiatus as not only unwise but also unfair and immoral. In this way ownership tends to approximate genuine possession.

Jealousy and Social Anomie

Unfortunately our treatment has been couched entirely in terms of the stable and integrated culture; there is not space to treat the complications arising when society has reached a state of disintegration or *anomie*. As the institutions of property in general disintegrate, sexual property follows suit. In extreme cases ownership may apparently disappear and be replaced entirely by custody, as when anarchy reigns.

Juxtaposition of contrary mores and rapid change have given our culture a certain amount of anomie, which is reflected in the emotions surrounding the distribution of sexual favor. None of our sexual institutions is sanctioned by all groups. Consequently, no matter how customary the sexual behavior, somebody can be found who is made jealous by it. For example those who are not used to dancing and who disapprove of it are apt to grow extremely jealous if a wife or sweetheart indulges. This, coupled with other traits such as our individualism and romanticism, has tended in the eyes of our intelligentsia to give jealousy a negative value. Yet among the juries of the land the so-called "unwritten law" is still a sanctioned reality.

Conclusion

It should now be clear that a genuine understanding of jealousy requires that it be studied and analyzed from a comparative sociological point of view. A theory of jealousy which derives its empirical facts solely from the manifestations of jealousy in our own culture can hardly be a satisfactory theory, no matter how plausible it may seem to people who live in our culture. When a comparative point of view is adopted it is seen that the situations calling forth a jealous response vary tremendously from one culture to another. Jealousy is an emotion which has a function as a part of an institutional structure. Not only is it normatively controlled but it gives strength to the social norms as well. To understand the social function of jealousy, to see the significance of its variable but inevitable appearance in different societies, one must have a conceptual apparatus at hand. One must, for example, have some conception of the cultural definition of social situations in terms of the statuses and roles of the participants; some notion of means, ends, and conditions; and some idea of processes of interaction such as rivalry, competition, and trespass. In this way one is able to state in fairly brief and definite fashion the major conclusions about jealousy as empirically observed in different cultures. Otherwise one has facts but little else. It is not contended here that the sociological approach to jealousy is the only one that is needed. Jealousy must also be studied from the point of view of the personality as a unit. But it is contended that for a full understanding of jealousy the sociological approach is indispensable because it addresses itself to a real and important aspect of jealous behavior—the social aspect. To test this statement the reader is invited to compare the usual treatment of jealousy with what he has read in this chapter.

References

Anatole France, *The Red Lily* (Le Lys Rouge, 1894).

Jealousy has always been an important theme in fiction. This novel, the most modern in type that Anatole France ever wrote, is an unusually penetrating and poignant study of jealous involvement.

David G. Mandelbaum, "Polyandry in Kota Society," *American Anthropologist*, Vol. 40 (Oct.-Dec. 1938), pp. 574-583.

An extremely lucid description of a social system in which brothers have access to one another's wives. The expression of jealousy as between brothers is socially taboo, but not the expression of it with reference to men who are not brothers. Thus jealousy bolsters the given marital institution, even though the arrangements are extremely different from ours.

Boris Sokoloff, *Jealousy: A Psychiatric Study* (New York: Howell, Soskin, 1947).

Treats jealousy as an atavistic, somewhat neurotic emotion, to be overcome if possible. Analyzes jealous reactions from a psychoanalytic point of view. Presents numerous case histories at considerable length. A good example of a non-sociological approach.

Rupert B. Vance and Waller Wynne, Jr., "Folk Rationalizations in the 'Unwritten Law,'" *American Journal of Sociology,* Vol. 39 (Jan. 1934), pp. 483-492.

The legal system in the United States does not generally sanction the killing of the wife's paramour. It upholds the sanctity of human life. But the so-called "unwritten law" actually guides many jury and court decisions, and this is a "law" which holds human life to be secondary to the sanctity of the home and the husband's property right in his wife. An excellent article.

Willard Waller, *The Family: A Dynamic Interpretation* (New York: Cordon, 1938), Part 2, "Courtship Interaction."

Except for one brief but illuminating passage (p. 268) this treatment of courtship as a personal relation is not focused on jealousy, and yet the author's extremely perceptive treatment of the competitive and emotional aspects of this relation, as they are influenced by social institutions and cultural definition, supplements the analysis given in the present chapter.

CHAPTER VIII

SOCIALIZATION

THE PARADOX of human society—that it has a unity and continuity of its own and yet exists solely in the minds and actions of its members—can be resolved only by understanding how the newborn individual is molded into a social being. Without this process of molding, which we call "socialization," the society could not perpetuate itself beyond a single generation and culture could not exist. Nor could the individual become a person; for without the ever-repeated renewal of culture within him there could be no human mentality, no human personality. Both the person and the society are alike dependent on this unique process of psychic amalgamation whereby the sentiments and ideas of the culture are somehow joined to the capacities and needs of the organism.

No one understands the process thoroughly. It is still as mysterious as photosynthesis or organic aging. Yet it is a common meeting ground of all the sciences dealing with man; for here in the problem of socialization, biology and sociology, psychiatry and anthropology come together. Each of the human sciences has something it wants to learn about the process, and each has something it can contribute. If a science is interested in man at all it is interested in the subtle alchemy by which the human animal is transmuted into the human being. If the essential mystery has not yet been solved, this does not mean that nothing is known about the process; much is known, and only a fraction can be suggested here.

The Roots of Personality

In addition to socialization there are other factors affecting the individual, and the relation of these to our topic must be considered. In this matter, however, there is much confusion because of the perennial failure to distinguish between an abstraction and a concrete entity. Out of this confusion grow such loose phrases as "the individual and his environment" and such fruitless questions as "Which is more important, heredity or environment?" One might as well discuss a book in terms of ideas versus ink, or plot versus format.

The flesh-and-blood individual is unique, for there is none other exactly like him. To explain him in all his particularity would be a never-ending task that no one working as a scientist would attempt. Instead some of his traits may be singled out, traits that he shares with certain other people, and these used as a basis of understanding. Thus if a woman has a peculiarly shaped nose, one may find the explanation in the fact that certain of her ancestors exhibit a similarly shaped nose. But notice that one is already in the realm of abstraction. The woman's ancestors cannot have identically the same nose, because her nose is unique. They merely have *similar* noses. Shape has been singled out for attention, and absolute size, complexion, powder, etc. have been ignored. Also, she and her ancestors have many other things in common in addition to nasal shape and genetic relationship. If genetic relationship has been picked out to explain the shape of the nose, the reason lies in a certain universe of discourse (the conceptual apparatus of genetics) which places in a logical system the empirical propositions concerning this kind of causation. The assumption is, or should be, that genetic relationship may account for the shape of the nose, not that it accounts for the entire flesh-and-blood organ.

Terms such as "heredity" or "environment" do not refer to anything tangible but to an abstraction. To treat them as if they were on the same level as the concrete individual, as in phrases like "the individual and his environment," is to invite complete muddlement. Of course "the individual" may be viewed as an abstraction, but in this case it is necessary to be clear as to what level of abstraction and system of discourse one is employing.

Any given individual is, in part, a product of two distinct modes of transmission, one hereditary and the other social. The first operates through the mechanism of genes, chromosomes, and human reproduction; it relates to the general level of reality designated as biological and is studied by a special branch of biological science called "genetics." The second operates through the mechanism of habituation, learning, and symbolic communication; it relates to the general level of reality designated as socio-cultural, and is dealt with by a branch of social science which may be called "the study of socialization" or sometimes "social psychology" or "psycho-sociology." The accompanying diagram attempts to give a simplified picture of the situation. Obviously no concrete individual is the product

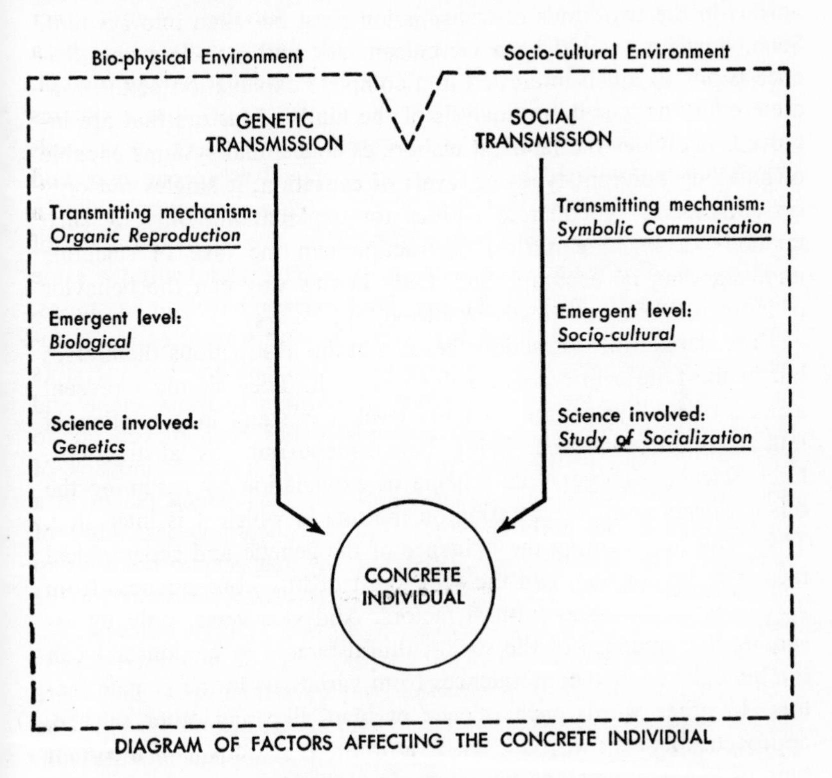

DIAGRAM OF FACTORS AFFECTING THE CONCRETE INDIVIDUAL

of either of these modes of transmission alone. He is always a product of both, and this means that both modes of transmission are mutually interdependent, each being a necessary condition of the other.

The complexity extends further than this, however. Not only is the individual a product of these two dynamic processes of transmission, but he is also a product of several different kinds of environment. Neither genetic nor communicative transmission can occur in man without a geographic, a biological, a cultural, and an interpersonal environment. For this reason the individual is just as much an outgrowth of the environments as he is a result of the two kinds of dynamic transmission.

Obviously if a complete explanation of the concrete individual is to be given, all the elements in the environments and all the mechanisms in the two kinds of transmission must be taken into account. Such, however, would be a Herculean task and a useless one. Science is not so much interested in a complete explanation of the concrete entity as it is in an analysis of the kinds of factors that are involved. It divides the labor; it elaborates conceptual systems capable of handling different types or levels of causation; it singles out only certain aspects of concrete entities for explanation. Only by such methods of logico-empirical abstraction can the task of scientific understanding be accomplished. Only in this way can the behavior of individuals be statistically predicted.

The danger of abstractions lies not in the abstractions themselves but in the failure to recognize them as such. They simply represent aspects of reality; on the concrete level they stand in a relation of mutual interdependence, being independent only as abstractions. Each science elaborates its scheme of explanation by assuming the other aspects and concentrating on the one in which it is interested. Thus only by assuming the influence of the genetic and geographical factors to be constant can the sociologist deduce consequences from variations in the socio-cultural factors. And vice versa, only by assuming the influence of the socio-cultural factors to be constant can the biologist deduce consequences from variations in the genetic factors. In other words each science of man, like any other science, approaches its task with an "as if" attitude. It reasons as if a certain type of factor were alone operative. In reality this is never the case, but it enormously speeds up scientific progress to make the hypothetical assumption. The main hazard is that the layman often forgets, as does the scientist occasionally, that the reasoning is hypothetical. He tends to assume that a given conceptual system describes concrete reality *in toto* and thus he lands in a kind of determinism, oversimplified and untrue. He then engages in futile battles with people who expound the determinism of other factors. Thus arises the war of the determinisms, a war of vague words and bad logic.

THE HEREDITY-ENVIRONMENT CONTROVERSY

The question, "Which is more important, heredity or environment?" illustrates the pitfalls. In the first place there is no such thing as "the" environment. There are many different environments, and what is environmental in one sense may be not so in another. Thus from the point of view of genetics the body is an environment in which the reproductive cells multiply and receive nourishment; whereas from the point of view of ecology the body is what the environment surrounds. In the second place the question wrongly assumes that environment and transmission are somehow opposed, so that if the one is important the other cannot be. Since, however, organisms are perpetuated through germ cells and nourished in an environment they obviously depend on both of these factors. In the third place the question makes a comparison without stating the terms of reference. It uses the term "important" but does not say for what. Finally, the question confuses necessary with sufficient conditions. A necessary condition is one that must be present if another factor is to operate. From the standpoint of a biologist a woman speaks because she has the organic capacity (it is assumed that somebody teaches her to speak). If, however, the question is why she speaks Chinese rather than some other language, this is not a sufficient explanation. Speaking Chinese is a cultural datum; and only a cultural explanation—in this case, the fact that she was reared in a Chinese society—can give a sufficient answer.

In trying to explain particular traits observers frequently commit what may be called "the family history fallacy." If the forebears exhibit the same trait as the descendant, one says that it "runs in the family." Traits, however, are transmitted from parent to child in two different ways—one by genetic transmission, the other by communicative transmission. If a child has an unusually flat head and his ancestors before him had the same sort of flat head, the likely conclusion is that this is a genetic trait, "in the blood." If it were an English child the conclusion would probably be correct. But if it were a Hopi child it would not be correct, because the Hopi Indians flattened the heads of their babies by tight lashing to the cradles. The Samoans, in turn, deliberately flattened the skull by the application of stones.

If the women in several generations of the same family have

been prostitutes, the fact is likely to be ascribed to a "hereditary taint," though it would seem much easier and less mystical to recall that mothers can teach their daughters to be prostitutes. In fact, occupations are frequently transmitted from parent to child, but never through the genes.

The family history fallacy arises from the fact that genetic transmission occurs only through the parent-child channel and that communicative transmission occurs very largely through this channel. For this reason one must always ask if the trait in question is the sort which *could* be physically inherited. If it is primarily symbolic, like language, one may infer that the sufficient cause lies in the social sphere. The fact that successive generations of a given family all speak English need not lead one to infer that this is a biological trait. If the trait is primarily physical, like the shape of the head, one may form the hypothesis that it is genetically caused (provided this does not blind one to the possibility of social causation). More crucial, however, is the necessity of asking whether or not the trait conforms to the known rules of genetic or cultural transmission. Does it appear for example in successive generations in such a manner as to conform to Mendelian principles? Or does it appear in such a manner as to indicate social transmission (e.g. in connection with social position and social norms)?

From a research point of view a great aid in overcoming the family history fallacy is the fact that social transmission is not limited to the parent-child relation. This makes it possible to separate the two kinds of transmission. Adopted children can be investigated to see in what ways they resemble their foster parents more than their biological parents; and identical twins can be studied to see in what ways they resemble each other more when reared together than when reared apart. Another great aid lies in cultural relativity. Since human beings are all of one species, any trait which varies from one culture to another is not likely to be adequately explained in biological terms.[1] The basic principle underlying all these methods is to hold one kind of factor constant while allowing the other kind to vary. This simply amounts to applying experimentally or statistically the abstraction practiced in theory.

[1] The converse, that any trait appearing in all cultures can be explained in biological terms, is not necessarily true because there may be purely cultural traits, transmitted by socialization, which are essential for human and societal survival and are therefore found in all cultures.

The Unsocialized Organism

A human being's dependence on the social environment begins long before he is born—with the folkways and mores governing his parents' courtship and marital selection, with the customs concerning pregnancy, with the whole system of cultural practices surrounding the family. His parents, socialized creatures when they conceived him, previously had to learn the sexual act. Conception took place in a socially defined situation important for the child's subsequent status. Techniques of prenatal care current in the community affected his chances of being born and of being healthy. In sum, the social circumstances preceding his birth not only made his life possible but also laid down to a great extent the kind of life he was to lead.

But it is not until birth that direct socialization begins. Hence it is worthwhile to inquire what the individual, as an organism, has at birth that is relevant to the process of socialization. The things he has may be divided into four admittedly overlapping categories: capacities, reflexes, "instincts," and urges.

1. *Reflexes.* Plainly, the severest limitation upon socialization is supplied by the automatic and rigid responses of the organism. Such responses, or reflexes, are attached to a given stimulus and, if learned at all, are acquired by a minimum of organic experience in relation to the physical environment. The pupil of the eye automatically contracts in strong light, the glands of the mouth salivate at the taste of sugar, the muscles of the arm contract at the prick of a pin, urination occurs with fullness of the bladder, etc. A catalogue of all the reflexes is impossible to make. The whole autonomic nervous system is reflex in character, including breathing, heartbeat, peristalsis, and digestion. Without its reflexes the organism could not live. Yet since the reflexes are automatic and rigid, they are unlearned and in many cases unmodifiable. They set limits on what the organism can and will do, but they are hardly the bases out of which socialization arises.

2. *Instincts.* Much debate has always attended the use of the term "instinct," especially as applied to human behavior. Biologists define as instinctive any behavior that originates in an urge or appetite, involves some sort of perception of the external world, is

peculiarly fixed and mechanical, is dependent on inherited structure and therefore characteristic of the species, and, though compulsory or necessary, is at the same time highly adaptive or functional (without the organism being aware of its ultimate significance).[2] It is plain why so much debate has surrounded the concept, for it is practically synonymous with the life process itself. Broad and complex, it embraces elements which need not occur together or which seem incompatible.

The human being at birth probably has no complete instinct but only certain elements of them, such as reflexes and urges. Given these plus his capacities, all of his subsequent behavior is partly learned and is hence not instinctive. Consequently the explanation of human behavior in terms of instincts is fallacious.

At one time almost any form of behavior was ascribed to some instinct. If a boy and girl fell in love it was due to the "instinct to reproduce the race." If they quarreled it was due to the instinct of pugnacity. If the quarrel resulted in a reconciliation it was due to the gregarious instinct; or if the boy fled, it was due to the self-preservation instinct. It was, in short, a type of explanation that explained everything (too much too easily). It was purely *post hoc;* it could seemingly "explain" why a thing had happened but could give no basis for predicting what had not yet happened. At its worst it was a redundant explanation, similar to the brilliant conclusion that opium causes sleep because of its dormitive powers or that sap goes up in trees because that is the nature of sap. At its best it was an explanation *obscurum per obscurius* (explaining an unknown by something still more unknown). To explain war, for example, as being the result of the "combative instinct" merely makes the problem harder. We know little enough about all the forms that human warfare has taken, but we know still less about this mysterious instinct. We have a rough idea in social and historical terms why war came to the United States in 1917 and 1941 rather than other years, but we have no idea why an instinct should suddenly have erupted at those times. Such an explanation, therefore, may be emotionally satisfying because the unknown is mysterious and hence magically superior, but it is not scientifically acceptable.

3. *Urges.* What is variously referred to as impulse, drive, tension,

[2] Wm. Morton Wheeler, *Essays in Human Biology* (Cambridge: Harvard University Press, 1939), pp. 38-39.

urge, or appetite provides firmer ground for analysis of human behavior. As previously noted, the organism has certain needs that must be met. Unless they are met it develops increasing tension and restlessness until it encounters a stimulus capable of relieving the tension. Thus the urges represent a dynamic force behind behavior. Whereas in the instinctive behavior of animals the satisfaction of the appetite is tied to only one or a few stimuli, in man it tends to be (except on the reflexive level) rigidly tied to none. A very wide range of stimuli can satisfy the various urges. Which stimuli do satisfy them becomes a matter of learning. The urges, not the reflexes, provide an organic bridgehead, a starting point, for the process of socialization.

4. *Capacities.* Intelligence is regarded as man's most important attribute because it enables him to compensate for the limitations of his body. He can run only so fast, lift only so much, fight only so well. He must therefore rely upon techniques that enlarge or extend what capacities he has. Though his learning capacity exceeds that of any other animal, it is nevertheless limited. Curiously enough, however, even this limitation can be overcome by the development of culture. Presumably his innate intellectual capacity could be increased by a eugenic program (itself a cultural phenomenon), but barring this the use of his capacity, in the sense of learning more and more, could still be increased by the development of new instructional and incentive techniques. Human mentality is like a box —the way to get more into it is to pack things systematically. No limit can be foreseen to the possible increase of man's intellectual efficiency through new techniques of socialization.

At present no human being learns as much as he could under more favorable circumstances, for his learning ability is never used to maximum capacity. Every society uses defective instructional techniques, appeals occasionally to wrong motives, taboos certain kinds of knowledge, and has a limited culture. The last factor—limited culture—may seem the most important cause for the failure to teach individuals all they can absorb, until it is recalled that no society ever transmits its whole culture to any one person. The amount that given individuals absorb is more a function of the techniques and incentives utilized than of the size of the culture. Actually the main societal consideration is not the maximum use of the individual's capacity in the sense of mere learning but the maximum incorporation of his productive effort with that of others. If the collective activities are well organized, a small but specialized contribution from each person will have more effect than a much greater individual contribution in a poorly integrated system. For this reason a lot depends on how much use is made of individual differences in amount and kind of capacity. All told, societies vary enormously in their waste of human learning ability, but they all waste it. Since modern scientists have such difficulty in perfecting teaching techniques, in measuring capacities and talents, and in motivating people to learn, there is little wonder that societies have also bungled the job.

Isolated Children: What They Show

One line of evidence showing the role of socialization in human mentality and human behavior and demonstrating how utterly limited are the resources of the organism alone, is afforded by extremely isolated children. Since with these individuals physical development has proceeded to an advanced point with practically no concomitant social influence, they reveal to what degree the stages of socialization are necessarily correlated with the stages of organic growth. They enable us to see what an unsocialized mind (and body) is like after developing beyond the point at which normal minds have been socially molded.

Two such cases have been seen by the writer.[3] The first was the case of an illegitimate child called Anna, whose grandfather strongly disapproved of the mother's indiscretion and who therefore caused the child to be kept in an upstairs room. As a result the infant received only enough care to keep her barely alive. She was seldom moved from one position to another. Her clothing and bedding were filthy. She apparently had no instruction, no friendly attention.

When finally found and removed from the room at the age of nearly six years, Anna could not talk, walk, or do anything that

[3] The material that follows is condensed, with permission of the publisher, from two papers by the writer: "Extreme Social Isolation of a Child," *American Journal of Sociology,* Vol. 45 (January 1940), pp. 554-564; and "Final Note on a Case of Extreme Isolation," *ibid.,* Vol. 50 (March 1947), pp. 432-437. The literature on feral and extremely neglected children has been summarized by J. A. L. Singh and Robert M. Zingg, *Wolf-Children and Feral Man* (New York: Harper, 1942). This source contains a full bibliography up to the date of publication. Since that time several articles have appeared, mostly devoted to the question of whether or not so-called "wolf-children" have actually existed. This aspect of the subject has been, in the writer's opinion, magnified beyond its importance.

showed intelligence. She was in an extremely emaciated and undernourished condition, with skeleton-like legs and a bloated abdomen. She was completely apathetic, lying in a limp, supine position and remaining immobile, expressionless, and indifferent to everything. She was believed to be deaf and possibly blind. She of course could not feed herself or make any move in her own behalf. Here, then, was a human organism which had missed nearly six years of socialization. Her condition shows how little her purely biological resources, when acting alone, could contribute to making her a complete person.

By the time Anna died of hemorrhagic jaundice approximately four and a half years later, she had made considerable progress as compared with her condition when found. She could follow directions, string beads, identify a few colors, build with blocks, and differentiate between attractive and unattractive pictures. She had a good sense of rhythm and loved a doll. She talked mainly in phrases but would repeat words and try to carry on a conversation. She was clean about clothing. She habitually washed her hands and brushed her teeth. She would try to help other children. She walked well and could run fairly well, though clumsily. Although easily excited, she had a pleasant disposition. Her improvement showed that socialization, even when started at the late age of six, could still do a great deal toward making her a person. Even though her development was no more than that of a normal child of two to three years, she had made noteworthy progress.

A correct interpretation of this case is handicapped by Anna's early death. We do not know how far the belated process of socialization might ultimately have carried her. Inevitably the hypothesis arises that she was feebleminded from the start. But whatever one thinks in this regard, the truth is that she did make considerable progress and that she would never have made this progress if she had remained isolated. Of course, she was not completely isolated. Had she been, she would have died in infancy. But her contact with others was almost purely of a physical type which did not allow of communicative interaction. The case illustrates that communicative contact is the core of socialization. It is worth noting that the girl never had, even after her discovery, the best of skilled attention. It took her a long time to learn to talk, and it is possible that once she had learned to talk well the process of socialization would have been speeded up. With normal children it is known that the mastery of speech is the key to learning.

The other case of extreme isolation, that of Isabelle, helps in the interpretation of Anna. This girl was found at about the same time as Anna under strikingly similar circumstances when approximately six and a half years old. Like Anna, she was an illegitimate child and had been kept in seclusion for that reason. Her mother was a deaf-mute and it appears that she and Isabelle spent most of their time together in a dark room. As a result Isabelle had no chance to develop speech; when she communicated with her mother it was by means of gestures. Lack of sunshine and inadequacy of diet had caused her to become rachitic. Her legs in particular were affected; they "were so bowed that as she stood erect the soles of her shoes came nearly flat together, and she got about with a skittering gait." [4] Her behavior toward strangers, especially men, was almost that of a wild animal, manifesting much fear and hostility. In lieu of speech she made only a strange croaking sound. In many ways she acted like an infant. "She was apparently utterly unaware of relationships of any kind. When presented with a ball for the first time, she held it in the palm of her hand, then reached out and stroked my face with it. Such behavior is comparable to that of a child of six months." [5] At first it was even hard to tell whether or not she could hear, so unused were her senses. Many of her actions resembled those of deaf children.

Once it was established that she could hear, specialists who worked with her pronounced her feebleminded. Even on nonverbal tests her performance was so low as to promise little for the future. "The general impression was that she was wholly uneducable and that any attempt to teach her to speak, after so long a period of silence, would meet with failure." [6] Yet the individuals in charge of her launched a systematic and skillful program of training. The task seemed hopeless at first but gradually she began to respond. After the first few hurdles had at last been overcome, a curious thing happened. She went through the usual stages of learning characteristic of the years from one to six not only in proper succession but far

[4] Francis N. Maxfield, "What Happens When the Social Environment of a Child Approaches Zero," unpublished manuscript.

[5] Marie K. Mason, "Learning to Speak after Six and One-Half Years of Silence," *Journal of Speech Disorders*, Vol. 7 (1942), p. 299.

[6] *Ibid.*

more rapidly than normal. In a little over two months after her first vocalization she was putting sentences together. Nine months after that she could identify words and sentences on the printed page, could write well, could add to ten, and could retell a story after hearing it. Seven months beyond this point she had a vocabulary of 1,500-2,000 words and was asking complicated questions. Starting from an educational level of between one and three years (depending on what aspect one considers), she had reached a normal level by the time she was eight and a half years old. In short, she covered in two years the stages of learning that ordinarily require six.[7] Or, to put it another way, her I.Q. trebled in a year and a half.[8] The speed with which she reached the normal level of mental development seems analogous to the recovery of body weight in a growing child after an illness, the recovery being achieved by extra fast growth until restoration of normal weight for the given age. She eventually entered school where she participated in all school activities as normally as other children.

Clearly the history of Isabelle's development is different from that of Anna's. In both cases there was an exceedingly low, or rather blank, intellectual level to begin with. In both cases it seemed that the girl might be congenitally feebleminded. In both a considerably higher level was reached later. But Isabelle achieved a normal mentality within two years, whereas Anna was still markedly inadequate at the end of four and a half years. What accounts for the difference?

Perhaps Anna had less innate capacity. But Isabelle probably had more friendly contact with her mother early in life, and also she had more skillful and persistent training after she was found. The result of such attention was to give Isabelle speech at an early stage, and her subsequent rapid development seems to have been a consequence of that. Had Anna, who closely resembled this girl at the start, been given intensive training and hence mastery of speech at an earlier point, her subsequent development might have been much more rapid.

Isabelle's case serves to show, as Anna's does not clearly show, that isolation up to the age of six, with failure to acquire any form of speech and hence missing the whole world of cultural meaning, does not preclude the subsequent acquisition of these. Indeed, there

[7] *Ibid.*, pp. 300-304.
[8] Maxfield, *op. cit.*

seems to be a process of accelerated recovery. Just what would be the maximum age at which a person could remain isolated and still retain the capacity for full cultural acquisition is hard to say. Almost certainly it would not be as high as age fifteen; it might possibly be as low as age ten. Undoubtedly various individuals would differ considerably as to the exact age.

Both cases, and others like them, reveal in a unique way the role of socialization in personality development. Most of the human behavior we regard as somehow given in the species does not occur apart from training and example by others. Most of the mental traits we think of as constituting the human mind are not present unless put there by communicative contact with others. No other type of evidence brings out this fact quite so clearly as do these rare cases of extreme isolation. Through them it is possible "to observe *concretely separated* two factors in the development of human personality which are always otherwise only analytically separated, the biogenic and the sociogenic factors." [9]

The Development of the Self

The heart of socialization is the emergence and gradual development of the self or ego. It is in terms of the self that personality takes shape and the mind comes to function.

The self develops out of the child's communicative contact with others. Contact is at first on a physical level, and in this phase the infant's stability and continuity seemingly come from several sources: his body, which furnishes a constant flow of internal stimuli and has regularly recurring needs; his external surroundings, which constantly bombard his awakening senses and have a certain stability; his attendants, who observe a certain regularity in ministering to him. Consequently the possibility for forming habits is there from the beginning. Such activities as sucking the thumb and swinging suspended toys tend to be done repeatedly in the same way, and later the child shows a strong tendency toward "ritualistic" conformity to behavior patterns already established, as every parent knows. Thus the element of persistence, of conservation, so essential for the notion of the self, is present from the start.[10]

[9] Kingsley Davis, in a foreword in Singh and Zingg, *op. cit.*, pp. xxi-xxii.

[10] Cf. Jean Piaget, "Principal Factors Determining Intellectual Evolution from Childhood to Adult Life" in *Factors Determining Human Behavior* (Cambridge: Harvard University Press, 1937), pp. 35-36.

The self, however, has a character different and apart from that of the physiological organism proper, a development and a structure of its own. It is not there at birth but arises in the interplay of social experience. Parts of the body—toes, teeth, tonsils—can be lost without any corresponding loss to the self. Only when the loss has a real social meaning (as when a young girl loses a leg or becomes facially disfigured, or when it involves the organism's capacity for thought and feeling—as when the brain is injured or a gland has a tumor) does the change make a difference for the self. In these cases the effect of the bodily change clearly illustrates the separate character of the self. The latter is a psychic, not a physical entity.

George H. Mead has pointed out that an essential characteristic of the self is its reflexive character.[11] By this he means that the self can be both subject and object to itself; it can reflect upon itself or, as we often put it, can be self-conscious. Mead then says that the essential problem of selfhood or self-consciousness is "How can an individual get outside himself in such a way as to become an object to himself?" He can do it only through others, by temporarily assuming the role of other persons and looking at himself, so to speak, through their eyes. He learns to imagine how he appears to others, to imagine how others judge this appearance, and then to react himself to this judgment as he imagines it. Unless the attitudes are in his mind they cannot affect the self; and unless they are attributable to others, they cannot be acquired. Thus by adopting toward himself the attitudes that others take toward him, he comes to treat himself as an object as well as a subject.

In acquiring the attitudes of others toward himself, the individual is not merely passive. He explores and finds out because the satisfaction of his wants greatly depends on others' attitudes toward him. In fact, the expression of attitudes by his fellows soon becomes so important to him that he wants and demands attention. He has a powerful incentive to understand their attitudes, because otherwise he could not predict or control what happens to him. The child early learns that one of the most important ways of controlling his destiny is by influencing the feelings of others toward himself. Since attitudes are matters of meaning, they can be known only through the mechanism of symbolic communication. Hence the child must learn

[11] *Mind, Self, and Society* (Chicago: University of Chicago Press, 1934), Part III. Much of the present section is paraphrased from Mead's brilliant discussion.

to utilize the symbols by which attitudes are communicated, so that he can conjure up the attitudes of others in his own imagination and in turn communicate his own reactions to others in the light of what he imagines their judgments to be. In order to communicate with others he must himself be able to respond to what he communicates, else he would have no notion of the meaning of what he says and does. Once he has acquired the attitudes of others as part of himself, he can judge how another person will respond by how he himself responds to the words he utters. He not only hears himself but responds to himself; he talks and replies to himself as truly as the other person talks and replies to him.

"The self, as that which can be object to itself, is essentially a social structure, and it arises in social experience." It could not conceivably arise outside of social experience. After it has arisen it contains the social system actively within itself, and so in a way can provide its own social interaction. The person can carry on a conversation with himself. What he says, or thinks he might say, calls out a certain reply in himself (as he takes the role of the other). This reply leads him to say something else, and so on. Thus a person, once he is socialized, can remain solitary for a long time without ceasing to enjoy a certain kind of social interaction. Eventually, however, he must have an audience. Otherwise he cannot check the accuracy of his own responses; his imaginings become barren, repetitive, and divorced from reality.[12] But the very process of thinking is simply an inner conversation in which the individual responds to what he himself says and in turn replies himself to his own response.

It is astonishing how early in life the infant learns to take the role of the other. By the age of two it plays at being mother, baby, or sister. In doing so it views the situation from the standpoint of the person in question, and acts accordingly. The attitudes thus imitated are often those taken toward the infant itself. Thus a child of two may examine a doll's dress, pretend to find it wet, reprimand it, and take it to the bathroom. Such a child has already internalized the attitudes of others. By putting itself in the role of the other it can then respond to its own words and acts in terms of the meaning they would convey to the other person. In this way the self develops and grows.

In an organized game, such as baseball, the child must be ready

[12] Mead, *op. cit.*, pp. 140-141.

to take the role of everyone else in the game. "He must have the responses of each position involved in his own position. He must know what everyone else is going to do in order to carry out his own play."[13] The organization of reciprocal responses is contained in the rules of the game. In so far as the child has grasped the rules of the game and thus can participate in the mutual responses that constitute the actual play, he has acquired within himself an organized system of roles. His specific response is controlled by his sense of the whole system of responses. These are not so much the responses of particular persons as of positions.

The community or social group, like baseball, has an organized character. And as it takes shape in the organization of the self, a process of generalization occurs. What were earlier for the child the attitudes of particular other persons, now become the attitudes of everybody in the given situations. This justifies Mead's term, "the generalized other." As the individual incorporates into himself the system of mutually related attitudes in the community with reference to the common activities and goals of the group as a whole, he becomes a complete self, a social product in the fullest sense.

Taking the attitude of the generalized other is, on the intellectual side, simply the process of abstract thought, while on the emotional side it is the process of moral reasoning. The rules of logic are universals applying to everyone who wishes to reason accurately. The principles of morality are equally universal, applying to everyone who wishes to live properly. Of course, not all of the attitudes acquired by the individual are equally general. Many of them apply to particular classes and groups, but even these are integrally related to the most general attitudes of the entire community. When a person puts himself in the place of the generalized other and thus judges his own conduct, he is reflecting in himself the organization of the community at large. The self, then, is a structure of attitudes, not a group of habits. There are some habits that have nothing to do with the system of attitudes, and the attitudes, while they may be habitual, are distinguished by the fact that they are acquired through communicative interaction with others. No sharp line can be drawn between our own selves and the selves of others, since our own selves function in our experience only in so far as the selves of others function in our experience also.

[13] *Ibid.*

The reflexive character of the self can be phrased in terms of the "I" and the "me." "The 'I' is the response of the individual to the attitudes of the others; the 'me' is the organized set of attitudes of others which one himself assumes," and to which the "I" responds. The "me" is what is remembered and reflected upon; the "I" is what remembers and does the reflecting.[14] The "me" is the self that one is aware of, the "I" is the unpredictable response. A player can throw the ball to another player because he knows what the rest expect of him. Their expectations are his "me." But exactly how he will respond—whether he will make a brilliant play or an error—neither he nor anybody else knows. The response at the moment of action is the "I"; it is the dynamic unpredictable aspect of the self. As soon, however, as the "I" has acted, it can be remembered and reflected upon; it then becomes a part of the "me." The player has in him all the attitudes of others calling for a certain response, and this is the "me" of the situation; his response at the moment when made is the "I." The "I," then, is always acting in that infinitely small moment when the future becomes the present. It always contains an element of novelty. It resolves in a partially unexpected fashion the conflicting elements of the situation. It is what gives the person a sense of freedom and initiative. The "me" calls for a response in a given situation but the exact character of the response is not completely determined, being morally, not mechanically, necessary. Plainly the "I" and the "me" are separate aspects of the same thing. Taken together they constitute the personality as it appears in social experience. If the self did not have these two aspects there could be no conscious responsibility, and there could be no novelty.

"The self is not something that exists first and then enters into relationship with others." It is something that develops out of social interaction and is constantly changing, constantly adjusting, as new situations and conflicts arise. It assumes the prior existence of a social order and yet is the vessel in which and through which the order continues.

DESIRE, CONSCIOUSNESS, AND THE SELF

The energy for the self comes from the organism but the use made of this energy is only partly organic. Organic desires and needs

[14] Mead, *op. cit.*, p. 175. *Cf.* the section on "Position and Role" in Chap. 4 above.

must be met, at least sufficiently to keep the organism running, and they are met largely through the assistance of others. The self, in taking over the attitudes of others, is therefore acting partially as an instrumentality for the organism. However, it is at the same time acting also as an instrument for the control of the organism. Since it is built out of the attitudes of others, the self cannot help but place a value on these attitudes apart from or in spite of organic satisfaction. This is especially true of one kind of attitude—the attitude of approval and disapproval; for this offers a key to much else. It is only through the approval of others that the self can tolerate the self.

To be sure, there is a selection among possible others of those whose opinions count most. Not everyone counts with equal weight, and the degree to which an attitude counts depends on the degree of identification between oneself and the person expressing the attitude.

In any case the others never give their approval for the complete and free satisfaction of organic desires. Some satisfaction is permitted, to be sure, but on the other hand much self-abnegation is also demanded. As a result there inevitably arises a conflict between the individual's bodily desires as they impinge on the self and the attitudes of others toward the self in relation to these desires. Of course, other people do not give their approval to the pursuit of their approval by any means whatsoever. The individual's striving for good standing must be undertaken according to certain standards. He is tempted to seek it by deceptive measures which if they became known to others would lead to the opposite result, just as he is tempted to satisfy forbidden organic desires by secret means. He is restrained, however, successfully or unsuccessfully, not only by the fear of detection but also by the fear of what he himself will think of himself.

All of this means that the self is perpetually in a state of uneasy equilibrium. It strives for superiority (approval of others) yet it fears inferiority (disapproval of others). It seeks what organic satisfactions it can and yet reacts toward these satisfactions with the moral attitudes acquired from others. The conflict between what it must do and what it wants to do acts as a constant stimulus to bring the warring parts together, to work out an adjustment. The self is therefore a dynamic system, the parts of which are functionally related but never completely integrated. It is always striving and seeking.

The conflict manifests itself in earliest childhood when frustration first makes its appearance. The infant begins with a completely egocentric reaction to the world—the demand to have its desires met. Gradually, as it begins the slow and difficult process of acquiring the attitudes of others, it learns that anger is met with anger, aggression with aggression. The attitudes of others are part of a restricting situation that cannot be brushed aside. The infant must therefore take account of these attitudes and try to manipulate them, even before they are understood. He takes cognizance of them at first in an absolute manner, as sheer imperatives, because he is unable to enter into the role of the commanding adult who issues them. This is what Piaget has called the stage of "moral realism." [15]

As time goes on, however, and the child increasingly adopts the attitudes of others toward himself, he becomes less egocentric. He learns to communicate and identify himself with others, and to participate in coöperative enterprises. Instead of being controlled by exterior constraint he is increasingly controlled by notions of what is right and wrong, proper and improper, which he applies himself. He develops a conscience that reflects not only the opinions of those immediately around him but also the attitudes of the generalized other, the moral voice of the community as a whole. Instead of an external struggle there develops an internal struggle. The conscious reflecting part of the self must somehow balance and reconcile three countervailing sets of forces: the acquired attitudes and goals, the organic urges, and the facts of the situation at any given moment. The conflicts can be resolved only with the help of suppression. Sometimes it is unpleasant facts in the situation that are suppressed, sometimes it is the moral imperatives, sometimes it is the organic desires. But though suppressed from consciousness, these elements still remain a part of the personality and still influence behavior. They manifest themselves in various ways which the trained observer can detect. For this reason the self cannot be understood simply as that which appears in consciousness but must also be understood as embracing much that, at least at any given time, does not appear in consciousness.

The unconscious part of the personality has been divided by the psychoanalysts into two parts: the "Id" (it wants) and the "Super-

[15] Jean Piaget, *The Moral Judgment of the Child* (New York: Harcourt, Brace, 1932). Chap. 2.

ego" (thou shalt not). The one is partly a reflection of organic urges and desires and partly a reflection of acquired goals which, in a given situation, may be illegitimate or pursued by illegitimate means. The other is a reflection of the moral imperatives of the community, the generalized other. Conceptualized in this way, a great deal of the behavior of the individual becomes comprehensible and to some extent predictable. As the normal individual becomes mature, a modus vivendi is worked out whereby some satisfaction is given to all parts of the self but no part is allowed to run away with the others and thus divorce the person from his social reality.

The abnormal individual is one who fails to work out such a modus vivendi as he grows to adulthood and who thus appears queer to his fellows.

Who Socializes the Child? [16]

The nature of socialization is obviously of such a character as to be greatly affected by the kind of persons who do it. It is furthermore of such importance to society that it has been institutionalized and regulated with regard to its form and personnel. In fact, from a societal point of view the child is valued more for what he will be than for what he is. His value is like that of a savings account, chiefly anticipatory. Any doctrine that views the child's needs as paramount and those of organized society as secondary is a sociological anomaly. Since it is socialization that turns the child into a useful member of the society and gives him social maturity, it is natural that the child's socialization has not been left to mere accident but instead has always taken place within an institutional framework and been controlled through institutional channels.

There are two quite distinguishable categories of persons from whom the child acquires the sentiments, beliefs, and knowledge of his culture. The first includes those who have authority over him, the second those who have equality with him. His training varies in content and significance according as it is acquired from one or the other. In fact, the two general types of morality distinguished by Piaget—that of constraint and that of coöperation—are mainly, as he indicates, the respective product of these two types of relationship.

[16] Most of this section is taken from the writer's paper, "The Child and the Social Structure," *Journal of Educational Sociology,* Vol. 14 (December 1940), pp. 217-229.

The morality of constraint is one of objective duty based on unilateral respect for persons in authority, its rules being felt as superior, external, absolute, and beyond comprehension. The morality of co-operation rests on mutual understanding between equals, the rules having no mystic superiority or absoluteness in themselves but simply being the working principles of association, capable of modification according to the rational considerations and needs of the participants.[17]

Of interest to us is the fact that these two types of socio-psychic relationship, both extremely important in the child's socialization, rest upon the bases of status ascription previously discussed.[18] Persons having authority over the child are generally older than he, and those having immediate and primary authority are also usually kin to him. Persons sharing equality with him, whether kin or not, are apt to be of similar age.

That there should be an authoritarian element in socialization seems easy to explain. The patterns of behavior expected in the culture are not innate but are in many cases contrary to biological inclination. Hence the persons charged with socializing the young must not only have something to transmit and the responsibility of transmitting it, but must also have the power to command obedience. The reason why older persons are given this power is obvious, for when the process of socialization is first begun the infant has no juniors and no capacity for associating with equals. Furthermore, socialization must naturally proceed from those who have more of the culture to those who have less; it must proceed from the mature to the immature. The fact that the particular adults first given the task are usually kinsmen (e.g. parents) arises out of the child's original close connection with them in the family system.[19] It is convenient though not necessary to have the persons responsible for reproducing and maintaining children also responsible for socializing them. With a wide age and experience gap separating the child from his socializers, he cannot "understand" fully the logic and nature of all that they transmit to him or achieve immediate insight into their minds. He has to accept some rules simply because his superiors stipulate them. In case he does not understand or, understanding,

[17] Piaget, *Moral Judgment of the Child.*
[18] Chapter 4, pp. 96-113.
[19] See Chapter XV, pp. 394-396.

does not wish to obey, he may be coerced—because from the point of view of society the essential thing is not that the child be "freed from taboo" in order to "express his personality" but that he be taught the folkways and mores, prepared for his adult statuses, and protected from himself during his period of childishness and dependence. Hence what the child absorbs at first is largely a morality of constraint. It is in this way that society, taking no chances, transmits the most valued and essential parts of its heritage. Ultimately, as we have already said, societal morality is not a matter of rational understanding but a matter of felt obligation. The official socializer—be he parent, educator, or master—is the representative of the greater authority of society.

The equalitarian element in socialization, although ubiquitous, is perhaps a bit more difficult to explain than the authoritarian element, because it is not so much the outcome of deliberate policy or the focus of official attention. Let us begin by asking why similarity of age, sex, and rank should be a basis for equalitarian relations, and these a source of the morality of coöperation. The answer is that persons related by similarity of status stand in the same relation to persons in authority. This being true, they are in a position to protect rather than to coerce one another. Any rule governing their mutual interaction, in so far as it is made by themselves, has no other *raison d'être* than the spontaneous realization that the rule is necessary for the continuance of the interaction. Age mates, for example, being at the same stage of socialization, can participate in one another's subjective attitudes because they look at the world through the same eyes. This makes it easy for them to understand why each one expects a given type of response and thus lays the basis for reciprocity. The same is somewhat true of sex and caste mates.

From such equals there are acquired some things that cannot be acquired from persons in authority. These include not only the coöperative morality already discussed but also some of the more informal aspects of culture—small folkways, shades of meaning, fads and crazes, secret modes of gratification, and forbidden knowledge. Such things are often socially necessary and yet socially tabooed. An example in our society is a knowledge of sex relations which, according to strict doctrine, is supposed to remain a closed book until marriage; if the doctrine were carried out to the letter, the performance of numerous functions would be much more difficult; and so sex knowledge is not excluded completely, but is transmitted as a part of the lore that passes from child to child, a part of the so-called "child culture." Leaving such things to equalitarian relations for transmission has the effect of controlling them because coevals, being almost equally ignorant, can transmit relatively little real information one to the other. The total amount of knowledge transmitted from child to child cannot be as great, potentially, as the total amount that can be transmitted from adult to child. Yet in so far as the child learns in the equalitarian group to understand the rules as part of a coöperative effort, in so far as he learns to stand up for his rights without the protection of authority or the abjectness of dependence, he acquires something that is very hard if not impossible to get in the authoritarian type of relationship.

In sum, both authoritarian and equalitarian relationships contribute to the socialization of the child, and both tend to be ascribed (at least initially) in terms of sex, age, and kinship. Things that involve discipline and responsibility in transmission are usually handed over to authoritarian relations, other things to equalitarian relations. We thus glimpse the manner in which ascribed statuses figure in the dynamics of socialization.

Education and Educational Theory in Modern Society

Until now we have discussed socialization as if it were the same in all cultures. This is true only in the most general sense. It now behooves us to consider the ways in which childhood varies in different cultures and to examine certain problems raised by our own society.

A small stable society, which utilizes ascribed status more than does a large changing one, has a simple form of socialization. Training in the universal features of the culture is accomplished in the day to day association with adults. Training for specialized statuses is accomplished through informal instruction given by persons already in those statuses, often members of the family. Certain rituals, fetishes, and emblems help emphasize changes of status, and the pattern of life for each individual is rather well defined from the start. The culture changes so slowly that the entire older generation forms a suitable agency for socializing the young.

A large changing society, on the other hand, cannot transmit its huge cultural heritage simply on the basis of informal and amateurish socialization. Nor can it fit persons into its complex and highly specialized statuses simply on the basis of sex, age, and kinship. Sex and age are so broad as to yield too few classes, and the inheritance of status is too static to fit a rapidly changing milieu in which hundreds of new statuses appear in each generation. The inheritance of parental position works best when the parent socializes the child. With increasing specialization, parental training becomes less and less adequate until reliance must finally be placed on socialization outside the family. This leads to the appearance of schools, separate agencies in the society to carry out the function of education. The schools have professional teachers, a physical plant, a large investment, and an aggregation of pupils. They can perform the complex tasks of education in a way that the parents could not. They, like the parent, are in an authoritarian position with reference to the child, but due to their professional interest in education as such and to their greater resources they can be more flexible in the kind of training they give and the newness of the knowledge they transmit. They are organized not only for the transmission of existing knowledge but also for the discovery of new knowledge. They instill scientific discovery and advancement, and hence change, as ideals.

It is little wonder that in such a large changing society status achievement encroaches upon status ascription, with sex, age, and kinship playing merely the role of limiting or fluid factors in the competition for achieved statuses rather than acting as direct sources of specific statuses. By the exercise of unusual ability and fortitude a woman may qualify for a man's occupation, a young man rise to an old man's professional rank, or a poor person climb to a position of wealth. In this way under complex social conditions, individuals of different sex, different age, and different origins compete for the same statuses. This means that it is the process of socialization itself, especially as found in the educational system, that is serving as the proving ground for ability and hence the selective agency for placing people in different statuses according to their capacities. Thus intense competition gives an incentive for intense effort in learning and, as if this were not enough, this effort is artificially stimulated in numerous ways. Furthermore, the existence of professional teachers with an interest in techniques of instruction and a high degree of specialization in their narrow fields enormously improves the effectiveness of instruction. The principles, the elements, the general guiding signposts of different subjects are ferreted out, reduced to a rational order, and taught in a short space of time. Libraries store knowledge in specialized compartments for ready reference. Mutual discussion among students helps reinforce what is learned. Thus the segregation of the educational function in a separate agency (the school) is necessary, in order to adapt the process of socialization to the needs of a society in which the achievement rather than the ascription of status is emphasized and in which complexity and change are paramount.

Each kind of society—the simple-stable and the complex-instable—has its peculiar problems. The problem of the simple one, with its ascribed statuses and rigid institutional patterns, is its lack of adaptability to changing conditions. It may pursue ancient custom to the point of ossification and disaster. The complex specialized society, on the other hand, runs the risk of uncontrolled individualism with consequent loss of social cohesion. Intense specialization leads to a failure of society's members to understand one another. A partial antidote to this tendency is the fact that each individual has many statuses, so that his allegiance extends beyond any specialized group. But within each individual, and between him and others, there must presumably exist some integration of the various statuses; otherwise both personal and societal order will disappear. The integration must be on an evaluative as well as a factual level. The more a society becomes dependent upon specialization and its statuses become accessible through individual achievement, the more tenuous becomes the integrating principle—unless (and this is the difficult part) the realm of sacred common values remains superior to the everyday world of competitive interest.

Specialized achieved statuses require generally that the individual master certain rational techniques. He must adopt something of a scientific attitude toward his work and his career, and the highest prestige often goes to those who are the most skillful in this. Hence obligatory norms that limit arbitrarily the means for gaining a position are subjected to criticism by people competing for positions. The nonrational beliefs and practices associated with the obligatory norms are apt to be scoffed at. Under these circumstances, in the face of individualistic motivation and scientific criticism, the central values and common ends of the society tend to crumble.

Organized education cannot escape this problem of the specialized society. In the liberal democratic United States it has intensified the problem in two ways: by trying to deny and minimize ascribed status, and by attempting to evade normative indoctrination. In neither attempt has it been wholly successful or consistent, but in philosophy if not always in practice it has stressed achieved and condemned ascribed status and has evaluated scientific truth above doctrine. In keeping with this it has stated its goal to be the scientific study and efficient satisfaction of the child's needs, has minimized ritual, and has skirted those of the nonrational norms that could not be somehow rationalized as "science." It has been individualistic in the sense of being preoccupied with "individual needs," positivistic in the sense of looking to science for ethical conclusions, and rationalistic in the sense of assuming the sole significant orientation to the world to be one of cognition.[20]

It may well be questioned, however, how far a society can dispense with ascribed status and nonrational belief, and still survive. To begin with, we have already seen that infants must be "placed" in the social structure before the process of absorption into this structure can begin; and since the aim is eventual placement in highly specialized adult statuses, it is hard to see how the infants could all, regardless of sex, age relations, and parentage, be given the same place to start with, especially as long as a familial mode of reproduction is maintained. Moreover, any persisting society is an example of change within constancy, in which ascribed status helps to provide the constancy, achieved status the change, both being indispensable. It is also no accident that a regime in which ascription is strong is also one in which nonrational beliefs and norms are strong. To fix persons in statuses independently of their personal qualities requires a firm system of institutional controls. Ascribed statuses are generally broad ones in which the technical aspect is not complicated; the important things are sentiment, custom, and ritual rather than ra-

20 It is realized, of course, that all thought in educational circles cannot be placed under one rubric. What is aimed at here is the description of a general tendency. It is surprising to what an extent even the violently opposed schools of educational philosophy take the same things for granted, their differences being more superficial than the basic similarities that give them the same general interpretation of social life.

tional skill. To dispense with ascribed statuses altogether would knock a powerful prop from under the common values and ends which give society its cohesiveness, especially if these were further destroyed by scientific criticism and individualistic motivation. Since, moreover, as our previous discussion showed, ascribed statuses are connected with socialization in authoritarian relations, and these with the transmission of cultural values and mores, a regime of purely achieved status would constitute a threat to authority and to the functions of authority. Finally, there is every reason to believe that the individual could not stand the insecurity, conflict, and turmoil which such a changeable and disparate society would produce. The integration of the personality reflects the integration of society, and a regime of pure competition would produce neither the one nor the other. In short, it seems that a society cannot travel always in the direction of specialization and status achievement, that eventually its loss of solidarity will reach the point where an internal revolution by a militant cohesive minority or an external conquest by a militant cohesive rival will turn it back in the direction of institutional rigidity.

What is said here is not meant to blame recent educational philosophy but to point out certain features of the child-and-society relation which liberal democratic educators are prone to ignore. The discussion has attempted to show that status ascription, far from being merely an anachronism from a predemocratic era, is a universal and systematic part of society on which the process of socialization and the maintenance of solidarity are both dependent. In handling the stream of raw material from which it must build the personnel for its differentiated social structure, a society has little to go on in ascribing the initial statuses which it must ascribe; but it makes the most of this little, and utilizing it as a basis for the authoritarian and equalitarian relationships in which socialization takes place, it transmits both the formal and the informal aspects of the culture in a manner conducive to structural integration. Unless these things are understood it seems that educational philosophy will concentrate too narrowly on the so-called needs of the child and not sufficiently on the equally real needs of the society, so that many fundamental customs will seem anomalous and worthless—customs which if they were eliminated, would leave the society strangely incapable of maintaining itself.

Socialization and the Adolescent [21]

Consideration of formal education and its problems leads us to the last period of intense socialization, the period of adolescence. It is a peculiar period in many ways and hence requires separate attention.

Whether publically recognized as a separate status or not, the adolescent period seemingly has one outstanding peculiarity: it is a time when the individual is attaining physical maturity without necessarily attaining social maturity. In terms of growth, strength, fecundity, and mental capacity, full maturity tends to be attained only a short time after puberty; but socially the adolescent still has a long way to go before full status is reached.

This tendency for the adolescent to be more mature physically than socially is most pronounced in those settled societies placing a premium on age; but it is a condition that is to some extent inherent in the nature of all human society. Evolving through uncounted millennia, culture has developed a complexity of principle and a fullness of content that require a long time for the individual to master. At the same time it has made possible a type of social organization in which power and advantage are dependent on knowledge, experience, reputation, and social position rather than brute strength or innate cunning. In so far as these things have anything to do with age, they are more likely to come with middle age or even old age than with adolescence. Even an army, which presumably depends par excellence on physical skill and strength, is controlled by elderly generals and colonels. The adolescent, despite his achievements in battles, sports, and tests, has long been forced to defer to older persons whose biological capacities are less than his. The latter, by virtue of having held a position early in life, are able (in a stable society) to continue to hold it later in life and by virtue of it to acquire other positions of even greater influence. Furthermore, because of the endlessness of the educational process they are in a way better qualified for responsible positions. Their qualification, however, is a socially acquired and not a biologically maturing qualification. It is based on knowledge and experience, both necessary for successful political and administrative decisions.

[21] Most of this section is taken from the writer's paper, "Adolescence and the Social Structure," *Annals of the American Academy of Political and Social Science*, Vol. 236 (November 1944), pp. 8-16.

In a sense (the physical sense) the community does not utilize its great men until they are already past their prime; but in another sense (the social sense) it utilizes them at the peak of their greatness —in what one might call their administrative or sociological maturity. The principle of seniority is therefore no accident, no empty form. The charge is frequently made that the old hang onto their positions as vested interests and that this is the explanation of the subordination of youth to age. That older persons seek to hold what power they have is generally true,[22] but their desire does not explain the fact that they *can* do so. They are able to hold their power because they have a kind of superiority—a superiority developed and buttressed by an organized society, but a superiority nonetheless.

There has consequently grown up a situation in which the adolescent, despite his physical equality with or even superiority to the older person, is nevertheless placed in a socially subordinate position. The result is a sort of disharmony which in times of social disorganization sometimes expresses itself in conflict between the generations.

If mental and physical maturity came between 30 and 35 years of age instead of between 15 and 20, there would be a much longer period of youthful plasticity during which an enormously enhanced amount of culture could be absorbed. As it is, especially in modern society, the individual must keep on learning after his capacity to do so has already begun to decline. Even though his sheer capacity has reached its peak during adolescence, his acquired knowledge, judgment, insight, and self-reliance are generally far from their peak.

The great extension of the average length of life in modern times, while it has afforded more scope and rationale to post-adolescent learning, has not lengthened the adolescent period itself. Instead it has prolonged the duration of adulthood and has consequently made adolescence a smaller fraction of the average life-span.

Also helping to make the complex heritage of modern culture possible is specialization. Each individual is not required to learn the entire culture but only that part of it which concerns him. This mechanism, however, like the extension of the length of life, has its

[22] See the description of the Arapesh in Margaret Mead, *Sex and Temperament in Three Primitive Societies* (New York: Morrow, 1935), pp. 77-78, for an apparent exception. Also the Japanese head of the family was given to retirement when his eldest son came of age. See Lafcadio Hearn, *Japan* (New York: Macmillan, 1928), p. 73.

limitations, as one can readily see by imagining a society with no general language but merely with a separate language for every occupational group.

Societies of course differ as to how freely they permit young people to accumulate knowledge and experience. Frequently, in order to transmit first the ideal elements of the culture the elders, as mentioned earlier, select the cultural content that is given to children and protect them from contrary experiences. To the extent that this happens it postpones social maturity to some stage beyond adolescence. In modern society, because of this protectiveness as well as other factors, even middle-aged people are commonly accused of being emotionally immature.

Adolescence, then, is ordinarily the time when the lag of social development behind physical development first becomes pronounced. As society grows more complex the lag becomes greater, and adolescence as socially defined extends farther into physical adulthood.

OCCUPATIONAL PLACEMENT

If training is required for one's occupation the choice of an occupation should be made by the time of adolescence at the latest, because this period represents the last stage of really rapid learning. Yet in a complex and changing society the decision as to occupation tends to be deferred until late adolescence or early adulthood, for the reason that occupational possibilities are altering so fast that decisions made earlier may be subsequently rendered inadvisable. But it is precisely in such a society that an elaborate training and hence an early decision are most essential.

If in a simple and stable society the occupation is ascribed or chosen early in life, if the training extends through childhood or is relatively simple in character, adolescence does not stand out occupationally as a period of any particular importance. By the time he reaches adolescence the individual may in fact be practicing his occupation and may be looked upon in this regard as an adult. If on the other hand the society is complex and changing, adolescence tends to become a time of difficult choosing and intensive training and hence acquires a pronounced importance as a socially recognized, eventful period of life. If there is a gradation within each occupation, the adolescent generally starts at the bottom rung. This tends to give him a distinctly subordinate status. If the element of competition is introduced, it acts as an individualizing force that makes of adolescence a period of strain and perhaps of deprivation at the same time that it raises the level of general achievement.

REPRODUCTIVE CONTROL

In its handling of the adolescent every society must somehow recognize the fact that the reproductive capacity first appears at the inception of adolescence. One crucial question is whether the adolescent shall be permitted to gratify his sexual desires through normal heterosexual intercourse or whether such gratification must be postponed. A second is whether the gratification, if permitted, shall be in marriage or in premarital relations; and if the latter, whether the illegitimate children shall be killed, disposed of to relatives, or kept by the girl. Finally, there is the question of whether marital choice is free or is controlled by others, and whether marriage establishes a separate household or merely an extension of the parental menage.

Among most peoples of the world, at least until recently, there was variation around a recurrent pattern. Either marriage occurred shortly after puberty or premarital intercourse prevailed. The choice of a marital partner was generally in the hands of parents or kinsmen, though the right of veto, in theory at least, supposedly belonged to the parties to the marriage. Wedlock did not usually imply a separate household and did not convey full emancipation from the parents. Although there were countless variations on this generalized pattern, the underlying theme was extremely widespread. Its main characteristic was that it gave a sexual and reproductive function to the adolescent but carefully controlled the exercise of this function.

By way of contrast, American society is unusual though not entirely unique in the following ways: It maintains the ideal of premarital chastity in the face of a long period of postponement of marriage after puberty. In connection with this it upholds the freedom of marital choice and fosters competition and the doctrine of caveat emptor in courtship. Finally it emphasizes the independence and separateness of the wedded couple. As a consequence the adolescent period becomes one of considerable strain. The young person is permitted to associate closely with the opposite sex but is put on his honor to remain virtuous, is supposed to choose his own mate independently but is in many ways still under the authority of the parents, and is forced to compete for love in a rating and dating system that interferes and gets entangled with his fortunes in that other competitive system, the occupational sphere. The strains are somewhat different for boys and for girls,[23] but only as different sides of the same situation.

CULTURAL ACQUISITION

Only the highly civilized societies, as previously mentioned, possess a specialized educational system forming a separate phase of life. For inculcating modern culture such a system is necessary. Its concentrated and abstract curriculum, professional staff, physical separateness, and internal organization all provide a rapid and systematic grounding in the principles of the civilization. But by virtue of the very qualities that make it efficient in teaching abstractions, it tends to divorce itself from the facts and experiences of everyday life. For years the pupil is drilled in principles, on the assumption that he will subsequently apply them in actual life. His childhood is thus treated as the preparation for life, not as real life itself.

The difficulty is of course that not everything can be taught in school. The person often emerges with a hoard of abstract knowledge but with little knowledge of the concrete situations he must negotiate in order to get along. The harder he studies, the more unfit he becomes for ordinary day-to-day existence. Above all, there is such a long interval between learning and application that the incentive to learn often flags and must be bolstered by an amazing system of planned competition and artificial rewards.

Out of ennui and practical necessity the average pupil finally begins to participate in a more vivid world, the world of youth culture. This in its adolescent phase is characterized by irresponsibility, "having a good time," athletics, sex attraction, and the repudiation of adult control.[24] One reason it takes this form is that it is "denied status by society at large, and is regarded primarily as a destructive and undesirable, a foolish and queer expression of the impulses of young people."[25] It has, in other words, no avowed

[23] See Talcott Parsons, "Age and Sex in the Social Structure of the United States," *American Sociological Review,* Vol. 7 (Oct. 1942), pp. 604-616.

[24] Parsons, *op. cit.,* pp. 606-608.

[25] Peter Blos, *The Adolescent Personality* (New York: Appleton-Century, 1941), p. 254.

function in the institutional structure but is interstitial, officially purposeless [26]—a phenomenon seldom found in other societies.

No wonder the cry of unreality is raised against the school system and reforms are proposed which have in view the reintegration of education and life. Some of the reforms, however, have missed the point. They have overlooked the efficiency of systematic instruction and have attempted to make education "grow out of real life situations," [27] not realizing that since modern culture rests on abstract knowledge, to confine all instruction to the applied and the concrete would soon produce stagnation.

The root of the difficulty apparently lies in the fact that while the young person is going to school he is doing little else of a responsible and productive nature. Therefore, the remedy is perhaps to give him an essential function in the world outside of school—i.e. to let him work—and to relate his schooling to this function. He could then receive his reward not solely in terms of grades, diplomas, honors and degrees, but also in terms of wages and things accomplished. Thus the learning of principles would be attached to actual situations, not by the radical method of reducing all learning to a clumsy empiricism and thereby bankrupting the culture, but by making the young person a citizen who produces to the limit of his natural and acquired capacities.

The objection that a thorough grounding in basic principles leaves little time for participation in economic and political activity is valid. But there are three directions in which this obstacle may be overcome: first, the invention of new educational technology; second, the elimination of irrelevances from the curriculum; and third, the overhauling of the incentive mechanism. New educational technology, such as the recent methods of improving reading habits, may make possible the absorption of the same amount of knowledge in a much shorter time. As to irrelevances in the curriculum, it seems clear that they are there because the purpose of schooling both for the society and for the individual is not clear. One way of eliminating the irrelevances would be to define more clearly the fundamentals in our culture and thus reduce the number and the variety of "liberal arts" subjects. An additional way would be to eliminate applied sub-

[26] See Frederic M. Thrasher, *The Gang* (Chicago: University of Chicago Press, 1927).

[27] See I. B. Berkson, *Education Faces the Future* (New York: Harper, 1943), Chap. 8.

jects such as manual training and shorthand, except in so far as they relate to the pupil's known vocation. This would require specialization earlier in the school career than is now in fashion, and would have the disadvantage of requiring the choice of an occupation when the individual is still young and hence incapable of choosing wisely; although under a planned economy vocational guidance by experts would be required in any case. Early specialization would allow the school work to be tied to actual life because the child would enter the first stages of his occupation while already going to school. This in turn would help to solve the incentive problem. If a child were already launched on the first stages of his occupation, if his school subjects had specific application to his job so that his wages, advancement, and so forth, depended on them, he would be more disposed to study.

YOUTH AND EDUCATION IN RUSSIA

Of all the countries that have experimented with educational policy, Russia has been most drastic and apparently most successful in solving some of the basic problems of adolescence.[28] In the first place, she has made education as well as economics the monopoly of a completely dictatorial state, thus clarifying the goals of education (greater production and more total allegiance) and facilitating the planned integration of education with political and economic organization.

Politically the official party associations—Cubs, Pioneers, and Comsomol (all neatly paralleling the stages of the school system) —give an official function to the youth culture by assigning students an active and responsible part in the school administration and the nation's political life, and by serving as the chief source of recruits for the ruling elite, the Communist Party.

Economically, through "polytechnization," the school is geared with productive life. Not only is every school attached to a production unit but it is, at least by the high-school level, highly specialized. Indeed, the technical institutes are administered and financed by the

[28] A. Steinberg, in Margaret Cole (Ed.), *Our Soviet Ally* (London: Geo. Routledge, 1943), pp. 149-172; Samuel Northrup Harper, *Civic Training in Soviet Russia* (Chicago: University of Chicago Press, 1929), Chap. 12; and *Making Bolsheviks* (Chicago: University of Chicago Press, 1931), Chaps. 1 and 2; W. Thacher Winslow, *Youth a World Problem* (Washington, D. C.: Government Printing Office, 1937), pp. 126-138.

factory trusts, and other forms of specialized training are controlled by the commissariats destined to employ the students upon completion of their courses. Often the student enters partial employment in his field while still going to school and remains partially a student after taking a regular job. His expenses are generally borne by the appropriate commissariat.

Finally, the Soviets rely for education as little as possible on the family. Not only do they relieve the family of the cost but they take the child extremely early for "preschool education" in communal crèches and kindergartens. By the time of adolescence, therefore, it becomes easy for the child to shake off the parental authority, already superseded by a state authority that does not expect to be shaken off.

The Soviet system suggests that to make the school an integral part of the political and economic structure and to give youth a productive role, central planning of the whole economy is necessary. Whether or not a democratic state can achieve such planning is a profound question. Apparently, however, it must either achieve it or go out of existence. The adolescent problems of America have been one price—high and possibly unnecessary—paid for an extremely individualistic, dynamic social order. In the future the growth of industrial culture and the competition of tightly organized giant states may force us to use more efficiently the brief span of human immaturity.

Summary

The stili mysterious process by which the young human organism acquires the culture and enters the structure of the society can be illuminated by several different approaches. One of these concerns the role of socialization as a whole in relation to the other determinants of personality. Viewed in this way, socialization has a peculiar nature characterized primarily by communicative interaction. Concretely it can never be completely separated as a factor, and for this reason the logic of scientific abstraction must be kept in mind. The nearest an observer can come to concrete separation of socialization from genetic factors is in the cases of extremely isolated children. These demonstrate that without cultural transmission there can be no human mentality.

A second approach to the problem of socialization concerns the development of the self. It appears that culture actually takes hold of the individual through his assumption of the attitudes of others. Through these the self gradually develops. The attitudes of others penetrate not only into the individual's consciousness, but they form part of the unconscious as well. The individual's psyche is largely a reflection of the attitudinal system and hence of the social organization of the community in which he lives. To be sure, the individual is not a passive receptacle for cultural influence. Instead he must somehow combine the capacities and urges of the organism with the acquired drives and the normative restraints of his society. For this reason the self is always at best an uneasy equilibrium.

A third approach concerns the agencies of socialization. Who does the socializing, and why? It appears that the task is accomplished both in authoritarian and in equalitarian social relations, each kind of relationship making a unique contribution. In complex changing societies much of the authoritarian socialization, particularly in the latter two-thirds of the child's career, is carried out by a separate educational organization. Here one problem is precisely too much separation from the rest of life. The adolescent has somehow to reconcile his physical maturity with his social immaturity, his reproductive capacity with his educational and vocational needs.

Modern society has still to solve some basic problems of socialization at all stages of childhood and youth. Indeed, it cannot be said that any society makes full use of the individual's capacities. The improvement of socialization offers one of the greatest possibilities for the future alteration of human nature and human society.

References

Peter Blos, *The Adolescent Personality* (New York: Appleton-Century, 1941).

One of the best, if not the best, general book on the adolescent personality in our culture.

James H. S. Bossard, *The Sociology of Child Development* (New York: Harper, 1948).

A general treatise on the status of the child in different societies, on the types of social situations in which socialization occurs, and on the social factors determining personality development. Contains a very extensive bibliography and many footnote references to the literature.

Abram Kardiner and Ralph Linton, *The Individual and His Society* (New York: Columbia University Press, 1939).

Psychoanalytic interpretation of comparative materials from primitive societies. Linton, the anthropologist, provides data from the Marquesan and the Tanala cultures. Kardiner, the psychoanalyst, gives the interpretation and elaborates a theory of "basic personality structure." Interesting if not quite convincing.

Susan Isaacs, *Social Development in Young Children* (New York: Harcourt, Brace, 1933).

An illuminating description of the social behavior of young children as observed in an English nursery school. The first part, which gives the observations, seems better than the second part which gives the interpretation in psychoanalytic terms.

Geo. H. Mead, *Mind, Self and Society* (Chicago: University of Chicago Press, 1934), Part III, "The Self."

An intricate and systematic interpretation of the self as a social product. Mead, a great philosopher, was a pioneer in the development of the newer attitude toward the growth of the individual mind in society—an attitude shared by Dewey, Cooley, Faris, and many others. Prepared posthumously (largely from student notes) the book is one of the best expressions of that attitude. It is an enduring classic, hard to read but essential.

Gardner Murphy, Lois B. Murphy, and Theodore M. Newcomb, *Experimental Social Psychology* (New York: Harper, 1937), Part 2, "Interpretation of the Process of Socialization"; Part 3, "A Genetic Study of Social Behavior."

Sums up and evaluates the results of a great number of studies of child development. One becomes lost in details in this encyclopedic work, but it is an invaluable reference.

Jean Piaget, *The Moral Judgment of the Child* (New York: Harcourt, Brace, 1932).

All of Piaget's empirical studies of children are important for the understanding of socialization. This one deals in an extremely cogent manner with the stages and conditions through which moral judgments are developed. Some of Piaget's interpretations are open to question but the facts, presented in a lucid manner, are always valuable and pertinent.

J. A. L. Singh and Robt. M. Zingg, *Wolf-Children and Feral Man* (New York: Harper, 1939).

Contains the diary of the Rev. J. A. L. Singh describing the so-called wolf-children of Midnapore, India, together with a discussion by Professor Zingg and others of the literature on feral and isolated children. Much scientific dispute has centered on this topic, mainly over the unfortunate term "wolf-children."

CHAPTER IX

PERSONALITY INTEGRATION

WHEN in 1524 Francisco Pizarro sailed from Panama toward an unknown southern destination, he began a venture that had meaning in two different contexts. On the one hand he was, as history now shows, expanding the Spanish Empire over a great new area, the magnificent realm of the Incas, and was thus spreading the civilization and expanding the society of Europe. This was the sociological (including the political, economic, and religious) context. On the other hand he was, as an experienced but still obscure captain in his early fifties, acquiring fame and fortune beyond the dreams of most men. An illegitimate son, a swineherd in his home town, an illiterate man of no education, he viewed his gamble as an avenue to the greatest glory in his life, a potential triumph of the most satisfying kind. This was the personal context.

Necessarily the two contexts are related. If Pizarro's venture had not been significant to others in a social sense, he would not have regarded it as important in a personal sense and would not have undertaken it. Yet despite their interrelatedness the two contexts are quite distinct. The political historian analyzes the action in terms of the first context, relating it to the other events in the world of national enterprise, events having nothing to do with Pizarro as a person. He knows that if Pizarro had not discovered and conquered Peru some other man, probably a Spaniard, would have done so. The biographer analyzes the action in terms of the second context, relating it to the thoughts and aspirations and other activities in the life of the great conquistador. In both cases, of course, the concrete event is the same; it is only the ways of looking at it that are different.

When one views behavior from the standpoint of the biographer or psychologist, the most profound problem concerns the total unity of the personality; just as, when viewing behavior from the standpoint of the sociologist, the deepest problem concerns the total unity of society or the group. Both personality and society are modes of abstraction, ways of organizing sensory impressions and of relating events to other events. Each mode of interpretation leads ultimately to the question of the structure and functions of the system as a whole. What is it that gives personality, for example, its coherence and continuity? What is it that enables us to place it in a certain category and give it a name such as "personality" or the "self"?

Naive people often say that there can be no general principles regarding personality because "every person is different." But this statement itself is a general principle, presumably applying to "every person." To think that it is the only universal principle about personality is fallacious, because the very use of the word "persons" implies that there are some things that all people have in common. Such naive propositions, which kill rather than foster inquiry, result (as mentioned before) from a confusion between the concrete and the abstract. To be sure, all persons are different; but just as surely, they are all alike. It depends on how they are regarded. Every apple is different but this does not preclude our making valid statements about apples in general. Indeed, we make valid statements about *fruit* in general and reduce them to a science called *pomology*. Francisco Pizarro was different from all other human beings, but in many ways he was like all other Spaniards and in some ways like all other persons.

Our first interest in the present chapter is to sketch the nature and structure of the human personality and to show the place of social interaction in it. Our second interest is to describe the ways in which persons differ from one another and to show the role of culture and social experience in causing the differences. Since socialization is so greatly responsible for the development of personality, our discussion of that topic has already accomplished much of the task. The present treatment can therefore be brief.

It is characteristic of human beings that they find it almost impossible to study themselves scientifically. In the case of personality as with other human topics, the first thing that catches the attention is not the normal behavior (which is taken for granted) but the abnormal. We therefore know more about personality *dis*integration than we know about personality integration. In fact we tend to define the integrated or normal person as one who has none of the characteristics of the disintegrated or abnormal. Integration therefore becomes a residual category into which we throw everything that is not disintegration. But from a scientific point of view such residual categories should not be allowed to stand unmolested.

Academic psychologists have done little toward clarifying the matter of personality integration. They have misinterpreted their task as that of explaining concrete behavior from every point of view—organic, psychic, and social—which has made them encyclopedic in their approach and confused in their methodology. Also they have been more interested in analyzing individual differences than in formulating a general theory of personality. As a result they have concentrated on personality traits rather than on the whole person.[1] The psychoanalysts and other branches of "dynamic" or "depth" psychology have done more than the academic psychologists to give us a workable theory of personality organization.

The term *personality,* as we use it, refers to a psychic phenomenon. It is neither organic nor social but is an emergent from a combination of the two. Since the psychic, or mental, is hard for people to visualize because it is subjective, there is a constant tendency to try to reduce it to something else. Our evidence for its existence comes from two kinds of behavior, both of which are indicative of mental processes but not to be confused with them. The first evidence is that of nonsymbolic behavior, as in eating; the second is that of symbolic behavior, as in speech and gesture. With these indices at our disposal we are capable of learning a great deal about the mental processes of others; and since we experience directly our own mental processes, we can put ourselves in the place of others and predict on the basis of a knowledge of the situation what they will do. We can do this with particular ease, especially with reference to persons in our own culture, because our own self has been formed by taking over the attitudes of others through communication. Social interaction, as we have seen, is always based on mutual prediction of one another's behavior and always assumes the operation of subjective mental processes.

The central focus of subjective mental processes and hence the thing to which all behavior can be related in terms of a system, is

[1] Gardner Murphy, Lois B. Murphy, and Theodore M. Newcomb, *Experimental Social Psychology* (New York: Harper, 1937), Chap. 7.

the self or ego. We have already tried to show how it is formed and to indicate that it has two polar aspects, the one organically derived and the other socially derived. Let us illustrate these aspects in terms of two perceptions—"sweetness" and "wrong." Given a normal organism, candy will ordinarily taste "sweet." The sweetness is not a quality of the candy as such because candy has no mind; nor is it a quality of the organism alone, because without something sweet the taste cannot emerge. The sweetness is a sensation, a psychic emergent, which appears when candy and tongue come together under proper conditions. It appears in consciousness and therefore can be related to other things that appear in consciousness—viz., the color and shape of candy, the name for it, the box in which it is contained, and the price and occasion of its presence. The sensation is thus connected mentally with other sensations, with factual knowledge and with moral evaluations. Suppose, for example, that the individual tasting the candy is an orthodox Mohammedan and that he is tasting it during a day when according to his religion he is not supposed to take food in any form. Added to the taste of sweetness in this case is another subjective state of a very different character, the feeling of doing something "wrong." Now the feeling of "wrong" resembles the sensation of sweetness in being a function neither of the external world nor of the organic structure alone; but, unlike sweetness, it does not emerge from the combination of external stimulus and neural receptor. Instead it depends completely on meanings derived from other persons and involves *an attitude taken toward* certain facts or certain sensations. Identically the same sweetness may be viewed as either good or bad, depending on how the situation is defined.

It is characteristic of subjective states, of whatever type, that they can be pleasant or unpleasant. If unpleasant, something must be done to alter the experience. If too much candy has been eaten and the sweetness becomes sickening, the individual usually gets rid of the sensation by stopping eating. On the other hand he may risk offending his hostess and consequently may keep on eating beyond the point of satiety. If he is doing something "wrong" he may stop or make atonement. In the case of the "wrong," however, the unpleasantness does not derive initially from the organism itself but rather from responses set in motion by the individual's conception of himself in the eyes of others. The ego, then, is in the position of having to control and reconcile the pleasures from different sources; it is this process of controlling and reconciling that forms the key to personality structure.

The Striving for Unity

The unity of the self does not come easily. It is threatened on all sides by new and often hostile elements which must be either warded off or assimilated. The individual must be able to foresee and predict what happens, to understand the world he lives in and thus prevent the occurrence of sudden disturbances. In order to have confidence and certainty, he must feel that he lives in a stable and intelligible world. His security is threatened not so much by physical injury as by unpredictability and misunderstanding, particularly in his social relations. Unpleasant or unforeseen experiences are imaginatively rehearsed again and again in the effort to understand and assimilate them.

The assimilation of the outer world depends upon a constant but purely subjective interpretation which creates an inner world.

> Immersed in an environment which he does not and cannot understand, the individual is forced to create a substitute world which he can understand and in which he puts his faith. He acts in consistency with that conception, derives his standards of value from it, and undertakes to alter it only when convinced by further experience that it fails to serve the goal of unity. Since this self-made scheme of life is his only guarantee of security, its preservation soon becomes a goal in itself. He seeks the type of experience which confirms and supports the unified attitude, and rejects experiences which seem to promise a disturbance of this attitude.
>
> The apparent stability of the habit system is therefore not to be interpreted as due to the fixation of pathways in the nervous system, but rather as the reflection of a stable system of values.[2]

When the person is faced with a social situation inconsistent with his conception of himself, he must either assimilate it by incorporating it somehow into his value system or else reject it. Conflict is thus

[2] Prescott Lecky, *Self-Consistency: A Theory of Personality* (New York: Island Press, 1945), p. 50. This small book is highly recommended as a compact and unusual statement of the structural-functional theory of personality. The present writer has drawn heavily on it in the paragraphs that follow.

a necessary factor in personality development, and progressive assimilation of new situations is the only means by which a stable organization can be attained. If the new element is too foreign to the established system, it may be rejected. In either case, whether by assimilation or by rejection, the explanation of the choice lies in the individual's existing organization of values. The ego is not influenced mechanically by each external stimulus, like a puppet in a Punch and Judy show, but experiences and reinterprets the stimulus in the light of the meanings already established; and the effort is always to maintain the subjective unity which alone makes life possible. Assimilation or rejection of new elements is often accompanied by emotion, a by-product of the painful or exciting readjustment to new values. The primary attention of the conscious mind is always directed toward the disturbing problem at hand, while past solutions of other problems form the unconscious basis for the solution of this one.

> All of an individual's values are organized into a single system the preservation of whose integrity is essential. The nucleus of the system, around which the rest of the system revolves, is the individual's valuation of himself. The individual sees the world from his own viewpoint, with himself as the center. Any value entering the system which is inconsistent with the individual's valuation of himself cannot be assimilated; it meets with resistance and is likely, unless a general reorganization occurs, to be rejected. This resistance is a natural phenomenon; it is essential for the maintenance of individuality.[3]

All human behavior can be interpreted as motivated by the need for unity. Particular motives are simply expressions of this main motive. The goals that the individual pursues are simply means to this more general result. Since the need for unity, however, never appears directly as a goal the individual is generally unaware of it. He is aware only of the specific ends he is seeking. The general tendency to maintain unity is therefore an abstraction of the observer, a way of understanding the specific behavior of the person observed. Such an abstraction is necessary if a scientific explanation of the person's behavior is to be obtained. A mistake of the mechanistic psychologists is to assume that the external stimulus, quite apart from its subjective meaning for the self, is a determinant of behavior.

[3] Lecky, *op. cit.*, p. 82.

A mistake of the dynamic psychologists is to assume that there are particular goals fixed in the organism which determine behavior. The Freudians, for example, posited sexual satisfaction as the fixed goal, but they were forced to admit that other goals such as the "death instinct" could on occasion take primacy over it. Thus they wound up by positing a set of mutually opposed "instincts" or goals, without realizing that this situation is comprehensible in terms of some more general principle of balance and adjustment among the alleged instincts. The need for integration or unity is this general principle; it alone can explain the mutual adjustments of the more specific ends.

Freud's scheme suffers from a low order of generality. He mistook the specific for the general. Thus the fact of repression was interpreted by him as the ego's attempt to keep the sexual desires from offending the moral principles acquired from the society, or vice versa. But this whole process is meaningless apart from a tendency to maintain a system of subjective evaluation built around the conception of the self. Anything, not merely sexual desires, can be repressed. That which is repressed is whatever might threaten the unity of the self if it were admitted to awareness. Repression is one of the means by which the ego protects itself from disturbing elements and maintains its integration. In like manner the emotions can be interpreted in terms of self-integration.

> Love is the emotion subjectively experienced in reference to a person or object already assimilated and serving as a strong support to the idea of self. Grief is experienced when the personality must be reorganized due to the loss of its supports. Hatred and rage are impulses of rejection and destruction felt towards unassimilable objects. The emotion of horror appears when a situation arises suddenly which we are not prepared to assimilate, such as the sight of a ghastly accident.[4]

Thus the scientific analysis of the personality as a system of values, ends, and attitudes built around the individual's conception of himself and having as its first necessity the establishment and preservation of its unity, gives the maximum degree of generality. It therefore affords the best approach to understanding personality. All other ap-

[4] Lecky, *op. cit.*, p. 94.

proaches, in so far as they are correct in their observations, can be reinterpreted as special subsystems of the more general theory.[5]

The Sources of Personal Unity

Some major sources of unity in the self seem to be the following: (1) physical continuity, (2) memory, (3) ends, (4) norms, and (5) statuses. The meaning of these will become clear upon discussion.

PHYSICAL CONTINUITY

Not only does the body furnish the capacity for psychic complexity and the energy for ego satisfaction, but it also supplies the locus or reference point to which the personality is attached. If John Smith is said to be "a different person since he got religion," he is still nevertheless attached to the same body. In the eyes of others and of himself he is located there. When his body dies, he dies too. True, the memory of him lingers on and his "stature" as a person may even grow, but the memories refer to a time when he had a body.

The organism itself possesses a high degree of structural and functional unity. It would be strange if this unity did not account, in part at least, for the unity of the self. The constancy of organic needs provides a certain consistency, a thread around which the habits of action are woven. The capacities provide automatic limits on the varieties of behavior. The persistence of habits once established gives a cumulative character to personal development. The rhythm of the organism helps to determine the regular changes of mood.

Moreover, the traits of the body tend to be given a certain meaning by others and hence by the person himself. Sex, age, and race are utilized in the ascription of status. Beauty, height, girth, strength, health, and alertness affect social relationships and, through these, the personality. Most of these socially noticed traits either change slowly or not at all; they therefore afford a certain stability to the individual's conception of himself.

MEMORY

The selectivity and scope of the human memory contribute greatly to personal integration. Through memory, events are related

[5] For a lucid statement of the nature of scientific advancement as a matter of progressive generalization, see Alfred N. Whitehead. *An Introduction to Mathematics* (London: Oxford University Press, 1911), particularly pp. 81-83.

one to another in chronological order, and the past lives in the present. What is remembered depends primarily on its relevance to the self, with the result that memory helps to produce order out of the chaos of experience.

Certain principles of memory do not vary much in different cultures. The curves for learning and forgetting, the mechanisms of primacy, recency, intensity, etc. are fairly uniform. But the content of memory is mainly social. We remember those things that are important in the social context and forget those that are unimportant. We generally remember what we are supposed to remember and forget what we are supposed to forget; we remember things that are favorable to the self and forget those that are unfavorable (with notable exceptions, of course). In many cases the act of forgetting is the result of a deliberate effort by the self; such suppression does not mean that the forgotten event ceases to affect the personality, but rather that the ego is attempting to maintain its integration in the face of disturbing elements. Both remembrance and forgetfulness serve to protect the self in its most vital aspect, the conception of its relative standing with reference to normative standards.

Events are easier to remember when they contain familiar elements. A sentence with only one new word is easier to remember, other things equal, than one with three new words. Bartlett recounts the results of a visit to England by a Swazi chief and his followers from South Africa. When asked what they remembered best among their English impressions, they recalled most vividly the London policeman regulating traffic with uplifted hand. The reason was that the Swazi greet their fellows in a somewhat similar manner, and the visitors were impressed by such an effective use of this gesture in a foreign country. Being one of the few things that fitted into the Swazi social framework, it was remembered.[6]

The social relevance of memory is easy to demonstrate. The Swazi, for example, remembered exceedingly well the characteristics of their cattle, presumably because of the importance of cattle in their lives, but their retentiveness in other regards was below that of white men. "Even the manner of remembering may be socially determined to a considerable degree. Bartlett reports that when he talked to a Zulu about the former military exploits of his people, the Zulu lived

[6] Otto Klineberg, *Social Psychology* (New York: Holt, 1940), p. 217, citing F. C. Bartlett, *Remembering* (Cambridge: Cambridge University Press, 1932).

through his memories with the greatest vividness and emotional excitement. A Swazi would tell about similar incidents in a stolid and unmoved manner. It was not a matter of differences in temperament, since the Swazi also could be aroused to violent interest by other questions, particularly those dealing with cattle, women, marriage, and children." [7]

It is through selective memory and forgetfulness that the ego organizes its experience and builds a conception of itself through time. Such selectivity helps to keep habit formation from being a purely mechanical process. The past does not determine the present automatically but only as sifted through and assimilated by the subjective mind.

THE HIERARCHY OF ENDS

The individual's conception of himself refers not only to the past but also to the future. Regarding certain ends as valuable, he strives to realize them. His striving is socially determined in at least two ways. First, the ends themselves are acquired from others. (Organic needs play a part, but the specific character of the ends is socially defined—e.g. one does not eat whatever would be nourishing but only what is customary.) Second and more important for us at the moment, the integration of the ends is also derived from the social milieu. We have seen that each person possesses a multiplicity of goals but only scarce means, and that consequently he has to allocate his scant resources according to the relative desirability of the various goals. How does he come to feel that some goals are more desirable than others? How and why does he acquire his hierarchy of ends?

If a society's survival requires that certain ultimate values be held in common, each individual must place these shared values at the top of his own private scale, at least in so far as he judges the behavior of others. This does not mean that the ends he seeks for himself will necessarily conform to these values but simply that he will judge others, and in return will be judged, according to the common values. Any competitive end he may pursue must therefore be limited by the more ultimate or coöperative goals of the group as a whole. His conception of himself is built from other peoples' conception of the ends which he in his status and in his situation

[7] Bartlett, *op. cit.*, p. 241.

should pursue. His hierarchy of ends is therefore individualized yet subordinated to the common ultimate values.

To say that the person's various ends should be compatible is to state an impossible ideal. Different ends are in the nature of the case incompatible, since their attainment requires the utilization of scarce means (time and energy). What is required for personal unity is an *organization* of the ends in such manner that the degree of preference between any two is felt distinctly. Necessarily this subordination of one end to another must have an upper point (the ultimate values) which is like the tip of a pyramid, and a lower or bottom layer (the purely instrumental ends) which is like the base of a pyramid. In any case a scale of evaluation and therefore a basis of choice must be present if there is to be any psychic integration.

An indication of personality disorganization is chronic inability to make a decision, because such a condition shows there is no orderly relationship between the ends (the Dr. Jekyll and Mr. Hyde, or split personality, type of adjustment). If ends are systematically arranged in a hierarchy, the claims of each and every one are recognized rather than ignored and a choice becomes possible.

Subordination of one end to another does not mean that the subordinate end has no claim in its own right but simply that the claims of the different ends are not all equal. It is impossible for a human being to treat all ends except one as if they had no claim of their own. The various ends are connected with different needs and functions that cannot be ignored if life is to go on. The necessity of each one depends on the particular situation, so that the hierarchy of ends reflects in a sense the total balance of situations in which the individual normally finds himself. Also there are different avenues to the realization of any given end. Assuming, for example, that the individual's goal is to have children, this goal may be satisfied in any of several ways—by adoption, kidnapping, artificial insemination, adultery, or married intercourse. Which method is chosen depends not on the goal itself but on the demands of other goals involved in the situation. In our culture the desire to appear respectable makes adultery and kidnapping unsatisfactory as a means of acquiring a child; and our emphasis on biological paternity makes adoption rather unsatisfactory. Thus in every phase of life we find that other ends limit the means that can be used in the pursuit of any particular end. The person's value system is therefore a network of sovereign but mutually dependent goals. He must know how to give each goal its due, which means that he must have a scale of preference; and his scale of preference comes from and is constantly modified by social interaction. In short, not only does he get his values and ends from others but also his preferences or *scale* of values and ends as well.

This acquisition of a value scale, however, is not mechanical. Other persons regard the individual's actions from the point of view of their own values, not from the point of view of his. Thus a man may act in such a way as to bring success to himself. He does this by doing something that others consider worthwhile because it helps to satisfy their ends. They are not interested in his success; in fact they may be envious of it, but they are interested in what he does. From their standpoint the success may be accorded as a grudging reward, but from his standpoint it is regarded as the achievement of a major goal.

As seen by an observer the effort of the individual is always to achieve integration—an integration built around the conception of the self as derived from others. But the actor seldom, if ever, regards himself as striving for integration as such. He is merely striving for certain ends, of which the most general is the good opinion of others or conformity to the standards of the generalized other. The integration comes from the largely unconscious balancing of the various ends. The preference system is a subjective thing. In a sense it is worked out by each individual himself. To aid him in working it out, however, he has (1) models in those around him, especially those with whom he identifies himself; (2) cultural patterns of preference; and (3) the fact of social compulsion. What compulsion does, of course, is to penalize or reward behavior in terms of the individual's own goals. If stealing appears to the actor to be a satisfactory means of acquiring property, the society can make it an unsatisfactory means by taking away legitimate or illegitimate property already acquired or by taking away the thief's liberty. Precisely because his fellows make so many demands on him, precisely because his organism is constantly calling for gratification, precisely because his situations are so many and so different, the individual is hard put to it to achieve a working integration of his ends. His integration cannot be only within himself but must also be between himself and others, because others are instrumental to the realization of his own ends.

NORMATIVE INTEGRATION

The moral imperatives appear to the individual either as desirable ends in themselves or as necessary obstacles to the attainment of other ends. In the first case the person must reconcile the moral goals with his other goals in order to give each kind of end some degree of attainment. In the second case he must observe or appear to observe the moral code sufficiently to prevent retaliation by others from blocking his realization of his private ends. No individual adopts exclusively the one attitude or the other. All of us are normatively motivated to a great extent, but all of us are also sceptically opportunistic in many regards. Neither attitude, of course, leads to complete observance of the social norms nor to their complete nonobservance. No matter how morally inclined a person is, he still finds it necessary to provide some outlet for nonmoral desires. Some of the greatest sinners have been at the same time the greatest believers. If temptation were not inherent in the situation there would be no sense to the rule. On the other hand, no matter how morally sceptical a person may be, he still derives his conception of himself from others and therefore has some convictions concerning what he ought and ought not to do. Scepticism, indeed, is usually superficial. The individual needs, and indeed seeks, deep convictions because these give him a basis for constructing his picture of himself. Yet he also needs a certain amount of scepticism, because no system of norms is entirely consistent with itself or entirely adequate for all emergencies; nor is it sufficiently tolerant of the individual's nonmoral ends. The norms have evolved through millennia of imperfect obedience and consequently are so adapted as to compensate for the tendency toward nonconformity. A society in which everyone suddenly conformed strictly to the norms would not only be utterly static and incapable of adjusting itself to changing circumstances, but it would make impossible demands on the individuals composing it. The norms are formulated in such a way as to give a certain stress or pull that would create incompatibilities and distortions if carried out to the letter. The situation is like the representation of objects in two-dimensional space, where certain distortions must be practiced on the canvas in order to achieve a true effect. Certain distortions must be present in the normative system in order to achieve functionally adequate behavior from the members. For example the norms place great emphasis upon the necessity of work, relatively little on the necessity of play—evidently because work, by definition, is irksome. Similarly, they encourage the rearing of children but do not particularly encourage, and sometimes actively discourage, sexual intercourse—on the assumption, presumably, that the latter will be indulged in anyway.

The particular system of norms transmitted to the individual occupying a given set of positions is therefore only an element in his personality, but it is an important element. He must somehow assimilate the moral imperatives into his total structure of ends and behavior patterns. He must avoid both the error of compulsive conformity (which would cause the other aspects of his personality to atrophy) and the error of compulsive violation (which would cause his relations with others to degenerate). He avoids these dangers primarily by keeping in mind the principles or general goals behind the specific normative rules; by correctly conceiving himself and his situation in the eyes of others so far as observance of the rules is concerned; and by bringing all the elements of his personality—his goals, behavior, positions, and knowledge—into one central picture of himself.

POSITIONS AND ROLES

It has often been noted that one's personality changes with the social position. A man regarded as meek and timid often turns out, when placed in a position of authority, to be aggressive and decisive. A man who becomes a dean in a university has not had a dean's personality all his life; he acquires it with the office. A girl who becomes a wife often changes her behavior and her attitudes with surprising rapidity. The same is equally true of the delinquent and the criminal.

If a change in a particular position can have such palpable effect, then the individual's total system of positions must play a great part in determining his personality. In fact, we may view the personality as a product of all the positions one occupies. From a sheer knowledge of the statuses and offices, without ever having seen the flesh-and-blood incumbent, one could construct the positional personality. This would not be the complete personality because the latter is a function of other factors as well, but it would form an important aspect of the personality.

It is easy to see why this should be. A status or an office is defined precisely by the expectations of others in a given situation. It fixes and organizes the expectations with respect to certain obligations and therefore represents the exact point at which social organization and individual behavior join together.

Directed toward the particular individual are expectations that are not directed toward every individual in the society, but only towards those like himself who occupy the same position. The position locates him in the total social context. Furthermore, since he occupies not one but several positions, and since few persons in the society occupy identically the same combination of positions, his total positional system gives him an individual identity; it specifies his unique, individual integration of societal elements. In this way he is able to build up a conception of himself in an organized fashion without being simply a replica of every other member of the society. The sociological determination of personality, therefore, does not imply a lack of individuality.

As a source of personal integration the system of positions is of course extremely important. In general a social system is so arranged that an individual does not occupy positions making incongruous demands on him. To be sure, it gives the same individual various competing positions in the sense that his time and energy cannot be given to any one of them as fully as its demands seem to require. Our culture in particular forces the individual to strain and extend himself to a maximum. Thus a man's occupational advancement often requires an amount of work that inevitably takes time away from his family; his duty to his country as a soldier often interferes with his occupational advancement; his love affairs interfere with his education; etc. But competing statuses are different from incompatible ones. Statuses may be incompatible because the duties are opposite. Thus a Protestant minister could hardly be the proprietor of a burlesque show. In one role he would be expected to defend the mores, in the other to give relief from them; and it is hardly credible that he could be equally sincere in both capacities. Other statuses are incompatible because, by social definition, they cannot be occupied by the same person at the same time. This is particularly true of positions that stand to each other in a relation of subordination and superordination. Thus an army officer cannot be at the same time a private, a king a commoner, or a pariah a Brahmin. Of course, the same person may be subordinate in one context and superior in another, but usually with different persons. One is a parent of one's own offspring but a child of one's parents; a scientist is an expert in his own field but a layman in another; a captain is superior to the sergeant but inferior to the general.

The individual exhibits great flexibility in adapting himself to different demands in different statuses, but there is a limit to which he can go in this direction. The social system usually helps him by virtue of its tendency to give some consistency to the statuses that one individual may occupy simultaneously. It also gives consistency and an orderly development to statuses that the same individual may occupy sequentially. In this way the person finds his psychic integration ready-made, at least in part. His effort is expended on simply living up to the expectations rather than choosing which expectations he shall want to live up to. The more his status is ascribed rather than achieved, the easier is his task.

Individual Differences

Social scientists (anthropologists and sociologists in particular) have often been accused by psychologists of overlooking individual differences. This is because the focus of the social scientist is on the social structure as a system rather than on the person as a system. If, however, as is usually the case, the psychologist thinks of "personality" as the concrete individual his notion of "individual differences" is likely to be heavily biological. The social scientist is interested in biological differences between individuals only in so far as they are somehow involved in social organization—as in the case of status ascription on the basis of sex, age, etc. But the main fact is that persons differ from one another not only because of biological variation but also because of sociological variation. The first great source of individual variation is cultural difference. One individual may differ from another because he has a different culture; it is largely for this reason, for example, that a Chinese is different from a European. Each culture tends to give a characteristic stamp to the personality of the people who share it; this stamp will differ from one culture to another.[8] Within a single culture, however, it will be found

[8] Abram Kardiner and Ralph Linton, *The Individual and His Society* (New York: Columbia, 1939), especially Chap. 4.

that individuals differ from one another, not primarily because of their organic differences but because of their differences of status. They differ as to occupation, family relationship, class, education, etc. No two individuals have exactly the same combination of social positions and social experience. For this reason one of the main contributions of the social scientists is a description and explanation of individual differences. Without a knowledge of the social system and of the places of individuals within this system, the psychologist cannot explain the major differences between one individual and another. His explanatory principles must come from social science on the one hand and from biology on the other.[9] This is to say that the psychologist himself has relatively little to contribute on the subject, except certain techniques of measurement and description.

Suppose that we stood on a corner in New York City and interviewed at random a hundred people. How would we explain the personality differences between them? Let the first one be a recently arrived Japanese. He would be different in countless respects from an American simply because he grew up in another culture and in another kind of social system. Some of the differences would be fundamental. The manner in which he had been socialized, the particular sentiments and attitudes he had acquired, the kind of family and class organization he had become accustomed to—these would have given him a peculiar kind of character resembling in a general way the character of all other Japanese.[10] It is in this sense that we can speak of "national character," being careful always to avoid any racialistic implication or any assumption that there is no further variation.

Let the next two persons be a native Negro and a native white man. Reared in the same culture they would have a great deal in

[9] The assumption that there is a special branch of psychology devoted to the study of "individual differences" is a strange one. Presumably any science that deals with human beings at all, from genetics to sociology, is devoted to such study. If one attempts to cover the whole subject of how individuals differ from one another, one winds up in a complete and hopeless encyclopedism. This is illustrated, for example, by Frank S. Freeman, *Individual Differences* (New York: Holt, 1934). The book sets itself no problem at all but presumably represents a treatise on individual differences in general. As such it is interesting for what it leaves out rather than for what it includes. It contains no treatment of cultural, class, and occupational differences, but instead devotes almost its entire attention to differences of intelligence. On this subject it is an excellent book, but why assume that it is devoted to such a broad and endless topic as "individual differences"?

[10] Ruth Benedict, *The Chrysanthemum and the Sword* (New York: Houghton Mifflin, 1946), Chaps. 3, 5-12.

common; but unless we kept the Japanese in mind as a contrast, we would tend to forget their common traits in our fascination with their differences. The Negro would inevitably reveal, either in exaggerated protest or in exaggerated humility, his conception of himself as a member of a lower caste. The white man would hardly be conscious of his own white caste status at all except in so far as he thought about his behavior toward Negroes. This freedom would give him an unreflecting security and a degree of self-confidence that the Negro could not enjoy with reference to race status. On other counts, of course, the degree of self-confidence might be reversed.

Suppose that the next two persons were a research physicist and a rural politician. Here the habits of mind engendered by the practice of two diverse occupations, by different kinds and degrees of training, by opposite kinds of daily routine, and by divergent forms of contact with others, would have a powerful effect on the whole personality and would make the two men unmistakably different. Yet on the basis of other social influences on personality they might be somewhat alike. It does not follow that *two* research physicists or *two* rural politicians would be exactly alike.

Suppose next that we found two persons, one of whom had been reared as an only child by a rich, indulgent, dominating, and overprotective mother, whereas the other had been reared in a large family by parents who were frugal, efficient, and well-balanced. Certainly there would be a difference of personality organization between these two. One of them might well exhibit a shut-in type of personality with a history of neurotic or psychotic behavior, while the other might be open and sociably inclined with no history of mental aberration whatsoever.

In this way we could go through the hundred persons, finding significant personality differences between each pair. To a surprising degree these differences would be due to differences of culture, status, occupation, training, or other factors in the social history of the individuals. Also, whereas we have discussed only one major source of difference in each pair, it is quite obvious that many different kinds of difference may be in operation at once. The Negro might be the research chemist, the white man the rural politician; the Negro might also be the child of an overprotective mother and the white man the child of well-balanced parents. The complete personality of any one of the hundred persons, therefore, even on its social side alone, would be a product of a large number of factors. No two persons in the entire hundred would be completely alike. This is why the description of individual peculiarities in a completely concrete sense would be a never-ending encyclopedic task. Scientifically we inevitably must deal in abstractions to some extent. Our interest in differences and similarities must be limited to certain aspects; it cannot embrace everything. It is the psychiatrist trying to restore the mental balance of a particular person, who must take account of the greatest number of factors; but even he must draw upon principles established by abstract analysis and statistical verification.

Conclusion

The self or ego can be regarded as a psychic system, the parts of which are functionally related to one another and to the system as a whole. It is a subjective system, involving values, ends, sentiments, and beliefs. Any theory of personality integration that tries to ignore the subjective aspect will prove a failure. The most general and universal motive, the motive behind all others, is the necessity of maintaining the unity of the system. Unless the individual can somehow fit his mental life together, he cannot maintain the continuity and efficiency necessary for ordered existence. The thread around which the parts are integrated is the conception of the self, which is derived from and maintained in a social context. Aiding him in attaining unity are the continuity of his organism, the selectivity of his memory, and the unity of the social organization from which his ends, norms, and statuses come. In this way and with these sources he builds up a personality, or character, that is unique in its entirety but is similar to others in its parts.

One individual differs from another in his degree of integration. He also differs, quite apart from integration, in the kind of traits that are incorporated into his psychic system. In both cases the difference is to a great extent determined by the social context and social experience in which he has been reared and to which he must continue to respond. For this reason the study of social organization and interaction is a necessary adjunct to the understanding of personality. The unity and character of the psychic system are dependent upon, but not identical with, the unity and character of the social system.

References

Gregory Bateson and Margaret Mead, *The Balinese Character* (New York: New York Academy of Science, 1942).

Interesting study of the relation between personality and culture through the medium of pictorial representation.

Charles H. Cooley, *Human Nature and the Social Order* (New York: Scribner's, 1902), Chaps. 5 and 6 on "The Social Self, the Meaning and Various Phases of 'I'"; Chap. 1, "Society and the Individual"; Chap. 10, "The Social Aspect of Conscience."

A sociological classic, still readable.

John Dewey, *Human Nature and Conduct* (New York: Modern Library, 1922).

A philosopher's interpretation of individual conduct in terms of habits acquired in a social milieu.

Ellis Freeman, *Social Psychology* (New York: Holt, 1936).

Originally written as a treatise on values this book was published as a text. Chap. 3 deals with individual experience as a function of the organism and the stimulus and with the difference between physical and mental levels; Chap. 4 with the normal individual's construction of his universe. Part 2, "Individual and Cultural Determination of Values"; Part 3, "The Psychology of Some Fundamental Social Values."

Karen Horney, *The Neurotic Personality of Our Time* (New York: Norton, 1937).

The integration of the self tends to become a problem only when it is absent. Consequently the literature relevant to the present chapter is scanty except as it deals with neurosis, psychosis, etc. Horney's book is a good example of the new tendency in psychoanalysis to take more account of social factors in personality disorders.

Everett C. Hughes, "Personality Types and the Division of Labor," *American Journal of Sociology*, Vol. 33 (1928), pp. 754-768.

Still one of the more suggestive articles on personality in relation to competition for occupational positions.

Clyde Kluckhohn and Henry A. Murray, *Personality in Nature, Society, and Culture* (New York: Knopf, 1948).

A well chosen collection of readings. Attempts to cover all the various determinants of personality but devotes most of its space to social determinants.

Clyde Kluckhohn and O. H. Mowrer, " 'Culture and Personality': A Conceptual Scheme," *American Anthropologist,* Vol. 46 (Jan.-March 1944), pp. 1-29.

A good statement of the theoretical problems involved in personality study. Maintains that no aspect of personality can be studied adequately without a conceptual framework that explicitly *recognizes the range of determinants and the variability of the components of personality.*

Prescott Lecky, *Self-Consistency: A Theory of Personality* (New York: Island Press, 1945).

An excellent and stimulating book. Published posthumously, it is one of the few books that focuses directly and cogently on the problem of the present chapter.

Henry A. Murray, *Explorations in Personality* (New York: Oxford University Press, 1938), Chap. 2, "Proposals for a Theory of Personality."

Technical and hard to read, but it wrestles with some of the major problems in conceptualizing and studying what is called personality by scientific techniques.

Leo W. Simmons, *Sun Chief: The Autobiography of a Hopi Indian* (New Haven: Yale University Press, 1942).

One of the few full life histories of an individual in contact with two cultures. The account is socially and culturally oriented, although the interpretation in terms of personality development is still incomplete.

CHAPTER X

PERSONALITY DISORGANIZATION

IF personality integration is in part a function of social factors, then so is personality *dis*integration. True, the organism is in both cases a necessary condition, but the variables or determinants often lie in the socio-cultural sphere. Just as a person may be physically sick without the cause lying in his psychic make-up (e.g. malaria), so he may be mentally ill without the cause lying in any physical malady (e.g. hysteria). Of course, physical illness may affect one's socio-psychic adjustment (as when the malarial sufferer grows inefficient, loses his job, and becomes depressed), and mental illness may affect one's physical equilibrium (as when acute anxiety produces diarrhea); but in neither case should the result be confused with the cause.

Fruitful insight into the dynamics of human mentality comes from the study of psychic disorders, because in such disorders the requirements of the ordinary personality are, by their absence, made conspicuous. Our present interest attaches, however, only to the social aspects and hence to the social causes of mental disorder. In trying to assess these we shall pursue the following three lines of reasoning: First, the definition of mental disorder is stated in social terms; second, the functioning of disordered minds refers to and in many cases arises out of social experience; and third, the incidence of certain mental disorders indicates socio-cultural causation.

The Concept of Mental Disorder

Most people believe they can tell when a person is insane or neurotic, but they seldom can give a clear definition of mental disorder. Their reactions to a deranged person are spontaneous, not based on logical classification but on a quick response to the individual's behavior in the social situation. Their definition is therefore an implicit one, and in order to understand it we must analyze not only the mental processes of the deranged person but also the mental process of the people who judge him.

In the last analysis the underlying criterion of mental derangement, the substance of every definition, is that of abnormality. But in what sense is "abnormality" to be taken? Does it refer to actions different from the statistical average? Decidedly not. There are, for example, very few diamond cutters in our society, far fewer than there are schizophrenics or paranoiacs; and yet we do not label the diamond cutters as insane and the schizophrenics as sane. A diamond cutter might be regarded as insane if his behavior differed from that of other diamond cutters—if, for instance, he tried to cut diamonds with his teeth or with a shotgun. This is closer to the truth because it suggests that people judge normality and abnormality with reference to a position and a social situation, not simply with reference to the population at large. But we must be careful. A diamond cutter who invents an improved cutting technique may thus deviate from the usual practice of those in his trade, but instead of being called crazy he is likely to be called rational and clever. It is not abnormality in a statistical sense that constitutes mental disorder, even when the deviation is with reference to a given status. Neither the genius nor the feebleminded person is ipso facto insane, any more than the king, the explorer, or the oboe player.

Does abnormality then refer to deviation, not from the statistically average but from the normatively expected? If so we are all mentally disordered, because each of us fails to observe the behavior ideally expected of us. Criminals are not regarded as necessarily insane; in fact, by the legal definition of crime no criminal could be insane at the time he committed his crime. Furthermore, many crimes are committed in the name of the right and the good regardless of the fact that they violate the law. For centuries the English persecuted dissenters of all types, yet the "crimes" of these worshipers were religious and hence highly normative in their motivation. We can only conclude that the mere fact of deviation from a normative rule is not itself the criterion ordinarily used in defining mental disorder.

Can the element of abnormality be dispensed with altogether? Can it be said, for example, that mental disorder consists of holding erroneous beliefs? Obviously not, because the concept of delusion so prominent in cases of derangement "refers not simply to a false belief, but to a false belief which a reasonable person would not hold. There are a great many false beliefs held by groups of normal persons" who have not had the opportunity to learn better but who are following traditional and religious authority.[1] A false belief that is understandable in the culture and in the situation is not a delusion in the psychiatric sense.

What really sets the mentally deranged apart as a class is their unpredictability. It has been previously noted that social life rests upon the mutual predictability of one another's behavior. By this is not meant predictability in the crude sense of merely an accurate statement of what the organism as a physical object will do next, but in the sense that the motives are understood by one's fellows and the resulting actions known in advance. Expectation in this refined sense rests upon communication, for it is through symbolic contact that people share what is in one another's minds. Even though a person does not conform to the obligatory norms, we expect him at least to be influenced by a knowledge of them. We expect him to realize, emotionally as well as intellectually, that certain norms apply to him in his situation. Above all we expect him to admit the norms as premises to his thinking, as ends, means, and conditions of action. If he does not, his behavior tends to become unpredictable (in the refined sense), communication breaks down, and we judge him to be mentally off balance. The clearest road to being considered insane, therefore, is to differ so systematically and persistently from the normative assumptions and mental habits of others that they cannot understand the motivation and hence do not know what to expect. In such circumstances communication becomes impossible. It is not so much deviation as an inability to explain satisfactorily the deviation to others (in terms that fit their assumptions) that leads to the judgment of mental disorder. The deranged person is not capable of being influenced by the communications of others; he is not "reasonable."

A person's conduct may be unpredictable because his culture or his situation is unknown to us. "Many actions of natives in preliterate societies, normal in their own cultures, would be regarded as evi-

[1] Robert E. L. Faris and H. Warren Dunham, *Mental Disorders in Urban Areas* (Chicago: University of Chicago Press, 1939), p. 156.

dence of insanity in our society. Actions which are normal in one culture are abnormal in others. This generalization is even true of such variations in culture as may be seen within one large nation. For example, certain types of religious fanaticism are normal in parts of the rural sections of Southern states, while the same behavior may be the occasion for commitment to a hospital in a Northern city. . . . Such eccentric behavior as attempting to push a peanut along a sidewalk with the nose may appear insane, until it is discovered that the performer is a college student, being hazed or the loser of an election bet." [2] Unpredictability becomes symptomatic of mental disorder, then, when it occurs in spite of a knowledge of the person's culture and his social situation and when the grounds of the behavior cannot be satisfactorily communicated to the ordinary persons within the group.

If a person violates one norm—e.g. by committing a crime—there is no indication that he is mentally unbalanced. It may be that his reasons are understandable to others even though others would have behaved differently in the same situation. Only if the crime is such that the motive remains incomprehensible will the sanity of the criminal be questioned. If an individual kills his best friend because he thinks the friend is trying to poison him (when in fact the friend was not in the least hostile) or if he kills people indiscriminately for no apparent reason, we suspect a motive hidden to himself and therefore not communicable. The psychiatrist may be able to understand his motivation, but not the layman.

For ordinary people, therefore, the class "crazy persons" is a residual class. Into it are put all those individuals whose conduct, in terms of motives, is quite unpredictable. In general the unpredictability derives from either a failure to "see" things as they are ordinarily seen in the group or a failure to communicate the reasoning process by which what is seen is connected with the results that emerge in behavior. If the individual believes that he is a famous personage when he is in fact an ordinary citizen, his actions may follow logically from this assumption and he may be able to communicate his motives based on the assumption; but if no amount of explanation by other parties will alter his conception of his own identity, if he builds up additional false beliefs and behavioral pe-

[2] Faris and Dunham, *op. cit.*, pp. 155-156.

culiarities to protect his conception, then he is regarded as mad. There is a point when communication no longer penetrates to his mind; he thus remains socially isolated in an important respect. In other cases practically no communication is possible at all, so that it is impossible to determine what the assumptions are, the individual being incoherent and unresponsive.

This peculiarity of the conception of mental disorder—namely that it is a residual category embracing all cases in which there is an extreme breakdown of communicative understanding—explains two widely known facts. First, the study of the causes of mental disorder in so far as these are socio-psychic rather than physiological is greatly handicapped by the difficulties of communication. The psychiatrist must communicate with the patient in order to understand the disorder, and yet, because of the disorder, he can hardly communicate with him. The techniques of the psychiatrist are designed to overcome this handicap but as yet they are meagre, embracing such things as hypnosis, narcosis, free association, suggestion, dream analysis, winning of affection, and experimental stimulation of interpretative responses (by playing meaningless records, showing meaningless ink blots, or noting the blocking or hypertension produced by an assortment of words). The second well-known fact is the aura of horror which surrounds the idea of insanity. Scarcely anything is more terrible to the ordinary person, nurtured and created as he is by a social milieu, than the spectacle of complete unpredictability based on inability to communicate. It reveals to the observer a human organism which at the same time is not human and suggests to him a bottomless pit of mysterious depth, a pit in which the realities by which he lives are reduced to shadows, strange parodies. His assurance, his security, his sense of his own reality are menaced by this anomalous spectacle.

The neurotic person, as opposed to the psychotic, is one whose motivational system is only partly removed from the comprehension of his fellows and whose unpredictability is therefore limited. For this reason more advance has been made in the study (on the psychosocial level) of neurosis than in the study of psychosis. In fact, as psychosocial techniques are worked out for the treatment of psychotic patients they are derived in the main from the easier work with more accessible neurotics.

The Dynamics of Mental Disorder

Though helpful, it is not enough to know the criterion by which mentally disordered persons are set apart. A further step is to examine the content of the disordered mind, the dynamic processes by which social reality is distorted and strange responses produced. These processes have been described at great length and under many names in the psychiatric literature dealing with neuroses and psychoses. In general the discussions of them have been more descriptive than analytical, and frequently the interpretations (as in the early stages of Freudian psychoanalysis) have been biological in character. In the present context we shall describe briefly some of the major maladjustment processes, but our main emphasis will be on showing how these processes arise from and relate to the socio-cultural system of which the individual is a part.

CONFLICT

In all scientific theories of mental disorder the notion of psychic conflict is fundamental, but the nature and source of the conflict are not always understood. All forms of mental conflict, we believe, can be stated in terms of the means-end schema, the logical possibilities of which are as follows:

(1) *Ends may be incompatible because they are opposite in character.* A man who wishes to be both a person of learned dignity and a popular clown is pursuing two mutually opposed ends. A soldier who wishes to escape from the dangers of battle and at the same time appear brave to his fellows is doing the same. In such cases one or the other end must be suppressed; the ego must create a hierarchy rather than an equality of antithetical ends. If the ends are strongly held, however, the effort to control one or the other may fail, giving rise to neurotic or psychotic symptoms.

(2) *Different ends may compete for scarce means.* The woman who loves her husband and children and at the same time loves her career will find that each makes demands on a scarce commodity, her time and energy. She must be prepared either to sacrifice one in favor of the other or to accept an incomplete fulfillment of both. If she can establish no such modification, then she allows the con-

flict to continue and to that extent becomes a disorganized person. As previously mentioned, all ends are competitive, but genuine conflict arises only when there is no distributive order, no hierarchy of ends in the individual's mind. As a yardstick in distributing his scarce means among his various ends, the individual has his feeling of preference. What leads him to prefer some ends against others is the strength of his organic urges on the one hand and the strength of his socially acquired desires on the other. Striving for any end presumably requires organic tension and satisfaction of the end implies release of the tension. But tensions having an organic origin, though their expression is socially learned, are different from those having a social origin, because attainment of the end usually causes temporary satiation and the demotion of that end to a lower status for the time being. Thus sexual gratification causes a temporary lull in sexual desire, so that the individual can turn his attention to other matters. Tensions having a social origin often lack any complete release. The rivalry for prestige and esteem, for example, is never-ending. Particular subgoals may be attained, with some relief of tension; but always there is the realization that one's own prestige and esteem are eclipsed by others. Moreover, it is the socially acquired tensions that take precedence over the organically stimulated ones, involving some control and suppression of the latter. The socially acquired goals thus create tension in a double sense—in their own right and by virtue of the tension created by suppressing and limiting the organic strivings. The social milieu is so organized as to make maximum use of the driving power of suppressed and controlled organic urges.

The organization of the individual's ends depends primarily on the social milieu in which he learns his ends. If there is no consistent hierarchy transmitted to him, he will have no means of adjusting the claims of the various ends, and conflict will result. Many psychiatrists believe that it is during the main period of socialization (during childhood) and in the main socializing groups (family, play group, and school) that the basis is laid for the personality disintegration subsequently manifested by neurotics and psychotics. Above all, inconsistent discipline by persons who themselves are disintegrated tends to produce mental cases. One investigator sums up the background of problem children as follows:

> There is no consistent adherence to any rules. The child may frequently indulge in unapproved or unapprovable behavior without any attempt at correction whatever. On the other hand, he may frequently be punished for behavior that is insignificant or at other times approvable.
>
> The criteria for correction appear to reside in the emotional state of the adult rather than in the conduct of the child or any social implications of his behavior.
>
> The discipline for similar behavior may range from nothing at all to the most severe physical punishment, and punishment of any grade or severity may follow in quick succession punishment of any other grade.
>
> When punishment is inflicted, it tends to be oversevere.
>
> In other words, the disciplinary setup is totally erratic and inconsistent, lacks pattern and tends to be severe in contradistinction to strict.[3]

Not only does the child in such a setting have no solution to problems, but no one else has either. The child cannot form habits that will uniformly protect him from punishment or guarantee him a reward. He must approach each new situation with apprehension and must find any decision extremely difficult. He acquires no principles of preference whereby he may distribute his energy between the various ends which he has. By the time he becomes an adult he may easily go to pieces in face of problems which another person might easily solve.

(3) *Conflict may arise from too great a disparity between ends and means.* If the goal is strongly desired and yet is impossible of achievement, frustration necessarily results. Repeated frustration tends to produce a generalized lack of confidence in one's ability to achieve *any* end, and a generalized conception of oneself as less efficient and less worthy than others. The main goal, the approval of others, is contingent upon the accomplishment of a wide variety of subordinate ends. Repeated frustration therefore means a breakdown with reference to those standards by which one evaluates oneself. Fortunately, approval by others does not rest entirely upon a high

[3] L. F. Woolley, "The Effect of Erratic Discipline in Childhood on Emotional Tensions," *Psychiatric Quarterly*, XI (April, 1937), 237-252. Quoted by Roy M. Dorcus and G. Wilson Shaffer, *Textbook of Abnormal Psychology* (Baltimore: Williams & Wilkins Co., 1939, Second Edition), p. 334.

order of achievement but in many cases it rests on achievement higher than that which the person can attain. What is expected is also limited by the position one occupies, so that one does not ordinarily compare one's lack of achievement with that of everybody else in the society. An advantage of certainty as to one's position is that one then knows exactly what is expected and suffers no remorse for not doing what is not expected.

Conflict, as viewed in terms of the means-end schema, reduces in practice to two possibilities: the lack of a consistent and assured order of preference between an individual's various ends and the failure of achievement of cherished ends because the means are lacking. These are not mutually exclusive possibilities but rather they tend to reinforce each other. Karen Horney has pointed out that the neurotic person continually stands in his own way.[4] His lack of order in his ends makes it hard for him to achieve any particular end. The methods by which he escapes from the conflict of ends and from the sense of frustration make it still harder for him to accomplish anything.

Since the rights and duties connected with social positions are translatable into the means-end schema, the conflict so far described is at the same time a conflict in one's system of statuses and roles. Presumably the system of positions a given individual occupies should be integrated if his personality is to be integrated. Care must be exercised, however, to make sure that what is externally chaotic does not hide an internally well-organized personality. The occupant of a given status may exercise the prerequisites of that status without having adopted them in his emotional complex. Thus a minister may simply preach for a living; he may not believe everything he preaches, and if his behavior in another position is incompatible with the proper attitudes of a minister this may represent merely a lack of intergration of the external social organization, not a similar lack in his own personality. The divergence between external role and internal attitude is usually present to a slight extent. It is least disorganizing to the person when the divergence is tacitly accepted and practiced by the social group in general—the so-called institutionalized evasion of institutional prescriptions. Theoretically an indi-

[4] *The Neurotic Personality of Our Time* (New York: Norton, 1937), p. 25-26.

vidual might occupy all his positions as a disinterested incumbent, merely playing the called-for roles as means to purely private ends.

A society does not inquire too closely into private attitudes so long as the overt behavior is satisfactory. If the responses of a person are always satisfactory, it is assumed that his attitudes are also correct. Such a completely Machiavellian adjustment, however, is logically impossible, for the reason that to use one's position purely as a means, one must have an end. The source of this end can only be the socio-cultural system of which the person is a part. Thus at some point the individual takes the prescriptions of his society sincerely. He wants certain things that he has been taught to want in his position. Furthermore, the price of insincerity is eternal vigilance. To act a false role in even a substantial portion of one's behavior is exceedingly tedious. Of course there are conventionally false roles that are played by everybody and which become habitual, but these in the last analysis are merely part of the social expectations and imply a deeper sincerity underlying the apparent insincerity. The crucial case is the playing of a false role to gain private ends which, if known, the society would not sanction. Individuals may and do play particular roles in this way, but that they should play any great number of roles in such manner is inconceivable. The ends would often not seem to justify the tediousness of keeping up the deception. Furthermore, the constant deception itself is impossible to maintain, for the reason that our deliberate control over our behavior seldom extends to all phases of it. We give ourselves away in some all too eloquent detail and the deception is off. In addition the actual attainment of an unsanctioned end is hard to conceal. Once the deception is discovered, the sanctions visited on a person for insincerity are such as to make the risk of incurring them inadvisable. At bottom, then, there is a close relationship between the system of roles that the person plays and the private ends that he cherishes. If the one is not intergrated, neither is the other. The main danger of interpretation lies in taking too simple a view of social organization—of mistaking the avowed moral norm for the actual norm.

Though not all ends are normative in character, practically all of them are relevant to the norms. One of the greatest conflicts is between ends that are tabooed or for which nearly all convenient means are tabooed, and those which are normatively required. Even tabooed ends are social in origin and tabooed means are socially learned (in addition to being parts of the actual social structure). For an end to be tabooed implies that somehow, if it were not tabooed, it would be strong in its own right. The source of it must therefore be something else than the normative order. It may be learned, to be sure, but once learned it is strongly motivated in a way that a sheer obligatory end would not be. To explain this fact, we must assume that the source of the tabooed end is either an inherent organic urge built into the organism genetically or a relation of this particular end to the total system of ends. A good example of an end deriving its strength from the organic source is the attainment of sexual gratification. This end is permitted but only when certain means are utilized. Once a child has learned how to satisfy this urge by masturbation he is strongly motivated to use the means, even though it is illegitimate. Its illegitimacy conflicts with the contrary norm which has been thoroughly ingrained in him and has acquired its own power over the organism. Guilt feeling may consequently develop as a result of the conflict and produce a state of acute discomfort.

An example of the second source of strength behind a tabooed end is the feeling which a person may have towards his mother-in-law. Normatively, in our culture, a person is supposed to show respect for his mother-in-law. Yet she often has no great appeal in herself, and owing to her past authority over the mate is a constant obstacle to the attainment of desired ends. There easily develops, therefore, an attitude of antagonism toward the mother-in-law, a desire to get her out of the way somehow. Most readily available means to this end, however, are tabooed. One may not poison her, turn her out of the house, insult her, buy her off, or disregard her. One is often forced to put up with her. In such a case there is no innate urge to be rid of the mother-in-law, but looking at the total configuration of positions and roles, she is a person who almost in spite of herself stands in the way. In a perfectly organized society, of course, the position of the mother-in-law would be integrated with all other positions, so that the required attitudes would flow naturally from the attitudes implicitly embodied in an individual's relations with all other persons in his social universe. But no society is ever so well integrated. Always there are numerous ends that are socially determined but are nevertheless tabooed. The conflicts to which they give rise in the subjective mind of the actor are just as real and powerful as the conflicts created by tabooed organic wishes.

SUPPRESSION

The core of mental disorder being conflict, it remains to see what defenses the personality erects to protect itself against conflict.

An obvious solution is to suppress one of the conflictful elements. Such suppression removes from consciousness the end or the memory of an act. If the end or the memory is in conflict with another end—say, a moral norm—the suppression of it will allow one to retain the feeling of self-approval so essential to a satisfied existence. Admittedly, suppression is a normal accompaniment of everyday life. It is one of the necessary features of social control, for if we acted on every impulse or idea that came to us, if we gave expression to every conflicting inclination, we would be incapable of conforming to social expectations. Our mind exercises a perpetual censorship, so that few observers suspect and we ourselves scarcely realize how varied and bizarre are the things that pop into our heads. Through repression the personality selects its ends and its actions, achieves consistency and integration. Unless, however, there were a set of socially derived obligatory norms, there would be no necessity of suppression. What the psychoanalysts have called the "super-ego," that part of the personality which is authoritarian and moral, which makes the individual feel guilty when he has done something wrong, is the socio-cultural system of norms as internalized in the particular personality. Unless in addition there were impulses and acts which did not conform to the norms, there would again be no need of repression. The phenomenon of repression is therefore a normal manifestation of the kind of socio-cultural creatures that human beings are.

The difficulty, however, is that suppression is not a perfect instrument. If the repressed thoughts could be completely eliminated, the conflict would come to an end. But in many cases there is strong motivation behind the suppressed ideas. Banishing them from consciousness does not banish them from the mind, nor does it banish them from influencing behavior. The individual may reveal the continued presence of the material in dreams, slips of the tongue, groundless anxieties, exaggerated goodness or modesty, unwarranted aggressiveness, unreasonable censure, patent rationalization, or what not. He may actually perform the forbidden behavior in disguised form or with an elaborate but false excuse. If he performs the forbidden behavior despite disguises and excuses, he is likely to feel doubly guilty, with the necessity of still more complex defenses against the memory or the repetition of the act. The following case, that of a woman of thirty-five, illustrates the suppression of forbidden ideas by amnesia.

> The patient had experienced several periods of from a half hour to several hours in duration for which she retained no memory whatever. She would start to town, for example, then sometime later would suddenly come to herself at a distant point without any memory for the events that took place in the interval. . . . It was decided to hypnotize her. In twenty minutes under hypnosis sufficient material was recovered to reconstruct almost completely several of the amnesic episodes, all of which occurred in relation to a love fantasy with a man other than her husband. It was suggested during the hypnotic state that these memories would be retained following it. She was then awakened, and the entire production reviewed with her. At this time she recognized the need of forgetting these episodes and everything connected with them because the idea of infidelity to her husband, even in fantasy, was intolerable to her. In this case there have been no recurrences for several years.[5]

If instead of living in a West-European type of culture (in America) this woman had been reared in a Chukchee camp in Siberia, such a conflict could not have occurred, because among the Chukchee sexual relations with men other than the husband are considered right and proper.[6] The *content* of the conflict—the forces that are opposed—thus varies considerably from one culture to another. But the psychic mechanisms once conflict has been started are presumably universal, being connected with both the universal physiological structure and the universal sociological structure of the human species.

RATIONALIZATION

Probably the simplest way of giving expression to unacceptable desires and of trying to avoid guilt feelings is to think up a good reason (i.e. one sanctioned in the social group by a moral evaluation

[5] Dorcus and Shaffer, *op. cit.*, pp. 414-415.
[6] M. A. Czaplicka, *Aboriginal Siberia* (Oxford University Press, 1914), pp. 78-80.

higher than that which forbids the tabooed topic). Thus a student who ought to study for an examination but feels disinclined to do so may tell himself that he needs exercise because exercise is essential to his health, and health is more important than passing a particular examination. He may then go out and spend the afternoon playing golf, enjoying himself immensely, and not suffering any remorse until after he has written a poor examination paper the next day. Even then he may still hide from himself the fact that he could have taken his exercise *after* the examination rather than before, with equal benefit to his health.

As a device for preserving one's self-esteem such justification of one's disapproved wishes by allegedly good reasons is a normal and necessary aspect of behavior. The individual has to protect himself against guilt-feelings deeply imbedded in his unconscious self as well as against the repressed desires the expression of which gives rise to these guilt-feelings. Otherwise he runs the risk of becoming overrepressed—more of a strict conformist than actual opinion demands and at a disadvantage as compared with those who have internalized the norms less drastically.

But if the conflict is severe rationalization may gradually merge into something further removed from normality, such as projection or anxiety.

PROJECTION

It is but a step from simple rationalization to a special and more complex form of it—namely, shifting the blame for untoward thoughts or actions to something else than oneself. The mother may hide her inability to manage her child by claiming that his mischievous propensities were inherited from his father. In this way she puts the blame primarily on the child himself (which helps to satisfy her resentment toward the child) and secondarily on the father (which helps to satisfy her resentment towards him). In truth, however, she has done both of them a wrong about which, if she admitted it, she would feel guilty. Her suppressed guilt may lead her to assume that the child and husband are both resentful toward her, so that by a complicated process she has come to project her own hostility towards them into their minds as hostility towards her. It can be seen to what extent projection is a matter of the interplay of conceptions of the attitudes of others and how, by a cumulative process, it tends to remove a person from an accurate notion of the real situation.

For many reasons other persons are the means to our ends. Yet we are restricted in the extent to which we may use them simply as means. The baker has bread which the hungry might like, a man has affection which a woman might like, the politician has power which a citizen might like, etc. Always human beings are necessary instruments to the achievement of our desires; and they and the rules they enforce also stand in the way of such achievement. All of us therefore have occasion to resent certain persons and wish that we could do things we really cannot do. If such thoughts arise, they offend our sense of what is right. Consequently we suppress them and the hostility emerges in ways that we do not recognize. We may express the resentment by blaming them. Since this is doing them a wrong, we may expect that they shall retaliate. Such projection of our feelings into their minds may lay the basis for a paranoid reaction to others, and if carried far enough may eventuate in a full-blown psychosis. Hostility breeds hostility even when it is suppressed. "A person who wants to injure, cheat, deceive others has also a fear that they will do the same to him,"[7] because he knows that if they knew about these thoughts they would retaliate and because he knows that he stands in their way as well as their standing in his way. His guilt feelings not only force him to project onto others the hostile thoughts that he himself really feels, but they also punish him by making him fear the consequences of these thoughts in terms of what others will do to him. Dorcus and Shaffer[8] describe the typical development of paranoia in the following way:

> The real difficulty may begin when the individual blames or condemns himself for some act or idea which conflicts with his ideals, and consequently he may persecute himself because his self-respecting sentiment demands it. It is now only a step further to project this persecution onto others . . . Thus his repression of the unacceptable acts or ideas leaves him with a feeling of self-condemnation which he in turn projects on others whom he now considers to be persecuting him. The activities and statements of those about him are now interpreted in terms of his feeling. . . . as being directed toward him. He is constantly looking for hidden meanings . . . ,

[7] Horney, *op. cit.*, p. 71.
[8] *Op. cit.*, p. 304.

> and since his desire for condemnation and persecution is so strong he has little difficulty in finding them. Gradually he may come to believe that large organizations are attempting to ruin him and even those who claim to be his nearest friends are secretly planning his downfall. It may, however, occur to him that an individual who is given so much attention and is persecuted to such a degree must be a very important individual. [He] may develop delusions of grandeur. If he chances to come upon the name of some great individual it is not unlikely that the name will become associated with his delusional content, and since he misinterprets most things as having reference to him, he may gradually develop the belief that he is this great person.

So ubiquitous is projection that its presence is not abnormal, but only its extreme manifestations.

ANXIETY

Realizing that this fear of others based on an unconscious notion of retaliation is really one form of anxiety, let us discuss other anxiety states and symptoms.

The fact that ends always relate to the future but that the circumstances are never completely under control introduces uncertainty into human life. This, plus the fact that the self judges itself in terms of past successes and failures, creates perpetual apprehension of what may happen next. When the apprehension is normal—when, that is, it is what one is expected to show in the given situation—it goes under the ordinary name of fear. When, however, the object feared appears too trivial or too imaginary in the eyes of others, when the intensity of the fear is disproportionate to the meaning of the situation, it is called anxiety. Fear and anxiety undoubtedly are present in every case of mental disorder, but we have now in mind those cases where there is a conscious realization of an unfounded phobia or compulsion. Since in such cases the explanation does not lie in the ordinary motivational terms of the society, an examination of the hidden and distorted mental content must be made.

The apparent basis of anxiety may be an unfounded fear (phobia), a fixed idea (obsession), or an involuntary and oft repeated act (compulsion). In any case the object of the phobia, obsession, or compulsion is not what it seems to be. Instead it is merely a symbol or diversion of the real source of the anxiety, which at bottom involves a conflict. The real source, because in some way humiliating, has been repressed and the manifest object simply stands for it or serves as a symbolic defense against it. The individual may be completely aware of the futility of it and unable to explain it, yet he cannot help himself.

It should further be noted that anxiety accompanies an escape (by means of repression) from the conflict of ends. When the repressed material threatens to influence one's behavior, anxiety is set up. The specific object of anxiety cannot be consciously admitted because it has been suppressed. Therefore, the conscious object of anxiety must appear as something else, presumably something that entails less feeling of guilt. The common purpose in every case is the avoidance of guilt-induced anxiety. For example, the most frequent symptom of compulsion neurosis is the constant impulse to wash the hands. The memory of some past act or wish, such as masturbation, has been suppressed, but unconscious guilt feelings continue to create anxiety. Our hands may have been involved in the forbidden act or wish. Washing the hands is a perfectly permissible act, and in our culture the association of sin with dirt and salvation with cleanliness gives the act a symbolic efficacy in relieving the anxiety. The thing feared, the guilt, is inside one. It cannot be avoided by flight (although actual flight is sometimes adopted) but it may be helped by such symbolic, essentially magical, practices. If the practice succeeds in allaying the anxiety and keeping the distressing memories from consciousness, it may be pursued repeatedly, obsessively. The powerful drive behind the compulsion or obsession is provided by the tormenting anxiety. Intense anxiety is one of man's most excruciating emotions. "Patients who have gone through an intense fit of anxiety will tell you they would rather die than have a recurrence of that experience." [9] The helplessness of the sufferer contributes to the terror.

Anxiety also lies at the bottom of hysteria which in one sense is the most rational of the psychoneuroses. The symptom or malady becomes a means of escape from something that would otherwise have to be faced. Almost any symptom may thus be utilized, from functional blindness, paralysis, vomiting, amnesia, and deafness to epileptoid seizures and somnabulistic episodes. The escape cannot be consciously adopted, however, for then the individual would suffer

[9] Horney, *op. cit.*, p. 46.

from guilt feelings. It must be real for the actor himself as well as for others, and there seems little doubt that hysterics actually suffer the symptoms they manifest.

Dorcus and Shaffer [10] recount the case of a Negro girl who over a period of years had suffered from convulsive seizures. These seizures had gradually become worse and more frequent, and occurred "whenever she had an unpleasant duty to perform." She was soon completely cured of the symptom by the following method: "She was told that her condition was due to her nerves and was given a bottle of asafetida which was described as a powerful nerve tonic that would build up her nerves very rapidly. She was to take a teaspoonful of it three times a day for a week and should cease having any seizures within that time. . . . If any time she felt a seizure coming on, she should take another teaspoonful of the medicine. . . . If she failed to do this and a seizure did occur, it would then be necessary for her to take it three times a day for a week as in the beginning." This spectacular and unpleasant treatment so impressed the patient that her seizures stopped within three days, with no recurrence of the symptom.

Not all hysterias are remedied so easily, because the conflicts are deeper and one symptom, if cleared up, will be replaced by another. What is necessary is to establish communication with the patient, bring the source of the basic anxiety to consciousness, establish new attitudes and new social situations, and thus reorientate the system of ends in such manner that integration is achieved. This is not easy, but the case mentioned previously of the woman who suffered from amnesia illustrates that it can be done.

SUMMARY

Mental disorder, in so far as it is a result of forces on the psychosocial level, may always be analyzed as a conflict of ends in the sense of a failure to achieve a distributive hierarchy among the various ends and a failure or frustration in the pursuit of ends. This conflict is not, as has been so often maintained, a conflict between biological drives on the one hand and social norms on the other or between the individual and society. It is rather a conflict between ends, whatever their source. The societal norms would be powerless to influence conduct unless they became ends; and to the extent that

[10] *Op. cit.*, pp. 408-409.

they become ends, they carry behind them a quantum of organic energy. Organic drives would have no influence on action unless they too became ends, and as ends they are always channelized and given direction—always, in a very real sense, acquired. The ends that represent the internalization of obligatory norms (such as taboos) as well as the ends that represent the internalization of socially acquired competitive aims (such as ambition), become imbedded in the unconscious layers of the mind; and their frustration by other ends may create just as much tension, just as much anxiety, as the frustration of ends more directly connected with innately structured organic urges.

There are various normal ways by which individuals resolve their conflicts—usually by conscious deliberation, frank discussion with somebody else, rationalization, and repression. But if the conflict is strong the milder methods become inadequate. Repression is redoubled, only to have the conflict manifest itself again in indirect and crippling ways. In such cases rationalization, projection, and anxiety develop to such an extent that the individual's behavior gets farther and farther away from reality (i.e. farther away from the motivational assumptions and habits of his fellows). The more he departs from reality, the poorer is his adjustment and the greater the conflict and frustration of ends, until eventually a crisis develops which jolts him back into some reorganization of himself or pushes him into a full-fledged neurosis or psychosis.

Everything therefore depends upon the type of socialization which the individual received and the type of social situation in which he lives. The integration of ends is closely though not rigidly dependent upon the integration of statuses and roles and the consistency of norms which have been given the individual. He will meet current crises well or poorly according to the kind of personality he has developed from past interaction. Some of the psychosocial interpretations of specific types of abnormal symptoms may be erroneous, but the general theory of the dynamics of mental disorder seems established. This theory is plainly sociological, for it is only through communicative contact with others in his society that the person can acquire ends and can therefore experience conflict. It can therefore be said of mental disorder that its content is always, and its cause is often, social.

The Social Incidence of Mental Disorder

Consideration of the dynamics of neurosis and psychosis has led us naturally to the third topic of our present discussion—namely, the incidence of mental cases in relation to social organization. If personality disintegration is socially engendered, the amount of it will vary according to the type of society in which people live, the position which they occupy in the society, and the particular series of experiences through which they live. This is in fact the case. Both the amount and the kind of mental disorder vary as the type of social milieu varies.

TYPE OF SOCIETY AND MENTAL DISORDER

Bronislaw Malinowski, in his observations of three different primitive societies, came to the conclusion that the type of culture determines the amount and kind of neurosis.[11] His Trobriand Islanders, because of their family organization, had few neuroses of the kind which could be traced to childhood conflicts, whereas the Amphlett Islanders some thirty miles south, "essentially similar in race, custom and language," but differing in social organization (with stricter sexual morals, taboos on pre-nuptial intercourse, lack of periods of sexual license, and a tighter family unit) exhibited considerable neurosis.

> In the Trobriands, though I knew scores of natives intimately and had a nodding acquaintance with many more, I could not name a single man or woman who was hysterical or even neurasthenic. Nervous tics, compulsory actions or obsessive ideas were not to be found. . . . The natives of the Trobriands know well and recognize that in the neighbouring islands of the Amphletts and d'Entrecasteaux there are other types of black magic which can produce effects on the mind different from those known to themselves, of which the symptoms are according to their accounts compulsory actions, nervous tics, and various forms of obsession. And during my few months' stay in the Amphletts, my first and strongest impression was that this was a community of neurasthenics. Coming from the open, gay, hearty and accessible Trobrianders, it was astonishing to find oneself among a community of people distrustful of the newcomer,

[11] *Sex and Repression in Savage Society* (London: Kegan Paul, 1927), pp. 85-90.

impatient in work, arrogant in their claims, though easily cowed and extremely nervous when tackled more energetically. . . . I at once found a number of people affected with nervousness whom I could not use as informants, because they would either lie in some sort of fear, or else become excited and offended over any more detailed questioning.[12]

On the South coast of New Guinea, Malinowski observed another tribe, the Mailu, who also differed from the Trobrianders in having a more authoritarian and repressive social structure and a greater amount of neurosis.

Ellsworth Faris found that the Congo Bantu of the Equatorial Rain Forest exhibited few or no psychoses, a fact which he attributed to their simple and integrated social organization.[13] Ruth Benedict came to the conclusion that the emotions, so far as their violence and direction are concerned, are determined by the type of socio-cultural system. Jealousy, envy, and hostility, love and dependence, and consequently neurosis and psychosis, differed in form and amount according to the type of society.[14]

Following these leads, Abram Kardiner and Ralph Linton made an attempt to compare primitive societies with respect to the type of personality which they tended to engender.[15] Several societies were compared, but two—the Polynesians of the Marquesan Islands and the Tanala of Madagascar—were given special attention, the aim being to show the connection between the stresses of the sociological structure and the strains in the personality structure. Though not entirely successful, mainly because of the inadequacies of psychoanalysis and the unfamiliarity of the main author (Kardiner) with sociology and anthropology, the attempt nevertheless shows the extent to which the internal dynamics of the personality are produced by the culture from which the personality arises.

From these comparative studies the conclusion may be drawn that societies differ in the degree to which their members are forced to play incompatible roles, to engage in disquieting scenes, and to submit to inconsistent norms—in short, they differ with respect to the

[12] *Ibid.*, pp. 87-88.

[13] *The Nature of Human Nature* (New York: McGraw-Hill, 1937), Chap. 24.

[14] *Patterns of Culture* (Boston: Houghton Mifflin, 1934). See also A. I. Hallowell, "The Social Function of Anxiety in a Primitive Society," *American Sociological Review*, Vol. 6 (December 1941), pp. 869-881.

[15] *The Individual and His Society* (New York: Columbia University Press, 1939).

conflict of ends which their members according to their statuses and situations acquire. Societies consequently differ as to the number, prevalence, and kind of neuroses which their members develop. This does not mean that, once given the conflict, the mental mechanisms are not similar to those which would occur in any other culture. We have already seen that the structure of the personality, as a universal trait of the species, is the resultant of bio-sociological constants. The types of neuroses and psychoses, the external symptoms and internal dynamisms, are probably the same everywhere.[16] But the *content* of the conflict varies as the culture varies, and this content is highly important in causation and in treatment. It has been asserted that there are culture-specific psychoses, as in the following account of the Eastern Cree:

> They are a particularly gentle, peaceful people. Among them bloodshed is severely frowned upon, and murder is entirely unknown. But they lead a precarious existence. When famine strikes them, as it often does, they become cannibalistic. Because of the strong taboos on human flesh and the essential gentleness of the culture generally, it is not surprising that mental conflicts should result from this situation. The principal disorder of the Cree is the Wihtiko psychosis, in which there is psychopathic craving for human flesh, accompanied by the delusion that one has been transformed into a Wihtiko, a greatly feared folklore being who is himself cannibalistic. . . . This disorder is not known to occur elsewhere.[17]

But such cases are defined by their content and the inciting situation, not by the mental mechanisms, which are the same as elsewhere.

Class Position and Mental Disorder

Within the same society one would expect mental disorder to vary in amount and kind according to the individual's place in the social structure. It should vary, for example, according to class

[16] Mental Breakdowns Occur on the African Veld, Too, *Science News Letter* (Feb. 11, 1939). Moving pictures were taken of Negro patients coming into an African hospital. They showed an astonishing similarity to cases in American hospitals. According to Dr. Winfred Overholser, superintendent of St. Elizabeth's Hospital at Washington, D. C., there is an amazing similarity of symptoms, the African patients being matched, case for case, by patients in the Washington hospital.

[17] Wm. F. Ogburn and Meyer F. Nimkoff, *Sociology* (New York: Houghton Mifflin, 1940), p. 223.

status. Yet extreme care must be exercised in making such deductions. In an integrated society the motivation of one stratum is understood by the members of other strata because every person, in conforming to his class or caste standards, is really conforming to the general standards of the society. Hence the ideology of one stratum is merely a specialized part of the central ideology. For this reason it is not necessarily true that the more a class ideology deviates from the average in a culture, the greater the incidence of mental derangement in this class. The ideological peculiarities of a particular class may be adequately provided for and incorporated in the central ideology.

Furthermore, from a mental health point of view it makes little difference whether the system of stratification is that of classes or castes. Neither type is inherently destructive of sanity. But it does make a difference whether or not the system, whatever it is, is unified by a nucleus of common values. Only a particular kind of deviation—a deviation from the norms governing the entire society—brings disorganization to a particular class. In this case the members of the deviant class find it hard to organize their lives and to achieve an integration of the self; but if the class has a strong organization within itself and a protected system of contacts with other classes, this tendency may be checked. The rate of mental disorganization is highest when a class is put in the position of desiring certain ends that the general society regards as possible and desirable for everyone, and yet is prevented by the organization of the society from being able to realize those ends.[18] In the United States, for instance, the Negro shares the avowed faith in equal opportunity for all and yet is denied such opportunity in fact. In India the social supremacy of the Brahmins, still satisfactory to the orthodox, is being challenged by the importation of political ideology from the West. The behavior of individuals caught in this frustrating situation manifests frequent attempts to escape an unbearable reality. Reality seems unbearable only when another reality exists as a conceivable alternative; and another is conceivable when it forms a part of the cultural ideology. Mental conflict is engendered, then, not so much by the vertical structure itself as by inconsistency within the structure.

[18] Cf. Robert K. Merton, "Social Structure and Anomie," *American Sociological Review*, Vol. 3 (1938), pp. 672-682. Revised as a chapter in Ruth Nanda Anshen (ed.), *The Family: Its Function and Destiny* (New York: Harper, 1949).

It might seem that an open class organization would affect mental health adversely because of the constant readjustments it requires of its circulating individuals. But the open class system is protected against this adverse result by the fact that as distinguished from a caste society the differences between the mores of different strata are small. If the differences were wide, vertical mobility entailing a shift from one set of mores to a radically different set would certainly have profound effects upon the person so shifting. But in an open class system the differences between classes take the form of an infinite number of small gradations and reduce themselves to superficial externalities; so that though vertical mobility places the strain of rapid change and adaptation on the individual, it compensates for this by the pulverization and externalization of differences. Furthermore, even in a mobile system most people do not move, and if they move they do not move far in the class scale.

Probably the feature of an open class system most often suggested as conducive to mental ill health is its competitiveness. Where there is competition, there is insecurity with its accompaniment of fear and anxiety. If a social system is sufficiently competitive to have an open class system, it is also competitive in other relationships—in courtship, in school, in athletics. The threat of competition therefore surrounds the individual, and almost everything he holds dear is subject to possible loss to others. No wonder the "inferiority complex" is a normal symptom in such a society. No wonder no social system can afford to be entirely competitive or to have an entirely open class system. Actually the individual is protected not only by his ascribed statuses but also by rationalizations for failure and by various aids extended to him by friends, relatives, and the community at large. In short, a competitive system has its own integrated system of values which helps it avoid the fatal consequences of its own competitiveness.

URBAN ECOLOGY AND MENTAL DISORDER

Evidence concerning the relation of class position to mental disorder can be obtained from urban studies. It has been found that in American cities some districts have much higher rates of insanity than others and that different types of derangement have different patterns of distribution. Faris and Dunham found that in Chicago the highest rates for schizophrenia (dementia praecox) occur in the hobo, rooming-house, foreign-born, Negro, and central business districts whereas the lowest rates occur in the residential, native-born, and high rental apartment-house districts. In general the high rates for this disease occur in and near the center of the city and low rates on the periphery of the city. The foreign-born living in areas apart from their own group show very high rates, and the foreign-born living in Negro areas show higher rates than those living in white areas. Different Negro areas show distinct rates according to the kind of neighborhood. Such evidence suggests that schizophrenia depends upon the social situation rather than upon race or place of birth as such, and that the main factor is the amount of social disorganization in the area.[19]

Not only does schizophrenia as a whole show a consistent pattern of distribution but the various subtypes—paranoid, catatonic, and hebephrenic—show peculiar distributions within the schizophrenic areas. The paranoid type predominates in the rooming-house areas, the catatonic type in the foreign-born and Negro areas, and the hebephrenic falls between the two.[20]

In contrast to schizophrenia, no striking pattern of distribution could be discovered for manic-depressive psychosis. There is a tendency for this disease to occur more frequently in areas with a higher cultural and economic level, but there is no correlation with race or nativity groupings.[21] Alcoholic psychoses, on the other hand, show a distribution similar to that for schizophrenia but unlike that of manic-depressive psychosis. The rates are highest in or near the center of the city, especially in the disorganized areas and particularly among racial and foreign-born groups not living in areas populated by their own kind. Drug addiction shows a somewhat comparable pattern, although the concentration is greater in apartment-hotel and hotel areas.[22]

These findings help to substantiate the view that social factors are involved in many of the psychoses. The ecological method cannot reveal all the ways in which social factors operate; it may well be, for example, that they are involved in manic-depressive as well as schizophrenic psychosis but that their nature is not revealed by ecological distribution. In the case of schizophrenia, the most com-

19 Faris and Dunham, *op. cit.*, pp. 38-57.
20 *Ibid.*, Chap. 5.
21 *Ibid.*, Chap. 4.
22 *Ibid.*, Chap. 6.

mon of all the mental diseases (accounting for a third or more of the total patient population in state hospitals), the ecological method strongly points to some influence by the social milieu. The kind of person most likely to develop schizophrenia is one who has a seclusive or shut-in personality. Those areas in which the rates of schizophrenia are high are precisely the ones in which the individual is least likely to form an ordered and consistent conception of himself in relation to the world. They are areas where conflicting cultures, high mobility, great poverty, family disorganization, and personal insecurity are to be found. Such areas may tend to produce confused, frustrated, and chaotic personalities, some of whom seemingly protect themselves by withdrawal from reality, resulting in behavior so bizarre and out-of-touch with ordinary social standards that it renders them helpless and leads to their hospitalization as insane. On the other hand, disorganized zones may have a high proportion of schizophrenics because they attract down-and-out persons. Ecological studies are not conclusive as to causation.

War and Mental Disorder

The two World Wars demonstrate in another way the role of social factors in mental disorder. The rate of derangement in civilian populations often declines during wartime due apparently to the mobilization of the citizenry behind a single purpose, giving new meaning and vitality to the common man.[23] In the armed services, however, the rate of mental derangement reaches phenomenal proportions. In spite of a vigorous attempt in World War II to reject draftees showing neurotic symptoms, the largest single class of disability discharge was neuropsychiatric. The proportion of all discharges falling in this class ranged from 20 to 50 per cent, depending upon the particular period of the war and theatre of action.[24] Most of these discharges were for neurosis rather than psychosis, but the neuroses were often profound and very disabling, plaguing many individuals long after their re-entry into civilian life.

The explanation of the high neurosis rate among combat troops is almost purely functional—in terms of a conflict between the desire to remain alive and the desire to be a good soldier. The men are

[23] Edward A. Strecker and Kenneth E. Appel, *Psychiatry in Modern Warfare* (New York: Macmillan, 1945), pp. 8-11.

[24] *Ibid.*, p. 12.

away from home, away from the accustomed grooves and the usual satisfactions of civilian life. They are thrown into new groups of men of roughly their own age, living closely and constantly with them and depending on them for companionship and security in new and dangerous surroundings. These groups are organized so as to produce high morale—intense devotion to the pursuit of a common cause through mutually beneficial coöperative endeavor. The individual thus becomes highly responsive to the opinions of others around him concerning his own behavior in dangerous situations. The safety of each person depends on the organization of the group and on the efficiency and bravery of every member under adverse conditions. The individual develops a conception of himself in terms of these expectations. He wants to be a good soldier, to be fearless, fair, accurate, cool, eager, and loyal. Yet on the other hand he also wants to remain alive, and the two desires are often in absolute conflict. He sees death and destruction all around him, things that he has been taught in civilian life to avoid. He sees his buddies die, often under horrible circumstances. He knows that his own chances are poor, and this is brought home to him by narrow escapes. He is sickened by fear, but he tries to suppress the fear because it conflicts with his conception of himself as a good member of the group. The suppressed fear, however, may be exacerbated by numerous narrow escapes, repeated loss of loyal and well-liked friends, by the evident trickery and might of the enemy, the increase of fatigue and loneliness, the feeling of guilt over not playing one's part and being afraid. Gradually the intense fear, in spite of the strong attempt to control it, may manifest itself in anxiety and tension which become so great that they tend to impair the performance and the personal relations of the soldier. A vicious circle may set in whereby the individual attempts to ignore and suppress his fear, which increases his (to him) inexplicable anxiety, which increases his inefficiency, which increases his fear and dissatisfaction with himself, which redoubles his effort to control himself and hence his anxiety, etc. Finally, various symptoms of his internal conflict may appear—such as a phobia against the kind of plane he usually flies, a loss of visual acuity in time of battle, or a severe intestinal or stomach disorder that incapacitates him for fighting. The effect of the symptom is to save him from dangerous combat, but he cannot admit this to himself because it would violate his conception of himself as a brave and loyal member of his combat unit. If his symptom seems like a real illness to him this in a sense resolves his conflict, but from the point of view of the war effort he becomes a loss, and the aim of psychiatric treatment is to restore him to active combat, usually by giving him insight into his inner conflict, pointing out to him that fear and anxiety are very common and understandable, giving him rest and recreation for awhile, and showing him that his fellows have a sympathetic understanding of his difficulties. The following case of conversion hysteria illustrates some of the mechanisms.

A 23 year old pilot, popular and competent as a combat flier, a member of a fighter-bomber squadron suffering heavy losses due to intense enemy action, had the misfortune on his twenty-fifth mission of seeing his best friend shot down. Saddened by this loss, he resolved to do his best to avenge it on the enemy. After his thirtieth mission, however, he began to notice a blurring of vision during flights. He could not see objects distinctly, especially when diving on his target and when strafing. In addition, he noticed that he was becoming restless and having vague and unaccountable feelings of apprehension. When he was told by his colleagues that his bombing was inaccurate, he went to his Flight Surgeon. Upon testing, he showed a defect in depth perception, but the cause seemed to be mental rather than organic. Accordingly he was referred for neuropsychiatric consultation.

In the interview he was quiet, well controlled, and coöperative. He described the uneasiness he felt on missions but could not account for his apprehensions. He would not admit that he was afraid of enemy action or that he had been unduly disturbed by the deaths of his friends. His conversation became much more detailed and lively when focused upon his visual trouble. He said that shortly after he penetrated enemy territory on missions, his vision became blurred. The blurring would clear on active winking, but he would then notice that his eyelids felt heavy, as if he were sleepy. On occasion, this sensation would become so pronounced as to alarm him lest his eyes should shut completely and not open again.

The patient was given a drug (pentothal) in order to get information about his suppressed thoughts and emotions. During the treatment he underwent a vivid emotional abreaction, freely acting out the anxiety which was his real response to the combat situation. He spoke of his friends who had been shot down and of his feeling that, if this had happened to them, it would certainly happen to him. He complained of all the things he had to watch for in enemy territory. There were so many dangers, so many things to look out for and to keep his eyes on, to avoid being taken by surprise. When he was in enemy territory, looking for German fighters and gun positions, he had to use his eyes to an inordinate degree.

As the effects of the narcosis wore off, and he became oriented to the present, he expressed considerable shame at having revealed such strong anxiety. He thought his reaction was very childish and weak, and asked what he could do about it. He was told that half the battle was in understanding it and that, now that he had insight into how he really felt, he could see for himself whether he could master his anxiety well enough to continue in combat. From this time on he made rapid progress. He was sent to a rest camp for a week and on his return showed a new buoyancy and increase of confidence. His depth perception improved. He was accordingly returned to his outfit, where he resumed combat flying and completed his tour of duty.[25]

Not all cases are this simple or have such a happy outcome. Many are complicated by guilt feelings growing out of family problems, sex matters, or other experiences only indirectly connected with the war. Nevertheless, the war situation tends not only to create a vivid conflict centering on the fear of death or injury and hence to produce neuroses in which the sex conflict of Freudian theory drops completely out of the picture, but it also brings many other potential conflicts to the surface. The total effect is enormously to enhance the rate of neurosis among military personnel in combat areas. In other words the current scientific view is not that some people will develop a neurosis and other people will not, but that everyone has his breaking point. There are strains that nobody, no matter how well balanced, can withstand. Military action, with its danger, uncertainty, horror, noise, and fatigue greatly intensifies the strain and therefore produces neurosis in a high proportion of otherwise healthy individuals. The strain, however, is primarily a mental one, a conflict between what the individual believes he ought to do and the suppressed desire to escape terrible danger. The causation of military neurosis, then, as with all other neurosis, lies primarily in the situa-

[25] Adapted from Roy R. Grinker and John P. Spiegel, *Men Under Stress* (Philadelphia: Blakiston, 1945), pp. 105-106. See their excellent work, Chap. 6, for the theory of combat neurosis.

tion as reflected in the mind of the individual rather than in the organism. In short, the etiology of neurosis is largely social as proven by changes in the rate of neurosis with a change of social circumstances.

Conclusion

Our interest in mental disorder is sociological, extending only so far as such disorder can be shown to have a social content and to be socially caused. Necessarily this is not the whole story, for there are obviously organic factors in addition; yet the past theories of mental aberration have so far overemphasized the organic, the instinctive, the purely individual factors that it is wise to insist on the sociological determinants as well.[26] We have approached this task in several different ways: first, by showing that the definition of mental disorder is itself social in character; second, by showing that the dynamic mechanisms of derangement (conflict, suppression, projection, anxiety, etc.) grow out of, reflect, and are concerned with culturally defined social relationships; third, by showing that the incidence of mental disorder varies according to the kind of social milieu (the social class, urban district, wartime experience) to which people are subjected. Individuals vary in the degree of social stress and strain they can bear without cracking, but everybody has some breaking point. What defines the breaking point is not the objective situation but the situation as it appears to the actor. How it appears to him is largely a function of his conception of himself as the events and the action unfold. In the last analysis it is the socially formed self which disintegrates and falls into what we call mental disorder; hence the disease process can be understood only when recognition is given to the self as an entity and to the social experience out of which the self is constructed.

References

Norman Cameron, "The Paranoid Pseudo-Community," *American Journal of Sociology*, Vol. 49 (July 1943), pp. 32-38.

The paranoid, through his growing failure to communicate with his fellows, builds up an imaginary community to which he reacts. The responses of the real community to his actions merely

[26] A work that stresses hereditary factors in mental disorder is Carney Landis and James D. Page, *Modern Society and Mental Disease* (New York: Farrar and Rinehart, 1938).

serve to reinforce his belief in the hostility of the imaginary one. The author has done much work along the line of reinterpreting disordered mentality in sociological rather than biological or purely psychological terms. His other contributions are cited in this article.

Robert E. Clark, "The Relationship of Schizophrenia to Occupational Income and Occupational Prestige," *American Sociological Review,* Vol. 13 (June 1948), pp. 325-330.

Finds that the Chicago schizophrenic rates (and presumably the incidence of schizophrenia) are negatively correlated with occupational income and prestige.

B. Dai, "Personality Problems in Chinese Culture," *American Sociological Review,* Vol. 6 (October 1941), pp. 688-696.

Shows that the Chinese are not so well adjusted after all. Gives an interpretation of mental disorders in a Chinese cultural setting.

Kingsley Davis, "Mental Hygiene and the Class Structure," *Psychiatry,* Vol. 1 (February 1938), pp. 55-65.

The theory of the relation between an open class system and the mental hygiene movement, based on an examination of mental hygiene literature.

Albert Deutsch, *The Mentally Ill in America* (2nd ed., New York: Columbia University Press, 1949).

This account of the amazing treatment of the insane in our country from colonial times to the present affords valuable insight into the way mental disorder is regarded by the so-called normal. The medical theories are quite as astounding as the popular ones.

H. Warren Dunham, "Social Psychiatry," *American Sociological Review,* Vol. 13 (April 1948), pp. 183-197.

Describes the interrelations between sociology and psychiatry, and cites a very wide range of research and theoretical literature on the social aspects of mental disorder.

Robert E. L. Faris and H. Warren Dunham, *Mental Disorders in Urban Areas,* (Chicago: University of Chicago Press, 1939).

An ecological study of the spatial distribution of mental disorder in Chicago and Providence.

Harrison G. Gough, "A Sociological Theory of Psychopathy," *American Journal of Sociology,* Vol. 53 (March 1948), pp. 359-366.

A restatement of the concept of psychopathy in terms of the sociological theory of role-playing.

Arnold W. Green, "The Middle Class Male Child and Neurosis," *American Sociological Review,* Vol. 2 (February 1946), pp. 31-42.

Based on first-hand knowledge, this article maintains that the lower class industrial family is in many ways the antithesis of the middle class family in its handling of the child. It does everything supposedly wrong. And yet the incidence of neurosis appears to be much less than in the middle class.

Arnold W. Green, "Social Values and Psychotherapy," *Journal of Personality,* Vol. 14 (March 1946), pp. 199-228.

A critical evaluation of various schools of psychotherapy on the ground that they implicitly assume certain social values in their work without realizing it. Mental health is dependent on a stable integrated social order; in so far as our social order is not stable or integrated, it is a major cause of neurosis, but one which psychotherapy is helpless to change.

Roy R. Grinker and John P. Spiegel, *Men Under Stress* (Philadelphia: Blakiston, 1945).

Probably the best single work on mental problems as seen in combat personnel in World War II. The authors are distinguished psychiatrists who served in a medical capacity with the Air Corps.

Norman S. Hayner, "Hotel Life and Personality," *American Journal of Sociology,* Vol. 33, (March 1928), pp. 784-795.

This article is interesting for the insights gained on the relationship of personality and social situation.

Karen Horney, *New Ways in Psychoanalysis* (New York: Norton, 1939).

"Dissatisfied with therapeutic results and certain phases of psychoanalytic theory, she attempts to bring psychoanalysis in line with the newer conceptions in sociology and anthropology and to substitute a 'sociological orientation' for an 'anatomical-physiological' one." (Dunham)

Clyde V. Kluckhohn, "The Influence of Psychiatry on Anthropology," in *One Hundred Years of American Psychiatry, 1844-1944* (New York: Columbia University Press), pp. 589-617.

"A competent and detailed account of the reciprocal influence of anthropology and psychiatry in the United States." (Dunham)

PART III

MAJOR GROUPS

PRIMARY AND SECONDARY GROUPS

RURAL AND URBAN COMMUNITIES

THE CROWD AND THE PUBLIC

CASTE, CLASS, AND STRATIFICATION

MARRIAGE AND THE FAMILY

CHAPTER XI

PRIMARY AND SECONDARY GROUPS

IN the classification of human groups one of the broadest and most fundamental distinctions is that between small and intimate groups on the one hand and large and impersonal groups on the other. In its formulation of this dichotomy American sociological theory has generally followed Charles H. Cooley's distinction between primary and secondary groups, as set forth in 1909 in his book, *Social Organization.*[1] European theory has followed a somewhat similar distinction formulated in 1887 by Ferdinand Tönnies between *Gemeinschaft* (close communal relationship) and *Gesellschaft* (organized impersonal relationship).[2] Other authors have stated the same dichotomy in one form or another, not only because it is an obvious fact but also because it is a fundamental one.

Cooley's classic definition runs as follows:

> By primary groups I mean those characterized by intimate face-to-face association and cooperation. They are primary in several senses, but chiefly in that they are fundamental in forming the social nature and ideals of the individual. The result of intimate association . . . is a certain fusion of individualities in a common whole, so that one's very self, for many purposes at least, is the common life and purpose of the group. Perhaps the simplest way of describing this wholeness is by saying that it is a "we"; it involves the sort of sympathy and mutual identification for which "we" is the natural expression.[3]

1 New York: Charles Scribner's Sons. Cooley did not employ the term *secondary* but it has become an apt and widely used name for what he had in mind.

2 *Gemeinschaft und Gesellschaft* (Leipzig: Fues's Verlag). There is now an English translation by Chas. P. Loomis, *Fundamental Concepts of Sociology* (New York: American Book, 1940).

3 *Op. cit.,* p. 23.

Two things in this quotation are worth noting: first, that the author means to designate a class of *concrete* groups (into which he puts families, play groups, neighborhood groups, and others); second, that he uses the phrase "face-to-face association" but places the emphasis upon particular *qualities* of the relationship such as "sympathy and mutual identification." These points have led to some confusion. It is generally agreed that *all* groups tend in some degree to possess consensus—to engender a "we" feeling in their members. This was implied by Cooley himself in his subsequent discussion of the necessary extension of "primary ideals" to larger groups. Without the "we" feeling large groups cannot retain their cohesion.[4] If primary association is thus conceived as a quality of all groups, it does not constitute a means for separating concrete groups into two types called primary and secondary. Furthermore, this particular quality cannot be said to be limited to "face-to-face" groups. There are relationships that are friendly and intimate but involve indirect contacts (such as the friendship of two distant scholars or the love affairs of soldiers and girls initiated through correspondence), and there are relationships that are formal and impersonal but involve face-to-face contacts (such as the military salute or the act of prostitution).[5] Close scrutiny of Cooley's statement seems therefore to reveal some ambiguity.

In order to clarify the nature of primary groups our discussion will stress the following points: (1) There is a primary, or *gemeinschaftliche,* type of relationship. (2) This type of relationship is characterized by a number of interrelated qualities. (3) It, with its distinctive qualities, is found more abundantly in some concrete groups than in others. (4) The particular groups in which it is found most abundantly are those most likely to rest upon certain physical conditions. Let us begin with the last point and work backwards.

The Physical Conditions of Primary Groups

Cooley's idea of "face-to-face" contact expressed an important fact, but he did not sufficiently analyze this fact to see both its broader implication and its narrower limitation. He should have realized that there are not one but three essential conditions which, when

[4] *Ibid.*, Chaps. 4 and 5.

[5] Ellsworth Faris, *The Nature of Human Nature* (New York: McGraw-Hill, 1937), Chap. 4.

present, tend to give rise to primary groups. The first of these is close (face-to-face) physical proximity of the group members; the second is smallness of the group; and the third, durability of the bond. All of these three conditions—closeness, smallness, and continuation—seem to be equally essential as well as mutually related. But note that they are *physical* conditions. They merely constitute the external setting in which a certain kind of social milieu is extremely likely to arise. It does not follow that this milieu will inevitably arise under these conditions, or that it may not arise under other conditions.

It often happens that a primary relation arises with only one or two of the conditions present. Thus "the historic friendships like that of Emerson and Carlyle did not rest on physical presence" [6] but they did rest on the fewness of the persons involved and the long duration of the acquaintance. The essential thing is not so much the physical conditions as the values, the regard for each other, that drew these persons together in spite of physical separation. It is necessary to keep the temporal and spatial conditions of primary association analytically separate from its social nature. Why each condition is so closely related to the social characteristics will be clear only after discussion of these characteristics, but for the present a word more should be said about each condition.

PHYSICAL PROXIMITY

In order for intimacy to arise it is necessary that people have rather close contact, and nothing provides such contact better than face-to-face association. Seeing and talking with each other facilitates the subtle exchange of ideas, opinions, and sentiments. It makes possible the "conversation of gestures" of which Mead speaks. So true is this that close contact has come to symbolize good feeling and identity between persons. Caressing, kissing, and sexual intercourse; eating and dwelling together; playing, traveling, studying together—all tend to be regarded as external symbols of close solidarity. True, these symbols may become formalized as in the handshake of a stranger or the kiss of a French general, but even such formal usages imply a certain element of mutual regard which ultimately stems from the role of face-to-face contact in primary groups. A part of our horror of prostitution apparently derives from our customary

[6] Faris, *op. cit.*, p. 38.

association of sexual contact with affection, and the significance of the "kiss of Judas" would be utterly nil without a similar association of kissing with affection.

Physical proximity thus provides an opportunity for the development of primary groups, but whether or not that opportunity will be utilized depends on the situation as defined in the culture. In the first place the normative order regulates the conditions under which physical contact may take place. As between individuals of different status there are usually barriers—e.g. between members of different classes and castes, different religions and occupations, different ages and sex. These barriers prevent physical proximity from providing an opportunity for intimacy to develop; they thus keep different strata and different groups distinct. The existence of such barriers serves, in the second place, to emphasize the fact that physical intimacy in other relations is normatively prescribed. For instance the customary ban on close physical contact between the sexes serves to emphasize the necessity and importance of such contact in marriage. In these two ways—by *pro*scribing and *pre*scribing it according to the situation—a social system controls physical proximity in the interest of the existing social organization. In some cases where physical contact is necessary but not socially prescribed, it is treated in a tolerant but not encouraging manner. Physical nearness in a packed subway, a crowded restaurant, or a public lavatory may be much greater than the parties would in ordinary situations consider correct, but it is recognized that the circumstances make it necessary. Such tolerated physical proximity sometimes develops into a social relationship but not often. The effect of close physical proximity on the social relationship depends in the last analysis on the cultural definition of the situation.

SMALLNESS OF THE GROUP

A face-to-face group must also be a small group, for it is impossible to be in sensory contact with many people at the same time. A speaker may address an audience containing thousands of persons, but this is under special conditions; and it illustrates perfectly the necessity of smallness in addition to proximity as a condition favorable to the development of intimacy. Other factors being equal (such as the nature of the occasion—whether a show, a lecture, or a funeral), the smaller the group the more intimate it is.

Undoubtedly the character of the group tends to change with its size, and interesting attempts have been made to demonstrate the relationship between the two.[7] As the group becomes larger each person counts less as a unique personality but more as a sheer cipher or unit; the group tends to acquire a more complex and formal organization; representative and substitute agencies arise in greater abundance; the rules of association become more explicit and the means of control more official; and the group increasingly acquires a character of its own apart from that of its specific members. With very small groups even the addition of one more member makes a difference. Thus a group of three is notoriously different from a group of two, and a group of four is different from one of three. But when the group numbers five or six the addition of one more does not necessarily change its character although the addition of several more will do so. With very large groups, of course, it requires a great addition to change the character of the group. There is not much difference between a city of 100,000 and one of 125,000, but there is a big difference between either of these and a city of 500,000.

In a small group the members can know one another personally and can all participate directly in group decisions. Furthermore, they can develop a group character and a group intimacy rather quickly (e.g. in a small boat). If the group is larger more time is required to establish full mutual acquaintance between the members. When people live together all their lives, however, as in a peasant village, it is possible for 200 or more to know one another intimately. This brings us to the time factor as a condition of primary group association.

DURATION OF THE RELATIONSHIP

Intimacy is largely a matter of the frequency and intensity of association. Other things equal, the longer the group remains together the more numerous and deeper are the contacts between its members. Social ties deepen in time through the gradual development of interlocking habits. An oft-repeated association, like any other experience, becomes part of one's way of life. Although a husband and

[7] See Georg Simmel, "The Number of Members as Determining the Sociological Form of the Group," *American Journal of Sociology,* VIII (July 1902), pp. 1-46, 158-196; Howard Becker and Ruth Hill Useem, "Sociological Analysis of the Dyad," *American Sociological Review,* VII (Feb. 1942), pp. 13-26.

wife may have quarreled for ten years, the very fact that they have lived together for that long makes it hard for them to do without each other. A nation is a durable entity but not a small or intimate one.

It thus becomes clear that physical proximity, small size, and long duration are the conditions most favorable to the development of intimate ties. It is possible for one of these conditions to be present without the other two, but the most favorable situation for the development of a primary group occurs when all three are present to a high degree. Let us now examine more closely the qualities of association that these conditions tend to develop.

The Character of Primary Relations

A primary relationship involves, first of all, an identity of ends as between the parties. Among the identical ends is of course the relationship itself, which is not regarded by the participants as a means to an end but as a good in its own right. This means that the relationship is noncontractual, noneconomic, nonpolitical, and nonspecialized. Instead it is personal, spontaneous, sentimental, and inclusive. A brief discussion of each of these major traits will indicate their importance.

IDENTITY OF ENDS

In a perfect primary relationship there is an interpenetration of ends in two different senses. First, the parties have similar desires and attitudes so that they are striving for similar things and can be together without disagreement. They look at the world through the same eyes. Two friends who are united by a common intellectual interest afford an example of this. Second, there is an interpenetration in a deeper sense: each party pursues as one of his ends the welfare of the other. He may superficially and in a given connection define the other's welfare differently from the way the other party himself views it, but in the last analysis he must accept the basic desires, the ends, of the other party as also his own ends. Thus a man who tries to dissuade his friend from a given line of conduct does so only on the ground that what the friend appears to want now is not what he will want later. He may explain to him, for example, that to throw up his job now in a pique at his boss will only cause him to regret the act later. This function—that of helping an individual interpret and understand his own welfare—is one of the great values of friendship, and it implies at bottom that the ends of one become by that very fact also the ends of the other. Another example is the behavior of a mother who injures her own health looking after that of her child. Not only is the child's welfare a supreme end for her but the joys and sorrows of the child are also her joys and sorrows, because she is in such sympathetic understanding with the child.

Seldom is the identity of ends complete. A man may distrust and resent his friend to some extent; a child may resist his parent. Seldom, moreover, is the relationship entirely mutual; it is usually a bit one-sided with one party entering much more than the other into the spirit of it. But at least we can visualize a theoretical asymptote—a complete and mutual identity of ends—which primary relations approach but do not attain.

The identification of ends is connected with a certain fusion of personalities within the group, so that what one experiences the other also tends to experience. This fusion can be observed, for example, in the case of stage-fright on the part of persons who are not actually on the stage but are close relatives of someone who is. They often experience the ordeal as vividly as if they were on the stage themselves, or even more so. There is the case of the mother of a student actress in a college play who when asked how she had enjoyed the play said she had not paid any attention to it, she was so worried when her daughter was on the stage. This fusion of personalities constitutes an important part of the "we" feeling that Cooley wrote about. It gives the relation an altruistic character, at least in one sense of the word. It does not mean that one party sacrifices his own interests for the benefit of the other, but simply that the other's interests are also his. If a mother injures her health in caring for her child, she is not going contrary to her own ends; rather she is avoiding the pain of seeing her child suffer. The child's needs become her ends.

THE RELATIONSHIP IS AN END IN ITSELF

A primary relationship, ideally considered, is not regarded by the parties as simply a means to an end but rather as a value or end in itself. It is in their eyes its own excuse for being. If a friendship is formed for a purpose—say, to make a sale—we do not regard it as a genuine friendship. If a marriage is made purely with an eye to economic gain, it lacks a certain quality which we think should go into marriage.

The intrinsic value attached to the primary relationship helps explain the sense of spontaneity and freedom felt by the parties. The relationship is not compulsory, not a means to a superior end, but is intrinsically enjoyable. From an objective point of view such a relationship may look like a subtle prison for the parties concerned. We speak of a couple being so attached to each other as to be oblivious to everything else; we speak of "fascination," "infatuation," "entanglement," etc. Yet subjectively the relationship seems spontaneous because it is purely voluntary. Only when a close relationship is forced on one or is simulated for an ulterior purpose does it become burdensome; and in this case scarcely anything can be more confining. A love affair in which one no longer feels any love but which cannot be broken off is exceedingly trying.

THE RELATIONSHIP IS PERSONAL

In the primary group the interest of each is centered in the others *as persons*—i.e. as objects of value. The relationship disappears if the particular person disappears from it.

> No offense is greater in a lover than this: that he should treat his love "impersonally.". . .
>
> The distinction between personal and impersonal relationships is a vital one in human affairs. Personal relationships, be they those of friend to friend or of husband to wife, be they motivated by love or by hatred, be they transitory or permanent, stand apart in a class by themselves. . . .
>
> The most obvious and inevitable quality of a personal relationship is that it is *not transferable.* It attaches to determinate individuals who cannot be duplicated nor replaced. A new personal relationship can be established, an old one can be abandoned, perhaps the driving force that initiated the relationship may give way to another, but no substitution can be made of one individual for another in the same relationship. If Helen leaves Menelaus and flees with Paris, it is absurd to describe the new situation as a continuation of the personal attachment of Menelaus and Helen, with Paris acting as a substitute. The personal relationship between Helen and Mene-

laus continues, with love changed to fear and resentment. The attachment of Helen and Paris is a new entity, a new relationship.

> On the other hand, any relationship which can be transferred from one individual to another is to that extent impersonal. When citizens enter and leave the allegiance of a State, when laborers enter and leave the employ of a factory, when men supplant each other in all the diverse functions of organized society, their personality is only incidental to the political, economic, or social tie which they assume or avoid. We consider that these relationships themselves are constantly in being, whoever may be the persons bound therein.[8]

The primary relationship is a matter of persons; it exists because of the person, not despite him. Cigarettes can be bought from anybody. Our attention is focused on getting them, not on the person who sells them to us. The less the seller intrudes his personality, the better. A vending machine will do just as well except that it will not cut prices. If one man or one machine will not sell us cigarettes, another will; and it makes no great difference which one does.

The personal nature of the primary relationship has a further consequence—namely, that things trivial in other contexts may be important in this one. "As every lover who is not a bungler knows, there is no external distinction between great things and trivial things in matters of love." [9] This is because, since the relationship is personal, whatever either party chooses to regard as important necessarily becomes important. The essential thing is the attitude of each person towards the other; and anything that reveals this attitude, be it small or large, has great significance attached to it. A careless gesture, an idle remark, may be sufficient to start a quarrel. Events are not important in themselves but rather as symbols of the subjective attitudes that each is taking toward the other.

THE RELATIONSHIP IS INCLUSIVE

The person in a personal relationship is not an abstraction. He is not merely a legal entity, an economic cipher, or a technological cog. He is all of these rolled into one. He is the complete concrete person and the relationship involves him in all his completeness, extending to his whole being. His value attaches not to any particular

[8] Robert C. Binkley and Frances W. Binkley, *What Is Right with Marriage?* (New York: Appleton, 1929), pp. 31-32.

[9] Binkley and Binkley, *op. cit.*, p. 34.

aspect or activity of himself but to his whole self. This is why long acquaintance and close contact are so essential to a primary relationship. Each person comes to know the other in all the details of his life. In this way the primary relation differs from all other social relations, because the others do not involve complete personalities.

THE RELATIONSHIP IS SPONTANEOUS

A purely primary relationship is voluntary. In this it does not differ from a purely contractual relationship, but in a contract the conditions are laid down explicitly and the other person is held to these conditions. Furthermore, the contract exists for an ulterior purpose and is not an end in itself. As a consequence the personal relationship, which depends always on the will of either party at any point in the interaction, is voluntary in a more complete sense; and as mentioned before, it therefore implies the greatest spontaneity on the part of the participants.

In actual groups, of course, the very inclusiveness and closeness of primary association means that great control over the person is exercised. Neighborhood and family control is very complete control, and the individual often wishes to escape it by getting into the anonymous and more impersonal life of a larger setting such as a big city. The truth is that such actual groups embody only imperfectly the primary relationship. They demand a great deal of loyalty and they have an element of status, of institutionalization, in them which makes them something less than spontaneous and free. Even so, the control is in general voluntarily accepted by the members of the group. One does not feel that a marriage relationship is onerous even though it imposes many limitations on one. If one does feel it to be onerous this is a sign that the relation is involuntary and therefore is not completely primary.

Concrete Groups and Primary Relationships

We have now described some of the essential qualities of primary relationships—the identity of ends, the intrinsic value, the personal, inclusive, and spontaneous character which they possess. We have also given the physical conditions which favor the occurrence of such relationships. It has become increasingly clear, however, that primary relationships as we have described them do not exist in concrete form. They are merely the extreme pole, the asymptote, toward which some actual forms of interaction tend but never reach. It has also become clear, as the preceding paragraph suggests, that in actual groups of a close and intimate kind certain characteristics of a type opposite to those we have described may be found. Thus the small and durable group may be characterized by hate and conflict rather than love and harmony. Obviously then there are some theoretical problems remaining that require clarification.

The groups embodying most completely the characteristics of primary relationship are those that are freest from any connection with social organization. They imply no larger obligation, no fixed status, no involuntary element. Such, for example, is the relation of two friends who come together simply because they want to do so and who are under no obligation to continue the bond if either loses interest. Even here some rudimentary sense of obligation is inevitably incurred and there is some cultural standardization of the relationship. In primitive societies friendships are often sealed with a ceremony and are expected to continue for life. In our own society they are remarkably free. If the number of friends is increased, the element of obligation and control becomes greater; yet the boy's gang, based on similar age and similar interests, embodies primary relationships to a high degree. Like friendship, the love relationship of a man and woman apart from any marital or parental ties has a strong primary character; but here the fact of potential connection with the family system of the society places the relationship on a precarious footing.

The truth is that every society is of necessity inimical to the full expression of primary association. If it is to control individuals, it must control their relationships. Even in the most personal affairs it must define mutual obligations. It must take advantage of personal affection, of the sense of spontaneity, of the identity of ends to furnish organization for the performance of societal functions. It cannot let individuals associate simply on the basis of personal attraction or on a purely voluntary basis. Instead it must use the propulsive power inherent in these, and in using them it must inevitably destroy them in part. Thus in countless ways it limits contacts in such a way that friendship will develop along functional lines that fit into the total organization. It tries to limit or at least control the boys' gang, because it recognizes in such a group an anarchic force. Similarly it limits and controls sexual love between man and woman in the interest of reproduction, child-rearing, and the continuity of the system of stratification. It recognizes in the voluntary unregulated liaison an anarchic force.

But if organized society is inimical to the full expression of primary relationships, it is also friendly to a partial expression of them. At the bottom of human society is the fact of communicative contact between one person and another. The self cannot develop on the basis of secondary contacts; it requires close, intimate, personal contacts. It requires the security of a stable and familiar group, the sense of identity with others, the sympathetic interest and personal evaluation which others show. The intricate process of socialization, then, is handled in those concrete groups—notably the family and the play group—where an emphasis is placed on the conditions and the qualities of primary association. Such groups are institutionalized and organized, giving their members mutual rights and obligations defined in the culture, and as such they are not purely spontaneous and voluntary; yet so far as possible an attempt is made to give them an identity of ends, an intrinsic evaluation of the group as such, a sense of personal closeness, and an unawareness of the impingement of social controls.

In the last analysis the society relies heavily on the physical conditions of primary group formation—proximity, smallness, and long duration—to provide some of the qualities of primary association despite their socially organized character. In this way the family and the neighborhood (the local territorial group) provide the archetypes of what may be called organized primary groups.[10] It happens that human beings throughout most of their history have lived chiefly in groups characterized by proximity, smallness, and durability. But precisely because so much of their lives was passed in such groups, these groups were thoroughly organized from a social point of view. For this reason familial relations and in fact all personal relations seem more formalized in primitive groups than among ourselves. It is only in modern society that secondary contacts have come to play an important role, and consequently some of the burden of social

[10] The nature of the human family is discussed more fully in Ch. XV below. Ralph Linton, *The Study of Man* (New York: Appleton-Century, 1937), pp. 210-228, has an excellent discussion of the primitive band, clearly bringing out the primary group elements present in it.

organization has been lifted from the small primary groups which have thus gained in spontaneity and informality.

Secondary Groups

Secondary groups can be roughly defined as the opposite of everything already said about primary groups. In the first place the conditions for their existence are mainly opposite in character. The secondary group covers such a wide area that no two of its members need live in close proximity, and it is so large that all of its members could not possibly know one another personally. Although it may have very long duration, the personal relations of its members may be brief. In the second place its characteristics generally appear at the opposite extreme from those of the primary group. It involves relationships that are not ends in themselves, not personal, and not inclusive. But this way of defining secondary groups is not entirely satisfactory. If an organized social group is to exist, it must have some of the elements we have cited in the case of the primary group. It must have to a certain degree an identity of ends on the part of its members; it must be conceived by its members as a value, an end, in itself; and it must have long duration. The modern nation, with millions of citizens, shows the necessity of these primary group characteristics; yet we think of it as a secondary group. The same is true of a large labor union, an army, or a scientific association; and it is true of any going group, no matter what its size. It is less true of a city, because under modern conditions the population of a city constitutes a group only in a very loose sense. In so far as the secondary group is a real organized group and not merely a statistical category, it has some of the elements we have already designated as possessed by the primary group.

Do we then have a distinction without a difference? No, because the real difference between primary and secondary association relates not to the groups as such but to the kinds of relationships that constitute the group structure. The nation is called a secondary group because its members, as members, do not have close, personal, warm relations. They have these relations in other contexts—as members of families, villages, fraternities, etc.—but not simply as citizens of the same nation. Only when two persons are in a foreign land, and often not even then, is common citizenship deemed a sufficient ground for intimate association. Yet somehow the nation must be personalized, symbolized, represented, and led if it is to operate as a group. It must have the loyalty of its citizens. And this means that there must be a common bond albeit an impersonal one between its citizens. They must feel themselves to be members of the larger group and be willing to make sacrifices for its welfare. At the nerve center of this group, of course, there must be a small unit of political leaders and officials who know each other personally by reason of their position in the group structure. But as between the great mass of citizens the expression of the common bond does not lie in close personal interaction but rather in impersonal and indirect communication through newspaper and radio, formal representation through the ballot, and devotion to leaders known only at a distance. The growth of such large and impersonal groups is one of the most fascinating chapters in the history of human society. In many ways it is a new chapter, for the degree to which life today is controlled by the impersonal group has never before been equaled.

The nature of secondary contacts is obvious. They may be face-to-face, but if so they are of the touch-and-go variety. The contact with the streetcar motorman, with the grocery clerk, or with the bank cashier is a perfect illustration. Many contacts are entirely indirect, being handled through long-distance communication, the two persons never seeing each other. Thus an insurance salesman may call a prospective client by telephone and handle the entire transaction by wire, mail, and check; or a scholar thousands of miles away may write for a reprint of a scientific paper which he has seen referred to. Actually a great part of the essential business of the modern world is handled through impersonal contacts, whether of the face-to-face or the indirect variety. Such contacts do not necessarily imply any identity of ends as between the parties concerned, any interest in the other party as an end in himself, any conception of the relationship as an end in itself, or any sentiment whatever attaching to the contact. They do not require that the parties know each other in an inclusive sense but only in a very special context, and when this context changes the relationship has no significance. One party may be substituted for another without affecting the relationship. The contact is viewed purely as a means to an end and is dropped as soon as the end changes. It, along with the other party, is treated in a rational context. In other words the secondary contact is entered into in the spirit of rational calculation—in the spirit of technological, economic, and political manipulation.

One of the clearest exemplifications of the secondary relationship is that of contract. (In fact, all secondary contacts could be viewed as contractual in nature, some of them merely being highly informal and ephemeral.) Each of the contracting parties enters the agreement for a definite purpose, and his purpose may have little relation to that of the other party. He intends to get all he can out of the contract, and he puts into it only so much of his own interest as he has to; his liability is limited. Everything is explicitly stated—what each of the parties contributes, what he gets, for what length of time, and under what circumstances. In case of dispute over the contract the law enforces only the terms of the contract. Anything that is not stated is not part of the contract. Sentiments and motives do not count. The parties may love or hate each other; they may know or not know each other; they may or may not share the same religion or the same class position. In short the contractual relation is a rational instrument. Neither it nor the other party is of any intrinsic interest to the individual entering the contract; the interest lies rather in the goal for which these are the means.

Obviously no organized group can depend exclusively on secondary or contractual attitudes among its members. Whether it is a labor union or an army, a priesthood or a university, it must receive from its members some loyalty and devotion to the group as a whole and some attachment to the institutional patterns that make its structure. Even a business concern, which is so structured that virtually every relationship is supposedly contractual, will not work without a certain identification of its members with the organization as a whole. No matter what the group, it must have some basis of allegiance and identity that will support the rules that make possible the secondary and contractual relationships. Unless contracts can be enforced they are worthless, and they can be enforced only through the will of the people as expressed in their courts. Unless the day-to-day contacts of strangers in a city are somehow reduced to rule, unless they are guided by considerations of honesty, fairness, courtesy, and convenience, chaos will result; and it is in the name of the collectivity and on the basis of sentiment that these rules are supported.

Attitudes of loyalty and identification do not develop automatically. They come as a result of communication from one individual to another, and especially the kind of communication that occurs in intimate personal relations. For this reason primary groups are essential to the existence of large secondary groups. It is in the primary group that the individual in his formative stages identifies himself with others and takes over their attitudes. There he acquires the sentiments of love, freedom, justice, and propriety later attached to the secondary group; there, in face-to-face and durable personal relations, these sentiments are constantly renewed and reinforced; and there the expression of the self in the "we" of the whole is achieved. This fact explains why the family is often said to be the foundation of society and the play group the best school for the future citizen.[11] Without these primary groups the large secondary group would be like a tree without roots; it would fall of its own weight.

For this reason the secondary group, no matter how big and impersonal, must be articulated with the primary groups. Its members must be associated not only in secondary contexts but also in primary contexts, and the two contexts must be structurally integrated. Hence we find that every primary group contains elements of formal social organization, just as every secondary group (at least so far as attitudes and sentiments are concerned) contains elements of primary association. The two kinds of group are symbiotic and interpenetrated.

The large group, however, does not depend exclusively on primary contacts to maintain allegiance and provide cohesion. It makes use of impersonal controls, indirect communication, and bureaucratic organization. Whereas in the primary group the individual is controlled largely by the informal expressions of others' attitudes—by gossip, ostracism, withdrawal of affection, frank discussion, etc.—in the larger group he is controlled in part by law and economic competition. He finds himself caught in a network whose operation is largely impersonal, touching him only in specialized contexts but in ways that are explicitly stated and quantitatively measurable. The rules apply to everyone in the group, and since they apply to large numbers they cannot take the whole man into account. They treat the man as a cipher, a statistical and legal but hardly a human entity. He gets his information about the group as a whole from impersonal sources—the newspaper, the radio, the lecture, the disembodied rumor. To be sure, this information is often about specific people,

[11] Cf. Cooley, *op. cit.*, pp. 32-50.

the officials or the elite of the group; and an effort is often made to personalize as much as possible the mass means of communication by radio addresses, gossip columns, lecture and handshaking tours, etc. The symbols of the group are made as concrete and colorful as possible and are manipulated in a manner calculated to appeal to mass sentiments. Still, in the last analysis the communication is addressed to so many people that it cannot help but be impersonal. Even though the leader's voice and face come into the home by radio, television, and rotogravure, even though the gossip columns recount his daily doings, he is still remote; he would not know his admirer if he met him on the street and certainly could not be intimate with him and all others like him. By every device the secondary group attempts to overcome the sense of impersonality while retaining the efficiency that impersonal organization gives. The success achieved can be measured by the vitality of secondary groups in the modern world. Though they occasionally fail, they represent, as a form of social organization, an outstanding achievement of modern times.

Conclusion

The distinction between primary and secondary groups suffers the danger of reification. A "group" in a literal sense designates a physical aggregation of people, such as a crowd at a football game. On the other hand the term is frequently used in the sense of a number of people involved in one or more kinds of patterned interaction; accordingly, the members of a state bar association constitute a group. The difficulty is that in this sense the same individual can be a member of several different groups, and consequently we have to give up thinking of groups as physical entities. In the foregoing discussion we have seen that not even groups in this non-physical sense can be classified as wholly primary or wholly secondary. It is much easier to classify contacts and specific relationships as falling in one or the other of these two categories, and this is largely what we have done. In the last analysis, however, we have found that the conditions and characteristics of so-called primary and secondary association are to a certain degree independently variable. The completely primary relationship is one which combines all of the conditions and characteristics that fall at the primary end of the scale. Such a relationship is an ideal-type which does not exist in actuality.

PRIMARY AND SECONDARY RELATIONSHIPS

	Physical Conditions	Social Characteristics	Sample Relationships	Sample Groups
PRIMARY	Spatial proximity.	Identification of ends.	Friend-friend.	Play group.
	Small number.	Intrinsic valuation of the relation.	Husband-wife.	Family.
	Long duration.	Intrinsic valuation of other person.	Parent-child.	Village or neighborhood.
		Inclusive knowledge of other person.	Teacher-pupil.	Work-team.
		Feeling of freedom and spontaneity.		
		Operation of informal controls.		
SECONDARY	Spatial distance.	Disparity of ends.	Clerk-customer.	Nation.
	Large number.	Extrinsic valuation of the relation.	Announcer-listener.	Clerical hierarchy.
	Short duration.	Extrinsic valuation of other person.	Performer-spectator.	Professional association.
		Specialized and limited knowledge of other person.	Officer-subordinate.	Corporation.
		Feeling of external constraint.	Author-reader.	
		Operation of formal controls.		

The same is true of the completely secondary relationship. Therefore, the groups that we call primary are simply those that are bound together by relationships having a preponderance of the primary conditions and characteristics; and the groups that we call secondary are those bound together by relationships having a preponderance of secondary conditions and characteristics.

For the convenience of the reader in summing up the points covered in the chapter, a table is appended giving the major conditions and characteristics of the two types of association, along with examples of groups that fall on one or the other side of the dichotomy.

References

R. C. Angell, *The Integration of American Society* (New York: McGraw-Hill, 1941).

This is a study of the effects of the multiplication and increasing differentiation of groups in American society. As such it has bearing on any discussion of secondary groups.

Albert Blumenthal, *Small Town Stuff* (Chicago: University of Chicago Press, 1933).

With most Americans now living in urban places the American small town, so characteristic of the past, is in danger of being forgotten. Blumenthal's account of one such town is both sociological and impressionistic. It nicely catches the flavor of the small community as a primary group.

Charles H. Cooley, *Social Organization* (New York: Scribners, 1920). Part I, "Primary Aspects of Organization"; Chap. 30, "Formalism and Disorganization."

The classic statement concerning the nature of primary groups.

Ellsworth Faris, *The Nature of Human Nature* (New York: McGraw-Hill, 1937). Chap. 4, "The Primary Group: Essence or Accident."

Already cited in the text, this well-written essay maintains that a group is primary because of the relations of its members, not because of spatial contiguity or temporal priority.

Earle E. Eubank, *The Concepts of Sociology* (New York: Heath, 1932), especially pp. 135-156.

The nature of groups ("human plurels") and the problems of classifying them.

Richard T. LaPiere, *Collective Behavior* (New York: McGraw-Hill, 1938), Chap. 5, "Conventional Behavior"; Chap. 6, "Regimental Behavior"; Chap. 7, "Formal Behavior"; Chap. 8, "Congenial Behavior."

Interesting observations on types of interaction, from extremely formal to extremely informal.

Robert M. MacIver, *Society* (New York: Rinehart, 1937), Chap. 12, "The Primary Group and the Large-Scale Association."

One of the better textbook treatments.

Robert Redfield, *Folk Culture of Yucatan* (Chicago: University of Chicago Press, 1941), especially Chap. 12.

While the whole book is concerned with the problem of increasing secularization of society in Yucatan, Chap. 12 summarizes the results of the study, indicating the degree of secularization and individualization and their accompanying characteristics.

Robert Redfield, "The Folk Society," *American Journal of Sociology*, Vol. 52, (January, 1947), pp. 293-308.

Describes the main characteristics of a folk society, including those which mark it as "primary." This article should be read together with Louis Wirth's article on Consensus.

Jerome F. Scott and George C. Homans, "Reflections on the Wildcat Strikes," *American Sociological Review*, Vol. 12 (June, 1947), pp. 278-287.

This article throws light on the nature of secondary organization by showing the role of faulty communication in the development of many wildcat strikes.

Frederic M. Thrasher, *The Gang* (Chicago: University of Chicago Press, 1936).

The most thorough, firsthand study of youthful gangs ever made —in the home of gangs, Chicago.

T. N. Whitehead, *Leadership in a Free Society* (Cambridge: Harvard University Press, 1936).

The role of primary group relations in the motivation and behavior of industrial labor. Makes a good case for the necessity of taking account of informal relationships in large industrial enterprises. (See also the references to Chap. 17, "Economic Institutions").

Max Weber, *Essays in Sociology* (New York: Oxford University Press, 1946, translated by H. H. Gerth and C. Wright Mills), Chap. 8, "Bureaucracy."

One of the outstanding statements of the nature of bureaucracy as a form of social organization.

Louis Wirth, "Consensus and Mass Communication," *American Sociological Review,* Vol. 13 (Feb., 1948), pp. 1-15.

A forceful discussion of the problem of consensus in a mass society. As such the article contributes much to the understanding of mass society and secondary relations.

William F. Whyte, *Street Corner Society* (Chicago: University of Chicago Press, 1943).

Primary and secondary groups in the Italian section of a large city. Extremely graphic description and interpretation based on participant observation.

Kimball Young, *Sociology: A Study of Society and Culture* (New York: American Book Company, 1942), Chap. 7, "The Primary Community."

A textbook discussion of the rural neighborhood as a primary community. Contains selected references.

CHAPTER XII

RURAL AND URBAN COMMUNITIES

LET us now turn to a particular kind of territorial group—the community—where membership is determined by the sharing of an immediate locale. Later, in connection with the state, wider territorial groups will be dealt with and at another point, in connection with the family, kinship groups will be considered. But for the present the local territorial group, universally important in human society, requires analysis.

What Constitutes a Community?

An attempted definition that encompasses all human communities meets the same dilemma that presented itself in the case of primary and secondary groups. There is both a physical criterion (in this case territorial proximity) and a social criterion. Since neither alone will define the community, both must be considered.

TERRITORIAL PROXIMITY

Never does a population spread itself evenly over a region. Always there are clusters of residences, and inevitably the people within one cluster find it easier to interact with one another than with people in other clusters. They may do business with outsiders, but they do more business with one another. They find it more convenient to visit, worship, play, work, and gossip with one another than with outsiders. The slower the means of communication, the more restricted is the area, the fewer are the people, and the greater is the amount of primary contact. On the other hand the more rapid the means of interaction, the larger is the potential size of the community and the more secondary is its social structure. Those people belong to a given community who live closer to its central cluster than to any other such cluster.

It is no accident that people cluster together. Nearness facilitates contact, furnishes protection, and makes easier the organization and integration of the group. Within the cluster, patterns of spatial distribution are created or evolved which serve to symbolize and make more efficient the group structure. Among the Serente, a primitive Amazonian people, the community site is shifted from time to time, but always each household has the same spatial location with reference to the other households (in accordance with its clan and moiety connections). A similar use of spatial patterning has been observed in other primitive societies. Malinowski has this to say of the Trobriand village:

> We pass the grove and find ourselves between two rows of houses, built in concentric rings round a large open space. Between the outer ring and the inner one a circular street runs round the whole of the village. The outer ring consists of dwelling-houses, the inner of store-huts in which the *taytu,* a variety of yam, which forms the staple food of the natives, is kept from one harvest to the next. We are struck at once by the better finish, the greater constructive elaboration, and the superior embellishment and decoration which distinguish the yam-houses from the dwellings. . . . Both these and the dwellings always face the centre. . . . A big yam-house belonging to the chief stands in the middle of [the central] space. Somewhat nearer the ring, but still well in the centre stands another large building, the chief's living hut.
>
> This singularly symmetrical arrangement of the village is of importance, for it represents a definite sociological scheme. The inner place is the scene of the public and festive life. A part of it is the old-time burial ground of the villagers, and at one end is the dancing ground, the scene of all ceremonial and festive celebrations. . . . The inner ring of store huts [surrounding the central space] share its quasi-sacred character, a number of taboos being placed on them. The street between the two rows is the theatre of domestic life and everyday occurrence. . . . The central place might be called the male portion of the village and the street that of the women.[1]

In American cities economic and social competition produce typical patterns of segregation of ethnic groups and class strata. In short,

[1] Bronislaw Malinowski, *The Sexual Life of Savages in North-Western Melanesia* (New York: Harcourt Brace, 1929), pp. 9-10.

although the form of the community varies from one society to another, there is always a community which utilizes in its social structure the possibilities of territorial proximity. Always there is a center, a place where events that are community-wide in interest and importance may be celebrated. It is here that the villager, without fully realizing it, comes to honor everything affecting the entire community.

Finally, the community is always the heart of a larger region of exploitation. This larger region, or hinterland, may or may not be settled. If settled, the people may simply be remote members of the community or they may be members of lesser communities. The degree of contact shades off imperceptibly as distance and other barriers remove the hinterland from the community. The larger the central cluster, other things equal, the greater must be the hinterland.

SOCIAL COMPLETENESS

The community is the smallest territorial group that can embrace all aspects of social life. Although the household is a smaller contiguous group, it is also more limited in scope. The community on the other hand is a local group broad enough to include all the major institutions, all the statuses and interests, that make a society. It is the smallest local group that can be, and often is, a complete society.

The community does not, as does the clan, gang, crowd, business, or church, require the existence of other groups outside and beyond itself. In most instances it forms part of a larger organization such as a tribe or a nation, but it need not; and even so, it remains true that most of the individual's social life is lived within his community. The common area of residence implies also a common life.

As a consequence, community ends are more ultimate than those of most other groups, for they embrace or transcend the ends of specific groups within the community. The community cannot be partial, cannot be identified with any particular institution or group by which it is constituted, for it consists precisely in the inter-institutional and inter-group connections that give to the whole its cohesion. The ends of the community are the standards by which the competing claims of its component groups are adjusted. This gives to community ends their transcendency and makes them at once more remote, more nebulous, and more pervasive than the specific group ends with which the individual is ordinarily in closer contact.

Types of Communities

In classifying communities one may use four interrelated criteria, as follows: (1) the size of the population; (2) the extent, wealth, and populousness of the hinterland; (3) the specialized functions of the community within the whole society; and (4) the kind of organization the community has. These criteria enable one to distinguish between various kinds of primitive communities, between primitive and civilized and between rural and urban communities.

PRIMITIVE BANDS AND VILLAGES

What distinguishes the local group in primitive as against civilized society is its smallness, its sparsely settled and undeveloped hinterland, its detachment from other communities, and its comparatively simple social organization. The smallness of the community and the undeveloped character of the hinterland are both connected with the primitive technology. Slow transportation limits the extent, and simple hunting or tilling techniques limit the intensity, of exploitation. It has ordinarily been assumed that gathering, fishing, or hunting peoples will naturally have smaller villages than herders and agriculturalists, but so many factors other than the technology enter the picture that generalizations on this basis alone are true only in a crude sense. Fishing villages near well-stocked waters may contain more inhabitants than agricultural villages on poor soil. Bearing in mind, however, that food-getting technology is likely to be related to other factors as well, we can agree with the following summary by Linton:

> Where there is no reliance on trade and manufactures, the upper limit for agricultural groups seems to be 350 to 400. Even this requires unusually good soil and well-developed farming techniques, and such a size is rarely reached. Taking the world as a whole the average size of the band for agricultural peoples is probably between 100 and 150. Herding peoples with well-developed transportation facilities may, by frequent movements, live in units nearly as large as those of agriculturalists. The bands of hunters and food-gatherers are usually much smaller. In regions of scanty food supply they may

be limited to ten or fifteen individuals, while under optimum conditions they rarely exceed 100 to 150.[2]

The hinterland of the primitive band may contain a great deal of space per person. The aboriginal population of California is estimated to have been only 150,000 (about 1 per square mile), that of Australia 250,000 (about 1 per 12 square miles).[3] Nomadism makes it possible for a small group to cover a large territory. Usually nomadic peoples do not wander aimlessly and perpetually in a straight line, but rather have a regular circuit. The community moves about its hinterland, re-establishing itself at different points. This enables the small band to exploit a wide territory despite otherwise poor means of communication and transportation.

The largest primitive villages are those practicing agriculture in rich alluvial valleys with inexhaustible soil. But many less fortunate agricultural communities are forced by soil conditions to move every few years, thus practicing a sort of agricultural nomadism. This was true, for example, of the Indians in the Amazon valley and the Veddahs in Ceylon.

Owing to its isolation the primitive community is more self-sufficient than the modern town or city, more of a society within itself, and for this reason is the purest type of community. The main sources of inter-community contact are marriage, kinship, and trade. Except through marriage there is little exchange of residents from one village to another. Though on ceremonial occasions several bands or villages may come together, the rule still holds that life is almost wholly restricted to the local sphere.

So far does this localism go that each band or village tends to have a slightly different culture from the others. Since the individual seldom leaves the band, his absorption of culture is derived mainly from intimate and constant contact with its members. His loyalty and interest are bound up with the local group where most of his close ties, including those of kinship, are usually to be found. Not infrequently the members of a village feel vaguely kin to one another and often they *are* kin to one another, as emphasized in extreme cases by "village incest" taboos.

[2] Ralph Linton, *The Study of Man* (New York: Appleton-Century, 1936), pp. 215-216.

[3] Robt. H. Lowie, *Introduction to Cultural Anthropology* (New York: Rinehart, 2nd ed., 1940), p. 13. The present density in the United States is approximately 46 per square mile; in Puerto Rico, 630.

One of the first steps as civilization develops is the breakdown of localism and the growth of inter-community contact. Some of the things usually missing or present only rudimentarily in the primitive community are laws, writing, science, and a special education system —all fundamental in civilized life. The institutions of the primitive community have an undifferentiated character, being all woven into the same concrete patterns and giving to the community an organic corporateness that many modern towns and cities lack. This is why it is easier to study primitive rather than modern communities as functional organic wholes. The modern community, which is more of a specialized part of a larger whole, cannot be understood in terms of itself alone. Each segment may be more closely linked with similar segments in other communities than with dissimilar segments in the same community. In college towns, for example, one of the reasons for town-and-gown conflict is the faculty's greater concern with nationwide academic opinion than with local opinion. Similarly, the middle-class suburb suffers from the fact that most of its inhabitants have a residential but not an occupational interest in the community. The primitive band or village is more of a functional unit in its own right. Small, isolated, and unspecialized, it is a primary group in every sense.

RURAL VERSUS URBAN

In modern society one of the great distinctions is that between rural and urban, between country and city. It is a distinction that has little to do with the primitive communities just discussed because the village or hamlet in our society, no matter how small, is still subjected to countless urban influences. Whereas the strictly primitive society is a completely rural society, free from any urban influence, the civilized society is always partially urbanized. The rural-urban differential is therefore a gradient (albeit an important one), with the rural end of the scale never even approaching absolute rurality.

Much ink has been wasted in trying to define "urban." The difficulty lies in the fact that as usual a physical condition (in this case, concentration of population) tends to give rise to but is not invariably correlated with a social phenomenon (urbanism).

One might think that all places with a high density of population are urban, but this is not true. Some of the agricultural villages of India, where land is so dear that as little of it as possible is used for residential purposes, have an average number of persons per room as great as have the crowded Indian cities. Yet nobody would think of calling these villages urban simply because of the density. They have too small an absolute population and too small an inhabited area. On the other hand, too large an area cannot be called a community or "place." One would not call Australia a "city," despite the fact that most of its people live in cities. The demographic distinction between rural and urban must therefore take account not only of the ratio between population and land (density), but also of absolute population and absolute area. Accordingly, the degree to which a place is urban can be defined as follows:

$$U = f\left(\frac{P}{A}, P, A\right)$$

when U = urbanity, P = population, and A = area. The question of weighting the three factors is arbitrary, and is settled differently in different countries. The usual practice is to reason mainly in terms of absolute population, tacit assumptions about density and area being made explicit only when necessary. Thus the United States Census Bureau sets a floor on population as the dividing line between urban and rural. It treats all incorporated places of 2,500 or more as urban, the assumption being that an "incorporated place" has a restricted area so that the inhabitants dwell close together. Obviously, however, not all "places" with 2,500 or more are incorporated; so the Census Bureau includes as urban the unincorporated places having a sizable population.[4] Within the urban category additional distinctions are made primarily on the basis of absolute population. Thus we speak of cities of 100,000 to 500,000 inhabitants, cities of 500,000 and over, etc. Nevertheless, although urban areas inevitably contain small parcels of uninhabited land, it is assumed that the area embraced should be generally one of high and continuous density. With the expansion of city populations beyond the municipal boundaries, it becomes necessary to redefine the

[4] Specifically, it includes "unincorporated political subdivisions with a population of 10,000 or more and a population density of 1,000 or more per square mile; and in the States of Massachusetts, Rhode Island, and New Hampshire, those towns (townships) which contain a village of 2,500 or more, comprising either by itself or when combined with other villages within the same town, more than 50 per cent of the total population of the town." *Statistical Abstract of the United States,* 1946, p. 2.

areas in non-political terms—hence the metropolitan district.[5] The factor of density is clearly demonstrated by the fact that in 1930 the 96 metropolitan districts (all with 100,000 or more population) embraced nearly half of the country's total population but only 1.2 per cent of the area.[6] In 1940 New York City, with 299 square miles, had an average density of 24,900 per square mile—more than 56 times the average density of the entire country.

But the floor of what is considered urban is not uniform from one country to another. It varies all the way from 1,000 in Argentina to 10,000 in Italy and Spain. Also the amount of area included is not uniform. The cities of Hungary, for example, embrace a tremendous agricultural area. The *municipios* of Latin America (somewhat similar to our New England townships) are often confused with towns and cities in the strict sense, though they include great amounts of rural countryside. Furthermore, the reporting of statistics for cities of various size classes is not standardized. Generally, however, the larger the population of the towns being considered, the more available is the information and the more possible is international comparison.

Socially speaking, the city is a way of life. The adjective "urbane" suggests this way of life very neatly; it indicates a wide acquaintence with things and people, a certain tolerance born of this acquaintance, and a somewhat suave and polished manner arising from diverse association in a cosmopolitan milieu. The urbane person has mastered the art of external comformity, of superficial politeness, which hides rather than reveals the internal motivation and state of mind. He has learned how to lead different lives in different contexts, to take advantage of anonymity and of special friendship as the occasion arises. He is the product of a peculiar kind of environment, the urban setting.

Now the question arises, to what extent is the urban way of life limited to the urban population? To what extent do the physical and

[5] Defined in 1930 as including, "in addition to the central city or cities, all adjacent and contiguous civil divisions having a density of not less than 150 inhabitants per square mile, and also, as a rule, those civil divisions of less density that are *directly* contiguous to the central cities, or are entirely or nearly surrounded by minor civil divisions that have the required density." [Fifteenth Census of the United States, *Metropolitan Districts: Population and Area* (Washington: Government Printing Office, 1932), pp. 5-6.]

[6] Walter F. Willcox, *Studies in American Demography* (Ithaca: Cornell University Press, 1940), p. 113.

the social definitions of urban correspond? The answer is that there is a causal connection between the two but not a one-to-one correspondence. The city, as a place where population is concentrated, inevitably gives rise to and depends upon certain features of social organization that we regard as urban. By its very nature it throws people into close contact with strangers, facilitates the rapid diffusion of news and fashions, permits a high degree of individualization, stimulates invention, social mobility, secularization, etc. At the same time it depends on a complex economic system which makes possible the quick transfer of goods and services, an elaborate division of labor, and a high degree of rational enterprise. But once these things have arisen, once we have actual cities, their influence can be carried far beyond the city boundaries and can thus characterize people who do not actually dwell in cities. In this way rural areas can become highly urbanized.

The fact that the city's effects are wider than the city itself means that we should speak not only of cities but of urbanized societies and regions. Yet when the term "urbanized" is used this way its meaning is ambiguous. It may simply describe the degree to which the population of the region is living in cities irrespective of other social traits, or it may refer to the diffusion of urban attitudes throughout the population. Generally the two correspond, but one country can be demographically more urban and yet socially more rural than another. Chile, for example, has a greater percentage of its population living in cities than does Canada [7] but its people, by almost any set of indices, are less urban.

Origin of the City

The problem of the origin of the city life is simpler than many other "origin" problems, because the first cities appeared recently enough to leave evidence of themselves. The archeologist, however, is not sure he has yet discovered the very first cities. Nor, assuming he has discovered them, is he capable of giving us the full social picture, because his evidence is limited to what he can dig up. Yet he does provide some valuable hints.

Since cities cannot exist without drawing an economic surplus

[7] Kingsley Davis and Ana Casis, *Urbanization in Latin America* (New York: Milbank Memorial Fund, 1946), p. 3.

from the hinterland, their emergence had to await the growth of technology to such a point that a surplus could be created and transported. This stage was not reached until settled agriculture had been attained in the late neolithic period some seven or eight thousand years ago. The most favorable spots were those where the climate was dry enough to be healthful and hot enough to provide sunshine, where the natural vegetation was thin enough to be cleared, the rainfall not so heavy as to leach the soil, and the soil itself so thick and rich as not to become easily exhausted with successive crops. These conditions were often found in rich alluvial valleys deficient in rainfall but with riverine flood waters to furnish irrigation.[8] Consequently, what appear to be the first cities arose in the Nile, Tigris, Euphrates, and Indus valleys. In the New World the first cities, apparently without influence from Old World cities, arose along the desert river valleys between the Andes and the Pacific, in the flat table lands of Guatemala, and in the Valley of Mexico.

Agriculture alone was not enough. Also required was an adequate system of transportation so that the surplus could be brought to the city. In this the invention of the wheel and the domestication of animals were a great help. The domestication of animals not only made possible use of pack animals and wheeled vehicles but also, as applied to agriculture, increased the ratio of crop production to human labor. In the absence of the wheel, as in the New World, pack animals could be used or, if the economic system were otherwise sufficiently well organized to release them (as among the Inca), human burden-bearers could be employed. Relatively dry alluvial valleys provided few obstacles to land communication, and the rivers themselves gave cheap transportation.

In order to get the surplus to the city, however, something more than the means of transportation was necessary. The city had somehow to offer services to, or have power over, the rural people. It accomplished this purpose through the trading of manufactured goods (hence the intense urban division of labor), through the offering of military protection (drawing upon concentrated manpower and using

[8] Ralph Linton, "Crops, Soils, and Culture in America," in *The Maya and Their Neighbors* (New York: Appleton-Century, 1940), p. 37. Paul Kosok, "The Role of Irrigation in Ancient Peru," *Eighth American Scientific Congress, Proceedings,* Vol. 2, Anthropological Series (Washington: Department of State, 1942), pp. 169-178. Kirk Bryan, "Pre-Columbian Agriculture in the Southwest as Conditioned by Periods of Alluviation," *ibid.,* pp. 57-74.

strong fortifications), through the provision of religious services (furnished by a professional priesthood), and through the offering of recreation and entertainment. In every case the city was admirably suited to provide these things. But it did not need to attract only; it could also demand. With a high concentration of numbers it was in a strategic position to attack and dominate any particular part of the rural region, even though the population of the whole hinterland might exceed that of the city by many times. With an elaborate division of labor it could equip its soldiers well. The city was consequently in a position to levy tribute on the countryside; or to put it another way, whoever could levy tribute over a wide area tended to create a city and to gain power therefrom.

Written records relating to the early cities of both the Old and New Worlds are available. For the Old World they are records written by the inhabitants themselves; for the New World they are records written by Europeans. We thus get a historical cross-view of some of mankind's earliest cities. Cuzco in the Andes reached a population of about 200,000.[9] Tenochtitlan (Mexico City) in the Valley of Mexico had approximately 60,000 houses and an estimated population of 300,000 when the Spaniards came.[10] Many Mayan cities were admitted by the Spanish Conquistadores to be "more considerable than Seville."[11] For people to exist in such large aggregates the conditions necessary for city life must have been well advanced. Descriptions of life in these cities—with their professional sports, their gambling, their class distinctions, their temples, fiestas, market places, prostitutes, and slang—all have a modern flavor. They attest that there is a social atmosphere common to all cities where-ever and whenever found.

As we move forward from the late Neolithic and early Bronze periods the record, at least so far as Europe and the Mediterranean world are concerned, becomes ever fuller. There is gradual improvement in technology, especially in the use of metals and in handicraft generally. The greatest strides were perhaps made in the field of symbolic inventions, the most outstanding of which was writing. Any-

[9] Geo. P. Murdock, *Our Primitive Contemporaries* (New York: Macmillan, 1936), p. 423.

[10] Edwin R. Embree, *Indians of the Americas* (Boston: Houghton Mifflin, 1939), p. 68.

[11] Franz Blom, *The Conquest of Yucatan* (Boston: Houghton Mifflin, 1936), p. 62.

thing that improves communication and the storing of culture also facilitates the growth of cities. The historian not only finds in his materials the record of the growth of cities—Athens, Carthage, Alexandria, Rome, Constantinople—but he also finds the record of the decline of cities.[12] The most interesting kind of decline was not that of particular cities such as Ur,[13] but the decline of urban life in entire regions. A regional decline is indeed the maximum that one can find, because once the inventions fundamental to city life were made they were never completely lost. Once cities appeared on the human scene they never disappeared again except in particular areas.

The Modern City and the Urbanized Society

The great impetus to the development of cities came with the industrial revolution. The application of mechanical power to textile and metal industries in the latter part of the eighteenth and early part of the nineteenth centuries enormously increased the economic surplus available for the support of urban populations. The new power could best be utilized with large machines and large plants; hence the factory with its requirement of numerous workers created the factory town and factory city. At the same time the agricultural system, stimulated by a rising urban market, constantly improved its techniques. And the application of mechanical power to water and land transportation enabled the agricultural produce to reach the cities quickly and cheaply. Improved transportation also facilitated the circulation of people and information. The introduction of the power press and machine manufacture of paper made possible an enormous increase in printed matter, thus facilitating technical education, scientific progress, and further innovations in all fields. The development of canning and refrigeration; of telegraph, telephone, and radio; of electric railways, automobiles, and airplanes—these and countless other inventions enormously increased the number and potential size of cities. Everywhere the urban population grew faster than the rural; everywhere the city increasingly set the

[12] It is this sort of interest that Henri Pirenne is following in the first chapters of his *Medieval Cities* (Princeton: Princeton University Press, 1939). Archeologists are still puzzled by the decline of the Mayan cities of the so-called Old Empire. See Thomas Gann and Eric Thompson, *The History of the Maya* (New York: Scribner's, 1931), pp. 61-66. Also Ralph Linton, *op. cit.*

[13] Sir Leonard Woolley, *Ur of the Chaldees* (Harmondsworth: Penguin, 1938), Chap. 7.

pattern of life, becoming the chief diffusion center as well as the main offspring of the new mechanical era.

With this rapid rise of cities there came into human life something new and important—the urbanized society. As long as most of the population remained rural, the urban way of life was not the only way of life. Only recently have the populations of large regions come to live preponderantly in cities. Only recently have urban attitudes penetrated deeply into the country. The change, though occurring rapidly, has only commenced. When the whole world becomes urbanized, as it seems it surely will, then human society will have undergone a major transformation. Table 1 gives the proportion of the population living in cities for selected countries of the world. In many countries over half the population now lives in urban places.[14]

Urban Growth in the United States

The growth of cities in the United States is a remarkable phenomenon. When the country embarked on its career as an independent nation in 1790 it had no towns of 50,000 inhabitants, and only 5 per cent of the population lived in places of more than 2,500. By 1920 more than half the population lived in urban centers, and by 1946 approximately 60 per cent did so (Table 2). No less than 53 per cent of the urban people, or 30 per cent of the total population, resided by 1930 in big cities of over 100,000 inhabitants. The phenomenon is best summed up in this way: by 1946 there were 15 times as many rural people in the United States as there were in 1790, but there were 420 times as many urban people.

With the rapid concentration of people in cities there was an actual shrinkage of the rural-farm population. "In 1920 the rural-farm population numbered 31 million and made up 29.7 per cent of the total population. By 1940 it had shrunk to a total of slightly over 30 million or 22.9 per cent of the population. By the end of 1944 the farm population had declined still further, to about 20 per cent of the national total." [15] The increasing rationalization of agriculture

[14] The precise number depends on the limit to what is considered urban. If a limit of 2,500 or 3,000 were set, many additional countries would prove to be heavily urbanized.

[15] Philip M. Hauser and Conrad Taeuber, "The Changing Population of the United States," *Annals of the American Academy of Political and Social Science*, Vol. 237 (January 1945), p. 17.

TABLE 1

PER CENT OF POPULATION IN CITIES, VARIOUS COUNTRIES

Country	*Date* *	*In Cities 5,000 +*	*In Cities 10,000 +*
Great Britain	C 1931	—	74
Japan	C 1935	64	46
Germany	C 1933	56	—
	C 1939	—	52
Uruguay	E 1941	56	52
U.S.A.	C 1940	53	48
Argentina	E 1943	49	47
Chile	C 1940	45	41
Canada	C 1941	43	38
France	C 1936	47	38
Cuba	C 1943	39	36
Sweden	C 1935	36	33
Greece	C 1928	36	—
	C 1937	—	30
Egypt	E 1939	—	27
Panama	C 1940	26	25
Mexico	C 1940	28	22
Puerto Rico	C 1940	26	21
Poland	C 1931	24	20
Venezuela	C 1936	22	18
Brazil	C 1940	21	18
Colombia	C 1938	19	15
India	C 1941	12	10

* "C" means that the figure is derived from a census, "E" that the figure is an estimate.

TABLE 2

GROWTH OF THE URBAN POPULATION IN THE UNITED STATES

1790 to 1946 *

Year	*Per Cent Urban*	*Percentage Increase in Per Cent Urban*
1790	5.1	——
1800	6.1	19.6
1810	7.3	19.7
1820	7.2	−1.4
1830	8.8	22.2
1840	10.8	22.7
1850	15.3	41.7
1860	19.8	29.4
1870	25.7	29.8
1880	28.2	9.7
1890	35.1	24.5
1900	39.7	13.1
1910	45.7	15.1
1920	51.2	12.0
1930	56.2	9.8
1940	56.5	0.5
1946 †	60.0	6.2

* Philip M. Hauser and Hope T. Eldridge, "Projection of Urban Growth and Migration to Cities in the United States," in Milbank Memorial Fund, *Postwar Problems of Migration* (New York: 1947), p. 162.

† Estimated.

has enabled a smaller and smaller proportion of the population to grow the food for all the rest. As late as 1870, 53 per cent of American workers were gainfully employed in agriculture, whereas in 1940 only 17 per cent were so employed. Clearly "in little more than a century our country has profoundly altered its mode of life and has been transformed from a rural frontier settlement into a full-fledged, urban industrial society." [16]

It will be noticed from Table 2 that the rate of urbanization in this country has been declining. The rate was fastest during the period from 1840 to 1870, and since then, with minor fluctuations due to economic conditions, has been gradually slowing down. Yet

TABLE 3

PROJECTIONS OF URBAN POPULATION AS PERCENTAGE OF TOTAL POPULATION

1950-2000 *

Year	*Per Cent Urban of Total Population*		
	Low	*Medium*	*High*
1950	60.1	61.2	62.2
1960	60.5	64.3	68.1
1970	60.8	67.5	74.6
1980	61.1	70.9	81.6
1990	61.4	74.5	89.4
2000	61.7	78.2	97.8

* Hauser and Eldridge, *op. cit.*, p. 165.

there is little reason to believe that urbanization will soon come to an end. On the contrary the United States is still less urbanized than several other countries, and the basic economic and social trends still point to more concentration in cities. Hauser and Eldridge have made projections of the future urban population which are given in Table 3. On the basis of their highest projections they find that 98 per cent of the population will be living in urban places by the year 2000. On the basis of their medium assumption the percentage will be 78, and on the basis of their lowest assumption it will be 62.[17] In the future the United States urban growth "will undoubtedly proceed at a slower rate than in the past. The average annual rate of growth of the urban population from 1900 to 1930 was about 3.2

[16] National Resources Committee, *Our Cities* (Washington: Government Printing Office, 1937), p. 2.

[17] Philip M. Hauser and Hope T. Eldridge, *op cit.*, pp. 159-173.

per cent (and higher in earlier decades), whereas between 1930 and 1940 growth averaged 0.8 per cent per year." Since 1940 the urban population has increased about 0.25 per cent per year. The reasons for the decreasing rate of growth lie in declining fertility, a declining rate of improvement in mortality, and declining immigration. Nevertheless, the urban population will in all probability continue to grow faster than the rural population.[18] There are still more people on farms than are necessary to grow the crops.

TABLE 4

PER CENT OF POPULATION IN CITIES OF 100,000 AND MORE 1820-2000 *

Year	*Per Cent in Cities*	*Percentage Increase in Per Cent in Cities*
CENSUS FIGURES		
1820	1.3	—
1830	1.6	23.1
1840	3.0	87.5
1850	5.1	70.0
1860	8.4	64.7
1870	10.7	27.4
1880	12.4	15.9
1890	15.4	24.2
1900	18.7	21.4
1910	22.1	18.2
1920	25.9	17.2
1930	29.6	14.3
1940	28.9	—2.4
MEDIUM PROJECTIONS		
1950	31.4	8.7
1960	33.2	5.7
1970	35.0	5.4
1980	37.0	5.7
1990	39.0	5.4
2000	41.2	5.8

* Hauser and Eldridge, *op. cit.*, pp. 170-171.

As between the various classes of cities the rate of urban growth in the United States has been fairly uniform. "The proportion of the population living in places of 100,000 or more inhabitants has increased in much the same way as the proportion living in all urban places. In most decades the increase in the proportion of the population in the large cities has proceeded at a more rapid rate than the proportion urban (see Table 4). The outstanding exception is

18 Abram J. Jaffe, "Population Trends and City Growth," *Annals of the American Academy of Political and Social Science,* Vol. 242 (November 1945), p. 18.

the decade 1930 to 1940 when the proportion in large cities actually decreased, and the proportion urban increased slightly." [19] In Table 4 medium projections for the proportion of the total population living in cities of 100,000 and over are given to the year 2000. According to these calculations "more than 67 million persons, or 41.2 per cent of the total population, will be living in cities of this size class by the year 2000, as compared with about 38 million, or 28.9 per cent in 1940." [20]

Confusion has arisen from talk about urban decentralization in America. It is a fact that the areas around big cities have been increasing more rapidly in population than the core cities themselves. In 85 metropolitan districts, for example, average annual rates of growth were as follows: [21]

	1920-30	*1930-40*
Central cities	1.9	0.3
Outside central cities	3.9	1.3

But this kind of "decentralization" is only natural. As the great urban agglomerations continue to grow they will not simply pile up an ever higher density at their center, but rather will add more people around the periphery. The periphery represents a much greater area, and with improving transportation, urban residents can live farther out and thus avoid the disadvantages of ever greater concentration at the center. Such decentralization does not mean, however, that urbanization is lessening. On the contrary it means that ever more people are flocking to the urban areas. This is shown by the following average annual rates of growth of 137 metropolitan areas: [22]

	1890-1900	*1900-10*	*1910-20*	*1920-30*	*1930-40*
137 Metropolitan areas	2.9	3.3	2.6	2.7	0.8
Balance of nation	1.6	1.4	0.7	0.7	0.6

Big urban agglomerations are like sandpiles: the more that is added at the center, the more the edge expands. Our so-called urban decentralization is really an accommodation by which an ever greater urbanization is accomplished. Urban growth is continuing, and this means that business and industry are not moving to the country.

[19] Philip M. Hauser and Hope T. Eldridge, *op. cit.*, pp. 170-171.
[20] *Ibid.*, p. 171.
[21] Jaffe, *op. cit.*, p. 21.
[22] *Idem.*

The Sources of Urban Population

The speed and scope of urbanization in the United States, remarkable as it seems, is by no means unique. Practically everywhere in the world there has been and is now occurring a marked increase in the number and size of cities. This tendency slowed somewhat during the great depression but nevertheless continued. In every country in Europe during the inter-war period the urban population was growing faster than the rural.[23] In India the percentage of the population living in places of 5,000 or more was 9.3 in 1881 but 12.8 in 1941. In Latin America, despite a lack of heavy industrialization, the cities are growing very rapidly, and the larger the city the faster it tends to grow.[24] All told, rapid urbanization is a world phenomenon.

For an understanding of this world-wide trend toward urbanization one must know the source from which the cities are getting their people. We know, for example, that almost without exception the fertility of city people is lower than that of rural people.[25] We know, too, that the mortality rate is more often higher in urban centers than in the countryside.[26] It follows that the cities have a lower natural increase than the country, and that consequently their faster growth can be due only to rural-urban migration. The rush of rural people to modern cities is probably the greatest human migration that has ever occurred. It means that the urban world is largely peopled by persons not reared in that world but brought up instead in a rural atmosphere. It means that urban growth must eventually come to a halt, because the massive size of the big conurbations will eventually preclude their absorbing enough migrants from the depleted countryside to maintain their rate of growth. As the rural

[23] Dudley Kirk, *Europe's Population in the Interwar Years* (Geneva: League of Nations, 1946), pp. 15, 29.

[24] Davis and Casis, *op. cit.*, pp. 1-22.

[25] A. J. Jaffe, "Urbanization and Fertility," *American Journal of Sociology*, Vol. 48 (July 1942), pp. 48-60. Kingsley Davis, "Human Fertility in India," *ibid.*, Vol. 52 (November 1946), pp. 244-246. P. K. Whelpton and Clyde V. Kiser, "Trends, Determinants, and Control of Human Fertility," *Annals* (January 1945), pp. 113-118. The studies of rural-urban fertility differentials are extremely numerous. Abundant citations will be found in *Population Index*.

[26] Edgar Sydenstricker, *Health and Environment* (New York: McGraw-Hill, 1933), Chap. 4. U. S. Bureau of the Census, "Mortality by Marital Status by Age, Race, and Sex, Urban and Rural, 1940," *Vital Statistics—Special Reports, Selected Studies,* Vol. 23, No. 2. Davis and Casis, *op. cit.*, pp. 14-17, 24-30. Noel P. Gist and L. A. Halbert, *Urban Society* (New York: Crowell, 1942), pp. 255-261.

population becomes an even smaller proportion of the total population, and as the pattern of low fertility diffuses from the city to the rural regions, the source of recruitment for the cities will dry up. At that point the cities must either stop growing or enormously increase their fertility.

Social Effects of the City

A great amount of speculation, most of it uncontrolled, has gone into the question of the city's social effects. There is a feeling that urban life is somehow new, perhaps unnatural, yet that it is dominant and that consequently it must have tremendous effects on civilization.[27] But concepts such as unnatural or abnormal, when applied to human society, tend to be normative or metaphysical rather than scientific. Certainly, for some millions of years after the first appearance of culture, human groups lived only in a rural setting. Most of them still do, despite the progress of world urbanization. In this sense cities are abnormal, but they are scarcely less abnormal than the numerous other cultural developments—such as agriculture and metallurgy—that originated in the last few thousand years.

The problem of city effects needs careful formulation prior to discussion or research. In the first place, the variable ("city") is difficult to isolate. In the second place, the "effects" are different according to whether we are talking about the people inside or the people outside the city. People need not live in a city to be affected by it. The city is a diffusion center, evolving traits which, though they could have arisen nowhere else, can nevertheless be spread to non-city areas. This means that the full effect of city life cannot be measured by rural-urban differences in contemporary society, because both sides of the comparison reflect city influence. A more complete measure of urban influence would require a comparison between a modern city and an isolated primitive society. Yet this would not show what in the city is to be attributed to the city itself. It is all too easy, simply because cities are tangible, to attribute to them social effects that are in reality a function of other factors.

What seem to be the effects of the city in one area often turn out,

[27] Elmer T. Peterson, *Cities Are Abnormal* (Norman: University of Oklahoma Press, 1946). Ralph Linton, *The Science of Man in the World Crisis* (New York: Columbia University Press, 1945), pp. 215ff.

on analysis of another area, to be due to something else. Thus in the United States we often attribute to the city effects which in reality are due to the newness of our social order, the influx of foreign immigrants, the diversity of groups, etc. By looking at England, an older and more fully urbanized area, we discover that many of the alleged effects do not hold true. For instance, the commonly assumed association of urbanism with high divorce and crime rates does not hold true in England as against the United States. Again, the frequent identification of high urbanization with heavy industrialization is not borne out in Latin America; [28] nor is the association between literacy and urbanization fully supported by a comparison of Egypt or Chile with Norway.

We cannot attribute the rise in living standards, the occurrence of the industrial revolution, and the growth of science all to the city, because the city is a result of these. But unless we watch ourselves carefully, we are likely to attribute to the city the effects of these basic changes. Lewis Mumford blames the modern metropolis for business cycles, imperialistic wars, bureaucracy, mental disorder, and in fact "the paralysis of all the higher activities of society." [29] If loose reasoning of this sort is to be avoided, some way of isolating the strictly urban variable must be found. The most satisfactory way seems to be to deduce the major social traits of the city from its demographic uniqueness—that is, the size and density of its population—and then to check with empirical findings. This is what is done in the following section.

THE URBAN SOCIAL STRUCTURE

(1) *Social heterogeneity*. The concentration of a large population in a small area requires social heterogeneity for the following reasons: Density maximizes the competition for space and for comparative advantage, and thus forces a striving for specialization. The population cannot support itself by agriculture but only by manufacture and trade, which flourish on specialization. The fact that goods must be brought from a wide area means contact with regional diversity. Since competition decreases the birth rate and therefore requires the continual recruitment of population from the countryside, the diversity of different regions is incorporated into the very texture of the

[28] Davis and Casis, *op. cit.*, pp. 2-22.
[29] *The Culture of Cities* (New York: Harcourt, Brace, 1938), pp. 272-279.

city. As a consequence the city has always been more heterogeneous than the rural community. It has "been the melting-pot of races, peoples, and cultures, and a most favorable breeding-ground of new biological and cultural hybrids. It has not only tolerated but rewarded individual differences. It has brought together people from the ends of the earth *because* they are different and thus useful to one another, rather than because they are homogeneous and like-minded." Indeed, "the greater the number of individuals participating in a process of interaction, the greater the potential differentiation between them. The personal traits, the occupations, the cultural life, the ideas of the members of an urban community may, therefore, be expected to range between more widely separated poles than those of rural inhabitants." [30]

(2) *Secondary association.* By virtue of its size the city cannot be a primary group. It must instead be a secondary group. People must associate constantly and at close quarters with strangers. Hence the purely rural reaction to strangers—a reaction of either hostility or hospitality—must be replaced by indifference. Although superficial manners of politeness and mutual convenience evolve in the city, they are mechanical; in general the urbanite treats the myriad of strangers he meets in daily contact as animated machines rather than as human beings. His behavior toward an acquaintance is different from that towards the surrounding sea of strangers, yet it is conditioned by the very presence of these strangers. He distinguishes, for example, between various degrees of acquaintanceship, gives only a small portion of his time to each acquaintance, and judges each by much the same external standards that he necessarily uses for quick judgments of strangers. "The urban world puts a premium on visual recognition." We see the uniform that denotes the function but are oblivious to the personal eccentricities lying behind the uniform.[31] We judge the person by how he looks, how he speaks, and how he acts—in a brief moment of time; because, not knowing him, not knowing anyone else who knows him, and not caring anyway, we can do nothing else.

[30] Louis Wirth, "Urbanism as a Way of Life," *American Journal of Sociology*, Vol. 44 (July 1938), pp. 10-11. Our discussion in the present section draws liberally upon this stimulating article. For a mathematical statement of the relation between population concentration and specialization, see Geo. K. Zipf, *Human Behavior and the Principle of Least Effort* (Cambridge, Mass.: Addison-Wesley Press, 1949), Chap. 9.

[31] Wirth, *op. cit.*, p. 14.

Even friends and acquaintances are likely to be known only in a particular context, in a particular segment of life. Urbanites, to be sure, are "dependent upon more people for the satisfactions of their life-needs than are rural people and thus are associated with a greater number of organized groups, but they are less dependent upon particular persons, and their dependence upon others is confined to a highly fractionalized aspect of the other's round of activity." [32] For this reason urban contacts are described as segmental. It is parts of persons, not whole persons, that are known.

(3) *Social tolerance.* Given the diversity of its population and the impersonality of its contacts, a certain tolerance characterizes the city. People rub elbows with and become indifferent to extremes of all kinds—extremes of opinion and interest, extremes of poverty and wealth, extremes of education and background. The indifference arises partly through necessity, partly through the superficiality and brevity of contacts, and partly through familiarity. If oddities and anomalies are seen often enough, they cease to seem odd and anomalous. The city dweller becomes blasé, no longer surprised by anything. This tolerance certainly has its limits; the city demands a certain amount of external conformity on grounds of decency and convenience. But the limits are wider than in a rural community, and they exercise less control over private life. Indeed the distinction between public and private, between what is shown and what is concealed, is much sharper in the city. It is the public behavior that the city regulates, the private behavior that it ignores. Its control is impersonal and general, that of the country personal and particular.

(4) *Secondary control.* The presence in the city of two social worlds—the world of physically close but socially distant strangers and the world of friends and acquaintances—gives the individual a double refuge. He can escape the oppressive control of any primary group when he wishes, simply by disappearing into the sea of strangers. This is the famous anonymity of the city, which frees the urban dweller from close moral control. On the other hand he can escape the impersonality and indifference of the city, as indeed he must, by becoming part of a primary group. He can recapture in the family, the gang, the circle of friends, his sense of emotional security, of being a human being rather than a mere cipher, and thus banish the intense loneliness that the city gives the isolated individual. Al-

[32] *Ibid.*, p. 12.

though a secondary group, the city is at the same time a congeries of interlocking and overlapping primary groups. These exercise considerable control over conduct, but not so thoroughly as in an exclusively rural society.

Because primary controls can be evaded, the city must ultimately have recourse to secondary controls. It must curb the spirit of mutual exploitation that arises from close, diverse contact between people having no sentimental or personal ties. The specialized policeman, the department store and hotel detective, the numerous civic bodies and planning commissions, all have a hand in regulating the complex and predatory relations between urbanites. Even religious control, in so far as it exercises an influence in the secular city, does so largely through secondary associations operating as legal entities and pressure groups. The larger the city, the greater becomes the problem of control and the more complex the agencies of secondary regulation. The city is therefore the place where legal control achieves its greatest day-to-day application, and where the mores and folkways, of themselves, can least be counted on to handle the situation.

(5) *Social mobility.* Just as the city requires and promotes great geographical mobility (of persons, goods, and ideas), so it requires and promotes great social mobility as well. Its elaborate division of labor, its competitiveness, its impersonality—all tend to emphasize the achievement rather than the ascription of status. Recruiting a heterogeneous population whose origins are obscure and rewarding them on the basis of uniqueness, eccentricity, novelty, efficiency, and inventiveness, it necessarily judges status according to what the individual does and how he looks rather than to whom he was born. The urban person can therefore raise or lower his status to a remarkable degree during his lifetime, and the competition for status (and with it the insecurity of status) becomes a perpetual preoccupation.

This does not mean that inequalities are less in the city. On the contrary, they are tremendous. It does mean, however, that the inequalities of the city are not exclusively inequalities of opportunity but also, and to an increasing degree, inequalities of achievement. Thus the purely caste element in social stratification is minimized. In the great and growing cities of India, for example, the caste system cannot be maintained.[33] In the Middle Ages the budding cities were

[33] See Chap. XIV.

places where serfs lost their unfree status.[34] Today the city is a place where social climbing is most prevalent. The ascription of status on the basis of kinship is too conservative, rigid, and slow a principle to serve the dynamic needs and alternative opportunities of the urban structure. Such ascription as remains tends to rest on readily observable traits such as sex, age, and race, but even these are notoriously hard to sustain as strict bases of status in the city. By ingenuity and industry the urban person can overcome almost any categorical definition of his status. The exercise of talent, the achievement of education, the accumulation and display of wealth—these are avenues to a high position in all the different spheres of urban life. It is characteristic of the city that nearly everything is professionalized, from sports and entertainment on the one hand to politics and business on the other. Status increasingly centers on the occupation, on the nature and competence of the activity, rather than on the accident of birth.

Although the city's competitively induced inequalities are great, ranging from the highest of the high to the lowest of the low, there are nevertheless limits peculiar to the city itself. One of these is the fact that the city gives greater voice as well as greater opportunity to the bottom strata. It brings a large number of lowly persons together and often segregates them in particular neighborhoods, where spatial juxtaposition strengthens common interest in creating class solidarity. As a result the stratification of the city appears to undergo a peculiar evolution. The erstwhile dominance of the higher commercial class slips increasingly into the hands of a higher governmental or bureaucratic class, giving rise to a new system of stratification more socialistic and collectivistic in character. Whether or not the new system contains less inequality than the other depends on the nature of the political system. The city can seemingly harbor democracy or totalitarianism with equal facility.

(6) *Voluntary association.* The sneer size of the urban population, its close proximity, diversity, and easy contact, make it the perfect setting for the voluntary association. No matter what a person's hobby or vocation, national background or religion, age or color, he can always find others with a similar basis of interest. For this reason nearly every kind of group tends to acquire a strongly

[34] Henri Pirenne, *Medieval Cities* (Princeton: Princeton University Press, 1939), pp. 122-123, 126-127, 154.

voluntaristic character, membership depending neither on the accident of geography nor the accident of kinship. Even primary groups succumb to this tendency, becoming both more voluntary and more specialized. Courtship becomes more open to individual choice; wedlock becomes easier both to enter and to leave; parenthood becomes more deliberate; and friendship becomes more segmented and ephemeral. In addition, entirely new kinds of groups arise, based on extremely specialized interests. Thus the number of group memberships per capita is extremely high in the urban population, and these are divided among a bewildering variety of cliques, clubs, nationalities, and neighborhoods having relatively little to do with one another except in an economic sense.

"Typically in the city, interests are made effective through representation. The individual counts for little, but the voice of the representative is heard with a deference roughly proportional to the numbers for whom he speaks." [35] The group must organize or its cause will perish. The emphasis on the collective pursuit of particular interests helps to explain why the city is hardly a genuine community. Not only is it not a primary group, it is not even regarded as a group by its inhabitants. It is rather a statistical, geographical, and minor political entity commanding little allegiance for itself.

(7) *Individuation.* Curiously, the aggregation of masses in the city has the effect, not of suppressing the individuality of each person, as one might expect, but of emphasizing it. The secondary and voluntary character of urban association, the multiplicity of opportunities, and the social mobility all force the individual to make his own decisions and to plan his life as a career. The concurrent variety of groups he may join and interests he may pursue make it unlikely that anyone else in the city will have exactly the same social personality. Moreover, the competitiveness of the city places him over against everyone else; he is not inexorably tied to any particular relationship or any particular cause. His awareness of differences in others and his knowledge of human relativity give him perspective on himself, so that he can view himself with greater objectivity and separate himself from the mass of those around him. The fact that he must manipulate others and must guard against being manipulated, forces him to distinguish clearly between himself and others. The net result is a sort of atomization of the constituent

[35] Wirth, *op. cit.*, p. 14.

individuals. On one side stand the individuals, highly self-conscious and unique, and on the other side stand the great associations and institutions of the city. There is nothing much in between. The individual stands over against the whole city, never completely absorbed by any one social group.

(8) *Spatial segregation.* The competition for space in the heterogeneous and dynamic city leads to a characteristic segregation of groups and functions, visible in the city's spatial pattern. The center of the urban area is of course monopolized by functions of basic importance to the whole city, such as finance and government. Most of the finance is paper work; it can be carried out in small space; but since it controls vast resources and is therefore high-priced, it can afford an exceedingly high rental in the center of the city. Similarly, the commercial activities that appeal to rare and expensive tastes and hence must draw their limited patronage from every sector—e.g. quality jewelry stores, big department stores, legitimate theatres, fine hotels—are also located in the center. The same is true of high-priced professional services—e.g. diagnostic clinics, law offices, accounting firms, government offices, etc. Such functions cannot be entirely dispersed to neighborhood areas, as is largely the case with retail grocery establishments, filling stations, cleaning and pressing shops, shoe repair shops, garages, and drug stores. Instead they need to be at the crossroads of the entire city, the point where they are nearest to the most people. Here the land is so costly that the buildings expand vertically, filling the center of the city with skyscrapers.

So high-priced are the activities at the center and so valuable is the land, that residential occupancy is excluded except in hotels and skyscraper apartment buildings. As a result the place of work becomes increasingly separated from the place of residence. The financial and commercial hub has chiefly a daytime population; at night the erstwhile occupants are sleeping in another place.

Since residence is a symbol and a result of one's social station, there arise in the city segregated residential areas where the inhabitants are distinguished by racial, ethnic, religious, occupational, or pecuniary characteristics. In general the higher the social status the more advantageous the residence from the point of view of space per person, architectural and scenic beauty, and freedom from nuisances such as smoke and noise. If such places are near the place of occupation—near the center of the city—they require huge outlays in cash rentals. It they are far away from the place of occupation—in the suburbs—they require, in addition to the purchase price or rental cost a steady outlay in time and money for transportation. Only persons enjoying a high social status can afford these great costs.

Spatial segregation offers a convenient means of understanding the city's social organization. The inhabitants of a given area tend to have not only a general social station in common but also many other characteristics. It is found that fertility, mortality and migration; crime, delinquency, divorce, and suicide; insanity and morbidity; illegitimacy, illiteracy, vice, pauperism, and many other indices of social behavior differ sharply from one area of the city to another. The study of social organization in terms of spatial distribution (so-called urban ecology) therefore provides a method of study that is highly objective and readily accessible. Of course it is true that no section of a city is absolutely homogeneous and that often it is necessary to relate different indices of behavior to the individual as a unit rather than to the area. Urban ecology is consequently only one among many general methods of sociological study. Yet its results, some of which have been utilized in the present book, are useful.[36]

THE CITY'S INFLUENCE ON ITS HINTERLAND

The point has already been made that, since city effects are wider than the city itself, we must speak not only of city dwellers but also of urbanized societies and regions; and that the degree to which a whole region is socially urbanized depends both on the proportion of the population living in cities and the degree of diffusion of urban traits from city to country. How can the latter be determined?

A purely physical measure of influence is the population of a city divided by the distance from it, on analogy with celestial mechanics and electrical magnetism. This way of measuring population influence has been analyzed by John Q. Stewart and has been applied

[36] For descriptions of urban ecology in the United States see Gist and Halbert, *op. cit.*, Part II; Stuart A. Queen and Lewis F. Thomas, *The City* (New York: McGraw-Hill, 1939), Part III. The pioneer work in urban ecology was done by the Department of Sociology, University of Chicago, under the able inspiration of Robert E. Park. See, e.g., Robert E. Park, Ernest W. Burgess, and Roderick D. McKenzie, *The City* (Chicago: University of Chicago Press, 1925).

to social data by him and George K. Zipf.[37] Such an approach seems perfectly reasonable because we know that, other things equal, contact between individuals is greater the closer they are. But the physical analogy is of no consequence itself, except as suggesting a hypothesis. Human beings do not exert magnetism or attraction according to their physical mass, but they do so through socio-cultural channels. Therefore, the question arises as to whether or not social influences of cities (or any other population aggregates) vary according to their population divided by the distance from the point being influenced. In general, as several studies suggest, this tends to be true. Thus the percentage of a large urban department store's charge accounts carried by persons in each of 96 surrounding towns and cities was found to be proportional to the population of the town or city divided by its distance from the department store. A similar relationship was found in the case of attendance at the New York World's Fair, the circulation of big daily newspapers, the trips of trucks and passenger cars, obituaries in the *New York Times,* and residential moves (migration).[38]

The relationship between influence, size, and distance has long been known in a general way. McKenzie proved conclusively that the influence of a city varies with its size and that it tends to wane with distance outward. He illustrated this with many different series of statistics. He also pointed out that influence on a certain point is conditioned by the competition of other large urban centers.[39] But the formulation of the matter in mathematical terms has received wide attention only recently. The advantage of a mathematical formulation is that it enables us to state exactly the generalized relationship which on theoretical grounds we can expect nearly all concrete cases of urban influence to approximate. Then we can state the exact amount of deviation from this norm in actual cases, thereby setting a further problem for explanation. In this way order and exactitude in the study of urban influence can be introduced. Obviously, for

[37] See John Q. Stewart, "Empirical Mathematical Rules Concerning the Distribution and Equilibrium of Population," *Geographical Review,* Vol. 37 (No. 3, 1947), pp. 461-485; and Geo. Kingsley Zipf, *Human Behavior* (Cambridge: Addison-Wesley, 1949).

[38] George Kingsley Zipf, "The Hypothesis of the 'Minimum Equation' as a Unifying Social Principle with Attempted Synthesis," *American Sociological Review,* Vol. 12 (December 1947), pp. 641-648. John Q. Stewart, *Coasts, Waves, and Weather* (Boston: Ginn, 1945), p. 163.

[39] R. D. McKenzie, *The Metropolitan Community* (New York: McGraw-Hill, 1933), Parts II and III. By courtesy of the publisher.

example, the political influence of Washington, D. C., is greater than its relative size and distance would indicate. But in order to know how much greater we must have a precise statement of the theoretical or expected norm from which there is a departure.

The conventional "center of population" in the United States, computed by the Census Bureau, lies on farm land in Indiana. The computation is made on the lever-arm principle, one man at a distance of 1000 miles counting as the equivalent of 10 men at 100 miles. Thus the greater the distance, the greater the influence. But we know that social influence really works the other way. The shorter the distance, the greater the influence. If accordingly a simultaneous application of the population-divided-by-distance rule is made, we get a measure of the total demographic force being exerted on any one particular spot by all the other areas. In the United States the maximum demographic force or intensity is found to center in New York. This has been true for more than a century. New York City is therefore the true center of population in this country.[40]

Every city dominates an area around it. Why it should dominate is explained by the demographic force just mentioned. Translated into social terms this means that the efforts of more people are concentrated in one spot than in any other spot within the region, hence this spot carries more weight than any other particular place in the region. Even though the hinterland may contain many times the population of the city, its people are spread out more thinly and thus lose the advantage of concentration. The city is the one strong among the many weak. Turning the explanation around, one can say that unless the city is dominant it cannot command the wherewithal for its survival. It must somehow, by exchange or by force, secure from the rest of the population a sufficient surplus to maintain large numbers in a small area. The fact that it exists at all is evidence of its dominance.

It is customary in dealing with urban areas to distinguish between the metropolitan community and the metropolitan hinterland. The first, embracing the suburbs as well as the central city, is an area of common life within commuting distance of the central city; it is "the 'built-up' area in which public services such as water, light, sanitation, and power become common problems." [41] The hinterland,

[40] Stewart, *Coasts, Waves, and Weather*, pp. 163-167.
[41] McKenzie, *op. cit.*, p. 84.

on the other hand, is the trade area under the domination of a given city. As compared with the metropolitan community, which in the United States is virtually synonymous with the Census Bureau's "metropolitan district," the boundary of the hinterland is hard to determine. Dominance in one respect may not coincide with dominance in another respect. Nevertheless, in the United States a useful demarcation of metropolitan hinterlands has been worked out on various bases, including the distribution of daily newspaper circulation. If a town reads a greater number of City "A" than City "B" newspapers, it can be placed in the sphere of City "A." Dealing with all towns in this way one finds that the whole country can be divided into a number of cultural and economic provinces, each with a single dominant city as its focus.[42] Since the newspaper is an important avenue of communication, supported primarily by advertisers who want business, it is not surprising to find that the regions thus delimited agree fairly well with those based on wholesale trade, farm marketing, telephone calls, railroads and bus tickets, and highway traffic counts.

> The city whose newspapers have the largest circulation is likely to be the city that sells the most goods in an outlying district. But the newspaper, although a business enterprise, is more than that. It carries stories and editorial comments about politics, sports, "society," prominent persons, and a host of items about religious, civic, economic, artistic, and other interests and events. As readers of a metropolitan paper, country people share these interests.[43]

Of course, the influence of the central city is not equal throughout its hinterland. It is strongest in the immediate suburbs and weakest at the hinterland boundary. Furthermore, cities are somewhat specialized, and with reference to their specialty the hinterland may be larger than ordinary. Los Angeles dominates the whole country with reference to the movie industry, Chicago with reference to meat packing, and Detroit with reference to automobiles. By virtue of its peculiar financial character, New York dominates the entire country in countless ways; and this accords perfectly with our previous state-

[42] Robt. E. Park and Charles Newcomb, "Newspaper Circulation and Metropolitan Regions," in McKenzie, *op. cit.*, Chap. 8. See also Gist and Halbert, *op. cit.*, pp. 118-122.

[43] Stuart A. Queen and Lewis F. Thomas, *The City*, copyright 1939 by McGraw-Hill Book Co., Inc., p. 249.

ment that it is the center of population. For New York, therefore, the whole country is the hinterland even though lesser cities have carved out subsidiary domains of their own.

Given the dominance of the city, it can be expected that many of its traits will be diffused to rural people, first in the areas closest to the city, then in the remote outposts.[44] The process will be faster the more the city is linked with its hinterland. The city and its hinterland become ever more closely interwoven as transportation and communication become more rapid and as distance is overcome by speed. "There is developing within the United States, and in fact throughout the modern world, a pattern of settlement which may be designated as city regionalism. This new city regionalism differs from the regionalism of former times in that it is a product of contact and division of labor rather than of mere geographic isolation."[45] National business concerns find it convenient to have branches in the key regional cities. So do many government agencies, including the Federal Reserve Banking System. Once a city has established itself as the center of a region it tends to expand and diversify its functions, becoming a true metropolis.

The city has continued to absorb people from the hinterland, often taking away more than the natural increase of the countryside and thus depleting the rural population. (Between 1920 and 1930, for example, 41 per cent of all counties in the United States declined in population.) But as it has drawn people from the hinterland the city has also expanded its metropolitan boundaries. The drift to the cities has been a drift to the suburbs, primarily to residential suburbs. If each metropolitan district is weighted equally, regardless of size, the average increase of population during 1930–40 in the United States was 29.7 per cent for suburbs, 6.5 per cent for the central cities.[46] Furthermore, those rural areas that are closest to the city have far outstripped the more remote areas in population growth. As a result of these twin processes—the drift of people to the cities and the expansion of the cities outward—the metropolitan community has come to play a greater and greater part in its total region. In short an ever larger portion of the population is living

[44] Empirical evidence is contained in Edmund de S. Brunner and J. H. Kolb, *Rural Social Trends* (New York: McGraw-Hill, 1933), Chap. 5.

[45] McKenzie, *op. cit.*, p. 313.

[46] Chauncy D. Harris. "Suburbs," *American Journal of Sociology*, Vol. 49 (July 1943), pp. 9-10.

in cities, exerting a constantly greater and closer influence on the diminishing remainder.

Future of the City

Most speculation about the city's future focuses either on beautifying the city or on dispersing its population. The first is primarily an engineering and architectural task. The second is unrealistic, because the only dispersion occurring is a movement of many people and some industry to the suburbs. Any large-scale dispersion of city people to the country would likely come, if at all, as the result of a cataclysmic event such as atomic warfare rather than as a gradual change. The truth is that the world is becoming ever more urbanized as regards both place of residence and point of view. Two great questions therefore stand out: First, to what extent can the entire world become urbanized? Second, what will be the effect on human society?

In thinking of these questions, one should bear in mind that we have been talking all along about three different things: (a) The growth and size of particular cities; (b) the percentage of the total population living in cities; and (c) the spread of urban attitudes and institutions throughout the whole population. These require separate consideration.

(a) It seems unlikely that the growth of existing cities will continue indefinitely. In advanced Western countries the growth of population in general is coming to a halt. This means that if existing cities are to continue to grow they must do so not simply by draining the rural population of its surplus, as they have done in the past, but also by drastically reducing the rural population. They will draw not only upon the interest but also upon the capital. If, therefore, the growth of existing cities does not stop rather soon, the second aspect of our problem will be raised in an acute form; for we shall all be living in the very largest cities, and eventually in New York City alone. But, as pointed out before, the central cities, as contrasted with the rest of metropolitan districts, are already showing signs of a coming halt in growth. They may actually lose population while the metropolitan districts continue to grow. It may be, therefore, that future metropolitan growth will involve such an expansion of area that the average density of the districts will be either stabilized or decreased.

(b) Even in the advanced industrial nations, already heavily urbanized, the percentage of the population living in cities seems destined to increase for awhile yet. Though in these nations the trend will eventually come to a halt the rest of the world, still overwhelmingly rural, will still have a tremendous urbanization ahead of it. Exactly what the saturation point will be is hard to say, but it is entirely within the bounds of possibility that the entire world will eventually reach the degree of urbanization now attained by only a few advanced industrial nations. Consequently it is possible that eventually 75 per cent of the world's population will live in places of 10,000 or over.[47]

(c) As for the diffusion of urban attitudes, it seems likely that the advanced countries will move ahead until their entire populations manifest most of the traits characterizing the city. When this happens, such countries will be completely urbanized. There is little reason why the same trend should not eventually affect all regions of the world. When these areas advance far enough to have numerous cities, they will manifest demographic and social patterns similar to those of the more industrialized countries today.[48] The main question is whether or not, when the saturation point of city development is reached, when almost the entire population has been urbanized from birth, when the rural background of most urban people today has been entirely replaced by an urban background, the problem of social order can still be solved. Can the anonymity, mobility, impersonality, specialization, and sophistication of the city become the attributes of a stable society, or will the society fall apart? How can devotion to a common system of values and a common set of mores be maintained in a highly literate, scientifically trained, individualistically inclined, and sceptically oriented population? The answer is not clear. Probably it can and will be done. England, with its high degree of urbanism, is a stable nation as compared to many rural ones. But in any case it seems certain that a completely urbanized world will be greatly different in its social structure from anything we yet know today. One difference for example, is that a world so technologically advanced as to be completely urbanized cannot

[47] This was the case in England, 1931 (Table 1).

[48] This is apparently the case in Japan, the most advanced Oriental nation. See Irene Taeuber and Edwin G. Beal, "The Dynamics of Population in Japan" in *Demographic Studies of Selected Areas of Rapid Growth* (New York: Milbank Fund, 1944), pp. 1-34.

exist as a collection of sovereign nations; it must either become one political world or destroy itself in Brobdingnagian conflict.

References

Ernest W. Burgess (ed.), *The Urban Community* (Chicago: University of Chicago Press, 1926).

A collection of sociological articles on the modern city. It was literature such as this that inspired much of the modern ecological research and sociological thinking about cities. See especially the chapter by Robert E. Park, "The Urban Community as a Spatial Pattern and a Moral Order," pp. 3-20.

Kingsley Davis, Harry C. Bredemeier, and Marion J. Levy, Jr., *Modern American Society* (New York: Rinehart, 1949), Part 2, "The New Urban Environment."

Selected readings on the growth of cities and the urban way of life.

Chauncey D. Harris, "Suburbs," *American Journal of Sociology,* Vol. 49 (July 1943), pp. 1-13; "The Cities of the Soviet Union," *Geographical Review,* Vol. 35 (1945), pp. 107-121; "A Functional Classification of Cities in the United States," *ibid.,* Vol. 33 (1943), pp. 86-99.

Interesting analyses of statistical data on cities. The one on suburbs describes the growth of suburbs in the United States by functional types, using 1930 and 1940 census data. Suburbs grew more rapidly than any other type of community, but residential suburbs grew faster than other kinds of suburbs.

Julius Jahn, Calvin F. Schmid, and Clarence Schrag, "The Measurement of Ecological Segregation," *American Sociological Review,* Vol. 12 (June 1947), pp. 293-303.

Application of mathematical and statistical techniques to the measurement of residential segregation in cities. Some acquaintance with statistical methods is necessary, but the paper is a good example of increasingly scientific procedures in the study of social phenomena.

Walter M. Kollmorgen, *Culture of a Contemporary Rural Community: The Old Order Amish of Lancaster County, Pennsylvania* (Washington, D. C.: Department of Agriculture, 1941), Rural Life Studies No. 4.

An able description of the rural society of a peculiar religious sect. See also the same author's article in the American Journal of Sociology, *Vol. 49 (Nov. 1943), pp. 233-241, and his chapter in Ralph Wood (ed.),* The Pennsylvania Germans *(Princeton: Princeton University Press, 1942).*

The Rural Life Studies of the Department of Agriculture afford excellent descriptions of varied types of rural communities.

Robert S. Lynd and Helen M. Lynd, *Middletown* (New York: Harcourt, 1929), and *Middletown in Transition* (New York: Harcourt, 1937).

Pioneers in the sociological study of the American town, the Lynds wrote two of the most readable and widely acclaimed community analyses that have ever been published.

R. D. McKenzie, *The Metropolitan Community* (New York: McGraw-Hill, 1933).

A thoroughly scientific account of the rise of the metropolitan community in the United States, the nature of urban regions and urban dominance, and the ecology of the city. This book represented a milestone in the study of the city.

Horace Miner, *St. Denis: A French Canadian Parish* (Chicago: University of Chicago Press, 1939).

A study of what Robert Redfield calls "peasant society." A land-locked community, with the parish as its basis, St. Denis is strongly familial and primary in its relationships.

Lewis Mumford, *The Culture of Cities* (New York: Harcourt, 1938).

A highly evaluative discussion of the modern city from an esthetic, moral, and welfare point of view. The author is naive with reference to economic and sociological facts, and the book is overrated.

Elmer T. Peterson (ed.), *Cities Are Abnormal* (Norman: University of Oklahoma Press, 1945).

The book is not quite so bad as its title sounds. It contains some interesting chapters by various kinds of journalists and specialists.

Calvin F. Schmid, *Social Trends in Seattle* (Seattle: University of Washington Press, 1944).

A very careful statistical study of what has been happening in Seattle.

Warren S. Thompson, *The Growth of Metropolitan Districts in the United States, 1900-1940* (Washington: Government Printing Office, 1948).

This report published by the Census Bureau is a very careful analysis of metropolitan growth trends during four decades. The author had to make a great many adjustments in the statistics. The result is instructive, though somewhat dry and hard to read.

George K. Zipf, "The $\frac{P^1 P^2}{D}$ Hypothesis: On the Intercity Movement of Persons," *American Sociological Review,* Vol. 11 (December 1946), pp. 677-686.

A technical article showing that the number of people moving between any two cities of the United States is proportionate to the product of the populations of the two cities (P^1 and P^2) divided by the shortest transportation distance (D) between them. A good example of quantitative generalization.

CHAPTER XIII

THE CROWD AND THE PUBLIC

TURNING from the stable and organized groups to the relatively unorganized, we come upon some curious manifestations of social life—crowds, publics, mobs, and masses, in all their diverse forms. The unanticipated, irrational, and often undesired behavior of these groups lends them fascination as an object of study, not only for the social scientist but also for the layman interested in the strange aspects of the life around him.

Although unorganized groups embrace many different types, most of them can be subsumed under two general categories representing opposite extremes, the crowd and the public. A consideration of the crowd and its variations will lead naturally into a discussion, later in the chapter, of the public.

The Crowd

It is extremely difficult to find human aggregates that are mere collections of physical bodies. Always people physically together are also to some extent socially together. Though they may congregate in the most casual way, on the street or in a railway station, the mere awareness of one another's presence starts a lively though silent interchange of mutual impressions. Their clothes, faces, and movements reveal much about one another's statuses. Their behavior makes allowance for the existence of the others, implying the unconscious sharing of certain sentiments and enforcement of common conventions. Even their apparent indifference to each other is a cultivated attitude, easily dispelled as soon as a change occurs in the situation. Let a bomb explode, a fist-fight develop, or an immoral act occur, the erstwhile indifference evaporates and gives place quickly to overt focused interaction. The aggregation has changed from a passive and nonfocused group to an active directional crowd.

It is not simply the amount of interaction but also its focus that makes a group. The people in the waiting room of a railway station hardly form a social unit at all, but a lynching mob is a definite unit. The difference is not simply that there is more interaction in the latter but that the interaction has direction; it is more clearly pointed toward a common end and is consequently more cumulative. The latter is a focused crowd, the main object of our present interest, while the former is a diffuse crowd or mere social aggregation. In describing the general characteristics of crowds we have in mind the focused crowd, although it actually occurs far less often than the mere aggregation.

GENERAL CHARACTERISTICS OF CROWDS

One criterion of the crowd is *physical presence.* It has been said that the size of a crowd is limited by the distance which the eye can see and the ear can hear. Without such physical presence there can be no crowd. Unlike a gang, a family, or a community, its existence ceases the moment it is dispersed. Since people can seldom remain physically present for any great length of time, this means that the crowd is a *temporary* and *ephemeral* social group. It is always a creature of the moment, with neither a past nor a future. Furthermore, its size is limited by the necessity of physical presence. When it gets beyond a hundred thousand it must be exceedingly close-packed to remain a crowd. The audience at an important football game represents about a maximum. The people watching a parade up Fifth Avenue, if spread the entire length of that street and numbering hundreds of thousands, hardly represent a crowd in the strict sense. Such a throng has some of the characteristics of a crowd but also some of the characteristics of a public. The size of the crowd is equally indefinite at its lower limit. The popular saying that three is a crowd puts the limit a little too low. Five or six is a better limit. But in any case the physical characteristics of the crowd —its size, closeness, and temporary nature—mean little unless its social characteristics are also present.

The crowd is *unorganized.* It may have a leader but it has no division of labor, no system of statuses. The implications of this trait are far-reaching. It means, in the first place, that to an exceptional degree the interaction is *uncontrolled,* therefore spontaneous, amorphous, and unpredictable. It means, in the second place, that everybody has the same status in the group, that the crowd is made up of *uniform units.* Whatever the statuses of the individuals in the larger social system, as members of a crowd they are alike because the crowd has no organization which can utilize the individual differences. This situation at once provides them with *anonymity,* for their social identity does not carry over into the crowd. It also robs the interaction of whatever unique qualities the individuals, as separate socialized personalities, may possess and gives to the interaction its notoriously crude and unrefined character—the ends and sentiments utilized being those of the *lowest common denominator.* In other words, the interaction takes place in terms of *generalized emotions* and sentiments that everybody possesses who happens to be in the group, no matter what his status; it therefore appeals to society-wide or stratum-wide norms rather than to those norms associated with particular positions, and has none of the qualification or hesitation which ordinarily attends the application of norms in organized social life. This explains why the crowd can be so *fanatical,* why it can pursue an end without any restraint or regard for consequences. Its participants have lost those parts of themselves which distinguish them as separate personalities, and have retained only that part which resembles all the other participants no matter how high or how low. For this reason, too, the crowd is *uninhibited.* Its participants not being identified as distinct persons, their ordinary statuses and roles being set aside in this temporary and unconnected situation, their sense of security and power being augmented by the immediate presence of others doing the same thing, they yield easily to impulses that otherwise would be restrained.

As a result the crowd when aroused tends to focus its attention upon one thing, an *idée fixe.* This gives expression to impulses that would not only otherwise be restrained but would in many cases be repressed from consciousness; hence the capacity of the group to give expression to *unconscious motives.* This effect is further enhanced by the well-known *cumulative* and *circular character* of crowd interstimulation. Because the participants in a crowd are all on one level, because their attention is focused on one thing, because their inhibited impulses find ready release in spontanous action, the crowd is highly suggestible. The participants react to one another's gestures, postures, and cries in an almost automatic animal-like way, with a swiftness that precludes thoughtful interpretation or rational foresight. Much of the reaction is in fact of an imitative type, each individual doing exactly what the others are doing. The effect of so many persons stimulating the actor in the same way and at such close range is to heighten his response. His heightened response in turn gives greater stimulation to the others, and their greater response stimulates the actor still more. This cumulative character of crowd interstimulation tends to make the behavior of the crowd ascend to a climax. The climax is passed only when physical exhaustion is reached or the common end is accomplished. The individual is for the moment "lost in the spirit of the crowd" and works himself up "to a high pitch." The members of the crowd as a whole are "beside themselves" and "don't know what they are doing." It follows that certain types of behavior such as fads, crazes, manias, riots, panics, and stampedes—are more characteristic of crowds than of other groups. The initial close aggregation of individuals may be oppressive. The close presence of others may cause shortness of breath, discomfort, tension, and depression until the crowd as a whole gets into action. Then there is a quickened heart beat, thrill, exhilaration, and expansion until the excitement reaches a peak. Sometimes the source of suggestion comes from some particular individual or nucleus of individuals who may be located near the center of attention or who are themselves the focus of attention. Once the dominance of a center is established, its reactions are communicated rapidly to the periphery. The power of suggestion in many cases is tantamount to hypnosis. Individuals are particularly susceptible to the display of excitement in others; they tend to respond to such exhibitions with excitement in themselves. Once the crowd gets going, however, it is not every suggestion that takes hold. Suggestions contrary to the dominant focus of attention and activity are ignored, while those fitting it are accepted.

To stop the formation of an acting crowd or mob or to disperse it after it has formed, it is often necessary to shift its attention. This can be done in some cases by calling to mind the identity of each person, reminding him of his everyday status and of the ordinary inhibitions by which his behavior is governed, etc. It can sometimes be accomplished by removing the object of attention, as when a Negro is spirited away from the jail in which the lynching mob hoped to find him. Again it can be done by strong measures that replace the original crowd emotion by a more powerful and discouraging one, as when a prison riot is broken up by gunfire from the guards. Occasionally it is possible to divide the opinion of the group and start them arguing instead of acting. There is the famous story, for example, of the college professor who was summoned before the board of trustees and accused of disbelief in God. He saved himself by asking them first to define God. Crowds, however, are seldom so sedate as a board of trustees, so that it is not easy to put them in an argumentative frame of mind.

THE SOURCE OF THE CROWD

The individuals who constitute any particular crowd, if it is purely a crowd, are together by accident. This does not mean that there are no causes which explain their coming together but rather that the causes do not flow from the group itself. Having no organization and being ephemeral, the crowd does not select its participants. The casual nonfocused aggregation is a constant feature of social life, especially in complex urbanized societies where secondary contacts are the order of the day. Necessarily, the members of these aggregations are drawn from all walks of life and are present in the situation only because, in pursuing their private ends, they have to make use of common conveniences (such as trains, subways, stadia, parks, restaurants, etc.). Most such aggregations never eventuate in any sort of acting crowd, but a crowd may grow out of them if the proper circumstances arise.

A focused crowd is formed, either out of an aggregation or a dispersed population, when some stimulus comes along that releases an existing tension. This stimulus may be nothing more than an individual doing something that others find they would like to do, such as dancing. Usually, however, it involves a more violent stimulus and a greater tension. A fire alarm, for example, may cause such panic to the occupants of a building that a stampede will result. The sight of an immoral or criminal act may arouse an aggregation to a high pitch of anger and punitive action. Societal mores and criminal laws could not exist unless they had emotional backing in the sentiments of the public. The open violation of these sentiments sets up a tension for which mob action furnishes a satisfying release. Crowds also give release to tensions created by social conditions considered unjust, so much so that some authors have considered the primary source of crowds to be social unrest.

TYPES OF CROWDS

The crowd is commonly said to arise in the interstices of social organization. Not being organized itself, it has no elaborate articulation with the rest of the social system. Having no permanence it can have no culture or tradition of its own. And possessing a certain spontaneity and unpredictability it has practically no measure of self control. The social norms seem often designed to prevent the formation of crowds or at least to keep them on the level of nonfocused aggregations. Thus the police take precautions against riots, marine officials precautions against mutiny, fire departments precautions against stampedes, and banks precautions against panics. It is indeed a case of an ounce of prevention being worth a pound of cure, for once a crowd goes into action it is a potent engine of destruction, hard to stop and hard to guide. There is in most thought on the subject an undercurrent of disapproval of crowds, the assumption being that they are destructive rather than constructive and that they make beasts out of otherwise normal men. Because of the mechanism of circular response the crowd's focus of attention narrows to only one end, pursued with ascending intensity and heedless violence; and we have seen already that the normative order requires a certain balance of ends. The primarily emotional rather than intellectual character of the crowd, connected with its lack of organization and internal control, renders it incapable of any complex accomplishment. It can destroy more easily than it can build. And since it often gives expression to inhibited impulses, it tends to ignore or offend the restraining mores. In short, there seems plenty of evidence that the crowd is often an unanticipated and undesired social phenomenon, an anarchical element in an ordered society.

But it would be amazing if such a potent force were not socially utilized in some way. In fact it requires but little reflection to realize that the crowd situation is constantly being planned for and utilized by every type of social system. In the last chapter, for example, it was pointed out that there is usually a central community area wherein community-wide gatherings take place. These gatherings are often of a crowd-like character. Especially noteworthy is the fact that the circular response and augmented excitement of the crowd is a highly effective device for instilling or re-emphasizing the transcendental ends, the group values, the sacred norms, and the traditional ideas by which the community lives. These ends, values, norms, and ideas cannot be maintained in the minds of the societal members simply in matter-of-fact ways, because they are not matters-of-fact but something added to and transcending factual (sensory) reality. Religion has always included the crowd situation among its most important devices for maintaining its hold upon the people. In some religions, especially those of primitive societies and the more muscular Christian sects, this is clearer than in others, but all of them make use of the device. The vociferous revivals and camp meetings of the rustic Baptists, Holy Rollers, Pentecostals, etc. are but extreme examples of crowd behavior characterizing the formative period of nearly every religious sect from the early Christians of Rome to the Jewish Chassids of the seventeenth and eighteenth centuries. But even the most staid and established church makes some use of crowd interstimulation and makes elaborate provision for it. Similarly, political parties thrive on crowd-like conventions; governments rely upon public displays and enthusiastic assemblages; and colleges whip up college spirit with pep rallies, shirt-tail parades, and goal-post demolition squads. The excited, yelling, sometimes hysterical throng is a perennial asset of large organized groups from the community to the nation.

Lest it seem that two irreconcilable views of the crowd are here depicted, let us reflect that social attitudes are always relative. The active crowd in the wrong situation is regarded as a menace because of its tremendous force whereas in the right situation, because of this selfsame force, it is regarded as a great asset. Yet there is one qualification that must be made. The nature of the crowd is seriously altered when it is made a part of social organization. On the one hand its spontaneity and unpredictability, its anonymity, transiency, and destructiveness are sharply curtailed. The religious congregation, for example, is a group that has met before, which reassembles "to repeat an experience that gave pleasurable, inspired feelings at previous times."[1] Its activity is guided by a body of memories and behavior patterns and is manipulated by the church officials. Often the exhibition of too much spirit is regarded as bad taste; the congregation is restrained by traditional decorum and is reduced to a passive audience. On the other hand, the skill with which the con-

[1] E. B. Reuter and C. W. Hart, *Introduction to Sociology* (New York: McGraw-Hill, 1933), p. 485.

gregation is manipulated may be such as to enhance the hysterical features of the crowd far beyond what could likely happen spontaneously. The minister may be a masterful leader, capable of evoking the highest emotionalism. His sermon may be interspersed with singing, injecting a rhythmic element into the circular response and giving the devotees a chance to participate actively in the meeting. Individual confessions of sin may further extend the mutual participation. The members of the congregation may have been so selected as to draw those with emotionally charged attitudes. In any case they have come with an attitude of expectancy of the exhilaration to come, with past habituation in this type of emotional self-abandonment. As the inflammatory oratory of the minister works up to a climax, as the music increases in tempo and volume, as the confessions grow more intimate and fervid, as the heat of the room increases and the panting becomes more audible, certain individuals inevitably break under the strain and give way to wild cries and physical contortions. These in turn stimulate the others to like behavior. Soon there are sobs, groans, shrieks, hysterical laughs, shouts of ecstasy, jerks, uncontrolled shakes, barks, wallowings, and what not. Visions and hallucinations may appear to the worshipers. They may flail and roll about. An intensity of crowd hysteria has been reached which would seldom if ever occur without a high degree of deliberate planning and manipulation of the conditions. Such frenzied worship may defeat the very purpose of congregational association, because the pleasure of the orgy may eclipse all other values, including those for which the gathering was called. But the opposite tendency, to make of the congregation merely a passive audience, probably also defeats this purpose.

It seems clear in view of these considerations that the first line of distinction in classifying types of crowds is that between crowds which are definitely provided for in the social organization and those which arise spontaneously and unpredictably. This is a distinction cutting across the others, for nearly every kind of concrete crowd may have both a planned and an unplanned form. The interacting situations in which people come together are infinite in their variety. Most of these involve persons with fairly well defined statuses with reference to one another. As such, they are not crowds. Some of them may accidentally become crowds while others engender a crowd spirit by design.

A second broad distinction is that between crowds determined by common or group ends and those determined by private ends. In the latter the private ends must be such as to bring the individuals together. They may be ends that are not even similar but which happen to bring numbers of individuals into the same restricted areas —as on a crowded street. Usually, however, the ends (at least on an immediate level), though disparate and perhaps opposed, are alike. For instance, the people who gather to see a fire are all motivated by curiosity: Everybody's end is alike. But the crowd as a unit is in no way embraced in or conducive to this end. Any particular person would be watching the fire even if nobody else were. In fact he could watch it better if he did not have to look over others' shoulders. The crowd is merely a by-product of the pursuit of similar but private ends. Doubtless the curiosity of each person is enhanced by the presence of others who are also curious, and there may be some thrill in simply being in a crowd. But the goal of each does not require or refer to the rest. There is a common external focus but no common end. How ends can be alike but separate is shown most clearly in crowds that are positive hindrances—when, for example, the members are seeking all at the same time and to the inconvenience of one another to buy tickets, to take advantage of exceptional bargains, or to board a train at the rush hour. Such a competitive crowd may manifest mutual ill will or mutual tolerance. It can in any case do little *as a crowd* except mill around. If it breaks out in united protest against some inconvenience which it suffers, it becomes something radically different—a common-end crowd. If it settles down to carry out some purpose by organizing itself and dividing its labor—in case, say, it decides to put out the fire it has been watching or to save the victims of some accident—it at once becomes an ordered group and ceases to be merely a crowd.[2]

With these distinctions in mind we can give, in outline form, some of the major types of crowds, as follows:

I. *Crowds articulated with the social structure*

A. Formal audiences: theatre audiences, sports audiences, religious congregations. These have central focus and like ends but are passive in character.

[2] Cf. R. M. MacIver, *Society* (New York: Rinehart, 1937), pp. 188-189.

B. Planned expressive groups: dancing crowds, party crowds, religious orgies. These have little focus but pursue a similar end which is the activity itself and the pleasure it gives. They serve the function of giving escape and release from the tension of routine activity. The presence of others through group interstimulation is a definite aid in the fulfillment of this function.

II. *Casual crowds*

A. Inconvenient aggregations: collections of people trying to share common facilities, such as a queue at a ticket window, a group trying to board a public bus, or a number of people caught in a traffic jam. In these crowds the presence of others is a handicap in reaching a competitive goal, and the interstimulation may take the form of mutual antagonism.

B. Panic crowds: persons fleeing from a building on fire, from a flood, from a battle, or from any other catastrophe. In these the interstimulation within the group is apt to heighten the sense of panic, to increase the irrational character of the response, and to be a positive handicap (indeed sometimes a tragic handicap) to escape from the common danger.

C. Spectator crowds: groups drawn together to witness a fire or other spectacular event. These resemble the audiences mentioned above, except that the occasion is unplanned and the activity largely uncontrolled. The focus is an accidental occurrence; group interstimulation plays a relatively small role except in drawing people's attention to the occurrence.

III. *Lawless crowds*

A. Acting mobs: lynching parties, looting gangs, rebellious crowds. The aim of the group is to achieve some purpose by physical force contrary to the ordinary rules of law and order. The presence of large numbers gives a sense of anonymity, heightens the emotions, and leads to actions that the individuals alone would hardly perform. There is usually the feeling that an injustice is being righted and that basic rights are being vindicated in the face of slowness, inefficiency, or inequity of the established legal system.

B. Immoral crowds: orgiastic assemblages, drunken brawls, riotous and destructive celebration. This type resembles the expressive groups mentioned above, but the release from tension goes so far as to violate the mores. Group interstimulation heightens the sense of release; anonymity provides a feeling of protection from possible punishment; the frustrations of ordinary life, especially sex frustrations, provide the motivation for seeking complete relief. The action of the crowd tends to end when a state of satiety is reached.

Such a classification as this is not complete or definitive. Other modes of classification would do just as well.[3] Furthermore, any actual crowd may represent more than one type. Lynching mobs, for example, sometimes have a definitely orgiastic character that suggests the immoral crowd as well as the mob. An attempt to classify crowds does show, however, the numerous ways in which the basic attributes of the crowd—close physical contact, mutual stimulation, temporary duration, unorganized interaction, and anonymity—manifest themselves in human society.

The Public

Unlike the crowd, the public is a dispersed group. Except in the case of small isolated communities, it never meets together. Its interaction must take place through indirect media—through long chains of private conversations, through rumor, gossip, news, via press, radio, newsreel, and television. Such indirect media enable the public to have a far larger membership than any crowd could have. In fact, one can imagine a great world public comparable in breadth of information and strength of cohesion to the public of a single nation today. Yet as a result of its size and dispersion the public cannot exhibit the milling process, the sharp focus, the emotional intensity, and the impulsive unanimity of the crowd. It is hardly an acting group at all but more of a feeling and thinking group—hence the linkage of "public" with "opinion." Any action by the public is done through representatives or through separate individual acts such as voting.

It follows that the individual as a member of the public is more aware of himself and his own interests, and less aware of the group, than he is as a member of a crowd. He is not carried away by the stimulating physical presence of others. "Instead of acting in response to the suggestions and excited stimulation of those with whom

[3] E.g. Herbert Blumer, "Elementary Collective Groupings," in Robert E. Park (ed.), *An Outline of the Principles of Sociology* (New York: Barnes & Noble, 1939), pp. 233-241.

he is in rapport, he acts in response to the object that has gained his attention and on the basis of the impulses that are aroused by it."[4] He is concerned with making decisions about current issues in the light of his own predilections and desires. The behavior of the public, then, is simply the summation of all the private decisions made and acted upon by the constituent individuals.

This raises the question of how the public achieves unity. If its members make their own decisions about every issue, how can any unison emerge? The fact is that decisions must be made on some basis. Even when individuals are thinking "for themselves"—that is, without any direct stimulation from anyone else—they are doing so in terms of mores, sentiments, and formulae that are part of the culture and in terms of information that is transmitted to them through others. Consequently there can be no public without to some degree a common culture, and none without common channels of indirect communication. The two great methods by which public support can be obtained for any line of action are: first, the appeal to the existing sentiments and traditions; second, the giving of false or true information. It is sometimes said that the public as contrasted with the crowd is a rational group, but this is nonsense. The process of making decisions does involve fitting the traditional formula to the current situation as known, but the formula itself is not necessarily the result of logical thought processes nor is the information necessarily accurate. It is precisely by being nonlogical —that is, by accepting feelings and attitudes ready-made and by selecting information according to desire rather than according to accuracy—that people with different interests come to hold similar views and the public becomes something more than a mere statistical concept.

THE EFFECT OF PUBLIC OPINION

The mass effect of a similar decision by thousands or millions of people, all acting privately, can be enormous. A shift in public taste may ruin one industry and enrich another. A strong public reaction may start a war or produce a revolution. Every government must foster a favorable public opinion or run the risk of being overthrown.

There is always an unpredictable element in public opinion. Polling experts may accurately predict, the day before the election, how

[4] Blumer, *op. cit.*, p. 243.

people will cast their ballots, but this is too late for anyone to utilize the prediction. A forecast made long before the election showing how people would vote *if the election were to occur the next day,* is valuable, not because it predicts the ultimate outcome of the real election but because it gauges what must be done by one side or the other to influence the real election. The very fact that there is an issue before the public indicates uncertainty. An issue that is settled is no longer an issue. It is only with respect to "live" issues—questions on which there is an active division of opinion—that public attention focuses. In such cases the outcome hangs in the balance. If a poll discloses the trend of public thinking or if a prediction is made as to the ultimate solution, this becomes merely another item of information in the controversy surrounding the issue. It would be possible, of course, to make an accurate prediction of what the outcome would be *if this prediction were not made* (or not given any publicity), but once the prediction has been made and publicized it will itself influence the ultimate result, often contrary to the outcome otherwise accurately foreseen. Seldom, however, are predictions decisively important in settling public issues. In fact predictions are constantly being made, not as scientific statements but merely as propaganda devices to try to influence the final result.

From the fact that public opinion and public action revolve primarily around issues, we see that the trend of public behavior is not automatically given in the existing social organization. At most the existing framework merely dictates the terms of the issue and reduces the number of possible solutions. In the United States the question is which *party* will *elect* the next *president*. Whether we shall have a president or a king is not an issue because that was settled long ago in the Constitution. Again, whether we shall have an election or a military coup is not an issue, for that too has been settled. It is clear that the existing social system takes care of the fundamentals. The issues are mostly on the surface, although a trend in the solution of issues as they arise can and does gradually influence the character of the social organization. When an issue is solved and the solution becomes part of the social organization, it is no longer in the forefront of the public consciousness. At that point public attention has moved on to something else.[5]

[5] *Cf.* A. Lawrence Lowell, *Public Opinion in War and Peace* (Cambridge: Harvard University Press, 1923), pp. 87-94.

PUBLIC OPINION AND PROPAGANDA

Public opinion is a collective product. As such it is not a unanimous opinion, nor is it exactly the opinion of a majority or even of any single person. It is more nearly a composite opinion, a sort of synthetic average, formed out of all the different opinions actually held by the public. Being a collective product it "does represent the entire public as it is being mobilized to act on the issue, . . . Public opinion is always moving toward a decision even though it never is unanimous."[6]

Necessarily public issues tend to be phrased in dichotomous terms—e.g. war or peace, protection or free trade, prohibition or saloons, freedom or slavery. This does not mean that each problem has only two facets but simply that public action can best be mobilized, a common denominator most easily struck, when there are only two sides. The most common formula is the "for or against" statement. People can be lined up according to whether they are for or against birth control, for or against price control, for or against immigration, etc. Often the individual is not on either side in a completely unqualified sense, but the heat of public debate and the necessity of mass action reduce the problem to its lowest common denominator, the simple dichotomy. Each pressure group tries to phrase the issue in a way that will marshal sentiment on its side. If one is "for divorce" then one must be "for the destruction of the home"; if one is "against religious education in the public schools," one must be "for atheism and moral decay." The final solution of the issue is often one that practically nobody actually desires but which represents the ultimate outcome in the struggle of conflicting pressure groups—a struggle in which the weapons of distortion, intimidation, censorship, misinformation, and irrelevancy play important parts. Only when a whole system of issues and solutions are observed does a semblance of order and consistency appear in public behavior. The solution of a particular issue often seems utterly chaotic and unrepresentative.

Not every member of the public is equally interested in a given issue. Those who have a real or fancied interest in the matter and are organized for action take the greatest interest; and these endeavor to win the support of the less interested groups. This puts the less

[6] Blumer, *op. cit.*, pp. 247-248.

interested groups in the position of arbiter; it is their reaction that usually determines which extreme will get most in the final outcome.[7] Yet, precisely because it did not play the main role in formulating the question and marshalling the arguments, the so-called passive public, in spite of its position as arbiter, is somewhat at the mercy of pressure groups. It has to decide on the alternatives presented to it, using such information and reasoning as come along, and hence often has to take one or the other of two evils. It does not usually set up the alternatives itself.

The tricks by which people are led to favor one alternative as against another are almost limitless. There is no point in describing them here.[8] Suffice it to say that they all involve either the control of fact or the control of interpretation. In reaching a conclusion about an issue, a person must have on the one hand what he thinks is an accurate account of the current state of affairs and its probable consequences and, on the other hand, a set of values by which he judges the consequences. If publicists can falsify the facts for him, lead him to make a wrong prediction, emphasize certain of his values as against others, or lead him to connect the facts with particular values that he would not otherwise consider relevant to the situation, they can influence his opinion. The use of all the tricks falling in these categories is what we call propaganda. In other words, propaganda is the use of reasoning or facts in which one does not believe, to persuade another person to favor a particular kind of action that he would not otherwise favor. If the publicist himself believes the reasoning or the facts, the process is not propaganda but education or indoctrination.

The most prevalent forms of propaganda in our society are those associated with politics and with commerce. The former is of great significance because it is linked with the exercise of power. The latter is of equal significance because it is linked with pecuniary advantage. In both cases the incentive is very great for the group in question, whether a pressure group, a government, a business firm, a church, or a labor union, to use all the tricks at its command. A part of the institutional machinery has the function of controlling the un-

[7] Blumer, *op. cit.*, pp. 248-249.

[8] See Clyde R. Miller, *The Process of Persuasion* (New York: Crown, 1946); Robert K. Merton, *Mass Persuasion* (New York: Harper, 1946); and Leonard W. Doob, *Propaganda* (New York: Holt, 1935).

inhibited use of propaganda, but in the nature of the case it can never be completely successful.

Censorship is merely negative propaganda. Through its use one seeks to control public opinion by forbidding access to certain arguments or facts.

GROWING IMPORTANCE OF THE PUBLIC IN MODERN SOCIETY

With the development of modern technology the public, in the sense used here, has assumed increasing importance. It has grown to massive numbers, embracing on some issues hundreds of millions of people. It has spread out in space, sometimes girdling the globe. The existence of such widespread public opinion on many issues means that news is circulating, that minds are meeting at least to the extent of debating an issue. The huge impersonal state, the great city, the huge corporation, the great ecclesiastical hierarchy, the mass-production plant—all would be impossible without the presence of a wide public. These agencies must reach and get favorable action from millions of people. Only by appealing to them through channels of mass communication, by public education, public debate, public propaganda, and mass advertising, can any semblance of unity and efficiency be achieved. Modern society rests preëminently on public opinion and public behavior. It is in fact a congeries of different publics, the size and character of each varying with the issue, with the means of communication, and with the degree of interest and education. Public opinion in all its various manifestations is the intellectual arena of modern society, helping greatly to give this society its dynamic quality.

References

William Albig, *Public Opinion* (New York: McGraw-Hill, 1939).

A standard textbook in the field.

Hadley Cantril, *Gauging Public Opinion* (Princeton: Princeton University Press, 1944).

Describes in readable fashion the ways in which public opinion is sampled, analyzed, and interpreted. Very fully illustrated from the author's rich storehouse of opinion research results. See also the same author's The Invasion from Mars *(Princeton: Princeton University Press, 1940) an account of the panic created by Orson Welles' famous broadcast.*

V. F. C. Hecker, *The Black Death, and The Dancing Mania* (Cassell and Co., 1888).

Remarkable examples of mass behavior in the Middle Ages.

Helen MacGill Hughes, *News and the Human Interest Story* (Chicago: University of Chicago Press, 1940).

A fascinating discussion of the social nature of news, with special reference to the human interest story in the newspapers.

Richard T. LaPiere, *Collective Behavior* (New York: McGraw-Hill, 1938).

Presents in brief, readable, and organized fashion the salient characteristics of different kinds of crowds and publics. Particularly good on recreational and escape types of behavior.

Paul F. Lazarsfeld, Bernard Berelson, and Hazel Gaudet, *The People's Choice* (New York: Duell, Sloan, and Pearce, 1944; reprinted, Columbia University Press, 1948).

A study of the behavior of the American public during a presidential election campaign, based on studies of voting behavior, opinion polls, and propaganda.

Gustave LeBon, *The Crowd* (London: Unwin, 1899).

This is the pioneer treatise on crowd behavior. LaPiere says of it: "Le Bon's analysis is stimulating but is often mystic and is frequently inconsistent. His central thesis, that an individual behaves differently in a group than he does in isolation, is incontestable. His explanations of this fact are, however, little short of Hegelian."

Walter Lippmann, *Public Opinion* (New York: Macmillan, 1922).

Already recommended as a masterpiece.

Robert K. Merton, *Mass Persuasion: The Social Psychology of a War Bond Drive* (New York: Harper, 1946).

An inquiry into the techniques and conditions by which Kate Smith, the radio star, sold some $39,000,000 of war bonds in the course of a single day. Based on careful study of listeners while the campaign was going on.

Arthur F. Raper, *The Tragedy of Lynching* (Chapel Hill: University of North Carolina Press, 1933).

A study of lynching as a social phenomenon.

Bruce James Smith, Harold D. Lasswell, and Ralph D. Casey, *Propaganda, Communication, and Public Opinion* (Princeton: Princeton University Press, 1946).

Contains 117 pages discussing the profession of public opinion analyst, the contents of communications, and the effects of communications. Then, in the next 264 pages, an annotated bibliography of 150 "outstanding titles on propaganda, communication, and public opinion."

Walter White, *Rope and Faggot* (New York: Knopf, 1929).

A Negro's critical analysis of lynching behavior.

CHAPTER XIV

CASTE, CLASS, AND STRATIFICATION

WHEN we think of castes and classes, and of social stratification in general, we have in mind groups who occupy different positions in the social order and enjoy different amounts of prestige. It should be noted, however, that not all differences of position come under the heading of stratification. For instance, no one regards all husbands as forming a social class, or all adolescents or grandparents; but one does regard all farm tenants as forming one.

The difference between stratified positions and unstratified ones seems to hinge on a difference with respect to the family. Those positions that may be combined in the same legitimate family—viz., positions based on sex, age, and kinship—do not form part of the system of stratification. On the other hand those positions that are socially prohibited from being combined in the same legal family—viz., different caste or class positions—constitute what we call stratification.

With reference to the class hierarchy the family is a unit: its members occupy the same rank. This is because one of the family's main functions is the ascription of status. It could not very well perform this function if it did not, as a family, occupy a single position in the scale. Children are said to "acquire their parents' status," with the implication that the two parents have a common status to transmit and that the child gets this status automatically as a member of the family. In the same way husband and wife are treated as social equals. In short, between members of the same family class antagonisms are felt to be inappropriate. This is why all wives do not constitute a social class opposed to all husbands. We know that there are wives in every social stratum, and that a wife is generally much closer to her husband in loyalty and interest than she is to other women, and certainly closer to her social class than to the feminine sex as a whole. It becomes obvious, then, that if different statuses may be combined in the same family and must be so combined in order to operate properly, they cannot form the basis of stratification.

Between persons of unequal status in the class hierarchy there is invariably a formal or informal ban against marriage and hence against the formation of legitimate family bonds. The marriage of a pariah and a Brahmin in India, of a Negro and a white in the United States, of an *hacendado* and a *peon* in Mexico, is strongly tabooed. But marriage within one's own stratum is encouraged. This means that members of the same class are drawn together by actual and potential family ties; whereas members of different strata are repelled by the nonexistence and impossibility of such ties. Consequently the system of stratified statuses often engenders stratum solidarity, whereas the other kind of statuses usually does not engender solidarity among those holding the same status. An open conflict between social classes may develop much more easily than an open conflict between different age groups or different sexes. The "battle of the sexes" is something of a figurative expression, whereas a class war is sometimes a reality.

This is not to say that nonstratified statuses lack an invidious element. On the contrary we attach a differential evaluation to male and female, to old and young, to married and divorced. But the "rank" of these statuses is not part of a graded series; and the persons occupying them, as we have just seen, are usually more closely identified (e.g., in the family) with others in different statuses than with those in the same status. Furthermore, the individual himself cannot easily alter his nonstratified status by his own efforts.

Class and caste positions, on the other hand, contain a stronger invidious element. The gradations are numerous and are arranged in a hierarchy. The relations between different grades are made impersonal by the exclusion of family bonds, whereas relations within one's own grade are made more solidaristic by the presence of family connections. Finally, there is always the possibility of changing, of improving or worsening, one's class position. It may be impossible to alter the class position very drastically, yet some change is always possible. Negroes in the United States can only rarely pass into the white caste, but they can greatly raise or lower their position within the Negro caste. For all of these reasons the preoccupation with prestige, emulation, and rank is greater in connection with one's stratified than in connection with one's nonstratified statuses.

The distinction between stratified and nonstratified statuses, as just given, serves two purposes. First, it separates the topic of stratification from the more general topic of status and role (already discussed in Chapter IV). Second, it suggests the crucial role of the family in understanding stratification. This second feature will become increasingly clear. For the moment, however, we wish to explain as fully as possible the causes of stratification in human society.

The Explanation of Stratification [1]

Looking at the cultures of the world one finds that no society is "classless," that is, unstratified. There are some primitive communities so small that no class strata appear, the social organization resting almost entirely on age, sex, and kinship; but even here chieftainship, individual prowess, and clan or family property introduce an incipient stratification. As soon as greater size and complexity are attained, stratification unmistakably appears.

At the same time, although the principle of stratification is universal, its concrete manifestation varies remarkably from one society to another. Consequently, the explanatory task requires two different lines of analysis—one to understand the universal features of stratification, the other to understand the variable features. Naturally the two lines of inquiry are indispensable, but in what follows, because of space limitations, the emphasis will be on the universals.

THE FUNCTIONAL NECESSITY OF STRATIFICATION

Men have always dreamed of a world in which distinctions of rank did not occur. Yet this dream has had to face a hard reality. Any society must distribute its individuals in the positions of its social structure and induce them to perform the duties of these positions. It must therefore solve the problem of motivation at two levels: to instill in the proper individuals the desire to occupy certain positions and, once in these positions, the desire to perform the duties attached to them.

[1] This general theory of stratification is taken largely from Kingsley Davis and Wilbert E. Moore, "Some Principles of Stratification," *American Sociological Review*, Vol. 10 (April 1945), pp. 242-247.

If the duties associated with the various positions were all equally pleasant to the human organism, all equally important to social survival, and all equally dependent on the same ability or talent, it would make no difference who got into which positions, and the problem of social placement would be greatly reduced. But actually it does make a great deal of difference who gets into which positions, not only because some positions are inherently more agreeable than others but also because some require special talents or training and some have more importance than others. Also, it is essential that the duties of the positions be performed with the diligence that their importance requires. Inevitably, then, a society must have some kind of rewards that it can use as inducements and some way of distributing these rewards differently according to positions. The rewards and their distribution, as attached to social positions, thus become a part of the social order; they are the stratification.

One may ask what kind of rewards a society has at its disposal in distributing its personnel and securing essential services. It has, first of all, the things that contribute to sustenance and comfort—the economic incentives. It has, second, the things that contribute to humor and diversion—the esthetic incentives. And it has, finally, the things that contribute to self respect and ego expansion—the symbolic incentives. In any social system all three kinds of rewards, as well as others, must be dispensed unequally as between different positions.

In a sense the rewards are "built into" the position. They consist in the "rights" associated with the position, plus what may be called its accompaniments or perquisites. Often the rights and sometimes the accompaniments are functionally related to the duties of the position. However, there may be a host of subsidiary rights and perquisites that are not essential to the function of the position and have only an indirect and symbolic connection with its duties, but which still may be of considerable importance in inducing people to seek the positions and fulfill the essential duties.

If the rights and perquisites of different positions in a society must be unequal, then the society must be stratified, because that is precisely what stratification means. Social inequality is thus an unconsciously evolved device by which societies insure that the most important positions are conscientiously filled by the most qualified persons. Hence every society, no matter how simple or complex, must differentiate persons in terms of both prestige and esteem and must therefore possess a certain amount of institutionalized inequality.

It does not follow that the amount or type of inequality need be the same in all societies. We are simply trying to explain the universal fact of stratification, regardless of its particular form. The varying kinds of stratification are a function of other factors in addition to the broad functional necessity under discussion.

The Two Determinants of Positional Rank

Granting the general function that inequality subserves, one can specify the two factors that determine the relative rank of different positions. In general those positions convey the best reward and hence have the highest rank which (a) have the greatest importance for the society and (b) require the greatest training or talent. The first factor concerns the relative functional contribution of the position as compared to others; the second concerns the relative scarcity of personnel for filling the position.

DIFFERENTIAL FUNCTIONAL IMPORTANCE

Actually a society does not need to reward positions in proportion to their functional importance. It merely needs to give sufficient reward to insure that they will be filled competently. In other words, it must see that less essential positions do not compete successfully with more essential ones. If a position is easily filled, it need not be heavily rewarded even though important. On the other hand, if it is important but hard to fill, the reward must be high enough to get it filled anyway. If it is unimportant and hard to fill, it will possibly be dropped altogether. Functional importance is therefore a necessary but not a sufficient cause of high rank being assigned to a position.

DIFFERENTIAL SCARCITY OF PERSONNEL

Practically all positions, no matter how acquired, require some skill or capacity for performance. This is implicit in the very notion of position, which implies that the incumbent must by virtue of his incumbency accomplish certain things.

There are ultimately only two ways in which a person's qualifications come about: through inherent capacity or through training. Obviously, in concrete activities both are always necessary; some capacity is necessary if training is to be effective, and some training is required if capacity is to express itself. But from a practical standpoint the scarcity may lie primarily in one or the other, as well as in both. Some positions require innate talents of such high degree that the persons who fill them are bound to be rare. In many cases, however, talent is fairly abundant in the population but the training process is so long, costly, and elaborate that relatively few can qualify. Modern medicine, for example, is within the mental capacity of most individuals, but a medical education is so burdensome and expensive that virtually none would undertake it if the position of the M.D. did not carry a reward commensurate with the sacrifice.

If the talents required for a position are abundant and the training easy, the method of acquiring the position may have little to do with its duties. There may in fact be a virtually accidental relationship. But if the skills required are scarce by reason of the rarity of talent or the costliness of training, the position, if functionally important, must have an attractive power that will draw the necessary skills in competition with other positions. This means, in effect, that the position must be high in the social scale—must command great prestige, high salary, ample leisure, and the like.

An Apparent Criticism

One may object to the foregoing explanation of stratification on the ground that it fits a competitive order but does not fit a noncompetitive one. For instance, in a caste system it seems that people do not get their positions because of talent or training but rather because of birth. This criticism raises a crucial problem and forces an addition to the theory. It does not, however, upset the theory.

In the first place it should be apparent that our analysis concerns the system of positions, not the individuals occupying those positions. It is one thing to ask why different positions carry different degrees of prestige, and quite another to ask how certain individuals get into those positions. Most of the literature on stratification has tried to answer the second question (particularly with regard to the ease or difficulty of mobility between strata) without tackling the first. The first question, however, is logically prior and, in the case of any particular individual or group, factually prior.

In the second place, the functional necessities responsible for stratification do not operate to the exclusion of all other functions. There are certain additional functions, equally necessary, which have the effect of limiting and guiding stratification. For example, the necessity of having a social organization—the family—for the reproduction and socialization of children requires that stratification be somehow accommodated to this organization. Such accommodation takes the form of status ascription. The child, as mentioned before, receives initially the class status of his parents. Even in a highly competitive system this helps or hinders him throughout the rest of his life in the acquisition of adult statuses. In a less competitive system, such as is possible in stable agricultural societies, the influence of the parental position may tend to last through life. Although this seems to exclude functional importance, training, and talent, it is nevertheless true, as we shall show below in the discussion of caste, that there is alwavs some competition required, and for most positions some capacity and some training. Consequently it is still possible to explain on the basis of functional importance and scarcity of personnel the general hierarchy of positions. Even though a high caste person occupies his high rank because of his parents, the reason for the high evaluation of the functions that his caste performs in the community cannot be found in this fact. The low estate of the sweeper castes in India, as compared with the priestly castes, cannot be explained by saying that the sons of sweepers become sweepers and the sons of Brahmins become Brahmins. There is a tendency for sweepers to have a low status and for priests to have a high status in every society. Thus the functional necessity behind stratification seems to be operative at all times, despite the concurrent operation of other functions.

Major Societal Functions and Stratification

In so far, then, as there are differences between one system of stratification and another, they are attributable to whatever factors affect the two determinants of differential reward—functional importance and scarcity of personnel—with respect to the various kinds of positions. Positions important in one society may not be important in another, because the conditions faced by the societies or their degree of internal development may be different. Yet owing to the universal necessity of certain functions in society, which require social organization for their performance, there is an underlying similarity in the kind of positions put at the top, the kind put at the middle, and the kind put at the bottom of the scale. For this reason it seems wise, before discussing the varieties of concrete systems of stratification, to take up some major functions in society and see what tends to give them their rank. For this purpose we shall select religion, government, economic activity, and technology.

RELIGION

A later chapter (Chapter XIX) presents an analysis of the social functions of religion. It tries to show that religion serves to express, reinforce, and rationalize the common values and group ends of the society. Through belief and ritual the common ends and values are connected with an imaginary world symbolized by concrete sacred objects. This world, in turn, is related in a meaningful way to the facts and trials of the individual's life. Through the worship of the sacred objects and the beings they symbolize, a powerful control over human behavior is exercised, guiding it along lines sustaining the institutional structure and promoting the ultimate values and ends.

If this conception of religion is true, one can understand why in every known society the religious activities tend to be under the charge of specialized persons who tend to enjoy greater rewards than the ordinary societal member. Certain of the rewards and special privileges may attach to only the highest religious functionaries, but others usually apply to the entire sacerdotal class if such exists.

There is a peculiar relation between the duties of the religious official and the special privileges he enjoys. If the supernatural world governs the destinies of men more ultimately than does the real world, its earthly representative, the person through whom one may communicate with the supernatural, must be a powerful individual. He is a keeper of sacred tradition, a skilled performer of the ritual, and an interpreter of lore and myth. He is in such close contact with the gods that he is viewed as possessing some of their characteristics. He is, in short, a bit sacred and hence free from some of the more vulgar necessities and controls.

It is therefore no accident that religious functionaries have been associated with the very highest positions of power, as in theocratic regimes. Indeed, looking at it from this point of view, one may wonder why it is that they do not get *entire* control over their societies. The factors that prevent this are worthy of note.

In the first place, the amount of technical competence necessary for the performance of religious duties is small. Anyone can set himself up as enjoying an intimate relation with deities, and nobody can successfully dispute him. Therefore, the factor of scarcity of personnel does not operate in the technical sense.

One may assert, on the contrary, that religious ritual is often elaborate and religious lore abstruse, and that priestly ministrations require tact if not intelligence. This is true, but the technical requirements of the profession are for the most part adventitious, not related to the end in the same way that science, for example, is related to air travel. The priest can never be free from vulgar competition, because the criteria of whether or not one has genuine contact with the supernatural are never strictly clear. It is this vulgar competition that debases the priestly position below what might be expected at first glance. That is why priestly prestige is highest in those societies where membership in the profession is rigidly controlled by the priestly guild itself, for such control creates an artificial scarcity. The threat of vulgar competition also explains why, in part at least, elaborate devices are utilized to stress the identification of the person with his priestly office—devices such as spectacular costume, abnormal conduct, special diet, segregated residence, celibacy, conspicuous leisure, and the like. Without these props the priest is always in danger of becoming somewhat discredited—as happens in a secularized society—because in a world of stubborn fact, ritual and sacred knowledge alone will not grow crops or build houses. Furthermore, unless he is protected by a professional guild, the priest's identification with the things of the other world tends to preclude his acquisition of the goods of this world. If he cannot accumulate worldly goods he loses one of the main symbols and supports of high status.

As between one society and another it seems that the priest receives the highest rank in the medieval type of social order. Here there is enough economic production to afford a surplus, which can be used to support a numerous and highly organized priesthood; and yet the populace is unlettered and therefore credulous to a high degree. Perhaps the most extreme example is to be found in the Buddhism of Tibet, but others are encountered in the Catholicism of feudal Europe, the Inca regime of Peru, the Brahminism of India, and the Mayan priesthood of Yucatan. On the other hand, if the society is so crude as to have no economic surplus and little occupational differentiation, so that every priest must at the same time be a cultivator or hunter, the separation of the priestly status from the others has hardly gone far enough for priestly prestige to mean much. When the priest actually has high prestige under these circumstances, it is because he also performs other important functions (usually political and medical).

In an extremely advanced society built on scientific technology the priesthood tends to lose status, because sacred tradition and supernaturalism drop into the background. The ultimate values and common ends of the society tend to be expressed in less anthropomorphic ways by officials who occupy fundamentally political, economic, or educational rather than religious positions. Nevertheless, it is easily possible for intellectuals to exaggerate the degree to which the priesthood in a presumably secular milieu has lost prestige. When the matter is closely examined the urban proletariat as well as the rural citizenry proves to be surprisingly god-fearing and priest-ridden. No society has become so completely secularized as to liquidate entirely the belief in transcendental ends and supernatural entities. Even in a secularized society some system must exist for the integration of ultimate values, for their ritualistic expression, and for the emotional adjustments required by disappointment, death, and disaster.

GOVERNMENT

Like religion, government plays a unique and indispensable part in society. But in contrast to religion, which provides integration in terms of sentiments, beliefs, and rituals, it organizes the society in terms of law and authority. It also orients the society to the actual rather than the unseen world.

Political action, by definition, implies authority. An official can command because he has authority, and the citizen must obey because he is subject to that authority. For this reason stratification is inherent in the nature of political relationships.

So clear is the power embodied in political position that political inequality is sometimes thought to comprise all inequality. But it can be shown that there are other bases of stratification, that the following controls operate in practice to keep political power from becoming complete: (a) The fact that the actual holders of political office and especially those determining top policy must necessarily be few in number compared to the total population. (b) The fact that the rulers represent the interest of the group as a whole rather than that of themselves alone, and are therefore restricted in their behavior by rules and mores designed to enforce this limitation of interest. (c) The fact that the holder of political office has his authority by virtue of his office and nothing else and therefore any special knowledge, talent, or capacity he may claim is purely incidental, so that he often has to depend upon others for technical assistance.

In view of these limiting factors it is not strange that the rulers often have less power and prestige than a literal enumeration of their formal rights would lead one to expect.

WEALTH, PROPERTY, AND LABOR

Every position that secures for its incumbent a livelihood is, by definition, economically rewarded. For this reason there is an economic aspect to those positions (e.g. political and religious) the main function of which is not economic. It therefore becomes convenient for the society to use unequal economic returns as a principal means of controlling the entrance of persons into positions and stimulating the performance of their duties. The amount of the economic return therefore becomes one of the main indices of social status.

It should be stressed, however, that a position does not bring power and prestige *because* it draws a high income. Rather, it draws a high income because it is functionally important and the available personnel is for one reason or another scarce. It is therefore superficial and erroneous to regard high income as the cause of a man's power and prestige, just as it is erroneous to view fever as the cause of a man's disease.[2]

The economic source of power and prestige is not income primarily, but the ownership of capital goods (including patents, good

[2] The symbolic rather than intrinsic role of income in social stratification has been succinctly summarized by Talcott Parsons, "An Analytical Approach to the Theory of Social Stratification," *American Journal of Sociology*, Vol. 45 (May 1940), pp. 841-862.

will, and professional reputation). Such ownership should be distinguished from the possession of consumer's goods, which is an index rather than a cause of social standing. In other words, the ownership of producers' goods is properly speaking a source of income like other positions, the income itself remaining an index. Even in situations where social values are widely commercialized and earnings are the readiest method of judging social position, income does not confer prestige on a position so much as it induces people to compete for the position. It is true that a man who has a high income as a result of one position may find this money helpful in climbing into another position as well, but this again reflects the effect of his initial, economically advantageous status, which exercises its influence through the medium of money.

In a system of private property in productive enterprise, an income above what an individual spends can give rise to possession of capital wealth. Presumably such possession is a reward for the proper management of one's finances originally and of the productive enterprise later. But as social differentiation becomes highly advanced and yet the institution of inheritance persists, the phenomenon of pure ownership, and reward for pure ownership, emerges. In such a case it is difficult to prove that the position is functionally important or that the scarcity involved is anything other than extrinsic and accidental. It is for this reason, doubtless, that the institution of private property in productive goods becomes more subject to criticism as social development proceeds toward industrialization. It is only this pure, that is, strictly legal and functionless ownership, however, that is open to attack; for some form of active ownership, whether private or public, is indispensable.

One kind of ownership of production goods consists in rights over the labor of others. The most extremely concentrated and exclusive of such rights are found in slavery, but the essential principle remains in serfdom, peonage, encomienda, and indenture. Naturally this kind of ownership has the greatest significance for stratification because it necessarily entails an unequal relationship.

But property in capital goods inevitably introduces a compulsive element even into the nominally free contractual relationship. Indeed, in some respects the authority of the contractual employer is greater than that of the feudal landlord, inasmuch as the latter is more limited by traditional reciprocities. Even the classical economics recognized that competitors would fare unequally, but it did not pursue this fact to its necessary conclusion: unequal control of goods and services, however it may be acquired, must give unequal advantage to the parties to a contract.

TECHNICAL PERFORMANCE

The exclusively technical sphere has to do with finding empirical means to single goals without any concern with the choice between goals. The explanation of why positions requiring great technical skill receive fairly high rewards is easy to see, for such positions offer the simplest case of the rewards being so distributed as to draw talent and motivate training. An engineer cannot be made out of just anybody, nor can he be made overnight. But why technical positions seldom if ever receive the very highest rewards is equally clear: the importance of technical knowledge from a societal point of view is never so great as the importance of goal integration, and goal integration takes place on the religious, political, and economic levels, not on the technological. Since the technological level is concerned solely with means, a purely technical position must ultimately be subordinate to other positions that are religious, political, or economic.

Nevertheless, the distinction between expert and layman in any social order is fundamental and cannot be entirely reduced to other terms. An individual must have access to training before he can become an expert, and the training requires effort. He cannot, therefore, simply purchase or inherit the position. The control of the avenues of training may inhere as a sort of property right in certain families or classes, giving them power and prestige in consequence. Such a situation adds an artificial scarcity to the natural scarcity of skills and talents. On the other hand, it is possible for an opposite situation to arise. The rewards of technical position may be so great that a condition of excess supply is created, leading to at least temporary devaluation of the rewards. Thus "unemployment in the learned professions" may result in a debasement of the prestige of those positions. Such adjustments and readjustments are constantly occurring in changing societies; and it is always well to bear in mind that the efficiency of a stratified structure may be affected by the modes of recruitment for positions. The social order itself, however, sets limits to the inflation or deflation of the prestige of experts: an over-supply tends to debase the rewards and discourage recruitment or produce revolution, whereas an under-supply tends to increase the rewards or weaken the society in competition with other societies.

Particular systems of stratification show a wide range with respect to the exact position of technically competent persons. This range is perhaps most evident in the degree of specialization. Extreme division of labor tends to create many specialists without high prestige since the training is short and the required native capacity relatively small. On the other hand it also tends to accentuate the high position of the true experts—scientists, engineers, and administrators—by increasing their authority relative to other functionally important positions. But the idea of a technocratic social order or a government or priesthood of engineers or social scientists neglects the limitations of knowledge and skills as a basis for performing social functions. To the extent that the social structure is truly specialized the prestige of the technical person must also be circumscribed.

Vertical Mobility and Immobility

The generalized principles here suggested are meant to explain the existence of stratification. Let us now turn, however, to another problem—the question of the degree of mobility between strata. This problem assumes that stratification exists, and simply raises the further question of the extent to which the person's occupancy of a position within the system is ascribed or achieved. The question has already been discussed with reference to statuses in general, but not specifically with reference to stratified statuses. As applied to stratification it immediately brings us to the topic of caste versus open class organization.

When the term "caste" is mentioned, one thinks of India, not because India has the only caste system in existence, nor even a complete one, but because she has the most extreme one. If the Hindu social order could be summed up in a single phrase, it would be this: It is the most thorough-going attempt known in human history to introduce inherited inequality as the guiding principle in social relationships. Such an attempt cannot completely succeed, any more than an attempt to introduce absolute equality can succeed. We must therefore think of India as an extreme but still imperfect embodiment of the caste idea.

It is possible to imagine two impossible social systems—one based entirely on inherited inequality, the other based entirely on equality of opportunity. They would both be stratified, but in the first every individual would have exactly the status that his parents had, whereas in the second every individual would achieve a status altogether independently of his parents' position. These two ideal types represent two theoretical poles. Any concrete social order may approach one or the other of these poles, but none ever actually reaches either pole. The Indian caste system approaches the first pole; the American class system approaches the second. Any actual system will prove upon analysis to be mixed, to have both principles in operation, though it may rely much more heavily on the one than on the other. In India there is considerable mobility up and down the social ladder despite the ideal of fixity; whereas in America there is considerable inheritance of status (especially as concerns the Negro-White racial statuses) despite the ideal of equal opportunity. To prove these assertions, let us consider each of the two societies in detail, beginning first with India.

THE INDIAN CASTE SYSTEM

The common features or tendencies which together distinguish Indian castes from other types of groups are as follows:

(1) Membership in the caste is hereditary. The child at birth takes the rank of his parents.
(2) This inherited membership is fixed for life, because, except in the sense of being outcasted, the individual cannot alter his caste by any effort of his own. He cannot change his status by good works, marriage, dissimulation, or any other strategem.
(3) Choice of marriage partners is strictly endogamous, for it must take place within the caste group.
(4) Contact with other groups is further limited by restrictions on touching, associating with, dining with, or eating food cooked by outsiders.
(5) Consciousness of caste membership is further emphasized by the caste name, by the individual's identification with his caste in the eyes of the community, by his conformity to the peculiar customs of his caste, and by his subjection to government by his caste.

(6) The caste may be, and in the past generally was, united by a common traditional occupation, although it may be united in addition or instead by the belief in a common tribal or racial origin, by adherence to a common religious sect, or by some other common peculiarity.

(7) The relative prestige of the different castes in any locality is well established and jealously guarded.

These features represent the ideal-type, symbolized in Indian ritual and rationalized in Indian religion. But in practice some modification of the theoretical system occurs, with the result that not all castes exhibit all the features mentioned. For instance, there are a few rare castes that admit new members; there are some that marry outside; and there are some that change their names to improve their status. Yet any group that is called a caste in India will exhibit most of the features listed.[2]

Because of the uncertainty in classifying castes, subcastes, and sections, and because of confusion in names, it is impossible to say exactly how many castes there are in India. In 1901, the last year in which a complete tabulation of all castes was attempted, the number of "main" castes and tribes was found to be 2,378.[3] Some of these had members running into the millions, others had a mere handful. The so-called main castes presumably did not include subcastes. How many of these there are cannot even be guessed, but it is safe to assume that any caste whose members run into the hundreds of thousands is divided into a large number of subcastes, and these are commonly endogamous groups having most of the characteristics of castes. In 1891, for example, the Jat and Ahir castes each had over 1,700 subcastes, and the Kurmi had nearly 1,500.[4] In 1931 over 15 million Brahmins were returned in the census, but to regard all of them as members of one caste would be erroneous. They are split into an immense number of separate groups and subgroups. In one province alone as many as 200 major castes of Brahmins have been counted, none of which permit intermarriage. These Brahmin castes even differ markedly in social standing. Some of them rank at

[2] E. A. H. Blunt, *The Caste System of Northern India* (London: Oxford University Press, 1931), Chap. 1. L. S. S. O'Malley, *Indian Caste Customs* (Cambridge: University Press, 1932), Chap. 1.

[3] *Census of India,* 1901, Vol. 1, Part 1, p. 537.

[4] Blunt, *op. cit.,* pp. 37-38.

the top of the social scale while others rank so low that even their own clients, members of low castes, will not take food in their houses.

Caste is, or was until recently, almost universal in India. The Hindus who are not members of some particular caste are few. Some reform groups, such as the Brahmo Samaj and the Arya Samaj, have professed to repudiate caste, but these have only tiny followings. Indeed, though provision was made in the 1931 census for a "nil" return, even the members of these reform groups tended to report their caste. Propaganda against the caste question on the census schedule was widespread in 1931, yet in all of India less than 1 per cent of Hindus failed to report their caste. Failure to report was usually due to ignorance, error, and unwillingness rather than actual lack of caste. Even among Muslims, whose religion supposedly denies caste, there are many castes. The census of 1911 listed 94 Muslim castes. Even among the six million Indians who have embraced Christianity, caste distinctions still generally prevail. In short, caste is extremely widespread and pervasive in India. It is present in all regions and affects nearly every person regardless of his religion.

So many castes jostle each other in India that they must somehow be grouped. In practice the people adopt a rule-of-thumb mode of classification. The chief line of distinction runs between the twice-born, or "clean," castes (embracing all the so-called caste Hindus) on the one hand, and the once-born, or "unclean," castes on the other. The line is by no means uniform from one locality to another, but in some form it seems to be everywhere present. It is the sharpest distinction in Hindu society.

There are several criteria of membership in the depressed castes. If, for example, a caste suffers all of the following disabilities, it is certainly in this class:

(1) Inability to be served by clean Brahmins.
(2) Inability to be served by barbers, water-carriers, tailors, etc., who serve the caste Hindus.
(3) Limitation on contact with caste Hindus because of possible pollution.
(4) Inability to serve water to caste Hindus.
(5) Inability to use public conveniences such as roads, ferries, wells, or schools.
(6) Inability to enter Hindu temples.
(7) Inability to dissociate oneself from a despised occupation.

These criteria admit of degrees and vary somewhat independently. A caste that suffers food and water restrictions may nevertheless be served by Brahmins of good standing. In Bengal there have been castes whom the barber would serve but whose toe nails he would not cut and whose marriage ceremonies he would not attend.[5] Furthermore, "a caste may be untouchable in one district and not in the next; and there are untouchable castes with touchable sections.[6] Nevertheless, it is possible to determine roughly the number of persons falling in the depressed category. In 1931 the number came to 50.2 million, which represented 21 per cent of the total Hindu population. India seems to have one of the largest bottom layers of any nation in the world. It is this bottom layer, the submerged fifth of the population, that must bear the brunt of the struggle for survival in an overpopulated, underdeveloped, poverty-stricken country.

The emphasis on the line between interior and exterior castes should not obscure the fact that within each of these there are sharp differences of rank. "It is not to be imagined that within the circle of untouchability," for instance, "there are no subgradations, and that all untouchables are equals among themselves. In the Madras Presidency alone . . . there are, it is said, no less than eighty subdivisions, those at the top regarding the less fortunate of their own brethren as untouchable. At the bottom of the scale come some classes, like the *Nayadis* of Malabar, whose very shadow is pollution." An address by Gandhi contained the following statement:

> All the various grades of untouchables are untouchable among themselves, each superior grade considering the inferior grade as polluting as the highest class of the caste Hindus regard the worst grade of untouchables. Further, among the same grade of untouchables there are sections, each considering itself different and distinct from any other, prohibiting inter-dining and intermarriage.[7]

But as in the case of other societies, public interest does not center on the gradations of rank in the lowest strata but rather on the gradations at the top. In this regard the main distinction is between the Brahmins and the other clean castes. The Brahmins represented 8.2 per cent of the total caste Hindus in 1931. Of the remaining

[5] *Census of India,* 1901, Vol. 1, Part 1, p. 541.

[6] Blunt, *op. cit.,* pp. 334-335.

[7] B. Shiva Rao, *The Industrial Worker in India* (London: Allen & Unwin, 1939), pp. 81-82.

caste Hindus an unknown number ranked close to the Brahmins as part of the aristocracy, while the others, the major portion, constituted a broad middle class embracing many kinds and degrees of gradation.

The Impossibility of an Absolute Caste System. Although its precise form has changed from time to time, the caste system in India has endured for some thirty centuries. It reached its peak at roughly the same time that the European feudal system reached its peak. The Muslim invasions then introduced a disturbing element but not a decisive one; the British introduced a more disturbing element but one still not decisive. Yet, as already mentioned, the caste system was never perfect. Long before the Muslims or the British, there were factors in India that worked against the system. These were factors that will militate against a complete caste system in any society; so their theoretical importance makes them worth discussing.

In the first place, any system of stratification must have certain standards of excellence. The social scale must be related to and presumably based on a scale of values. Hindu culture, like any other, has such standards. It places a high value, for example, on the seclusion of women, on the celibacy of widows, on the purity of diet, on the purity of occupation, on the ownership of land, on freedom from manual labor, and on the knowledge of sacred literature. It follows that any group (be it a local caste group or even a family) that manages to improve itself with respect to any of these standards, will also improve its social status. And inevitably some groups will strive to improve themselves, because they believe in these values and because they can thereby raise their social status. Thus the objective scale of values behind caste stratification itself induces people to violate the main principle of caste, the fixity of status.

Blunt gives numerous examples of changes of status by change of occupation.[8] The Pasi caste practices the despised occupations of hunting and fowling. A part of the caste has turned to cultivation and fruitselling, a more honorable calling. Consequently this part has become a new caste, adopting a new name (Phansiya) and acquiring a higher social status than the remaining Pasi.

[8] *Op. cit.*, pp. 236-238.

> The Kayastha caste, as a whole, stands in high repute. But the numerous class of *patwaris* (keepers of the village revenue records) consists almost entirely of Kayasthas: and as the *patwari* has a bad name for chicanery, the better class Kayasthas affect to despise this occupation. Some years ago many Srivastava [Kayastha] families . . . refused to have any relations, whether connubial or commensal, with *patwira* families; and the Kayastha *sabha* [association] had some difficulty in preventing the consequent formation of a "patwari" subcaste.[9]

The Indian scale of values emphasizes the observance of certain taboos and moral rules. Castes that relax the observance of these rules lose status, while castes that tighten such observance gain status. The Biyahut, or "Married" Kalars, are a particular branch of the Kalars. They are distinguished by the fact that they prohibit the remarriage of widows, saying that a woman is married once and for all. As a consequence they rank a little higher than the other Kalars, who permit widow remarriage.[10]

Since the observance of most of the rules is costly, the more sucsessful the caste is in an economic sense the more it can improve its conformity. Economic competition cannot be wholly eliminated. The acquisition of wealth can never be made exactly proportional to one's inherited social status. In every case some connection of course exists between inheritance and acquisition. In India prior tc British rule, the untouchable castes in many areas were not allowed to own land. They are still handicapped in education, occupation, etc., and so do not have an equal chance to acquire wealth. Nevertheless, in so far as there are property rights not governed by inheritance (and they cannot all be) and in so far as there is manufacture and trade, the possibility of acquiring or losing wealth is present, and with it the possibility of rising or falling in the social scale. In India even lowly or unclean occupations may in some cases afford a nice profit. Customarily the profits are invested in land; the families thereupon become landholders, abandoning their old occupation and achieving a new station in life. Some of the marks of high status may on the other hand carry an economic penalty. Thus it is said that one can always tell which farms belong to Brahmins and which

[9] *Ibid.*, p. 222.

[10] Robert V. Russell, *Tribes and Castes of the Central Provinces of India* (London: Macmillan, 1916), p. 73.

to non-Brahmins, because the Brahmins, unwilling to do manual labor, must hire their work done by others, and the work is always inferior to that which a farmer would do for himself.

It seems clear, then, that the Hindu attempt to construct a system of absolute social inequality is inherently contradictory. The very scale of values or standards by which one stratum is judged better than another motivates people to try to improve themselves with reference to these standards; in so far as they succeed, the community is bound to recognize their achievement by giving them more or less prestige. A change of occupation, a shift of economic fortune, an alteration in the observance of moral rules and taboos—any or all of these will affect the standing of the group in the eyes of the general community.

So far the argument has been confined to an internal contradiction in the principle of caste. Now it can be shown that the ideal of absolute inequality is not only internally inconsistent but also incompatible with basic societal needs. To be practicable, the ideal would require a completely static social order. The moment there is social change there is also social mobility, for two reasons: (a) Any society, simply by the interaction within its structure, generates internal frictions that inevitably lead to a change of the structure. (b) The external conditions in which the society lives and to which it must adjust if it is to survive, are constantly changing.

If, for example, we wished to have each caste and subcaste performing its own unique occupation and occupying the same rung generation after generation, a uniform rate of population replacement would be necessary in every caste. But the very notion of caste implies that there are different caste customs, and some of these customs will unavoidably affect fertility and mortality. This being true, some castes will expand in population and others will contract. For those that expand, some new occupations must be found because the caste members would be crowded out of employment in the old. For those castes that contract, replacements from other castes must be found because otherwise the necessary occupation would not be practiced. Differences in natural increase therefore prevent absolute immobility.

Similarly, geographical changes require social adaptations. Hindu society has from its inception been an agricultural and pastoral society. The very practice of these arts introduces changes in the physical setting. As the countryside fills up, forests are depleted and fields eroded. New diseases and calamities appear. New economic and political developments become possible. The social system must adjust to these changing conditions, and such adjustment inevitably entails a certain amount of social mobility.

Enough has been said to indicate that there are always factors that contravene the caste principle of absolute fixity of status. This is why the caste ideal has never been perfectly put into practice. The Indian social order (prior to Western influence) makes an extraordinary effort to put it into practice, creating as complete a caste system as can be found. Yet theory and practice are two different things in India, for we find that absolute fixity of hereditary status is not and has never been maintained perfectly.

CASTE IN THE UNITED STATES

If the term "caste" be taken analytically rather than descriptively, it will be plain that any society has a caste element in it. So long as the individual family has major responsibility for the child, the principle of inheritance of status from parents, which is the essence of caste, will be present. In this sense the United States has definitely an element of caste, for the position of the father has a great deal to do with the position of the son. But since another principle is also at work, namely the achievement of position, giving rise to mobility between strata, we do not describe the American social order as "a caste system."

In one segment of its social organization, however, the United States does have a rather full embodiment of the caste principle. In the South as everyone knows, Negroes and whites constitute two castes set apart. Nearly all the features of Indian caste are perceptible in the relations of these two groups. Outstanding among these is the ideology of pollution. In both India and America this magical concept serves to justify the caste structure. It is somehow contaminating to sit beside a Negro, to touch his hand, or to drink from the same cup. Children are told at five-and-ten-cent stores not to blow the whistles and horns because some Negro may have put his mouth to the same instrument. Toilet, eating, hotel, and nearly all other public facilities must be separate for the two groups.

The fundamental rule is that Negroes and whites shall never associate in any relation of intimacy that implies equality. Consequently, most of the restrictions imposed on the untouchables in India (already listed) can be roughly matched with reference to the Negroes in the southern part of the United States. One of the most fundamental of these restrictions is of course the ban of intermarriage. This ban indicates (in the United States) that the racial integrity of the upper caste is to be strictly maintained, to the degree that all persons of mixed racial qualities shall be placed unequivocally in the lower of the two castes. To permit intermarriage would be to give the hybrid offspring the legal status of its father and would soon undermine the racial basis of the caste order. Hence either intermarriage must be strictly forbidden or racial caste abandoned. Thirty states forbid intermarriage and thus align themselves legally on the side of racial caste.[11]

Thus in every walk of life the American untouchables are set apart. The fundamental division is based on the most obvious of characteristics: skin color. Since this trait is handed down genetically from parent to child, it satisfies the first requisite of caste, namely that the division shall be strictly hereditary. Only if a Negro is so light as to "pass" may he hope to escape from his debased status, but even then a chance discovery is apt to catch up with him and push him back into the cellar of his dark ancestry.

Open Class Stratification

Modern Western society is identified on the whole with an open class type of stratification. This type comes nowhere near approaching the theoretical pole of absolute equality, which would mean no stratification at all. Rather, it assumes that inequalities will exist, and simply stresses equal opportunity to take advantage of them. The strata are "open" because individuals may presumably move into or out of them according to their merit. Pushed to its logical extreme the system supposedly gives all individuals an equal chance to advance in the social scale. But what is an "equal chance"? Strictly defined, it would mean that all significant differences are equalized at the start. This interpretation, however, would make it totally impossible to explain subsequent differences in achievement, except on a free will basis. What seems to be meant is that *social* factors shall

[11] Kingsley Davis, "Intermarriage in Caste Societies," *American Anthropologist*, Vol. 43 (July-September 1941), pp. 388-389.

be made equal at the start, leaving the field open to biological differences which, with appropriate effort, the individual can transmute into social advancement. Thus the inheritance of wealth is socially given—the individual did not earn it. True, he did not earn his high I. Q. either, but this is something over which society has no control (except through a conceivable eugenic program). Equal opportunity therefore implies that the social chances are made equal, thus giving capacity and effort an unrestricted opportunity to be rewarded by social advancement.

Such seems to be the real meaning of democracy, expressed over and over again in statements of our ideals. But, like the idea of caste, this idea is never fully embodied in actual practice. The reason is that in every human society the family is the reproductive unit, so that the parental status unavoidably affects the status of the child. A boy reared by professional parents in a suburban home, sent to a good high school, enrolled in a good university, and given a stake when he starts his career has an inestimable advantage over the boy born in the slums. His mode of speech, his manner of dress, his fund of knowledge, his confidence in himself, his acquaintances and contacts —all give him an overwhelming advantage in the struggle for prestige. This is why, for example, the highly distinguished people in America come mainly from professional and business families. In proportion to the number of each class in the population, professional families contribute twice as many notables as do business families, 20 times as many as do farming families, and 45 times as many as do unskilled labor families. Our system has, then, a caste element that keeps it from being entirely open, despite our democratic ideal.[12]

It should be made clear, however, that the fact that the ideal is not perfectly embodied in practice does not mean that it has no effect on stratification. As long as there is *some* opportunity to advance, as long as there are some counterweights to family influence, the individual has hope and incentive to do his best. Although everybody knows that the son of a minister has a better chance to become a governor than the son of a farmer, nobody can deny that they both have some chance. To a degree the presence of differential social opportunity, just like the presence of differential biological quality, puts a premium upon effort. The farmer's son, if he works

[12] Stephen S. Visher, *Scientists Starred, 1903-43, in "American Men of Science"* (Baltimore: Johns Hopkins Press, 1947), p. 424.

hard enough, may overcome his initial handicap and beat out the minister's son. The less the opportunity, the greater the merit of success. The son of the rich man is therefore to be pitied, because he begins life with such an advantage that his winning the race is no proof of merit, no proof that the virtues of thrift, abstinence, and hard work have been exercised.

One of the anomalies of the social structure of the United States is the coexistence of a strongly democratic ideology on the one hand and a bi-racial caste system on the other. This anomaly has given rise to much social and psychic tension, and for many decades has made the race issue one of our great social problems. One of the striking manifestations of this tension has been not only the outpouring of literature on the question but also the phenomenon of lynching.

Summary

Our discussion of stratification began with a definition of the phenomenon to be considered. We said that those statuses were stratified which normally could *not* be combined in the same family. Whereas the possibility of family bonds tends to hold members of the same stratum together, the impossibility of such bonds tends to set members of different strata apart. Thus one of the basic rules in a rigidly stratified society is class endogamy, the taboo on intermarriage. The more open a society is, the less objection it has to intermarriage between classes.

We next undertook to explain the universal presence of stratification in human society. We said that it came from the fact that every society has to pay some attention to functional importance and to scarcity of personnel (in terms of talent and training) in filling its positions. In order to satisfy these requirements, differential rewards must be given for different positions—and these differential rewards are precisely what we call stratification. We held, however, that the functional necessities behind stratification are not the only necessities with which a society is faced. There is also, for example, the necessity of a reproductive organization, which means that the family, with its influence running counter to the competitive principle behind stratification, is always present.

The family implicitly gave us our cue for distinguishing different types of stratification. At one theoretical pole is the type which we might call absolutely closed, at the other pole the type which we might call absolutely open. The first would be one in which inheritance of the parental status (and hence the influence of the family) is complete; the second would be one in which there is no inheritance of the parental status and hence no family influence. Obviously, neither pole has ever been realized in practice. It is impossible to eliminate all competition for status, just as it is impossible to eliminate all ascription of status. In other words the role of the family in this matter is never absolute, nor is it ever nil. Thus the stratified systems we actually find in human society are mixed types. They have both the caste element and the open class element in them. But some of these systems approach much more closely to one pole than to another, and they do this much more in their ideals than in their practice. This does not mean that they are not different. There is an extreme disparity between the caste system of India and the open class system of the United States. But it does mean that the difference is not so great as we might theoretically imagine or as their pure ideologies might suggest.

References

Romanzo Adams, *Interracial Marriage in Hawaii* (New York: Macmillan, 1937).

Why has Hawaii, a United States Territory, been relatively free from race prejudice? Why has mobility rather than caste prevailed? This excellent book, on the basis of thorough investigation, holds that intermarriage is a key factor in explaining the phenomenon.

Dewey Anderson and Percy E. Davidson, *Ballots and the Democratic Class Struggle* (Stanford University Press, 1943), Chap. 2, "Occupational Status and Political Behavior"; Chap. 4, "Class Consciousness and Political Behavior."

Extremely interesting conclusions drawn from statistical analysis of voting behavior in relation to social and economic characteristics of the voters.

E. A. H. Blunt, *The Caste System of Northern India* (London: Oxford University Press, 1931).

In many ways the most systematic and lucid dissection of the caste order in existence.

John H. Burma, "The Measurement of Negro 'Passing,'" *American Journal of Sociology,* Vol. 52 (July 1946), pp. 18-22. "How Many Negroes 'Pass'?" *ibid.* (May 1947), pp. 498-500.

Two different attempts, using different kinds of statistics, to determine the proportion of persons who leave the Negro caste and join the white caste in the United States. The results indicate that past estimates have been grossly exaggerated.

Richard Centers, *The Psychology of Social Classes* (Princeton: Princeton University Press, 1949); "Occupational Mobility of Urban Occupational Strata," *American Sociological Review,* Vol. 13 (April 1948), pp. 197-203.

To what degree does the United States have an open class system? By studying the occupations of fathers and their sons, the author shows quantitatively that there is vertical mobility in our social system.

Percy Erwin Davidson and H. Dewey Anderson, *Occupational Mobility in an American Community* (Stanford University Press, 1937).

Analysis of occupational inheritance, career patterns, and geographical and vertical mobility among men in San Jose, California. A good example of statistical investigation in the field of social stratification.

Allison Davis, Burleigh B. Gardner, and Mary R. Gardner, *Deep South* (Chicago: University of Chicago Press, 1941).

A sociological analysis of the two racial castes in a Southern town, together with a study of the classes within each of these castes.

Kingsley Davis, Harry C. Bredemeier, and Marion J. Levy, Jr., *Modern American Society* (New York: Rinehart, 1949), Part 4, "Our Class System," and Part 5, "Race versus Democracy."

Three chapters of selected readings on our class system and four chapters on our race relations.

G. S. Ghurye, *Caste and Race in India* (London: Paul, Trench, Trubner, 1932).

A general book on the Indian caste system written by an Indian sociologist. Particularly good on modern changes.

August B. Hollingshead, "Selected Characteristics of Classes in a Middle Western Community," *American Sociological Review,* Vol. 12 (August 1947), pp. 385-395.

Statistical differentia and observations on five social classes in a small Middle Western town. Good example of applied research on this subject.

J. H. Hutton, *Caste in India: Its Nature, Function, and Origins.* (Cambridge: University Press, 1946).

A general treatise on the caste system by a man thoroughly acquainted with it. Contains a chapter on "Analogous Institutions Elsewhere," a glossary, and a bibliography.

Carey McWilliams, *Brothers under the Skin* (Boston: Little, Brown, 1943).

"The story of how we treat our minorities—Indian, Chinese, Japanese, Negro, Mexican—who want, not charity, but democracy to begin at home"—advertisement. Racy but responsible journalism.

Gunnar Myrdal, *An American Dilemma: The Negro Problem and Modern Democracy* (New York: Harper, 1944), 2 vols.

Probably the most comprehensive and controversial study of American Negro-white relations. Representing as it does a collaborative effort on the part of a great many American scholars, both Negro and non-Negro, it contains a wealth of information, facts, and figures, together with an extensive bibliography on pp. 1144-1180 of Vol. 2.

Donald Pierson, *Negroes in Brazil* (Chicago: University of Chicago Press, 1942).

An interesting and accurate account of race relations in a country where the position of the Negro is fundamentally different from that found in the United States.

Stephen Winsor Reed, *The Making of Modern New Guinea* (Philadelphia: American Philosophical Society, 1943).

An illuminating and thorough study of the making of a caste society. In New Guinea stratification is still in the making. Reed's description of this process in societal evolution is enlightening.

Pitirim Sorokin, *Social Mobility* (New York: Harper, 1927).

Written when Sorokin was still content to be a scientist, this comprehensive comparative study of social mobility is a classic in the sociological literature.

Edgar T. Thompson (ed.), *Race Relations and the Race Problem* (Durham: Duke University Press, 1939).

An unusually good collection of scientific essays on Negro-white relationships. Special mention should be made of the editor's own chapter, "The Plantation: The Physical Basis of Traditional Race Relations"; of Copeland's paper on "The Negro as a Contrast Conception"; and of Stonequist's contribution on "Race Mixture and the Mulatto."

CHAPTER XV

MARRIAGE AND THE FAMILY

ANYONE turning his attention to the family soon encounters a strange paradox. On the one hand, all the manifestations of popular thought disclose an intense and continuous interest in family affairs. Nearly every short story, moving picture, novel, and play weaves its plot around romantic love. Humor, gossip, and mass journalism play ceaselessly on the infinite variations of sex and family relations. Solemn books harp constantly on the family's importance in personality development and social well-being, assuring us *ad nauseam* that the family is the most fundamental and universal of all institutions. Yet, on the other hand, in the world of social science a completely different picture presents itself. There the family is neglected. Whereas economic, political, and educational institutions are studied intensively, there is scant place for the study of the family. These other branches have names such as "economics" or "political science," but there is no name for the science of family relations. What is called "domestic science" is really a study of household technology and has little to do with the family as a social institution.

How can this paradoxical contrast between popular interest and scientific disinterest be explained?

One item is this: The social sciences devote their attention primarily to the instrumental aspects of social life—to those aspects that are deliberately manipulated to achieve accepted ends. Family affairs, however, are not instrumental but final or ultimate. Love is a supreme emotion, not a means to an end. The obligations of parents, of husbands and wives, are among the highest in the moral hierarchy. The idea of analyzing them from a scientific point of view seems repellent or perhaps ridiculous. The main reason why family relations are so closely identified with morality is that they involve the control of the sexual impulse—an impulse so anarchic that the strongest sentiments are required to keep it in line. Family patterns therefore are regarded as sacred and are removed by taboo from free investigation and discussion. Birth control is not a simple technological matter but a great moral issue. Such treatments of the family as occur are often moral exhortations or inspirational orations rather than scientific analyses. Most social research into the family has had an immediate moral purpose—to eliminate deviations like divorce, desertion, illegitimacy, and adultery—rather than a desire to understand the fundamental nature of social institutions. The subject has acquired the reputation of being either moralistic or pornographic, and reputable social scientists therefore shy away from it. A man who writes a treatise on the industrial corporation is judged to be a regular fellow, but one who writes a treatise on the family is thought to be a little queer.

Another item explaining the neglect of the family in social science is the small size and intimacy of the family unit. So close to the individual is the family that it is sometimes felt to be not social at all. The classical economists, when they claimed that each man pursues his own self-interest by rational means, did not mean that each man treats members of his own family simply as buyers and sellers on the market. Instead, these economists *assumed* that the economic man is also a family man carrying out his domestic obligations in a spirit different from that of rational calculation; but they did not state this assumption because they felt the family to be more individual than social. Like the economists, most social scientists have simply assumed rather than studied the family. They have relegated its study to biology, medicine, and psychiatry. The family's decreasing significance as an economic and political unit and its rise as an emotional matter have contributed to this result. Any given family is connected with the rest of society in only a limited sense. Its sphere of influence, as a family, is small. A government may on the other hand extend its authority to every corner of the society, and a business firm may sell its product to and draw its materials from the whole world. In this sense the family seems socially unimportant. It is only the *pattern* of family relationships and the effect of this pattern in millions of homes, that influences the total society.

It seems clear that the very qualities which have made family affairs a subject of extreme popular interest have also made them a subject of neglect in social science. Yet nothing illustrates more sharply the inadequacy of traditional social science as a means of understanding an entire society. In any study of human society as a whole, marriage and the family cannot be omitted. Their fascination for the popular mind and their identification with morality both attest their social significance, even though it is not the sort of significance that lends itself to being understood by rationalistic social science. Only in social anthropology where the study of primitive society has revealed the profound influence of kinship, and in sociology where the attempt to see society as a totality has made marriage and the family inescapable, have family groups and institutions received attention.

The present chapter gives a condensed account of the family in relation to the social order. It is not concerned with the "problems" of the family (usually defined in terms of current moral issues) or with the abnormalities and deviations from proper family behavior, but with the normal and accepted system of family relations. The normal and regular require explanation just as much as the abnormal and irregular. Consequently, the discussion will deal first with the functions of the family, then with the kind of structure (family organization) that has evolved to fulfill these functions, and next with the forces that are necessary to support this structure. Finally, it will deal with the historical changes in family organization that have accompanied the development of modern society, and with some of the stresses and strains involved in the modern family system.

Social Functions of the Family

It has already been pointed out that a society, in competition with other societies and with nature, can survive only if its members, through their activities, perform certain social functions. These functions will not be performed except as the activities are organized. Hence any existent society will be found to possess an institutional structure through which its functions are performed, and any particular part of the structure will be adapted for the performance of certain functions. In the case of the family we have an institutional complex adapted to meeting the societal need for continual replacement of the societal membership. This replacement has several aspects. It involves the physical reproduction of new individuals, the nourishment and maintenance of these individuals during infancy and childhood, and the placement of these individuals in the system of social positions. We may characterize the main social functions of the family, then, as falling in four closely related divisions: reproduction, maintenance, placement, and socialization of the young. These have many ramifications and can be broken down into a host of subsidiary functions, but they nevertheless do not embrace all the functions that the family performs. Like any other organized group the family in any given society will be found to perform, at least in part, certain other social functions such as economic production, care of the aged, political control, and physical protection. But its role in performing these other functions is usually a by-product of its primary role of reproduction; other institutions are usually better adapted than is the family for meeting the other great societal needs. Other institutions also contribute to the performance of family functions. Formal educational systems, for example, may share with the family a large part of the socialization and placement process. Finally, the family helps to meet the needs of the individuals who compose it. We have seen that a social system must somehow meet the organic needs of its members, not only for the survival of its members but also to motivate them in such a way as to induce them to perform the activities necessary for meeting societal needs. The family, like any other institutional complex, therefore performs individual functions by helping to meet the organic and acquired needs of the persons in the society. Thus it contributes to the individual's sexual gratification, psychic security, affection, guidance, etc. Its individual functions are a corollary of its societal functions. From a sociological point of view we are mainly concerned with the social functions, and consequently we stress the four functions mentioned —reproduction, maintenance, placement, and socialization—as being the core functions with which the family is always and everywhere concerned. There may be great variation from one society to another in the precise manner and degree of fulfillment of these functions, but the four mentioned seem to be the ones which universally require a family organization.

The interesting thing about these four functions is not simply that they are universally the province of the family but that the combination of them has certain structural implications. To see this we need only realize that no necessary connection exists between the four functions. Procreation can be accomplished by persons who have nothing to do with the subsequent socialization of the child—a possibility proved by the prevalence of adoption, which among some peoples reaches an extreme frequency. Likewise, the economic cost of rearing children may be borne by someone other than the progenitors or the socializers—as illustrated when children are placed in foster homes and paid for by a social work agency. There is of course a close connection between socialization and status ascription, but again not a necessary one. All of these functions could therefore be accomplished independently of one another. The fact that they are not performed separately but are accomplished by one and the same group means that this group, whatever its name, must have a peculiar and unmistakable structure. It must, in the first place, be a biological group because reproduction requires that there be sexual relationships between two, and biological relationships between all members of the group. It must, in the second place, be a working group with economic solidarity and division of labor between the members, because the care and support of children demand this. It must, in the third place, be a group whose initial and later members have a similar class status with common class sentiments and advantages, because status ascription and training for a status require such homogeneity. It must, in the fourth place, be an intimate group having a common habitation and enduring for a long time, because the human reproductive span and the period of dependency in the offspring are both long, capable of occupying together as many as forty years of the parents' lives. After the long period of procreation and child care the group partly breaks down by the withdrawal of the offspring to found similar groups of their own; but in the meantime the biological interconnection between the members, the coöperative labor, the common class status, the long and close living together, and the shared sorrows and gratifications must have increased the primary solidarity and deepened the sentimental ties until the group is one of the most fundamental in the lives of its members and in the society of which it is such an essential part.

Thus, from a sheer analysis of the concurrent functions themselves, we can deduce the kind of group which performs them. The group which has just been described is, in every particular, the family group. It could be no other kind of group and perform this peculiar combination of major functions as its main societal task.

Family Structure

The first characteristic of family structure to bear in mind is its biological constitution. This does not mean that the family is determined by instinct or that it is somehow more "natural" than other institutional groups. It means simply that its members are related to one another through the process of reproduction, and that this relationship serves as the basis for the social definition of the group and the assignment of rights and duties as between the members. The fact of biological interconnection we may call consanguinity, and the social recognition of such interconnection we may call kinship. The family is a group of persons whose relations to one another are based upon consanguinity and who are therefore kin to one another.

Of course the family is not the only kinship group. Since human beings represent one interbreeding species they are all biologically related, and a society may utilize consanguinity for purposes of social organization to a degree that goes beyond the family. Thus the clan and the joint household are also kinship groups. What distinguishes the family is the closeness of the biological connection. Its members are more closely related to one another through the process of reproduction than are the members of any other group. Husband and wife are biologically related through intercourse and joint reproduction; parent and child are related through direct filiation; and brothers are related through common parents. Strictly defined, then, the family consists of parents and children. It is the smallest kinship group. Its capacity for expansion is more limited than that of any other kinship group.

This does not mean that every family is actually a biological group. There are some married couples who never have children, yet they constitute a partial family. There are many children who are adopted, yet they are members of the adoptive family. "In parts of Melanesia, for instance, the family to which a child belongs is not determined by the physiological act of birth, but depends on the performance of some social act; in one island the man who pays the midwife becomes the father of the child and his wife becomes the mother; in another the father is the man who plants a leaf of the cycastree before the door of the house." [1] There are societies in

[1] W. H. R. Rivers, *Social Organization* (New York: Knopf, 1924), p. 52.

which apparently the physiological role of the male in reproduction is not understood, so that our notion of the biological connection between father and offspring is not part of the cultural ideology. There are other societies in which the connection is understood but little or no significance is attached to it, the husband simply regarding any child born to his wife as his own.

What is meant by the consanguineous character of the family is that in all societies, barring extremely unsettled conditions and aberrant individuals, the assumption prevails that the members of the family are related through the process of reproduction. Always and everywhere, for example, the married pair are expected to have children, and children outside of wedlock are discouraged. In many cultures the marriage is not regarded as full-fledged and permanent until after a child is born. Moreover, always and everywhere the husband is expected to have sexual relations with his wife. Other men may also be permitted to have relations with her, but the right of the husband is generally regarded as primary and is never questioned. Whatever children are born or adopted are regarded as his, and he has a socially defined interest in them. The myths and religious beliefs concerning the inception of children in the mother's body include the father as somehow connected with the process, even when the children are physiologically derived from another male. Thus there is always a sense in which the family is viewed as a kinship group based on connection through birth.

The seeming exceptions to this principle really prove it. In adoption, for instance, the adoptee is treated *as if* he were actually related to the adopters, an assumption which implies the prior existence of kinship as the basis of family organization. Even relationship by affinity bears out the principle; for although the married pair may have no common ancestry (in many societies, on the contrary, they are required to be closely related) they are nonetheless related by the birth of their common offspring.

Contrary to the belief of early scholars who talked about "primitive promiscuity" and "sexual communism," the immediate family is everywhere and at all times set apart and socially recognized. It may not be set apart as sharply as it is in our culture, but it is recognized nonetheless. Involved in its structure are three fundamental relationships that are always socially defined—the marital, parental, and sibling relationships. These are complicated by two other biological factors running through them: age and sex. The parent-child and sibling relationships are differently defined according to the sex and relative age of the parties concerned. Bearing in mind the complications which age and sex introduce, there are in the immediate family (as mentioned in Chapter VI) at least fifteen different biological relationships that may be socially recognized. Thus even this small group, simple as it may seem, offers complex possibilities for institution building. Some of the profoundest differences between one society and another lie in the kind and number of uses made of these elementary relationships.

Every normal individual acquires membership in two different family groups. This is because he participates in two species of birth: first when he himself is born, second when he procreates another individual. The first of these families we may call the family of orientation, because it is in this family that Ego is socialized and linked through his parents with the rest of the social organization. The second we may call the family of procreation, because it is here that Ego has children of his own. Ego is the sole link—the sole overlapping member—between these two families. It is necessary to look through the eyes of a participant (Ego) and thus to keep these two family groups separate, because the connections between them are of considerable importance. For instance, the departure of Ego from his family of orientation and his formation of a new family offer the possibility of strain and conflict. Societies differ greatly as to the manner in which the transition is accomplished.

It is plain that the extended kinship universe is composed of interlocking families. The chain of connection always involves the three basic relationships—marriage, parenthood, and siblingship—and the family units are the cells out of which the larger whole is constructed. To understand kinship in general it is therefore essential to understand the immediate family.

The Principle of Legitimacy

The structure of the human family is rooted not in biology but in the folkways and mores. This is why the exact form of the family varies significantly from one culture to another. Since the functions of the family are centered on reproduction, the institutional organization must utilize biological principles and these set certain limits on the amount of cultural variation. The mores cannot require that men become pregnant or that women have fifty children each. But within limits the cultural organization can emphasize and suppress, add and subtract, guide and control, until it has created a family system that is functionally and structurally related to the rest of the social order. Without an institutional system for the performance of the family functions, these functions would not be performed. We have already seen that man as a species can survive only in a cultural milieu. There is nothing about the family, including sexual intercourse and the handling of the newborn child, that does not have to be learned. There is nothing about it that does not involve social definition and mutual rights and obligations. It is necessary, therefore, to examine some of the basic mores that support the structure of the family and which are as ubiquitous as the family itself. The first of these is what may be called the principle of legitimacy.

The weak link in the family group is the father-child bond. There is no necessary association and no easy means of identification between these two as there is between mother and child. In the reproductive groups of monkeys and apes the male parent is held in the group not by any interest in the offspring but by his interest in the female. Among human beings a bond is created between the father and his children by a complex set of folkways, mores, and laws. Similarly, a durable relation is created between him and the mother. The mother's relation to the child is also socially regulated, but in this case the bond is more easily established and maintained.

The social definition of fatherhood we may call, following Malinowski,[2] the "principle of legitimacy"—the universal social rule that "no child should be brought into the world without a man—and one man at that—assuming the role of sociological father, that is, guardian and protector, the male link between the child and the rest of the community." [3] Without this general rule, to which many others are subsidiary, there would be no family; hence it is as uni-

[2] Bronislaw Malinowski, "Kinship," *Encyclopedia Britannica,* 14th Ed., p. 406; "Parenthood—the Basis of Social Structure" in V. F. Calverton and S. D. Schmalhausen, *The New Generation* (New York: Macauley, 1930), pp. 134-146; *Sex and Repression in Savage Society* (London: Harcourt, Brace, 1927), pp. 212-214.

[3] Malinowski, "Parenthood—the Basis of Social Structure," *loc. cit.,* p. 137. Cf. Kingsley Davis, "The Forms of Illegitimacy," *Social Forces,* Vol. 18 (October, 1939): 77-89; and "Illegitimacy and the Social Structure," *American Journal of Sociology,* Vol. 45 (September, 1939): 215-233.

versal and fundamental as the familial institution itself. It prevails no matter what other conditions prevail. Children may be an asset or a liability, prenuptial and extramarital intercourse may be forbidden or sanctioned, still the rule runs that a father is indispensable for the full social status of the child and its mother. Otherwise the child is illegitimate and the mother disesteemed.

Obviously the principle of legitimacy implies to some extent the control of sexual relations, since sex relations are a necessary condition of procreation. But all communities make distinctions between the various links in the procreative process. Most societies, for example, dissociate coitus and parenthood. "Broadly speaking, it may be said that freedom of intercourse though not universally is yet generally prevalent in human societies. Freedom of conception outside marriage is, however, never allowed, or at least in extremely few communities and under very exceptional circumstances;"[4] and if allowed it is likely to be interrupted with abortion or the resulting offspring may be eliminated through infanticide. In those societies where prenuptial intercourse is regarded as perfectly legitimate, marriage is yet a *conditio sine qua non* of legitimate children. Persons having free intercourse in such societies either escape pregnancy or parenthood by one means or another, or they marry when pregnancy occurs. Liberty of sexual intercourse is therefore *not* identical with liberty of parenthood. "Marriage cannot be defined as the licensing of sexual intercourse, but rather as the licensing of parenthood."[5] The early anthropologists, who were so interested in the question of whether or not extramarital intercourse was permitted in the tribes they studied, would have done better to ask the more profound question of whether or not unmarried parenthood was allowed. A positive answer to the second question would have unhinged our notion of social organization far more than a positive answer to the first question.

The Incest Taboo

There are various ways in which the principle of legitimacy may be violated. The offense is simple when the man and woman are unmarried to anyone, because by subsequently getting married to each other they may legitimize their illicit offspring. But if either of

[4] Malinowski, "Parenthood," *loc. cit.*, p. 138.
[5] *Ibid.*, p. 140.

them is already married to another party, the illegitimacy is adulterous and may be defined as either unimportant or exceptionally bad, depending on how much importance the culture attaches to physiological paternity as against sociological fatherhood. If the two parties are closely kin to each other (members of the same family) the illegitimacy is incestuous and is everywhere (except in ancient Egypt and in certain royal lines) considered horrible.[6] Obviously if a society is to have a family institution it must condemn illegitimacy, but why is incestuous illegitimacy or simply incestuous intercourse an object of such special condemnation? Why, in other words, do incest taboos exist? No one can claim a scientific understanding of the family, or indeed of society, without an answer to this question.

The family is an *organized* group. Its members occupy a definite set of mutual statuses, interact according to definite behavior patterns, and are motivated by reciprocal attitudes and sentiments. Without this institutional organization the family's performance of the four main functions mentioned above could not be accomplished. Sheer animal mating alone would not produce a new generation—not even in the physical sense, much less in the social sense. It is through the institutional organization that the sexual urge is harnessed to the work of creating a new generation, that the procreators are held responsible for the welfare and socialization of the young. Through this organization the offspring are provided with a peaceful and protected milieu in which they safely reach maturity and from which they are well launched into the competition of the larger society. Should the different statuses and relationships in the family become confused, the organization and functional efficiency of the family would be lost. The incest taboos confine sexual relations and sentiments to the married pair alone, excluding such things from the relation of parent and child, brother and sister. In this way confusion is prevented and family organization is maintained. The incest taboos therefore exist because they are essential to and form part of the family structure.

Suppose that brothers and sisters were allowed to violate the incest taboos. Consider first the effect of the sexual rivalry which would develop between brothers and between sisters. If, for example, there were two brothers and only one sister in the family, sexual

[6] For an analysis of the causes and kinds of illegitimacy, see Davis, "The Forms of Illegitimacy," *loc. cit.*

jealousy would probably destroy the brotherly attitudes supposed to prevail; the conflictful situation that would result would not be sufficiently peaceful for satisfactory socialization. Since siblings are generally reared in the same household, such rivalry would be stimulated very early and would be very intense. Moreover, since the number and sex distribution of siblings in different families is impossible to control, no standard institutional pattern could be worked out so that jealousy would be a support rather than a menace. Consider next the confusion that would result when children were born of such brother-sister relations. The brother would be not only his child's "father" but also his "uncle;" the sister would be not only her child's "mother" but also his "aunt." In addition there would arise a family within a family, a cancerous growth upsetting the original group and leading to an extreme concentration of each family within itself.

If sexual relations between parent and child were permitted, sexual rivalry between mother and daughter and between father and son would almost surely arise, and this rivalry would be incompatible with the sentiments necessary between the two. Should children be born the confusion of statuses would be phenomenal. The incestuous child of a father-daughter union, for example, would be a brother of his own mother, i.e. the son of his own sister; a stepson of his own grandmother; possibly a brother of his own uncle; and certainly a grandson of his own father. This confusion of generations would be contrary to the authoritarian relations so essential to the fulfillment of parental duties. The daughter receiving attention from her father, furthermore, would be in a weak position. Whereas sexual relations usually connote equality of status between the parties, father-daughter incest would put the daughter in a position of subordination. While she was still immature the father could use his power to take advantage of her.[7] Her position vis-à-vis the parent is one of dependence and submissiveness. Legitimate sexual relations ordinarily involve a certain amount of reciprocity. Sex is exchanged for something

[7] This is what happens in actual cases, where the daughters are often less than ten years of age. See Jacob A. Goldberg and Rosamond W. Goldberg, *Girls on City Streets* (New York: American Social Hygiene Association, 1935), pp. 185-217. Svend Riemer says nothing about the age of the daughters in Swedish court cases but analyzes the life histories and motives of the offending fathers; the father's use of his superior power and authority is quite apparent in the cases described. "A Research Note on Incest," *American Journal of Sociology*, XLV (January 1940): 566-575.

equally valuable, not squandered or extorted. A woman is expected to use her attractiveness to gain certain legitimate ends such as recognition, status, and a husband. The family stands back of her and helps her to make a respectable bargain. Monopoly by the father and his jealous resentment of outsiders would jeopardize the girl's opportunity. The child must be protected from parental aggression during her immaturity and enabled to make use of her status as a female upon something like equal terms. But such protection is not easy, because the temptation presented by a young and attractive member of the opposite sex in the same household is very strong. Only the most stringent taboos can restrain the parent from the thought and the deed. The taboo on incest is one of the strongest mores in existence.

When we think of the family's functions, its peculiar structure, and its reciprocal sentiments and roles, we can understand why the prohibition of incest is absolutely indispensable to its existence as a part of social organization. Since no society can get along without an efficient reproductive unit we find that incest taboos are everywhere imposed, their violation viewed with a horror so profound that some observers have mistakenly judged it to be instinctive.[8]

Family Transmission

Each immediate family is created by marriage, perfected by the birth of offspring, and ended by death or another marriage. It is thus a durable group that persists through and is responsible for major changes affecting the persons who compose it. But it is not a permanent group, for it lasts always less than a lifetime.

The impermanence of the family does not preclude a certain continuity between families in successive generations. Necessarily, each individual carries over into his family of procreation the things he has acquired in his family of orientation and transmits them to his own offspring. Among the things transmitted are the following: the family's own peculiar version of the general cultural heritage; its own mannerisms, attitudes, and history; its own membership in

[8] A fuller analysis of incest taboos will be found in Brenda Seligman, "Incest and Descent: Their Influence on Social Organization," *Journal of the Royal Anthropological Institute*, LIX (Jan.-June 1929), pp. 231-272. Reo Fortune, "Incest," *Encyclopedia of the Social Sciences;* and Bronislaw Malinowski, *Sex and Repression in Savage Society* (London: Paul, Trench Trubner, 1927).

wider groups such as clan, sect, class, and nation; and its own property. The overlapping personnel between successive families thus amounts to a cultural overlapping as well.

Not everything is transmitted. In the first place, each new family of procreation represents not a recrudescence of one family of orientation but a fusion of two, because husband and wife (by the law of incest) necessarily come from two different households. In the second place, to the extent that there is social mobility and social change, each new generation is different from the old. Between the old and the new generation, in fact, there may be conflict and estrangement.[9] Yet enough is transmitted to give a recognizable continuity. The transmission of the general cultural heritage and the family's own culture we call *socialization;* the transmission of membership in wider social groups, *descent;* the transmission of property, *inheritance;* and the transmission of status, *succession.* Necessarily these forms of transmission are mutually interrelated and overlapping, but it helps to clarify the family's function in society to treat them separately.

THE FAMILY AND SOCIALIZATION

The topic of socialization has already been dealt with in Chapter VIII. In the present context our interest attaches merely to the peculiar role of the family in this process. The family has several characteristics that give it a strategic importance in socialization, as follows:

(1) The family gets the child first. The child is born into the family a social blank, more plastic than he will ever be again. The initial steps of socialization therefore begin within the home. Other agencies come later and must build upon the groundwork already supplied by the family.

(2) The family is the most persistent factor in the child's life. Friends are dropped easily, teachers changed annually, playmates forgotten readily, but the parents retain their close contact with the child throughout most of his early life. For this reason the influence of the family is deep and abiding.

(3) The family is a primary group. It has a spontaneity and freedom that comes from complete mutual habituation within a small circle. It gives a sense of mutual identification as "we" which

[9] See Kingsley Davis, "The Sociology of Parent-Youth Conflict," *American Sociological Review,* Vol. 5 (August 1940), pp. 523-535.

is not simply the product of socialization but also a catalytic agent for it. The more there is a feeling of "we" the fewer are the barriers to the transmission of attitudes and sentiments.

(4) The family is connected with the satisfaction of all the needs of the child, from the most material needs such as food and drink to the most spiritual such as security and affection. The dependence of the child upon the family for the satisfaction of his needs is most complete at birth and gradually diminishes—with varying rates of speed in different societies—until a certain minimum is reached. But taking *all* of the child's needs into account we can say that no other group seriously rivals the family.

(5) The family furnishes both kinds of relationship—the authoritarian (as between parent and child) and the equalitarian (as between siblings)—within which socialization can take place. In this it differs from play groups and cliques, which are almost purely equalitarian. Each type of relationship supplies a unique and necessary element in socialization; and the fact that the family provides them both in a small circle gives it a special completeness in performing this function.

(6) The members of the family are identified with one another by the general community. The first identification the child has is with his family, and this identification determines many other forms of belonging. It is in the family that the child is first placed, so to speak, for the purpose of incorporating him in the social structure. The identification with the family persists throughout life. It may be modified by the emergence of a superior and competing allegiance when the child marries and founds a family of his own, but by that time the process of socialization has already been virtually completed.

Consideration of these peculiar contributions enables us to understand the family's outstanding role in socialization. The fact that it is the first, the most persistent, the most intimate, and the most complete agency dealing with the child explains why it is so essential in the formation of personality. It gives a sense of security which psychiatrists allege to be essential for mental health. It supplies a constancy of emotional attitude and social response, a confidence concerning future regularity. This is why the family plays such a part in mental balance and imbalance.

Since socialization is intimately linked with everything the child does in life, we can understand why the family occupies a key place in social organization. We can understand why every society gives the parents considerable authority over the child and why the family is a universal basis of status ascription, economic solidarity, and sentimental allegiance.

DESCENT AND THE CLAN

When identity with a certain family gives one membership in a wider group, the process is called descent.[10] All kin groups acquire their membership primarily in this way, one of the most prominent being the clan. Theoretically the clan is an organized body of kinsmen descended from the same ancestor, though actually many clans become so large that their common ancestor is either mythical or forgotten. Since the clan represents the expansion of the immediate family, tracing its descent in theory from an original pair, its members would at first be prohibited by the incest taboo from intermarrying. It could be expected that as the size of the clan grew this taboo would be correspondingly extended, so that even very old and populous clans would not permit their members to intermarry, no matter how distant the actual kinship. This supposition is borne out by the facts, for an almost universal characteristic of the clan is exogamy. Furthermore, the kinship terminology associated with clan systems reveals the same tendency. Ego often must call his father's brother, not "uncle" but "father." And since he calls his father's brother by this term and his mother's sister "mother," then the children of these persons, who belong to the same clan as himself, are called "brothers" and "sisters" rather than cousins. In addition to calling clan members by the same kinship terms as used for members of the immediate family, Ego tends also to treat them to some extent as family members. He is, for example, forbidden to have sexual intercourse with or marry his classificatory "sisters."

Being exogamous the clan cannot count its membership through both parents but through only one. Ego is a member of either his father's or his mother's clan, but not of both. If descent is through the father the clan is patrilineal; if through the mother, matrilineal. In either case it is important to note that the clan transcends the immediate family. Whereas the family is necessarily a small and impermanent group, the clan is indefinitely expansible and presumably immortal. There are clans in China said to contain as many

[10] W. H. R. Rivers, *Social Organization* (New York: Knopf, 1924), p. 86.

as 200,000 to 300,000 members.[11] Clans may therefore perform many functions that the immediate family cannot perform, such as military protection against outsiders, political and juridical regulation, accumulation of large capital reserves, development of economic specialization, and organization of religious activities.

In addition to transcending the immediate family in size and duration, the clan is also partially in conflict with it. Husband and wife, being from different clans, possess inevitably a divided allegiance. In a matrilineal clan system, for example, the father's children will be members of his wife's clan. His sister's children will be members of his own clan, and he may owe more allegiance to them than to his own children.[12] Furthermore, the clan tends to usurp some of the functions of the immediate family. Never does it usurp the function of reproduction because clan exogamy prevents that, but it does encroach on the economic, educational, and status-ascribing functions. In societies with well developed clans the immediate family (though always necessary) is often weak.

Clans are found very widely in the world. They occur in the exceedingly primitive tribes of aboriginal Australia as well as in the highly developed civilization of China. Primitive hunting and food gathering societies may have either matrilineal or patrilineal clans, as may also certain agricultural peoples such as the Trobriands and the Zuñi, but in the more developed civilization such as those of ancient China, Greece, Rome, and India, the clans tend to be patrilineal. In our own society there are no clans strictly speaking, but there are powerful family lines such as the Rockefellers, the Du Ponts, the Roosevelts, the Lowells, the Cabots, and the Adamses.[13] Also our family names descend patrilineally, giving each person an identification with his male line. So much does this influence our thinking that we often talk of the inheritance of traits exclusively in terms of the male ancestry. A young man named Boone, for example, may proudly say that he has inherited his ancestor Daniel's pioneer spirit—entirely ignoring all the females who have married Boones in the meantime and contributed an overwhelming percentage to the present Boone's inheritance. Similarly, the Nazis tried to show that

[11] Ralph Linton, *The Study of Man* (New York: D. Appleton-Century, 1936), p. 201.

[12] Bronislaw Malinowski, *Crime and Custom in Savage Society* (London: Kegan Paul, 1932), pp. 100-111.

[13] See Ferdinand Lundberg, *America's 60 Families* (New York: 1937).

President Franklin D. Roosevelt was a Jew, because he was, they said, descended centuries ago from a Hollander named Rosenfeld. Even if the allegation were true, it would not follow that the President had Jewish "blood" in him, because the great number of gentile females marrying into the line would long since have diluted to virtually nothing the fabled Jewish "blood."

There are various kinds of clan systems, some weak and some strong, some with numerous clans and some with only two. When they are well-developed the clans can dominate the whole pattern of social organization, weaving almost every major institution into their texture. They tend to arise in a stable, rural society and to disappear when urbanism and industrialism arise. They have played a tremendous role in the history of human society, and even today millions of persons live in clan societies, and many more in societies with a clannish tendency. But the clan cannot itself perform the function of reproduction. That the family alone can do, and it is through the family that the individual's clan affiliation is determined.

INHERITANCE OF PROPERTY

For property which the clan owns (land, buildings, and perhaps cattle) the problem of inheritance does not arise, because the clan in theory never dies. The surviving members as a group continue to operate the clan holdings. But familial or individual property raises the inheritance question in an acute form. When the family is broken by death such property must usually be received by one or more surviving members. Only the most individualistic societies (e.g. present-day English-speaking countries) allow property owners to will their property to nonkinsmen, and even there the right is restricted. Ordinarily inheritance is a kinship institution reflecting the dominant pattern of family organization in the society. Natural as this may seem it nevertheless creates a troublesome source of conflict because, since each individual can procreate several offspring, inheritance is a one-to-several proposition. The necessity constantly arises of "dividing the property" by some scheme, and no scheme has ever done full justice to all the parties concerned.

The testator is in a peculiar position. Alive, he wishes to control his property after death. Such control, indeed, gives him power while alive. He can for example threaten the young with disinheritance if they contravene his wishes. Yet since he will be dead, he must depend upon others (living persons) to carry out his wishes. The interest of these others, however, is not always his interest. The community is inclined to respect the wishes of the dead but not if they injure the living. It looks with suspicion upon whims born of petty quarrels, upon freak wills, and upon efforts to bind the heirs in perpetuity. It also has great respect for the claims of kinship, often regarding the owner more as a representative of the family than as a sole owner. For the protection of state, church, and family, it generally favors some standardization of inheritance custom. The beneficiaries, for their part, are often in the embarrassing position of being close relatives and yet competitors for the inheritance. If the community can standardize its custom it will avoid unseemly conflict between them; yet the discriminations involved in any scheme, no matter how standardized, are great.

In most civilized societies testation is neither completely free nor completely automatic. The testator is permitted to exercise a choice with respect to part of his wealth, but the other part must be divided according to definite rules among prescribed relatives. There is usually, for example, a *legitim*—a "legally enforceable claim of widows and children to at least a part of the dead husband's or father's estate." [14] The law of the old Spanish codes (carried to most Latin American countries) illustrates this compromise. The estate is usually divided into three *un*equal parts: the first and largest (the *legitima*) is for legitimate children or other near relatives and cannot be willed to anyone else; the second (the *mejora*) is an extra portion to be given to certain children, often one or more sons, sometimes the elder; and the third is available for free testation—often for the benefit of the church.[15] The extra portion usually represents the land and buildings from which the family derives its sustenance.

"In all peasant countries there is still a strong tendency to think of real property at least as belonging to the family rather than the individual. It is the family's means of life, from which no member can be shut out except for positive misconduct." [16] But normally there will be not one new family in the next generation, but several.

[14] G. D. H. Cole, "Inheritance," *Encyclopedia of the Social Sciences,* p. 36.

[15] Kingsley Davis, "Changing Concepts of Marriage," in Howard Becker and Reuben Hill (eds.), *Marriage and the Family* (New York: D. C. Heath, 1942), p. 103. See also Salvador Minguijon Adrian, *Historia del Derecho Español,* 2nd ed. (Barcelona-Buenos Aires: Editorial Labor, S. A., 1933), pp. 158-167.

[16] G. D. H. Cole, *op. cit.,* p. 36.

They may find it impossible all to live on the family holding, and yet if the holding is divided it may lose its efficiency. The heirs may, however, keep the holding in common and seek to enlarge it. This custom approximates a joint family system, popular in India and some Slavic countries. In more individualistic cultures, however, equal inheritance quickly leads to division of property (gavelkind, or partible inheritance). An alternative to this is the custom of impartible inheritance, whereby only one son is given the family holding. This son may be the oldest (primogeniture) or the youngest (ultimogeniture, or Borough English), or he may be chosen by the father according to ability. Each custom, found in various localities, has had its advantages and disadvantages. Inheritance by the eldest son has meant that he would more probably be mature at his father's death and could give the most help to the younger brothers who would eventually have to leave the holding. If the father lived to a ripe old age, however, the older children (unless guaranteed something) would long since have departed, and only the younger would be left to take over the family property. In any case the theory has been that those deprived of a chance to inherit the real property did at least get portions of the movable property—the daughters marriage portions and the sons money for education. The system has tended either to put too much responsibility on one son or to deprive the other sons of too much security. It has worked best in an expanding society where the noninheriting sons could find plenty of opportunities away from the homestead. The system of primogeniture among the British aristocracy filled the civil service, the clergy, and the army with brilliant younger sons.

The question of inheritance among the offspring reaches its most acute form when for one reason or another the property is indivisible. It may be indivisible because of its physical character. A house cannot be easily taken apart and distributed room by room. A farm may not be efficient if it is reduced in size beyond a certain point. Today in India, for example, the subdivision of agricultural land by heirs has reached an extreme degree, so that the average holding is too small not only for efficient cultivation but also for the adequate support of a family.[17] In France action had to be taken against "morcellement." But property may be indivisible for another reason—the

[17] G. T. Garratt, *An Indian Commentary* (New York: Cape and Smith, no date), pp. 27-33.

desire to maintain an estate intact and thus retain the power that goes with it. It is this desire that has given rise among many aristocracies to devices aimed at holding the property together. One such device is inheritance by one heir as mentioned above. But even this device does not guarantee perpetuity unless a restriction upon sale or division of the property is placed upon the heirs. Such a restriction, called "entail" in English and *mayorazgo* in Spanish, was formerly quite common in Europe and was brought to certain colonies in the New World.

> The kings of Spain encouraged the transplanting of this Old World system to the New . . . A number of mayorazgos were created among the holders of large properties in Chile, the estates being thus preserved against subdivision. Although the number of these mayorazgos was not great, they represented a power and an influence far beyond their numerical strength. They not only held intact a number of great estates, but they also set a pattern that was followed by the majority of Chilean haciendas. It became the custom to hold properties unbroken from one generation to another and to pass them undivided to the oldest son. This practice greatly strengthened the system of large holdings, tending still more to concentrate land in the hands of a few. It made more permanent the properties based on grants of land to the early colonists. . . . Formal entailment of property began in Chile near the close of the seventeenth century and continued for several decades after independence had been won. It survived longer in Chile than elsewhere in the Spanish colonies or even in Spain herself. The more democratic government established in Spain in 1812 brought with it the abolition of such oligarchical institutions in that country, and echoes of this action were heard in America in the enactment of measures leading to the same end. In Mexico the mayorazgos were finally abolished in 1823. After surviving in Chile until the middle of the nineteenth century, they were finally ended by the laws of 1852 and 1857. Even then the custom of holding the large properties intact did not cease but continued to characterize Chilean agriculture for many years and to exert a powerful influence on the entire life of the nation.[18]

It can be seen that in both industrial and landed economies, when instruments of production are privately owned, inheritance becomes an important basis of class distinction, especially if it is

[18] Geo. McCutchen McBride, *Chile: Land and Society* (New York: American Geographical Society, 1936), pp. 111-112.

of the impartible type. But as family holdings in the urbanized industrial society of modern nations have grown more fluid, consisting of money, stocks, and saleable capital, it has become easier to divide the inheritance. In the United States today, in case of intestacy, the children both male and female share equally in the inheritance.[19] But in state-centered economies such as that of Soviet Russia, where ownership applies only to consumption goods, the inheritance of property does not serve as a basis for class distinction. As a matter of fact the transmission of property at the death of the owner has always been seized upon as a convenient time for the community at large to encroach upon private ownership. In the Middle Ages both the church and the Lord of the Manor took an interest in such transmission, and managed in one way or another to benefit at the expense of the heirs.[20] In modern times the state is taking an ever larger share through graduated income taxes.

SUCCESSION

Not only are possessions transmitted along kinship lines, but so are specific offices and statuses. Such ascription of office we call succession. British kings, for example, succeed according to the principle of primogeniture, whereas British prime ministers achieve their position according to the principle of election. Succession to various types of statuses—political, occupational, religious, and class—along the line of filiation is an ancient solution to the problem of fitting each new generation into the social organization. We have dealt with it under the heading of ascribed status, so no more need be said about it here except that the same "one-to-several" conflict sometimes arises in succession to office as arises in the inheritance of property. If an office such as the kingship or chieftainship is limited to one person at a time, the system of succession must discriminate among the children of the defunct according to some principle. The history of many monarchies is red with the blood of brothers murdered by brothers, because the principle was either not clear or not accepted. Most inherited statuses do not require discrimination among siblings; nevertheless there is a sense in

[19] Chester G. Vernier, *American Family Laws* (Stanford: Stanford University Press, 1936), Vol. IV, pp. 113-116.

[20] Geo. C. Homans, *English Villagers of the Thirteenth Century* (Cambridge: Harvard University Press, 1941), Chaps. 8, 9-11, gives a lucid description of medieval English inheritance customs.

which even these statuses are affected by the "one-to-many" difficulty. General class and occupational statuses cannot always be open to all the children of all the persons in these statuses, because the number of children may be too numerous. Let us suppose for example that occupations were hereditary, but that the birth rate for priests was twice what was necessary to maintain the proportion of priests in the population. The society would come to have more priests than it could use, or some priests' children would have to find other occupations. Kinship succession obviously requires, if it is to work, either a very stable society and an even balance of births and deaths in all strata or else a method of discrimination among siblings. A regime of rapid change that emphasizes achieved status gives little play to succession. Such a regime will necessarily give the child advantages and disadvantages according to where his family stands in the class hierarchy, but these are mainly advantages or disadvantages with reference to subsequent competition. They do not completely guarantee his ultimate status.

The Great Transition

Our discussion has been dealing with universal features of the family. It has mentioned variations around these universals only incidentally. Now, however, the variations must themselves receive attention; for the form of the family differs greatly in different cultures.

So numerous are the possible variations in family organization that space does not allow us to treat them all. Below is an outline of some of the principal points of variation, classified under the three basic relationships of the family:

I. *Marital Relation*
- A. Number of mates
  - Monogamy
  - Polygyny
  - Polyandry
- B. Kind of mates
  - Marriage
  - Concubinage
- C. Degree of authority
  - Equalitarian

Patriarchal
Matriarchal

D. Strength of bond
  Temporary
  Loose (easy divorce)
  Unbreakable (no divorce)

E. Possibility of remarriage
  No remarriage after death or divorce
  Permissive remarriage
  Mandatory remarriage

F. Age at marriage
  Early (child marriage)
  Late

G. Choice of mate
  Who determines choice
    Free selection by young persons (courtship)
    Controlled selection by parents
  Bases of choice (endogamy and exogamy)
    Kinship
    Caste
    Class
    Region
    Religion

H. Exchange at marriage
  Brideprice
  Groomprice
  Equal exchange

I. Residence after marriage
  Matrilocal
  Patrilocal
  Independent

II *Parent-Child*

A. Number of children born
  High fertility
  Low fertility

B. Degree of parental authority

C. Duration of parental authority
  Until death of parent
  Until retirement of parent
  Until some fixed time
    (e.g., puberty or marriage of child)

D. Disposition of child
   At death of parent
   At divorce of parents
   After illegitimate birth

E. Handling of illegitimacy
   Types of illegitimacy recognized
   Assignment of responsibility
   Possibility of legitimation

F. Type of descent
   Matrilineal
   Patrilineal

G. Type of inheritance
   Testamentary
   Non-testamentary

III. *Siblings*

A. Strength of the bond

B. Share of inheritance
   Equal inheritance
   Primogeniture
   Ultimogeniture
   Sex limitations on inheritance

C. Duration of common residence

D. Kind of mutual obligations

This list is not meant to be exhaustive but simply illustrative. It shows how complex must be any full-scale treatment of family institutions in different cultures.

Is there no way, the reader may ask, of reducing the variations in family organization to some pattern? Is there no key factor which determines all the rest and which, once understood, enables us to grasp the whole configuration in each case? The answer must unfortunately be in the negative. There is no such key. But one factor does come fairly close to meeting the purpose. It does not appear in the preceding list because it concerns a wider sphere than the immediate family itself, but it plays a crucial role in determining the nature of the immediate family. This factor is the relation of the family of procreation to the two families of orientation—or, in other words, the relation of the family formed by marriage to the original families of the husband and wife. The importance of this factor can be understood by considering two polar types, the one in which the family of orientation completely dominates the family of procreation and the other in which such dominance is completely absent. The first we shall call a familistic society, the second a nonfamilistic (or individualistic) society.

If the immediate family is controlled by the extended family—if, that is, the society is familistic—a number of consequences follow. Referring to the points of possible variation listed above we can say, for example, that plural mating (in the form of either polygyny or concubinage) is very likely to occur, because in a kinship dominated society any means of enlarging the family contributes to one's power and prestige. We can say, too, that authority within the kinship system is not likely to be equalitarian, for there is clearly great power of the older generation over the younger and often great power of the husband over the wife. In addition, the age at marriage is likely to be quite young and marital choice to be determined by the parents rather than the young persons themselves. This means that romantic love is ruled out as a basis of marriage. The economic exchanges in connection with marriage are apt to be complex, embracing not only a wide range of goods and services but also a wide circle of relatives. The newly married couple will tend to live with the parents rather than in a separate household, for the joint household facilitates parental control. The newly married couple will tend to give birth to a large number of children, because in a static familistic regime a high death rate prevails and therefore a high fertility must also prevail. Although the customs will encourage the bearing of numerous progeny, this does not necessarily mean that families will be huge. Infant mortality will take away between a third and a fifth of the babies born, and heavy child mortality will take additional ones. The individual family may in fact be a small and weak unit, the clan being the all-important group. In this case inheritance is not important because clan property is generally inalienable; but even if there is no clan system, inheritance is apt to be rather strictly along kinship lines. In any case the tie between siblings is likely to be very strong, since siblings have to hold the kinship group together after the death of the parents. At the same time, in order to hold the property of the family line together, there may be unequal inheritance as between one sibling and another. The emphasis of all institutions, indeed, is upon the perpetuation of the clan or family line. The individual family, being only a cell in this larger group, has its independence greatly curtailed by the claims of extended kinship.

Clearly the relation of the immediate family to the extended kin offers a key to the understanding of family organization. It enables us to classify societies into two broad types, each with characteristic patterns. Historically one of these types—the familistic—has prevailed to a much greater extent than the other. This is because human beings have generally dwelt in small isolated villages or bands. Such communities were cemented by long association into intricate primary groups, where mutual knowledge, standard opinion, ubiquitous gossip, and ancient tradition gave a fixed character to the culture. Status was largely ascribed on the basis of kinship, age, and sex. The extended kin adhered together; the old controlled the marriage and early family life of the young. So long as the local community remained supreme, with hunting or agriculture the main occupation and rusticity the main attribute, familism prevailed. But when the modern nation began to evolve, bringing millions of strangers into a common milieu, fostering a dynamic technology, a mobile class structure, a complex division of labor, and a dominant urbanism, kinship began to lose its importance as a basis of social organization. The political, protective, and economic functions of the clan passed to other agencies; the household lost its role as a productive unit; and little was left for the family except the core functions. Marriage became increasingly a private matter beyond the control of the parents, and each new family unit tended to be independent of its predecessors. With the decline in mortality, fertility also declined. The small family, occupying its own small living space and moving as a free unit, became the dominant pattern. This small family system originated in Western industrial civilization and is now being diffused, along with other features of industrialism, to the rest of the world. It seems likely that eventually the whole of mankind will have a family organization roughly similar to that found in the United States today.

The Hindu Family

As an example of a familistic system let us take the Hindu family as it was encountered by the British in the eighteenth century. At that time India was exclusively an agricultural and handicraft country. The population dwelt in virtually self-sufficient villages rooted in tradition. The three main institutions were the village itself, the joint family, and caste—all of them closely interwoven. The joint family consisted of males having a common male ancestor, female offspring not yet married, and women brought into the group by marriage. All of these persons might live in a common household or in several households near to one another. In any case, so long as the joint family held together, its members were expected to contribute to the support of the whole and to receive from it a share of the total product.

In the Hindu conception of marriage little attention was paid to the wishes of the young persons. Marriage was regarded as compulsory. The parents were morally obligated to find mates for their children, and the children to accept the parental choice. Involved in an intricate system of religious beliefs, caste restrictions, and communal controls, the parents would exert extreme effort to marry their children. Indeed they often married them at a very early age, in infancy or childhood, and the marriage was consummated as soon as the girl reached puberty. The marriage contract was regarded as an agreement between two joint families rather than between the two young people.[21]

In such circumstances there was no room for romantic love as a basis of marital selection. In fact there was no room for courtship, because the young people never saw each other prior to marriage. The Hindu ideal of marriage had no regard for individual taste or inclination—it was, rather, afraid of them. Manu did recognize selection by mutual choice (*Gandharva*) as a possible form of marriage, but he placed it far down the list of preference and regarded it as highly undesirable.[22] One Hindu woman said: "Though the visiting missionaries used to tell me of love before marriage I was careful enough to pay no attention to such unexamined assertions. I held to my mother's sentence: 'True love is the *result* of marriage.' "[23] Instead of being attracted by the personal qualities of the future mate, each party had simply an ideal of what a mate should be, and the emotions felt toward the ideal mate were expressed as a matter

[21] The description of the Hindu family given here is taken mainly from the writer's chapter in Becker and Hill (eds.), *loc. cit.*, pp. 93-100. Citations to literature will be found in that chapter.

[22] Rabindranath Tagore, "The Indian Ideal of Marriage," in *The Book of Marriage*, Hermann Keyserling, ed. (New York: Blue Ribbon Books, 1920), p. 104.

[23] Dhan Gopal Mukerji, *Visit India with Me* (New York: Dutton, 1929), p. 189.

of natural duty toward the actual mate. In this way the Hindu social system controlled individual impulse and subordinated marital choice to group ends.

Since marriage was held to be compulsory, it was also universal. Everybody was married at an early age. "Anyone making gifts to, or taking gifts from, a Brahmin who remains a householder, but does not marry, goes to hell." [24] Marriage was also held to be indissoluble. It was a sacrament, an indestructible and secret union. So indestructible was it, in fact, that a second marriage (at least for the wife) was abhorred, and the lot of the widow condemned to celibacy was notorious. Marital devotion received its supreme expression in the rite of *sate* (or *suttee*), whereby the widow joined her husband in death by casting herself on the funeral pyre. In ordinary cases, however, the widow simply remained celibate. Since marriage occurred at an early age, there were many child widows doomed to spend the rest of their lives without a husband. Such women remained with the deceased husband's family, where they were little better than servants. Their condition was alleviated if they had borne children, especially male children, but at best it was unfortunate.

Both polygyny and concubinage were permitted but did not occur frequently. Also religious and secular prostitution occurred. These institutions allowed the male but not the ordinary female to escape the rigorous limitation of indissoluble wedlock.

The married couple went to live with the husband's family. Indeed, upon completion of the betrothal the young girl often went to her husband's household long before she reached puberty. There she was at the beck and call of the older women in the household. She frequently returned to her own household (usually in another village) to bear her first child, but she was otherwise a member of her husband's family for life. Furthermore, the Hindus had borrowed from the Muslims the custom of secluding their women (*purdah*). The women of the household, at least in the higher castes and especially in the northwest of India, remained in the *zenana,* or women's quarters. These quarters, usually at the back of the house, were forbidden to men other than the husband and, under proper conditions, his near male relatives. Some women boasted that not even the eye of the sun had seen their face.[25]

[24] Tagore, *op. cit.*, p. 101.
[25] Frieda H. Das, *Purdah* (New York: Vanguard, 1932), pp. 102-103.

Patrilocal residence made child marriage feasible, because by going to live with the husband's family the young couple were spared the necessity of setting up a separate household or depending on the bridegroom's earnings. There was thus no economic objection to the marriage of children; and when one remembers that the little bride brought with her a sizeable groomprice and was treated as an unpaid servant, one sees that there was an economic incentive to such marriage. The rule of residence also helps explain the "low" position of Hindu women. Since daughters were destined to leave the household at an early age, they were not valued as highly as were the permanent male members. The incoming daughters-in-law, young strangers from another household, were equally disvalued. They were felt to be of a lesser order than the males of the household. Not until they bore a son did they gain respect in their adopted home. Pride in their son became the main consolation of their life but attendance upon their husband remained their chief duty.

The young wife was expected to bear offspring as soon after puberty as possible. The Hindu religion required every man to have at least one son and grandson to perpetuate the family line, because only they could perform the ceremony essential to his salvation after death. Without this *sraddha* ceremony the successive reincarnations of the deceased would operate to impede his progress heavenward. Since mortality among Hindus was very high (the average expectation of life being less than thirty years), each man wished to have as large a number of offspring as possible in order to be sure of having at least one son and one grandson living at the time of his death. The Hindu birth rate was thus extremely high, and as a result the population grew rapidly whenever circumstances permitted.

Childlessness, regarded as a great calamity, was blamed upon the woman and attributed to sinful living in the previous incarnation. The misfortune, however, was lack of sons, not daughters. Should the newborn child be a girl there was cause for mourning and invective, and a chance that death would be allowed to claim her.[26]

Basic to the Hindu joint family was patrilineal descent. Children were identified in name and allegiance with the family line of their father. Property descended patrilineally, but since real property did not belong to individuals but to the joint family as a unit, the question of inheritance as we understand it did not arise. When an indi-

26 Das, *op. cit.*, p. 53.

vidual died the property still belonged to the family. Every male child acquired at birth "a vested interest in the ancestral property, becoming a co-owner with his father, brothers, and other male relatives." [27] The males represented the family in the *panchayat* (caste council), directed the economic affairs of the family, and dealt with the outside world. Their dominance was reinforced by the seclusion of the women and by greater freedom and education.

This description of the highly integrated Hindu family was never entirely true in practice. There were always regional and caste variations. Moreover, it applies more aptly to the India of two centuries ago than to India today. Some of the features described have practically vanished, others have become surreptitious, and still others flourish only in orthodox homes. British overlordship brought more than new control to India; it brought a widely different way of life. The change has been accomplished partly by education but mainly by alteration of the general social organization upon which family life is dependent. Hindu familism was best suited to an agricultural society where mobility was slight, specialization simple, status fixed, science rudimentary, and custom immutable. It required that kinship be a major basis for status ascription, and since kinship is independent of personal achievement it required a static society. The description thus serves to depict the kind of social order represented by familism, although it should not be inferred that every familistic system is like that of India. India's social order is unique in many respects, but there is a certain basic resemblance of its family organization to that of other agricultural civilizations (such as that of old China and old Japan). The contrast between such family systems and that of modern America is sharp indeed.

The Modern Family

Modern society, characterized by an elaborate industrial technology, a high degree of urbanization, and a great amount of geographical and social ability, has sheered away the extended kinship bonds. The sole effective kinship group is now the immediate family, and even this unit has lost in size and function. True, the immediate family has gained in importance by being freed from the control of extended kindred, but it has declined in importance in other ways.

[27] L. S. S. O'Malley, *India's Social Heritage* (Oxford: Clarendon Press, 1934), p. 123.

Factory production has destroyed the system of complementary activities within the home by substituting a new division of labor integrated outside the home. The demand for technically trained personnel has led the school increasingly to take over the function of education and status placement. Urbanism has affected not merely the externals, such as size of the home, but also the essentials of family life. It has forced individuals to coöperate with countless persons who are not kinsmen. It has also encouraged them to join special interest groups, thus drawing them out of the unspecialized and heterogeneous family with its wide sex and age differences. It has substituted legal controls for the informal controls of the small community and has subjected the family, with its archaic combination of intimacy and conventionality, to two kinds of competition—one the competition of impersonal associations pursuing particular interests in a rational manner, the other the competition of unconventionalized intimacies entailing no long-run obligations. The anonymous city has thus turned business, recreation, sex relations, and in fact nearly all activities into possible competitors of the family. Social mobility has cut still deeper. In so far as individuals improve their class status by virtue of their own achievement rather than by birth, an intrinsic function of the family (status ascription) is lost to it. In a completely open society where all vertical positions were filled purely by individual accomplishment, there could scarcely be a family organization; each family member would tend to find himself in a different social stratum from the others, and the invidious sentiments thus brought into the family circle would prove incompatible with family sentiments.

The tendency of modern society to sheer away extended kinship ties and to reduce the size and functions of the immediate family has gone farther in middle class urban America than anywhere else. Since the urban middle class, because of its size and its economic dominance, sets the family pattern for the rest of America, since the family in other classes and indeed in the whole world seems to be moving toward this standard, the key to the future family lies here. What we find is that the family unit has been reduced to its lowest common denominator—married couple and children. The family aspect of our culture has become couple-centered, with only one or two children eventually entering the charmed circle. Even this smallest possible family unit, however, has shown a tendency toward instability. The divorce rate has risen to a dizzy figure. Women have come as near achieving equality with men, and children emancipation from parents, as in any nation at any time. The idea of immediate personal happiness as the primary aim of matrimony has become widespread; even college courses on marriage advertise themselves as "a guide to happiness." Mass romanticism—the deification of romantic courtship—has reached its pinnacle, as witness the preoccupation of motion pictures and popular literature with the trials of adolescent love. The ideal of a separate living space (room, apartment, or house), as private for each couple as walls and separate conveniences can make it, has achieved a new intensity. The use of contraception has become ever more effective, the number of children born during a marriage ever more reduced. Ceremony and religion have lost almost all connection with the home as an entity, and ideological conflict has reduced the uniformity and certainty of the family mores. The individuation of family members has seemingly reached a point beyond which it can go no farther.

Most of the so-called family problems of today are due not to the perversity of human nature but to our new kind of family organization. In order to see this let us consider three such problems—divorce, the declining birth rate, and parent-youth conflict.

DIVORCE

Following World War II the divorce rate in the United States rose to its highest peak, approximately one in every three marriages ending in divorce during that period. This was not necessarily the world's highest divorce rate (the rate in Egypt is higher), but it was one of the highest. In a culture that places as much emphasis on marriage and marital happiness as ours does, this proclivity for divorce may seem strange. Yet actually our very emphasis on marital happiness is the main explanation of the high divorce rate. In the first place our puritanical mores attempt to confine sex expression to marriage. In the second place our free and open courtship makes personal attachment the main basis of marital choice. The two things together give rise to the romantic complex in which the force of suppressed sex desire and the whims of personal feeling combine to induce a maximum amount of irrationality. In many quarters the parties are expected to remain "technically virginal" until marriage. As a result the unconsummated intimacy of "necking" and "petting" during courtship creates so much sex tension that marriage as a means of gratification seems overwhelmingly desirable. Once married, however, sexual satiation and routine living wear off the romantic halo. Then the couple discover whether or not they really like each other. If it turns out that they do not like each other after all, the marriage has no excuse for continuing, because it was undertaken in the first place merely on the basis of personal feeling. The surrounding community in the urban setting no longer forces the couple to continue an unwanted marriage. Our divorce law still implies that one party (the guilty one) does not want a divorce and that the other party (the innocent one) wants it only as an escape from a greater evil, but it does not work out that way in practice. Supposedly granted for an unbearable offense by one party against the other, most divorces today are actually given on the basis of mutual consent. The alleged "ground" for divorce is merely a convenient legal fiction.

But why do we emphasize marital happiness? The answer is that there is nothing else in modern marriage to emphasize. Wedlock has so far lost its connections with the rest of the social order that it has become merely a vehicle for sexual gratification and companionship. Outside this sphere it has no significance that would give it stability. It is no longer an economic partnership, a political alliance, a communal matter, and a religious sacrament. A divorce no longer interferes seriously with a person's main activities. For purposes of companionship a new marriage may serve better than the old; at least it is worth a try.

The popular sociological view is that factory, city, school, specialized associations, etc. have taken over most of the family's so-called institutional functions but that the affectional functions—sexual gratification and companionship—still remain. A recent textbook on the family exemplifies this view. Entitled *The Family: From Institution to Companionship,* it states its main thesis as follows:

> The basic thesis of this book is that the family has been in historical times in transition from an institution with family behavior controlled by the mores, public opinion, and law to a companionship with family behavior arising from the mutual affection and consensus of its members.[28]

[28] Ernest W. Burgess and Harvey J. Locke (New York: American Book, 1945), pp. 26-27.

The present writer disagrees with this formulation on two grounds. First, the theory states that mores, public opinion, and law are ceasing to control family behavior. But this is sociologically impossible. Marriage and family relations are socially defined. They are institutions. (There is a difference between even modern marriage and a liaison.) It is therefore impossible for the family to exist without normative control. If the modern family emphasizes companionship, it is not because the mores no longer have anything to do with it but because the mores have changed. We now have a different normative system with reference to the family, and a different social setting in which the system is applied. Second, the theory under discussion implies that the institutional functions can disappear (and the family thus cease to be an institution) but that the so-called affectional functions can remain as strong as ever. But affection is not based on thin air. If marriage does not somehow involve the partners in common activities—functions—apart from sexual intercourse, it cannot hope to produce a satisfactory companionship or attain any stability. In short when the social functions of the family are all lost, affection within the family and in fact the family itself, will also be lost.[29] One cannot be retained without the other. The instability of modern marriage clearly shows that it is becoming deficient as a source of emotional security.

There is one function remaining to the family that is clearly institutional and incapable of being shifted to any other institution without a revolutionary change in society. This is the bearing and rearing of children. The current emphasis on companionship and happiness in marriage has lost sight of the main social function of marriage. If marriages were not for the purpose of having children there would be no purpose in them at all, because companionship could be had without the formalities of wedlock.

As a matter of fact the main concern over divorce in our culture is a concern over the children. In our small family system the child of divorced parents has nowhere to turn except to one parent or the other. In contrast to a culture with a joint family system, our culture cannot provide a stable domestic milieu that continues after divorce.

[29] More extensive discussion of this point will be found in the writer's paper, "Reproductive Institutions and the Pressure for Population," *Sociological Review* (British), Vol. 29 (July 1937), pp. 289-306.

Divorce is therefore more serious for the child among us than among most cultures.[30]

Having become for us the sole important kinship unit, the small family exhibits an unusual emotional concentration within itself. Its members, living apart from other kinsmen and surrounded by temporary acquaintances or strangers, can rely only upon themselves to share the feelings of family solidarity. The resulting intensity is sometimes extremely great, if not stifling. Consequently any marital discord not only affects the mates acutely but also involves the children, subjecting them to divided loyalty and emotional insecurity. Furthermore, the equalitarian principle in wedlock makes the disposition of the child problematic. In a society where clans exist there is little question as to the child's custody and residence, but in our society the court must decide custody in each case of divorce. The welfare of the child is supposed to be the main basis of the court's decision, but the criteria of "welfare" are not standardized. Sometimes the child is forced to divide his time between two different households, with consequent stresses and strains upon his personality. In any case he is, after the divorce, the sole remaining link between the former mates, and too often therefore becomes the only instrument through which they can express their mutual resentment. A study of the divorce child in Nebraska showed that "often the part-time child is used as a weapon by one or both parents," that "in a few cases youngsters stated they had procured information for one parent against the other," that the situation afforded "the father an opportunity to find out how his former wife is spending his alimony, whom she is 'stepping out with,' and so forth," that "the mother may likewise question the child when he comes 'home' from father," and that in some cases "the child is bribed in order to get this information" and is thus taught by his own parents "to lie, spy, and blackmail." [31]

It is fortunate that in America most divorces are granted to couples who are childless. Not only has the birth rate been declining but divorces have been increasingly occurring in the earliest years of marriage. The modal divorce now occurs in the third year of mar-

[30] The present discussion of divorce in relation to the child is taken from the writer's article, "Children of Divorced Parents: A Sociological and Statistical Analysis," *Law and Contemporary Problems* (Summer 1944), pp. 700-720.

[31] T. Earl Sullenger and DeLene Brownlee, *Children of Divorce* (Omaha: Municipal University, 1934), p. 9.

riage. So the increased divorce rate has not meant a corresponding number of children affected. Approximately two-thirds of the couples divorced are childless, and the majority of the remaining one-third have only one child. The conclusion therefore seems justified that much of the public alarm over the rising divorce rate is exaggerated. In any case it would seem that a far greater problem, especially so far as children are concerned, is nonlegal separation and desertion; but because statistics are almost entirely lacking these problems are not given much attention.

THE DECLINING BIRTH RATE

Evidence that the middle class urban family is functionally inadequate is contained in the low birth rate. During the five years preceding the 1940 census our cities were replacing their population by births to the extent of only 74 per cent. This means that with the same fertility and mortality they would, unless aided from the outside, ultimately lose 26 per cent of their population per generation. Since the period mentioned the urban birth rate has risen, but few expect it to be high enough in the long run to replace the urban population. Not only is the urban birth rate as a whole low, but the middle class has fewer children than the strata lower in the social scale. This inverse differential fertility, although customary with us, is socially anomalous because it means that persons better placed in society and hence presumably more highly regarded are not having a proportional share in rearing the next generation.

PARENT-YOUTH CONFLICT

The modern urban family is also beset by an unusual amount of conflict between parents and their adolescent offspring. The conflict is due essentially to the competition of other agencies in dealing with the child, the rapidity of social change which makes the parents obsolete, the lack of any clear definition and ceremonial recognition of the change of authority as the child approaches maturity, and the conflicting folkways and mores governing adolescent behavior. Again it is our social system that is responsible, because adolescence in many other cultures is not a time of conflict. The stress and strain in our culture is symptomatic of the functionless instability of the modern small family.[32]

[32] See Kingsley Davis, "The Sociology of Parent-Youth Conflict," *American Sociological Review*, Vol. 5 (August 1940), pp. 523-535.

Conclusion

In what has been said here about the American family, it is the middle class urban family that has been the focus of attention. The farm family and the Negro family are variations that require separate interpretation. It is clear, however, that we do have a new kind of family system, different by far from the familistic systems of stable agricultural societies. It is clear, too, that both kinds of systems have certain basic similarities. The immediate family has basically the same structure wherever it is found and carries on the same core functions. The small family system of our society, however, has had its structure weakened by a growing lack of integration with the rest of the social order. Consequently, marriage is becoming increasingly unstable and the core functions are being performed only inadequately. Eventually a new form of integration may appear, but it is hard to predict exactly what form such integration will take.

References

American Journal of Sociology, Vol. 53 (May, 1948), pp. 417-495.

This whole issue is devoted to articles on "The American Family." Regional patterns, ethnic patterns, social change, and research trends are featured. Most of the articles are mediocre but some are interesting.

Nels Anderson, *Desert Saints: The Mormon Frontier in Utah* (Chicago: University of Chicago Press, 1942), Chap. 15, "Social Implications of Polygamy."

Informed discussion of the development and objectives of Mormon polygyny.

John S. Bradway (ed.), "Alimony," *Law and Contemporary Problems,* Vol. 6 (Spring 1939), pp. 183-320.

An entire volume of an excellent journal devoted to the most mercenary side of marriage.

John S. Bradway (ed.), "Children of Divorced Parents," *Law and Contemporary Problems,* Vol. 10 (Summer 1944), pp. 697-866.

By far the most complete and diversified discussion of this subject in the literature.

Alfred Cahen, *Statistical Analysis of American Divorce* (New York: Columbia University Press, 1932).

The United States has the poorest divorce statistics of any civilized nation. Here a maximum amount of information is ingeniously squeezed out of such statistics as we do have.

Arthur W. Calhoun, *A Social History of the American Family* (New York: Barnes and Noble, 1945).

First published in 1917-19, this three-volume history of the American family from colonial times to the present is the standard and by far the best work on the subject. Here the domestic foibles of our ancestors, together with their peculiar laws and bizarre ideas, are recounted with faithful attention to detail.

Leonard S. Cottrell, Jr., "The Present Status and Future Orientation of Research on the Family," *American Sociological Review*, Vol. 13 (April 1948), pp. 123-136.

An evaluation of present research with suggestions for future work.

Kingsley Davis, Harry C. Bredemeier, and Marion J. Levy, Jr., *Modern American Society* (New York: Rinehart, 1949), Part 9, "Modern Marriage and the Family."

Selected readings on "American Family Organization," "Courtship and Mate Selection," "Parent-Child Relations," and "Divorce."

John D. Durand, "Married Women in the Labor Force," *American Journal of Sociology*, Vol. 52 (November 1946), pp. 217-223.

An extremely able article on the extent, trends, and significance of the employment of married women in the United States labor force. The author, formerly employed by the Census Bureau, is an authority on the labor force. This whole issue of the Journal *deals with various aspects of family life.*

Morris Fishbein and Ernest W. Burgess (eds.), *Successful Marriage* (Garden City, N. Y.: Doubleday, 1947).

An omnibus symposium on everything from "Premarital Sex Relationships" to "Are You Going to Have a Baby?" One of the better exemplars of this type of literature.

E. Franklin Frazier, *The Negro Family in the United States* (Chicago: University of Chicago Press, 1939).

The most definitive history and sociology of the Negro family yet published, by a distinguished Negro sociologist. Not only are the special features of the Negro family explained in clear language, but through the history of the family we are given an unusual and valuable view of the Negro in America.

Paul C. Glick, "The Family Cycle," *American Sociological Review*, Vol. 12 (April 1947), pp. 164-174.

An exceptionally illuminating article on the quantitative aspects of different stages in the family cycle, by an official of the Census Bureau. Shows the median duration of each stage, the average age at first marriage, average age at birth of first child, average age of parent when first child is married, age of wife when husband dies, etc.

Willystine Goodsell, *A History of Marriage and the Family* (New York: Macmillan, 1935).

A more general history than Calhoun's, covering family development throughout Western civilization.

Margaret Jarman Hagood, *Mothers of the South* (Chapel Hill: University of North Carolina Press, 1939).

Not quite but almost as fascinating as Tobacco Road, *this study of white tenant farm women, made by a well-known sociologist, will open the eyes of anyone who is not a white tenant farm woman.*

Alfred C. Kinsey, Wardell B. Pomeroy, and Clyde E. Martin, *Sexual Behavior in the Human Male* (Philadelphia: Saunders, 1948).

This is the famous "Kinsey report," the first volume in a series on the sex life of Americans. Directed by a biologist, the investigation is aimed at discovering the facts about actual sex behavior independently of what the mores say the facts ought to be. The reader's interest in sex can be counted on to take him through the somewhat heavy statistics.

Bronislaw Malinowski, *The Sexual Life of Savages in North-Western Melanesia* (New York: Harcourt, Brace, 1929).

Sold as pornography on Sixth Avenue, this is really one of Malinowski's greatest books. Analyzes in detail the interrelations between sex, kinship, morals, and social organization.

Leon C. Marshall and Geoffrey May, *The Divorce Court*, Vol. 1, *Maryland;* Vol. 2, *Ohio* (Baltimore: The Johns Hopkins Press, 1932, 1933).

Here an economist and a student of law combine their efforts in a statistical study of the cases in the divorce courts of two states during the course of a year. The result is the best empirical discussion of divorce litigation in American literature.

I. Schapera, *Married Life in an African Tribe* (New York: Sheridan House, 1941).

> *A detailed and intimate description of courtship, marriage, and family customs among the Kgatla of Bechuanaland Protectorate. Includes changes under European contact.*

Leo W. Simmons, *The Role of the Aged in Primitive Society* (New Haven: Yale University Press, 1945).

> *Variations and similarities in the adjustment of the aged in different types of societies.*

Willard Waller, *The Family: A Dynamic Interpretation* (New York: Cordon, 1938), Part II, "Courtship Interaction"; Part III, "Marriage Interaction"; Part IV, "Parenthood"; Part V, "Family Disorganization."

> *After a slow start this becomes one of the most interesting textbooks ever written. The intimate interaction in courtship, marriage, divorce, and parenthood is analyzed with rare insight by one whose spectacles were* not *rose tinted.*

PART IV

MAJOR INSTITUTIONS

SCIENCE, TECHNOLOGY, AND SOCIETY

ECONOMIC INSTITUTIONS

POLITICAL INSTITUTIONS

RELIGIOUS INSTITUTIONS

CHAPTER XVI

SCIENCE, TECHNOLOGY, AND SOCIETY

MODERN man, who lives in a technological wonderland, finds it easier to point out specific techniques than to define technology in general. He not only confuses technology with science on the one side and economics on the other, but sometimes even identifies it with things in themselves. This last error is exemplified in the distinction commonly made in anthropology and sociology between "material" and "nonmaterial" culture.[1] Axes, knives, and spears presumably fall into the former category; myths, dogmas, and marriage into the latter. But the trouble is that material objects are not parts of culture because they are "material" but rather because they are comprehended, desired, altered, thought about, and used by human beings. It is their meaningful, not their material aspect which makes them cultural in character. Culture, as we have seen, is a sociopsychic level of reality. The aspects of culture cannot be divided into material and nonmaterial, and this distinction in no way helps us to understand the nature of technology.

For the American Indians coal was not a cultural object, but for the white settlers, who found it lying on the surface, it was definitely such. Physical nature merely furnishes the materials for technology; culture furnishes the knowledge and patterns of use. Science is that part of the cultural heritage which represents a systematic knowledge of nature, and technology is that part which contains the applications of this knowledge. Much technology, however, is the application of rule-of-thumb rather than systematic knowledge, so that science is not necessary for at least a rudimentary technology.

[1] See, for example, Wm. F. Ogburn, *Social Change* (New York: Viking Press, 1926); F. S. Chapin, *Cultural Change* (New York: Century Co., 1928); Clark Wissler, *Man and Culture* (New York: Thos. Y. Crowell, 1923), pp. 74-75. A critique of the distinction is contained in R. K. Merton, "Civilization and Culture," *Sociology and Social Research*, Vol. 21 (Nov.-Dec. 1936), 103-113.

The end of scientific activity is truth, but technology has a utilitarian goal. Technological ends are always empirical ends—ends the attainment of which is possible and demonstrable in this world. There is, for example, no technique for attaining absolution from sin. There is to be sure a "ritual technique," but this is a different species of technology; an external observer, watching a man go through the purifactory ritual, could not grasp the connection between the means adopted and the end pursued. Not only is the end subjective, otherworldly, and hence unobservable, but there is no intrinsic relation between it and the ritual means. Seeing the ritual gives no clue to the end, and knowing the end gives no clue to the ritual. The only relation between the two is a symbolic one, so that unless the symbolic connection is already known nothing can be deduced concerning the action. True technology, on the other hand, is distinguished by the presence of intrinsic connections between the means employed and the end pursued. A man who builds a boat and rows across to the other side of a river has achieved an immediate end by the application of an intrinsically appropriate means. The boat's relation to the goal is not symbolic but physical, a matter of gravity, motion, and friction. To achieve the end requires an application of physical laws regardless of whether or not these laws are explicitly known.

The technological end is not thought of as competitive with other ends but as purely instrumental. This gives it an "immediate" quality. It cannot be an ultimate end, not only because ultimate ends by definition are not instrumental but also because they tend to be nonempirical. Economic and political action, on the other hand, always involve the balancing of competing ends. Of course, for both kinds of behavior the control of techniques or "means of production" is of tremendous advantage. A capitalistic economic order, for example, is one in which individuals in their private capacity own the instruments of production. Some control over instruments of production is necessary if there is to be any production—technology can never stand alone; but private ownership is not the only mode of control. There may be control by the political group as an entity. Even under capitalistic laissez-faire there is considerable state control over the rights and use of private property. The common confusion between economics and technology is partly due to the fact that both are close together in the means-end chain and hence to the fact that economic interests involve an immediate control over technology. Economic behavior too is rational and pursues a proximate rather than an ultimate end. The difference between economy and technology, however, is equally as fundamental as the similarity and should never be ignored. The industrial system is a network of highly interrelated productive mechanisms; capitalistic business is a system of control over this network, determining through the patterns of price and profit the distribution of the products. Identically the same network of productive mechanisms can operate under an entirely different system of control—for example, under the Soviet system of state socialism.

If the end of scientific action is always truth, then to the extent that any other end intrudes itself the action ceases to be scientific. If, for example, a moral end takes precedence over truth in a piece of research, the research becomes scientifically worthless. A man who, under the guise of investigating the chemical effects of various germicides on sperm and mucous membrane, had chiefly in mind the aim of condemning contraception would be acting not as a scientist but as a propagandist. Having truth as only a secondary goal he might distort his findings in order to prove that contraception is "harmful." This truth indicates a deep and inevitable conflict between science and morality. It is not a complete conflict, because the normative order must somehow be related to the factual order and consequently a systematic knowledge of the factual order may often prove essential to the normative sphere. In other words, scientific truth is often instrumental to moral values. But it remains true that the search for truth, if pushed far enough, runs counter to the moral interpretation of phenomena. Scientists, as concrete persons, are not and need not be always nonmoral and unemotional. Scientific activity need not be divorced from moral aims. Yet in so far as a man is a scientist, that part of his behavior that is called science must be guided by the canons for establishing empirical fact. His ultimate purpose may be the glorification of the ways of God, but his more immediate purpose must be strictly the search for truth. The conflict really becomes acute only when the search for empirical truth becomes an ultimate value too and therefore competes with religious and moral values. This is very likely to happen because the pursuit of science can become a way of life for those who engage in it. Indeed it becomes a way of life for an entire professional fraternity and hence for this group a common value sacred in its own right.

In this circumstance the scientist is likely to collide with the theologian, the moralist, and the common man, all of whom are less emotionally bound to empirical truth. Thus it is not really science and morality that are in conflict but the morality of science and the morality of ordinary behavior.

Technology encounters less conflict with morality in one sense because it is always aimed at achieving a utilitarian goal. Without the goal, technology would be meaningless. Therefore, the usefulness of technology is always readily apparent, whereas the usefulness of the search for truth is not so apparent. Yet technology is limited precisely by the limitation of its goals. It cannot develop except where the goals are held, and the goals may not be held because of moral attitudes. If one group in a society has a given goal in view, it can develop a technology for reaching this goal; but the endeavor may be blocked by another group which holds a different goal. The conflict between the two groups then becomes political and moral and has nothing to do with technology, except to limit its development. The very divorcement of science from everyday pursuits protects it from many of the limitations of moral conflict, whereas the relevance of technology for these pursuits makes it, or at least its products, of greater moral significance. In this sense technology stands as a buffer between science on the one hand and social control on the other. Science fares better if it is regarded as the handmaid of technology rather than the handmaid of morality, because the rational and intrinsic connection between means and end in technological action is compatible with the search for empirical truth. The technological goal may serve as a spur to scientific endeavor by giving point to the goal of knowledge. It may thus save science from the accusation of being a useless ivory tower and yet at the same time bear the brunt of moral limitations.

If the absence of a particular and demonstrable utilitarian goal is taken as a condemnation of science, or if the relation between research and practice is construed too narrowly, then science is hampered. There is a tendency to say, because one does not *see* the relation between research and a practical goal, that there is no such relation. Actually if one could see the relation with absolute clarity there would be no need for research; the problem, the very task of the research, would be known. It took business men a long time to see the value of laboratory research in industry because, not being scientists or technicians, their conception of the relation of research to practical goals was exceedingly narrow. They thought that in order to apply science it was necessary that each and every operation have a direct relation to the utilitarian end; whereas in truth the more remote the research from a particular utilitarian end, the more valuable it is for an entire *range* of goals (other things equal).

There is certainly a technology as well as a science of social relations. But in social phenomena the balancing of different ends is so important that sheer technology seldom exists in practice. Because other people are seldom allowed to be treated as sheer means, we either condemn or ridicule attempts to technologize social relations. To be sure, if the social relations dealt with are secondary rather than primary a considerable amount of calculation is permissible—in labor management, government and administration, and sales policies, for example. But such attempts are usually rationalized as being for the "benefit" of the laborers, the citizens, or the customers, and in general the action is more hemmed in by normative restriction than is the treatment of nonhuman materials. Our attention is therefore directed in the present chapter to technology as the application of knowledge to physical phenomena, deferring any discussion of "social technology" to other chapters.

Types of Technological Systems

No society can live without a cultural adjustment to its environment. Even the crudest society must therefore possess a technology though it need not possess a science. There are, however, extreme differences between technologies. The history of man's cultural evolution is mainly a technological history, because it is primarily man's material devices (tools, shelters, vessels, etc.) that have been recovered from the dim past. Moreover, the fact that technology is somehow tangible and rational makes it readily describable, so that students of simple and archaic societies can give us accurate descriptions of it. Finally, the importance of technology is universally admitted, especially by modern thinkers. It follows that the information about technology is quite abundant and unusually exact. The social or institutional aspects, however, are not so clearly known.

Chapple and Coon have pointed out that at least four elements are involved in any technique.[2] These are the type of implement, the kind of operation, the source of power, and the nature of the social interaction required. "It is impossible," they point out, "to weave without a loom, or to grind grain without some kind of a mill," and each process varies according to the kind of machine used. In the case of weaving there is a definite progression depending on whether a one-bar, two-bar, or two-beam loom is used; and in the case of milling, a tremendous difference depending on whether a simple hand mill or a more efficient rotary device is used. As for the operations, the weaver performs a sequence of three—"shedding, wefting, and battening; the potter goes through a larger number—grinding and sifting the clay, adding tempering matter, wetting the tempered clay to a desired consistency, shaping the vessel, and firing it." Different men may perform the operations separately, and the amount of training and skill required varies greatly with the kind of operation performed. "In the case of the simpler techniques, one man usually knows several; with the more difficult ones, specialists are needed. Yet even in the case of specialists there is a definite limit to the amount of manual skill which the average human being can acquire, the California Indian woman who makes a feathered basket may be just as skillful as the machinist in the Ford plant who grinds valve-seats in new motors. The whole point about machinery is that you put the skill of the gifted worker into the designing of the machine, and the ordinary worker who operates the machine need not be highly trained. Thus mass production requires less training than hand work; employees in a shoe factory are not as skilled as hand shoemakers, yet they produce many more shoes per capita, by means of simpler sequences of action."

The third element, *the source of power,* is as important as the type of implement or the sequence of operations. "Most techniques, particularly in the simpler groups, are performed by hand; the force employed is that of the technician's own muscles. Thus the hand-loom weaver and the potter, with or without his wheel, are hand-power operators. In some societies, however, people have devised means of using the power of animals instead. This is an advance in that it frees the operator from the machine, in that most animals are stronger than men, and in that the man so freed can tend many

[2] Eliot D. Chapple and Carleton S. Coon, *Principles of Anthropology* (New York: Holt, 1942), pp. 138-140.

machines at once, or leave the animal working while he does something else. A far greater advance is the use of natural forces through machines, as in case of windpower, waterpower, steam, and electricity." The three steps in the utilization of power—human, animal, and mechanical—enable the single individual to produce increasingly large quantities of materials per working hour.

The fourth element, the *interaction* involved, relates the technique to a group situation. "Some techniques, like weaving, are solitary tasks and in their simpler forms inhibit interaction; others, like house-building among the Gallas, can be done by large work gangs of men, and offer an opportunity for much interaction; still others, like the construction of a modern office building in an American city, not only permit interaction, but make it necessary, since a large number of men performing different skilled tasks must work together if the job is to be done. . . . The techniques which people practice, therefore, have much to do with the determination of the complexity and character of their institutions." And we may add, *vice versa.*

Attempts have been made to relate types of societies to technological systems.[3] Such attempts have not been completely successful, but they raise the question of the relation of technology to society in an interesting form. Generally the classifications of technological systems give a central place to the methods of getting sustenance, assigning only secondary importance to the methods of securing clothing, shelter, etc. On this basis the main distinction is between a society that depends exclusively on gathering and one that depends upon plant and animal domestication. Obviously, however, these are broad categories. Some primitive groups depend more on hunting than simple gathering, and some depend on fishing. Also there is, for more complicated technologies, a distinction according to whether they emphasize agriculture or emphasize herding. Agriculture can be practiced with practically no use of domesticated animals, and herding can be practiced with no devotion to agriculture, although generally the two go together. Agriculture may also be settled or it may be nomadic. In the latter case the group abandons a given site within a year or two (as soon as the cleared land,

[3] E.g., L. T. Hobhouse, G. C. Wheeler, and M. Ginsberg, *The Material Culture and Social Institutions of the Simpler Peoples* (London: Chapman & Hall, 1930); Chapple and Coon, *op. cit.,* Part II.

as in many tropical areas, loses its fertility). Finally, there is a broad distinction between industrial and nonindustrial technologies, and this again involves various subtypes. In any case it is plain that a rough progression from one type to the next can be generally observed. Each new type keeps some of the techniques of the old and merely adds to them. An industrial society obviously relies on agriculture and animal husbandry, but it introduces a new type of manufacturing process and a more intensive commerce. This progressive aspect indicates that we are here dealing with a type of social evolution.

The kind of technology places certain limits on the kind of social organization that is possible. It does not determine the exact form of society—the marriage patterns, the political system, the property relations, etc.—but it does rule out certain possibilities that may be realized with a different technology. For instance a gathering or hunting technology means that the population must usually be sparse and communication consequently poor. This means in turn that each community is likely to be isolated, with the community itself often being the widest social unit. Settled agriculture, on the other hand, enables a larger number of people to exist in a smaller area, giving rise to more cultural interchange and a more extended political organization. With industrial technology the social horizon expands remarkably, enabling world-wide cultural interaction and the nation-state to arise.

When the writer first visited Latin America he had the feeling of being hemmed-in. He first attributed this feeling to the laziness and inefficiency of the Latin Americans themselves, and he thought that a person from the United States should be able to show them how to get things done. He soon discovered, however, that he could do no more than they, and that indeed the difficulty did not lie in the people themselves but in the technology they had to work with. The telephone equipment was antiquated, the roads were poor, the automobiles scarce, the water systems inadequate, the factories absent, the buses slow. The individual from the United States, accustomed to a slightly more advanced technology, soon discovered that he could get no more done than the local people. Technology definitely limits what is possible.

It should not be assumed, however, that the technology determines the social order. This is an attractive assumption because, as mentioned before, technology seems to have a definiteness and tangibility that make us fall easily into the habit of assigning it causal primacy. But technology is a part of culture and is in equilibrium with the other parts. It is as much a result as a cause.

Social Factors Fostering Technological Development

Behind any technological system lies an institutional order. The rapidity and nature of technological advance therefore depend as much upon the institutional order as upon the previous stage of technology itself. What, then, are some of the institutional factors favoring rapid technological development?

One outstanding determinant lies in the sphere of social values. It concerns the climate of opinion toward change in general and toward technological change in particular. If the social order places a positive value upon change, if it regards with an open mind the utilization of new devices, it will necessarily give a wide scope to technological innovations. Of course, such open-mindedness is always relative in degree, because no society will welcome all changes simply for the sake of change. People inevitably tend to place the burden of proof upon the new device, and find rationalizations for rejecting something that requires the inconvenience of new adjustments.

> The Dyaks were accustomed to felling trees by peeling them down strip by strip, and when shown the quicker and better method of cutting a V-shaped notch with an axe were unwilling to make the change. Pasteur's discovery of germs as a cause of disease was bitterly opposed by the medical profession for a long time. Harvey's discovery, in the first part of the seventeenth century, that the blood circulates was strongly opposed, especially by the physicians and scientists of the time. Harvey claimed that no man over forty accepted the doctrine of the circulation of the blood when it was first presented. . . .
>
> The use of coal was prohibited in England in the reign of Edward I, and a citizen was tried, condemned, and executed for burning "sea cole." A bill was introduced in the House of Commons at the instance of the British Admiralty forbidding the use of steam power in the British Navy. . . . Chauncey Depew warned his nephew not to invest $500 in Ford stocks because "nothing has come along to

> beat the horse," and J. P. Morgan and Company refused a large investment in a company that was later very successful as General Motors. Commodore Vanderbilt opposed the adoption of air brakes, and told Westinghouse, the inventor, that he had no time to waste on fools.[4]

Yet we find great differences between one society and another in the degree to which resistance to change represents a central value. Modern society, no matter how much it may resist a particular innovation, has as one of its chief dogmas the doctrine of progress—the belief that *this world* can be made a better place by the constant application of empirical knowledge to our material and human resources. It is consequently committed in principle to the value of change. Hindu society, on the other hand, before the influence of the West made itself felt, had no such doctrine. It was inherently suspicious of change, and focused its attention upon the individual's improving his position *in the other world* through the rigid observance of custom in this one.

Values, however, must be instrumented by a social organization before they can become effective. A second factor favorable to technological change is consequently the appearance of institutional methods for rewarding the inventor and diffusing his techniques. A system that fosters competition and social mobility is at the same time one that fosters technological accomplishment, because competitive advantage can be gained only by finding some way around those who are already entrenched. The legal guarantee of competitive advantage flowing from innovation lies in patent and copyright law, whereby the inventor is given exclusive rights to the use of his invention for a long time. It is assumed that he can derive a profit from his innovation only by making its fruits available to the public. He is therefore rewarded not merely for making the invention but also for diffusing it. The reward may not lie exclusively in monetary terms. Scientific ideas are generally not patented and often not copyrighted. The scientist's recompense for making his discoveries may come from enhanced salary but it may also come, and often more importantly, from the prestige he receives among his colleagues and in the world at large. Einstein's compensation for the hard work of

[4] Wm. F. Ogburn and Meyer F. Nimkoff, *Sociology* (Boston: Houghton Mifflin, 1940), pp. 824-826. Citations to basic literature on this subject will be found on these pages.

making his revolutionary discoveries can hardly be measured in monetary terms. Yet, as in technology, scientific innovations cannot bring any sort of reward unless they are also diffused. The incentive to scientific work depends upon the social conventions among scientists—conventions which give recognition to priority of discovery, which utilize ceremony (honors, titles, etc.) and position within scientific organizations to symbolize the prestige of the outstanding discoverer. Science itself is a competitive system, and like any other form of competition it requires rules. The rules, together with their enforcement, constitute the institutional structure that makes scientific advance possible.

A third factor is specialization. Significant changes of technique are most apt to be made by one intimately acquainted with a particular field. Since each innovation combines old elements, the person most likely to discover it is the one whose mind has long weighed the mutual implications of these elements. The total heritage grows far beyond the power of any one man to grasp. Since life is short and the intellect limited, each man can hope to contribute only in the restricted sphere of his particular competence. Thus there is specialization not only of the technician and scientist from the rest of the population, but also of one technician or one scientist from another. A university faculty is composed of people who cannot speak one another's language and who have only the vaguest idea of what one another is doing. The history of scientific and technological advance is a history of ever narrower specialization.

Finally, methods of storing and transmitting ideas also foster technological advance. Writing enables the highest achievements of any generation to be stored for the next. Printing facilitates the easy spread of ideas to the whole population. Libraries facilitate the accumulation of knowledge in specialized fields and thus aid the process of specialization. It follows that the more literate the population, the more accessible it is to the absorption of technological innovation.

Obviously our consideration of factors favoring technological advance has moved toward technology itself as a factor. We began by pointing out the role of the value system; then we mentioned the importance of an institutional order facilitating competition, mobility, and specialization; and now we have cited such things as printing and libraries. This requires us to admit that technology itself is a strong factor in technological advance. Since each stage of development is dependent on previous stages, the interpretation of any one stage must rest to some extent on what went before. But our question has really called for the social factors that make possible an orderly advance of technology as a whole, not the factors responsible for reaching a particular stage. The intrinsic evolution of technology can be speeded up only in a favorable social environment. Technology itself cannot guarantee its own progress.

Social Factors Hindering Technological Development

To make the matter clearer let us consider some of the social factors obstructing technological advance. The simplest way to characterize them would be to say that they are the opposite of the favorable factors mentioned above, but this would not be particularly helpful. Still another oversimplification would be the statement that technological advance is held up by "social conservatism." This is circular, for it tells us nothing more than that resistance to change results from resistance to change. What we want to know is the nature and function of social conservatism.

The distrust of change has deep roots because every social system requires stability. The individual must feel somewhat secure in his future expectations if he is to coöperate efficiently with others. The knowledge of the past must somehow serve as a guide to the future. Even a competitive order requires some stability. Each person must feel that contractual arrangements will be carried out, that the rules and laws governing competition will not change overnight. If the structure breaks down, then competition is likely to turn into conflict. Similarly, science itself requires stability. There must be political stability so that some people can devote themselves to the pursuit of knowledge. There must be economic stability so that a surplus of goods can be accumulated for the support of these men and their laboratories. There must be stability in the rules of science itself—in the criteria of validity, the ethics of credit and recognition, the devotion to truth, etc. If scientific theory were sheerly a matter of fashion, there would be no science. Any society is therefore on its guard against change. The question is why one society can nevertheless tolerate considerable technological change, while another cannot.

One common feature of the fixed society is what might be called diffuse otherworldliness—the tendency to fix attention on the transcendental world and to view the material world primarily as symbolic of transcendental realities. Since technology and science deal with the intrinsic relations between phenomena, the insistence upon a supernatural interpretation in every detail is a serious obstacle. If the supernatural is interpreted as being exceedingly remote, interfering with the things of this world only indirectly and in a broad way, then specific events can always be interpreted in scientific terms without hindrance. Or if the ways of God are thought to be revealed by scientific method, another avenue to freedom is found. But if each and every event in the palpable world is thought to be fraught with immediate religious significance of importance to the soul of the participant, scientific and technological advance is greatly hindered. The following incident from India illustrates the effect of such diffuse otherworldliness.

> This tract of country [a jute-growing area in Bengal] was proverbially unhealthy. Something had to be done about the malaria, fever, what not! And the mill owners, with new zeal for better health conditions, tackled the problem. The drainage, they discovered, was at fault. They offered to replace it with an entirely new system, which they laid down at their own expense. It made an immediate difference to the health of the countryside, and the Progressive-Indian Secretary of the District Board devoted a high-sounding paragraph to this fact in the Annual Report.
>
> "The malodorous waste matter from the mills no longer clogs our drains," he read out to the meeting.
>
> The President of the moment was an orthodox Hindu.
>
> "Stop!" said he. "Where does it go?"
>
> It was a startling question, but the Secretary was equal to the occasion. "Where all drainage goes, into the river, and thence," he added after a pause—"out to the sea."
>
> "The river—you mean Ganga Ma?"
>
> "What else?"
>
> "The sacred river, our Ganga Mata, to receive malodorous stuff from the jute mills!"
>
> . . . And, regardless of the feelings of the mill owners (mostly Scotsmen), he insisted on scrapping the new drainage, getting a majority for a resolution requiring its instant removal.[5]

[5] Cornelia Sorabji, *India Recalled* (London: Nisbet, 1936), pp. 175-176.

Along with the diffuse otherworldly attitude goes a lack of interest in technological advance. In such circumstances there is no doctrine of progress, or if there is it relates to progress in the next world rather than this one. Hence there is no particular reward for the innovator and no social mechanism for stimulating and aiding him.

But how, you may ask, does a society happen to get into this religio-conservative frame of mind? One answer is isolation. Seemingly essential for the emergence of inventions and for the seculiarized environment in which it can take place, is cross-cultural fertilization—the circulation of diverse ideas and customs because of the contact of cultures. If the local community is isolated as a virtually self-sufficient entity, if the strata in society are water-tight compartments with little cultural interchange, if communication, transportation, and trade are poor, diffuse religiosity and an absence of technological advance are likely to be the result. Furthermore, the small isolated community cannot embody the specialization, accumulate the economic surplus, and store the knowledge necessary for technological advance.

Clear now should be the fact that technology and the rest of society are intimately related. Not only, for example, is isolation inimical to invention but this condition itself results from a lack of invention. Social isolation and technological innovation are mutually antithetical. Similarly nearly every social trait has some mutual interdependence with nearly every technological trait, and vice versa. It follows that technology cannot be interpreted purely in terms of itself. A sociological interpretation of it is also necessary.

Perhaps the quickest way of seeing the interrelation between technology and society is *not* to raise the question of change as we have done in this chapter, but to raise the question of who controls the technology. This carries us straight to the subject of economic and political institutions—a subject to be dealt with in the next two chapters.

References

J. D. Bernal, *The Social Function of Science* (New York: Macmillan, 1939).

Somewhat evaluative and not based on empirical study, but contains rather interesting discussions of the relationship of science to social order.

Ansley J. Coale, *The Problem of Reducing Vulnerability to Atomic Bombs* (Princeton: Princeton University Press, 1947).

This study sponsored by the Social Science Research Council, concludes that it is not easy to get away from atomic bombs.

S. Giedion, *Mechanization Takes Command* (New York: Oxford University Press, 1948).

Traces the manner in which mechanization has come to pervade the pattern of our life and discusses its impact on individual and collective life.

Richard T. LaPiere, *Sociology* (New York: McGraw-Hill, 1946), Chap. 9, "Technology"; Chap. 13, "Science and the Arts."

Good treatment of technology as a component of the social system and science as an element in the ideology.

Robert K. Merton, *Science, Technology and Society in 17th Century England* (Bruges: "Osiris History of Science Monographs," 1938).

An excellent sociological study of factors contributing to the rise of science at the time and place when science was really getting under way.

Robert K. Merton, "The Sociology of Knowledge" in Georges Gurvitch and Wilbert E. Moore (eds.), *Twentieth Century Sociology* (New York: Philosophical Library, pp. 366-405).

Comprehensive analysis of the nature and developments in this special field of sociological inquiry. The footnotes plus a list at the end comprise an elaborate bibliography.

National Resources Committee, *Technological Trends and National Policy* (Washington: Government Printing Office, 1937), Part 1, "Social Aspects of Technology"; Part 2, "Science and Technology."

Prediction of inventions, social effects of inventions, resistances to technological innovations, the relation between science and technology.

Wm. F. Ogburn, *The Social Effects of Aviation* (Boston: Houghton Mifflin, 1946).

Treats not only the changes that have already taken place but also those that are likely to occur. A good example of the difficulties of predicting social consequences of a single invention.

S. M. Rosen and L. F. Rosen, *Technology and Society* (New York: Macmillan, 1941).

An interesting discussion, although resting on the questionable assumption that a disequilibrium now exists between a rapidly changing technology and a more slowly changing social system.

Richard H. Shyrock, *The Development of Modern Medicine* (New York: Knopf, 1947).

A history of medicine from the 17th century, stressing the close relationship with general social history. The author is outstanding in this field.

William Vogt, *The Road to Survival* (New York: Sloane Associates, 1948).

The untoward effects of our technology upon our resources, their relation to population and social welfare. Extremely well written and incisive, though highly controversial.

E. P. Wigner (ed.), *Physical Science and Human Values* (Princeton: Princeton University Press, 1947).

A symposium of papers presented in the nuclear science session of the Princeton Bicentennial Conference. Includes papers devoted to (a) the relations between scientific and governmental institutions and (b) the influences which scientific work and the scientist himself should *exert on society.*

CHAPTER XVII

ECONOMIC INSTITUTIONS*

IT IS not sufficient that human society use its technology to produce the means of life. What is required in addition is that it distribute the instrumentalities and the products among its members in an orderly and efficient way. If men obtained goods solely through unrestrained cunning and ruthless struggle, there would ensue a state of social chaos in which actually they could obtain no goods at all—for technology, security, in fact all culture would have disappeared. If a man dared not leave his home for fear someone else would immediately take possession, if he dared not use his car for fear of having it stopped and appropriated, if he could not count on his firm still occupying the office when he arrived for work, if he could not count on receiving any wages or having any agreement fulfilled—if he could dare nothing and expect nothing, he could likewise contribute nothing. Such a society would produce only privation and death. Contrary to the dreams of some utopians, therefore, the problem of human society can never be reduced simply to a matter of technology. Equally as important as a productive system and yet far more difficult, is a distributive system—an allocation of rights and duties with respect to the fruits of technology. If, like the solitary wasps, each man produced enough for his own sustenance there would be no question of distribution. But in human society the very nature of cultural adaptation implies division of labor and specialization, which in turn imply the necessity of exchange; and the inevitable scarcity of goods means that the system of exchange, whatever its form, will give to the societal members less than they want and certainly less than they might conceivably have. It is on the distributive level that one man's

* This chapter was written with the valuable collaboration of Mr. Harry Bredemeier, who wrote some sections in substantially their present form.

interest is opposed to another's interest; and yet despite this opposition some order, some feeling of rightness, some mutual tolerance must be maintained. The more complex the society, the more its destiny rests on the distributive relationships: its members have more goods but they also have more wants, and their specialized interdependence makes their lives rest increasingly upon the exchange as opposed to the production of goods. The basic ideas, norms, and statuses which govern the allocation of scarce goods in any society, whether the society be primitive or civilized, we call its economic institutions. Of these the most fundamental and universal are the institutions of property and contract.

Property

Property is essentially the distributive system in its static aspect. It consists of the rights and duties of one person or group (the owner) as against all other persons and groups with respect to some scarce good. It is thus exclusive, for it sets off what is mine from what is thine; but it is also social, being rooted in custom and protected by law.

So ingrained in human thought is the fallacy of misplaced concreteness that property is often regarded as the thing owned rather than the rights which constitute the ownership. In popular speech property is the material object, while ownership is the state of having the object. Property conceived in this way is usually thought of as something tangible, like land and furniture. Indeed, not until the end of the nineteenth century did the United States Supreme Court recognize that property refers to rights and is not identical with a tangible object.[1] Rights and duties are not tangible in a physical sense, and the tangibility or intangibility of the thing owned is of no great consequence. What is important is the exchange value of the object, the nature and completeness of the rights, and the number and characteristics of the owners.

THE NATURE OF PROPERTY RIGHTS

If property is nothing more than rights and obligations with respect to something scarce but valuable, how then can we dis-

[1] John R. Commons, *Legal Foundations of Capitalism* (New York: Macmillan, 1924), p. 14.

tinguish it from other foci of rights and duties? A woman has, as against other women, certain rights in her husband. She has acquired him by a legitimate transaction and has a slip of paper somewhat resembling a deed to prove it. Whether or not she actually possesses him at the time (some other woman may be "using" him), she nevertheless continues to have the legal rights in him. Her rights are legally protected against trespassers, and he may not leave her except after a duly enacted legal process. Is he then her property? If so, property is such a broad concept that any right is a property right. The concept, to be useful, must be narrower than this.

One way to approach the problem is to ask, "What is the difference, from a property point of view, between a husband and an automobile?" The proper answer (viewing both as sheer objects, of course) is that there is no difference. As a sheer object either one can fit into a property situation. The distinction between what is property and what is not does not lie in the character of the object but in the nature of the rights. If we talk of rights then there is a difference between a husband and an automobile, the difference lying precisely in the society's definition of what the woman can do with her car compared to what she can do with her husband, and (really part of the same thing) how other people must behave with respect to each of these "things." Her rights in the automobile include the right of transferring it to a third person, but the rights in the husband do not. Furthermore, the husband is acquired by an agreement that makes no effort to state the "consideration" involved or to list the precise obligations entailed. In a commercial contract the parties are not obligated to do anything not stated in the document, whereas in a marriage the two parties have countless obligations defined in custom and law but not stated in any agreement. For these reasons the wife's rights in her husband are not property rights but rather what we call "marital rights."

The first characteristic of property rights, then, is their transferability. The assumption is that these rights may be exchanged whenever such an exchange seems mutually profitable to the parties concerned. In some cases property is inalienable in the sense that it cannot be sold; but this does not preclude its being transferred, for at the very least it must be transmitted from one generation to the next. Such inalienability applies to particular groups (e.g., the local clan unit) and is perfectly compatible with transfer from generation to generation within the group. Furthermore, the taboo against selling the property often applies merely to individual members of the group; in many cases the group as a whole, if it decides to, may dispose of the common property. In any event the conception of property always implies that except for some taboo on sale or transmission it *could* be so transferred. This characteristic helps us to distinguish a property right from, say, the possession of a skill. A physician can transfer his automobile to someone else by gift, sale, or will, but he cannot convey his skill. He can, of course, *teach* his skill to someone else provided he has the ability to teach and the other person has the ability to learn; but this is not true transference, because the physician still retains his own skill and the pupil has another one like it. The physician can transfer his rights in either his automobile or his practice to someone else; and these, then, are his property; his rights in neither his wife nor his skill can be so transferred (for different reasons), and they are not, therefore, property rights.

Connected with this transferability is a second characteristic—namely, that property rights in an object do not necessarily imply actual use and enjoyment of the object by the owner. The object may be stolen by another to use and enjoy, borrowed with the owner's consent, or rented at a cost. In other words there is an important distinction between ownership and possession—a distinction that gives rise to some of the greatest human problems, notably robbery and fraud on the one hand, debt slavery and bondage on the other.

Closely related to this is a third characteristic of property—its power aspect. The possession of exclusive rights to something that is scarce and valuable necessarily implies the possession of power over others who also desire the scarce and valuable things. Indeed, it is only because certain things are both scarce and desired by many persons that they are valuable; and the more complete and exclusive the rights of one individual or group in the thing, the greater is the control which can be exerted over other individuals, other groups, or the members of the group in which ownership resides. The amount of power which property gives to the owner depends not only upon the definition of his rights but also on the intensity of others' needs for that which is owned. A man's ownership of several suits of clothes for example, although it is quite complete, does not ordinarily give him any power over other members of his community. But if he were to have the same kinds of rights in all clothing factories, his power over others would be great. Since this is the case, it is clear that no society can afford to leave to chance either the distribution of property rights or their definition.

It is sometimes suggested that another, fourth, characteristic of property rights is that they refer to a concrete external object. This seems to limit too narrowly the range of property rights, however; for while it is true that concrete entities may be part of a property situation, it is also true (a) that not all concrete objects are the focus of property rights and (b) that some foci of property rights are not concrete objects. What property really refers to in all cases is the right to demand certain kinds of behavior from other individuals, including the right to demand that public officials enforce certain behavior on others. In the case of the sale of a company's "good will," for example, what is the object involved? There is no object, really; what happens is that the former owner of the good will agrees not to compete with the buyer by using the name of the product or the name of the company, or even his own name if that has become known to the customers as part of the company. It is a right not an object which is scarce and valuable in this case, the right to the "loyalty" of the customers. Similarly, if I own a home in a residential suburb, my property rights refer not only to the physical house and lot but also to the *expectation* that a glue factory will not be erected next door.[2]

This is the question of tangibility again. The nature of property, we have said, is to be found in the institutionally defined rights, not in the physical properties of the object. But there is one characteristic of the property-object worth mentioning—namely, that it is usually nonhuman. This means that the object has no rights of its own but is simply the impassive object of such rights and obligations on the part of the interested parties and the public at large.[3] It is the owner's will, his discretion and advantage that are served by the object. This is one reason why we do not think of a woman's

[2] This has not, to be sure, always been a part of my property right. The change is as clear an illustration as any of the relative nature of the norms defining property.

[3] Domestic animals, of course, are frequently protected against cruelty and other abuses. This is because in some respects they resemble human beings. They are animate and can be hurt.

husband as her property. He is a party to the situation and his will helps to govern it; he is not a passive object but has a few rights of his own.

The reader may say that slavery violates the generalization just made because the slave, though a human being, is defined as property. He has an owner; he may be bought and sold; he is at the disposal of his owner; he is therefore in much the same position as a domesticated animal. From the point of view of the institution of property, slavery is extremely interesting precisely because it does attempt to fit human beings into the category of objects of property rights. Later in the present chapter, in the section dealing with labor systems, an attempt will be made to show that even though slaves are *theoretically* defined as objects of property they are seldom exclusively so in practice. Always the slave is given some rights, and these rights interfere with the attempt to deal with him solely as property. Always, too, slavery seems to be a temporary institution resting upon a racial and cultural diversity that necessarily disappears after a generation or so. Thus slavery is an apparent exception that nonetheless proves the rule. By showing how difficult it is to treat the slave as a property object and as a person at the same time, it confirms the rule that full property rights apply only to those things, whether tangible or intangible, which have no rights of their own—e.g. nonhuman objects.

TYPES OF PROPERTY

Terms such as "private," "public," and "communistic" when applied to property are apt to be catchwords that arouse great emotion but convey little meaning. Sometimes the whole genus, Property, is implicitly identified with some particular species of it, as when people speak of "abolishing property" or of "subordinating property rights to human rights." Property in general is no more capable of being abolished than the weather (though particular species of property certainly are), and property rights *are* human rights (though they do not embrace all such rights). The first thing to bear in mind in clearing up such confusion is that all property is social in character, being a part of and dependent upon the social system. The second point to keep in mind is that all property is exclusive—preventing others from enjoying the *same* rights in the same object. This dual character—its sociality and its exclusiveness —sets a fundamental conflict. Property is forever a paradoxical thing, a blending of opposites, producing a perennial confusion of words and emotions.

Several variables in the property situation should for the sake of clarity be kept separate. One of these is the number and identity of the persons doing the owning. Another is the number and quality of the rights constituting the ownership. And a third is the size and nature of the entities owned. The following discussion of "private" and "public" property will try to keep them distinct.

The term "private" sometimes refers to the strongest and most complete rights in property and sometimes to the fact that a single individual holds these rights. The two, however, are not correlated. The most complete ownership is achieved not by individuals but by families, firms, tribes, and nations. Preferably the term "private property" should apply to rights held by individuals or groups acting in their own interest, and "public property" should apply to rights held by the community at large and administered by individuals or groups acting as agents of the community. The distinction, an important one, turns on the locus of ownership, but it also has certain implications for the kind of property rights exercised. Whereas private property rights are subject to regulation by the sovereign political group, the rights of this group itself as against other sovereign groups are subject to no regulation other than that of force. As between sovereign groups, then, we find the strongest and most complete rights. No property lines are clearer, none more exclusive and unyielding, than territorial boundaries. *Within* the sovereign group, however, the system of property relations among private interests is subject to supervision, regulation, and enforcement by the total political unit. They are not so complete because they may be suspended, confiscated, or limited, yet they are true property rights. No tribe or state can garner all such rights to itself as an entity. There must be some system of distributive rights among the societal members in their private capacities. Whether these distributive rights apply widely or narrowly, however, is another question. In some societies the basic instruments of production—the things on which the entire community depends—are objects of private ownership. In other societies it is mainly consumption goods that are so owned.

Plainly the distinction between private and public property is a distinction in terms of the kind of owners, but it is inevitably connected with the nature of the rights exercised and the kind of things owned. Keeping in mind the three variables—which may be succinctly phrased as, *Who* exercises *what rights* in *which things?*—let us consider some concrete kinds of property systems.

Collectivistic Land Tenure. In isolated primitive communities land is sometimes held in the name of the village or band as a whole. This condition, once thought to be widespread, led social theorists of the so-called evolutionary school to posit communal ownership as the original prototype of all land tenure. But Lowie, after an exhaustive survey of anthropological data,[4] came to the conclusion that such examples of complete communal ownership are few and that they are marked by one or both of two features, viz., the identity of clan and village, and the hunting or pastoral nature of the economy. For some hunting peoples (the Plains Indians, the California Maidu) there are no land rights for groups, so that instances of ownership residing in clans or households within the larger sovereign group are more numerous. Complete tribal or communal ownership of land, when it does occur, is likely to be found among hunting and pastoral societies. In about half of the thirteen hunting and pastoral societies reported by Lowie, land rights resided in no group smaller than the entire tribe. This was true for the Plains Indians, the California Maidu, and the Thompson River Indians (all with hunting economies), and for the Masai, Toda, and Hottentot (all with pastoral economies). Other hunting tribes, however, such as the Algonkians, Eastern, and Central Canadian Indians, the Coastal tribes of British Columbia, the Kariera of Australia, the tribes of Queensland, Australia, and the Vedda of Ceylon, broke up the tribal territory into holdings owned exclusively by smaller groups within the larger unit. Among the Vedda, whose tribal territory was guarded by professional archers who inflicted death on the trespassers, this decentralization of property rights was carried so far that it was possible to map the holdings of specific families. "A man would not hunt even on his brother's land without permission; and if game ran into an alien region the owner of the soil was entitled to a portion of its flesh." [5]

[4] Robert H. Lowie, *Primitive Society* (New York: Liveright, 1920), Chap. 9.
[5] *Ibid.*, p. 214.

The rights that went with "ownership," however, were highly variable even in these societies. No Vedda tribesman, for example, could transfer "his" land to someone else without the consent of every adult male in the family. Again, among the Kariera ownership rested in the male portion of the father-sib, and any individual could hunt over the entire tract at will; transfer of the land, however, except through descent, was inconceivable.[6]

Pastoral peoples generally do not split the communal land up into lesser properties. They have a highly developed sense of private ownership as regards livestock but not with reference to land. "A Masai shares pasturage with all the other inhabitants of his district and when the grass is exhausted there is a general exodus." The Kirgiz alternate between communal and family ownership of grazing grounds, depending both on the kind of animal involved and the season of the year. The tribe as a whole owns the camel pasturing land; but for other animals (sheep, goats, cattle, and horses), each family owns the winter pastures, which are scarce, while summer pastures are owned by the entire community.[7]

Among agricultural peoples communal property occurs only in the rare cases when the joint family happens also to constitute a village. Family and clan ownership represent probably the most frequent pattern of primitive land tenure.[8] This doubtless results from the fact that in simple economies, especially agricultural ones, the household group is an effective economic unit. "The loose household group, constituted by the three principles of blood, marriage, and adoption, is bound together by common ties of everyday living. This common life involves a certain participation in the production, distribution, and consumption of native wealth." [9] The utilization of land is not easily carried out by a single person or, with inferior techniques of cultivation and administration, by a large group. The household gives sufficient division of labor and is sufficiently permanent and cohesive (being drawn together by day-to-day living and close identity) to constitute an ideal unit of land utilization for agricultural purposes. When ownership follows utilization, as it often does, then the household becomes the most likely land-owning

[6] *Ibid.*, p. 213.

[7] *Ibid.*, pp. 215-216.

[8] Ernest Beaglehole, *Property* (London: Allen & Unwin, 1931). Table IV would seem to indicate this, although the table confuses different types of ownership and has relatively few cases.

[9] Beaglehole, *op. cit.*, p. 233, with reference to Samoa.

unit. In many cases, however, a family's ownership is limited to the exclusive use of the land and is inalienable. In other words, the family's property rights usually consist in the right to use the land for purposes of production; they do not generally include the right *not* to use the land, nor the right to transfer it at will.[10]

Another form of collectivistic land tenure, which is not usually felt to be collectivistic but is so in principle, is *feudalism*. Theoretically at least, feudalism assumes the ownership of all land to be vested in the state. The central political authority then parcels out large tracts to exalted persons, who may themselves parcel it out once more—always in return for services of one kind or another. The feudal structure, therefore, is anything but equalitarian yet it is communal in its main principle of state ownership. Where the central government is weak, however, as is usually the case in primitive groups and as was the case during the Middle Ages in Europe, it often loses control over the feudal nobility, who accordingly exercise extreme property rights within their respective domains.

The highest development of feudalism in primitive society occurs in Africa. There the king is frequently strong enough to regard all land as part of the royal property but not strong enough to retain complete control. Among the Thonga, for example, the king lets the land out to his nobles, or headmen, who in turn let it out to individual cultivators. The cultivators then have rather complete rights in their plots, in the sense that they and their heirs continue to use it. Even the grantor—the headman—must secure the cultivators' permission before so much as picking rotting fruit off the ground. If the cultivator should move away, however, the land automatically reverts to the grantor who then reallocates it. Similarly, if the headman himself should move, the land under his control cannot be sold or otherwise transferred; it also reverts to the state.[11] In Uganda the peasants are obliged to work and render military service to the feudal chiefs in return for their patches.[12]

Feudalism in more complex societies has some affinities with the primitive type but is more intricate. It rests usually upon the *theory* that a central power, the king or priest-king, has supreme

[10] This appears to be Lowie's inference, although several far-reaching exceptions to such a generalization are described by him, further illustrating the extreme variability of cultural definitions of property rights. See especially *loc. cit.*, pp. 227-232.

[11] Lowie, *op. cit.*, p. 221.

[12] *Ibid.*, p. 227.

power over an entire national territory. But in practice the means of communication are so poor, the bureaucracy so crude, and the connection between government and people so remote that effective control must be on a regional basis. Furthermore, the source of sustenance being primarily agricultural, money scarce, and trade slight, the four main valuables on which the regime can operate are land, work, food, and military service. The central government attempts to maintain itself by granting land (fiefs) to powerful allies (often relatives of the emperor, military aides, and religious officials). In return these allies, the feudal barons, are supposed to give financial support and military service to the central government. To get such support and service, the barons must also use the main stock-in-trade. They must grant land to vassals, who are expected to provide food and armed men when the occasion demands. There may be several grades, but at the bottom a class is reached (serfs or peasants) who actually work the land, eat most of the produce, and in return for the privilege furnish extra food to the lord, work the lord's domain, and occasionally take up arms (usually not as cavalry but as infantry). Land, as the primary instrument of production, is thus made the axis around which the whole hierarchy revolves. In theory the system is communistic but in practice there is a strong centrifugal tendency. The feudal baronies become kingdoms in themselves, capable of defying the central power. The serf or peasant class, by virtue of its numerical superiority, is capable of holding out for rights of its own—above all, the right to treat the land it works as its own for many purposes. A feudal system may therefore disintegrate, an individualistic system of small family holdings emerging. But an ordered society can grow out of this disintegration only if the state has maintained itself and has changed its character somewhat. If, for example, the government can establish direct relations with the now free peasantry, it may eliminate the intermediate feudal grades and exercise the regulatory, tax-gathering, policing functions itself, leaving most of the actual rights of ownership (sale, purchase, inheritance, and use) in the hands of the farmers themselves.

The third type of communistic land ownership, coupled with collectivistic ownership in even more important goods such as factories and transports, is exhibited by the modern totalitarian state. Here the theory is that the national territory is owned by the state, not by private persons, families, or corporations. Instead of farming out tracts to individual chiefs, however, the work of cultivation is managed by a political bureaucracy, the official remuneration of which is determined by salaries. This allows a much greater centralization and more direct control. The system is carried farthest in Russia but there was a similar tendency in Italy and Germany. In Russia land ownership was abolished and every effort made to institute collective farms. In the Fascist countries, on the other hand, the idea of ownership was retained but as government limitation of rents, income, planting, size of house, mobility, and disposal of produce became ever more rigid, such ownership became ever more reduced in scope.

Property Rights in Productive Technology. We saw in the last chapter that every society has a technology. The control of this technology, like the control of land, forms an important element in the economic structure. Even in primitive societies there are various kinds of capital equipment in which rights must be defined and protected. Spears, arrows, boats, fruit trees, herds, storage baskets, etc. must be distributed in an orderly and agreed upon manner. Two principles seem to govern the distribution of ownership in such movable objects: the principle that the producer of the pottery, or basket, etc. should be its owner; and the principle that the most effective user of the object tends to own it. Thus "Each Yukaghir owns his clothing, the hunter owns his gun, the woman her sewing implements." Since, however, the most effective users as well as the makers may be a group, these principles sometimes lead not to individual but rather to collective ownership. Among the Yukaghir, for example, boats, houses, and nets are considered to be the joint property of the family.[13]

It often happens, moreover, that property rights are divided among various groups within a tribe or community in a way that is difficult for Westerners to comprehend. While one man or family might own a certain tract of land, another might own the trees on the land, as is the case in Fiji. Or, as among the Maori, the family might own the right to gather shellfish or berries in different places, and another the right to hunt birds in certain areas. Sometimes "one

[13] Lowie, *op. cit.,* p. 234.

family had the right of digging fern-roots in a certain place, while another hunted rats in the same area."[14]

With regard to what is sometimes called "incorporeal property" private ownership is widely recognized in many groups. Magical incantations, songs, or even legends, for example, may be owned exclusively by one individual, with sometimes the right of selling and sometimes the restriction of nontransferability except through inheritance. The Dobuans of Melanesia consider the magical formulae for growing yams to be such highly valuable property that it must be taught by a man to his sister's son and to no other."[15]

In the face of extreme variability in property conceptions, it becomes clear that one must beware of assuming either the "naturalness" of private property or the "inevitability" of communism. But with reference to rights in productive instruments it seems safe to say that there are always two mutually contradictory principles at work: (1) the tendency of men to retain their rights in productive property but to let others work it for them; (2) the tendency of those who work the property to acquire rights in it. The first is made possible by the separability of use and ownership, the second by a counteracting affinity between the two.

It has been previously mentioned that possession and ownership are two different things, that persons who actually control, work, or use a given piece of property may not hold the major property rights to it. This is the situation, for instance, of the landlord and his sharecropper tenant. The sharecropper, by definition, owns nothing. The man who owns the farm furnishes him with mules, plows, and land, and usually takes half of the crop. An extreme is reached in complete absentee ownership. A modern corporation, for example, is "owned" by the stockholders, but many of these have no idea of and no contact with the actual plant of the corporation. The numerous widows who own stock in the Pennsylvania Railroad have property rights in it, but they have only the slightest inkling of what railroading involves.

There are thus in society two contrary forces at work, the one tending to separate possession from ownership, the other tending to keep them together. The first of these apparently results from the previously noted fact that an inevitable concomitant of property

[14] *Ibid.*, p. 229.
[15] Reo Fortune, *Sorcerers of Dobu* (New York: Dutton, 1932), p. 70.

rights is *power* over other persons. When, as often happens, the thing owned is so valuable and important to others that they are willing to pay the owner for the privilege of using it, there begins to appear a separation of ownership from use. Looked at from the point of view of the owner, the thing owned is so valuable that a *part* of the product can be given to somebody else as an inducement for him to use and exploit it. The owner can then enjoy the rest of the product without doing any work: the simple fact that he owns the productive instrument is sufficient to support him, and he may have to do no work at all. In many cases people thus released from work in connection with their property constitute a leisure class having governmental, scholarly, and religious functions. In some cases, on the other hand, they are an essentially idle class parasitic in character.

Now, from the point of view of societal survival it is advantageous for every class to contribute something to the operation of the society. This does not mean that a society is at a disadvantage if some of its members are not doing manual work; on the contrary the administrative, scholarly, and religious functions are highly important. But it does mean that the statuses and roles must be so arranged that everybody is functionally contributory. Noncontributory statuses must be eliminated and parasitic individuals made useful.[16] One way in which this is unconsciously accomplished in the process of social evolution is to counteract the tendency of owners to become divorced from the actual operation of their property. This counteraction we call the *affinity between use and ownership,* and there are several circumstances which produce the affinity. In the first place, there often appears a general ethical disapproval of absentee ownership which tends to justify depriving such owners of their property. Such an ethical principle is, however, partly an expression of the very affinity which we have mentioned and hence not really an explanation of it; furthermore, it runs counter to another ethical principle—namely, the sacredness of property rights—which is not easily contradicted. We have then to look below the ethical plane for further explanations of the affinity between ownership and use.

[16] Perhaps it should be emphasized at this point that we do not intend the phrase "must be" to be taken in the sense of either an ethical judgment or an inevitable mechanical "law." Always understood is the phrase, "if the society is to survive in competition with other societies which might have a margin of advantage in this particular respect."

Presumably productive instruments will operate best if particular individuals or groups are held responsible for them and receive, as a reward, a recompense in proportion to how well the instrumentality works—i.e. how much it produces. Now, being "held responsible" for productive instruments in this sense can mean only that the individual or group concerned has the right to make the important policy decisions and share in the product.[17] Such a right is an element in what is called "ownership." Quite apart from rights we know that the persons who are actually connected with productive instruments —land, transport, factories—are in an excellent position to use them for their own advantage as against the advantage of a titular owner. If the owner is absent and ignorant of the whole productive process, he is then dependent on his managers and workers. These, by virtue of being both familiar with and necessary for the productive process, are in a key position to give themselves advantages as against the titular owners. In other words, the share of the product that goes to capital may not always be forthcoming if the persons who furnish the capital (or whose ancestors furnished it) stand apart from the production itself.

In most primitive societies the property rights in productive instruments are closely aligned with functional performance. The affinity between ownership and use expresses itself. In a feudalistic system, as we have seen, the ownership of land rests presumably in a central government or crown. But it is an attenuated ownership, diluted through two or more lower ranks of owners. In practice many of the great fief-holders were remote from the cultivation of the land itself. The persons closest to it were the serfs who tilled the soil. Well known is the fact, repeated in the histories of many feudal systems, that in time the serf's connection with his land became hereditary and that he slowly acquired more rights in it until it was finally regarded as his property in freehold. This would seem to illustrate the principle that ownership and use tend, in the absence of contrary forces, to come together. In the year 1350 in England more than half the population were serfs attached to but not owning

[17] Soviet Russia has learned this lesson well. Whereas in the first years after the revolution the plant manager's authority was divided with the Party cell and the local labor unit, the stress has since then been steadily in the direction of giving him more complete authority and rewarding him more directly in accord with the productive efficiency of his plant. See Gregory Bienstock, Solomon M. Schwarz, and Aaron Yugow, *Management in Russian Industry and Agriculture* (New York: Oxford, 1944), Chaps. 1-9.

the soil on which they lived. By 1600 there was not a serf left in the entire country.[18] This remarkable revolution in land tenure occurred partly as a result of the Black Death of 1348-49 and the growth of a money economy, but behind these can be seen the gravitation toward a close relation between use and ownership of the land, such as had prevailed in early Anglo-Saxon times before the kings of the eighth century and afterwards had allotted fiefs to the church, army commanders, knights, administrative officials, and favorites.[19] Not every feudal system goes through precisely this evolution. Many of the fief-holders perform genuine managerial and administrative functions and retain ownership for centuries. Moreover, the central government is always in need of allies and is inclined under certain circumstances to re-grant land that may have fallen to the peasants.

But whenever property rights in productive instruments come to be exercised by individuals who are too far removed from the instruments to operate them efficiently, the rights tend to get transferred to users and possessors. What rights the absentee owners retain (for property rights are highly divisible) depend upon a variety of factors, of which two are of special significance: (1) the social functions performed by absentee owners apart from any specific connection with their property, and (2) the intensity of the society's struggle for survival either against other societies or against nature. The contribution of a genuine leisure class—one that gets paid for simply owning rather than for doing any kind of work—is of course nil; but a class may happen to be released from manual labor by virtue of owning property and thus contribute either to the overall management of that property or to the society at large. In this matter, however, it is necessary to be on guard against rationalizations, as when we say that a land-holding aristocracy "contributes to the development of literature and the arts." Such contributions, if genuine, can be rewarded in other ways than by giving individuals a direct right to the produce of given productive instruments. Artists may be paid through sale of their works. Governing officials may be paid through taxes. In fact, the Soviet Union illustrates well enough the fact that

[18] H. S. Bennett, *Life on the English Manor: 1150-1400* (Cambridge: University Press, 1937). p. 277.

[19] Heinrich Cunow, "Land Tenure—Western Europe, British Empire and United States," *Encyclopedia of the Social Sciences*, p. 87.

all essential functions in society can be performed without anybody having the rights of private ownership in productive technology.

It appears, then, that the two opposed principles—the tendency toward absenteeism and the tendency toward on-the-spot control—are always at work. Generally, where productive enterprises are complex there must be a separation between different functions—manual labor, management, etc. In the Middle Ages the feudal baron performed necessary services in terms of military and political protection, overall direction, and adjudication. But pure absenteeism, in which the owner has nothing to do with the things that he owns except to derive revenue from them, is usually unstable; and if it is accompanied by no other essential function on the part of the owner (i.e. unconnected with the property in question though otherwise significant), it is sociologically anomalous. The size of a completely idle group that society can support depends upon how seriously pressed the society is by other groups or by natural scourges. This again depends upon the society's technological apparatus in comparison with that of other groups. America, for instance, could support a larger leisure class if her foremost competitor were Cuba rather than Germany, Japan, or Russia.

So far, though, we have been considering only the problem of "ownership vs. use and control" without raising the question of the *content* of the ownership or the control. It is to this aspect of property that we must now address ourselves.

THE ETHICAL RESTRICTION OF PROPERTY RIGHTS

Private property is perpetually a source of inequality. This fact, along with the preceding discussion, discloses an inherent ambivalence in human society. On the one hand differentiation, both in a functional and in an invidious sense, is necessary. The very existence of norms shows this, for we must esteem persons differently according to how well they fulfill the norms. Also presumably we must attach greater value to persons according to the scarcity and essentiality of their qualities.[20] By apportioning property rights, and often other rights as well, differentially among the members of the society we reward them for contributing according to their capacities and efforts. But on the other hand, we have seen that property rights also give power; and in the absence of restraining influences

[20] Cf. Chaps. 4 and 14.

there is every likelihood that the power will be used for the personal advantage of its wielders or of the group with which they identify, independently of functional performance. The maxim that "To him that hath shall be given and from him that hath not shall be taken away" constitutes a recognition, imbedded in folklore, of this essential attribute of property. What it means is precisely that, *ceteris paribus,* the more A has that B wants the greater are the demands that A can make of B.

Since what is to the immediate advantage of one group or one individual in a society may not and usually will not be necessarily to the advantage of the society as a whole, there always develop restraints upon deleterious property uses. The business man who might wish to exercise his "private" property rights by adulterating his food products is prevented from doing so; and the restaurant that refuses to wash its "own" dishes will be closed. The business organization that provides gas and electricity to a community is not permitted to withhold its services from groups it may not like, nor is it permitted to exercise its power over consumers by charging them what it pleases. These examples of restrictions on property rights could be multiplied indefinitely from our own society and then multiplied again by reference to other societies. We shall content ourselves with two more specific cases selected to illustrate the close dependence of property rights on other (ever-changing) norms and values of a society.

Until 1915 in the United States the property rights of a corporation included the right to hire or not-hire a worker; and it was thought that this was balanced by the right of the worker to sell or withhold his labor power. The question arose of whether or not the property rights of the corporation included the right to require the worker to drop his membership in a union before accepting employment. The legislature of the state of Kansas thought that property rights should not be defined in this way; and the Supreme Court of Kansas agreed. The case was appealed to the Supreme Court of the United States, however, and it was there decided that both the legislature and the Supreme Court of Kansas had been wrong and that the corporation had the right to make such a stipulation.[21] Twenty-six years later the Supreme Court of the United States decided

[21] Coppage v. Kansas, 236 U.S. 1, 9 (1915). quoted in Commons, *op. cit.,* p. 58.

precisely the opposite.[22] It is obvious that there was never any "correct" answer to this question; property rights were defined in each case in accordance with prevailing sentiments of how rewards should be distributed and how this distribution should be arrived at.

The same principle may be observed in the field of housing legislation. That rights in dwelling structures owned by individuals are "private property" is a dictum that is close to the core of American values; but the concrete definitions of those rights have undergone drastic changes over a period of years. Before 1887, for example, it was a right of a landlord to provide or not to provide running water on each *floor* of a tenement in New York City. His power over his tenants was in other words so defined that if they desired the use of the scarce thing which he "owned" (shelter) then they could be forced to do without an inside water faucet. In 1887, however, the New York Tenement House Act *re-defined* property rights so as to make it necessary for a landlord to provide a running water outlet on each floor of a tenement. The point made above, that what is defined as the best interests of the collectivity as a whole may conflict with an individual's definition of his own interests, is vividly illustrated in this case by the fact that the 1887 law was bitterly contested in the courts until 1895 by the Trinity Church Corporation of New York City. One of the major grounds offered by the Corporation for refusing to comply with the law was that it was " 'a burden imposed upon landlords for the ease and comfort of tenants and clearly in violation of constitutional guarantees' "[23]—that is, Trinity's definition of the natural identity of interests did not coincide with the community's.

The distribution and definition of property rights unequally among groups and individuals, then, appear to be limited by the ethical precepts and values of the society. This factor, plus what we

22 Phelps Dodge v. National Labor Relations Board, 313 U.S. 177 (1941), quoted in Wilbert E. Moore, *Industrial Relations and the Social Order* (New York: Macmillan, 1946), p. 388, note 18.

23 Quoted by Charles Abrams, *The Future of Housing* (New York: Harper, 1946), p. 193. The dependence of property upon changing ethical valuations is further sharply illustrated by the Court's elaboration of its decision, which upheld the Health Department. " 'The learned counsel for the defendant asks where this kind of legislation is to stop. Would it be contended that the owners of such houses could be compelled to furnish each room with a bathtub. . . ? Is there to be a bathroom and water closet to each room. . . ? To which I should answer, certainly not. That would be so clearly unreasonable that no court in my belief could be found which would uphold such legislation. . .' " (p. 194).

have called the affinity between use and ownership, must be recognized as the controlling principle integrating property with the rest of societal institutions.

Contract

Since many of the things we have learned about property apply equally to the phenomenon of contract, we need spend less time on this than we did on the former. A contract is essentially an agreement between two or more individuals to behave in a certain specified way for a certain specified length of time in the future. What distinguishes a contractual relation from most other relationships is the fact that the reciprocal rights and obligations are limited to those specified in the contract. Thus the relationship between members of a family can hardly be said to be contractual, since there is no detailed listing of the number and duration of the rights and duties; there is usually the presumption that any particular member of the family will go far beyond his normal responsibilities in case of an emergency involving another member. The relationship which we call friendship is similar in nature. A contractual relationship, on the other hand, sharply demarcates what the respective parties to the contract may expect from one another, what rights they have with respect to one another and what obligations.

In its pure form the contractual relationship assumes no common end on the part of the contracting parties. They may, to use MacIver's terms, have *like* interests in the sense that each seeks to make a coöperative effort successful, each for the sake of his private goals; or they may have *unlike* interests in the sense that a loss for one is a gain for the other; but a *common* interest in the sense of an emotional identification with one another is conspicuously absent from a purely contractual relation. The stockholders in a corporation may be said to have like interests in the profitability of the business, as indeed may the employees and the managers. But insofar as their relations are contractual, they are interested in the corporation's profits only for the sake of their own rewards. A contract between a buyer and a seller, on the other hand, or between a lender and a borrower, involves unlike interests: a high price or a high interest rate is favorable for the seller or the lender, unfavorable for the buyer or the borrower.

A contract is impersonal. To a salesclerk it is immaterial who his customer is or how faithful she is to her husband, so long as the sale goes through. When, however, the salesclerk leaves his store and considers whom he should invite to his home for dinner, personal considerations may become relevant. The terms of the contract are universally applied to all persons; they are not particularistic. In so far as this is not true, the relationship is not purely contractual.

Closely associated with this characteristic is the further element of rationality. The impersonal nature of the contract situation as a means to a private end implies the rational weighing of alternatives and a search for the "least cost" method of obtaining the desired goal. In considering a contractual loan one asks what is the largest safe return I can get on this investment. On the other hand, if it is one's son who requests the loan one perhaps asks what effect will this have on his character, but more importantly, where can I get the money?

The *pure* contractual relation is virtually nonexistent in actual practice. There are always noncontractual elements in every contract situation; salesclerks judge people in their occupational roles, as may be observed in the average white salesman's treatment of a Negro customer; and managers of corporations sometimes hire their brothers-in-law when others are more qualified. While these departures from the ideal-type contract situation are interesting in themselves, there are other and more pervasive noncontractual elements which are frequently overlooked. The first of these is the fact that the ends of the contracting parties are beyond the scope of the contract. Thus, the rational weighing of alternatives does not extend to a consideration of whether or not the seller *should* seek the highest possible price from the buyer; the seller unthinkingly follows this pattern which is customary in his culture. Any departure from this behavior, while it might be admired for other (ethical) reasons, will be condemned as "poor business sense" unless there is a personal reason for it. On the other hand the bargain is not supposed to be merely shrewd but is also supposed to result in increased wealth for the entire society. In so far as the moral approval of shrewd business practices is strong, then, so-called "sharp" and often ruthless trading may be winked at or even applauded. But no society can tolerate for long behavior which enriches individuals without enrichening society, and there tends consequently to be a certain amount of moral indignation directed at contractual arrangements which do not add to the community's wealth.

The second noncontractual element in contract is the fact that every contract is hedged about with many restrictions not appearing in the terms of the contract itself. Thus, the contract is not enforceable if it is made with a minor, if one of the partners is "coerced" into the agreement, or if the terms of the contract put one of the partners in a condition of servitude.

Finally it must be noted that the contractual relationship itself, as an approved type of interaction, depends upon a highly special and complex web of norms and values which define such impersonal, rational, secular, and self-interested behavior as Right, Proper, and Good. This set of institutional prescriptions is the complex system which we call capitalism; and since capitalism is peculiar to contemporary Western civilization, we can expect to find much less close approximations to the purely contractual relationship in other societies. So long, for example, as the only known kind of relationship among individuals is a personal (particularistic) relationship of reciprocal rights and obligations, contract in the modern sense cannot develop. A debtor-creditor relationship or any sort of promise by one individual to another was in the Middle Ages, for instance, such a personalized matter that the transfer of the obligation to a third person was inconceivable. It was a "personal promise of oath and fidelity" arising out of the mutual confidence the two parties to an agreement placed in each other. In our society such a promise may as easily be the focus of transferable property rights as may a house; promises to pay a certain amount or deliver certain goods are bought and sold daily, as are promises to play baseball or to sing or not to sing. The nature of the contract can be illustrated by comparison with marriage. As John R. Commons has put it, "A promise to marry cannot be assigned by the promisee to a third party, nor negotiated upon the market,"[24] but a genuine contract can be.

This suggests that there is a fourth characteristic of a contractual relationship which distinguishes it from other types of relations—viz., its negotiability. This really flows from the other characteristics mentioned above—the *impersonal* nature of a contract, its *universalistic* character, and the secularized rationality with which it is viewed. All of these together comprise the important features of

[24] *Op. cit.*, p. 251.

contract; but as we have seen, institutional controls and directives are as operative here as they are in the simplest of societies where contract in its modern sense is unknown.

Modern Economic Institutions

We have already observed that the contractual relationship as a conspicuous characteristic is highly peculiar to Western societies over the last 300 or so years. It is intimately associated with a complex division of labor in which the interdependence of specialized groups requires a certain precision in the coördination of efforts. To erect a building efficiently, for example, it is necessary that the concrete be delivered at a certain date, that foundations be finished by the time the steel-workers start to work on the girders, which must by that time have been manufactured and delivered, which assumes that coal has been mined, iron smelted, both transported, and so on and on—not to mention the services required for all the workers or the intricate interconnections which produced a need for the building in the first place. A series of contracts, specifying obligations and rationally negotiated, is a vital necessity for such an organization of economic activity. But another necessity is inextricably connected with the division of labor, as suggested above. This has been clearly summarized by Commons, whom we have quoted before. Everything, he points out, which the individual consumes,

> passes first through the hands of many other persons, and each person depends on predecessors to select the best of the elementary utilities, to give to them the best form and to bring them regularly to the needful places. As this interdependence enlarges with commerce, the ignorance of each individual enlarges, and each depends more and more on confidence in the honesty, diligence, promptness and good management of others. In short, confidence in others is the largest of all the utilities, for without it each person would need to satisfy his own wants directly from nature or thru a small family or tribe whose members he could see and control.[25]

Reliance for the successful formation or emergence of this "largest of all the utilities" upon a natural identity of interests, upon Adam Smith's "invisible hand" leads to food adulteration, monopoly prices, fraudulent advertising, and flimsy construction; and as a

[25] *Op. cit.*, p. 204.

consequence, "as early as 1850 the visible hand of the court had begun to stretch the writ of trespass in order to protect the reputation of a manufacturer who had built up a business on the confidence he had inspired in customers as to the quality of his goods." [26] That is, the confidence of customers (otherwise known as "good will") comes itself to be a highly valued locus of property rights. A "confidence inspired in customers," however, may or may not be well-placed, and there tends to be a closer and closer supervision of standards and performance by societal agents. One characteristic of modern economic institutions, then, is a steady growth of the role of the government, the only organization presumed to represent *all* members of a society, in controlling economic activities. The investor, the consumer, and the worker all are protected more and more explicitly by a multiplication of laws and a proliferation of government agencies.[27]

In the field of labor-management relations the institutions governing the distribution of income and defining property rights are seen dramatically to be in a state of rapid flux. Two conspicuous aspects of this phenomenon are the development of powerful corporations on the one hand and the growth of large labor unions on the other. The extent of the former development is well known and need be only briefly reviewed here. It is clearly seen in the fact that in 1933 the 200 largest nonfinancial corporations controlled 59.9 billion dollars worth of instruments of production out of a total of 93.4 billion dollars worth controlled by all nonfinancial corporations. This is over 64 per cent.[28] In addition to the massing of production facilities in a relatively few large organizations, a furthur characteristic of modern economic institutions is the change occurring in traditional conceptions of property rights in the productive instruments. It is clear that the nominal "owners" of the corporation—the stockholders—have very little direct control over the instruments. The possibility that other corporations may own stock, or for that matter that a corporation may purchase all its own stock and thus "own" itself independently of "real" persons, plus the development

[26] *Ibid.*

[27] For a competent review and discussion of these controls, together with a valuable bibliography, see Wilbert E. Moore, *Industrial Relations and the Social Order*, Chap. 23, especially pp. 510-521.

[28] National Resources Committee, *Structure of the American Economy* (Washington, D. C., 1939), p. 106, Table V.

of holding companies and "pyramiding"—all these factors point to the conclusion that most of the property rights are vested in managers and directors whose stockshares usually represent but a small fraction of the total value of the corporation.[29] Decisions on what is to be produced, by what techniques, prices to be charged, wages to be paid, expansion policies, purchases, sales, etc.—all these "rights" are vested in managers and directors. The problem for the society then becomes one of insuring that these rights are exercised for the benefit of the society as a whole. What this means essentially is that the eternal necessity of institutionally motivating individuals to behave in such a way that societal functions as well as individual purposes get satisfied, tends to be focused around a relatively few key individuals who exercise the most important property rights. This problem of the institutional constraints and other factors governing (or failing to govern) management decisions is an extremely complicated one.

In economic activities there are usually distinguished four major groups, involving a good deal of over-lapping membership: investors, managers, workers, and the public. We have already spoken briefly of the problem of integrating investors', managers', and the public's ends; we must now point out the difficulty of securing a consensus among laborers and employers (managers-directors-investors) on distributive norms. A "union-management conflict" represents precisely a breakdown in the distributive norm. That this breakdown is a characteristic of our society presumably needs no documentation for the reader of daily newspapers. Nor is it necessary to point out that the mutual opposition of large groups, corporations and labor unions, as contestants in an issue where common ground is weak, can result only in a power struggle. Since one of the immediate consequences of such an absence of institutional regulation is likely to be a cessation of the coöperative process, it becomes increasingly necessary for the government to play a direct role in the resolution of industrial conflict.

From several different points of view (the regulation of prices, standards, labor-management relations), we have noted the increasing role of government in economic affairs as a characteristic of contemporary institutions. We might have added to our inventory the direct participation of the State in such activities as low-cost

[29] See *Ibid.*, Chap. 9, and Moore, *op. cit.*, Chap. 5.

housing, reforestation, TVA, atomic research, and so on. Having been led to this point by our study of economic institutions, however, we shall pursue the matter no further here but turn instead to the next logical phase of our analysis of human society—the nature of political institutions.

References

Thurman W. Arnold, *The Folklore of Capitalism* (New Haven: Yale University Press, 1937).

A racy satire describing the myths, prejudices, and legal fictions of the capitalist system, by a law professor who later became the "trust-busting" Assistant Attorney General.

A. A. Berle, Jr. and G. C. Means, *The Modern Corporation and Private Property* (New York: Macmillan, 1934).

One of the classics in this field. Treats the concentration of economic power, the separation of ownership and management, and the causes and consequences of these developments.

Robert A. Brady, *Business as a System of Power* (New York: Columbia University Press, 1943).

Big business organization under totalitarian governments in Germany, Italy, Vichy France, and Japan; and under liberal democratic governments in England and the United States. The economic, political, and social aspects of this organization. A thorough study.

Colin Clark, *Conditions of Economic Progress* (London: Macmillan, 1940).

A fundamental treatise beyond the capacity of the ordinary student but well worth the effort of those who can master it because of its intelligently empirical character.

W. Fred Cottrell, *The Railroader* (Stanford University Press, 1940).

A sociological study of an occupation.

Wilbert E. Moore, *Industrial Relations and the Social Order* (New York: Macmillan, 1946).

A comprehensive analysis of industrial organization (from both the managerial and the labor sides), of industrial relations, and of industry as a whole in relation to the rest of the society. Each chapter contains an unusually adequate bibliography.

Wilbert E. Moore, "Sociology of Economic Organization" in Georges Gurvitch and Wilbert E. Moore, *Twentieth Century Sociology* (New York: Philosophical Library, 1945), pp. 438-465.

The interrelations between sociology and economics carefully explored. Contains many bibliographical citations.

Otto Nathan, *The Nazi Economic System* (Durham, N. C.: Duke University Press, 1944).

This is probably the best and most thorough study of the Nazi economic system prior to World War II. It discusses in detail the techniques and organizations used by the Nazis to control the activities of industry and agriculture for purposes of a military economy. Contains a wealth of references.

F. J. Roethlisberger, *Management and Morale* (Cambridge: Harvard University Press, 1941).

An extremely readable and convincing presentation of the reasons for considering human relations as an important factor in industrial success.

R. H. Tawney, *The Acquisitive Society* (New York: Harcourt, Brace, 1920).

One of the classic critiques of capitalist economy as an institutional structure. Extremely readable and still relevant.

Thorstein Veblen, *The Theory of Business Enterprise* (New York: Huebsch, 1923).

No bibliography on economic institutions would be complete without mention of Veblen, who was in a way the agnostic founder of institutional economics. This is one of his most systematic books, but all of his others, if one can endure his archaic style, are relevant.

Max Weber, *The Protestant Ethic and the Spirit of Capitalism,* tr. by Talcott Parsons (London: Allen & Unwin, 1930).

Max Weber's famous and much debated thesis that religion can have something to do with economic trends—specifically that the Protestant Reformation had something to do with the rise of capitalism.

T. N. Whitehead, *Leadership in a Free Society* (Cambridge: Harvard University Press, 1936).

A general discussion of our economic system from the point of view of the human aspects of industry as revealed by studies in an industrial plant.

Wm. Foote Whyte (ed.), *Industry and Society* (New York: McGraw-Hill, 1946).

Chapters on the factory as a social system, the relation of the plant to the community, the connection between class status and occupational status, and the conflict between labor and management.

CHAPTER XVIII

POLITICAL INSTITUTIONS*

IMPATIENT of governmental restraints and perplexed by the tragic contrast between the desire for freedom and the universal subjection to authority, men have at times dreamed of abolishing political institutions altogether. They have reasoned that since government is neither divine nor natural but simply a creation of man himself, it can be eliminated; this would leave people free to pursue their natural inclinations and find their true happiness.

Propounded countless times, this anarchistic argument has always exerted a strong appeal so long as attention was fixed on the restraints that government imposes. But it has lost its force whenever reflection has turned instead to the help and protection that government gives. Such help and protection cannot arise from raw nature, but only from political organization. The checks and restraints of government are therefore the unavoidable price that must be paid for the functions it performs. Political efficiency requires that the price be low in relation to the services rendered, but the idea of eliminating the price altogether is a utopian dream.

Political Control

Political authority constitutes but one aspect of social control, and to understand its peculiarities one must distinguish it from the other aspects. Control can be looked at from two points of view: first, that of the person in control and, second, that of the person being controlled. It seems more convenient to take the latter point of view and to discuss the kinds of control as they affect the individual's sense of freedom.

* This chapter originally appeared in Spanish as "Reflexiones sobre las instituciones politicas," being published as Vol. 47 of *Jornadas* (Mexico, D. F.: El Colegio de Mexico, 1945).

THE SENSE OF FREEDOM

The term "freedom" may have a legalistic meaning, as when a free man is distinguished from a slave, or it may have a purely psychic meaning as when "freedom from fear" is mentioned. In general an individual's freedom, but not necessarily his *sense* of freedom, is limited by reducing his choice of means to his ends. (The determination of his ends also limits his conduct, but there is in this case no standard by which the degree of limitation can be judged.) The sense of freedom, however, is not directly influenced by the absolute freedom. It is a subjective and relative matter. Like other subjective states it is heightened by contrast: A criminal just released from prison or a slave from servitude feels freer than the ordinary citizen. The feeling does not depend on the absolute range of choice but on the impression of the range. Some persons who have actually a wide choice feel themselves restrained, while others who have actually a narrow choice feel unrestrained. If an individual wishes to exercise no more means than he may, he experiences the sense of freedom; otherwise he suffers a feeling of oppression.

It is an error, though a very common one, to treat this subjective frame of mind as if it referred to an objective phenomenon, or in other words to confuse subjective with absolute freedom. Such reification tempts the observer—be he democrat, fascist, or anarchist—to project his own feelings on to others. He unconsciously places himself, with his customary range of choices, in the position of other people and assumes that they feel as he would feel in their position. In this way he comes to think that certain peoples are not "free" enough—they are "in bondage"; and that still others are "too free"—they are licentious. The peoples in question, however, do not usually have the feelings imputed to them, and consequently the observer's predictions of their future behavior prove inaccurate.

During World War II, for example, it was common on the Allied side to think that the German people resented the Hitler regime because it restricted the things they could say and do, and that consequently the regime was sustained only by force. Strategy based on this assumption, however, proved fruitless, because the German people had been trained to accept their narrow range of choices as beneficial and to regard any wider range as merely the licentiousness of decadent democracy.

In short, subjective freedom does not necessarily correspond with absolute freedom. The same is true of other political concepts that have both a subjective and an objective side—such as "liberty," "exploitation," "justice," etc.[1]

LIMITATIONS ON FREEDOM

A proposition such as "All men desire freedom" is either tautological or untrue. If it maintains simply that all men desire the means they desire, it is tautological: it says simply that all men desire a *sense* of freedom, which is true by definition. If instead it holds that all men desire the widest *absolute* choice of means, it is untrue.

There are at least four important controls that limit choice but are nonetheless subjectively acceptable. They are: (1) ignorance, which prevents certain means from being desired because they are unknown; (2) moral conviction, which eliminates other means because they are contrary to the feeling of what is right; (3) religious belief, which rules out certain means because they are supposedly contrary to the will of supernatural beings and will receive supernatural punishment if violated; and (4) the multiplicity of ends, which makes it impossible to utilize all the means at one's disposal on any one end alone. These controls are of course interrelated and overlapping. Although they impose the greatest limitations on choice, they are not *felt* as limitations; or at least they are not regarded as deriving from the will of other persons but rather seem to arise from oneself or from the nature of God and the universe.

There remains a fifth control that, considered alone, does infringe the sense of freedom—namely, the determination of one's conduct by other persons having superior power over one. The range of choice in this case (assuming no overlapping with the previous four) is not limited to what the individual can visualize or desire, but is narrowed to the point where he must choose either to obey the rule or risk the penalty imposed. The penalty does not arise from nature, God, or his own conscience but from the contrary will of other persons; it is consequently against this will that one's resentment is directed.

This fifth form of control may be split into several subtypes, depending on the kind of power the other persons have over the individual. The first subtype is the control exercised by the *opinion*

[1] For an excellent analysis of possible ambiguities, see David Riesman, "Civil Liberties in a Period of Transition," *Public Policy*, Vol. III (1942), pp. 33-96.

of others. This is probably the most profound form of social control, for each person is perpetually preoccupied in work and play with "what other persons will think." Sometimes this kind of control overlaps with the next two kinds, economic and political. If, for example, the other person is an employer, his opinion may carry extra weight. In any case the employer generally has *economic* power in the sense of determining some of the conditions of work. Finally the third subtype, *political* power, is present when a person has authority over one.

It will be the purpose of the rest of this chapter to explore the nature of political control. Such control is by no means the only regulating mechanism, as shown by what was said about other social controls. In fact the main limitations on political control are to be found precisely in these other forms of social influence on conduct.

The Function of Government

Political control involves not only authority but *ultimate* authority, backed at some point by the use of force. The question then is this: Why does a society require such ultimate and extreme authority? Why can it not get along simply with the types of nonpolitical controls described above?

Certainly in some primitive societies there is an almost complete absence of differentiated political institutions. There is no law (strictly defined), no legislative council, no chief executive, no formal court. One might therefore assume that in such societies the nonpolitical types of control are adequate for the maintenance of social order. Yet this would not be quite accurate. It can be shown in such cases that the *need* for political control is present and that what are normally nonpolitical institutions are made to serve this need, whereas in other societies the need is met by a specialized political structure.

THE BANTU OF KAVIRONDO

Let us take as an example two Bantu tribes of Western Kenya, the Logoli and Vugusu.[2] These tribes, with populations of 45,000

[2] The following account is taken from Günter Wagner, "The Political Organization of the Bantu of Kavirondo," in M. Fortes and E. E. Evans-Pritchard (editors), *African Political Systems* (London: Oxford University Press, 1940), pp. 197-236. Although the author employs the past tense to describe those conditions superseded by the influence of European suzerainty, we shall employ the present tense throughout in order to avoid confusion.

and 40,000 respectively, practice a shifting type of agriculture and cattle raising. Each occupies a continuous stretch of territory and possesses the myth that all members are descended from one remote tribal ancestor. Each is divided into several exogamous, patrilineal clans subdivided into subclans and lineages.

The surprising thing about these tribes is that they possess no formal political organization and yet manage to maintain a certain amount of social order and unity. Such political control as exists is largely expressed through the clan rather than through the tribe. The tribe exercises no central authority over the clans in either external or internal affairs. One might infer that the real political unit is the clan rather than the tribe, but the clan does not have a formal political organization any more than the tribe does. The tribe does in many ways function as a social unit. Since the members of a clan must marry outside the clan but inside the tribe, interclan bonds are established. These bonds, connecting every clan member with his maternal and connubial relatives in other clans, constitute a tribal-wide network so strong and intricate that it operates "as if there were a central authority overruling that of the clan." [3] Furthermore, the cult of a common tribal ancestor and the occurrence of collective sacrifices and circumcision rites create a sense of tribal unity and coöperation. Although the tribe does not act as a political unit against outsiders, its members are more closely tied to one another than to outsiders. In short, the tribe is the largest group that feels as a unit and on certain occasions acts as one, but it is not a complete political unit, for it lacks a political structure and performs its political functions only indirectly, yielding to the clan a more definite role in this regard.

The fact that in this society certain political functions are fulfilled without a political structure serves to emphasize and clarify the nature of the functions themselves. The primary and essential functions appear in their pristine form, unalloyed with secondary functions contingent upon existence of a governmental organization.

One indispensable function is the final enforcement of the mores when ordinary methods have failed. Among the two Bantu peoples, violations of the mores are ordinarily met by restitutive and punitive requirements. For intentional injury to the person or property of

[3] *Ibid.*, p. 200.

another, a double indemnity must be paid. For breach of a taboo an appropriate sacrifice or purification ceremony must be performed. Ordinarily the nonpolitical controls are adequate to induce the offender to make the proper amends. Not only is he unsophisticated with respect to possible alternatives, but he himself believes in the rightness of the restitutive and punitive requirements. Instead of questioning the validity of the tribal norms, he interprets his initial violation as weakness, oversight, or evil on his or somebody else's part. He believes that deviation from established norms will evoke punishment by the ancestral spirits. Finally, since he must depend on others economically, even as he depends on them emotionally, he finds their formal ostracism (required by custom in the case of crime) hard to bear.

Thus every form of nonpolitical control operates to keep each person in line. But there are occasional violators who will not yield to these pressures, persons presumably consumed by passionate desire or hatred. What does the group do in such instances? It does what any other group would do. It uses force. The clan expels the offender and withdraws from him all protection. When caught in the act of committing his next offence he may then be killed by anybody. He is most likely to be lynched by a large and mixed group, spontaneously. The application of force is thus made without any formal procedures. The most definite step is taken by the clan when it expels him. Without his clan the individual is helpless.

A situation harder to handle than habitual violation of the mores is one in which two parties are at loggerheads, each believing that he is right, each having supporters, and each ready to battle for his side. This is particularly serious in a society lacking in centralized authority, for it is exactly such cases that centralized authority is supposed to settle.

In the initial stages of such a dispute the wronged party usually resorts to self-help. He recovers a stolen object or redraws a disputed boundary, or he resorts to a curse or to a shaman's magical services. If these measures fail he appeals to the old men of his subclan, and the accused, *if he belongs to the same subclan,* appears before them to defend himself. The old men listen to the two disputants and their witnesses. Any one of the old men can announce the decision because, given the facts, there is only one possible judgment known to all in common. If the evidence cannot be established satisfactorily, an ordeal is administered. After this no further action is required, for the ordeal is supposed to administer justice automatically.

The elders of the subclan are not a political body. They sit around every morning in a pasture discussing the news and the previous day's gossip. It is therefore easy for a person to come to them. If fighting breaks out, it is their duty to intervene by separating the parties and persuading them to return to reason. The ability of certain men to carry through such intervention forms one of the main criteria of leadership. A serious dispute involving injury or death quickly brings the elders of the entire clan to the scene. A meeting is held *ad hoc,* not formally organized but with strong personalities predominating. If one of the parties opposes a decision unanimously approved by the elders, the latter appoint a number of men to secure *by force* the required indemnity or the stipulated conduct. In case the clan elders themselves cannot agree, the weaker section is likely to secede from the clan, either joining another clan or migrating elsewhere and thus forming a new clan. Further conflict is thus solved by mutual avoidance, sometimes lasting for a generation or two.

Disputes between clans are harder to solve than those within the clan. In such cases the wronged person appeals to the elders of the offender's clan. His appeal may be reinforced, in serious instances, by elders and warriors from his own clan. If no agreement can be reached, the two clans break off relations and enter a state of vendetta, which lasts until the aggrieved clan exacts retribution sufficient to restore the pre-existing equilibrium. The elders in each clan then work for reconciliation by lamenting the deplorable consequences of the feud and appealing to the neighborliness and common ancestry of the two clans. Their efforts are aided by the elders in neutral clans who, by virtue of kinship and marital bonds and the weakening effect of interclan strife on tribal coöperation in warfare, are anxious to heal the conflict. If both clans prove willing, a feast of reconciliation and sacrifice is arranged, after which good relations are resumed. There is, however, no legally binding force behind the arbitration. The tribe has no official machinery for coercing a clan.

The external relations of the tribe reflect its internal situation. Enmity and warfare with other tribes is frequent. Yet the actual fighting or raiding is not conducted on a tribal scale. It is conducted by each clan or group of neighboring clans acting on its own account. The clans living nearest the dangerous sections of the border acquire leadership in warfare. This does not imply domination of the other clans, however, for there is no "calling up" of warriors or any hierarchical organization. All raids are one-day affairs and are done on a voluntary basis.

Since neither the tribe nor the clan has a governmental organization, leadership and authority do not rest upon formal political office. Instead they rest, first, upon the rights of inheritance pertaining to the first-born son and especially to the first-born son of a first-born son; second, upon wealth; third, upon a combination of personal attractiveness, good judgment, and strength of character; fourth, upon reputation as a warrior; fifth, upon possession of magico-religious virtues; and sixth, influence as clan elders. The clan elders have no definite political rights such as the right to collect tribute, to enact laws, to recruit soldiers, or to grant or refuse residence to strangers. Nor are they formally appointed or installed in their positions.

Yet the tribe manages to have certain politico-legal functions performed. These are, internally, (1) the final enforcement of the tribal mores and (2) the ultimate regulation of disputes; and externally, (3) the protection of the tribe. For each of these functions the tribes must rely heavily upon the clan, which at least has a crystallized structure based on patrilineal descent. Under this arrangement the tribal mores are well enforced, because the clan can coerce its members by spontaneous but highly effective measures. The regulation of disputes is also performed well, as long as the disputants are members of the same clan. But when they are members of different clans, open conflict cannot always be avoided even though it weakens the tribe. In warfare, too, the tribe must depend primarily on the clan. In short it appears that the tribe has gone about as far as it can in the development of social unity without political machinery. It is ready for or on the verge of the next step—a governmental organization that would enable it to coerce the clans when necessary and protect itself more systematically. One does not have to go very far in that part of Africa to find tribes that have taken this step, that have evolved into complex kingdoms, as for example the Kingdom of Ankole in Uganda.[4]

[4] Fortes and Evans-Pritchard, *op. cit.*, pp. 121-164.

INTERNAL FUNCTIONS

In most societies there are differentiated political structures that help to meet at least three major internal needs—the enforcement of norms, the balancing of ends, and the planning and direction of collective action. These needs are not met by political structure alone; in fact, we have just seen that they can be met without a distinct political organization. The peculiarity of the political organization is, first, that it exists primarily for these needs and, second, that it has reference to a particular aspect of them—namely, their *ultimate* and *authoritarian* aspect. This can be seen when each function is analyzed in turn.

Ordinarily the social norms do not need political enforcement because, as described above, they are internalized and obeyed through ignorance, moral conviction, fear of god, or economy of effort. But no matter how simple the society or how thorough the indoctrination, there is always the possibility that these controls will not restrain everybody. This is because of the constant pressure against the norms in any society. Each individual in pursuing his own ends is forced to compete with other individuals trying to capture the limited available resources to attain their ends. Consciously or unconsciously, he tries to find a way around the restraining norms. He forgets the rule, misconstrues its intention, denies that it applies in a given situation, and rationalizes his violations. He thus tends to repudiate certain norms as they apply to him, at the same time attempting to hold his competitors (whether in love or business) to those selfsame norms. Against this constant pressure purely moral, religious, and informal controls are not always adequate, because they depend on subjective emotion which the individual can often manipulate to his own satisfaction. There is required a more sinister control, exercised by an agency that pays no attention to how the individual feels about the rules but requires conformity nonetheless. Such an agency, prepared to restrain the individual by force if necessary, reinforces the other types of control and thus discourages the ordinary individual from treating the rule as a mere instrument rather than as a moral obligation. It also takes care of the exceptional cases of repeated and flagrant violation.

One may ask why, since they are man-made, any norms ever arise that are contrary to what people really want to do. The answer is that being "man-made" does not imply that they are deliberately invented. Rather, they arise unwittingly as a result of societal necessity in an exacting environment. Only those societies survive which evolve an efficient normative order. Furthermore, it is not possible for all members of a society to decide suddenly that the whole normative order is oppressive and thereupon to do away with it. For one thing, the normative order has become a part of the personalities of these members. The norms limit their absolute freedom, but do not limit their subjective freedom to the same degree. At any one time most of the norms are internalized; only a few are treated as purely external. Moreover the same norm may be emotionally significant to some people and emotionally neutral to others. Gangsters find murder an acceptable means to wealth and prestige, while others find it terrible to contemplate. It is virtually impossible to find any norm which everybody would regard as simply imposed by outside authority. Hence the failure to punish the violators of a norm offends those who cherish the particular norm in question. In addition, the attitude when other persons are the offenders is different from what it is when the offender is oneself. Since every individual stands to lose if the rules are not enforced, he has a stake in the observance of the norms by others. If he is a violator himself, he may attempt to justify himself and make a bid for leniency by discounting the value of the norm he has violated. But the number of his violations is always fewer than the number of his conformities. Consequently, no matter what his own behavior, every person favors enforcing the bulk of the social norms. Thus is explained the paradox that men support a political authority that makes them obey even when they do not wish to obey.

Any normative system, however, leaves plenty of room for honest differences of opinion. Generally these differences are settled through the *ordinary* give-and-take of social intercourse. People are allowed some leeway in holding contrary opinions; they frequently win or lose at the bar of public opinion; and those who cannot agree often resort to the expedient of avoiding each other. But sometimes the differences, reflecting strongly opposed interests, give rise to open conflict between segments or strata of the society. In this case, since conflict tends to weaken the society, some agency is required which is strong enough to settle the issue. This agency must represent the society as a whole, not some special part of it. In the Bantu society just described the elders of the clan represented the clan informally. In a larger and more complex group the representation must be more definite and formalized—an agency that operates as a balancing or adjudicating body. Such an agency really has no authorization apart from the attitudes and desires of the societal members. It merely serves as the instrument of their ends—the ends which they conceive *for the group* (i.e. group goals). At the same time the society's members have private or distributive goals that are contrary and competitive one with the other; and there is no automatic way in which these will naturally harmonize. Yet they must be made to harmonize in behalf of the group goals. In short, the group goals must take precedence over the purely distributive goals. This precedence is expressed in the supremacy and authority of the political agency, which is charged with the power to enforce arbitration in order to prevent conflict.

The unified behavior of a social aggregate is for the most part the result of the unplanned and unrealized integration of individual activities. Yet some planning and direction in behalf of the aggregate are also required, especially in time of crisis when the ordinary equilibrium is upset. Such planning and direction cannot be performed by a multitude but only by one or at most a few individuals. Furthermore, it would be worthless unless the few had the power or authority to see that the plans were carried out by the many. The planning and direction must consequently be done by the same agency that is authorized to enforce the norms and to arbitrate between conflicting interests. None other will do.

EXTERNAL FUNCTIONS

The ability of the group to meet external dangers is largely a result of its internal efficiency and the brilliance of its planning. Naturally, therefore, the same agency that represents the society in internal affairs tends to represent it in external matters as well. Indeed, an agency that did not control internal affairs could not really represent the group in external affairs, because it could not guarantee any commitments that it made or marshal the forces of the group in time of peril. The handling of war and diplomacy, therefore, is preëminently the function of the political agency.

SUMMARY

The major functions of government have now been delimited. They are, internally, the ultimate enforcement of norms, the final arbitration of conflicting interests, and the overall planning and direction of the society; and externally, the handling of war and diplomacy. In fulfilling these functions a government may undertake an almost limitless variety of services and activities. It may take a hand in education, poor relief, armament production, price regulation, etc., but it does so always in behalf or on the excuse of its major functions.

Political Structure

It has proved impossible, as one might expect, to discuss the functions of government without also suggesting some of the structural principles appropriate to these functions. The Bantu, who have no political organization, helped us to delineate function without discussing structure, but it soon became apparent that among these people the clan and subclan serve as substitutes for political organization. Now, however, we are ready to consider in more complete fashion the underlying principles of differentiated political structure.

THE AGENT OF THE ENTIRE SOCIETY

A distinct political organization is necessary because, in a complex society, the general and spontaneous action of the members cannot alone fulfill the political functions. A special group—the rulers for the time being—must discharge the necessary duties as the agent of the entire society. An important part of the institutional machinery, therefore, consists in defining the positions that convey rulership, specifying how persons are chosen for the occupancy of these positions, and emphasizing the connection between the ruling group and the society as a whole. Great importance is necessarily placed on symbols—symbols that link government and society, that connote prestige and power, and that attest the right of particular persons to occupy given positions. Necessarily the duties and obligations are not the same for all governmental offices but are differentiated one from another in a mutually dependent, interlocking system. In a complex society these may be divided into branches—executive, legislative, administrative, judicial, military. The heads of these branches constitute the real rulers in the sense of those who determine policy, but all government employees, even the most lowly clerks or policemen, share some of the characteristics of official status. As the agent or representative of the group, the government supposedly occupies a neutral position with reference to the competing interests within the society. The legal and symbolic systems often are designed to ensure this neutrality—to ensure that political action is always not only in the name of the entire society but actually in behalf of the societal as distinct from the private ends.

Unfortunately, however, the peculiarity of political power is that it may be exercised without being legal. Once having delegated the right to act for the whole group, a society finds it hard to keep control over the rulers who, by virtue of their very authority, can bear down upon the common citizen. Furthermore, any group that can elicit sufficient power and support may overthrow the legally constituted government. If it does, it becomes *ipso facto* the ruling group. So rulership is in the last analysis *de facto* rather than *de jure*. Even though illegal, however, a government still represents the group. It does so in the sense of acting for and in the name of the entire collectivity, whether the collectivity desires this or not. It does not necessarily do so in the sense of pursuing the ends which the citizens conceive as desirable for the society; but, in an effort to clothe itself in legitimacy and hence to acquire very necessary popular support, it generally *proclaims* that it is pursuing those ends. Its avowed purpose is the furtherance of the collectivity. Any government, licit or illicit, which fails to profess this aim or fails utterly to carry it out, ceases to be a government. The very necessity the rulers feel to give themselves legitimacy shows the force that normative controls exercise in a society. There is no exception to the principle then that the ruling group, either by right or by might, speaks for the entire society.

THE MONOPOLY OF FORCE

The government's well-known monopoly of force is a corollary of its regulative functions. The monopoly does not mean that the government alone uses force. It may delegate this use or fail in particular instances to control it. Nor does the monopoly mean that the government employs force on every occasion. It means, rather, that the government has the inherent prerogative to use physical coercion when necessary for the performance of its functions. (It also generally means that the government has the power to use force even when such use is *not* necessary.) Above all it has the right, or the obligation, to suppress any unauthorized use of force by an individual or a particular group.

Any nongovernmental agency which succeeds in using force on a large scale becomes itself a *de facto* government and automatically acquires at least a limited legitimacy. This is illustrated by the case of the revolutionary government of Argentina in 1930. The president of the new government, General Uriburu, sent a communication to the Supreme Court stating that a provisional government had been established by the revolution, and that this provisional government was in possession of the military and police forces necessary for peace, safety, and order. "The Court recognized the provisional government as a *de facto* government on two fundamental grounds: first, that the facts stated in the communication unquestionably characterized it as a de facto government; second, that, according to national and international doctrines concerning the acts of de facto officers, their acts were valid no matter what defects or vices were inherent in their appointment or election, and that no one could test the validity of their appointment when they were in apparent possession of the powers and functions of goverment." But the Court also added "that the acts of such government would be subject to judicial review as if it were a de jure government." [5]

THE TERRITORIAL SCOPE

Can a monopoly of force be limited in any way and still remain a monopoly? Obviously it cannot be limited with reference to any social factor because, by virtue of functional necessity, no other social agency can completely limit governmental power. A clan whose members were scattered in different areas, for example, could not possess a sovereign government, because some of its members would be living amongst members of other clans where they would be a clear minority, subject really to the power of these other clans. In the same way a linguistic or an occupational group could hardly

[5] Santos P. Amadeo, *Argentine Constitutional Law* (New York: Columbia University Press, 1943), p. 86.

serve as the limit of an independent government. True, there is actually considerable distribution of political authority along cultural lines. There was political representation of linguistic groups in the Austro-Hungarian Empire. There is religious and caste representation in India today. There is the right in America of bar associations to "disbar" members of the legal profession, and the *de facto* right of craft unions to monopolize an industry. But in practically every such case there are two things to notice: (1) the authority is not ultimate but is delegated by a higher authority; (2) the higher authority is territorially defined and hence automatically sets a geographical boundary to the operation of the functional authority. In brief the monopoly of force always resides, ultimately, in a territorial unit. The Catholic church presumes to speak with final authority to its parishioners in many matters, but it divides its jurisdiction on a territorial basis. Furthermore, it has no power of physical coercion. Ultimate political power involves a monopoly of force within a given territory.

THE UBIQUITY OF GOVERNMENT

Connected with the government's power and territorial exclusiveness is the individual's inability to avoid political control. Ordinarily an adult can avoid family life, can resign from an association, and can refuse to affiliate with a religious group. But he cannot cease to be under the authority of some political entity such as a nation. He may be able, with express permission, to change from one governmental jurisdiction to another, but he cannot escape such jurisdiction altogether. There are, to be sure, "stateless" persons who are without the normal protection, services, etc. granted to recognized citizens, but they are nonetheless subject to the laws of the land wherein they reside. Resident aliens are also subject to the laws of the land, but they are protected to some degree by the sovereign state of which they are recognized citizens. No part of the inhabited world is free from political jurisdiction, whether primitive or civilized. Isolated men may escape to uninhabited areas where no jurisdiction reaches, but the moment a group of such men come together in social interaction, political relationships arise. If a man wishes to participate in human society he must sooner or later submit to some political authority.

SOVEREIGNTY

The characteristics of political structure just described—namely, its role as the agent of the entire group, its final monopoly of force, its territorial exclusiveness, its inescapability—all give it that self-completeness and independence which is called sovereignty. Supreme in its own domain, it acts as an independent bargaining unit in its dealings with other political entities. It may be a weak entity and have actually little power on the outside, but so long as it is not definitely conquered it has legal sovereignty. The status of Cuba, for example, is different from that of Puerto Rico.

The Nature of Political Action

Looking at political life from an interactional point of view, certain observations may be made. Whereas economic behavior implies a certain voluntariness and reciprocity in the relationship (e.g. in a contract), political action implies the opposite. Behaving politically "A" commands because he possesses authority and "B" obeys because he is subject to that authority. The latter may claim that "A's" alleged authority is not legitimate, either because his supposed office does not exist, because he acquired the office in an illegal manner, or because the jurisdiction does not apply to "B's" case. But once he admits the legality of the demand, he has no alternative but to obey or risk the consequences. If he is caught disobeying, the consequence may not be merely restitutive but may be punitive as well, for the state has jurisdiction over his person. In practice he may of course successfully evade the consequences of disobedience. He can do this most safely if he has another source of power to balance against "A's" political authority. Yet, though political position is by no means the only source of power, any other source can at best guarantee only a partial and usually temporary immunity to governmental action. To persist in power any government must see that the price of disobedience is sufficiently high to induce most of the populace to obey the bulk of the laws most of the time.

"A," in seeking to coerce "B" into a certain line of conduct, is not supposed to pursue his own ends in contradistinction to those of the group. The fact that he is in authority gives him a certain power, to be sure, because he enjoys the control of force, but it also places limitations upon him. Were he to utilize his position simply to pursue his private ends, the result would be absolute coercion beyond any legitimate limits, and the basis of his position would soon deteriorate. As a sheer individual he cannot possibly match the combined strength of his fellows; his position of authority must have support, and in order to retain support he cannot use the position exclusively for his private ends. Even a conquest state professes to govern in the interests of the governed and thus involves itself in questions of legitimacy. Furthermore, even though the governing personnel is not responsible in equal degree to all elements in the population, it is usually highly responsible, as we shall see, to the elite.

Therefore, although "A" would be permitted in business to seek his own profit, in political office he is forbidden to do so except within the limits prescribed by his office. To be sure, if he is to be induced to accept responsibility he must be rewarded in some way. If the position is among the highest, the reward will have to be commensurate in order to attract capable candidates.[6] One crude form of reward is to allow the official to collect all he can from the very persons over whom he exercises his authority. This breaks down, however, because it is more profitable *not* to enforce the rules than to enforce them. Efficient government therefore demands that the rate of pay be fixed in some way independent of the authority in question. It must be a reward for adherence to certain standards of performance, and any unauthorized use of the official position must be a cause for punishment. Otherwise the person in authority enjoys an advantage which in a strictly economic sense no ordinary person can enjoy. He can divest others of their goods as effectively as if he were robbing them—an ironic and unstable situation, since he is supposedly representing the group and governing in its behalf.

The Central Political Problem

The possibility of corrupt political action poses the central problem of all government: how to ensure that those who represent the group, who protect and regulate it, actually use their authority to

[6] Geo. E. G. Catlin, *Principles of Politics* (London: Allen & Unwin, 1930), p. 184, speaks of men whose unusual energies are devoted solely to the acquisition of power for its own sake. These are, he says, "to an extraordinary degree political men, as the capitalist is to an extraordinary degree the economic man."

further its ends rather than their own when the two conflict. Every actual political system, no matter what its form, represents an effort to solve this problem. None has ever been completely successful, and yet none that has endured has been completely unsuccessful.

Most political theory, dominated by Western traditions, has assumed that the only system that can solve the problem is a democratic one. But the evidence is clear that some democratic governments have not come as near solving it as some autocratic ones. This is because the fidelity and efficiency of a government does not depend upon its form alone, but upon the relation of that form to the rest of the social structure. To see this, it is necessary to explore the connection between political organization and social stratification.

Government and Stratification

The notion of absolute equality cannot be applied to politics. One can imagine an economic system in which everybody would receive exactly the same income, but one cannot even conceive a political system in which everybody would exercise the same authority. No matter what its form, political organization implies by definition that one person has authority over another.

It is also of the nature of political authority that it is exercised by a few over the many. In the first place the task of government is only one among many that must be performed by specialized personnel. In the second place political authority is hierarchic and pyramidal in principle, with one or at best a few individuals at the top. Even when the governmental personnel constitutes ten per cent of the working population, as it is alleged to do in some bureaucratic regimes, it still is dominated at the top by an infinitesimal group who make the ultimate decisions and bear the final responsibility. The reason for this is that the thinking and planning necessary to guide the whole society can only be done, like all thinking and planning, by one or at most a few individuals. This is true no matter how large the population to be governed. There must in short be a "head" of any government; and when the governmental organization is large it is only those in the top positions who constitute this "head." The separation of administration from policy determination receives its clearest expression in the civil service, where governmental personnel is expected to be strictly nonpolitical. In speaking of a government or of a ruling group, it is necessary always to bear in mind the stratification within it, and at least to make the distinction between the "head" and the "body."

Granting that political authority is necessary in every society and that absolute political equality is therefore impossible, the search for equality must be placed on some other than the absolute level. It must be placed on the level of opportunity. If a few must govern and the rest must obey, one form that equality can take is the opportunity of the masses, at their own desire and out of their own ranks, to replace the rulers. This exposes the rulers to the most effective kind of accountability, the risk of losing office. It is a kind they ordinarily seek to avoid, but since death eventually takes them the problem of replacement arises anyway. The most unequal system, in this respect, is one in which the rulers replace themselves without any reference to the subjects. This ideal of immortal power is seldom realized, however, because the group of actual rulers is too small to impose its will after death. The nearest approach is the royal family line, but everyone knows that the hereditary monarch is more frequently the symbol than the essence of government, and that he usually depends on competent aides rather than kinsmen in the highest positions.

Actual inequality of opportunity more frequently expresses itself in another way—the tendency of one group or class within the larger society to choose the ruling personnel. The persons holding the highest positions are so few that they must depend for continuance in office upon the traditions and consent of some larger body, such as the elite class, the army, or the whole society. The tendency is to play these off one against the other as expediency demands. The army is handicapped by its specialized character, internal hierarchy, and its usual failure to constitute a well-rounded community. The government that leans on it alone is on shaky ground. The per capita influence of the elite, like the army, is greater than that of the mass, but the mass is more numerous. Such are the ambitions and gifts of those born in the common ranks, and such the deficiencies and conflicts among those born in the elite rank, that the latter are generally at least threatened with the possibility of replacement unless they guard their position by performing at least some of the functions they are supposed to perform. The small governing personnel, threatened on all sides, must also perform some of the functions it is supposed to perform, as well as pay due regard to the varying influence of the organized interests. It and the elite, no matter how autocratic they may be, no matter how absolute their alleged authority, must still devote some attention to the needs of the society in which and on which they live. Otherwise they cannot survive.

The right to elevate and to depose the rulers, whether the privilege of a special class or of the whole society, may be a part of the legitimate political organization of the society. But the power to elevate and depose may nevertheless be present regardless of the legitimate structure. A violation by the rulers of the rights and obligations defined in the political structure may bring theoretically illegal but ethically justified retaliation from all or some of the subjects. Indeed, the governed are never without some power; since the ruling group is small and is therefore helpless once the populace organizes against it, this power may become quite adequate to throw the government out of office. The opposition may take the form not of violence but of noncoöperation. The commoners too can violate rules and pursue their own interests in opposition to those designed by the government.

While the threat of deposition is the most powerful restraint upon governmental corruption and the opportunity of replacement the greatest form of political equality, there are other restraints and other forms of equality. So long as those in power really pursue the ends that the people cherish for the group, the masses will have the feeling of freedom and a sense of participation. It is therefore important to ask what, aside from the threat of deposition, can lead them to pursue those ends.

For one thing, the persons in authority are themselves motivated partially by sentiments and values acquired as members of society. Though political scientists often assume that such persons pursue power in a purely Machiavellian frame of mind, the assumption is heuristic rather than descriptive. Power as an end in itself can hardly outweigh all the other ends for which men live. It tends rather to be used as an important means to other ends, though not the sole means because some ends cannot be attained through power alone. The fact, therefore, that persons in authority have sentiments, moral convictions, and a multiplicity of ends places a limitation upon the abuse of their authority. In addition they are limited by ignorance of possible alternatives and above all by failure to foresee the consequences of their own acts. In fact they are limited by the same social controls that limit other members of society.

In view of these other controls it is not surprising that a government, even though not replaceable in the democratic sense of the term, may nevertheless satisfy the people. So long as it meets its institutional obligations in a satisfactory manner—so long as it satisfies the expectations of the people—it may remain in power. The people may, in fact, conceive an absolute regime as the best instrumentality for achieving their ends. This can be seen by taking an extreme example, the government of India under the caste system.

GOVERNMENT IN INDIA UNDER CASTE

Political organization in highly stratified societies has always puzzled democratic theorists. Ordinarily they have taken as a model the European feudal order, but for the sake of more general political theory it is wise to consider non-European examples as well.

In the case of India the first thing to notice is the extraordinary prestige of the priesthood. The Hindu religion, though it underwent numerous changes in the course of centuries, never lost its high evaluation of asceticism and the sacredness of the Brahmin. It conceived human society as a hierarchical and hereditary system of strata with the Brahmin caste at the top. The social position of the other castes was determined primarily by the degree of contact they had with the holy Brahmins. At the bottom of the ladder were castes that had no contact with Brahmins at all, and were therefore impure, untouchable, and incapable of entering the temple. For ordinary Hindus the doctrine of reincarnation held forth the possibility that if the rules of behavior appropriate to one's status were observed, especially in so far as the feeding and worship of Brahmins were concerned, there would be a chance of spending the next life in a higher caste.

This exaltation of the priesthood seems significant, because it is found not only in India but in virtually all stratified social systems—ancient Egypt, ancient Peru, and feudal Europe. Is there any connection, then, between a stratified order and an exalted priesthood?

The answer seems to lie in the affirmative. The fact that the hierarchical differentiation of status produces great absolute inequalities means that there must be compensating subjective justification of these inequalities. In short, the sense of freedom must compensate for the absence of absolute freedom. Without a strong system of ritual and belief to justify, rationalize, and enforce the inequalities, open competition for wealth and prestige would develop and vertical mobility would be substituted for hereditary immobility. In accordance with the importance attached to religious ritual and belief, then, the priesthood, as the body representing the people in religious matters, must necessarily enjoy an exalted position. When the priesthood is hereditary a situation comparable to that of hereditary rulers is created. The masses themselves have no chance to become priests. Made of inferior clay, they can prove their worth and imbibe a little of the sacred lustre only by doing honor to the men of god.

Precisely because of the power of the priesthood, the potential conflict between this class on the one hand and the governing personnel on the other becomes extremely crucial in a stratified social order. The priesthood exercises a claim that surpasses the sensory world and therefore has supremacy over the secular authority. Indeed, since the latter rules on the basis of a legitimate right sanctioned by the highest values and ceremonials, the priesthood is the body which in theory grants and confirms the right to rule. Yet, by definition, the government is the one that exercises final authority and disposes of physical force in the real world. It therefore enjoys a factual supremacy over the priesthood that stubbornly resists mere theory. In these two kinds of supremacy, in these two claims to power, the basis is laid for conflict. Unless the inherent conflict is avoided by some institutional device, the stratified order is subject to disorganization.

One solution—as in Egypt, the Inca Empire, and Japan—is to combine the priestly and secular functions in one person or group. This, however, is an apparent rather than a real solution, because in any civilized society the two functions are incompatible. Even if the emperor and the high priest are one and the same person, this person must inevitably delegate most of his functions; and one of the first steps is the delegation of priestly activities to certain officials and secular activities to others. The struggle then begins anew, one step down in the hierarchy.

Another solution lies in the rigid distinction of the two functions with little mutual interference; the priesthood lends religious sanction to the secular power, the rulers give civil sanction to the priestly prerogative.

Hindu society was peculiar in that, first, it carried the principle of hereditary status to its greatest extreme and, second, it gave the priesthood supreme power. The resulting conflict between the Brahmins and the Kshatriyas endured for centuries. The Brahmins supposedly were forbidden to occupy governmental positions and to accumulate wealth, but they violated this rule and succeeded in establishing the theory that the government existed for their benefit. No privilege, no indulgence was too great for them. In this situation the Kshatryas were pushed to the wall and ultimately disappeared.[7]

The Brahmins, by driving out the normal rulers provided in the Hindu caste structure, might be assumed to have established themselves as rulers. While this may have happened in some cases, the Brahmins generally retained their priestly identification. Their grip upon the political functionaries, however, made the society vulnerable. The rulers came to be either local upstarts, who might come from any caste and whose claim to legitimacy was slight, or foreigners. The system could not produce a stable, large-scale government. The only governments that gave stability were those imposed by conquerors or those that were purely communal. Everyday government was chiefly a local affair. The social norms were caste norms enforced by the local caste group.[8] Economic cooperation between the castes was on a village basis, and each village was largely self-sufficient, united against the dangers arising from the absence of orderly centralized government. The supremacy of the priesthood was therefore compatible with local but not with central political stability.

The case of India illustrates the importance of ritual and morality in the maintenance of a stratified system. The Hindus, poor and unequal as they were, did not accept the system because physically forced to do so. To them the Brahmin caste was the representative of the gods on earth and had a natural monopoly of sacred ritual and learning. Doing homage to Brahmins was the surest way of guaranteeing one's own spiritual and even material future. The supremacy of the Brahmin caste seemed entirely natural and right to

[7] G. S. Ghurye, *Caste and Race in India* (London: Kegan Paul, 1932), pp. 81-83.

[8] L. S. S. O'Malley, *Indian Caste Customs* (Cambridge: University Press, 1932), Chap. 2. E. A. H. Blunt, *The Caste System of Northern India* (London: Oxford University Press, 1931), Chaps. 4 and 15.

the other castes, and the duty of the political rulers lay in upholding it. The government was thus limited in its actions by the demands of the society it governed. It happened that the demands were not democratic demands but the opposite. They were caste demands, the strongest being that the hereditary priesthood should enjoy extreme privileges. How else could the community prosper? As the representative of the entire society the government was constrained to grant special favors to one part of that society—the part that stood in the highest reverential esteem.

THE MYTH OF THE CLASS STATE

The theory that the state is the instrument of a particular class, pursuing the interests of this class against the will of the rest of society, is never true in practice. It comes nearest to realization in the conquest state, where the conquerers constitute a dominant stratum, furnish the governing personnel out of their own ranks, and diverge culturally from the conquered. However, such a bifurcated society does not last long. Not all the conquerors can serve as rulers. There thus arises within the conquest stratum a distinction between officialdom and nonofficialdom. The conquered class thereupon becomes a tertium quid and acquires power as such. In the second place as time goes by the culture of the two groups, not to mention the blood, tends to merge, and the distinction between the two classes becomes hard to maintain. Consequently the hegemony of the conquering group disappears, at least in any sense antithetical to the wishes of the general population.

The case of India again serves as illustration. The Aryan invaders made an extraordinary effort to keep themselves distinct from the darker indigenous peoples whom they conquered. But their own ranks were split into four major strata, between two of which—the Brahmin and the Kshatriya—there was conflict. Despite the most rigid rules of endogamy, amalgamation with the native population took place, beginning first in the lower strata; and notwithstanding the most rigid limitations on social intercourse, cultural assimilation occurred. What was at first a conquest state finally turned into a solidaristic society, united under one religion and one priesthood but split into extremely exclusive though mutually dependent castes.

If the conquest situation cannot furnish an example of the class state, it is fruitless to look elsewhere. The Brahmins of India were not a "ruling class" but a stratum especially favored by the government. The top-most class is almost invariably, and of necessity, larger than the governing body itself. The latter, at least at the policy-determining level, is necessarily small. There grows up, then, a distinction between the members of the elite who actually govern and the rest who do not govern. This dichotomy inevitably expresses itself as a conflict of interest, and each side appeals for support to the lower classes.

The principle can be illustrated in many places. In Latin America, for example, the elite is eternally split into factions, each trying to gain governmental posts. A government is seldom able to satisfy the entire elite for long, even though drawn from its ranks.[9] Everywhere the struggles of politics are the struggles of one small group to obtain the support of the mass against another small group.[10] Even in a democracy the ordinary person is too preoccupied with other matters to compete for the reins of government or to determine its policies in detail. Active competition for political position is left to a small section of the citizenry, not all of whom can be in power at the same time. Only in a period of crisis will a larger portion of the populace interest itself in government and then only for a short time. The purpose of most rebellions is not to change the form of government but simply to change its personnel, which for the multitudes is often of no importance. So long as the political structure conforms to the sentiments and ends of the people, it is not felt to be oppressive no matter how absolute its character.

Of course, even when the governmental structure is justified in the mores and the possession of office conforms to legitimate practice, there still may be some envy and resentment. This arises from the fundamental human ability to put oneself in another's place and feel vicariously how he must feel. The member of an inferior stratum cannot help being fascinated by the doings and privileges of those in a superior status, and cannot help contrasting them with his own restricted activities. It is inevitable that occasionally this contrast should result in illicit efforts to overcome the barrier and put oneself in the superior position. Thus does absolute inequality tend constantly to infringe on the sense of freedom. But curiously, the social

[9] Kingsley Davis, "Political Ambivalence in Latin America," *Journal of Legal and Political Sociology*, Vol. I (October 1943), pp. 127-150.

[10] Catlin, *op. cit.*, p. 366.

controls are generally strong enough to suppress this tendency—controls that are by no means limited to force. This is illustrated by the reaction of the lower strata themselves to those of their members who try to gain a higher position or otherwise disrupt the system. They are often the first to experience a feeling of outrage and to punish the culprit, albeit at the same time they secretly understand his motivation and wish that in his place they might have succeeded. Mixed with their sense of competition and unwillingness to see one of their own number get ahead is the greater sense of impropriety. Cases inevitably arise in which the treatment of the lower strata is felt to be unjust by the standards prevailing, in which case a public reaction occurs;[11] but this is not the question at issue.

The Concept of a World State

The term "state" gives rise to some confusion. On the one hand it is often defined abstractly; on the other hand, concretely—usually in the form of the modern nation. It seems better to accept the first usage and designate the state as the institutional structure through which supreme authority within a given territory is exercised. The "government" then can be defined as the personnel or party that is filling the positions in this structure at a given time. The structure presumably possesses "legitimacy," in the sense that it is part of the organization of the entire society, conforming to the sentiments, values, and norms. Since, however, a group may seize power, the possibility of an illegitimate government must be recognized. Such a group and its partisans will inevitably try to acquire legitimacy and may succeed in doing so, even with a minimum change in the basic structure. Even in a stable system there is nearly always some conflict of opinion with respect to whether certain forms are legitimate or illegitimate, but deep-rooted conflict concerning the legitimacy of the entire structure tends to disorganize a society and hence seldom lasts for a long period. Those who question the whole system are usually members of a small coterie, the "lunatic fringe."

According to this mode of definition, the term "state" when used concretely needs qualification. It may be a tribe-state, a city-state, or a nation-state. Furthermore, it becomes possible to imagine a kind of state that has never yet existed—namely, a world state.

[11] See the poignant case of the King's concubine and the priest in Margaret Landon, *Anna and the King of Siam* (New York: John Day, 1943), Chaps. 30 and 31.

Like most imaginary entities the world-state is vague in its details. Its main outlines are constructed by analogy, often being pictured as simply the nation-state writ large. But the analogy cannot be perfect. There are some features of the nation-state that could not possibly characterize the world-state. The nation-state, for example, has the duty of protecting its people against the economic and military inroads of other nations. It must uphold the prestige, honor, security, and integrity of its citizens against those of other countries. To what extent this function has dominated all previous forms of the state, from tribe to nation, can be realized by recalling well-known facts. "There are exceedingly few human societies known to us in which there is not some form of warfare, and at least a good half of the history of political development is in one way or another a history of wars." [12] Boundary disputes have used up an enormous amount of national effort.[13] The world-state, on the other hand, will be entirely devoid of the function. It will have no other wars than civil wars, and no other boundaries than internal ones.

In addition the world-state will lose the function of treaty making. A treaty, being an agreement between sovereign states, cannot be made by a world-state. Present-day agreements between nations will be superseded by statutes and rules that will regulate interregional relations but will be internal in the world-state.

Along with these functional changes will go a change of outlook. The emotion of patriotism, if it remains at all, will certainly be so changed as to seem queer to the present generation. Patriotism has been associated with the conflict of one state against another. Transferred to a world-state its character will change radically. It may become a worship of the status quo, because the only foe of the world-state will be internal (the threat of revolution) rather than external. Or patriotism may become a mildly competitive attitude associated with region, class, or culture, but not deep enough to be subversive.

There will probably also be a diminution of the martial virtues such as bravery, cunning, endurance, and loyalty in combat. Since these virtues have been associated with human society since its origin, the world-state will thus effect a major change in human

[12] Fortes and Evans-Pritchard, *op. cit.*, p. xix.

[13] On the great attention devoted to boundary disputes in Latin America, see Wm. L. Schurz, *Latin America* (New York: Dutton, 1941), pp. 255-260.

emotions and evaluations. But the exact form of the change is not easy to predict.

The world-state may come by deliberate creation, peaceful evolution, or conquest—possibly by a combination of the three. Should one nation seize global power, the world-state would then be a conquest state. If our previous thesis is correct, however, it would not long remain a conquest state but would give place to a new legitimacy as wide as the world.

Once the world-state is established on a legitimate basis by whatever means, there will be no further reforms possible by consolidation of sovereignties. All reformist activity will presumably be directed toward the internal rectification of political ills. It will no longer be possible for politicians to deflect the people's attention from domestic reforms by pointing to foreign enemies. This fact may counterbalance the tendency to worship the status quo. In fact, it is just possible that external security will allow the greatest development of individualism ever known—individualism in the sense of a greater range and freedom of choice among means for each person. It is possible, on the other hand, that a cult or philosophy will gain supremacy and thus standardize the whole world; but in time, through sheer success, its rigor would probably relax.

There is a tendency to assume that if international wars are abolished, human conflict will virtually disappear. This is not a safe assumption. Quite possibly the total amount of *armed* conflict may diminish, but it will probably not disappear. Finally, emotional, political, and economic conflict will persist and possibly even increase. The world-state is therefore a widespread and very realistic goal, but it is not a panacea for human happiness.

Conclusion

The purpose of this chapter has been to differentiate political control from other types of control, and to suggest certain ways in which the other controls limit the political type. This has not been done by denying that the state has the characteristics usually associated with it. It does in fact seem to have the function of enforcing the norms and protecting the group, and its services are subsidiary to this function. A government acts in the name of the group, exercises a monopoly of force, rules a designated territory, and possesses the attribute of sovereignty. Furthermore, political action differs from economic action in the inherent inequality of the relationship. But an attempt has been made to get behind these functions, to understand why they are necessary and to envisage their implications. In this attempt consideration has been given to the central problem of all government: how to insure that the governing personnel will use its legitimate power to pursue what the people believe to be the group goals rather than its (the personnel's) private goals.

Different kinds of political organization represent different ways of solving this problem. An outstanding way is the democratic, in which the political structure is so arranged that the people can select the governing personnel. Another is the highly stratified type, in which the governing body is hereditary or is selected by a permanent elite that symbolizes the values of the entire society and accordingly has special privileges. This stratified type does not necessarily imply a feeling of oppression on the part of the masses, because in one way or another the structure gives expression to their values. In fact, concepts such as "freedom" and "liberty" are not descriptive terms but subjective and relative ones; and though useful in the realm of controversy, they must be used with extreme care in the analysis of actual political behavior. For this reason the present discussion has attempted to distinguish between absolute freedom and the sense of freedom, holding that the two do not always correspond.

Upon the analogy of the nation-state it is possible to imagine a world-state. While such a state would have some of the essential characteristics of all governmental organization, it would also have some unique features never before exhibited by any political entity. These unique features may be imagined by taking into account the special conditions that would prevail, but the details must necessarily remain vague. For this reason the idea of the world-state is like the idea of the airplane before the plane was actually invented.

References

Thurman W. Arnold, *The Symbols of Government* (New Haven: Yale University Press, 1935).

Provocative debunking of our political myths and semantic foibles. The author is particularly good at showing the absurdity of our traditional court practice and judicial theory. What he leaves unexplained is why people engage in such absurdities.

Geo. E. G. Catlin, *Principles of Politics* (London: Allen & Unwin, 1930).

A thoughtful and suggestive book. Somewhat hard to read but superior to the usual treatise in political theory. See also Catlin's other works.

R. A. Humphreys, *The Evolution of Modern Latin America* (New York: Oxford University Press, 1946), Chap. 4, "Democracy and Dictatorship."

The strange case of Latin America, where democracy and dictatorship play hide-and-seek with each other. See also J. Fred Rippy, "Dictatorships in Spanish America," in Guy Stanton Ford, Dictatorship in the Modern World *(Minneapolis: University of Minnesota Press, 1935).*

V. O. Key, *Politics, Parties, and Pressure Groups* (New York: Crowell, 1942).

A textbook in political science which is more realistic than the usual kind and which consequently provides more material for a sociological understanding of politics.

Hans Kohn, *The Idea of Nationalism* (New York: Macmillan, 1945).

"The most complete account of the nature and early history of nationalism"—MacIver. See also Carlton C. J. Hayes, The Historical Evolution of Modern Nationalism *(New York: R. Smith, 1931).*

Paul F. Lazarsfeld, *The People's Choice: How the Voter Makes Up His Mind in a Presidential Campaign* (New York: Duell, Sloan & Pearce, 1944).

Shows how modern empirical investigation and statistical analysis can get behind the votes to the motives and social conditions behind the vote.

A. D. Lindsay, *The Modern Democratic State* (London: Oxford University Press, 1943), Vol. 1.

A very penetrating and clear discussion of the theory of democracy and its relation to social and economic changes. See also the same author's small book, The Essentials of Democracy *(Philadelphia: University of Pennsylvania Press, 1929).*

Robert M. MacIver, *The Web of Government* (New York: Macmillan, 1947).

Here a leading sociologist turns his attention to a comprehensive analysis of the nature and kinds of government.

John M. Maki, *Japanese Militarism: Its Cause and Cure* (New York: Knopf, 1945).

Written by an American of Japanese ancestry, this study of the evolution of government and militarism in Japan is remarkably clear.

Franz Neumann, *Behemoth: The Structure and Practice of National Socialism* (New York: Oxford University Press, 1942).

Any student interested in the comparative sociology of government should read many realistic descriptions of government in totalitarian (Fascist and Communist), liberal-democratic, and traditional-monarchical countries. The present one is a good account of the Nazi system.

Lincoln Steffens, *Autobiography* (New York: Harcourt, Brace, 1931), Part 2, "See New York First"; Part 3, "Muckraking"; Part 4, "Revolution."

The fascinating story of how a journalist got and published the inside information on political corruption in the United States. Raises some real questions concerning the relation of government to the people.

CHAPTER XIX

RELIGIOUS INSTITUTIONS

SO UNIVERSAL, permanent, and pervasive is religion in human society that unless we understand it thoroughly we shall fail to understand society. Consequently, the purpose of the present chapter is to offer a scientific explanation of religion. We want to know what religion is and why it occurs; to comprehend its elements and its various forms; to grasp its functions and its structure. If we succeed, the most difficult step in our analysis of major institutions will have been completed.

The task is certainly not easy. No societal phenomenon is more resistant than religion to scientific explanation. Just why it should be so resistant will become clear as the discussion unfolds. Suffice it to say now that there are two chief sources of error, first an emotional and second a rational bias. The emotional bias springs from the fact that religion by its very nature involves ultimate values, making it almost impossible to view with a disinterested attitude. The investigator, whoever he may be, is irresistibly drawn into holding either that religion is a thoroughly pernicious force which dupes the mind, promotes ignorance, and delays progress, or that there is one true religion (his own) which is highest and best. Once the investigator has taken one of these paths, no matter how carefully he camouflages his opinion under scientific trappings, the fact of his bias shows through—in the first case as "debunking" and in the second case as special pleading. Even when the scholar's purpose is genuinely scientific, even when he avoids either debunking or justifying religion, he nevertheless tends to fall into another error—a rationalistic approach. He tends to assume that his fellows, in their religious behavior, are trying to fit means to ends in the same logical manner that he as a scientist would employ. This rationalistic explanation works fairly well with reference to technological and economic behavior, because in such behavior the element of rationality is maximized; but with respect to religion, which involves transcendental ends, strong sentiments, and symbolic instruments, it is fallacious. It attributes the existence of religion simply to ignorance and error, and assumes that when these are eliminated there will emerge the completely rational (i.e. completely nonreligious) man. It thus views religion as a mere epiphenomenon, an accident. Some upholders of this view, when finally disillusioned by the continued nonappearance of the rational man, have fallen back upon a biological interpretation: they hold that religion is an expression of instinctive emotions. Such a solution is as false as the other. Simply because religious behavior is nonrational the conclusion does not follow that it must be instinctive. The very nonrationality of religious behavior is the thing that gives religion its vitality in human life.

Outmoded Theories of Religion

To illustrate the rational bias, a review of two evolutionary theories of religion—animism and naturism—will suffice. Early anthropologists were mainly concerned with the "origin" of religion. Saturated in evolutionism, they sought to explain social institutions by describing their hypothetical beginnings.

According to Tylor and Spencer [1] the idea of the soul is central in religion. Early man hit upon this idea as a result of a simple error. Because in his dreams, while his body remained in one place, his self wandered about and did various things, he deduced that there must exist within himself two beings. Also since in his dreams he saw and talked to other persons whose bodies were not in the places dreamt about, he concluded that they too must have two beings within themselves. He thus gradually formed the notion that each individual has a double, another self, which has the power of leaving the body and traveling at a distance. This double resembles the person but is distinguished from it by several peculiar traits. "It is more active, since it can cover vast distances in an instant. It is more

[1] E. B. Tylor, *Primitive Culture* (London, 1903), Chapters XI-XVIII, Herbert Spencer, *Principles of Sociology* (London, 1882-96), Parts I and VI. The present account is abbreviated from that of Emile Durkheim, *The Elementary Forms of the Religious Life* (London: Allen & Unwin, 1915, trans. from French by J. W. Swain), Chaps. II and III. Durkheim's summary is more convincing than the original theories themselves.

malleable and plastic; for, to leave the body, it must pass out by its apertures, especially the mouth and nose. It is represented as made of matter, but of a matter much more subtile and ethereal than any which we know empirically. This double is the soul." [2]

But how did the soul, thus conceived, attain the status of a spirit—a detached soul-like entity not inhabiting a human body? Another error—this time a misinterpretation of death—provides the answer. Early man, thinking of death simply as a long swoon or prolonged sleep, observed that instead of waking, the body finally disintegrated. He was thus forced to assume that the soul became free and constituted a disembodied spirit. As the number of dead persons augmented with time, a population of spirit souls formed around the living population. These spirits were thought to have the needs, passions, and interests of men and to concern themselves with their living companions of yesterday, either to aid or to injure them. Possessing extreme fluidity, they could enter into the body of the living and cause all sorts of disorders or else increase the body's strength and vitality. Early man thus formed the habit of attributing to the disembodied spirits all those events of life which varied from the ordinary. The spirits constituted an ever ready supply of causes, so that one was never left at a loss for an explanation of an event. Did a man appear inspired, did he speak with energy, was he lifted outside himself and above the ordinary level of men? It was because a good spirit was animating him. Was he struck by an attack of illness or seized by madness? It was because an evil spirit had entered into him. Thus the power of souls was increased by all that men attributed to them, and in the end the living found themselves the prisoners of this imaginary world which their own imagination had created. For if the spirits were the givers of health and sickness, of good and evil, it was wise to conciliate and appease them when they were irritated. Hence arose offerings, prayers, sacrifices, and in a word all of the apparatus of religious observance.

Here was the soul transformed. From a simple double animating the body of a man, it had become a spirit, a good or evil genius, or even a deity. But since it was death which brought about this apotheosis, it was to the dead, to the souls of the ancestors, that the first cult known to humanity was addressed. Thus the first rites were

[2] Durkheim, *op. cit.*, pp. 50-51.

funeral rites; the first sacrifices were food offerings destined to satisfy the needs of the departed; the first altars were tombs.[3]

To explain animism Tyler formulated the theory that early man's limited intelligence could not distinguish animate from inanimate objects but endowed all things, even inanimate objects, with human characteristics and consequently with souls. Whereas the souls of men were thought to govern the world of men, the souls of other things were thought to govern the external world—the flow of rivers, the movement of stars, the germination of plants, the reproduction of animals, etc. Early man found himself even more dependent on these cosmic spirits than on the spirits of his ancestors, for whereas the ancestors were only imaginary the external things inhabited by spirits were quite real. He implored their assistance with offerings and prayers. Thus a completely animistic view of the world came into being; the ancestor cult was supplemented by a nature-worshiping cult.[4]

Spencer did not agree with this theory of the origin of animism. Regarding Tyler's assumption concerning early man's stupidity as too drastic, he substituted another hypothesis—that early man, in giving names to individuals, often chose the names of inanimate objects and thus came to regard these objects as having human qualities, as being in fact the ancestors of human beings. Early man "soon lost sight of the fact that these names were only figures, and taking them literally, he ended by believing that an ancestor named 'Tiger' or 'Lion' was really a tiger or a lion."

NATURISM

Max Müller and other students of Sanskrit accepted in general Tylor's theory of the soul's origin, except that they placed more emphasis on death as the source rather than dreams. They believed, however, that this development was only secondary in importance. The true source of religion they sought in another direction—the influence of external nature on man. Early man deified the most important and striking aspects of nature. "At first sight," wrote Müller, "nothing seemed less natural than nature. Nature was the greatest surprise, a terror, a marvel, a standing miracle, and it was

[3] This and the previous paragraphs are paraphrased from Durkheim, *op. cit.*, pp. 51-52.

[4] Durkheim, *op. cit.*, pp. 52-53.

only on account of their permanence, constancy, and regular recurrence that certain features of that standing miracle were called natural, in the sense of foreseen, common, intelligible. . . . It was that vast domain of surprise, of terror, of marvel, of miracle, the unknown, as distinguished from the known, or, as I like to express it, the infinite, as distinct from the finite, which supplied from the earliest times the impulse to religious thought and language." It is from this sensation of the infinite "that religions are derived."[5] But religion arises only when these natural forces are no longer represented in abstract form but are transformed into personal agents: spiritual beings or gods. This result was brought about by early man's stupidity again—this time his linguistic confusion. Language can refer not only to existent but also to nonexistent objects. It originally referred to human acts, and when applied to external nature it gave the names of human acts to natural objects. Hence a spirit had to be attributed to the objects in order to account for the acts which were confounded with them in their names. Language thus superimposed upon the material world as revealed to the senses, a new world composed of spiritual beings created out of nothing and felt to be the causes of physical events.[6] Once invented, the vocabulary representing this spirit world was capable of indefinite expansion, so that a pantheon, a hierarchy of deities could be created. The idea of a man's own soul was a secondary growth, and the religion of ancestor worship was a reflection of the more important nature worship.[7]

CRITIQUE

These evolutionary theories, now generally outmoded in scientific circles but still prevalent in popular accounts, are susceptible to two kinds of criticism. First, their general point of view can be assumed and a question raised as to which details are most plausible. Second, the entire point of view can be subjected to scrutiny.

Stating the problem as the evolutionists conceived it, we can raise the question of whether or not known primitive men do confuse the waking with the dreaming state, or animate with inanimate nature. The answer is that they do not. They can explain dreams

[5] Quoted by Durkheim, *op. cit.*, p. 74.
[6] Durkheim, *op. cit.*, p. 77.
[7] Durkheim, *op. cit.*, p. 78.

(assuming that they have any urge to explain them—which they seldom do) in any number of ways without resorting to the double,[8] and they always distinguish animate from inanimate objects. Rational techniques of dealing with nature, such as stupefying fish with poison or burning the ground before seeding, exist side-by-side with magical practices for securing a good catch or insuring a good crop.[9] The latter practices therefore do not depend on, and presumably do not originate with, a confusion between animate and inanimate. Ancestor worship is by no means universal, nor is it prior to other types of worship; if anything, it is a late development in human history. Neither is animism universal. Nowhere in Melanesia is there "a belief in a spirit which animates any natural objects, a tree, waterfall, storm or rock, so as to be to it what the soul is believed to be to the body of man." [10] In so far as contemporary primitives furnish evidence on the beginning of religion, the dream-and-double theory is open to question.

The theory of naturism seems more a reflection of our own culture than that of early man. We take an emotional attitude toward "natural beauty." Many primitive peoples—for instance, the American Indians—regard this attitude as rather silly. Also, Müller's belief that the application of humanistic language to inanimate objects created animism is hardly a satisfactory theory of religious origin; it assumes that when religion appeared language and society were already well developed, whereas a different analysis suggests that religion, language, and society are all inextricably related and must have developed simultaneously, not serially. Müller's investigations were based primarily on a *written* language. To assume that such a language reveals anything about the *origin* of a basic institution is a long assumption indeed, and certainly an erroneous one. The so-called mysteries of nature to explain which early man supposedly invented religion are not rare or unusual. The sun rises and sets every day, the moon waxes and wanes every month, the seasons follow each other regularly, and life pursues a normal course. Most religion is concerned not with the spectacular but with things as normal and expectable as sunup and sundown, winter and summer, birth and death. The idea of mystery or abnormality is something

[8] Durkheim, *op. cit.*, pp. 56-57.

[9] Ruth Benedict, "Animism," *Encyclopedia of the Social Sciences*, p. 65.

[10] R. H. Codrington, *The Melanesians* (Oxford, 1891), p. 123. Quoted by Durkheim, *op. cit.*, p. 67.

attributed to, not an inherent characteristic of, nature; and primitive man is not so prone to make this attribution as we are.[11] Instead of being impressed by his dependence on external phenomena, primitive man is more likely to have the feeling that external phenomena depend on him. If his feeling of frailness in face of mysterious and overwhelming nature were the source of religion, we would expect the most impressive natural phenomena to be deified—oceans, winds, mountains, sky, moon and sun. Sometimes they are but in many cases such things as ducks, rabbits, kangaroos, lizards, worms, cows, and frogs are given religious significance.

One could criticize particular accounts of religious origins indefinitely. Since such accounts are highly speculative, based on analogy and imagination rather than direct evidence, nearly any theory can be made to appear as plausible as any other. Thus it would be possible to defend a theory which based the origin of religion on property. When men were not around to protect their property, they invented a deity to protect it for them and told others about the powers of this deity and the possible punishment if trespass occurred; and gradually there grew up a pantheon of gods to protect not only property but all other rights as well, etc., etc. All that is required is a vivid imagination and a set of implicit assumptions. We are not primarily interested, therefore, in whether this or that evolutionary speculation is correct but whether the whole point of view, the whole system of implicit assumptions, can yield a scientific explanation of religion.

Unacceptable today is the idea that social institutions are explained by an account of their origin. The objection is not due solely to the impossibility of recovering traces of the earliest social beginnings. Certainly, since institutions are not tangible like stones and cannot be dug up, any evidence concerning their origins must be indirect and inconclusive. Contemporary primitive societies and ancient Vedic documents furnish no evidence, because they are as many thousand years away from the beginning as ourselves. But what really makes the evolutionary theories so naive is their lack of scientific sociology. The evolutionists put the cart before the horse: they tried to understand present-day institutions (about which they could secure data) in terms of remote beginnings (about which they could secure no data). Their chief clue to the remote past was

[11] Durkheim, *op. cit.*, pp. 84-85.

a knowledge of contemporary societies, both civilized and "primitive." But instead of studying these societies first as going systems, they elected to "explain" them by speculating about origins. Understanding so little of the nature of human society, their speculations contained many false premises. What they needed was a thorough knowledge of the functional and structural operation of real societies before they speculated about the beginnings of society.

A perfect illustration is contained in the doctrine of survivals. Tylor, thinking in terms of geology, assumed that in each culture there exist certain social survivals which originated and functioned in a previous stage of society but have no function in the present stage. By putting these vestigial remains together he thought he could reconstruct the bygone stages.[12] But the great difficulty is how to tell a survival from a working part of society. It is perhaps fairly easy to identify a vestigial organ in the human body by showing that, homologous with similar organs in lower forms, it has lost its function. But the identification of vestigial social structures is difficult. Our rationalistic bias may lead us to assume that anything not instrumental in attaining our ends has no function. We are apt to confuse individual utility with social function and consequently to treat a great many highly important elements in society as if they were simply hangovers from the past. Nowadays we know that many of the things once considered by the evolutionary theorists as cultural fossils have great functional significance in contemporary society. Religion is one of these. Thus we return to our main point that in order to understand origins, in order to distinguish survivals, the scholar must understand the structure and operation of contemporary societies.

The evolutionary school indulged not only in a fruitless search for origins but also in a rationalistic mode of explanation. It regarded social institutions as deliberate conscious adjustments to the environment. Religious beliefs, however, are obviously nonrational. How

[12] The idea of cultural fossils is borrowed, via analogy, from the biological and geological notion of evolution. This is shown by Tylor's famous geological argument, in which he maintained that "the institutions of man are as distinctly stratified as the earth on which he lives. They succeed each other in series substantially uniform over the globe, independent of what seem the comparatively superficial differences of race and language, but shaped by similar human nature acting through successively changed conditions in savage, barbaric, and civilized life." "On a Method of Investigating the Development of Institutions," *Journal of the Royal Anthropological Institute,* XVIII, 245-272. This passage is quoted by R. H. Lowie, *Primitive Society* (New York: Horace Liveright, 1920), p. 169.

then did they arise? According to the evolutionary point of view, such beliefs either had utility to begin with (though they might now be "survivals") or they resulted from "error." The critic will point out, in contradiction, that the alleged original utility is a figment of the evolutionists' imagination, and that if religious beliefs survive beyond the period of their utility then there must be some other factor at work more powerful than utility itself. Moreover, in so far as error is involved, it is regarded by the evolutionists as resulting solely from the kind of mistakes a scientist might make in observing and interpreting his data and as being consequently subject to constant correction by the progress of knowledge. In short, the logical conclusion from the evolutionary theory is that religion will ultimately disappear, being replaced by science. An underlying assumption in this attitude is that the sole significant relation of the individual to his environment is a cognitive one. Does he have correct knowledge or has he made a mistake? But surely the role of religion in human affairs cannot be determined solely on the basis of the scientific accuracy or inaccuracy of religious beliefs.

Let us recall how religion actually operates. Our reaction to the death of a deeply loved friend or relative is not simply one of cognition. We are not satisfied merely with knowing how he died. We want something more satisfying than this cold knowledge. Our emotional equilibrium has been upset, our hopes and desires frustrated. We need, in short, an interpretation in terms of sentiments and values. Such an interpretation may not conflict with the factual understanding of death at all. We may know perfectly well that the deceased was killed in an airplane accident, and we may understand the mechanical fault that caused the accident. Still we feel the need of an additional interpretation that will enable us to accept the death emotionally. We may dwell on his sterling character or the idea that he would not have us grieve; we may take refuge in the ritualistic expression of sorrow or in the condolences of others who know our affliction; and we may find comfort in the belief that in another life we shall be reunited with him, or that God will somehow make things right in the end. Since bereavement occurs to nearly everyone, in every society there are these sentimental interpretations of death. They are not mere "errors" soon to be eliminated. They are functionally necessary for the type of creatures human beings are—feeling as well as knowing creatures. Unless we understand the personal and social importance of nonrational belief, we fail utterly to understand religion.[13]

Traditional evolutionary theory is individualistic. It is a sort of Robinson Crusoe theory of religion. All that is required is a single individual sleeping, dreaming, looking at nature, and speculating. It takes no account of the fact that religion is something held in common by a group of people, that it is traditional and institutional, that it is a part of culture. It omits the phenomena of collective ritual and worship. These aspects of religion cannot be explained as the result of idle attempts by individuals to explain their dreams or analyze nature. For an analysis of religion in relation to society we must look elsewhere than in the faded pages of evolutionary theory.

The Functional Theory of Religion

In making scientific sense of nonscientific belief and practice, in explaining religion, myth, magic, and ritual, there has been one trend of social theory more successful than the rest. This is the functional-structural type of sociological analysis developed by William Robertson Smith, an early Scottish student of Semitic society, by Emile Durkheim and his school of sociology in France, by A. R. Radcliffe-Brown and Bronislaw Malinowski and their followers in English and American anthropology, and recently by Max Weber, Talcott Parsons, and other students of German sociology. The mode of analysis toward which all of these men were driving, and to which they all contributed, assumes that society is an emergent whole determined by the organization of its parts and that, being something different from the mere sum of its parts, it cannot be understood in purely individualistic and utilitarian terms. Also, the parts of society cannot be understood apart from but only with reference to the whole. The comparative method, for example, though absolutely necessary in a science of society, must be used with a knowledge of the entire societies whose parts are compared.[14]

[13] Cf. Talcott Parsons, *The Structure of Social Action* (New York: McGraw-Hill, 1937), pp. 666-672.

[14] See Robertson Smith's treatment of adoption, inheritance, residence at marriage, acceptance rites, clan names, and feuds in *Kinship and Marriage in Early Arabia* (Cambridge: University Press, 1885), and his *Lectures on the Religion of the Semites* (London, 1894), pp. 3-4, 16, 17. This idea of the emergent whole was more explicit in Durkheim than in Smith, but did not receive full methodological exposition until Radcliffe-Brown's *The Andaman Islanders* (Cambridge: University Press, 1922), Chaps. 5 and 6, and his article, "On the Concept of Function in Social Science," *American Anthropologist*, XXXVII (July-September 1935), 394-402.

These authors held, sometimes implicitly and sometimes explicitly, that there are certain necessary conditions for the existence of any society, and that in order to survive societies have had to develop an internal organization of their members capable of meeting these conditions. Hence, in contrast to the evolutionists, these scholars did not explain social institutions in terms of their historical origins but in terms of the part they play in satisfying societal needs. They realized, of course, that the human personality also requires certain conditions for its existence, but they held that the person is partly an organic and partly a social product. Individual needs, therefore, refer to an emergent system different from that to which societal needs refer. Though closely related to the needs of a society, they are not synonymous and indeed are sometimes in conflict with them.

Among the societal requirements, the necessity of ideological and sentimental cohesion, or solidarity, is outstanding.[15] "A society depends for its existence on the presence in the minds of its members of a certain system of sentiments by which the conduct of the individual is regulated in conformity with the needs of the society." [16] The reasons people give as to why they hold these sentiments are not to be accepted as scientific explanations but rather as rationalizations or justifications. The efficacy of the sentiments in producing social cohesion in no way depends upon the understanding of this function by the members of society. In fact the sentiments prove more effective if they are not scientifically understood by the average person. One of the functions of religion is to justify, rationalize, and support the sentiments that give cohesion to the society.

Certain observations bear out this interpretation. In the first place, religion is a part of society. It is common to the group; its beliefs and practices are acquired by each individual as a member of the group. The relationships of people to the gods and the relations between the gods parallel those in the society itself. The worship of the gods is a public matter, supported by the community and performed for communal purposes. The priest has a recognized status, and in complex societies the priesthood forms a recognized class. Finally, the communicants or adherents of the religion are united by other bonds as well, so that community and church often include

[15] Smith, *Kinship and Marriage*, pp. 1, 21-25, 36-39, and *Lectures on the Religion of the Semites*, pp. 29, 258-259.

[16] Radcliffe-Brown, *The Andaman Islanders*, pp. 233-234.

the same persons. In the second place, the expression of common beliefs through collective ritual seems to enhance the individual's devotion to group ends. It strengthens his determination to observe the group norms and to rise above purely private interests. It reinforces his identification with his fellows and sharpens his separateness from members of other tribes, communities, or nations.

The functions of religion, however, cannot be thoroughly grasped until its structural principles are understood. In this connection there are several distinctions that must be considered. These are the distinctions between the sacred and the profane, between the empirical and the superempirical, between belief and ritual, and between religion and magic.

The Sacred and the Profane

In every society there is a sharp distinction between the holy, the ordinary, and the unholy. The first are things set apart by a peculiar emotional attitude, usually of respect and awe. They are imbued with special powers either advantageous or dangerous. They are not to be used in an everyday utilitarian context, but are reserved for special occasions and hedged about with taboos and restrictions of all sorts. The *ordinary* embraces whatever is not viewed with these emotions or hedged about with these restrictions. It embraces those ideas, persons, practices, and things that are regarded with an everyday attitude of commonness, utility, and familiarity. It is that which is not supposed to come into contact with or take precedence over the sacred. The *unholy* includes whatever, in the circumstances, is thought to contaminate the holy. It is the denial or subordination of the holy in some way. The attitudes and behavior toward it are charged with negative emotion and hedged about by strong taboos. Clearly the holy and the unholy are closely related because of the highly emotional attitude toward them. They both stand in contrast to the ordinary. For this reason the usual distinction between the sacred and the profane is ambiguous. It is not always clear whether the unholy is included in the sacred or the profane. A threefold distinction therefore seems preferable.[17]

[17] When the term "sacred" occurs here, it is employed as a synonym of "holy." When the term "profane" occurs, it is used to embrace both the ordinary and the unholy. This usage is followed because the unholy generally consists of an unauthorized contact between the ordinary and the holy. This is what is meant by "profanation."

It is the holy in the first place and the unholy in the second place with which religion is chiefly concerned. Religious beliefs—embracing ideas, myths, legends, and dogmas—are notions concerning holy and unholy things. Religious rites are ways of paying respect to holy things and avoiding unholy things. The important question in the study of religion therefore becomes, "What is the source of the sacred?" The question is baffling but not incapable of solution.

The Superempirical

What has sidetracked many observers in their efforts to account for the sacred is the fact that the sacred thing is often, though by no means always, something tangible—a physical object such as a plant, a flag, a color, a word, a place, an act, the sun, the wind, or whatnot. Hence the observer has all too frequently tried to derive the sacred from the things themselves. He has classified and analyzed sacred objects to see why they should be called sacred. Müller, for example, attempted to account for the deification of natural phenomena in terms of the mystery and impressiveness of these objects, but the worship of the cow among the Hindus or of the water-hole among the Murngin would hardly fit this explanation. Wallis attempted to deal with religions according to the kinds of objects they worship—cow-worshiping religions, tree-worshiping religions, sun-worshiping religions, fire-worshiping religions, etc.[18] But the criterion of the sacred is clearly an attitude, not the intrinsic property of the objects toward which this attitude is fortuitously directed. It requires little reflection to see that sacred things are *symbols,* and that their significance lies in what they symbolize rather than in what they are. They are utilized in a sacred context because of their symbolic rather than because of their intrinsic properties. When sacred wine is drunk, it is not drunk simply for the purpose for which ordinary wine is drunk. It is drunk, rather, as a symbol. When a cow is worshiped, it is not worshiped because of the kind of animal the cow is, for the cow (from a physiological and anatomical point of view) resembles many animals which are not worshiped. If we are to understand the source of the sacred, we must turn not to the

[18] Wilson D. Wallis, *Religion in Primitive Society* (New York: Crofts, 1939), Chaps. 3-7.

objects themselves but to the meanings that they symbolize. What are these meanings?

In some cases sacred objects seem to symbolize little more than the attitude of respect itself. But generally it will be found in such instances that the *situation* in which the sacred object is employed gives the clue to a symbolic reference. This reference is either to other tangible objects or to intangible entities such as values, social forms, or superempirical beings. Undoubtedly symbolism plays an enormous role in religious life, and the chief reason would seem to be that the realities with which religion deals are intangible realities. If they are to be represented at all in the sensory world, they must be represented symbolically. Christian baptism is nothing at all when taken literally. Sprinkling water on people's heads is not ordinarily a religious rite, but when done in a particular situation and accompanied by certain attitudes, it acquires a religious significance because it then symbolizes certain sacred but intangible "realities." How else could these "realities" be made real, definite, simple, and comprehensible except by some mode of representing them in the sensory world? The sensory world, in and of itself, is not sacred but profane or ordinary. Only that part of it which in one way or another represents the intangible world of sentiments and values, souls and deities, powers and potentialities, acquires the sacred quality—a quality which is added to and apart from, and certainly not deducible from its sensory attributes.

We now glimpse the importance of the nonsensory, or superempirical, world. Religious belief and practice are primarily directed toward superempirical realities; these for purposes of definition and convenience may be classified under three heads: subjective states of mind (peace, salvation, nirvana), transcendental ends (immortality, purification), and imaginary creatures and objects (gods, spirits, centaurs, heavens, hells). The characteristic of these realities is their intangibility. Since they cannot be observed directly, they can only be represented or symbolized by sensory reality. Concrete objects which happen to be sacred are not sacred because of their sensory qualities but because of their symbolic connection with the superempirical realities.

Our answer to the question, what are sacred things, leads naturally to two additional questions. First, why should human beings harbor beliefs about imaginary entities and cherish transcendental ends? Second, why should they feel a peculiar attitude of reverence and rightness, fear and subserviance, toward these entities and ends? It is the insight of certain great sociologists that the answers to these questions cannot be found in the organic individual, nor yet in the external environment, but only in society. But the important consideration is *how*. How are the superempirical realities and the attitudes of respect and awe toward them related to society specifically?

A rough and not quite adequate account of the connection is the following. Society, on which the individual is absolutely dependent, which has an existence before and beyond the individual, yet which exists only by becoming a part of each individual's inner consciousness, is in the last analysis the only thing that has the power to inspire the feeling of awe. Since it (society) has a nature peculiar to itself and different from the individual, it attains results that are special and necessary to itself. But since it cannot attain these results except through the activities of its members, it requires the unconscious cooperation of these members. It requires that, forgetful of their purely organic interests, they make themselves its servitors; and it submits them to every sort of inconvenience, privation, and sacrifice without which society would be impossible. At every instant the members are obliged to submit to rules of conduct and thought which they would otherwise neither make nor desire and which are sometimes even contrary to the most fundamental inclinations and instincts.[19] But society is not sufficiently concrete, not sufficiently particular and simple, to become the direct object of reverential submission; so the individual feels his dependence not directly but in a number of indirect ways. One way is in the feeling of dependence toward everything important to the maintenance of society—the essential norms, the system of statuses, and the group ends. Another way is in the feeling of reverence toward an imaginary symbol of society, such as God—the superiority of God to man unconsciously representing the superiority of society to man. And a third way is in the feeling of awe or respect toward a concrete symbol of the imaginary symbol of society—e.g. the figure of Jesus on the cross standing for God.

[19] Durkheim, *Elementary Forms of the Religious Life,* p. 207. Radcliffe-Brown, *The Andaman Islanders,* pp. 257-258, 319.

This account (attributable primarily to Durkheim), striking though it may be, is not quite adequate. It undertakes to identify society as the empirical reality that sacred symbols symbolize. But obviously sacred objects do not symbolize society at all. They symbolize nonexistent entities—creatures and principles of the other world. The relation of these to society is not a symbolic relation but only a functional one: the effect of the beliefs and rites with respect to sacred symbols is to create a more cohesive society.

When Americans use the term "cow" they are using a symbol that refers to a given kind of animal. When a Hindu uses the term, however, he refers not merely to this animal as such but also to a host of superempirical characteristics which this animal is imagined to represent. The following passage makes this clear.

> "The cow is of all animals the most sacred. Every part of its body is inhabited by some deity or other. Every hair on its body is inviolable. All its excreta are hallowed. Not a particle ought to be thrown away as impure. On the contrary, the water it ejects ought to be preserved as the best of holy waters—a sin-destroying liquid which sanctifies everything it touches, while nothing purifies like cow-dung. Any spot which a cow has condescended to honor with the sacred deposit of her excrement is forever afterwards consecrated ground, and the filthiest place plastered with it is at once cleansed and freed from pollution, while the ashes produced by burning this hallowed substance are of such a holy nature that they not only make clean all material things, however previously unclean, but have only to be sprinkled over a sinner to convert him into a saint."
>
> To this it should be added that on certain occasions cows receive divine honors and are treated as if they were real and present deities. They are garlanded, water is poured on their feet, oil and yellow powder are placed on their foreheads. Further, the expiatory rite prescribed for grave social and religious offences consists of tasting a mixture of the cow's five products, . . .[20]

Obviously the Hindu cow does not symbolize Hindu society. It symbolizes those things that its devotees believe it symbolizes. But the fact that the Hindus all reverence the cow gives them a common bond. Cow worship, according to Mr. Gandhi, is "the central fact

[20] L. S. S. O'Malley, *Popular Hinduism* (Cambridge: University Press, 1935), pp. 15-16. The quotation in the first paragraph is taken from M. Monier-Williams, *Brahmanism and Hinduism* (4th ed., 1931), p. 318.

of Hinduism, the one concrete belief common to all Hindus." [21] It is therefore a rallying point giving cohesion to Hindu society. Furthermore, it furnishes definite rules of conduct for Hindus and thus constitutes an element in their social organization.

> According to a verse in the Mahabharata all who eat, kill, or permit the slaughter of, a cow are doomed to rot in hell for as many years as there are hairs on her body. The killing of cows formerly rendered a man liable to capital punishment, and it is still a penal offence in some States under Hindu rulers; in Kashmir, for example, the maximum penalty is seven years' imprisonment. It is not a penal offence in British India, but the Hindu community outcastes any man who kills a cow or eats her flesh: an exception must be made of some untouchables who will eat the flesh of a cow which has died a natural death. A man whose cow dies not through any deliberate act of his, but through his neglect or carelessness, is obliged to make atonement by means of a penance; one penance which is designed to make the punishment fit the crime is for the delinquent to leave his home for a certain time, and beg his daily bread by lowing like a cow, without using human speech.[22]

In addition, cow worship sets the Hindu community off from others that do not view the cow as sacred.

> Strong men will be moved to tears by the thought that a cow will be or is being sacrificed by Muslims, even though this is done in strict seclusion so as not to offend Hindu susceptibilities. The sight of a cow being openly led away for sacrifice often rouses Hindus to fanatical frenzy, resulting in bloody riots: in one of the districts of the United Provinces in 1931 eleven Muslims were brutally killed by a crowd of Hindus, simply because a Muslim landholder sent a haunch of venison to one of his tenants and the villagers, quick to imagine evil, thought that it was beef.[23]

The cow as a sacred symbol thus contributes to the ethnocentrism and hence to the solidarity of the Hindus. It also ramifies into the technology and the economy of Hindu society. The unwillingness to breed cattle scientifically, to kill them or to eat them, handicaps rural India in many ways; but to the Hindu these consequences are

[21] *Ibid.*, p. 14.
[22] *Ibid.*, pp. 16-17.
[23] *Ibid.*, p. 17.

less important than the otherworldly aspects. It is only as a sacred symbol that the cow serves social unity. If the symbol were not the cow, then it would be some other concrete object. Every cohesive social group has such symbols. It is not the object itself but the superempirical meaning attached to it that is sociologically significant.

Ultimate Ends and Religion

Preceding chapters have viewed the problem of social order as the peaceful allocation of scarce means to competitive ends. Repeatedly the fact has emerged that individuals are not permitted, and cannot be permitted, to pursue their private ends by whatever means their ingenuity might suggest. We have seen that political authority arbitrarily adjusts and enforces the rules of distribution, and that it does so not in the name of any private interest but in the name of the group as a whole. Group ends are and must be superior to private ends. Now we must ask what is the source of the ultimate group ends, and what is the role of religion with reference to them.

The question can be put in the form of a paradox: Since ends exist only in the minds of individuals, how does it happen that individuals do not place their private ends uppermost? Obviously each person is strongly indoctrinated with group ends in his youth. But the real question is why and how societies come to stress this indoctrination, and how its effects are maintained long after the period of youth is over. We know that if societies did not do this, they could not survive; but the question is how.

The ultimate ends are not inherited. They are not found in external nature. They must, therefore, arise as a cultural emergent. They must spring from the dynamics of communicative interaction in a group that maintains itself by cultural adaptation. Since they are not derived from biological urges on the one hand or from logical reasoning on the other, they have a subjective and a transcendent quality—an existence only in the indoctrinated mind.

But inevitably, since the actor has physical urges and must act in the factual world, his ultimate values and ends must be related to physical reality in some way. They cannot be left simply *in abstracto* in his mind, but on the contrary must be related very definitely to his needs, drives, capacities, and to the conditions of his environment; for it is these things that the ultimate values and ends control. To the external observer, not sharing in the subjective states of the actor (as when a Westerner observes a Hindu), the ultimate values appear unreal, but they are real to the actor and are real in their consequences. The actor's sense of their reality is enhanced by an imaginary world which he believes to exist but which he cannot see or touch. This imaginary world—the supernatural or super-empirical—can then appear to him to be a source of his ultimate values and ends. It is to this imaginary world, indeed, that they are in his mind intimately related; through it they become plausible and necessary.

The unseen world is of course fictitious, but it must appear real to the actor if it is to accomplish its function of rationalizing and justifying his ultimate group ends. The proof of its reality, for him, lies in what he believes to be its manifestations in the tangible world. Certain phenomena of the tangible world are taken as indices or symbols of the supernatural. There is thus a triangular relationship. At one corner are his ultimate values. At another corner are the supernatural entities which he imagines to explain and require these values. And at the third corner are certain phenomena in the sensory world which he believes to manifest and validate the supernatural entities. The last are what we have called sacred objects. Between them and the imaginary entities there can be no intrinsic or causal relation in the scientific sense, but only a symbolic relation. The connection is established only by faith, not by observation. But once having established by indoctrination a symbolic connection between the two, the individual can then relate his ultimate values directly to the sacred objects. They come to symbolize his values and serve as a rallying point for all those who share the same values. Furthermore, the sacred objects (as distinct from the unseen entities which they represent) are tangible, capable of being seen, heard, felt, and tasted. They therefore convey a sense of reality not only as concerns the supernatural world but also with respect to the values themselves.

Since the ultimate values and ends control the organic urges, they must acquire a powerful grip upon the individual. The belief in the supernatural world and the preoccupation with sacred objects help to tighten this grip. Such belief is made possible by the suggestibility of the human mind, which can acquire fictitious ideas through communication and can then react to these as if they were real. The human mind can acquire the point of view of others toward itself and can consequently project itself beyond the limits of time and space. It can, in short, become a part of the socio-cultural emergent. The infant learns the concepts of the superempirical world and the meanings of sacred objects just as he learns the concepts and meanings of the sensory world. Conceived along lines analogous to the real, the supernatural world is easy to grasp; and being imaginary, it can be easily played with and manipulated by the mind. It is much more flexible than the sensory world which is resistant to human desire and insensitive to human values. Furthermore even organically derived ends, gratifiable in the empirical world, become in the mind of the individual even more attainable through the agency of the superempirical world; for the powers of the supernatural world are superior to those of the sensory world. It is no wonder then that the individual comes to view this illusory realm with profound emotion, that he conceives the ultimate values and ends and the sacred objects not merely in an intellectual manner but also in an emotional and sentimental way, and that he pursues these ends and values even when his organic urges are being deprived. It is in this way that, though in a sense fictitious, the group ends and values nevertheless become real, ascendant, and ultimate to the believer.

The imaginary world, unsupported as it is by organic drives or factual knowledge, would be in danger of losing its grip on the mind if it were not constantly renewed by frequent contact with others holding the same transcendent beliefs. Consequently, collective communication is the best method of renewing the otherworldly beliefs and the values that go with them. Thus interaction in a form containing the utmost suggestibility and crowd interstimulation—public ritual, symbolic, expressive, rhythmic, repetitive, conventional, and colorful, with much use of sacred objects—becomes the chief instrumentality for reviving the actor's devotion to ultimate values and his belief in the fictitious world.

As applied in conduct the ultimate values and ends of course lead to the observance of the mores. They are the goals which the mores are thought to achieve. Moreover, the supernatural world is a convenient one for imagining that the good is inevitably rewarded and the bad inevitably punished. The same attitude of respect that is directed toward the ultimate values, superempirical entities, and sacred objects is also directed toward the mores. The latter, like the values themselves, receive their final justification and rationalization in terms of the superempirical world.

We are now back at the point where we left the Durkheimian theory of religion. We had raised the question, why the superempirical and why the attitude of emotion toward it? Having now brought the analysis of ends and means to bear on the problem, we are in a position to improve on Durkheim's solution. He had said that sacred objects symbolize society. We now see that they symbolize the things of the unseen world, and that the unseen world gives the actor a source and final justification for his group ends—ends that he shares with other members of his society.

Religion, then, does four things that help to maintain the dominance of sentiment over organic desire, of group ends over private interest. First it offers, through its system of supernatural belief, an explanation of the group ends and a justification of their primacy. Second it provides, through its collective ritual, a means for the constant renewal of the common sentiments. Third it furnishes, through its sacred objects, a concrete reference for the values and a rallying point for all persons who share the same values. Fourth it provides an unlimited and insuperable source of rewards and punishments—rewards for good conduct, punishments for bad. In these ways religion makes a unique and indispensable contribution to social integration.

Anthropomorphism and Moral Determinism

That part of the superempirical realm which is composed of fictitious entities—the supernatural, strictly speaking—has two features that confirm our interpretation: first, it is conceived anthropomorphically; second, it is regarded as causally dominant over the sensory world.

Why the supernatural should be anthropomorphically conceived seems clear. Being "human" is essentially a matter of feeling human emotions, sharing human values, and responding to human communication. Since the function of the fictitious world is to bolster the ultimate common values, the supernatural entities—whatever their external form is conceived to be, whether as inanimate objects, animals, spirits, men, or strange combinations—should be endowed with something like a human will and hence be responsive to human communication and guided by basically human motives. Moreover we conceive causation most easily in terms of the agency of human action. Accordingly if the imaginary world is to take causal primacy over the sensory world as its function requires, its creatures must be visualized as having an essentially human outlook.

In primitive and peasant societies supernatural beings exercise a powerful influence on thought and behavior. Not only are they constantly and dramatically real, but they are ultimately responsible for whatever happens. Men die because of evil spirits or black magic. Crops grow because of magic, prayer, or right living. Thus arises a sort of spiritual hegemony, a dominance of the spirit world over the actual world. Since the denizens of this spirit world, being anthropomorphically conceived, are responsive to men's deeds, they punish the violation of taboos and reward the observance of the mores. In this way the hegemony of the spiritual over the factual world implies a sort of moral determinism, which at bottom makes the morality of man the final cause of events in the physical world.

The assumption of moral determinism is firmly rooted in the human mind. Piaget experimented by telling a child about a man who had done something wrong. When this person was later crossing a bridge, the bridge fell down. Piaget asked the child why the bridge had collapsed at this moment. The response was that it had fallen because of the bad thing the man had done. "How many simple souls still think," says Piaget, "that even in this life people's actions are the object of equitable rewards and punishments, and would rather assume some hidden fault to explain a neighbor's misfortune than admit the fortuitous character in the trials that befall mankind." [24]

The spiritual realm naturally operates as a powerful instrument of social control. When an individual sins, he feels guilty; and by the well-known process of projection he unconsciously assumes a hostile attitude on the part of the supernatural beings. Their retaliation may be reserved for the next life or it may come in this life. Innumerable are the cultures in which some form of sickness is thought to result from a violation of certain norms. Among some tribes in Africa, for example, it is believed that if the relatives of

[24] Jean Piaget, *The Moral Judgment of the Child* (New York: Harcourt, Brace, 1932), p. 261.

an orphan do not give the child its rightful social position, the ghost of the child's father may inflict disease upon them.[25] The gods are most concerned with the rites and taboos with reference to themselves and to sacred objects, but they usually keep the general mores in mind too. Not only injury but also benefits may come from spiritual forces. If one wants something, the best way to get it is through the supernatural agency. Fish may be caught by fish magic, women by love magic.

This moral determinism, so essential in giving weight and sting to the ultimate values, is possible only by fiction; for the empirical world is not in fact morally determined. Human acts, sins, and virtues have far less effect upon external events than such determinism claims. To create the illusion of moral determinism it is necessary to invent a supernatural realm. Once created, this realm is of such consequence that its forces must be dealt with in some definite way, not left to mere chance or inexpert handling. Therefore the services of a professional practitioner—a shaman, medicine man, magician, priest, or seer—must be secured.

Religion and Personality

Religion helps to integrate not only the society but also the personality. The human mind, it will be recalled, is in large part a social product. Through communication with other minds each person acquires a system of goals that channelize the energies of the organism. At the apex of this system are certain ultimate goals. Some of these such as salvation, divine grace, eternal bliss, immortality—transcend factual experience and hence clearly imply religious belief. Others, such as national glory, the advancement of knowledge, the relief of suffering, or the diffusion of a faith, more clearly relate to this world but transcend the individual himself. Still others, such as prestige, esteem, and affection, relate to the individual in this world but are limited as to means by religious and moral considerations. It turns out, then, that the ultimate goals either have a direct religious reference and transcend the individual, or they are limited as to means by religious and moral restrictions. It is these ultimate goals that give the individual his life organization.

[25] W. H. R. Rivers, *Medicine, Magic, and Religion* (New York: Harcourt, Brace, 1924), p. 71.

So long as one's goals relate to this world, frustration is possible. If the aim is to propagate a faith, persecution may bring failure. If the aim is to achieve world mastery for one's country, a disastrous war may bring hopelessness. If the aim is to achieve fame, a mediocre career may bring disillusionment. With a multiplicity of goals no individual can escape frustration. Yet the ego can stand only a certain amount of frustration. Often it attempts to restore the balance by aggression, but the way of aggression is frequently blocked. In that case another avenue is open to him. The culture which drives him to seek goals that he cannot reach also, for the sake of sanity, provides him with goals that anybody can reach. These are goals that transcend the world of actual experience, with the consequence that no evidence of failure to attain them can be conclusive. If the individual believes that he has gained them, that is sufficient. All he needs is sufficient faith, and faith feeds on subjective need. The greater his disappointment in this life, the greater his faith in the next. Thus the existence of goals beyond this world serves to compensate people for the frustrations they inevitably experience in striving to reach socially acquired and socially valuable ends. It replaces a possibly dangerous aggression with a benevolent faith in the unseen. By giving him a world beyond this one, a sort of invisible shell around the factual sphere, the culture enables the individual to interpret any catastrophe as intermediate and secondary, leaving the road open to ultimate happiness.

But superempirical goals would be difficult to hold if there were not at the same time some belief in the actual existence of a superempirical realm in which the goals can really be reached. This belief in the superempirical would in turn be difficult if there were not concrete objects and concrete acts which constantly remind the individual of the existence of this realm. Thus the presence of sacred objects and participation in sacred ritual serve to comfort the individual, to reassure him in his faith. Common worship, prayer, and meditation, singing hymns, counting the rosary, making offerings, contemplating the Crucifix—these are all familiar means of renewing the faith and gaining comfort in Christianity.

Religion thus gives release from sorrow and release from fear. It also provides release from the very thing it instils, guilt. The social norms require behavior that no individual can completely live up to, because he has an organism that cannot be completely regimented and because the norms themselves are in conflict. The ego cannot stand too strong a sense of sorrow or of failure. Again nonempirical goals and the nonempirical world come to his aid. Ritual means are freely provided for wiping away guilt, so that one can count on divine grace.

Finally, religion gives the individual a sense of identity with the distant past and the limitless future. It expands his ego by making his spirit significant for the universe and the universe significant for him. When he changes his status—when for example he reaches puberty, gets married, has a child, becomes a widower, or lapses into old age—the expression of religious sentiment through ritual contact with sacred objects helps to reconcile him to the change if it is saddening and to impress its importance upon him if it is cheering.

In these ways religion contributes to the integration of the personality. But like other medicines it can sometimes make worse the very thing it seeks to remedy. Innumerable are the psychoses and neuroses that have a religious content. The superempirical world is so elastic, so susceptible of manipulation by the imagination, that the disordered mind can seize upon it to spin itself into almost any kind of bizarre pattern. It is a prop which takes courage to do without but which one dares not lean on too heavily.

Belief and Ritual

It has become evident that the holy or sacred is the heart of religion. What makes a thing holy, however, is nothing inhering in the thing itself but simply an attitude inhering in the mind. It is an attitude packed with emotion and sentiment, a feeling that certain things are above and apart from the ordinary matters of everyday life. Resting on this subjective attitude are two different aspects of the holy—namely, belief and ritual.

Religious belief is the cognitive aspect of religion: it attempts to explain the nature and origin of sacred things and implicitly assumes that they exist. It refers in the first place to the superempirical world, telling us what this world is like, what kind of creatures inhabit it, and what their past history and present interests are; above all, it tells us how this world is related to the one we actually live in. This means, in the second place, that religious belief tells us also what the nature of sacred objects is and how these objects relate to the superempirical world. In both cases—whether it refers to the invisible things beyond the senses or to the sacred objects within plain view—the belief rests upon an attitude, not upon observation. It is belief based upon faith rather than upon evidence; it is in Biblical language the substance of things hoped for, the evidence of things not seen. Even the sacred object, tangible as it seems, would be just an ordinary object if it were not for the belief, because its sacred character is not observable to the senses. There is nothing to distinguish a sacred cow from any other cow, except the faith of those who regard her as sacred.

Religious ritual is the active side of religion. It is behavior with reference to superempirical entities and sacred objects. Like the belief itself, it comes to have a quality of sacredness attached to it. It is highly circumscribed as to time and place, expressive of the internal attitude, symbolic of the unseen powers. It can include any kind of behavior known, such as the wearing of special clothing, the recitation of special formulas, and the immersion in certain rivers; it can include singing, dancing, weeping, bowing, crawling, starving, feasting, reading, etc. The religious character of the behavior, as in the case of sacred objects, does not come from the behavior itself but from the attitude taken toward it. The same motions, the same acts, may be holy in one context but either ordinary or unholy in another. Ritual helps to remind the individual of the holy realm, to revivify and strengthen his faith in this realm. It enables him to give expression to his religious sentiments and thereby to achieve an emotional catharsis. Ritual is especially effective if performed by several individuals, because then the factor of group stimulation (plus dramatic continuity) heightens the emotionality and makes the subjective impression all the more vivid. Since, however, isolation from the group is an unusual circumstance, advantage may be taken of the rarity of this circumstance to incorporate such isolation as part of religious ritual. By communing with himself, the individual communes also with God.

Both belief and ritual must be understood if religion is to be understood. One of the faults of the older theories was that they emphasized the intellectual aspect of religion and ignored the ritual aspect. They continually posed the problem of whether or not religious beliefs are true; and if not true, how they came to be held. Our analysis has attempted to show that the question is secondary. Religious beliefs are certainly not true in any scientific sense, but their social function does not depend on their being true. It merely depends on their being held. In fact, their untruth—the fact that they transcend experience—offers the main key to their social function. They are effective precisely because they are scientifically false. This brings us to the conflict between religion and science.

Religion versus Science

Viewed in one way there is no conflict between religion and science, but viewed another way there is implacable conflict. Both views are correct; they merely stress different aspects of the relationship. Let us discuss each in turn.

The no-conflict view points out that religious beliefs refer to the world beyond the senses. Therefore if they cannot be proved by the methods of science, neither can they be disproved. Another way of expressing it is that religion deals with first causes, science with immediate ones. A scientist can believe in God and yet be a perfectly good biologist; he merely sees the facts and principles of biology as so many manifestations of God's handiwork. His behavior in the laboratory can be appropriate to the scientific situation and his behavior in church appropriate to the religious situation, with no feeling of incongruity.

This is all right as far as it goes, but we know in fact that although many great scientists have been pious men, many others have been atheists; and we know too that many of them, both pious and impious, have had serious trouble with organized religion because of their scientific views. The root of the difficulty is in part this: The boundary between the unknown and the known is a shifting one. What was unknown yesterday is known today. Only a short while ago the origin of man on the earth was unknown to the human intellect. Religious belief filled in the gap by giving a very precise account of man's origin. The account was believed because it was thought to be divinely revealed. Eventually, however, scientific investigation began to bring the earthly origin of man into the factual domain. Here, then, there was serious conflict. The scientist could not accept the religious account as literally true and still be true to his science. Furthermore, he lived among people who were not scientists and who consequently held tenaciously to the old view long after science had disproved it. This situation created tension between him and the ordinary layman or the religious official. So long as the frontier between the known and the unknown is a shifting one, so long in other words as science is expanding, there will be conflict between religion and science. Neither one will be vanquished by this conflict, for as religion loses the battles it merely retreats to higher levels. The religious ideology grows more and more vague, more and more philosophical, and less and less anthropomorphic. It changes from fundamentalist to liberal, from dogma to philosophy.

Another root of conflict lies in the fact that science, like any other organized pursuit, possesses a faith of its own. It develops habits of mind and ethical attitudes different from those prevailing in the traditional religions. The scientific pursuit of empirical truth as the highest goal is exactly the opposite of the religious pursuit of nonempirical truth. The scientist develops an ingrained scepticism about existential propositions, by whomever made. He is thus likely to view with some scepticism statements about the nature of heaven, the life after death, the harmfulness of sin, the occurrence of miracles, and the revealed character of the Bible. Religion retreats from such scepticism by re-interpreting its propositions, making them symbolic and allegorical rather than literal. It also retreats by emphasizing the importance of religious sentiments as against religious beliefs. But it never surrenders.

The sharpest conflict between religion and science comes when religion itself is subjected to scientific analysis. Dependent as it is upon subjective faith, religion withers like a leaf before a flame when the scientific attitude is brought to bear on it. Thus the man who goes to church not with the idea of worshiping but with the idea of analyzing the causes of the behavior he observes will not find himself in tune with the occasion. He is similar to a man who goes to a football game not with the intention of watching the play but with the intention of watching the strange cries and antics of the crowd. If everyone in the crowd took the same attitude there would be no enthusiasm, no spirit to the thing. Systematic analysis is the opposite of crowd enthusiasm. If the public in general undertook an analysis of religious behavior, using systematic research tools, it would be the death of religion. Needless to say, such an eventuality is not likely. Most scientists will attempt to analyze everything else before they will ever tackle religion, and most laymen cannot even understand the statement of the problem. What passes for religious study is usually the history of religious doctrine, not the scientific explanation of religious behavior itself.

Religion and Magic

Since the spiritual world is conceived to be causally ascendant over the physical world, its powers are inevitably used for private as well as for public ends. Indeed these powers may even be used for ends not sanctioned by the group, but in this case the individual is indulging in black magic, a dangerous art that must be secretly and carefully handled. The relation between religion on the one hand and magic (whether white or black) on the other is necessarily a close one, yet the two spheres can be distinguished.

What we have been calling religion represents really one pole of a range of phenomena which, at the other pole, shades into magic. Thus we should not think of the difference between magic and religion as a rigid dichotomy but rather as a wide gradation involving several rather independent variables.[26] What they have in common is the reference to a supernatural realm, but they differ with respect to (a) the kind of ends pursued, (b) the type of attitudes involved, (c) the particular kind of supernaturalism required, and (d) the pattern of behavior exhibited. Let us consider the variation with respect to each of these.

The magical as distinct from the religious pole implies that a definite end is being pursued and that this end is immediate, practical, and usually private. Much of religion has no definite end. It is not used as a means but stands as an end in itself. In those instances when religious behavior or holy objects are used to attain an end, the end is either ultimate (lying outside the practical world) or public, held by the group in common and relating to group destiny. When a person prays to God to absolve him from his sins and help him to attain immortality, we do not hesitate to call the behavior religious although it is a private end that is being pursued. Similarly, when the members of a village come together in a temple to pray God for rain, we do not scruple to call the behavior religious

[26] Cf. Wm. J. Goode, *The Sociology of Primitive Religion* (unpublished doctoral dissertation at The Pennsylvania State College), Chap. 5, pp. 145-168.

although it is a practical end that is being sought. The following behavior, however, would appear more magical than religious.

> Among the Northern Chins, a sick man believing his bad luck due to the agency of an angry deity, offers a young fowl or small dog in sacrifice. If he recovers, it is a sign that the divinities are propitiated.[27]

The end in this case is both private and practical.

In religion emphasis is placed on the subjective attitude of the participants. Feelings of awe, reverence, elevation, and inspiration are experienced with reference to the holy. In magic, on the other hand, the attitude is more matter of fact, being much the same kind of attitude one would hold when using any ordinary technological device. E. E. Evans-Pritchard, in describing the Zande people of the upper Nile, says:

> In asking a medicine to act on his behalf a man does not beseech it to do so. He is not entreating it to grant a favor. He tells it what it is to do, just as he would tell a boy were he dispatching him on an errand. Most spells are spoken in normal, matter-of-fact voices and the medicines are addressed in a casual manner that has often surprised me.[28]

As previously mentioned, religion brings into play an entire supernatural world with creatures in it who are capable of responding to human wishes and human sorrows. Magic may accomplish its effects through the agency of these creatures, but on the other hand it may accomplish its effect simply by automatic action. In magic, in other words, the supernatural agency may be nothing more than an imaginary force or principle, imputed to certain objects because of some superficial analogy.

> In order to secure long life for themselves, the Eskimo sew to their clothing bits of the hearth stone, which has proved its enduring qualities by resisting the fire. Similarly, to make a boy a great hunter, they sew on the talons of the hawk, the greatest hunter of the Arctic.[29]

[27] Cited by John Lee Maddox, *The Medicine Man* (New York: Macmillan), p. 178.

[28] *Witchcraft, Oracles and Magic among the Azande* (Oxford: Clarendon Press, 1937), p. 452. Quoted in Goode, *op. cit.*, p. 154.

[29] Ruth Benedict in Franz Boas *et al., General Anthropology* (Boston: Heath, 1938), p. 635.

The intellectual content of magic is thus narrowed by its highly utilitarian purpose. In some cases, as when the principle of like cures like is being followed, it is narrowed to the vanishing point. The intellectual content of religion, on the other hand, is wide because of the kind of questions it poses and the kind of ends with which it is connected. It includes myths as to the origin of man and his major institutions, accounts of the gods, elaborate rituals and ceremonies. In some instances magic relates to these too and thus comes close to being religious, but in other instances this whole intellectual world is absent from the situation; instead there is merely a reliance upon some supernatural property acting automatically.

When a magician is involved, magical behavior may become almost purely a commercial transaction. Trickery and deceit become possible; the magician's customer must be on his guard against it. The practitioner is supposed to deliver a real service and though in most cases he can conceal his failures and parade his victories, he is sometimes held to account.

> Among the Bari people, the doctor who does not succeed in bringing rain when it is needed, loses not only his reputation and practice, but also his head. In 1859 the people experienced a terrible famine, and they demanded of the rain doctor that he bring rain at once. He exerted all his powers but in vain. The drought continued. Thereupon the indignant people killed him.[30]

Magic diverges most from religion when it is used to accompish aims not sanctioned by the group. It may be employed to achieve vengeance, to acquire property illegally, to steal another man's wife, to commit murder, etc. In such cases it has to be carried out in secret. The members of the group are apt to fear black magic, and in societies where it is part of the culture the members of the community must so conduct themselves as not to be accused of it. A disaster is likely to be blamed on someone's secret sorcery, and the person blamed may consequently be made the scapegoat. It has not been very long since witches were burned in Europe and America. In India such behavior is more recent as the following shows:

[30] Maddox, *op. cit.*, p. 152, citing A. G. Ellis, *Tshi-Speaking Peoples* (London: 1887), p. 124.

> The witch is in a different category from the exorcist. The latter has a recognized profession and his services can be hired and put to good use in driving away evil spirits. Witches, on the other hand, work secretly for evil ends and they are charged with the wickedness attributed to witches all the world over. They have the power of the evil eye; they cast spells; they make images of the persons they desire to kill or torture and pierce them with pins and needles, thorns and nails; they assemble at night at places of burial and cremation, strip naked, and chant unholy incantations. Women believed to be witches are consequently feared, hated, and sometimes put to death; there were nine murders due to this cause in Bihar in the year 1928. In Malabar . . . the sorcerers, who are known as Odiyans, are drawn mainly from two low castes, the Paraiyans (Pariahs) and Panans. There is also a class of men called Mantravadis, who make and deal in magic spells which can be used either against an enemy or for self-protection against a sorcerer's machinations.[31]

Black magic sometimes contributes to a sense of social well-being when a scapegoat can be found and held responsible for a group tragedy. It contributes to social cohesion when it is attributed to members of an enemy tribe or nation. Also, in some rare instances, accusations of black magic can be used as a means of bringing grudges into the open and submitting them to public opinion.[32] But in general it must be viewed as a cultural aberration. It is the penalty paid at the magical pole for the societal functions achieved at the religious pole.

One of the most popular theories of magic is that it is a type of primitive science. This is because it pursues practical ends, conceives certain effects to follow automatically from certain conditions, takes a nonemotional or impersonal attitude toward the causation, and has little to do with morality. Despite such analogies, however, magic is in many ways the opposite of science. Above all it departs from science in positing supernatural causation. Between the spell, rite, or object and its effect there is assumed to be a mystical power or spiritual agency which produces the effect. Furthermore in magic the facts are not used to test the theory as in science, but rather the theory—the magical procedure—is always assumed to be right.

[31] O'Malley, *op. cit.*, pp. 162-163.

[32] The Azande, previously mentioned, are a case in point. Evans-Pritchard, *op. cit.*, shows clearly the role of sorcery in the solution of conflict and the maintenance of the normative system among these people.

Here the element of faith and wishful thinking enters. A failure is therefore attributed to a failure to carry out the procedure correctly, not to the procedure itself. The tricks of the magician are used to hide failure and to give his client a false confidence in the efficacy of the performance. In fact the function of magic is to give confidence and a sense of security, and for this reason the individual must have a nonrational faith in its adequacy. Accordingly it can exist side by side with perfectly good technological and scientific practices. During World War II, as everybody knows, many of the aviators, trained in science and flying the most complicated machines that science had invented, carried along rabbits' feet, crosses, animals, articles of clothing, mystic numbers, or other articles that were supposed to give them luck. Science is always tentative and partial. It deals in probabilities, not in absolutes. Magic deals in absolutes and can therefore give confidence in a way that science cannot. It therefore does not disappear as technology and science advance, though it becomes less important.

In summary it can be said that some of the elements of magic overlap with science and some overlap with religion, but that as a whole it is different from either. Any given behavior may have elements of all three in it. The primary function of magic is apparently to give one a sense of confidence and security in the prosecution of one's mundane affairs. This function can often be quite useful, as when it helps to inspire a group for warfare or helps to overcome a neurotic ailment. It sometimes serves as a scapegoat mechanism. But it can also hold back scientific advance and can cause fear and strife within the community. Its functions are less essential than those of religion on the one hand and of science and technology on the other.

Religion in Modern Civilization

So long as one attributes religion merely to an error in reasoning, its future seems dim. One simply imagines that science will increasingly expose the error and religion will then disappear. One may even cite the decline of religion in modern society as evidence for this contention.

But this rationalistic point of view itself falls into an error. It fails to see that the nonrational character of religion performs a function for both the society and the personality, and that therefore it will not be overcome simply by substituting scientific explanations for religious explanations of the universe. A boy who is in love will not necessarily cease to be in love because he is told that his girl is merely a bundle of cells like any other mammal.

Admittedly there is a limit to which a society can go in non-rationality. It has to adapt itself to the actual world; consequently it must achieve a minimum ability to control and predict the events of this world. There is thus a limit on the extent to which a society can be guided by illusion and continue to operate. But, turning the question around, we can see that there is also a limit to which a society can be guided by sheer rationality. Rational thought refers to the application of means to ends; it cannot determine the ends themselves. A thief may behave more rationally and indeed more successfully than an honest citizen; the two differ not in rationality but in their moral attitudes. We have seen that one of the functions of religion is to justify and rationalize the ultimate ends of a society's members. This is a necessary function because a group must share certain values and goals in common, and this cannot be done by simply being rational. It seems unlikely, then, that science and technology can entirely replace religion, any more than the latter can entirely replace them.

This statement is not meant to imply, however, that there can be no change in the character of influence of religion as the rest of culture changes. On the contrary the study of religion shows that it changes along with the rest of society. As humanity moves from small isolated societies in the direction of huge, complex, urbanized ones, the following changes can be noted: *First,* the gods tend to be gradually withdrawn from the local scene. With diverse regions and diverse classes embraced under one religion, the gods can no longer be thought of as attached in some peculiar way to the trees, hills, and rivers of a particular locale or to the customs and habits of a particular town. The gods must necessarily become more remote. *Second,* anthropomorphism tends to diminish. The cruder conceptions of spirits and gods as definite physical types living, eating, and sleeping at some definite location in the invisible realm and closely in contact with concrete sacred objects, tend to be replaced by more abstract and generalized conceptions. *Third,* religion tends to be increasingly separated from everyday affairs. Whereas in the preliterate village religion seems to permeate nearly every act, being inextricably bound up with technological, economic, and political behavior, it is in the modern city withdrawn and put in a category by itself. The time devoted to ritual becomes lessened and segregated, the preoccupation with the supernatural becomes limited only to certain situations. *Fourth,* religious homogeneity tends to diminish. A complex civilization is also a diverse one, characterized by high mobility and the interpenetration of different groups and cultures. In this situation religious beliefs and practices jostle one another. Since the people must live together a modus vivendi is worked out, involving a certain amount of mutual tolerance in religious matters. Even the most doctrinaire religions, such as Islam, develop sects which must live side by side. Such tolerance is contrary to the absolutistic spirit of religion; in so far as it occurs it tends to weaken the complete acceptance of religious dogma. Scepticism, atheism, and apathy arise. *Fifth,* the religious system tends to become fragmented. Some of the essentially religious sentiments and ceremonies become attached to the state, which has an organization separate from that of the church. The stage is set for church-state conflict. The state either uses religion for its own ends (as was the case with Shinto in Japan and the Orthodox Church in Soviet Russia) or it relegates the church to survive by its own devices. The state may, as in the United States, undertake to foster public education in which no specific religious instruction is given at all.

All of these tendencies can be summed up under the heading of secularization, and one may ask how far secularization can go. The answer, I think, is that it can go a long way but that there is ultimately a limit. If the population becomes too matter-of-fact in its attitudes, too calculating in its behavior, too sophisticated in its values, it is likely not to stick together sufficiently to maintain order and protection. The resulting social disorder may give rise to new religious sects that preach a return to the pristine values and promise salvation if the people will listen to the message of the supernatural. The rise of Christianity in Rome was at the start just such an emergence of an obscure sect preaching its doctrine to a sophisticated civilization. Within a remarkably short time it was the state religion of the Empire.

A related question is how far the religion of the future may dispense with the supernatural. Can a society rely on the acceptance of certain ethical and moral principles without believing in the existence of a spiritual world? If by spiritual world we mean one peopled by the crude anthropomorphic imagination, it would seem to be possible to dispense with it, although admittedly no society has ever done so. If on the other hand we mean simply beliefs that transcend experience, the answer is no. These include ideas such as the master race, manifest destiny, progress, democracy, the classless state, justice, etc. They are essentially metaphysical as to intellectual content, and emotional as to motivation. They have heretofore been bolstered with anthropomorphic conceptions, but these have sometimes been pale and nebulous and it seems conceivable that the ideas, nonrational as they are, could survive without them.

A Brief Summary

This chapter began by considering some outmoded theories of religion. These appeared too evolutionary, rationalistic, and individualistic to explain the facts of religion. They concentrated too heavily on belief and did not pay enough attention to ritual and emotion. They needed correction by application of the sociological point of view.

In using a sociological approach we tried to show that religion exists in every known society because it performs important societal and personal functions. It provides, in its imaginary realm, a supposed reality to which the ultimate group values are tied. It thus rationalizes and strengthens the group values and thus overcomes the disintegrating tendency that an exclusive preoccupation with competitive ends would create. It also furnishes the individual with a cushion whereby the frustration, fear, anger, and insecurity growing out of failures in this world can be compensated for. In its ritual it provides a medium for the expression of religious feeling and for the interstimulation and renewal of religious sentiments. Sacred objects lend the supernatural an air of reality, and furnish convenient symbols for ritualistic and ceremonial manipulation. All told the sacred, or holy, performs such an important function in society that it will probably never disappear. The anthropomorphic conception of the nonempirical realm may possibly disappear, but not necessarily. The tendency toward secularization probably cannot continue to the point where religion entirely disappears. Secularization will likely be terminated by religious revivals of one sort or another. The precise nature of the revivals is impossible to predict. The details may resemble nothing we know now, but it is safe to assume that they will perform the same functions and have the same basic principles that have heretofore characterized all religion in all societies.

References

Ray H. Abrams (ed.), "Organized Religion in the United States," *Annals of the American Academy of Political and Social Science,* Vol. 256 (March 1948).

Contains sketches (mostly sympathetic) of the main religious groups; discussions of the relation of religion to class and family structure; accounts of social action programs adopted by religious bodies; and delineations of major trends and future prospects. Contains a sizeable bibliography.

Ruth Benedict, Chap. 14 in Franz Boas et al, *General Anthropology* (Boston: Heath, 1938).

An admirable and thorough chapter on primitive religion, with emphasis on cultural variation.

A. R. Brown, *The Andaman Islanders* (Cambridge: University Press, 1922; reprinted, 1948, by Free Press, Glencoe, Ill.).

Radcliffe-Brown's classic functional study of religious ceremony among a very primitive Negrito people has had a great deal of influence in diffusing the sociological approach to religion among anthropologists.

Hadley Cantril, "Education and Economic Composition of Religious Groups: An Analysis of Poll Data," *American Journal of Sociology,* Vol. 48 (March, 1943), pp. 574-579.

On the basis of 14,000 persons the conclusion is drawn that the proportion of Protestants increases with increasing income and education.

Michael Choukas, *Black Angels of Athos* (Brattleboro, Vermont: Stephen Daye, 1934).

A remarkably readable but nevertheless scholarly and first-hand sociological picture of one of the age-old strongholds of monastic celibacy, Mount Athos, off the coast of Greece.

Emile Durkheim, *The Elementary Forms of the Religious Life,* tr. by J. W. Swain (Glencoe, Ill.: Free Press, 1947).

The pioneer treatise on the sociology of religion, this book has not been surpassed; it is one of the greatest classics in sociological literature.

Five Great Encyclicals (New York: The Paulist Press, 1939).

Here are the Papal pronouncements on labor, education, marriage, communism, and the reconstruction of the social order. They reveal in striking fashion the mental processes by which supernatural absolutism is applied to social issues.

Horace L. Friess and Herbert W. Schneider, *Religion in Various Cultures* (New York: Holt, 1932).

A comparative treatment of all the main religions. Necessarily the handling of each religion is brief and the authors do not have a sociological point of view, but for a first view of comparative literature it is helpful, especially since there are elaborate bibliographies.

Walter R. Goldschmidt, "Class Denominationalism in Rural California Churches," *American Journal of Sociology,* Vol. 49 (January 1943), pp. 348-355.

On the basis of occupational data and church affiliation in a California town, the author shows that the Protestant sects represent different social classes. He explains why each denomination is associated with the particular class.

William Howells, *The Heathens: Primitive Man and His Religions* (Garden City, N. Y.: Doubleday & Company, 1948).

A fascinating book, sympathetically written yet objective. The author does not claim to cover the topic exhaustively, but he explores topics like the nature of religion, mana and taboo, magic in its various forms, divination, disease, witchcraft, etc.

William H. Melish, "Religious Developments in the Soviet Union," *American Sociological Review,* Vol. 9 (June 1944), pp. 279-286.

The survival of religion in Russia despite systematic governmental persecution has been remarkable. This article shows what adaptations to the situation have been made by the devout. It is part of an entire issue of the Review *devoted to Soviet Russia.*

L. S. S. O'Malley. *Popular Hinduism* (Cambridge: University Press, 1935).

A masterpiece of descriptive detail concerning one of the world's most inchoate but influential religions, by one of the most renowned students of India.

Liston Pope, *Millhands and Preachers* (New Haven: Yale University Press, 1942).

A study of the role of the church in labor relations in Gastonia, N. C., with an account of the "famous" strike in the Gastonia mills.

W. L. Sperry, *Religion in America* (New York: Macmillan, 1946).

A highly intelligent, lucid description of religion in the United States, written for the purpose of explaining the subject to Englishmen by the Dean of Harvard's Theological School.

Herbert Hewitt Stroup, *The Jehovah's Witnesses* (New York: Columbia University Press, 1945).

Sociological analysis of this small but vocal Fundamentalist sect. It helps to elucidate the principles underlying sectarian group behavior.

R. H. Tawney, *Religion and the Rise of Capitalism* (New York: Harcourt. Brace, 1926, reprinted as a Mentor book in 1948).

A remarkably stimulating and readable book dealing with the same topic that Max Weber handles (the relation of religion to economic institutions), but in a more popular fashion. See also Christen T. Jonassen, "The Protestant Ethic and the Spirit of Capitalism in Norway," American Sociological Review, *Vol. 12 (December 1947), pp. 676-686, which maintains that the Weberian thesis applies to Norway.*

A. S. Turberville, *The Spanish Inquisition* (New York: Holt, 1932, No. 45 in Home University Library).

A scholarly account of this remarkable institution which, as a technique for eliminating and impoverishing those who do not agree, is rivaled only by the instrumentalities of modern Fascism and Communism.

Joachim Wach, *Sociology of Religion* (Chicago: University of Chicago Press, 1944).

A general work by a former student of Max Weber. Hard to read and somewhat confused, but has a wealth of references and some good ideas.

W. Lloyd Warner, *A Black Civilization* (New York: Harper, 1937).

A functional interpretation of religion and magic among the Murngin, a tribe of Australian aborigines. An impressive study.

Max Weber, *The Protestant Ethic and the Spirit of Capitalism.* Translated by Talcott Parsons (London: George Allen & Unwin, 1930).

John Milton Yinger, *Religion in the Struggle for Power: A Study in the Sociology of Religion* (Durham: Duke University Press, 1946).

An attempt to study religion empirically as a factor in inter-human behavior—Jensen. It contains an extensive bibliography.

PART V

POPULATION AND SOCIETY

THE DEMOGRAPHIC EQUATION

WORLD POPULATION IN TRANSITION

CHAPTER XX

THE DEMOGRAPHIC EQUATION

THE SCIENCE of population, sometimes called demography, represents a fundamental approach to the understanding of human society. Because of its statistical character, it has unfortunately acquired the reputation of being dismal and dry; but with modern data and modern techniques it can be fascinating.

The primary tasks of demography are (1) to ascertain the number of people in a given area, (2) to determine what change—what growth or decline—this number represents; (3) to explain the change, and (4) to estimate on this basis the future trend. In explaining a change in numbers the populationist begins with three variables: births, deaths, and migration. He subtracts the deaths from the births to get "natural increase" and he subtracts the emigrants from the immigrants to get "net migration" (either number may be negative). If P_1 is the population of a given area at an earlier time, and P_2 the population at a later time, then

$$P_2 = P_1 + (\text{Births} - \text{Deaths}) + \text{Net Migration}$$

In order to compare the population growth in different areas or in different times, the demographer finds it necessary to substitute ratios for absolute numbers. Thus he relates births to the population in various ways to get birth *rates,* and he does the same with deaths and with migrants. In this way he can state his variables in terms of processes (fertility, mortality, and migration) and he can talk about the *rate* of growth or decline in the population. If "r" is the rate of growth, then the following formula holds:

$$r = (F - M) + (I - E)$$

where "F" is fertility, "M" is mortality, "I" is immigration, and "E" is emigration. In other words, the rate of population growth is determined by the natural increase plus the net migration. If the area in question includes the whole world, migration drops out of the formula; for in that case only fertility and mortality need be considered. But if the area includes less than the whole world, then migration must always be taken into account.

It is clear that any factor influencing the number of people must operate through one or more of the variables mentioned. In no other way can a population be changed. For this reason we may call the four variables "the primary demographic processes." They represent the core of population analysis. The demographer consequently requires not merely census returns (enumeration of the population at one point in time) but also registration statistics (continuous recording of births, deaths, migration, etc.).

If the populationist stopped here, however, his work would have little to do with social science but would be merely a branch of bio-statistics. What gives his subject interest to the social scientist, and social science interest to him, is in the first place the fact that fertility, mortality, and migration are all to a great extent socially determined and socially determining. They are the inner or formal variables in the demographic system, whereas the outer or ultimate variables are sociological and biological. Whenever the demographer pushes his inquiry to the point of asking why the demographic processes behave as they do, he enters the social field.

Population concerns social science in the second place because the demographer studies the number of people not only with reference to area but also with reference to their *characteristics*. He clings always to some definite area, but at the same time breaks down the total population within this area into groups or statistical classes, each having some definite, measurable attribute. Thus, for example, he may undertake to state the number of males and females in the population of the United States. He may go further and attempt to subclassify each of these groups according to age—say in five-year age intervals.

There are, of course, innumerable characteristics. One might count the number of people with long noses, with brown shoes, or with pretty wives. The demographer must therefore employ some criterion of relevance in choosing the traits he wishes to count. Unconsciously he tends to adopt two criteria: (1) the importance of the traits in the social organization; (2) the importance of the traits for the purely demographic processes. Often, as one might suspect, both criteria lead to the selection of the *same* traits.

From a strictly demographic point of view *age* and *sex* are the primary characteristics. Not only are they important bases for the ascription of social status, but they are biologically related to fertility and mortality, and indeed to migration as well. For this reason birth and death rates become most meaningful and are really strictly comparable only when the age and sex composition of the population is taken into account.

Most of the other significant traits selected for study by the populationist are not only socially important but are socially rather than biologically defined—e.g. marital status, literacy, citizenship, occupation, religion, income.

One should notice that the characteristics with which the populationist is concerned are in general those obtained in censuses. For instance, the United States census in 1940 secured data on all the traits mentioned above except religion. In addition it obtained information on many other subjects, including migration (1935 to 1940), age at marriage of married women, and number of children born to married women. The census therefore yields information that is both socially and demographically important.

Mutual Dependence of Population and Society

Deeply rooted in traditional population theory has been a biologistic approach, resting on the implicit or explicit belief that the dynamics of population can be explained by finding a fixed universal relationship between man's instinctive nature on the one hand and his physical environment on the other. The formula has been different with different authors. Sometimes it was a fixed equation between population and food supply (Malthus), or again between fecundity and density (Sadler), or between fertility and organic degeneration (Gini). But regardless of the specific formula, the underlying assumption was the same—that the secret of population lies in the relation of the human species to its physical environment. Other theories have emerged, but they have not had the vogue that the biologistic point of view has enjoyed.

Such biologistic determinism, though applicable to animal populations, cannot be applied to human beings; because, as we have abundantly seen in the present book, the cultural factors in human behavior must always figure in any theory designed to explain human action. A so-called law of population stated only in terms of man's physical nature and physical environment is at best merely an abstraction. To make it descriptive of reality it must be widened to include culture. But even so it is doubtful if the numerous factors governing population can be reduced to a single "law."

A human population cannot exist apart from a social order, because human beings cannot survive apart from socio-cultural interaction. Furthermore, as just seen, human populations are not defined exclusively by area but also by characteristics—many of them *socially defined*—so that it would hardly make sense to attempt to analyze these populations solely in biological terms. For example, to interpret changes in the population of the professional class in America as a function of a general relationship prevailing between food supply and fecundity would be fantastic.

It follows that society is both a necessary and a sufficient cause of population trends. We may state the relationship in the following way: Some of the elements in society, if they alone were operative, would greatly augment the population. Other elements in the same society, if alone operative, would greatly deplete the population. Any actual social system establishes a balance between these two contrary forces each of which limits the other; and the final result tends to be the maintenance or slight augmentation of the population. Why this should be true seems obvious on reflection. Any society, to have maintained itself in the struggle for existence, must have developed certain institutional mechanisms for insuring the procreation of each new generation and guaranteeing the survival of enough of this generation into the reproductive period to repeat the process. Since natural calamities are unpredictable, the "normal" way of life must be such as to build up a slight population reserve—so that in the long run maintenance will be assured. But the society is seldom in a position to foster unlimited growth because, as in any equilibrium, no one variable in the situation can move indefinitely in the same direction without corresponding changes in the others. Thus a continued population increase with no corresponding increase in the food supply would obviously end by increasing mortality and thereby stopping the population growth. Similarly a steady increase in the food supply, with no corresponding population growth, would soon lead to a wasteful and inconvenient situation in which the effort to raise food would no longer be expended and the increase in its abundance would be stopped. The principle of limits is effective no matter which variable is taken. A moving equilibrium presumes that all variables move together, none remaining fixed unless the others do.

We can state the same truth in another way by pointing out that since a social system is necessary for the life of a population, the effort of the society is not simply in the direction of increasing the number of people but also in the direction of maintaining the social order. If the growth of numbers threatens the social order, then restraints to such growth automatically arise. Too rapid an increase of population may take away the energy and attention needed for other societal functions, and thus become just as great a crisis as a rapid decrease would become.

When, for whatever reason, the adjustment between the rate of population growth and the social conditions is destroyed, certain "crisis mores" are brought into play which tend to restore the balance between augmenting and depleting forces. Such readjustments may not come into operation for some time after the original crisis; they may in fact represent a gradual change, but they are nonetheless a response to the critical situation that has developed.

To illustrate and verify this abstract discussion, let us now see how the demographic processes—fertility, mortality, and migration—are socially determined. The question of total population growth and its ramifications will be saved for the next chapter.

Social Determinants of Fertility

To most of us the endless succession of human births presents no intellectual problem. Procreation is simply one of the great facts of existence, and any speculation about it falls naturally into the realm of poetry, religion, and ethics rather than social science. Whatever study it requires is ordinarily conceived as applying to particular cases. One person wants to know how he can overcome his sterility; another, how he can stop having children; another, how he can be sure to have a boy next time. And such problems are felt to be medical, not sociological. To pose the question in general form and in non-medical terms raises a smile, because everybody knows that the explanation of human fertility, given sound bodies and natural urges, is as obvious as the sun's movement around the earth.

But the truth seems to be that fertility has always, in every kind of society, been socially controlled. Accordingly, a simple instinctive explanation of the birth rate is fallacious. Human beings who have been smart enough during thousands of centuries to build fires, fashion weapons, employ speech, and regulate behavior have also been smart enough to separate sexual pleasure from procreation. The anthropological and historical evidence on this score is quite convincing.[1] Not only crude contraceptives but also abortion and infanticide have been used to prevent families larger than those desired.

Like other forms of human behavior, procreation will not occur unless it is motivated—i.e. performed with ends in view. Ever since the development of culture some millions of years ago, human societies have not relied simply on biological instinct to provide children. They have also relied upon induced motivation within a social organization—upon definitions of the situation, upon customs and mores, upon institutions such as marriage and religion. An illustration of unconscious social motivation may be drawn from our own society. When a married couple attempt contraception but have a child anyway, we say that the child owes its existence to their inefficient contraception. But an equally important cause is the fact that their moral code did not sanction abortion or infanticide. Their procreative behavior therefore cannot be explained in terms of instinct or ignorance alone but also in terms of socially transmitted values and ends.

So ingrained is the old biologistic approach to human fertility that social factors, even when admitted, are felt to be superficial and limited primarily to modern society. It is believed that in most societies the actual reproduction (fertility) is about as high as the biological capacity to reproduce (fecundity). Thus we are told that the birth rate is low in the United States but that in India people reproduce to the limit of their biological capacity, and that this is somehow "natural." What is overlooked, however, is the fact that the alleged biological capacity could not exist without a socio-cul-

[1] See Clellan S. Ford, *A Comparative Study of Human Reproduction* (New Haven: Yale University Press, Yale University Publications in Anthropology, No. 32, 1945).

tural system, since human beings do not live, much less reproduce, apart from society. The so-called biological capacity is therefore an abstraction which, if embodied in practice, would require a maximization of all the social forces favorable to fertility. Actually there is no culture wholly favorable to fertility.

Why does culture always rest at a point below maximum favorableness to fertility? One answer might be that the means of subsistence are limited and that consequently human beings use some foresight in controlling their numbers. This does not seem to be true, for it is generally the poorest peoples who have the highest birth rates. A less rationalistic explanation seems more accurate. It appears that a good share of the resources of a society must go not to the mere sustenance of its population in a quantitative sense, but to the maintenance of its social structure. Resources that could be used for sustenance are spent for religious, educational, artistic, recreational, and governmental purposes. In so far as these things are necessary for the society—more necessary than a sheer increase of numbers—the social system evolves in such a way that they are partly taken care of by depressing fertility below what it might otherwise be. Paradoxically, unless some resources were used for social functions, the social order itself would disintegrate and fewer people could actually be supported than if all the resources were used merely for sustenance. The conclusion seems clear that the other functions set limits upon, at the same time that they are necessary to, the function of physical maintenance. It is the social and not merely the physical creation of a new generation that concerns society. Socialization, status ascription, and social placement, for example, are more efficiently carried out when children are not reproduced to the absolute limit of bio-social capacity.

Social Impediments to Maximum Fertility

The social controls over fertility are to a great extent unconscious, at least so far as the quantitative result is concerned. The people have other ends in mind than the limitation of numbers yet their behavior nevertheless achieves this result.

(1) *Taboos on the Association of Males and Females.* There are powerful social hindrances keeping men and women apart, especially when for one reason or another their association could

not eventuate in a legitimate marriage or could injure an existing one. We have already discussed incest taboos and their functions. Such taboos merge into various kinds of avoidances, some between relatives, others between persons of opposite sex in given situations. The avoidance in some instances amounts to seclusion, whereby females have contact with only a few males. The extreme example is *purdah* in Hindu and Mohammedan countries. Less extreme is the well-nigh universal restriction upon the association of wives with men other than their husbands—a protection against adultery. Another extreme form of avoidance is celibacy. On the famous monastery island of Mount Athos, for example, total exclusion of the female sex extended to the animal kingdom, and even males below eighteen years of age were not permitted on the premises.[2] The Catholic church, which in general favors high fertility, nevertheless maintains a celibate priesthood and a system of nunneries. Finally, there are always financial and class barriers which greatly limit the mutual association of the sexes.

(2) *Taboos on Sexual Intercourse*. Though contacts between the sexes are limited, they are not nearly so limited as sexual intercourse. Our culture allows much contact between brother and sister, for example, but brands intercourse between them as incestuous. In most societies the great bulk of association between the sexes is supposed to be devoid of sexual significance. It is safe to say, therefore, that taboos on intercourse have a greater effect in cutting down fertility than do taboos on association, although the two are related. Even between husband and wife there are often periods when the culture requires abstinence. The frequent taboo on intercourse after the birth of a child may last for a year in some cultures, and a violation may be thought to bring disease or bad luck on the child already born. Such a taboo helps to space children and also emphasizes for the parents the significance of the child (a modified couvade).

The great role of abstinence, however, occurs not within marriage but outside it. Taboos against fornication and adultery, the view that women are sexual property to be jealously guarded—these are the great restraints on intercourse, and they undoubtedly reduce the total fertility of the society. Thus the very institutions which are

[2] Michael Choukas, *Black Angels of Mount Athos* (Brattleboro, Vt.: Sociological Press. 1934), p. 200.

devoted to procreation (marriage and the family) are in part checks upon fertility. The customary age at marriage, coupled with the usual rule that reproduction must occur only within marriage, means that a certain portion of each woman's reproductive span is removed from the chance of pregnancy. In our civilization the average age at marriage comes several years after puberty. During the last three decades in Italy, for instance, the age at first marriage averaged about 24 years for women.[3] If, as Pearl shows,[4] the average age at menarche is about 15 years, we see that the custom whereby marriage for the woman is postponed in Italy to age 24 reduces the total number of years which the average matron devotes to reproduction by about 9. Since Pearl maintains that the usual age at menopause is 46 years,[5] making a total reproductive span of 31 years, the loss of nine years represents a 29 per cent reduction in the effective reproductive life of the average Italian woman. Italy is not an extreme case; there are other countries where the age at marriage is substantially later—e.g., Sweden and Ireland.[6] Nearly all cultures postpone marriage for some time after puberty. The customary age at marriage, therefore, plus intramarital and extramarital taboos, serves to restrict greatly the range and amount of coitus in which women may engage. India is a country noted for early marriage, but it practices a peculiar form of celibacy—namely, a taboo on the remarriage of widows. The effect of this institution in reducing fertility in India has been calculated as about 15 per cent.[7]

It should be pointed out, too, that a rigid insistence on monogamous wedlock may doom one mate to infertility if the other is sterile. Not every society allows divorce for sterility or permits the taking of a concubine.

(3) *Restraints on Conception.* In past ages celibacy and abstinence have often held the spotlight of public interest, but now contraception and sterilization overshadow these. Contraception is a purely deliberate method of permitting the enjoyment of intercourse

3 Warren S. Thompson, *Population Problems* (New York: McGraw-Hill, 3rd ed., 1942), p. 162.

4 Raymond Pearl, *The Natural History of Population* (New York: Oxford University Press, 1939), p. 49. There is reason to believe that the age which Pearl gives is too high.

5 *Ibid.*, p. 52. Since the average woman is more fecund in the earlier part of her reproductive span, the total loss in potential reproduction is greater than 29 per cent.

6 The average age at first marriage for women in the United States is 22.

7 Kingsley Davis, "Human Fertility in India," *American Journal of Sociology*, Vol. 52 (Nov. 1946), pp. 251-253.

without the penalty of pregnancy. Sterilization is similar, except more drastic and permanent. The argument in their favor, as against abstinence, is that they permit sexual pleasure; and as against abortion and infanticide, that they are less wasteful. Consequently, in an advanced stage of civilization when rational techniques are abundantly utilized to accomplish personal ends, contraception tends to be widely practiced. But it is by no means limited to advanced civilization. The Bantu tribes of Africa, for example, practiced a highly efficient form of contraception.[8] In any culture, for economic, moral, or medical reasons, there are situations in which pregnancy is not desired. Numerous societies, for example, permit extramarital intercourse but forbid illegitimate children; others permit marital intercourse but forbid pregnancy during certain periods. In these situations the culture, so to speak, calls for the use of contraception as a possible way out. It has been shown that even crude methods of contraception may result in a very substantial reduction of fertility.[9]

(4) *Abortion.* Even after conception has occurred, individuals may still seek to avoid childbirth. Voluntary abortion under certain circumstances is sanctioned in almost all societies, and under other circumstances condemned; but whether sanctioned or condemned, it occurs anyway because it enables the pregnant woman to avoid the unfavorable consequences of her situation. This is as true of the married woman who has had three children and secures an abortion to avoid a fourth as it is of the single woman who secures an abortion to avoid illegitimacy.

(5) *Infanticide.* The unmitigated disapproval with which our culture regards infanticide is exceptional, because most cultures (especially primitive ones) permit or encourage infanticide under certain circumstances. One circumstance is frequently the occurrence of a plural birth; another the appearance of unwanted females; another the wish to escape illegitimacy; another the desire to limit family size; and another the occurrence of deformity or sickliness in the child. In so far as infanticide is practiced merely to evade the responsibility or burden of children it is of course exceedingly wasteful, because contraception could accomplish the same end

[8] I. Schapera, *The Bantu-Speaking Tribes of South Africa* (London: Routledge, 1937), p. 95.

[9] Regine K. Stix and Frank W. Notestein, *Controlled Fertility* (Baltimore: Williams & Wilkins, 1940); Gilbert W. Beebe, *Contraception and Fertility in the Southern Appalachians* (Baltimore: Williams & Wilkins, 1942), pp. 97-109.

without the cost of pregnancy and the danger of parturition to the mother. But for other purposes it cannot be replaced by contraception or abortion. For instance one cannot know beforehand that a girl, a monster, or a set of triplets will be born. If one therefore wishes to avoid such children, infanticide in some form is a necessary means.

Though deliberate infanticide may not be practiced, the social customs governing infant care may nevertheless be so unhygienic as to produce many infant deaths and thus create an effect similar to the lowering of fertility by contraception, abortion, or infanticide.

Social Encouragements to Fertility

At the same time that a society limits fertility by its institutions and customs, it also encourages fertility within the limits of these institutions and customs. It offers inducements to its members to marry and to beget children within marriage. It thus integrates reproduction with the other patterns in the culture. Marriage and parenthood become advantageous to the individual not only emotionally but also economically, politically, and spiritually.

We often find for example that the permissive enjoyment of sexual intercourse, the ownership of land, the admission to certain offices, the claim to respect, and the attainment of blessedness are made contingent upon marriage. Though celibate groups may purposely remain unwed, the disvalue placed on the old maid and the old bachelor among ordinary people may amount almost to horror. The state of wedlock tends to be idealized, especially by the still unwed. Given such integration of marriage with the individual's conception of his own role, it is little wonder that he winds up in matrimony.

Marriage accomplished, the more specific encouragements to fertility apply. In familistic societies where kinship forms the chief basis of social organization, reproduction is a necessary means to nearly every major goal in life. The salvation of the soul, the security of old age, the production of goods, the protection of the hearth, and the assurance of affection may depend upon the presence, help, and comfort of progeny. This arrangement, this articulation of the parental status with the rest of one's statuses, is the supreme encouragement to fertility. Any departure from this pattern in the direction of individualism and functionless families weakens the motivation to procreate.

The cultural heritage also includes practices designed to overcome physical obstacles to married fertility. Towards impotence, sterility, miscarriage, and stillbirth it fosters an attitude of dread and combats them with numerous magical and medical remedies. In addition it often inculcates an attitude of disapproval toward cultural practices that impede fertility (e.g. nonmarriage, contraception, abortion) when used for purely private ends. Finally it extols virility and engenders the false belief that a sure proof of one's virility is the number of one's children.

With us marriage has become a medium of personal affection and sexual gratification rather than primarily a vehicle of procreation; the parental bond has lost most of its connections with the rest of society. Children have consequently become a burden and means are found, whether sanctioned or not, to avoid too many of them. The difference between primitives and ourselves is not that they procreate by "instinct" and we by "plan," but that their society rewards reproduction more abundantly than ours.

Social Determinants of Sickness and Health

Birth and death are but two sides of the same thing—transience. Between them stands the solid part, life itself, the preservation of which, for awhile at least, is essential to the species. The maintenance of life is therefore as great a cultural value as fertility. But it is a different kind of value. When one contemplates procreation as a future act, it is always someone else who is going to be created; but when one contemplates death, it is one's own extinction that is involved. The interest in procreation is often not such at all but an interest in sexual pleasure; when the two are separated, as they may be in any society, the motivation to procreate must be a derived or acquired motivation, dependent upon one's conception of the value of children. The desire to live is on the other hand more intrinsic to the organism, more purely individual and self-centered. It requires less external stimulation. Yet from a societal point of view both interests are equally essential. The society must contrive to motivate as well as implement reproduction, whereas it can remain content merely to implement the desire to remain alive.

The intrinsic interest in preserving one's own life is not simply an interest in sheer existence (though people will go to astonishing lengths merely to remain alive), but also an interest in good health. The suffering that accompanies poor health creates a constant imperative desire to improve it. An interest in the health of others, however, must be culturally engendered. Yet even this task would seem easier than the creation of an interest in procreation. To witness the suffering of intimate friends and relatives is hard, and to see them die is harder. With them a person has already established bonds of affection, whereas in contemplating procreation one is thinking of beings who are not yet real. Unless an individual is powerfully conditioned by cultural indoctrination, a failure to procreate is not so saddening as a failure to maintain his own health or that of his intimates. For this reason a powerful indoctrination is built up around procreation, and the failure to reproduce is in many societies felt to be life's greatest failure. In short, the cultural apparatus supporting the procreative interest must be somewhat more elaborate than that supporting the interest in longevity. The latter requires mechanisms to support it and therefore confines itself more easily to the rational pursuit of the best means available. The instrumentalities for providing health may be more elaborate than those for implementing reproduction, but the formation of the end itself (the desire for health) needs less cultural apparatus.

In an individualized society where individual wants are stressed, the interest in health and longevity becomes highly developed whereas the interest in fertility wanes. When scientific techniques are first developed, they are applied to the control of mortality rather than to the control of fertility. The latter is hedged round with more nonrational attitudes and lends itself less readily to scientific implementation. When people are too objective about it, the spiritual myths and social institutions supporting the desire to procreate dissolve. In this way is explained the paradox that the civilization with the best medical techniques for aiding procreation has the weakest desire to procreate.

In a sense, because death will eventually take us all it possesses a biological inevitablility that seemingly transcends social influences. We know that we can control the number of persons born—at least negatively in our own lives; but we cannot evade the fact that individuals finally die. But although we do not control death in the sense of eliminating it, we do control it through postponement. Such control takes much the same form as the control of fertility. There are socio-cultural forces tending to maintain life or improve health, and others tending to do the opposite. These factors are for the most part traditional and nonrational, though the goal is so universal and immediate and consequently so little supported by social myth and dogma, that scientific means are fairly readily adopted when these become available. The greatest social mythology is required not for the preservation of life but for its sacrifice; whereas the greatest mythology is required not for the sacrifice of fertility but for its maintenance. In the postponement of death the search is for the proper means of achieving the goal, not for the means of maintaining the goal itself.

It should be remembered, however, that health and life are not the only values that human beings cherish. The person who devotes all his time simply to keeping well is a crank with a special name, and is as unproductive and unliked as any other crank by any other name. There are other social needs and other values, and though these do not always clash with the goal of health they are nevertheless often in competition with it. There are occasions when the risk of death becomes a virtue and self-preservation a sin.

Social Impediments to Health and Longevity

So fully do we accept life as a value that we overlook ways in which death or ill health is socially caused. There are situations in which, by definite social prescription, death or physical injury is required. More numerous are the situations in which, though not planned that way, the individual is forced by rivalry and mental conflict to injure his own health or take his own life. Still more frequent are the situations in which the aim is to promote health but the result, through superstition and error, is to accomplish exactly the opposite. And innumerable are the situations in which actions regarded as irrelevant to health nevertheless injure it. Let us consider all these cases and then raise the deeper question of why society should act as a source of death.

(1) *Situations Defined as Calling for Death.* Sometimes, by cultural prescription, individuals may be put to death or injured for reasons beyond their own responsibility. The abandonment of the

aged and infirm, the exposure of deformed children, the execution of twins, the killing of female infants, the elimination of the painfully diseased, and the sacrifice of individuals for ceremonial purposes—all of these have been practiced by one society or another. Murdock writes of the Witotos of the Amazon valley:

> The reigning law of the jungle is the survival of the fittest, and there are no sentimentalists to oppose its corollary, the elimination of the unfit. Hence all who cannot pay their own way in society—the aged, the infirm, and the incurably sick—unless they have something of great value to offer in their wisdom or experience, are removed from society. They are not, to be sure, killed outright; they are simply abandoned in the bush to die.[10]

Some readers will recall that in Peter Freuchen's novel, *Eskimo,* the hero's mother-in-law is finally left behind in an igloo built for her, with food and with full knowledge that her departing relatives were abandoning her nonetheless. Freuchen's picture is true to life among the hard-pressed, migratory Eskimos. On the opposite side of the earth the Tasmanians practiced a similar custom, and the Hottentots of Africa and the Iroquois of North America in times of emergency did the same. In civilized societies, however, the old are likely to be preserved as long as possible. They carry an enormous amount of culture in their heads and consequently, to the extent that the culture is complex, acquire value as walking encyclopedias. Furthermore, in a stable traditionalized society where leadership depends not upon physical strength but upon sagacity and formal position, the old tend to retain their past authority.

The exposure of deformed infants is more frequent, the destruction of female infants still more frequent. Where hypergamy is practiced as in India, where the patriarchal pattern is extremely strong as in China, where polyandry is permitted as in Tibet, or where the conditions of life are extremely hard as in the Arctic, we are likely to find female infanticide occurring.

Human sacrifice has occurred in many societies and in several different forms, but seldom of course on a large scale. Sacrifice is of such character that unless the object sacrificed is of some value, the sacrifice is not genuine. Hence for supreme ceremonial occasions what could be better, what could have more value, than the life of a

[10] G. P. Murdock, *Our Primitive Contemporaries* (New York: Macmillan, 1936), p. 467.

human being? But precisely in so far as something is valuable, people are reluctant to sacrifice it. They find it hard to part with an adult member of the group in good standing. Often a compromise is reached whereby the person sacrificed is a slave, servant, wife, concubine, or captive. The sacrifice may be made in some critical emergency, as among the Bangala [11] and the Maori, or it may be made as a tribute to an important personage upon his death. If the immolated are wives or concubines the sacrifice is called by the Indian term *suttee,*[12] though the practice was found not only in India but also among the North American natives and elsewhere. Another type of human sacrifice is illustrated by the Chagga practice of burying two children at each entrance to the tribal territory to ward off attack, by the ancient Israelite practice of sacrificing the first born, and by the annual sacrifice of the Pawnee. But the most elaborate sacrificial ritual was developed by the Aztecs of ancient Mexico, who pleased the gods with constant human slaughter.[13] Cannibalism, sometimes undertaken for ritualistic purposes and sometimes for lack of food, is another member of the same series. It has been a bona fide custom in many societies.[14]

There are circumstances under which someone may be killed or injured as punishment or retaliation—e.g. warfare. During World War I the total number of deaths due directly to military action was estimated to be in the neighborhood of 10.6 million.[15] Though such a loss represented only a small percentage of the total population of the countries engaged in the war, it did affect some age groups very seriously. Homicide is a minor cause of death in every society. In the United States in 1941, for example, 7,929 persons died from this cause, more than seven times the reported deaths from typhoid fever. Capital punishment adds its bit. In 1939-41 in the United States an average of 132 persons were executed each year, more than a third of the number (373) killed by lightning.

[11] J. H. Weeks, "Anthropological Notes on the Bangala of the Upper Congo River," *Journal of the Royal Anthropological Institute,* Vol. 39, p. 454; cited by W. I. Thomas, *Primitive Behavior* (New York: McGraw-Hill, 1937), pp. 395-403.

[12] Edward Thompson, *Suttee* (London: Allen & Unwin, 1928).

[13] Murdock, *op. cit.,* pp. 393-400. W. I. Thomas, *op. cit.,* pp. 304-305.

[14] For an excellent discussion of cannibalism among the Eskimo, see E. M. Weyer, *The Eskimos* (New Haven: Yale University Press, 1932), pp. 117-124.

[15] Samuel Dumas and K. O. Vedel-Persen, *Losses of Life Caused by War* (London: Clarendon Press, 1923), pp. 137-182. Cited by Warren S. Thompson, *Population Problems* (New York: McGraw-Hill, 1942), p. 46. The figure does not include increased disease mortality resulting from the war, estimated at 4.0 million.

Whatever our attitude toward war, homicide, lynching, and execution, the fact remains that practically every society is prepared to defend itself against enemies without and criminals within, even to the point of taking lives. In every case the killing is conceived to be a means to an end, either legally or illegally. Thus the very forces that preserve social order and therefore life and property also act to take away life.

In some circumstances the individual is socially required to take his own life. The best known cases are *harakiri* in Japan, *suttee* in India, and the captain's going down with his ship in the West. In India suicide was once institutionalized in a peculiar form known as *kur* and *traga*. The political strife and rapine from which India suffered through most of her history caused the subjugated masses to evolve strange protective practices. Sometimes (*kur*) "a pile of wood was erected, on which was placed a cow or a calf or an old woman, and it was announced that the pile would be set on fire unless the grievance was redressed." Sometimes in west India a still more dreadful expedient (*traga*) was practiced, whereby the Bhats killed themselves to vindicate claims of right.[16]

From institutionalized suicide it is but a short step to the risk of death against complete odds—e.g. by the "suicide corps" of an army or the "virtual suicide" of the condemned martyr. Such spectacular events make us realize that human beings are not mere organisms each fighting for its own survival, but social creatures with ideals and sentiments.

In the other kind of suicide—individualistic suicide—the individual takes his own life in defiance of social prescription, because somehow he cannot achieve his ends and prefers death to the feeling of frustration. If others have been instrumental in defeating his ends, he may view his suicide as a cause of remorse to the others. Such use of suicide to achieve an end otherwise unobtainable is indeed strange, and shows again the cultural nature of human motivation. After the suicide the individual is of course not there to enjoy the end that has been gained; in fact, he is not there to enjoy any end. And yet this use of suicide is extremely common. One may kill himself in order to "get even" with an unresponsive lover, a scolding parent, or a scoffer.

[16] L. S. S. O'Malley, *Modern India and the West* (London: Oxford University Press, 1941), p. 32.

Whether of the institutionalized or the individualistic variety, suicide is an important cause of death. Dublin and Lotka treat it as one of the ten principal causes in the United States although this country, among civilized nations, does not have a high rate.[17] As many deaths are attributed to suicide as to syphilis.

(2) *Practices Intended to Give Health, but Having the Opposite Effect.* So keen is man's desire to feel well and live long that he has originated countless medical practices; but so complicated is his anatomy and so limited is his intelligence that these practices often thwart rather than further his goal. Whereas a disinterested observer would brand the previous instances of suicide and sacrifice as non-rational because the end pursued was not "real," he would brand the present practices as irrational because the means selected are inappropriate. The practices may achieve some other end than health; they may make the practitioner wealthy or give the patient a false sense of security; but since they fail to achieve the avowed aim of good health and longevity, they are failures.

Some health practices in any society are of course beneficial, but the proportion is generally less than we imagine. It might be claimed that the bulk of them are neutral, doing no good but also no harm. Yet a "neutral" health practice is self-contradictory because it is tantamount to doing nothing, and doing nothing may be a cause of death. Of course, since about 90 per cent of sick cases recover anyway, a "neutral" health practice is not fatal and the patient thinks it has cured him; but in other cases the "neutral" practice takes the place of treatment which might have been beneficial, and the patient never knows what killed him.

Health practices leading to death are less numerous than those leading simply to more ill health. For one thing the practitioner, if one is involved, cannot afford to be credited with too many deaths, especially sudden ones. Also a person who has died cannot, except by posthumous testimonials in the newspapers, spread the word around that the medicine he took is excellent, whereas one who has recovered can do so and thus perpetuate his remedy. Since most people recover anyway, they constantly increase and reinforce the heritage of "sure" cures.

The first step in understanding these practices lies in a review

[17] Louis I. Dublin and Alfred J. Lotka, *The Length of Life* (New York: Ronald Press, 1936), Chap. 5.

of the folk theory which underlies them. The principal fact is this: folk theory throughout human history has practically always regarded disease and death as caused by spiritual—religious, magical, and moral—forces. These forces have taken various forms, but recalling the chapter on religion we know that they are anthropomorphic, at least in the sense of responding to human desires and human acts, and that they make possible a sort of moral determinism. As applied to the treatment of disease they make sickness and health appear as resultants of moral events. Through them illness is interpreted as somehow springing from conduct contrary to the moral norms or the machinations of an enemy, while health is interpreted as flowing from the correct observance of the norms or from the social group as against its natural and human enemies. In short, the prevailing theory of disease has made the physical well-being of the individual appear to depend upon the moral well-being of the group.

Excellent illustrations can be found in almost any primitive society. Let us take as an example the Azande, an African people. Every ailing Azande attributes his sickness, whatever its nature, either to witchcraft (magic used against him by someone with a more or less justified grievance) or to sorcery (magic used against him by someone without a just grievance). All Azande believe that an unknown number of their fellows are witches possessing in their bodies a substance which can harm others. They attribute most misfortunes to the action of these witches and the rest to the bad magic of sorcerers. When, therefore, an Azande wants to know whether a misfortune will occur in the future he consults an agency which can reveal the forces of witchcraft and sorcery—a witch-doctor, oracle, or both. And when misfortune has already occurred such as illness, he calls upon the same agency to diagnose and combat the magical cause.[18]

If this were all there would be little of sociological interest in Zande magic. But the big question is this: Who are the witches and why do they exercise their harmful potentialities? The ordinary Azande does not know who the witches are; he merely knows they are among his neighbors, acquaintances, relatives, etc. He knows too that even if they possess the magical substance of witchery, they will not use it upon him without a *motive*. Behind all the acts of

[18] E. E. Evans-Pritchard, *Witchcraft, Oracles and Magic Among the Azande* (Oxford: Clarendon Press, 1937), pp. 148-149.

witchcraft lie the common emotions and sentiments—malice, jealousy, greed, envy, etc. When misfortune strikes, therefore, the stricken Azande turns over in his mind as possible witches all those with whom he is on bad terms. Consulting his medicine man, he gives him the names of these persons. The medicine man, well acquainted with local gossip and existing frictions, tells him after several hours of ceremonial dancing who the witch is. The diagnosis generally seems true. The medicine man "divines successfully because he says what his listener wishes him to say." He often discloses the witch's name implicitly rather than explicitly, and fills his seance with gesture and tricks calculated to inspire confidence in his divinations.

If the misfortune is serious enough, the witchdoctor's identification of the witch will be taken to one of the oracles for confirmation. The most important of these, the poison oracle, consists in administering poison to a fowl and noting the bird's reactions, particularly whether it lives or dies.[19] This oracle is not considered simply a matter of chance, as when we flip a coin to decide an issue, but is thought to have a mystical capacity for divining witchcraft. Furthermore the oracle has a ritualistic side. Unless the person who first gathered the poison and the one who administers it both have observed the proper taboos, and unless the oracle is properly addressed in putting the question, the procedure is worthless.

Once the oracle has confirmed the witchdoctor's identification of the witch, the client may bring the accusation to the person thus identified. This he does by presenting him, through a prince's official, with a wing of the fowl that "died in his name." The presentation constitutes a public request that the witch withdraw his baneful influence. "Almost invariably the witch replies courteously that he is unconscious of injuring anyone, that if it is true that he has injured the man in question he is very sorry, and that if it is he alone who is troubling him then he will surely recover, because from the bottom of his heart he wishes him health and happiness, in sign of which he will blow out water." He then blows water over the chicken's wing and repeats his good wishes.[20] If the sick man shows signs of recovery, his relatives praise the oracle for having picked out the witch so promptly. If he continues to remain ill, a fresh round of oracle consultations is begun to find out whether the witch was only

[19] *Ibid.*, pp. 93-94. [20] *Ibid.*, pp. 93-94.

pretending repentance or whether some new witch has meanwhile started to aggravate the sickness.

Plainly, the treatment of illness among the Azande is part of a general system of handling misfortunes by magical means, and this general system is at the same time an important instrument of social control. It is at bottom a system of criminal and civil procedure. The procedures described are the everyday usages of every section of Zande society in situations of sickness. By their routine character, by their status as established norms of behavior, they lessen the chance of violent quarrels. The authority of the poison oracle, the employment of an intermediary who obviates a meeting of the parties during the whole affair, the social standing of the prince's official who acts as intermediary—all minimize friction. "It is, moreover, to the interest of both parties that they should not become estranged through the incident. They have to live together as neighbors afterwards and to cooperate in the life of the community." The witch should be put in a good humor by politeness and "ought to feel grateful to the people who have warned him so politely of the danger in which he stands . . . for if he had been allowed to murder the man, all the while ignorant of his action, he would inevitably have fallen a victim to vengeance." [21]

The Azande have also less elaborate, more palliative magical treatments. The witchdoctor, summoned to treat a sick man, will generally make a poultice and place it on the affected part after one or two slight incisions. "He then massages the part with his hands and eventually withdraws the poultice and searches in it—with invariable success—for a bone or piece of charcoal or some such object, which he shows to the sick man's family." The object is believed to have been shot into the sick man by a witch.[22] But of course, unless the witch himself is made to desist from his enmity, he can shoot another bolt into the patient's body; so the treatment in this instance is merely palliative in its effect.

Though Zande treatment gives primacy to magic, it does not utterly ignore empirical causes. The symptoms of disease are recognized and separately distinguished, and the actual situation in which

[21] *Ibid.*, pp. 96-97.

[22] *Ibid.*, p. 90. This mode of treatment, which produces tangible evidence of the magical influence operating in the body, is typical of primitive society and reminds us once again that tangible symbols play an exceedingly important role in objectifying and concretizing the religo-magical surreality.

the disease occurs is observed. The Azande doctors are skillful in detecting the early symptoms of disease and in predicting its normal course. The factual situation is often so obvious that the Azande cannot help seeing its connection with the malady—as when a lion attacks or boiling water scalds a man—but such a factor is without a motive and therefore inadequate as an explanation. The true explanation goes back ultimately to human motives which, since they seldom in fact cause illnesses, must be conceived to cause them through the fiction of magic. In the treatment of the illness there may thus be an empirical element, as when a wound is washed with warm water or a burn coated with honey, but the main part of it and often the only part is likely to be in terms of magic. Many treatments employ sympathetic magic, as when elephantiasis is treated by making incisions in the swollen limb and rubbing ashes from a burnt elephant's leg.

The more serious the sickness, the greater the prominence given to motivated magic. In slight injuries or illnesses the matter is hardly worth the effort of bringing into play the whole witchcraft complex. But when the indisposition brings acute pain or threatens the life or economic productivity of the individual, the forces of witchcraft and sorcery must be coped with.

Behind the empirical cause, in Azande eyes, lies the mystical or magical cause derived unconsciously from the social relationships in which the patient lives. Since in any community there are innumerable lines of friction, the magical explanation in terms of motives arising in the social context is always in a sense an adequate explanation. It also gives force to the normative system of the community. Grievances between tribesmen are not grievances unless one of them has violated the rule of what ought to be the proper behavior. Each Azande must watch his step to see that he does not give his fellows too much cause for offense, and when he falls ill he must pick out the man who bears a grudge and straighten the matter out with him. In this way, through the magical theory of disease, serious illness becomes an occasion for examining social relationships, and its treatment an instrumentality of social control. The function of remedying the physical disease may not be attained but another and perhaps more important one is attained.

The very cultures in which modern medicine had its obscure beginnings, the Egyptian, Babylonian, Jewish, and Greek, were saturated with spiritual and magical theories of disease. For the Jews all sickness, all suffering was punishment for violation of God's law and the proper remedies were atonement, prayer, and right living.[23] Sickness, or ritual impurity, was regarded as contagious in a magical sense and hence might be readily transmitted to a man's family or clan.[24] This meant that the group as well as the individual took an interest in minimizing sinfulness. Purification could be carried out and health regained through priestly ministration, prayer, and sacrifice.

Early Christian medicine stressed faith healing. The "gift of healing" came not from knowledge but from the spirit of God. The elders of the church prayed over the ailing man, anointing him with oil in the name of the Lord.[25] The best healer was the priest, and by the same logic anyone who could heal the sick was likely to have attributed to him priestly or spiritual qualities.

The notion of ritual illness and the tradition of ritual cure continue, of course, into our own day. When the Americans took over the Philippines from the Spanish, they found the task of bringing health to the inhabitants extremely difficult. Spanish theologians had taught the Filipinos that illness and deformity were manifestations of divine wrath. The people were resigned to their angry God, used to his punishments. The practical consequences were sometimes both horrible and humorous together, as the following incident during a cholera epidemic reveals.[26]

> The people were often, in their pitiful ignorance, hastening their own destruction. One morning I came down to my office. My first glance, as always, was towards the big map on the wall. I was startled to see that, according to the arrangement of the colored flags which marked the location of every case, cholera had suddenly burst forth in little isolated groups all over Manila.
>
> An investigation was begun at once. This soon revealed that two days earlier a fisherman had come in from the Bay with a marvelous story of how he had seen bubbles rising in the salt water which, as they rose, formed the vague outline of a great cross. He

[23] Henry E. Sigerist, *Medicine and Human Welfare* (New Haven: Yale University Press, 1941), pp. 8-9.

[24] *Ibid.*, pp. 37-38.

[25] *Ibid.*, p. 18.

[26] Victor Heiser, *An American Doctor's Odyssey* (New York: Norton, 1936), pp. 103-104.

> had tasted the water and found it sweet. Crossing himself, with wonder in his heart that he had been chosen to discover this portent, he paddled furiously to land. Others at first incredulous, tasted and then believed. The fisherman escorted to the spot a priest, who blessed the water and declared it a miracle. . . . Dwellers along the shore poured themselves out on the Bay in anything that would float and eagerly scooped up the holy water in bottles, jugs, pans, and pails.
>
> Together with the Manila health officials I was soon on a launch, which nosed its way through the conglomeration of native craft. A glance was enough to show us that this was no miracle but a dire calamity. The sewer line, which emptied far out in the Bay, had broken. If access to the miracle were shut off immediately, we knew that, in the prevailing state of incipient rebellion against health measures, the believers would feel deeply outraged and would be ready for any violence; the health service would be attacked for interfering with divine providence itself. On the other hand, action was imperative if cholera were not to run riot in the town.
>
> We went to the Governor General and asked for constabulary to patrol the area and keep the people from committing mass suicide . . . The police and the constabulary prevented the collection of the water until the sewer was repaired, . . .

In all civilized countries today faith healing is practiced in one form or another. Prayers and sacred shrines are still regarded as cures of sickness. The shrine of Sainte Anne de Beaupré near Quebec has received trainloads of ailing pilgrims and the words "Sainte Anne, Mère de la Vierge-Marie, priez pour nous" have been breathed by countless souls. In the *Annales de la Bonne Sainte de Beaupré,* the monthly journal published by the Redemptorist Fathers who manage the shrine, the various cures are recorded, of which the following is a sample:

> Ironwood, Mich., July 28th, 1911.—For nearly two years I had suffered from ataxia and the doctors had pronounced my case incurable. But on my first visit to the shrine, July 24th, I was partly cured and left one crutch; and on July 25th, I ceased to use the other. Heartfelt thanks to Ste. Anne.[27]

[27] John Lee Maddox, *The Medicine Man* (New York: Macmillan, 1923), pp. 172-173.

A popular twentieth-century misconception is that science has replaced magic and superstition in the field of medicine. But when thinking of something as having "replaced" something else in human culture, it is wise to ask what were the functions once performed by the thing supposedly replaced. If the new acquisition cannot perform all these functions, it has not fully replaced the old practice. In the present case it seems clear that scientific medicine cannot fulfill all the functions which religio-magical medicine can. At any rate we find in our midst today an important body of religio-magical medicine.

A study made just prior to 1932 under the auspices of the Committee on the Costs of Medical Care[28] found that approximately a fifth of all persons professionally treating the sick in the United States were not scientifically trained physicians but imposters of one type or another. The amount of money paid these "healers" amounted to 125 million dollars, or 12 per cent of the total annually expended for the service of qualified physicians. The following table gives the salient facts:[29]

Practitioners	*Number*	*Amount Spent Annually for Their Services*
Osteopaths	7,650	$42,000,000
Chiropractors	16,000	63,000,000
Naturopaths & allied groups	2,500	10,000,000
Christian Science & New Thought healers	10,000	10,000,000
Total	36,150	125,000,000

Each of these healing cults is identified with a particular theory, the founder having launched his philosophy as an explanation and taught his procedure as a cure of all disease. In each instance the theory runs counter to the established facts of medical science. Each cult exhibits an unwillingness to scrutinize rigorously its central hypotheses; it clings to them with a fervor more characteristic of evangelism than science. The practitioners have a vested interest in their particular creed. If it is found invalid, their livelihood no longer exists. "It is this closed-mindedness, this devotion to a particular belief, which justifies the title 'cult' or 'sect' for all these groups."[30]

[28] Luis S. Reed, *The Healing Cults* (Chicago: University of Chicago Press, 1932).
[29] *Ibid.*, p. 1.
[30] *Ibid.*, pp. 2-3.

The founder of osteopathy was Andrew T. Still, "frontiersman, farmer, healer, amateur philosopher, uneducated, unpolished, eccentric, withal shrewd and bright in his way."[31] Without formal schooling except for a brief sojourn at the Kansas City School of Physicians and Surgeons, he had an inspiration late in life that the cause of all disease is structural maladjustment and that consequently drugs and vaccines are worthless. Since in his view the chief locus of structural maladjustment is in the spinal cord, he advocated as the best treatment the manipulation of the vertebrae.

As time has elapsed since its founding, the osteopathic cult has undergone an interesting and typical process of secularization. The original theory has not been thrown overboard entirely but has been restricted and qualified. Instead of explaining all disease it now pretends to explain only some disease; and its treatment has ceased to be a cure-all. Concomitantly, osteopaths have gradually adopted one by one the therapeutic procedures of medical science: surgery, diet, serums, vaccines, drugs.

This process of broadening has been the cause of much discord within the osteopathic camp. "The 'old doctor' opposed it to the end. Periodically, he exhorted his followers to hold to the 'fundamentalist' doctrine, to osteopathic manipulation pure and simple, and excoriated those who had departed from the early faith."[32] But the liberal wing gained steadily, until today osteopathic colleges are teaching most of the things ordinarily taught in medical schools and osteopathic practitioners are using, in states where the law allows, practically all the procedures of regular medicine.

But the absorption of osteopathy into the main stream of scientific medicine does not imply the disappearance of healing cults in general. On the contrary there have been such cults in the past and there will continue to be such in the future. Never has the United States been without one or more prominent ones.

At present both chiropractic and naturopathy, offshoots of osteopathy, though much more backward and cultish, are apparently also showing signs of secularization. Not so, however, certain other types of unscientific healing—Christian Science, New Thought, Episcopalean practice, etc.—which continue the early Christian tradi-

[31] *Ibid.*, p. 6.

[32] *Ibid.*, p. 13. The excellent account of osteopathy is contained in Chap. 2, pp. 5-31.

tion of the priest as a healer of the sick. In 1930 there were 8,848 Christian Science practitioners in the United States, the number having increased steadily since 1906. The total number of adherents at this time is estimated at 700,000, with the sect flourishing in England, France, and Germany. As a religion it is essentially a therapeutic system. "The vitality of the movement can be explained only on the ground of the actual or supposed efficacy of Christian Science in healing disease; the movement's appeal to new converts is the promise of health." [33]

In addition to Christian Science other religions have their form of faith healing. Jewish Science, an imitation of Christian Science, founded in 1922, bases its healing techniques on the same affirmations of goodness and health and prayerful communication with the Divine Mind. Its practitioners offer prayers for the patient and induce in him a religious, hopeful attitude.[34] The Episcopalean Church carries on healing services in many of its churches, largely inspired by the Society of the Nazarene founded in 1909. The Catholic Church, as always, has relics which the sick may touch, encourages prayers and sacrifices to the saints for healing purposes, maintains its healing shrines, holds special healing services, etc.[35]

The Explanation of Irrational Health Practices

There are five creditable theories as to why these unhealthful health practices are so exceedingly pervasive and persistent in human society. They are as follows: (a) the "error" theory, (b) the "really right" theory, (c) the "fraud" theory, (d) the "psychiatric" or "mental aid" theory, and (e) the "functional" theory. These theories are not mutually exclusive but supplementary. Each becomes wrong only when advanced as the sole explanation, as if none of the others could be right.

(a) *The "Error" Theory.* The dominant theory is that health practices which do not achieve their end are due to ignorance and error. According to this view, man simply lacks the knowledge and logic necessary for the complex task of dealing with sickness. As he develops science, however, ignorance and supersitition will be dispelled and the treatment of disease will become logico-empirical.

[33] *Ibid.*, pp. 72-75. [34] *Ibid.*, pp. 84-85.
[35] *Ibid.*, pp. 93-97.

Undoubtedly correct as far as it goes, this view is yet redundant. By definition a nonrational health practice is one which adopts the wrong means. We need to know not *that* an error occurs but why—why rational beings are superstitious and ignorant. Above all we need to know why particular kinds of superstition recur constantly. Since the universe is full of an infinitude of things irrelevant to a given illness, why are particular things chosen as the instruments of irrational treatment? Why, for example, does the devout Christian choose prayer rather than a watch-fob to cure his diabetes? By itself the "error" theory is inadequate.

(b) *The "Really Right" Theory.* A romantic explanation of folk medicine maintains that although such medicine does not seem efficient at first sight, it is actually so; that medicine men really have a secret knowledge of herbs; and that our own doctors would do well to study these folk practices. Such a view is hard to refute until a statistical study of the effectiveness of folk remedies is made, but the observations of historians and anthropologists suggest that most of the practices are "neutral" and that a few are definitely harmful. Doubtless a few remedies succeed in spite of wrong theory, but the success of such remedies is not expansible. Whereas a scientific theory constantly originates effective new treatments, an erroneous theory does not. Indeed, in nonscientific medicine the ritual element is more likely to be generalized than the empirical element. Thus the view that disease is caused by evil possession may be accompanied by beneficial massage in one case, by harmful gouging in another. There is no escaping the fact that some practices designed to improve health actually injure it and that the batting average, the percentage which really achieve their end, is exceedingly small. The "really right" theory is not, therefore, an adequate explanation. Superstitious health practices do not exist because they cure disease and prolong life; they exist for some other reason requiring a different kind of explanation.

(c) *The "Fraud" Theory.* Less romantic but equally rationalistic is the view that magical remedies are frauds practiced by shamen and priests upon a credulous community. Most students do not take such a Voltairian interpretation seriously, and yet they can hardly doubt that the deceptive legerdemain, artistry, and showmanship of the shaman help significantly to perpetuate nonrational treatments. Anthropologists, inquiring into the extent to which shamen believe in their own diagnoses and remedies, usually report both sincerity and subterfuge—sincerity with reference to the efficacy of magic in general, subterfuge with reference to particular dealings with patients. This, however, is true of "professionals" everywhere; occupying a special status they do not share exactly the same attitudes as their clients and hence inevitably practice some deception.

No one can deny the widely recognized cupidity of the shaman or that the beliefs and practices regarding health are usually so arranged as to give him a good return for his effort. The pharmacopia of ancient Egypt, for instance, included many ointments and emollients based on animal fat, but instead of easily available ox-fat or goose-grease the prescriptions called for the fats of many rare animals such as the lion, oryx, hippopotamus, snake, and lizard. Since no patient could obtain these himself, he had to buy them from his healer who willingly sold him "gallipots labelled as the fat of such and such an animal, whilst the pots actually contained, probably each and all of them, nothing but the homely goose-grease with perhaps a little coloring-matter added." [36]

The "fraud" theory therefore possesses an exterior plausibility but its weakness, as in all theories of the sort, lies in its inability to answer the question of why the people allow themselves to believe. If the shaman is motivated by cupidity, presumably the laymen are too, and they would not give their money for nothing. The truth is that unless there were already present in the public the need, will and habit of belief, the shaman's trickery would have no effect. Therefore, while admitting the shaman's showmanship as a factor in the situation, we still must explain independently the community's compulsion to believe.

(d) *The "Psychiatric" Theory*. Closely allied to the "really right" interpretation is the view which maintains that although folk medicine is physically erroneous it is mentally efficacious and therefore curative. Spiritual or magical treatment, it is claimed, gives the patient a confidence that helps him get well, especially when his ailment is imaginary or mentally caused.

This explanation is characteristically functional. The patient, and in most cases the practitioner too, must be unaware of the way the treatment actually works: he must have *faith* in the way it is *supposed* to work. In short this kind of treatment, in order to be

[36] Warren R. Dawson, *Magician and Leech* (London: Methuen, 1929), pp.65-66.

successful, *must* be nonrational, based on illusion. Health is attained not by the means in which the patient has faith, but by the faith itself. The moment he consciously employs faith as a means of getting well, so that he pretends to believe in something he knows to be false, the remedy loses its effect. Magico-religious doctrine provides the necessary element of illusion. By definition it fosters faith rather than scepticism. It assumes that the treatment works by some mysterious automatic process or by virtue of some spiritual intercession. The explanation, though childish, is emotionally satisfying, bars further investigation, and lulls the patient into confidence.

In accepting the truth of the "psychiatric" theory we must, however, make two essential qualifications. First, there are many ailments which are not mentally caused and in which suggestion is not a crucial factor. The disease gets worse or better despite the attitude taken toward it. Sufferers from tuberculosis are noted for their cheerful optimism; yet they die from the disease nonetheless. Conversely, grouchy or pessimistic people are not always ill, and if they are ill it is not necessarily because of their disposition. Second, though the process of mental healing is beautifully functional, it is only so in an individual sense. A patient's illusory beliefs may play no part in restoring him to health and yet they may still perform a function—in this case a social function. This leads us to a less frequent and less explored type of explanation, namely the "socio-functional" theory.

(e) *The "Socio-Functional" Theory*. How is it that societies survive despite a heavy burden of erroneous folk medicine? Can it be that erroneous medical practices constitute a societal advantage? The answer is yes. In the first place if the means of subsistence are scanty it may be advantageous to have a high mortality from disease rather than starvation, because starvation is more disruptive to social organization than ordinary disease and injury. In other words, if we admit that it may be necessary for societies to restrict their numbers, we must admit that this is likely to be done by custom rather than rational planning. Magical medicine makes it possible to believe in the value of life, to try to save it, and yet to increase the mortality. If the medicine men kill off a certain number of their patients and thus save the community from the conflict and demoralization contingent upon starvation, they have made an unintended communal contribution and at the same time have reinforced the sentiment in favor of prolonging life.

In the second place, and more importantly, nonrational folk medicine contributes to social solidarity by strengthening the system of religio-magical belief and culturally-engendered motivation. Each person's intrinsic desire to avoid the pain of sickness and to postpone death is a strong motivational force. If society can somehow harness the strong intrinsic desire and use it to control the individual in behalf of group strength, it has achieved much; and it can best do this by making the individual *believe* that health depends upon the correct observance of the mores, upon the spiritual forces that symbolize the society, and upon the ritual treatments which call these forces into play. We saw, in the case of the Azande, that the treatment of sickness was interwoven with the whole belief system of the society and operated to keep the members of the community under social control. The strongly individualistic desire for health and life is made the unconscious instrumentality for group cohesion and efficiency. If death sometimes occurs, the loss is real but the general gain is worth the particular cost. Actually, since "80 to 90 per cent of all patients get well under any treatment, or none," and since they invariably attribute their recovery to the treatment followed, the society does not lose in lives as much as it gains in confidence. It can make up for the loss of life by a high fertility, if necessary.

These explanations, all related and all partly true, when taken together clarify the extreme ubiquity and persistence of superstitious medicine. The desire to be well is so germane to the organism as to create a powerful motivational force; yet so complex are the factors governing health that they are seldom understood, and the sick person, left to ignorance, is ready to grasp at any straw. He is ready to believe those things which give him most hope—such as the colorful ministrations of the medicine man. The latter, avaricious and shrewd, stands ready with his tricks to encourage the patient's wishful thinking. But the illogical reasoning is not random; instead it conforms to a pattern, a pattern furnished by the culture. By thinking in this pattern the patient is led to feel his dependence upon the community for health and life and is motivated to observe the rules and pursue the values for which the community stands. In every society the same underlying phenomenon is at work, and it is for this reason that superstitious medicine is universal in the human species.

In modern civilization science has not wholly replaced magic and religion in the treatment of the sick. It will probably never do so, because the two kinds of treatment serve different functions, heal different maladies. Science cannot always give the particular kind of confidence which religio-magical medicine offers. The man of science must often admit failure, whereas the healer, part priest and part doctor, claims omnipotence. The scientific physician may lie to his patient in order to give him a helpful confidence in his recovery, but he cannot lie to his colleagues and the patient's relatives; and consequently he cannot build up a whole mythology in which the people believe. A cheery bedside manner and a hopeful face are about the limits to which he can go. The medical profession is rightfully committed, in fact, to "educating the public"; its approach is intrinsically antagonistic to a social mythology of disease and consequently cannot give the same confidence as the latter. It can give a general confidence in "scientific progress"—the improvement of human health over a long period; yet wishful confidence becomes crucial not in the long-run case of the nation or humanity but in the immediate case of the person suffering or about to die. It is the latter, with his friends and relatives, who needs hope—a sure hope which only the supernatural can provide.

Neither can scientific medicine supply the social functions which religio-magical medicine supplies. It cannot proclaim the value of life and yet unintentionally increase mortality. It cannot contribute to the strengthening of social solidarity by reinforcing the normative structure. In so far as a purely scientific attitude toward health is adopted, it is amoral. It may, to be sure, point out that human beings are dependent on each other for their health or ill health and encourage an attitude of preventive regulation and submission to governmental authority; but at the same time it may show that hallowed customs are unhealthful and the pursuit of certain social values is antagonistic to health. Indeed, in so far as health is accepted as a supreme value it implies a degree of individualism which is socially disintegrative. Because pregnancy is dangerous to health (during the 1930's in the United States over 5 women died out of each 1000 giving birth), should women stop having children in order to avoid this risk? Because war obviously causes death and disease, should a nation refuse to protect itself? Unconsciously we value other things higher than mere health and longevity. These other things are reinforced by magic and religion. But occasionally there is a conflict when scientific medicine, with its emphasis on health, opposes one or more of the traditional mores. An example is the long conflict between the demand of medical schools for bodies to dissect and the sentiment that dead human beings are sacred. There is still today a conflict over the medical technique of contraception. It is only a short while ago that the moralists (many physicians among them) gave up the fight against painless childbirth. There is always a no-man's land of conflict between scientific medicine and social mythology, but not when the medicine is itself mythological.

(3) *Practices Considered Irrelevant to Health, but Nevertheless Injuring It.* Nearly everything people do affects their health, but in most cases the influence is so small or so complicated that it goes unrecognized. For centuries Orientals ate polished rice without recognizing that it caused their beriberi, and for decades the Filipino betel chewers dipped their hands in jars of betel nuts without realizing that this spread cholera. Probably the most drastic way in which society regularly acts as a cause of death is precisely through its large heritage of unconsciously injurious customs—customs which govern diet, exercise, contact, and all the other avenues through which disease may be spread or injury inflicted.

A classic example of a social movement innocently conceived but tragically fatal is provided by the Medieval crusades. Whereas the local isolation of the manor had given some protection against transmissible diseases, the crusades established a line of travel for men, beasts, parasites, and bacteria; and the result was a holocaust of epidemics. Smallpox, leprosy, diphtheria, and bubonic plague came home with the armies and stayed to scourge Europe for decades and centuries.[37]

Another classic example is the common use of rivers for a dual purpose—sewage disposal and water supply—with the resulting transmission of typhoid, cholera, dysentery, and other diseases. So long in fact have such customs prevailed that certain species of

[37] Howard W. Haggard, *The Lame, the Halt and the Blind* (New York: Harper & Brothers, 1932), pp. 14-15.

bacteria and protozoa, through long evolution, have become biologically adapted to them.

Other illustrations include the tight-laced corsets of the Victorian era, the white bread for which the working classes of Europe fought, the use of human excreta as garden fertilizer, the habitation of swampy mosquito land, and the habit of barefootedness on polluted soil.

The harmfulness of such practices goes unrecognized for two reasons, both of which bolster and perpetuate each other: first the complexity of the causal chain, and second the emotionality and ritualism of the attitude toward sickness. Incomprehensibility fosters magic, which in turn fosters ignorance. When the injuriousness of a folkway is pointed out, people do not immediately abandon the practice; on the contrary they almost invariably defend it for a time, and sometimes forever. Modern society not only contains many unhealthful customs not recognized as harmful but also many known to be deleterious and yet not abandoned—for instance the enormous consumption of sugar in the United States.[38] Scientific medicine has railed constantly against the obstinate refusal of human beings to promote their own physical welfare.

In citing specific customs one is likely to lose sight of larger aspects of social organization which may also, in their ultimate effects, be physically harmful. Political weakness or disintegration, for instance, gives rise to fatal conditions. Where there is anarchy in every aspect of society—in short, where there is no society—there is no human life. While complete breakdown of social life is seldom if ever found, political disorganization is painfully frequent. An illustration of its effects can be found in China during the period of transition from the declining Manchu dynasty of the nineteenth century to the unstable Republic which followed. Political disruption caused banditry and a breakdown of communication and storage facilities, with consequent famines and extremely high mortality.[39]

Social Aids to Good Health and Longevity

If we have dwelt so long on the ways by which society causes death, it is because few attempts have been made to treat system-

[38] New York Academy of Medicine, *Preventive Medicine in Modern Practice* (New York: Paul Hoeber, 1942), p. 101.

[39] Walter H. Mallory, *China, Land of Famine* (New York: American Geographical Society, 1928).

atically this aspect of mortality. People generally think of society as promoting health because this is a strong and definite aim; and they explain away and dismiss as "superstition" the social factors in sickness and death.

It is certainly true, however, that even in societies with extremely high mortality the social system also operates to keep this mortality below the point of annihilation. Any society, if it is to continue, must somehow reduce its long-run mortality to what its fertility can replace. Our question then becomes: How is this control over mortality accomplished?

A resumé of the societal factors which promote good health would show that every basic institution is involved. Certainly those rules and practices by which food and shelter are produced, distributed, and consumed are essential for life—not all of them but a considerable minimum of them. The political structure by which protection is afforded also preserves life, as do the customs of regularity and rhythm in sleeping, playing, working, defecating, etc.

The following generalization seems to hold true—that in most of the societies of human history the practices specifically designed and consciously applied to the curing of sickness and prevention of death have been only slightly successful. The really advantageous institutions have been those which give human beings the essentials of life—which in short satisfy the needs designated in Chapter II as organic. It is primarily through institutional means of satisfying these needs that society contributes to health and longevity, not through specific health practices.

There is, however, one great exception. This is the development of scientific medicine in modern society. Scientific medicine, in both its therapeutic and its preventive aspects, has reduced human mortality more than any other single factor. It involves two essential features: first, a logico-empirical point of view toward the body and its disorders; second, an increasing array of instruments for observation, dissection, analysis, and treatment. The first has not been completely acquired even today and probably never will be; but there is an ever-widening sphere defined as "purely medical" and therefore buttressed against the intrusion of moralistic and mystical thinking. This empirical point of view rests of course upon the general cultural background which underlies all our science. It owes something to cultural cross-fertilization and increasing mobility in

Western society. In the growing atmosphere of logico-empirical thought medicine has found its place. Improved technology has given it better instruments and improved biology has given it better theories. Though the science and the practice of medicine have remained separate, both have advanced pari passu as one discovery has led to another with accelerating momentum.

The most significant medical trend today is the growth of preventive medicine. It is a late trend, because it requires a high level of public education and support of medical research. To convince a healthy citizen that he must spend money for community health measures is not easy. Unless some emotional stimulus is provided he tends to remain indifferent; and unfortunately the measures required to insure community health are exceedingly prosaic. Preventive medicine must depend upon organized campaigns, bureaucratic machinery, long-range planning, and a substantial economic subsidy. This is why the movement did not really begin until the nineteenth century, and why its pioneers were social reformers rather than doctors. It seems miraculous that it should ever have happened at all. But having happened it has created a major demographic revolution.

Human Migration

The "causes" of human migration have never been systematically understood. When people speak of them, they often have in mind either the motives that migrants carry in their heads or the conditions they face. It is not always realized that both kinds of "causes" are relevant and mutually interdependent. Except when forced to do so (as in slavery) no one migrates without an end in view. At the same time, however, the effect of an end with respect to migration cannot be known until the conditions are understood. The same end may be satisfied at one time by one kind of behavior and at another time by an opposite kind, depending on the situation. So in understanding migration it is not sufficient to deal with motives or with conditions alone; it is necessary to deal with both.

What complicates the picture is not simply the interplay between ends and conditions but the fact that these relate to different peoples and different territories. In all cases there are two territories to consider—the territory of origin and the territory of destination. So complicated and variable are the factors involved that the lack of systematic formulation is not surprising. Social scientists explain particular migrations in terms relevant to the given case; they do not discover laws or general rules covering all migration.

Always in migration there is an element of emotional and economic cost. It is not easy to leave one's friends, relatives, and familiar surroundings to take up residence in a strange land. Nor is it easy to accumulate the capital necessary to make the journey. It follows that the advantage must seem greater than the cost of moving. In general the further one moves, physically and culturally, the greater is the cost and the greater must be the advantage. Circumstances, however, may cut down the cost. If the migrant already has friends and relatives abroad, if he has a sure job, if his expenses are paid by the government or by a future employer, the way is smoothed for him. The decision to migrate rests then upon a rough calculus in which the relative advantages are balanced against the cost. This sounds as if the decision were a rational one, but one must remember that the ends are given and these ends differ from one period and one class to another. One must also remember that the migrant may be in error both as to the actual cost and as to the relative advantage of the move. The records of migration to America reveal that the migrants nursed many irrational fears and many irrational hopes. Interested parties played upon these fears and hopes, attempting by propaganda to influence the potential migrants. The hazards of communication made difficult an intelligent assessment of the advantages and costs. Many a utopian settlement in the new land, founded on wishful thinking rather than knowledge of the facts, resulted in disaster. Many a boat reached its destination with more than half its human cargo dead. Many a migrant wished he had never left home.[40]

The attitudes of nonmigrants toward migration depend on a host of circumstances. In some cases those in the home country do not want people to leave, because they fear some disadvantage to themselves or their country through such departure; in other cases they want people to go, thinking that perhaps this will leave more land, jobs, or wealth for those who stay. In the case of the receiving territory the inhabitants may be so weak or sparse (e.g. primitives) that their attitude toward immigrants is unimportant. Occasionally

[40] Marcus Lee Hansen, *The Atlantic Migration, 1607-1860* (Cambridge: Harvard University Press, 1941), Chaps. 4-10.

the people in the receiving territory, though capable of preventing immigration, see some advantage in it. Seldom do they like the immigrants but they may want laborers, soldiers, customers, and co-religionists in greater abundance. Never are they willing to take just any kind of immigrants. They prefer some against others on the basis of race, religion, language, health, economic status, and political philosophy. It follows that migration is always selective. In the first place not all persons in one area are equally impelled to move to another; and in the second place not all persons are equally permitted or welcome to come.

TYPES OF MIGRATION

Types of migration may be delineated in different ways according to the elements one cares to emphasize. Today, in an age of nationalism, the basic distinction is whether or not the migration involves the crossing of an international border. If it does not, it is called *internal* migration; if it does, it is called *external* migration. Since in popular thinking the terms "emigration" and "immigration" are associated with international changes of residence, these terms are not generally used for internal migration. Nevertheless even internal migration involves movement out of one area and into another; so the terms *out-migration* and *in-migration* have been utilized.

The demographic importance of internal migration exceeds by far the importance of external migration. Within a country few barriers are opposed to the free flow of persons, goods, and capital from one place to another, with the result that there is much internal migration. Some of this movement covers greater distances than some external migration. The great movement of millions of Chinese for hundreds of miles from the east coast to the interior during the Sino-Japanese conflict (1937-45) was a tremendous migration, stimulating social change in China on a grand scale.[41] The movement to the West Coast in the United States was equally great, as was the movement of Russians to Siberia. Yet because external migration is legally regulated it looms much larger in our literature and our thinking than internal migration.

Undoubtedly the chief form of internal migration, and hence the world's greatest movement of people, has been the rural-urban

[41] Ta Chen, *Population in Modern China* (Chicago: University of Chicago Press, 1946), Chap. 6.

migration of the last two centuries.[42] The growth of cities has been described in another chapter and need not be recapitulated here, except to repeat that this growth has rested more on migration than on natural increase and has consequently involved the movement of hundreds of millions of people.

Extant classifications of migration generally confine themselves to international movements and usually stress the relation between the migrants and the receiving people. In this vein five possibilities suggest themselves:

(1) *Conquest.* The migrant group, because of either superior culture or superior military strength, may come as conquerors. Their superior position however, tends to be temporary, for intermarriage usually produces biological amalgamation and cultural assimilation.[43] This happened to the Moslems in Spain just as it is happening today to the Spaniards in Mexico. It also happened to the Aryans in India, the Germans in Europe, and the Turks in Asia Minor.[44]

(2) *Displacement.* Conquest implies that the natives remain as a subordinate people in the conquered territory, forming either a majority (South Africa) or a minority (New Zealand) in the new regime. But sometimes they are completely displaced, either by being wiped out or by being pushed to a new territory. Many Indian tribes in North and South America were wiped out completely by the firearms, alcohol, and diseases of the Europeans. Others were driven to remote parts where they managed to make a stand. The mountains and jungles of southern and southeastern Asia are strewn with remnants of primitive peoples pushed back by the invasion of more progressive migrants who took the fertile valleys and plains.

(3) *Forced Labor.* Sometimes people move, not because they want to leave but because they are pulled out by a more powerful group who want their labor. Thus slavery has always been a basis for migration. The greatest period of such movement undoubtedly occurred during the three centuries between 1550 and 1850, when something between 10 and 20 million Negro slaves were transported from Africa to the newly discovered territories in the Western

[42] To be sure, some rural-urban migration is international in character, a fact seldom realized; but most of it is internal.

[43] Ralph Linton, *The Study of Man* (New York: Appleton-Century, 1936), pp. 243-252.

[44] Louis Halphen, "Migration—Ancient and Medieval, "*Encyclopedia of the Social Sciences,* p. 426.

hemisphere.[45] When slavery was gradually abolished throughout the European world in the nineteenth century the need for cheap plantation labor in new areas did not cease, however. Instead it continued and was met by another device for transporting people from backward areas. This was indenture, by which a poverty-stricken person bound himself to serve a master for a number of years in return for payment of his passage. Though a supposedly contractual arrangement, the inequality of the agreement often entailed virtual slavery for the person transported. This was particulary true when persons of non-European culture, with no education and little conception of the new situation, were induced to go to a far-away land where the customs and language were strange to them, where their race was conspicuous, and where the masters were leagued together and were dominant in a government closed to the indentured laborers. In such cases penal sanctions were imposed for breach of contract, and strong pressure was put on the hapless worker to re-indenture himself at the expiration of his original period. In this manner millions of East Indians, Javanese, and Chinese were transported to agricultural estates all over the world, especially between 1830 and 1910. In those cases in which Europeans indentured themselves, as they did in North American colonies, the similarity of race and culture between masters and workers was such that the arrangement proved only a mild and temporary servitude. With the Asiatics, however, it was at best a condition of semi-slavery.

(4) *Free Individual Migration.* When we think of "immigration" we usually think of the mass movement of Europeans to Australia, New Zealand, South Africa, and the Americas during the last two centuries. This movement was unique in many ways. It involved greater ocean travel over open waters, greater numbers (some 50 million), longer distance, and more voluntary, individual, and peaceful movement than had ever been known before. It was a phenomenon new to the world and one not likely to be seen again. Yet its very massiveness and recency colors much of our thinking about human migration.

(5) *Controlled Migration.* Gradually this free individual migration of the last two centuries is giving way to another kind—controlled migration. The rise of nationalism, with increasing state regu-

[45] Frank Tannenbaum, *Slave and Citizen: The Negro in the Americas* (New York: Knopf, 1947), pp. 29-39.

lation, has inevitably led to a greater control of human movement across national boundaries. Each nation now wants to regulate the number and kind of persons leaving as well as the number and kind arriving. With such control at both ends, with the earth much more heavily inhabited than it has ever been before, it is no wonder that the amount of migration has greatly diminished.

The United States, which received more immigrants than any other nation in the world, began to erect barriers against the influx in 1921 when the first quota law was enacted. Since that time our laws have become progressively restrictive.[46] Most other nations also now have strict legislation aimed at controlling the quantity and kind of immigrants admitted. Even Latin America, which professes to need immigrants, generally excludes Asiatics and wants only Europeans of certain types.[47]

Japan was one of the pioneer countries in controlling emigration as distinct from immigration. Her primary motive being the expansion of her Empire, she wanted her people to leave in such a manner that political penetration into new areas would be assured. To this end, after 1907, she sent approximately 200,000 Japanese to Brazil. These came under the auspices of Japanese companies enjoying government support. The migrants settled in carefully planned and regulated colonies where births and deaths were registered on Japanese forms, where books, magazines, and school classes were in Japanese, where life was as nearly like the Japanese home life as it could be made, and where close ties with the homeland were maintained. During World War II Brazil awoke to find it had an organized monster in its midst, and since that time the resistance of the Japanese colonists to assimilation has been as dogged as it has been ingenious.[48] Italy tried controlled colonization in Ethiopia and Abyssinia. Nazi Germany did not promote much organized emigration but did try to organize and use for nationalistic ends the German communities already located in many lands.

The reaction to the use of emigration as a means of political penetration was to heighten the tendency to limit and control the

[46] United States Immigration and Naturalization Service, *Our Immigration* (February, 1947).

[47] Kingsley Davis, "Future Migration into Latin America," *Milbank Memorial Fund Quarterly,* Vol. 25 (January 1947), pp. 44-62.

[48] J. F. Normano and Antonello Gerbi, *The Japanese in South America* (New York: John Day, 1943), Chap. 2. T. Lynn Smith, *Brazil: People and Institutions* (Baton Rouge: Louisiana State University Press, 1946), pp. 278-283.

entry of foreigners. No nation wanted a fifth column in its midst. At the same time, as an aftermath of the period of mass migration, many areas were plagued by problems of ethnic, religious, and racial minorities. Increased nationalism, fear of cultural diversity, resentment of the foreigner, fear of substandard competition, and increasing density of population, all combined to promote a policy of exclusion throughout most of the world.

The history of "displaced persons" after World War II illustrates the difficulty of migration under conditions of nationalistic control. Everybody felt that these unfortunates should have a place to go, yet few nations stepped forward to welcome them. Each nation busily searched for some other nation that would accept them. As time dragged on the problem solved itself more by mortality than by emigration from Europe.

The nationalistic control of migration has led to a peculiar world situation. Demographically the potential migration pent up in today's world is enormous. Not only is the earth's total population increasing at the fastest rate ever known, but the increase is extremely unequal as between different regions. Generally the fastest growth is occurring in the poorest regions, the slowest growth in the richest. As a result the previous inequalities of population distribution are being aggravated rather than alleviated. Certain backward, primarily agricultural regions are glutted with people and are showing signs of even greater glut in the future, while other areas, primarily industrial, are casting about for means of increasing their birth rates. Between the two kinds of areas the differences in level of living are fantastic. What more natural than to expect the destitute masses of the underprivileged regions to swarm across international and continental boundaries into the better regions? Like the atmosphere, the earth's human population is characterized by high and low pressure areas, and one expects an inevitable current of migration from one to the other. Actual migration, however, is not governed solely by high and low pressure. It is governed by economic costs, political barriers, ethnic attitudes, and limited horizons. These barriers have slowed down migration to a snail's pace. One wonders how long the inequalities of growth between major regions can continue without an explosion that will somehow quickly restore the imbalance. This problem will receive further consideration in the next chapter.

Summary

If this chapter has been long, it is for two reasons: First, the connection between society and the components of population (fertility, mortality, migration) is a complex one. Second, this complexity has been largely overlooked by those dealing with population. Both popular and scientific thinkers have generally shown a strong biological bias in their demographic theory. They have generally made population a function of instincts on the one hand and resources on the other. If they have admitted cultural factors at all it has generally been in the form of technology. But there is much more to culture than technology and much more to human society than economic behavior. Our survey has explored some of the ways in which the peculiar nature of human society affects the demographic processes. It has tried to show that every social system represents a balance of forces, some tending to heighten the rate of births, deaths, and migration, and some tending to lower it; and that the balance itself is related not only to the individual needs of the people but to the societal needs as well.

References

Gilbert W. Beebe, *Contraception and Fertility in the Southern Appalachians* (Baltimore: Williams & Wilkins, 1942).

A careful, technically sophisticated study of the consequences of offering contraceptive service to families in the Appalachian coal mine region of West Virginia. The author relates the region, its culture, and its past fertility history to the degree of acceptance and use of contraception.

Louis I. Dublin and Alfred J. Lotka, *The Length of Life* (New York: Ronald Press, 1936).

Unravels the intricacies of the life table with great clarity and discusses the major conclusions about the human life span to be drawn from such tables. Rather technical in spots.

Julius Isaac, *The Economics of Migration* (New York: Oxford University Press, 1947).

The most systematic treatment yet published of the interrelations between migration and economics. Deals mainly with free individual migration under the conditions of capitalist economy. Closely reasoned and tightly written, the book is meant for the professional economist and sociologist.

Raymond Pearl, *The Natural History of Population* (New York: Oxford University Press, 1939).

Mostly devoted to the factors determining fertility. Sums up a great amount of research by the author and others. Good reading although meant primarily for a professional audience.

E. F. Penrose, *Population Theories and Their Application* (Stanford University, California: Food Research Institute, 1934), Part 1, "Theories of Population"; Part 2, "Population and Resources."

One of the best discussions of population theory in the literature. Contains some very clear thinking with respect to Malthus, the optimum theory, and the relation of resources to population.

T. Lynn Smith, *Population Analysis* (New York: McGraw-Hill, 1948).

A textbook that stresses the characteristics of the population and elementary demographic techniques.

Regine K. Stix and Frank W. Notestein, *Controlled Fertility* (Baltimore: Williams & Wilkins, 1940).

Study of patients at the Margaret Sanger birth control clinic in New York City—their past fertility history, the effectiveness of untutored contraceptive practices, the use of the clinic's methods, and pregnancy wastage. Sets forth a new technique of measuring the effectiveness of contraception, and finds that nearly any birth-control method tends to reduce fertility substantially.

Warren S. Thompson, *Population Problems* (New York: McGraw-Hill, 1942).

The standard textbook on population. The author is a well-known authority in the field.

CHAPTER XXI

WORLD POPULATION IN TRANSITION[1]

VIEWED in long-run perspective, the growth of the earth's population has been like a long, thin powder fuse that burns slowly and haltingly until it finally reaches the charge and then explodes. For a million or more years our species increased with infinitesimal slowness, flourishing temporarily in some areas, hardly getting started at all in others. Throughout at least 99 per cent of its history it remained extremely sparse. Sustenance was obtained by hunting, fishing and gathering, which required huge areas for few people, sometimes as much as 200 square miles per person.[2] Not until the beginning of the Neolithic era some eight to seventeen thousand years ago, when agriculture, domestication of animals, pottery, and textiles were invented, did greater density become possible. After that time cultural evolution moved at a faster pace, for eventually metallurgy and writing were invented and agriculture and transport improved; but still the world's population, as distinct from that of particular areas, grew so slowly as to seem stationary by modern standards.

The first real burst of world population growth came with the latest stage in cultural progress—the Industrial Revolution. Not only did this change, considered in its broadest sense,[3] give an unpre-

[1] Most of this chapter is adapted from the writer's paper, "The World Demographic Transition," *Annals of the American Academy of Political and Social Science*, Vol. 237 (January 1945), pp. 1-11. For further information the student should read other articles in this issue of the *Annals*, which is entirely devoted to "World Population in Transition."

[2] A. B. Wolfe, "The Fecundity and Fertility of Early Man," *Human Biology*, 5 (Feb. 1933), pp. 36-39; Grahame Clark, *Archaeology and Society* (London: Methuen, 1939), pp. 174-182. Clark believes the population of Mesolithic England and Wales could not have exceeded 3,000-4,000 persons.

[3] The term "Industrial Revolution" should not here be construed narrowly, because it involved economic, social, and political changes equally as fundamental as the technological. Louis W. Moffit, *England on the Eve of the Industrial Revolution* (New York: International Publishers, 1925); Abbott Payson Usher, *The Industrial History of England* (Boston: Houghton Mifflin, 1920), Chaps. 4 and 10.

cedented impetus to population growth in Europe, but its rapid diffusion to other regions extended its influence around the globe. For the first time the world's entire population could be regarded as a single entity responding in varying degrees to one dynamic process. For the first time the movement of human masses across large oceans became feasible. For the first time a new type of balance between births and deaths, a balance less wasteful than the old, began to manifest itself. And finally, also for the first time, the arts of demographic accounting became sufficiently exact to yield a reasonable estimate of the earth's total inhabitants.

Modern Increase of Numbers

Although no reasonable estimate of the world total can be made for dates earlier than the seventeenth century, various scholars have worked out figures for subsequent times. These estimates are by no means exact and indeed the world's population is not known accurately today, but they are sufficiently accurate to give us a notion about the rate of growth for the globe and for the various continents.[4]

The accompanying chart depicts the relative growth of the world population and its continental components from 1650 to 2000. The projections to the year 2000 for each continent are tentative, especially for Africa, South America and Asia, but they give some notion of potential trends.[5] Table 1 gives the historical growth of the world population and the average annual rate of increase for different periods.

TABLE 1

Date	*Estimated World Population (Millions)* *	*Annual Per Cent Growth During Preceding Period* †
1650	545	——
1750	728	0.29
1800	906	0.44
1850	1,171	0.51
1900	1,608	0.63
1940	2,171	0.75

* Figures except that for 1940 are taken from Carr-Saunders, *op. cit.*, p. 42. The 1940 estimate is taken from the League of Nations Statistical Yearbook for 1941-42.

[4] World estimates have been re-examined by A. M. Carr-Saunders, *World Population* (Oxford: Clarendon Press, 1936), Chaps. 2 and 3.

[5] The projections are described by Frank W. Notestein, "Population—The Long View," in Theodore W. Schultz (ed.), *Food for the World* (Chicago: University of Chicago Press, 1945), pp. 36-57.

† Average geometric rates calculated by the exponential formula.

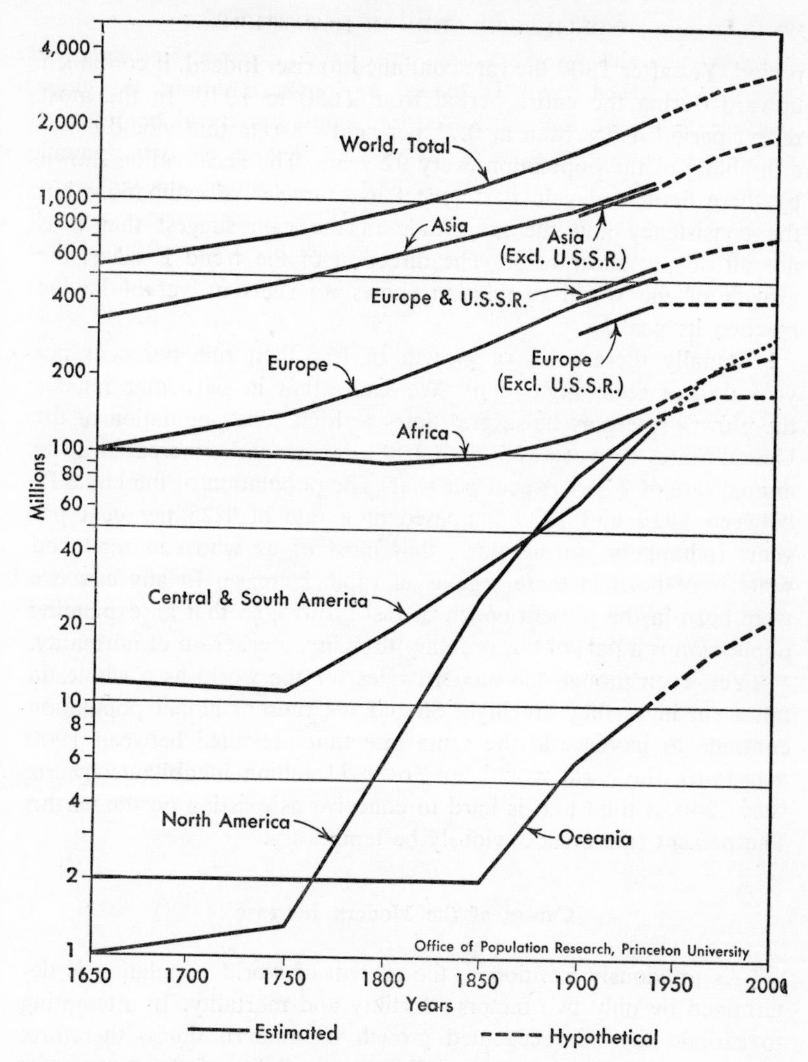

Estimated Population of the World and of Continental Areas, 1650-2000.

It appears that between 1650 and 1750 the rate of growth was already so high (0.29 per cent per year) that it could not have been in effect very long. The strange thing, however, is that this rate of growth, though probably unprecedented in the world's history, was the lowest rate for any major period in modern times. From 1750 to 1800 the rate climbed to a figure half again that of the earlier period. Yet after 1800 the rate continued to rise. Indeed, it continued upward during the entire period from 1650 to 1940. In the most recent period it has been at 0.75 per cent—a rate that would cause a doubling of the population every 92 years. The acceleration shown by these figures may in part reflect inaccuracies of estimation; but the consistency and the magnitude of the gain suggest that it is not all due to sheer error. The direction of the trend is clear; the growth of the world population shows no signs as yet of having reached its peak.

Actually these rates of growth of less than one per cent per year do not seem high to us. We know that in particular regions the growth rate may be several times as high. The population of the United States between 1850 and 1900, for example, increased at an annual rate of 2.36 per cent per year. The population of the U.S.S.R. between 1927 and 1939 increased at a rate of 1.25 per cent per year. It happens, furthermore, that most of us who can read and write were born in these regions of rapid increase. In any case we were born in the present epoch of fast growth; so that an expanding population is a part of our ordinary thinking, a criterion of normality.

Yet, even though the modern rates for the world as a whole do not seem high, they are high. Should the present global population continue to increase at the same rate that prevailed between 1900 and 1940, the earth would hold over 21 billion inhabitants by the year 2240, a total that is hard to conceive as existing on the earth.[6] The present rate must obviously be temporary.

Causes of the Modern Increase

As previously mentioned, the growth of world population is determined by only two factors—fertility and mortality. In attempting to explain the unprecedented growth of modern times, therefore, one must first ascertain the relative responsibility of these two variables.

[6]Robert R. Kuczynski, who discusses various estimates of the ultimate population the world can hold, believes that 11 billion is about the maximum. *Population*, Harris Foundation Lectures, 1929 (Chicago: University of Chicago Press, 1930), pp. 283-286. Most such estimates rely upon calculations of the world's potential food production. They are unrealistic for two reasons: first, it is impossible to guess what technological improvements will be made during the next few centuries; second, it is by no means certain that the maximum population will be determined by the food supply. It may well be that comfort and convenience will determine the limit.

The evidence all points to declining mortality as the major cause. No proof is available that in any significant part of the world birth rates have risen, but there is plenty of proof that in most advanced countries fertility has declined. In Europe as a whole there was apparently a tendency toward decline in the nineteenth century. The drop gathered speed as time went on, slackening only after 1933.

If birth rates did not rise but fell instead, then the expansion of population must have come from a decline in mortality—a decline great enough not only to compensate for lowered fertility but also to furnish a greater natural increase than ever before. The recorded statistics prove that this was the case, for in the now industrialized countries the average expectation of life has doubled since the seventeenth century.

The reduction in mortality was at first gradual and began primarily with a more abundant, regular, and varied food supply which came with peace and commercial prosperity. Protection from disease through public sanitation and scientific medicine had little influence until the nineteenth century and was tragically slow for the first fifty years of that period. It eventually did have a remarkable effect, however. In northwestern Europe the decline in mortality reached its fastest pace during the half century from 1880 to 1930.

Behind the revolutionary increase in longevity there was the general and all-inclusive change of European society from illiterate agriculturalism to literate industrialism. The change took centuries and even in Europe is still incomplete. Yet the decline in mortality was not merely a result but also a cause of the social transformation, for it facilitated a more efficient use of human energies.

Though fertility also declined, it did so more slowly than mortality. A curious fact of human behavior is that, in the transition to a modern regime based on fewer babies and longer lives, the decline of fertility lags behind that of mortality. This is because the struggle for survival has forced all societies to place a high value on both reproduction and the preservation of life. With the coming of a more deliberate, innovative control over human affairs, a movement to limit reproduction in unaccustomed ways meets strong opposition as being contrary to an established value; whereas an effort to preserve life, even in unaccustomed ways, generally receives approval as *favoring* an established value. Only after the successful preservation of life has resulted in larger families and these larger families have proved an embarrassment in the highly urbanized and mobile structure of modern society, does the individual seek a way around the practice of his high fertility mores. He leaves the public attitude intact but tends to violate it in his own private behavior. Thus the lag of birth control behind death control is implicit in the growing rationalism of modern life, which first attacks the negative value (death) and later the positive value (high fertility).

The New Demographic Balance

Because of this lag of fertility decline behind mortality decline, the early phases of industrial progress are always marked by a phenomenal increase in numbers. But when the competitive, individualistic, urban society has arisen as a result of this industrial progress, large families become a handicap rather than a blessing. Then the same rational approach that was applied to the limitation of deaths is also applied to the limitation of births, and population ceases to grow. A balance is once again achieved, but it is a different and remarkably more efficient balance.

For instance, the European population after 1800 tripled itself at the same time that it sent millions overseas. Yet as the birth rate dropped to lower levels, northwestern and central Europe reached a point in 1930-40 when the growth of population began once more to approach zero. Indeed such growth as remains is more apparent than real, because there is still an abnormal number of people in the reproductive ages. Age-specific fertility trends show that a stationary or a declining population will soon eventuate. Further reductions in mortality can no longer compensate for lowered fertility.

Thus in advanced areas such as Europe and places where Europeans settled, the Industrial Revolution has been accompanied by an intimately related demographic transition. The result is a new type of demographic balance representing an astounding gain in human efficiency. Under the old regime of high fertility and high mortality women experienced the drain and danger of pregnancy often to no purpose, because a large proportion of the offspring died before reaching maturity. Too much effort was spent in trying to bring each new generation to adulthood; too much energy was lost in sickness, malnutrition, and mourning; too much time was taken for mere sustenance. The new type of demographic balance released a large part of this energy—a tremendous amount of human energy—for other things.

Expansion and Diffusion from Europe

By virtue of having originated the Industrial Revolution and the demographic transition, European peoples acquired the means of world dominance. They increased at a much more rapid rate than the rest of the world's population. Within three centuries they multiplied themselves more than seven times while the other peoples increased only three times. In 1650 the Europeans numbered about 100 million; in 1933, scattered throughout the world, they numbered approximately 720 million, of whom some 200 million lived outside Europe. Their proportion of the world's population rose from 18 per cent at the earlier date to 35 per cent at the later one.[7] This numerical expansion was accompanied by an enormous geographical expansion, for the Europeans settled the sparsely populated "new" lands that they discovered. The movement was greatest in the nineteenth century and involved, between 1846 and 1932, an emigration of more than 50 million, the bulk of whom remained overseas.[8] Thus both European stock and European culture were transplanted to huge new continental and island areas—Australia, New Zealand, Siberia, South Africa, North and South America. Displacing sparse native populations and applying their advanced techniques to virgin soil, the Europeans achieved an abundance of food sufficient not only for their own maintenance but for huge exports as well. In most of the new areas they eventually began to industrialize, first on borrowed and then on domestic capital. Freed by geographical distance from the traditions and handicaps of the home environment, they made rapid progress in the modernization of life. They began with rapid population growth—the most rapid ever known—but reached the point of a stationary or declining population at about the same time as northwestern Europe. This was pre-eminently the history of North America, Australia, and New Zealand.

In areas where the native population was more abundant or where the transplanted European culture was not that of northwestern Europe, the transition was not so rapid. In Latin America,

[7] Carr-Saunders, *op. cit.*, pp. 42-45.
[8] *Ibid.*, p. 49.

for example, economic development and population growth proceeded at a slower pace. This region, with its high proportion of Indians and its transplanted Portuguese and Spanish culture, is now in the midst of an expanding growth cycle instead of at the end of it.

Even in regions where the Europeans did not settle in large numbers, they exerted their dominance and diffused their culture. In Asia, for instance, they found indigenous civilizations of an advanced and complex type with populations already massive in size. Whether they "conquered" or merely dealt with these people, they managed to dominate them politically and economically. Using their own capital and skill the Europeans organized trade in the ports and commercial agriculture in the hinterland. The native peoples served as a rural proletariat, working often for bare subsistence, occupying a dependent position, and thus reaping few of the potential advantages of participation in the world economy.

Although other factors were also responsible, there is little doubt that the economic position of the Asiatics tended to retard a balanced absorption of Western civilization. This was true despite the fact that the advanced stage of this civilization would otherwise have made rapid diffusion possible. The net result was that certain elements were diffused rapidly, others slowly. The techniques of reducing death rates (medical science, sanitary engineering, agricultural improvement, and better transport) were imported for both humanitarian and economic reasons, and proved one of the most acceptable features of European culture. The effect was counterbalanced in some regions (more in Africa and the southwest Pacific than in Asia) by the transmission of European disease, but eventually death rates in most areas touched by European contact began to improve.

Fertility, however, was not correspondingly reduced, first because reduction proved a less acceptable feature of Western culture, and second because the Asiatics, being for the most part a rural proletariat under European dominance, were on the more fertile side of the differential birth rate. The usual class differentials received in this case geographical expression—the Europeans representing the low-fertility upper stratum, the Asiatics the fertile lower stratum.

There has thus been repeated the usual lag of fertility decline behind mortality decline, and the inevitable result has been the commencement of a tremendous expansion of the Asiatic population

—the first phase of a growth cycle apparently similar to that which the European peoples are just completing. Most of the Asiatic countries—notably India, Java, and Malaya—are already well into the heavy growth phase. One country, Japan, is just beginning to foresee the end of it. Others, such as Iran, China, and Borneo, have hardly started yet. Since there are already teeming millions in Asia, the future increments will be staggering. Coming at a time when the Western peoples are already reaching a point of stability, the increase will inevitably raise the proportion of Asiatics in the world.[9]

It becomes clear that the Europeans, by originating the Industrial Revolution and spreading it to the rest of the world, have enormously strengthened their position but have finally laid the basis for a possible weakening of it. Whereas they formerly enjoyed a rising dominance, they now face an imminent decline in world power.

Population and National Power

Strictly speaking, not all European peoples are in the same boat. It is possible, as Notestein and Thompson have done,[10] to divide all countries into three classes: (1) Those of "incipient decline"—already past the cycle of rapid growth, with birth and death rates at very low levels, faced by declining or stationary populations during the next few decades: e.g. United States, Canada, Australia, New Zealand, and all of Europe except certain parts. (2) Those of "transitional growth"—now in an early stage of the industrial cycle, with birth rates still high but declining, having populations that will eventually, after a steep increase in the next few decades, reach a point of stability or decline: e.g. Russia, Japan, southeastern Europe. (3) Those of "high potential growth"—still to become industrialized and hence likely to have, under conditions of peace and economic expansion, an exceedingly long and fast growth based on traditionally

[9] Latin America is also destined to have a great increase, and Africa too. But in both cases the base population is so much smaller than that of Asia that the absolute increments will not be comparable, at least for a century or two. See Kingsley Davis, "Population Trends and Policies in Latin America," in *Some Economic Aspects of Postwar Inter-American Relations* (Austin: University of Texas Press, Latin-American Studies, II, 1946), pp. 25-46.

[10] Frank W. Notestein, Irene B. Taeuber, Dudley Kirk, Ansley J. Coale, and Louise K. Kiser, *The Future Population of Europe and the Soviet Union* (Geneva: League of Nations, 1944); Warren S. Thompson, *Plenty of People* (Lancaster: Vagues Cattell Press, 1944), Chap. 6.

high birth rates and improved mortality, but may possibly have, under conditions of political disruption and continued poverty, virtually no growth at all: e.g. India, China, Java, most of Africa.

Our knowledge is more exact for countries in the first two classes. For many of them reasonable projections of future population have been made. Using these projections but allowing for assumptions and subsequent developments not incorporated in them, it is possible to say something concerning the role of future population growth and national power.

CLASS I. INCIPIENT DECLINE

Beginning with the first class it is possible to find one country (France) where the decline of population, apart from immigration, has already begun. In others (Great Britain, Austria, Belgium, Switzerland, Sweden) it will probably begin in ten or twenty years. In the remainder the turning point will occur still later—in some cases not until the 1980's or 1990's. Regardless of these differences, the countries of Class I are all in a similar situation. They formerly enjoyed the greatest share of world power and experienced the fastest growth of population. Now, however, they face a decline of relative power as well as growth. At present they contain approximately 400 million people. By 1970 they will likely have hardly any more than that. Their share of the world's population will therefore, it appears, decrease substantially.

The United States is the most favorably situated of the Class I countries. Its current population exceeds 140 million. According to recent estimates based on medium assumptions, the 1970 figure will be 157 million; the peak will occur in 1985 with 161 million, then a gradual decline will set in.[11] Nobody pretends that these estimates will actually materialize in detail, but the trend they represent seems highly probable. In numbers the United States will be far behind Russia, China, and India; yet the fact that our area is second only to Russia and Brazil and our technology second to none, will make the population sufficient for us to retain strong national power. Still, as time goes on we can depend less and less upon sheer numbers or indeed upon industrial advantage, but must depend instead on good will and diplomatic skill.

[11] Warren S. Thompson and P. K. Whelpton, *Estimates of Future Population of the United States, 1940-2000* (Washington: National Resources Planning Board, 1943), p. 29.

Germany's demographic prospects are much poorer. Up to 1910 she had the highest birth rate in northwestern and central Europe, but by 1933 one of the lowest. If the 1933 rates had remained fixed she would have eventually begun losing 30 per cent of her population each generation. The Nazis introduced an elaborate population program and succeeded in raising the birth rate. Yet the change was so limited that only a stationary population could have been expected. Now, with the highest proportional war losses of any belligerent in the last war, with a reduced area and a wrecked industrial system, Germany will likely have fewer people in 1970 than she had in 1940. Few of her recent enemies can take comfort from this fact, for they share a similar prospect. The British Isles face an imminent and almost certain decline, so that in 1970 they will probably have fewer than 45 million (less than Italy today). France, without substantial immigration, will be lucky to have 35 million. Germany, with perhaps around 60 million, will still remain the most populous country in Europe (excluding Russia).

CLASS II. TRANSITIONAL GROWTH

The second class—countries of "transitional growth"—embraces today approximately 435 million people, but by 1970 it will exceed 550 million. These are the countries whose populations will increase most rapidly. The most important is Russia.

Two centuries ago Russia seemingly had fewer inhabitants than did France. Today, with more than 170 million, she has over four times the population of France and over twice that of Germany. By 1970 she will have, according to the projections of the Office of Population Research, something like 250 million. She seems destined to have about three and a half times the population of Germany by 1970. Combined with rapid technological advances and a fuller utilization of rich resources, Russia's population growth will make her a true giant among nations. Her only possible rivals will be the United States, China, India, and the British Empire. Of these, China and India will probably lag behind in technology, resources, and political unity, so that the very size of their populations will prove a handicap. The British Empire is obviously falling apart and the pieces that will remain will not amount to a great deal demographically. The United States remains the only real contender. It will have a smaller population and a lesser domain than Russia, but it will not run a serious risk of overpopulation, which is a possibility in Russia.

The Japanese also belong to Class II. Among all the Asiatic peoples they are the only ones to get far in the transition to a modern demographic pattern. In 1870 they were an agrarian people, isolated in their island kingdom and numbering only 35 million. By a series of rapid and successful wars they quickly acquired an empire. By 1940 their homeland population had grown to 73 million, the empire population to 105 million. This was fast growth, the result of rapid industrialization and urbanization, with mortality declining before fertility. The growth resembled that of England in the nineteenth century. But now the industrialization and urbanization show an unmistakable tendency to force fertility ever lower. If Japan regains her place as a modern industrial nation, she will have a stationary population sometime after the turn of the century; but in the meantime, barring new catastrophes, her population will grow very fast for awhile. The chances are that by 1970 she will have over 85 million on the home islands.

CLASS III. HIGH POTENTIAL GROWTH

Also in Class II are Chile, Argentina, southeastern Europe, and possibly one or two other areas. But by far the major portion of the world, including 60 per cent of the area and over 60 per cent of the population, belongs to Class III. This is the class with the most uncertain future, because everything depends on the kind of social and economic conditions that will prevail. If the very high mortality is brought down, the extremely high fertility will yield enormous growth. If the high mortality remains, there may be no growth at all. The level of mortality is irregular and unpredictable.

Some of Class III regions—such as most of South America—have plenty of room for expansion. These can absorb a heavy population growth and at the same time raise their level of living. But others—such as India, Java, and Egypt—have already grown until swarming millions are crowded on the land. India alone added 83 million to her population during the twenty years between 1921 and 1941. If political stability and economic progress continue, these regions will have fantastic numbers. Yet their density is already so great that it seems unsafe to predict peaceful progress. China's civil war, India's religious war, Java's independence war—these do not suggest peaceful progress. If internal strife should reach the point at which health services are disrupted, transport ruined, irrigation destroyed, and trade upset, the result would be such a resurgence of high mortality that huge losses of population would be experienced. The potentiality for rapid increase is there but its realization is highly uncertain. It may be that the Industrial Revolution will come to these areas only when the surplus population has been eliminated by catastrophe. In that case it will bring fast population growth but will start from a smaller base than that now existing.

By way of summarizing this discussion let us glance at the relative positions of certain Great Powers in 1940 and 1970, omitting (because of their uncertainty) the Class III countries. Taking the leading six powers and expressing their populations as a percentage of the combined total, one gets the following:

	1940	*1970*
U.S.S.R.	32.5%	39.6%
U.S.A.	24.5	25.0
Japan	13.6	13.5
Germany	12.9	9.5
Gr. Brit.	8.8	6.8
France	7.7	5.5
	100.0	100.0

If these "best guesses" for 1970 are roughly accurate, Russia will enhance her demographic position much more than any other country. The United States and Japan will hold their own. Germany, Great Britain, and France will lose heavily. These changes may not entail similar shifts in national power but they will exert some influence.

Military manpower, for example, roughly parallels total population. But the countries in Class I are faced not only with stationary or declining but also with aging populations; while those in Class III are burdened with heavy proportions of children. The highest ratio of military manpower to total population is found in Class II countries.

The important thing about manpower is not only what is available now but what will be available in the next 15 years. The ratio of males under age 15 to males aged 20-34 is therefore an index of replacement possibilities. The larger the ratio the greater the potential increase in manpower. Below are the ratios, as of the early 1940's, for some leading nations:

Japan	1.59
Russia	1.43
U.S.A.	1.03
Germany	0.99
United Kingdom	0.92

Not only will Japan and Russia gain population more rapidly than the others, but they will increase their military manpower even faster.

The increasing burden of aged persons in Class I countries is serious. In 1850 the United States had only 3 per cent of its population over 65 years of age. By 1940 the percentage stood at 7, and by 1970 it will be about 10. Nobody knows exactly what kind of a society will accompany a population with an extremely high average age, because such a phenomenon is quite new and unique in the world. It will doubtless be an efficient society, because only such a society can have a death rate low enough to give a high proportion of aged people. But it may also have certain defects as against societies with younger populations.

Impact of World Population Shifts on the West

As Western civilization spreads from its present centers to the rest of the world, carrying with it a wave of population growth, the present regional balance in the world will be greatly changed. The possibility that Asia's teeming millions will double or even triple within the next few decades, acquiring at the same time Western industrial and military techniques, appears as a Frankenstein appalling to many observers. Recent events in Asia do not lighten the somber picture. But, as usual, many fears have arisen that are based on illusion rather than fact. A few neglected points may help to dispel the gloom.

THE RACIALISTIC FALLACY

One groundless basis of fear is racialism. People feel that the Asiatic races are inherently different from Europeans, and that if they become dominant they will "reduce" the whole world to the Oriental level. This view overlooks the independence of race and culture. If the Asiatics make the changes that will give them dominance, they will (though racially the same) lose a great part of their Oriental mode of life. Their culture will become more European and they will eventually show a declining fertility. Japan is a good illustration, for she went further than other Oriental people in borrowing Western culture and thus increasing her power; but, as a consequence, her fertility also began to drop. The existing civilization of the Orient is not fixed in the genes of the Asiatic races. It is rather a historical stage resembling in some respects the medieval civilization of Europe, destined to pass irretrievably as the Asiatics become westernized.

To think that the Asiatics can borrow and utilize successfully the instrumentalities of the West without also borrowing its other features is to commit a sociological error. The techniques of controlling death, for example, cannot be fully acquired and put into effect without also acquiring the science that underlies them and hence acquiring the morality of science, the competitive selection of talented personnel, the capitalization of public education, the idea of free research, and the other insitutions of modern society. Western civilization is not an airtight system whose parts fit together as neatly as the parts of an organism, but it is a socio-cultural system in which most of the parts are functionally related. It may be borrowed piecemeal as long as the borrowers are a rural proletariat under European masters, but it cannot be borrowed piecemeal in such a way as to give dominance to a people. The Japanese were powerful because they borrowed much of Western culture, but they lost because they did not borrow enough of it. In short, if Western civilization is to be diffused around the globe, as is apparently happening, there is no reason to fear that an increase of Asiatic *races* is going to cause the whole world to "sink" to the level of present-day Oriental civilization.[12]

INVASION BY MIGRATION

Not only is it feared that the Asiatics will gain world dominance by population increase and technological acquisition, but also that they will demand the right to migrate to regions now held by Westerners.[13] This problem, however, has two solutions. If the

[12] Of course, it must be admitted that if other peoples acquire our civilization, and *if* they become our enemies, they will be formidable by virtue of their acquisitions. But this has nothing to do with race as such. It is unlikely that future conflicts will be along racial lines unless our own prejudice fosters them.

[13] For an expression of this demand, see Radhakamal Mukerjee, *Migrant Asia* (Rome: Tipografia Failli, 1936).

Asiatics come with the traits of modern civilization, there is little reason to exclude them more than any other people—unless their nationalism or our prejudice makes loyalty to the new land peculiarly difficult. If, on the other hand, they come as representatives of a less efficient civilization, there is good reason to exclude them except to the extent to which they can be fully assimilated.

An invasion of advanced areas by people with high mortality and fertility can scarcely be justified from the point of view of the people already in these areas. The region from which the migrants come will not be greatly benefited, and the area which they invade will be retarded. A mere extension of current Asiatic civilization to new areas does not solve any problem, and to avoid such a result the European peoples would be justified in holding the lands they have, no matter how "vacant" these lands appear to the Asiatics. As Fiji, Trinidad, Formosa, Natal, and the Guianas illustrate, the Asiatics are capable of installing in new lands the same wasteful demographic balance that they preserve at home. On the other hand as the cases of Hawaii [14] and the United States illustrate, it is possible for migrants to lose the cultural traits that gave them high fertility. It would seem, therefore, that the maximum limit on Asiatic migration into a Western country is the number who can be rapidly assimilated. Yet the confusion between race and culture makes assimilation difficult in some countries and thus gives rise to economic conflict and minority problems.

A BEEHIVE WORLD?

The fear of a beehive world in which ten to twenty billion people eke out a bare livelihood rests on illusion rather than probability. It overlooks the inherent antinomy between a rising standard of living and a *proportionate* increase of numbers. It falsely assumes that the resources of an advanced civilization may all be turned in the direction of feeding ever greater numbers. Most modern inventions, however, are not designed to increase the amount of food but simply to add to our standard of living in other respects. The peculiar thing is that once a society abandons the subsistence idea it can actually support more people than otherwise. This is because technological advance, developed in many cases with no immediate thought

[14] Andrew W. Lind, *An Island Community* (Chicago: University of Chicago Press, 1938), pp. 107-116.

of increasing the food supply, eventually turns out to help in this way too. But this enhanced food supply goes to support more people *better,* not more people at the same level. The main point is this: Having increased the food supply by means of technological advance, the society cannot retain this supply without also retaining the advanced standard of living—i.e. the high per capita consumption. It cannot sink back to mere subsistence, because its food-producing capacity depends on all its other capacities which would disappear under subsistence conditions.

Let us take as an illustration the United States today. It has low death and birth rates; but suppose that its fertility began to rise until it reached say 45 per 1,000, a figure which under present conditions of mortality would double the population every twenty years. What would happen? Obviously at some point there would come a time when the demand for nourishment would take precedence over other things. One convenient thing to reduce would be education, because then the manpower of adolescents could be used to produce food. Another would be recreation, because this involves a waste of energy, food, and time. Still another would be the publication of books and magazines not only because the population would not have the time or even the capacity to read, but also because books and magazines cannot be eaten and their production takes valuable energy.

To keep people from starving, economy after economy would have to be introduced. For a while the country might gain in efficiency, but eventually it would begin to lose it, primarily because real cultural advance would stop. The medical profession for example would soon begin to go downhill, because it would be without the aid of research in pure science and thorough education of its members, and yet would have an increasingly heavy task on its hands as the standard of nourishment went lower and the number of pregnancies grew. Agricultural progress would be halted for the same reasons. In the end the very economies that were enforced to secure adequate nourishment would curtail advances in food production. The death rate would begin to rise and would eventually reach the point where it balanced the high fertility. The population would then be "adjusted" to its environment but the adjustment would be that of subsistence, not that of advanced civilization. Furthermore, the actual population would probably be less than that supported formerly at the higher standard of living.

The real danger is not that there will be a beehive world, but that cultural progress will stop at some point short of a complete transition from subsistence agriculture to industrial civilization. It is a contradiction to think that all the energies of the latter can be used simply to support the maximum population capable of being fed. One is prone to reason that with a given amount of resources and a given technology more people can live if they use their resources for the production of food than if they use them for other things. Such reasoning, however, bears testimony to the confusion which a Malthusian approach introduces into population theory. Actually, technology and consumption are not separate variables. The most advanced technology requires a wide range of consumption. To narrow the latter necessarily involves narrowing the former. This is why an advanced society cannot use its cultural paraphernalia simply to support a huge population at the sustenance level.

The fear of a beehive world is clearly illusory. "But," one will say, "there are millions in Asia who are either actually starving or so badly nourished that they easily succumb to disease. Even in our own country there are many whose diets are below the minimum for good health. Surely this means that a great increase of population, particularly in the already heavily peopled areas, will mean mass starvation. Surely it means that the world's population is already exceeding its food supply." This, however, is also illusion. The very fact that numbers are increasing indicates that the means to support them is increasing too. Otherwise mortality would have risen and the population would never have grown to its present size. To think of the world's population as "outrunning" its normal food supply is like thinking of the hind feet of a horse outrunning the front feet.

It is true that one of the causes of mortality is still starvation, whether coming occasionally as famine or regularly as undernourishment. Such starvation, however, does not arise from the inherent limitations on potential food production but from present patterns of distribution and consumption. It seriously affects only certain classes in particular areas, and is a relative rather than an absolute matter in the world today. If these classes in certain areas were given plenty of food, *and if nothing else in their lives were changed,* they would suffer a lesser mortality and their numbers would consequently grow. They would build their population up to new food supply and start starving all over again, with more people to starve this time. For this reason the population problem in backward areas such as India and Egypt cannot be solved simply by food relief. It can be solved only by reducing fertility. If fertility is high, then in the long run mortality must also be high. To reduce mortality without also reducing fertility is at best a temporary and hazardous expedient.

In those countries where all classes limit their fertility a minimum standard of nourishment can be set and achieved, but not in those where fertility remains uncontrolled. If, for example, the rest of the world were willing to feed them, the Hindus would probably multiply until they were rubbing elbows. If later the relief were suddenly withdrawn, millions of them would starve and the population problem would be back where it started. Such a situation cannot characterize the whole of the modern world. Food relief, with nothing else done to change the way of life, is a product of those nations that do limit their fertility, that do advance their technology, and that do have a high per capita consumption. If long-range food relief or any other means of reducing deaths, is applied to particular areas without any fundamental changes in the economic and social organization of those areas—changes that will reduce fertility—they are futile.

The possible catastrophe is not a beehive world or a starving world, but a world that steadfastly refuses to lower its fertility. Such a world would be one in which cultural progress had stopped short of a complete transition from subsistence agriculture to industrial civilization, and in which the demographic transition begun by Western peoples never spread to the rest of the globe. It would mean a return to the old balance of high birth rates and high death rates, and life would once more be wasteful, brutish, and short. Fortunately this prospect, though possible, is not probable.

Future Prospects

Statistical indices of nearly all sorts indicate that today throughout most of the world cultural development is going ahead faster than population growth. This suggests that the Asiatic peoples, and others as well, will acquire modern civilization in time to check their fertility and thus achieve an efficient demographic balance, instead of multiplying so fast that such acquisition would be impossible and a stationary but wasteful situation would be made permanent. We are inclined to think of future population increases as formidable. Actually such increases can hardly occur on a purely agricultural basis. They require Westernization. This being true, the prospect that there will eventually be too many people in the sense of too many to support at a higher level of living is not likely. Nor is it true that the world's natural resources will likely be exhausted. No one knows the future miracles of technology but, as the use of atomic power suggests, it seems safe to conclude that technical advance will go ahead rapidly, and that it will find new ways to use those of the world's resources that are constantly renewable rather than those that are exhaustible.[15]

LITERACY

An excellent index of modernization is literacy. According to census returns and systematic estimates, about 59 per cent of the world's population aged 10 and over was illiterate in 1930. The continents, however, were extremely uneven in this regard, as Table 2 shows. Four per cent were illiterate in North America as against more than 80 per cent in Asia.

Most of these figures are crude composite estimates, but they suggest that the countries enjoying the highest literacy have in general the lowest birth rates. This indicates that when the now illiterate countries undergo the social changes that reduce illiteracy, they will also experience a corresponding decline in fertility.

How long such changes will take we do not know, but there is some evidence that it will not take long. In 1875 Chile's population

TABLE 2

LITERACY, FERTILITY, AND DEPENDENCE ON AGRICULTURE FOR THE WORLD AND THE VARIOUS CONTINENTS, 1930 *

Region	*Per Cent Illiterate (Age 10 & Over)*	*Per Cent Dependent on Agriculture*	*Crude Birth Rates*
World	59	60	39
North America	4	25	20
Oceania	14	30	23
Europe †	15	36	23
U.S.S.R.	40	67	45
South America	54	65	41
Central America & Caribbean	59	72	44
Asia †	81	69	44
Africa	88	77	48

* The figures represent the weighted average obtained by combining the official or estimated rates for all of the countries within the area.
† Exclusive of the U.S.S.R.

[15] Kirtley F. Mather, *Enough and to Spare* (New York: Harper, 1944).

was 77 per cent illiterate; by 1930 it was only 44 per cent so. In 1897 Russia's population age 9 and over was 76 per cent illiterate; by 1939 it was only 19 per cent so.

DEPENDENCE ON AGRICULTURE

Another excellent index of civilizational advancement is the proportion of the population dependent on agriculture. In 1930, judging by census returns and estimates, approximately 60 per cent of the world's people were dependent on this pursuit. Again, as Table 2 shows, the continents were unevenly divided.

It is believed that only a small portion of the population (say 20 per cent) need be engaged in agriculture to furnish the total population with food under full use of existing techniques. The possibility of rapid industrialization in Asia, South America, South Africa, and the Near East, is more than a dream. Already India, China, Brazil, Argentina, Mexico, Israel, and Turkey have made a definite start. With these prospects in view, a rapid growth of the world's population for the next few decades need hold no terrors. It need not imply perpetual growth or ultimate catastrophe. Already in what were once the world's fastest growing areas the population has approached a stationary or a declining state. It seems likely, then, that the next century will see a general reduction in fertility and the peak of the world's population growth reached. Then the new demographic balance will be spread throughout the world.

This is an optimistic conclusion, based on the belief that the sweep of social change will brush aside the impediments to controlled fertility (including its opponents). It does not overlook the real problems that lie ahead—the pains, imbalances, struggles, and injustices that inevitably attend the process of industrialization on the one hand and the differences of regional growth on the other. As the cases of Russia (in retrospect) and India (in prospect) illustrate, it is virtually impossible to make the transition from agriculture to industry without dislocating and disorganizing great sections of the population. The best that can be done is to use modern knowledge to make the transition as quick and smooth as possible. At the same time the powerful nations of the past must adapt themselves to new giants created by technological diffusion and demographic expansion. In this and in the handling of industrialization, an intelligent world population policy can be of immense service. As such it must be a policy based on facts rather than prophesies of doom or visions of paradise. It must realize that a nation's feeling of being "overpopulated" is not a legitimate ground for war or for appeasement. It must insist that if mortality is to be controlled, fertility must also be controlled—that there is no other way, no possible alternative, if the world's population problem is ultimately to be solved.

References

Kingsley Davis (ed.), "World Population in Transition," *Annals of the American Academy of Political and Social Science,* Vol. 237 (January 1945), pp. 1-203.

Population trends, characteristics, and resources in the major regions of the world, and aspects of population change. Most of the articles are written clearly and concisely.

W. D. Forsyth, *The Myth of Open Spaces* (Melbourne: Melbourne University Press, 1942).

The open spaces of the world are gone. The places that appear to be open to settlement have disadvantages such as bad climate, lack of resources, distance from markets. Migration in any case has changed its character. The modern migrant from Europe goes to a city, not to a farm. A cogent analysis of modern migration by an Australian.

David V. Glass, *Population Policies and Movements in Europe* (Oxford: Clarendon Press, 1940).

The most complete analysis of population policies yet published. Contains exhaustive treatments of German, French, Swedish, and Italian experiences, based on careful research.

Marcus Lee Hansen, *The Atlantic Migration, 1607-1860* (Cambridge: Harvard University Press, 1941).

A remarkably authentic history of the early migration from Europe to America. The human side of the migration, the motives and conditions, are brought out in extremely clear fashion. Social history at its best. It is a tragedy that the author did not live to finish his second volume on the migration after 1860. He did, however, study the migration from Canada to the United States in The Mingling of the Canadian and American Peoples.

Eva M. Hubback, *The Population of Britain* (New York: Penguin Books, 1947).

A popular but sound account of current population trends, problems, and policies in Great Britain.

George H. Knibbs, *The Shadow of the World's Future* (London: Ernest Benn, 1928).

The world's population is growing at a rate much too fast to continue long, because the world's resources are limited. An original and cogent consideration of world population changes by an eminent Australian statistician.

Frank W. Notestein, Irene B. Taeuber, Dudley Kirk, *et al., The Future Population of Europe and the Soviet Union* (Geneva: League of Nations, 1944).

Exposition of the science of making population projections and application of this science to the demographic future of the European nations to 1970. Somewhat technical and compact, but an extremely able work.

W. B. Reddaway, *The Economics of a Declining Population* (London: Allen & Unwin, 1939).

The assumed economic effects of a stationary or declining population. Consists mostly of fine-spun speculation, since virtually no modern countries have actually experienced such a trend.

Irene B. Taeuber, Edwin G. Beal, Kingsley Davis, *et al., Demographic Studies of Selected Areas of Rapid Growth* (New York: Milbank Memorial Fund, 1944).

Despite the formidable title, most of these papers are readable. They deal with the pressure of population growth on resources in such overpopulated areas as Japan, India, southeastern Europe, Egypt, and the Near East. They represent a commentary on the tragic failure of large segments of mankind to control their reproduction.

Irene B. Taeuber, Kingsley Davis, Dudley Kirk, *et al., Postwar Problems of Migration* (New York: Milbank Memorial Fund, 1947).

A collection of papers on migration in different parts of the world, on immigration into the United States, and on internal migration in America. Most of them are based on careful research rather than off-hand speculation.

Warren S. Thompson, *Plenty of People* (New York: Ronald Press, 1948).

Popular treatment of present trends in population growth and distribution throughout the world and particularly in the United States. The author is an outstanding authority on population.

Rupert B. Vance, *All These People* (Chapel Hill: University of North Carolina Press, 1945).

A careful and comprehensive study of the South's human resources as compared with the other regions of the United States. Population trends in relation to agriculture, industrialization, education, race, etc.

PART VI

SOCIAL CHANGE

THE MEANING OF SOCIAL CHANGE

CHAPTER XXII

THE MEANING OF SOCIAL CHANGE

TO SEE a picture of the strange clothes that were worn only yesterday, to read the history of the queer customs and ideas that once were current, to hear predictions of the marvels that are destined for tomorrow—to do these things is to realize the incessant changeability of human society. Individuals may strive for stability and security; societies may foster the illusion of permanence; the quest for certainty may continue unabated and the belief in eternity persist unshaken, yet the fact remains that societies, like all other phenomena, unremittingly and inevitably change.

This fact of change has long fascinated the keenest minds and still poses some of the great unsolved problems in social science. What, for instance, is the *direction* of social change? Is it toward some goal, toward some catastrophe, or toward mere extinction? . . . What is the *form* of social change? Is it more rapid now than in the past, and will it be more rapid in the future? . . . What is the *source* of social change? Is it a matter of borrowing or a matter of independent invention? . . . What is the *cause* of social change? Is it some key factor that explains all change, a prime mover that sets everything else in motion, or is it many different factors operating together? . . . And finally, what is necessary for the *control* of social change? Can we regulate and guide it in the direction of our heart's desire? . . . These are the tantalizing questions—tantalizing not only because of their difficulty but because of their human significance. Since men are social creatures, social change means human change. To change society is to change man.

For obvious reasons social change has been a perennial happy hunting ground for spurious theories and illogical beliefs. It has been approached too often with the reformer's zeal and with a philosophical or religious question uppermost. The strictly scientific literature on it is scant indeed, and none too good. If the following discussion can clarify some of the issues and suggest a few truths, it will have achieved its purpose. Necessarily social change has been discussed in various connections in early parts of the book. The present chapter aims merely to state the problem and define the major theoretical issues.

Social versus Cultural Change

By "social change" is meant only such alterations as occur in social organization—that is, the structure and functions of society. Social change thus forms only a part of what is esentially a broader category called "cultural change." The latter embraces all changes occurring in any branch of culture, including art, science, technology, philosophy, etc. as well as changes in the forms and rules of social organization.

To illustrate, let us cite on the one hand the rise of organized labor in capitalistic society and, on the other, the occurrence of systematic sound shifts in the Indo-European languages. The first represents a basic alteration in the relation of employer and employee, and has had repercussions throughout the economic and political organization of modern civilization.[1] The second is just as definitely a change. The sound shifts in the various languages after separation from the original and long extinct Aryan mother-tongue were strikingly regular and parallel, so that the philologists could reduce them to a few basic principles such as Grimm's Law.[2] But this phonetic change neither arose from nor affected the social organization of the peoples who spoke the Indo-European languages. It was purely a linguistic phenomenon, a cultural rather than a social change.

Cultural change is thus much broader than social change. Since our interest is focused on the narrowed topic we shall not become involved in such matters as the evolution of phonetic sounds, the history of art forms, the transition of musical styles, or the development of mathematical theory. Of course, no part of culture is totally unrelated to the social order, but it remains true that changes may

[1] See references in Wilbert E. Moore, *Industrial Relations and the Social Order* (New York: Macmillan, 1946), Chap. 17.

[2] Leonard Bloomfield, *Languages* (New York: Holt, 1933), Chaps. 20-21.

occur in these branches without noticeably affecting the social system. Sociologically, therefore, we are interested in cultural change only to the extent that it arises from or has an effect on social organization. We are not interested in it for itself apart from social change.

Change versus Interaction

From the standpoint of atomic physics an iron bar is not quiescent. Instead its protons and electrons are constantly active. Yet the shape of the bar remains relatively fixed, altering only when it is smelted, bent, rusted, broken, welded, etc. Similarly the individuals in a society are constantly interacting, yet the structure governing such activity—the forms and rules of interaction—may remain relatively stable for long periods of time. The activity itself should not be confused with changes in the structure, which alone comprise social change.

For example, the principle of monogamous wedlock has remained fixed in American law from the beginning. Marriage has changed in many ways but not in this one particular. Yet many millions of Americans have entered wedlock under this principle and have left it through death or divorce. Each such step has meant an important change to them as individuals but not a change in the social order. Just as linguistic change does not refer to the activity of speaking but rather to the forms of speech, so social change does not refer to social interaction but rather to the normative conditions of interaction.

Certainly there is a close connection between social interaction and social change, for it is mainly through interaction that change comes about. The development of organized labor occurred, in part at least, because of strains in the interaction of employer and employees under the old system. In other words interaction is possible because there is a structure, and change is possible because there is interaction.

The distinction between interaction and change may seem elementary, but in practice it is not always clear. For instance, where does the phenomenon called "the circulation of the elite" belong? Pareto, who has discussed this phenomenon at great length, seems to believe he is discussing social change.[3] Yet if the conditions by which

[3] Vilfredo Pareto, *The Mind and Society* (New York: Harcourt, Brace, 1935), Vol. IV.

the elite are recruited remain the same, there is no social change but merely social circulation or "metabolism." If, on the other hand, as Pareto seems to intimate, the displacement of one elite by another alters the social structure, it is social change—even though it may occur in cycles.

Short- versus Long-Run Changes

It seems wise to emphasize fairly long periods—generations or centuries at least—in first approaching the topic of social change. This helps to eliminate the confusion between interaction and change, and saves us from too great a preoccupation with the ephemeral present. What seems important today, what seems a vital change, may be nothing more than a temporary oscillation having nothing to do with essential trends. This is what historians mean when they say that time alone can place the events of the day in their true perspective. In any case, in discussing social change, one should specify the length of time one has in mind.

Whole Societies versus Parts

Any social system differs in different epochs. Some of its parts may remain virtually stable but as a whole it changes. This fact has led many authors to try to delineate types of societies and to interpret social change as the successive shifting from one type to another.[4] The task has proved extremely difficult, because societies differ in such myriad ways that any typology seems rough and vague. Scholars have been forced to talk about the "spirit," the general "ethos," or the "essence" of one society as against another. The very names they have given the alleged types disclose the nebulous and sometimes metaphorical character of their speculations. For instance Spengler distinguishes "Faustian," "Apollonian," and "Magian" cultures; Sorokin, "Ideational," "Sensate," and "Idealistic;" and Ruth Benedict, "Apollonian" and "Dionysian."[5] MacIver points out that these terms are so indefinite that the same ones are applied to the most advanced societies (e.g. by Spengler) and to the most primitive ones

[4] Oswald Spengler, *The Decline of the West* (New York: Knopf, 1926); W. M. Flinders Petrie, *The Revolutions of Civilization* (London: Harper, 1911); Pitirim Sorokin, *Social and Cultural Dynamics* (New York: American Book, 1937).

[5] Benedict, *Patterns of Culture* (New York: Penguin, 1934).

(e.g. by Ruth Benedict).[6] In addition different scholars looking at the same society are apt to characterize it differently, according to which particular traits they emphasize.

Perhaps the analysis of change in the parts of society may throw light on changes in the whole. As we shall see later, the way the different parts of society figure in the process of change is by no means clear, however.

Description versus Analysis

The poorest way to understand social change is simply to recapitulate all past changes. Twenty tomes would not suffice for such recapitulation, nor would any amount of repetition give it relevance.

> Information, no matter how reliable or extensive, which consists of a set of isolated propositions is not science. A telephone book, a dictionary, a cookbook, or a well-ordered catalogue of goods sold in a general store may contain accurate knowledge, organized in some convenient order, but we do not regard these as works of science. Science requires that our propositions form a logical *system,* that is, that they stand to each other in some one or other of the relations of equivalence and opposition already discussed.[7]

If a mere narrative were adequate for an understanding of social change the best means would be a moving picture of everything that happens. This film could then be run off whenever the subject of social change arose. The only trouble would be that showing the picture would take as long as it took the events to happen in the first place. We would have to repeat life in order to understand life.

The study of social change has often tended in the direction of sheer history, with no real light on causation; or, discouraged by the avalanche of facts, it has tended in the direction of sheer generalization, with mere citation of examples instead of systematic proof or disproof. To strike a golden mean requires that the facts be marshalled, organized, and dealt with in terms of theoretical proposi-

[6] Robt. M. MacIver, *Social Causation* (New York: Ginn, 1942), p. 276. Benedict was aware of this problem. *Op. cit.,* pp. 72-73. She was not primarily interested in the problem of social change.

[7] Morris R. Cohen and Ernest Nagel, *An Introduction to Logic and Scientific Method* (New York: Harcourt, Brace, 1934), p. 128.

tions susceptible of verification. Only in this way, by a *method* of analysis, can this kaleidoscopic phenomena of history be reduced to scientific order.

The Rate of Change

One must conceive of a balance of opposed forces, some favoring change, others opposing it. To the extent that they cancel each other, stability reigns. To the extent that forces favoring change prevail, a rate of change results.

But the "rate of change" has two different applications according to whether one thinks of whole societies or of parts. In the first application the rate refers to the rapidity of change in different societies or in the same society at different times. Thus modern Europe is commonly believed to have changed more rapidly than Medieval Europe and, in the nineteeth century, the United States more rapidly than Latin America. In the second application the rate refers to the rapidity of change in various parts of the same society, usually in the same period. Thus it is a disputed question as to whether in Western civilization during the last three centuries, economic and political institutions have changed more rapidly than familial and religious institutions.

No matter in which context, the comparison of rates of change is exceedingly difficult. To begin with, there are few ways of measuring change in an entire society. By what procedure, for example, can one prove statistically that the Roman society of the first century A.D. was changing more or less rapidly than the Greek society of the fifth century B.C.? It seems best to break the problem down into component parts. One may compare the changes in religion in the two places at the specified times, and also the changes in government, kinship, business, and what not. This has the advantage that in each case things of the same order are being compared—government with government, business with business, etc. In the end one may arrive at a tentative summation of the relative rates of change in the two societies during the two periods, although the techniques of measurement in the various fields would be hard to contrive.

When a comparison is made between different parts of society, an important basis of comparability is lost. How can it be proved, for instance, that the replacement of private by public ownership of railroads is a greater or lesser change than the passage of a prohibition amendment, or that the development of air transportation is a greater or lesser change than the spread of college education? It may seem absurd to speak of relative rates of change in such noncomparable matters—like asking if a giraffe moves faster than a cell divides—but it is sometimes done.

It is extremely difficult if not impossible to prove that in fact the rate of change in a particular part of culture is faster than the rate in other parts. On logical grounds we suspect that any such diversity of rate, if it occurs at all, occurs for a very limited time. The notion of "lag" implies that in order to have an "adjusted society" all parts of culture must eventually "catch up" with the most rapidly changing parts; and since a society must be fairly well "adjusted" in order to keep going, the size of the lag cannot grow continually larger. If there were a permanent difference in the rate of change, no matter how small, it would eventually produce a gap that would be intolerably wide. This reasoning suggests that over a long period the rate of change in two different parts of culture cannot be very different. We must conclude, therefore, that comparisons of rates of change between different parts of social organization have at best a dubious validity, and that comparisons between different whole societies, though difficult, may have a better claim to validity.

The Direction of Change

Though it appears difficult to say that within a given period a change from believing in three gods to believing in one is faster or slower than a change from horse-drawn to motor-drawn vehicles, one possible way of making the two comparable is to take into account the direction of change. If the ultimate result is going to be a belief in six gods, a change from a belief in three to a belief in one is not speed at all but retrogression. If in the same society the ultimate vehicle is to be a sun-driven motorcar, a change from horse-powered to gasoline-powered vehicles may be a step toward that result and therefore "faster" than the other change. Thus changes in different parts of culture could be compared with respect to the rapidity with which they approach the eventual result.

In most discussions of social change some direction is assumed. Often, however, this assumption is not inherent in the facts but is contributed by the wishes of the observer. The direction is interpreted as tending towards some goal that the individual would like to see reached, and it is against this goal (not the actual end-result) that "speed" or "slowness" is measured. Frequently it *is* possible to discern a consistent trend in changes that have taken place in the past —for example, the trend of modern technology toward greater productivity. But such a trend may not continue forever. It may reverse itself, in which case there would still be change but in the opposite direction. Again, the length of time under discussion must be kept in mind.

Attempting to take account of the direction of change is a necessary procedure both in organizing the facts and in arriving at causal principles. But a trend cannot be extrapolated unless there are logical and empirical grounds lying outside the given phenomenon for expecting a continuation of the trend. For instance, the fact that a given population has been growing rapidly does not mean that it will continue to grow at the same rate. An analysis of the various demographic and social factors affecting population growth may indicate that it will grow even more rapidly or considerably less so.[8] When "factors" are mentioned we are obviously in the realm of causal analysis, which is fundamental both for a consideration of rates and for a consideration of direction.

The Forms of Social Change

Closely linked with the question of direction is the problem of the *form* of social change. This seemingly boils down to a single issue—namely, whether change is cyclical or linear. An extreme statement of the cyclical hypothesis would be that social phenomena of whatever sort (whether specific traits or whole civilizations) recur again and again, exactly as they were before. An equally extreme statement of the linear hypothesis would be that all aspects of society change continually in a certain direction, never faltering, never repeating themselves. Put so baldly, neither of these statements would prove acceptable to most people. Yet what sort of an answer can be given? Is there any sort of compromise? Yes, if we confine ourselves to what is known rather than to the eternal, there is a possible compromise.

It is quite obvious that any trend will show minor fluctuations, for nothing changes at identically the same rate from one year to

[8] See Chaps. 20-21.

the next; and it is equally obvious that recurrences will not be absolutely perfect, for nothing returns to exactly its original state. Proponents of the linear or the cyclical view really take refuge in the unknown. They argue that although fluctuations and trends are both observable, social change is "ultimately" one or the other. Their opinions thus become philosophical dogmas rather than scientific hypotheses.

We cannot know anything about *all* of social change. We can know only about the social change that is observable. At best we have reasonably full data concerning a few thousand years of human history, out of millions of past years and no telling how many future ones. Any claim that a mode of change has always persisted and always will persist clearly goes beyond empirical knowledge. The question of what is the ultimate nature of social change is therefore simply a philosophical puzzle that has no place in social science. When we confine ourselves to what is knowable, we find both trends and fluctuations. Indeed, whether a given change is cyclical or linear depends largely on the span of time under consideration. A decline in business appears as a trend if only a few years are taken, whereas in a larger time context it appears as merely one phase of the business cycle.

The Source of Social Change

For a long time a controversy raged in cultural anthropology as to which is the more important, invention or diffusion.[9] Though not quite dead, it is a dying controversy—not because one side is winning but because the question is proving pointless.

The emphasis on diffusion was in the main a protest against the evolutionary point of view, which had implied that culture develops through a series of self-generating stages. The diffusionists pointed out that independent invention occurs with extreme rarity. The fact that a particular society has a given cultural trait is not usually due to its having evolved to that stage, but to the fact that it borrowed the trait from another society. Indeed, by the simple process of borrowing, a primitive society may become civilized within a century or so (as the Maori are doing today in New Zealand) and thus jump

[9] A. L. Kroeber, "Diffusionism," *Encyclopedia of the Social Sciences*. G. Elliott Smith *et al., Culture: The Diffusion Controversy* (New York: Norton, 1927). Robt. H. Lowie, *The History of Ethnological Theory* (New York: Rinehart, 1937), *passim.*

across a cultural chasm that took thousands of years to bridge by independent invention.

The diffusionists were correct in their criticism of the extreme evolutionary point of view. Yet they too overstated their case. Some of them went so far as to claim that two similar traits in two different societies could not possibly be due to invention in both places. The civilizations of South and Central America, for example, could not have arisen by themselves, but must have obtained their civilized traits from Egypt by way of India, Java, and Polynesia.[10]

Obviously, the opposition between these two points of view is much like that between environmentalists and hereditarians, or linear and cyclical theorists.

> As usually happens in the perpetration of scientific fallacies, the error has been introduced into the framing of the question. Hence we are tempted at first sight to jump to the erroneous answer. The correct reply to the . . . question, however, must insist that the very opposition, sharp and precise though it appears, between diffusion and invention, is really misleading.
>
> Let us inquire, then, what precisely an "invention" is. In the case of every modern invention, we know that it is invariably made and re-made time after time in different places, by different men along slightly different roads, independently of one another. It is enough to mention the famous disputes about the discovery of the infinitesimal calculus, the steam engine, the telephone, the turbine, the wireless; the endless priority wrangles in science; the difficulties of establishing rights to a patent; and so on. The fact is that each invention is arrived at piece-meal, by infinitely many, infinitely small steps, a process in which it is impossible to assign a precise share to any one worker or still less to connect a definite object and a definite idea with a single contribution. In the wireless, for instance, the man to whom the invention is popularly ascribed has little more than commercialized the already existing practical appliances. The real work can be traced back through Righi, Braun, Hertz, Clerk-Maxwell, Faraday, Ampere, and so on back to Galvani and Galileo. But these are only the summits—illuminated by the flash-light of sensational coincidence and the limelight of success as well as by the elevation of their genius. The real pathway of ideas and achievements goes through hundreds and thousands of humbler workers and laboratory

[10] Reprinted from Culture: *The Diffusion Controversy* by G. Elliott Smith *et al.*, by permission of W. W. Norton & Company, Inc.

mechanics, and mathematicians and engineers who jointly make the final success possible. Thus the invention of the wireless can be treated as a single event and ascribed to one man or another only after its nature has been completely misconceived.[11]

In the same way "diffusion" turns out to be a complex abstraction, not a separate entity. No idea, no practice, no technique ever passed from one society to another without some modification being added to it. The borrowed culture trait must be somehow modified and adapted so as to fit into the existing cultural context. It follows that diffusion and invention are always inseparably mixed. To oppose them as if they were mutually exclusive is to raise a false issue.

The Causes of Social Change

None of the questions so far discussed strikes the central one—the question of causation. It is now time to raise this question directly, to ask what brings social change and what retards it.

THE FALLACY OF DETERMINISM

Most popular among the causal theories are the determinisms. At their best they hold that because "A" varies as "B" and "C" vary, the variations in "A" are the cause of the variations in "B" and "C". Furthermore, they assume that "A" *always* causes the changes in "B" and "C" and that the causal influence does not run the other way. Sometimes "A" is held to be the causal agent even when its variations are not correlated with observable changes in "B" and "C". In other words the theorist picks one factor that is always present. He then explains changes in the whole of society by reference to this one factor. He often thinks of all sorts of reasons why his explanation is correct. Such theories are called "deterministic," not simply because they assume social changes to be susceptible of causal analysis (as any scientific theory must do) but because they assume the whole causation to be attributable to one factor alone.

There are two types of deterministic theories, one of which selects a nonsocial, the other a social, factor. The quickest way to disprove the first type is to show that concomitant variation between this factor and the social system does not occur. The second type is much harder to disprove.

[11] *Ibid.*, p. 28 (Malinowski's chapter).

A good example of the first kind of theory is geographical determinism, which holds that the geographical setting ultimately governs the form of society and hence explains social change. But the geographic environment, unaffected by man, changes very slowly and therefore cannot explain most social changes. Nothing much happened to the climate of Europe during the last five centuries, yet the social system was tremendously transformed by the Industrial Revolution. The same geographical environment may support extremely different civilizations, and similar civilizations may exist in quite different geographical settings. In most cases in which geographical change is alleged to produce social change, it will be found that the alleged geographical setting is in part man-made and therefore itself socially determined.

A good example of deterministic theory on the strictly social level is economic determinism or "the materialist interpretation of history." Proponents of this view protect their weak logical flank by refusing to make clear just what they conceive the "economic factor" to be. Sometimes they seem to include technology and again they seem to include political elements. Marx and Engels appear to have included technology when they declared that "the mode of production determines the character of the social, political, and intellectual life generally." (They did not say how the changes in the productive system were initiated, but apparently assumed that they generated themselves and operated as a first cause.) At the same time they included political elements when they interpreted "economic interests" to mean social relations and class interests rather than "individual self-interest." When the definition of the economic factor is left so ambiguous, it is easy to "prove" economic determinism and very hard to disprove it, because the proponent of the theory can shift the basis of this argument at will. When the argument requires, he can take the "economic factor" to mean a mode of production or, when he is pressed in another way, he can take it to mean the whole of social organization. Thus thousands of articles and books have been written about an issue that is primarily a verbal dispute.

The feeling that the economic interpretation is hard-headed and realistic, whereas any other is idealistic and fanciful, turns out to be the opposite of the truth. If this interpretation means that every individual is at bottom out for himself and that social ideals are mere camouflage, the view is not realistic at all, but fanciful. As mentioned previously, it is necessary to ask when discussing the pursuit of self-interest, what the "self" is. It is not simply a biological entity that feeds and spawns through instinct, but a human being formed by the inculcation of beliefs, attitudes, knowledge, and values. The pursuit of self-interest, therefore, may well involve the pursuit of ideals, if these have been incorporated as part of the self. The desire of Muslims in India to have a separate nation was not determined by their economic interest. On the contrary, since Pakistan was known in advance to be a poor area on which to found a nation, it was bound to prove economically very costly; yet the Muslims, by virtue of their religious motivation, were willing to bear the economic cost. This was a clear case in which religious sentiment determined economic behavior rather than the opposite. The same relationship can be found in countless other cases. Spain, for example, was determined to be a completely Catholic country and as a result lost heavily both in an economic and political sense. There seems no reason to believe that either her rulers or her citizens regarded this as a bad bargain, because to them Catholicism came before all else.

Equilibrium and Social Change

In their quest for simplicity most deterministic theories try to state a law of social change, as if the whole complex subject could be summed up in a single formula. All of them contain a grain of truth but they try to travel too far on one grain. The simplicity they introduce is a false simplicity which does not explain but explains away this problem. Let us abandon, then, the quest for a single law of social change. The subject requires instead an entire system of generalizations such as the notion of social equilibrium makes possible.

In previous parts of this book an attempt was made to set forth the necessary preliminaries to considering a social system as a moving equilibrium. The first step was to differentiate the socio-cultural level of phenomena from the biological and chemical levels—stressing for this purpose the role of communicative interaction between individuals. The next step was to delineate the chief elements composing the socio-cultural level. Among these were (1) the elements of social action—sentiments, values, and ends; means; and conditions; (2) the different kinds of action in which these elements are combined—technological, economic, political, religio-moral, expressive, etc.; (3) the normative prescriptions regarding the application of these kinds of action in varying situations—folkways, mores, laws, and institutions; and (4) the processes of interaction that manifest and maintain these principles—contact, conflict, competition, accommodation, etc. With some such conceptual apparatus it is possible to treat any given society as an approximation to an equilibrium. One can say that in the absence of outside interference a society will manifest a trend in a direction determined by the state of the socio-cultural variables at a given moment. Furthermore this equilibrium is in part self-restoring: it resists deflection.

It should be evident how inadequate a deterministic position is. By the equilibrium approach it does not make much difference which variable one starts with. Since the variables are mutually dependent, an examination of a change in one variable will inevitably lead to an examination of changes in other variables. If, for example, one starts with technology one soon finds oneself discussing related economic changes, because business firms either foster or withhold inventions according to which is profitable. Asking how withholding is possible, one next gets involved in the patent laws and hence in the political structure. And so on. In the end, in order to explain the total change in a society, one would have to consider the main variables constituting the social equilibrium.

In understanding the relations between the chief variables determining the social equilibrium, we naturally focus on the stresses and strains. But these stresses and strains are what they are precisely because of the character of the entire social order: they are, in short, stresses and strains *of* the whole social system. We also focus on any impingements from outside which may alter the equilibrium either permanently or temporarily, and we give careful attention to the forces within the society tending to restore the equilibrium.

It is only in terms of equilibrium that most sociological concepts make sense. Either tacitly or explicitly anyone who thinks about society tends to use the notion. The functional-structural approach to sociological analysis is basically an equilibrium theory. It is usually phrased in static terms, but as soon as the element of time is added it alludes to a moving equilibrium.

Not only is the concept of equilibrium a useful tool in general sociological analysis, but it is useful in any particular branch of social science. The various elements which may be employed for sociological purposes turn out to be not single items but whole congeries of variables within themselves—what we might call sub-equilibria. The social field in which the concept of equilibrium has been most fruitfully applied, for example, is economics. It therefore seems worthwhile to quote an eminent economist with reference to the value of the concept in the understanding of economic change.

> We have seen, first of all, that the theory of equilibrium . . . gives us, as it were, the bare bones of economic logic which, however abstract or remote from real life it may be, yet renders indispensable service in clearing the ground for rigorous analysis. The best way to convince oneself of the value of this service is to try to define such phenomena as overproduction, excess capacity, unemployment, maladjustment. . . . These terms, as commonly used, do not carry any precise meaning at all, and the fact that they do not explains the inconclusiveness of much argument that goes under those headings. As soon as we try to find such precise meaning for them and to fit them for the task of identifying definite states of the economic organism, the necessity of falling back on equilibrium relations becomes apparent.
>
> Although, in the second place, every event impinges on an economic world that is already disturbed and in disequilibrium, our understanding of the way in which the organism reacts to any given new event is unavoidably based upon our understanding of those equilibrium relations. . . .
>
> Third, the concept of a state of equilibrium, although no such state may ever be realized, is useful and indeed indispensable for purposes of analysis and diagnosis, as a point of reference. Actual states can conveniently be defined by their distance from it.[12]

If the concept is useful in this special branch of social science, we would expect it to be even more useful in the study of human society as a whole. A number of authors have made use of it (notably Pareto and Talcott Parsons) for this purpose, but the general theory of societal equilibrium is far from being well worked out. The exposition of it in the present volume is frankly tentative and incomplete,

[12] Joseph A. Schumpeter, *Business Cycles* (New York: McGraw-Hill, 1939), pp. 68-69.

but the aim is to suggest an approach to the problem of social change which will be creative in the sense of leading to further research and a growth of theoretical knowledge.

References

Brooks Adams, *The Laws of Civilization and Decay* (New York: Macmillan. 1916).

A classic which has proved to have unexpected vitality.

Crane Brinton, *The Anatomy of Revolution* (New York: Norton, 1938).

In addition to this study, previously cited, there are several other comparative analyses of revolutions, e.g. those by Lyford P. Edwards, R. B. Merriman, and Pitirim A. Sorokin.

M. C. Burkitt, *The Old Stone Age* (Cambridge: University Press, 1933)

A lucid and authoritative description of what is known about Paleolithic times. Especially good on the art of the period, and its social significance. See also her book, Our Early Ancestors *(same publisher, 1926), which covers the Mesolithic, Neolithic, and Copper periods.*

William Howells, *Mankind So Far* (Garden City, N. Y.: Doubleday, Doran. 1945).

The evolution of man, mostly organic but with some consideration of cultural evolution as well. Very readable and quite competent. For the cultural side see the Warden references in Chap. 1 of the present book, and the Burkitt books above.

A. L. Kroeber, *Anthropology* (New York: Harcourt, Brace, 1948), Chap. 9. "Culture Processes"; Chap. 10, "Culture Change"; Chap 11, "Some Histories of Inventions"; Chap. 12, "Culture Growths and Spreads"; Chap. 13, "Story of the Alphabet."

Readable discussions of cultural change.

Andrew W. Lind, *An Island Community: Ecological Succession in Hawaii* (Chicago: University of Chicago Press, 1938).

The economic and social history of our rapidly changing polyracial Garden of Eden in the Pacific, analyzed from an ecological point of view. An excellent study.

Ralph Linton, *The Study of Man* (New York: Appleton-Century, 1936) Chap. 18, "Discovery and Invention"; Chap. 19, "Diffusion"; Chap. 21, "Historical Reconstructions."

A better than average brief discussion of invention-diffusion topics.

Bronislaw Malinowski, *The Dynamics of Culture Change: An Inquiry into Race Relations in Africa* (New Haven: Yale University Press, 1945).

As is usual with Malinowski's books, this one has too ambitious a title. Neither the main title nor the subtitle describes it accurately. It is a collection of papers on miscellaneous topics concerned with cultural theory and with African cultures. Here are some of the titles: "Theories of Culture Change," "The Value of History and Its Limitations," "The Principle of the Common Factor in Culture Change," "Scientific Principles and Instruments in the Study of Culture Change."

Robert M. MacIver, *Social Causation* (Boston: Ginn, 1942).

A profound discussion of the different meanings of causation and approaches to its study with reference to social change. See also the same author's discussion in Society: A Textbook of Sociology *(New York: Rinehart, 1937), Book 3.*

Margaret Mead, *The Changing Culture of an Indian Tribe* (New York: Columbia University Press, 1932).

A readable account of the social disorganization accompanying acculturation of a tribe of North American Indians. The demoralization of the tribe, the breakdown of social controls, the loss of values, is vividly described. Social change accompanying acculturation has been widely studied—see Kroeber, Linton, and Malinowski items in the present list.

William F. Ogburn, *Social Change* (New York: Viking, 1938—originally pub. by Huebsch, 1922).

This is the book that first formulated the "cultural lag" hypothesis which subsequently gained wide popularity in American sociology.

N. L. Sims, *The Problem of Social Change* (New York: Crowell, 1939).

A superficial book, but it at least has chapters on some of the main aspects of social change and contains considerable bibliography.

Pitirim A. Sorokin. *Social and Cultural Dynamics* (New York: American Book, 1937-43), 4 Vols.

Monumental in size and scope, somewhat disappointing in execution. The author attempts systematically to survey human history and trace the fluctuations from one type of sociocultural system to another. Defective as it is, it is superior to Spengler, Toynbee, and a host of other works that attempt a similar broad survey and typology.

Abbott Payson Usher, *The Industrial History of England* (Boston: Houghton Mifflin, 1920).

Any student of social change should be thoroughly acquainted with the Industrial Revolution. The book mentioned here is a good history, but there are many others.

INDEX

NAME INDEX

"r" indicates reference at end of a chapter, "n" indicates a footnote)

SUBJECT INDEX

(Page numbers in bold face type indicate main treatments)